World
LITERATURE

Cultural Influences of Early to Contemporary Voices

James P. Stobaugh

HIGH SCHOOL LEVEL
STUDENT

First printing: November 2012
Fourth printing: March 2018

Master Books®, P.O. Box 726, Green Forest, AR 72638

Master Books® is a division of the New Leaf Publishing Group, Inc.

ISBN: 978-0-89051-675-1
ISBN: 978-1-61458-270-0 (digital)
Library of Congress Catalog Number: 2012951017

Cover design by Diana Bogardus.
Interior design by Terry White.

Please consider requesting that a copy of this volume be purchased by your local library system.

Printed in the United States of America

Please visit our website for other great titles:
www.masterbooks.com

For information regarding author interviews, please contact the publicity department at (870) 438-5288.

Dedication

This Book is gratefully dedicated to Karen and our four children: Rachel, Jessica, Timothy, and Peter.

He has given us a ministry of reconciliation . . . (2 Corinthians 5:18).

Master
Books®
A Division of New Leaf Publishing Group
www.masterbooks.com

Contents

READING LIST: The following is a list of additional books and texts not included within the study that are needed for this course. It is strongly suggested that students read most, if not all of these books during the summer before taking this course. Most will be available at local libraries or as free downloads at The Online Books Page (onlinebooks.library.upenn.edu/lists.html), Project Gutenberg (www.gutenberg.org/wiki/Main_Page), or Bartleby (www.bartleby.com/).

Augustine, *Confessions*

Dostoevsky, *Crime and Punishment*

Goethe, *Faust*

Homer, *The Iliad*

Homer, *The Odyssey*

Paton, *Cry, the Beloved Country*

Tolstoy, *War and Peace*

Virgil, *The Aeneid*

Using Your Student Textbook

How this course has been developed:

1. **Chapters:** This course has 34 chapters (representing 34 weeks of study) to earn two full credits; writing and literature.

2. **Lessons:** Each chapter has five lessons, taking approximately 45 to 60 minutes each.

3. **Student responsibility:** Responsibility to complete this course is on the student. Students must read ahead to stay on schedule with the readings. Independence is strongly encouraged in this course, which was designed for the student to practice independent learning.

4. **Grading:** Depending on the grading option chosen, the parent/educator will grade the daily concept builders, and the weekly tests and essays. (See pages 7 and 8.)

5. **Additional books and texts:** A list of outside reading is provided after the table of contents. Students should try and read ahead whenever possible. Most readings are available free online or at a local library.

Throughout this book you will find the following:

1. **Chapter Learning Objectives:** Always read the "First Thoughts" and "Chapter Learning Objectives" to comprehend the scope of the material to be covered in a particular week.

2. **Daily warm-ups:** You should write or give oral responses for the daily warm-ups to your educator/parent. These are not necessarily meant to be evaluated, but should stimulate discussion.

3. **Concept builders:** You should complete a daily concept builder. These activities take 15 minutes or less and emphasize a particular concept that is vital to that particular chapter topic. These will relate to a subject covered in the chapter, though not necessarily in that days lesson.

4. **Assigned readings:** Remember to read ahead on the required literary material for this course. Students should plan to read some of the required literature the summer before the course.

5. **Weekly essays:** You will be writing at least one essay per week, depending on the level of accomplishment you and your parent/educator decide upon. These are available in the teacher guide.

6. **Weekly tests:** These are available in the teacher guide and online.

Earn a bonus credit!

Easily integrate related history curriculum for an additional credit, a combination study done in less than two hours daily! History Connections are shown on the chapter introduction page to help students study these texts consecutively, exploring literature and history in unison. (The *American*, *British*, and *World History* curriculum is also written by James Stobaugh and published by Master Books®.)

What the student will need each day:

1. Notepad/computer: for writing assignments.
2. Pen/pencil: for taking notes and for essays.
3. A prayer journal. As often as you can — hopefully daily — keep a prayer journal.

Increasing your vocabulary:

Part of the reason for reading so many challenging literary works is for you to increase your functional vocabulary. Your best means of increasing vocabulary is through reading a vast amount of classical, well-written literary works. While reading these works, you should harvest as many unknown words as you can, and try to use five new words in each essay you write.

Create 3x5 Vocabulary Cards

FRONT	BACK
Adversity	Harmful, Evil Adversity is a Noun The adverse effects of smoking are great.

When you meet a strange word for the first time,

- Do your best to figure out the word in context,
- Check your guess by looking in the dictionary,
- Write a sentence with the word in it.

Use the illustration above to formulate your vocabulary cards of new words.

About the Author

James P. Stobaugh and his wife, Karen, have four homeschooled adult children. They have a growing ministry, For Such a Time As This Ministries, committed to challenging this generation to change its world for Christ.

Dr. Stobaugh is an ordained pastor, a certified secondary teacher, and a SAT coach. His academic credentials include: BA, cum laude Vanderbilt University; Teacher Certification, Peabody College for Teachers; MA, Rutgers University; MDiv, Princeton Theological Seminary; Merrill Fellow, Harvard University; DMin Gordon Conwell Seminary.

Dr. Stobaugh has written articles for magazines: *Leadership, Presbyterian Survey, Princeton Spire, Ministries Today,* and *Pulpit Digest.* Dr. Stobaugh's books include the *SAT Preparation Course for the Christian Student,* the *ACT Preparation Course for the Christian Student,* the *Skills for Literary Analysis,* the *Christian Reading Companion for 50 Classics,* as well as the *American History, British History,* and *World History* high school curriculum.

Preface

World Literature is a rhetoric-level course. Two things are distinctive about rhetoric-level courses: they are content driven, and they presume higher-level thinking. In most cases, you are going to have to read in excess of 200 pages per lesson. Therefore, it is highly advisable that you read most of this material the summer before you begin this course.

Theologian Walter Bruggemann, in his essay "Blessed Are the History-Makers," reminds us that culture is created, history is made, by those who are radically committed to obeying God at all costs (Walter Brueggemann, *Hope within History* [Atlanta, GA: John Knox Press, 1987], chapter 3). Will you be counted among that number? Be smart, but above all, be obedient to the Word of God. For the first time in 300 years, in your generation I observe the marriage of smart minds and born-again hearts. This combination is potent indeed and has revolutionary implications for the 21st-century world. Now, as only once before (i.e., during the Puritan era), this generation is both smart and saved; in other words, it is a Spirit-filled elite, and the ramifications are exciting to say the least.

There is much need. Social critic Os Guinness, in his seminal work *The Dust of Death* prophetically argues that "western culture is marked . . . by a distinct slowing of momentum . . . a decline in purposeful-ness" (Os Guinness, *The Dust of Death* [Downers Grove, IL: Intervarsity Press, 1973]). Guinness implies that the ideals and traditions that have been central to the American civilization are losing their compelling cultural authority. There is, in short, no corpus of universally accepted morality that Americans follow. As Dallas Willard in *The Divine Conspiracy* states ". . . there is no recognized moral knowledge upon which projects of fostering moral development could be based" (Dallas Willard, *The Divine Conspiracy* [San Francisco, CA: HarperCollins Publishers, 1997]).

You are part of one of the most critical generations in the history of Western culture. Indeed, only the generation of which Augustine was a part comes close in importance to your generation. In both cases — today and during the life of Augustine, Bishop of Hippo — civilizations were in decline. Young Augustine lived through the decline of the Roman world; you are living through the decline of American cultural superiority. However, the barbarians conquered Rome; the Christians conquered the barbarians. My prayer for each person who reads this course is:

I kneel before the Father, from whom his whole family in heaven and on earth derives its name. I pray that out of his glorious riches he may strengthen you with power through his Spirit in your inner being, so that Christ may dwell in your hearts through faith. And I pray that you, being rooted and established in love, may have power, together with all the saints, to grasp how wide and long and high and deep is the love of Christ, and to know this love that surpasses knowledge — that you may be filled to the measure of all the fullness of God. Now to him who is able to do immeasurably more than all we ask or imagine, according to his power that is at work within us, to him be glory in the church and in Christ Jesus throughout all generations, for ever and ever! Amen (Eph. 3:14–21).

Sumerian, Egyptian, and Hebrew Literature (Part 1)

(3000 B.C.–300 B.C.)

First Thoughts The story of Mesopotamia is the story of the very genesis of civilization. There is some debate about where people stopped merely herding their livestock and started farming and building cities and therefore creating a civilization. However, there are some strong arguments that it began in Mesopotamia. Mesopotamia, meaning "between the rivers," lies between the Tigris and Euphrates Rivers. It is located in the general vicinity of the present nation states of Iraq and Syria.

In fact, there is strong evidence that Mesopotamia is, in fact, Eden, where God placed the first man, Adam, and the first woman, Eve (Genesis 1). Again, there is strong evidence that the land between the Tigris and the Euphrates is this very place.

Chapter Learning Objectives In chapter 1 we may be visiting the Garden of Eden, but, in any event, we examine an amazing culture that wrote some of the best and earliest epic literature in world history. At the same time, it is more than coincidental that a different culture in another location records the same historical events that occurred in the Bible.

As a result of this chapter study you will be able to . . .

1. Write a process essay that speculates on how the *Epic of Gilgamesh* moved from an oral to a written form

2. Compare and contrast the Gilgamesh Flood narrative with the biblical Flood story (Genesis 8).

3. Compare and contrast the *Enuma Elish* (translated by N.K. Sanders) with Genesis 1 and 2.

4. Compare the gods and goddesses with the gods and goddesses that Elijah encountered.

Weekly Essay Options: Begin on page 273 of the Teacher Guide.

Reading ahead: The Book of Esther, author unknown

9

Epic of Gilgamesh

(c. 1200 B.C.)

Background Mesopotamia's oldest known communities date from 7000 B.C., although that date is much debated. Most biblical scholars argue for a much sooner date (c. 4000 B.C.). Several civilizations prospered in the region until, in the 6th century B.C. it became part of the Persian Empire, the largest empire in the world up to then (see Dan. 5).

The first city-states ("city-state" is defined as an autonomous, self-contained urban center, surrounded by a dependent agricultural area) in the area were the Sumerian cities Eridu and Uruk, among others. Abram emigrated from the Sumerian city of Ur.

Sumerians developed a system of writing by imprinting on clay tablets using a stylus. A form of printing was a similar first: they carved "negative" images onto "cylinder seals." These were stone cylinders, usually from 2 to 6 cm long, which could then be repeatedly rolled over fresh clay to produce the "positive" inscription. As forerunners of the rings used to imprint wax seals in later times, they were used to identify possessions such as pottery, to seal written tablets to guarantee their authenticity, and to protect other valuables via clay stoppers on containers such as bottles, urns, and leather bags. Sumerians also invented the wheel and therefore improved transportation endeavors and building programs. Other contiguous people groups took note of these wonderful things.

They were not slow to follow. About 2330 B.C. Sumeria was conquered by Sargon I, king of the Akkadians. The Gutians, tribespeople from the eastern hills, ended Akkadian rule about 2200 B.C., and, a few years later, the Sumerian Ur arose to rule much of Mesopotamia. Finally, Hammurabi of Babylon (reigned about 1792–1750 B.C.) conquered the whole Mesopotamia area. The Hittites nearly conquered the whole area, but it was ultimately the Persians who dominated the entire Mesopotamia area to the end of our era.

I will concentrate on only two of these Mesopotamian civilizations: Sumerian and Persian.

Mesopotamian peoples produced highly decorated pottery and clothing. They also invented musical instruments such as the harp and lyre that were used to accompany the recital of their many epic literary works (e.g., *Epic of Gilgamesh*). They developed the concept of the library, assiduously collecting and cataloguing their mass of not only literary works. These works were the basis of some in vigorous public and private debates.

Furthermore, scholars are convinced that the Sumerians in particular had a form of assembly for making key political decisions using a consensual approach. They held courts to make legal judgments. They were the first people to develop a code of law and therefore used precedent to determine later court cases. That they also developed some understanding of economics is attested by evidence of price-setting agreements and openly advocated urban planning. The word suburb is mentioned for the first time in a Sumerian text.

The Sumerians used many metals in the construction of buildings and jewelry; these included gold, silver, tin, lead, copper, and bronze. They, were not, however, able to develop iron weaponry — a shortcoming that ultimately hindered them militarily when invading armies brandished iron swords and chariots.

Sumerian religions were polytheistic. The gods played a crucial role in the Sumerians' lives, both as a nation and as individuals. Most Sumerians, for instance, had a personal god or gods with whom they forged a special relationship. They were "good luck charms." They looked to them for protection and assistance in all things, while also blaming them when things went wrong. These gods continued to be worshiped right through to the late Babylonian period.

- Warm-up: What are three distinctive components of Sumerian Civilization?

- Students should complete Concept Builder 1-A.

- Students should review the required reading(s) before the assigned chapter begins.

- Teachers shall assign the required essay. The rest of the essays can be outlined, answered with shorter answers, discussed, or skipped.

CONCEPT BUILDER 1-A
Active Reading

Read this excerpt from the *Epic of Gilgamesh*, and respond to the following:

Shurippaka city which thou knowest,
(And) which on Euphrates' banks is set
That city was ancient, (as were) the gods within it,
When their heart led the great gods to produce the flood.
There were Anu, their father,
Valiant Enlil, their counselor,
Ninurta, their herald,
Ennuge, their irrigator.
Ninigiku-Ea was also present with them;
Their words he repeats to the reed-hut:
Reed-hut, reed-hut! Wall! Wall!
Reed-hut, hearken! Wall, reflect!
Man of Shuruppak, son of Ubar-Tutu,
Tear down (this) house, build a ship!
Give up possessions, seek thou life.
Despise property and keep the soul alive.
Aboard the ship take thou the seed of all living things.
The ship that thou shalt build,
Her dimensions shall be to measure.
Equal shall be her width and her length.
Like the Apsu thou shalt sail her.
I understood, and I said to Ea, my lord:
Behold, my lord, what thou hast thus ordered,
I shall be honored to carry out.
But what shall I answer the city, the people and elders?
Ea opened his mouth to speak,
Saying to me, his servant:
Thou shalt then thus speak unto them:
I have learned that Enlil is hostile to me,
So that I cannot reside in your city,
Nor set my foot in Enlil's territory.
To the Deep I will therefore go down,
To dwell with my lord Ea.
But upon you he will shower down abundance,
The choicest birds, the rarest fishes.
The land shall have its fill of harvest riches.
He who at dusk orders the hush-greens,
Will shower down upon you a rain of wheat.
With the first glow of dawn,
The land was gathered about me.
(too fragmentary for translation]
The little ones carried bitumen,
While the grown ones brought all else that was needful.
On the fifth day I laid her framework.
One (whole) acre was her floor space,
Ten dozen cubits the height of each of her walls,
Ten dozen cubits each edge of the square deck.
I laid out the shape of her sides and joined her together.

What is the setting?

Who is the protagonist (main character)?

What crisis is the protagonist facing?

How does he handle this crisis?

Religion

The Sumerian pantheon was called the Anunnaki, although another name, the Igigi, was also used. These gods appeared to be polarities; thus the first evidence of dualism entered worldviews. There were, in other words, good gods — the Anunnaki — and bad gods — the Igigi.

Originally, Marduk was the city god of Babylon, but in 1800 B.C., he became the supreme god of the Mesopotamian pantheon. In fact, he was the god of the Palestinian provinces — and many think he was the god that Elijah confronted on Mt. Carmel (1 Kings 18). As such, he was recognized by the gods of the cities that were subjected by the Babylonian kings. According to myth, Marduk defended the other gods against the diabolical monster Tiamat. After he had killed it, he brought order to the cosmos, built the Esagila, and created mankind. This is clearly seen in the *Epic of Gilgamesh*. In the poem "Enûûma êêlišš," it is stated that all other gods are just manifestations of Marduk.

Marduk and other gods and goddesses were worshiped at ziggaruts or temples. In fact, one, named Etemenanki, the foundation of heaven on earth, is considered by most scholars to be the Tower of Babel of Genesis 11.

When the Babylonians celebrated New Year (the so-called Akitu festival), they remembered how Marduk had created order in the universe. The heart of this cosmos was Babylon, and the Esagila shrine was, therefore, the center of the universe. The Babylonian Marduk was embraced by the Persian invaders.

In October 539 B.C., with the Jews in exile, the Persian king Cyrus took Babylon, the ancient capital of an empire covering modern Iraq, Syria, Lebanon, and Israel. Babylon was, by this time, the ancient world's capital of scholarship and science. The subject provinces soon recognized Cyrus as their legitimate ruler. Since he was already ruler of modern Turkey and Iran, it is not an exaggeration to say that the capture of Babylon meant the birth of the first true world empire. The Persian Empire was to last for more than two centuries, until it was conquered by the Macedonian Greek king Alexander the Great. Cyrus allowed the Jews (who were exiled in Babylonia) to return home. The *Gilgamesh Epic* is one of the most remarkable pieces of literature in the Western world. It is full of intricate story lines and flamboyant characters. It probably was created in oral form around 7000 B.C. To give one perspective, this epic was written around 5,000 years before the Jewish exodus from Egypt. Most scholars believe it was recorded on the Gilgamesh Tablets in 1200 B.C.. The existence of this remarkable secular account of the biblical Flood (Gen. 8) by a pagan civilization is remarkable and offers more evidence for the historical validity of the Bible.

Gilgamesh is the best known of all ancient Middle Eastern heroes. Numerous tales in the Akkadian (i.e., Sumerian/Babylonian) language have been told about Gilgamesh, and the whole collection has been described as a spiritual journey — the journey of a king who seeks immortality.

The complete text of the *Epic of Gilgamesh* is on 12 incomplete tablets and can be found today in the British Museum.

The *Epic of Gilgamesh* story/plot is really quite simple. The hero Gilgamesh is Ulysses, Oedipus, and Davy Crockett rolled into one. He is the quintessential hero. He has one major flaw: he is a selfish, self-centered prig. At its core, the Gilgamesh Epic is more than a story about Gilgamesh — it is a journey, a quest for truth. It would be the Sumerian version of John Bunyan's *Pilgrim's Progress*. Although no one had any sense of the subconscious, ego or id in 1200 B.C., the *Epic of Gilgamesh* is a story of a man who finds himself. The outward plot is mirrored by an internal human journey.

The story is straightforward and simple. The heroes and villains are easily identified. This epic would be the "Star Wars Trilogy" of 1200 B.C. The reader knows, without a doubt, who the good guys are and who the bad guys are. This is no *Iliad*, by Homer, where the reader is not quite sure if Hektor is a villain or hero. The reader knows that Gilgamesh is the good guy.

In order to curb the good king Gilgamesh's harsh rule, the god Anu creates Enkidu, a wild man who at first lives among animals. Enkidu meets Gilgamesh in Enkidu. Tablet II describes Gilgamesh defeating Enkidu. In Tablets III–V the two men pursue Huwawa. In Tablet VI, Gilgamesh is tempted by romance. Tablets VII

One of the 12 clay tablets containing a portion of the Epic of Gilgamesh.

and VIII are the story of Enkidu's death. Afterward, the much wiser, but grieving, Gilgamesh (Tablets IX and X) searches for Utnapishtim, the survivor of the Babylonian flood, in order to obtain eternal life. He finally reaches Utnapishtim, who tells him the story of the flood and shows him where to obtain eternal life (Tablet XI). Gilgamesh, though, fails in his pursuit. An appendage to the epic, Tablet XII, relates the loss of some sacred objects given to Gilgamesh by Ishtar. The epic ends with the return of the spirit of Enkidu.

Assignments

- Warm-up: Describe Sumerian religion
- Students should complete Concept Builder 1-B.
- Students should review reading(s) from next chapter.
- Students should outline essay due at the end of the week.
- Per teacher instructions, students may answer orally, in a group setting, the essays that are not assigned as formal essays.

A report is an informative essay where the reader communicates information to a reader. Plan your report: List your specific group-related ideas under topics, arrange your ideas in order, make an outline, and write your report.

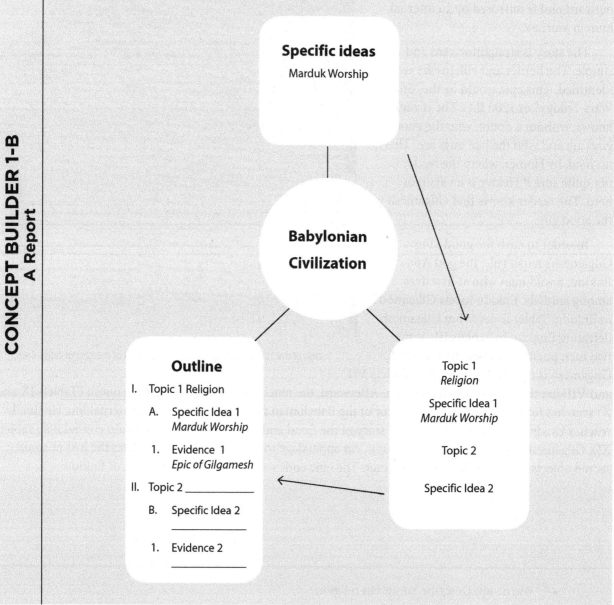

Specific ideas
Marduk Worship

Babylonian Civilization

Topic 1
Religion

Specific Idea 1
Marduk Worship

Topic 2

Specific Idea 2

Outline

I. Topic 1 Religion

   A. Specific Idea 1
      Marduk Worship

    1. Evidence 1
       Epic of Gilgamesh

II. Topic 2 _____

   B. Specific Idea 2
      _____

    1. Evidence 2
      _____

Biblical Parallels

Gilgamesh makes an arduous journey to learn how Utnapishtim (another hero type) acquired eternal life. In answer to his questions, Utnapishtim tells the following story.

Once upon a time, the gods destroyed the ancient city of Shuruppah in a great flood. Utnapishtim, forewarned by one of the gods, managed to survive by building a great boat. He did as commanded and survived the flood. As a reward for his faithful obedience, he was granted immortality by the gods.

In the following excerpt, identify as many biblical parallels as you can.

Shurippaka city which thou knowest,
(And) which on Euphrates' banks is set
That city was ancient, (as were) the gods within it,
When their heart led the great gods to produce the flood.
There were Anu, their father,
Valiant Enlil, their counselor,
Ninurta, their herald,
Ennuge, their irrigator.
Ninigiku-Ea was also present with them;
Their words he repeats to the reed-hut:
Reed- hut, reed- hut! Wall! Wall!
Reed- hut, hearken! Wall, reflect!
Man of Shuruppak, son of Ubar- Tutu,
Tear down (this) house, build a ship!
Give up possessions, seek thou life.
Despise property and keep the soul alive.
Aboard the ship take thou the seed of all living things.
The ship that thou shalt build,
Her dimensions shall be to measure.
Equal shall be her width and her length.
Like the Apsu thou shalt sail her.
I understood, and I said to Ea, my lord:
Behold, my lord, what thou hast thus ordered,
I shall be honoured to carry out.
But what shall I answer the city, the people and elders?
Ea opened his mouth to speak,
Saying to me, his servant:
Thou shalt then thus speak unto them:

I have learned that Enlil is hostile to me,
So that I cannot reside in your city,
Nor set my foot in Enlil's territory.
To the Deep I will therefore go down,
To dwell with my lord Ea.
But upon you he will shower down abundance,
The choicest birds, the rarest fishes.
The land shall have its fill of harvest riches.
He who at dusk orders the hush-greens,
Will shower down upon you a rain of wheat.
With the first glow of dawn,
The land was gathered about me.
(too fragmentary for translation]
The little ones carried bitumen,
While the grown ones brought all else that was needful.
On the fifth day I laid her framework.
One (whole) acre was her floor space,
Ten dozen cubits the height of each of her walls,
Ten dozen cubits each edge of the square deck.
I laid out the shape of her sides and joined her together.
I provided her with six decks,
Dividing her (thus) into seven parts.
Her floor plan I divided into nine parts.
I hammered water-plugs into her.
I saw to the punting-poles and laid in supplies.
Six 'sar' (measures), of bitumen I poured into the furnace,
Three sar of asphalt I also poured inside.

Three sar of the basket-bearers transferred,
Aside from the one sar of oil which the calking consumed,
And the two sar of oil which the boatman stowed away.
Bullocks I slaughtered for the people,
And I killed sheep every day.
Must, red wine, oil, and white wine
I gave the workmen to drink, as though river water,
That they might feast as on New Year's Day. . . .
On the seventh day the ship was completed.
The launching was very difficult,
So that they had to shift the floor planks above and below,
Until two-thirds of the structure had gone into the water.
Whatever I had I laded upon her.
Whatever I had of silver I laded upon her,
Whatever I had of gold I laded upon her,
Whatever I had of all the living beings I laded upon her.
All my family and kin I made go aboard the ship.
The beasts of the field, the wild creatures of the field,
All the craftsmen I made go aboard.
Shamash had set for me a stated time:
When he who orders unease at night
Will shower down a rain of blight,
Board thou the ship and batten up the gate!
That stated time had arrived:
He who orders unease at night showers down a rain of blight.
I watched the appearance of the weather.
The weather was awesome to behold.
I boarded the ship and battened up the gate.
To batten up the (whole) ship, to Puzar-Amurri, the boatman,
I handed over the structure together with its contents.
With the first glow of dawn,
A black cloud rose up from the horizon.
Inside it Adad thunders,
While Shallat and Hanish go in front,
Moving as heralds over hill and plain.
Erragal tears out the posts;
Forth comes Ninurta and causes the dikes to follow.
The Anunnaki lift up the torches,
Setting the land ablaze with their glare.
Consternation over Adad reaches to the heavens,
Turning to blackness all that had been light.
The wide land was shattered like a pot!

For one day the south-storm blew,
Gathering speed as it blew, submerging the mountains,
Overtaking the people like a battle.
No one can see his fellow,
Nor can the people be recognized from heaven.
The gods were frightened by the deluge,
And, shrinking back, they ascended to the heaven of Anu.
The gods cowered like dogs
Crouched against the outer wall.
Ishtar cried out like a woman in travail,
The sweet-voiced mistress of the gods moans aloud:
The olden days are alas turned to clay,
Because I bespoke evil in the Assembly of the gods,
How could I bespeak evil in the Assembly of the gods,
Ordering battle for the destruction of my people,
When it is I myself who give birth to my people!
Like the spawn of the fishes they fill the sea!
The Anunnaki gods weep with her,
The gods, all humbled, sit and weep,
Their lips drawn tight. . . . one and all.
Six days and six nights
Blows the flood wind, as the south-storm sweeps the land.
When the seventh day arrived,
The flood (carrying) south-storm subsided in the battle,
Which it had fought like an army.
The sea grew quiet, the tempest was still, the flood ceased.
I looked at the weather. stillness had set in,
And all of mankind had returned to clay.
The landscape was as level as a flat roof.
I opened a hatch, and light fell on my face.
Bowing low, I sat and wept,
Tears running down my face.
I looked about for coast lines in the expanse of the sea:
In each of fourteen (regions)
There emerged a region (mountain).
On Mount Nisir the ship came to a halt.
Mount Nisir held the ship fast,
Allowingno motion.

[For six days the ship is held fast by Mount Nisir.]
When the seventh day arrived,
I sent forth and set free a dove.

The dove went forth, but came back;
There was no resting-place for it and she turned round.
Then I sent forth and set free a swallow.
The swallow went forth, but came back,
There was no resting-place for it and she turned round.
Then I sent forth and set free a raven.
The raven went forth and, seeing that the waters had diminished, He eats, circles, caws, and turns not round.
Then I let out (all) to the four winds
And offered a sacrifice.
I poured out a libation on the top of the mountain.
Seven and seven cult-vessels I set up, Upon their plate-stands I heaped cane, cedarwood, and myrtle.
The gods smelled the savour,
The gods smelled the sweet savour, The gods crowded like flies about the sacrificer.
As soon as the great goddess arrived,
She lifted up the great jewels which Anu had fashioned to her liking:
Ye gods here, as surely as this lapis
Upon my neck I shallnot forget,
I shall be mindful of these days, forgetting (them) never.
Let the gods come to the offering:
(But) let not Enlil come to the offering, For he, unreasoning, brought on the deluge And my people consigned to destruction. As soon as Enlil arrived,
And saw the ship, Enlil was wroth, He was filled with wrath against the Igigi gods:
Has some living soul escaped?
No man was to survive the destruction!
Ninurta opened his mouth to speak,
Saying to valiant Enlil:
Who other than Ea can devise plans?

It is Ea alone who knows every matter.
Ea opened his mouth to speak,
Saying to valiant Enlil:
Thou wisest of the gods, thou hero,
How couldst thou, unreasoning, bring on the deluge?
On the sinner impose his sin,
On the transgressor impose his transgression!
(Yet) be lenient, lest he be cut off, Be patient, lest he be dislodged
Instead of thy bringing on the deluge,
Would that a lion had risen up to diminish mankind!
Instead of thy brining on the deluge,
Would that a wolf had risen up to diminish mankind!
Instead of thy bringing on the deluge,
Would that a famine had risen up to lay low mankind!
Instead of thy bringing on the deluge,
Would that pestilence had risen up to smite down mankind!
It was not I who disclosed the secret of the great gods.
I let Atrahasis see a dream,
And he perceived the secret of the gods.
Now then take counsel in regard to him!
Thereupon Enlil went aboard the ship.
Holding me by the hand, he took me aboard.
He took my wife aboard and made (her) kneel by my side.
Standing between us, he touched our foreheads to bless us:
Hitherto Utnapishtim has been but human.
Henceforth Utnapishtim and his wife shall be like unto us gods.
Utnapishtim shall reside far away, at the mouth of the rivers!
Thus they took me and made me reside far away,
At the mouth of the rivers.

Assignments

- Warm-up: Compare the Sumerian hero Gilgamesh to a modern hero (e.g., Spider-man).
- Students should complete Concept Builder 1-C.
- Students should write rough drafts of assigned essay.
- The teacher may correct rough drafts.

CONCEPT BUILDER 1-C
Process Essay

A process paper either tells the reader how to do something or describes how something is done.

What are you trying to explain?

↓

Why is this process important to you?

↓

What is the process?

Enuma Elish: Tablet One

When there was no heaven,
no earth, no height, no depth, no name,
when Apsu was alone,
the sweet water, the first begetter; and Tiamat
the bitter water, and that
return to the womb, her Mummu,
when there were no gods

When sweet and bitter
mingled together, no reed was plaited no rushes
muddied the water,
the gods were nameless, natureless, futureless, then
from Apsu and Tiamat
in the waters gods were created,
in the waters
silt precipitated,

Lahmu and Lahumu,
were named;
they were not yet old
not yet grown tall
when Anshar and Kishar overtook them both, (i.e.,
born after)
the lines of sky and earth
stretched where horizons meet to separate
cloud from silt.

Days on days, years
on year passed till Anu, the empty heaven,
heir and supplanter,
first-born of his father, in his own nature
begot Nudimmud-Ea,
intellect, wisdom, wider than heaven's horizon,
the strongest of all the kindred.

Discord broke out among the gods although they were
brothers, warring and jarring in the belly of Tiamat,
heaven shook, it reeled with the surge of the dance;
Apsu could not silence the clamour, their behavior
was bad, overbearing and proud.

But still Tiamat lay inert till Apsu, the father of gods,
bellowed for that servant who clouds his judgment,
his Mummu,
'Dear counselor, come with me to Tiamat.
They have gone, and in front of Tiamat they sit down
and talk together about the young gods, their first-
born children; Apsu said,

Their manners revolt me, day and night without
remission we suffer. My will is to destroy them, all of
their kind, we shall have peace at last and we will sleep
again.

When Tiamat heard she was stung, she writhed in
lonely desolation, her heart worked in secret passion,
Tiamat said,
Why must we destroy the children that we made? If
their ways are troublesome, let us wait a little while.

Then Mummu advised Apsu, and he spoke in malice,
Father, destroy them in full rebellion, you will have
quiet in the daytime and at night you will sleep.

When Apsu heard, the die was cast against his
children, his face flamed with the pleasure of evil; but
Mummu he embraced,
he hung on his neck, he sat him down on his knees
and kissed him.

The decision was known to all their children;
confusion seized them and after, a great silence, for
they were confounded.

The god who is the source of wisdom, the bright
intelligence that perceives and plans, Nudimmud-Ea,
saw through it, he sounded the coil of chaos, and
against it devised the artifice of the universe.

He spoke the word that charmed the waters, it fell upon
Apsu, he lay asleep, the sweet waters slept, Apsu slept,
Mummu was overcome, Apsu lay drowned, undone.

- Warm-up: Compare Apsu to YHWH, God.
- Students should complete Concept Builder 1-D.
- Students will re-write corrected copy of essay due tomorrow.

CONCEPT BUILDER 1-D
Compare/Contrast Essay

Compare and contrast the Gilgamesh epic and the biblical account of the Flood (Genesis 8).

	The Flood	
	Epic of Gilgamesh	**Bible**
Setting	Ancient Middle East, perhaps in the Euphrates River Basin	Euphrates River Basin
Characters		
Plot		
Diety(ies)		

Compare Two Flood Narratives

Utnapishtim's flood-story in the *Epic of Gilgamesh* and the story of the Flood in the Bible are two differing accounts of the same historical event. There are numerous parallels between the two accounts, as well as several contrasts.

In the *Epic of Gilgamesh*, the gods, spurred by the counselor Enlil, decided to deluge the earth with a worldwide flood, scourging mankind for their sinfulness by decimating his race completely. However, Ea, choosing to be merciful in judgment, forewarned Utnapishtim that he should construct an ark so that he alone of all men (with his family and friends) should survive the flood. "Man of Shuruppak, son of Ubar-Tutu, tear down (this) house, build a ship! Give up possessions, seek life. Despise property and keep the soul alive. Aboard the ship take thou the seed of all living things" (*Epic of Gilgamesh*).

In the biblical Flood account, God, observing the wickedness of man, purposed to wipe them out with a flood. But willing that the human race should not be entirely cut short, he selected the single righteous man among them, Noah, and commanded him to build an ark, so that he alone of all men (with his family) should survive the Flood. "So God said to Noah, 'I am going to put an end to all people, for the earth is filled with violence because of them. I am surely going to destroy both them and the earth.' So make yourself an ark of cypress wood.' . . . 'But I will establish my covenant with you, and you will enter the ark — you and your sons and your wife and your sons' wives with you. You are to bring into the ark two of all living creatures, male and female, to keep them alive with you' " (Gen. 6:13–19).

In only seven days, Utnapishtim had finished his ark. It is unclear how long Noah took in his construction, but interestingly, God commanded him to board his ark seven days before he sent the Flood. Utnapishtim's flood lasted for seven days, and his ark remained where it landed upon Mount Nisir for another seven. So the number seven plays a part in each flood account, although Noah's Flood was far longer, lasting 150 days. The number seven continues to repeat itself in both accounts.

As the water level began to recede, both Utnapishtim's and Noah's arks came to rest on mountains. Utnapishtim docked on Mount Nisir and Noah on the mountains of Ararat. Then, yearning to find proof of land, both Utnapishtim and Noah released birds, knowing if they did not return that they had found a safe spot of landing.

"When the seventh day arrived, I [Utnapishtim] sent forth and set free a dove. The dove went forth, but came back; There was no resting-place for it and she turned round" (*Epic of Gilgamesh*).

"Then he [Noah] sent out a dove to see if the water had receded from the surface of the ground. But the dove could find no place to set its feet because there was water over all the surface of the earth; so it returned to Noah in the ark" (Gen. 8:8–9).

"Then I [Utnapishtim] sent forth and set free a raven. The raven went forth and, seeing that the waters had diminished, he eats, circles, caws, and turns not round" (*Epic of Gilgamesh*).

"He [Noah] waited seven more days and again sent out the dove from the ark. When the dove returned to him in the evening, there in its beak was a freshly plucked olive leaf! Then Noah knew that the water had receded from the earth. He waited seven more days and sent the dove out again, but this time it did not return to him" (Gen. 8:10–12).

After it was safe to exit, Utnapishtim, in gratitude to the gods for sparing his life from their wrath, offered sacrifice on the top of Mount Nisir. "Then I let out all to the four winds and offered a sacrifice. I poured out a libation on top of the mountain. Seven and seven cult — vessels I set up, upon their plate-stands I heaped cane, cedar wood, and myrtle. The gods smelled the savour" (*Epic of Gilgamesh*).

Similarly, upon exiting the ark, Noah built an altar to the Lord on top of the mountains of Ararat. "Then Noah built an altar to the LORD and, taking some of all the clean animals and clean birds, he sacrificed burnt offerings on it. The LORD smelled the pleasing aroma and said in his heart: 'Never again will I curse the ground because of man, even though every inclination of his heart is evil from childhood. And never again will I destroy all living creatures, as I have done'" (Gen. 8:20–21).

Finally, upon observing the sacrifice offered by Utnapishtim, the great goddess removed her lapis and, holding it high, declared, "'Ye gods here, as surely as this lapis around my neck I shall not forget, I shall be mindful of these days, forgetting them never" (*Epic of Gilgamesh*). Therefore, the great goddess's beautiful lapis of jewels stood as a sign that she would never forget the destruction caused by the Flood.

Correspondingly, God, as a sign of His covenant with Noah, that He would never again destroy the world with a flood, set His rainbow in the sky. "Whenever I bring clouds over the earth and the rainbow appears in the clouds, I will remember my covenant between me and you and all living creatures of every kind. Never again will the waters become a flood to destroy all life" (Gen. 9:14–15). Therefore, the great goddess of the *Epic of Gilgamesh*'s lapis and God's rainbow, were parallels of one another, serving the same purpose.

In conclusion, both the *Epic of Gilgamesh* and Genesis contain the story of a worldwide Flood, sent from heaven to decimate all of the earth. However, one man, the hero of the story, is spared, that he might preserve life on earth. Both Utnapishtim and Noah construct arks, in accordance with the orders given to them, and, when the floods come, they are secure inside their vessels. They both offer sacrifices to their respective divinities and are assured by signs that they will never be forgotten by them.

The main contrasts between the narratives lie in the divinities themselves. In the Genesis Flood account, God, in His perfect wisdom, does not decide, but declares, according to His unfaltering plan, that he will wipe out mankind from the face of the earth. When all is completed, He regrets nothing. The gods of the *Epic of Gilgamesh*, however, are discombobulated. They allowed themselves to be swayed against their better judgment by Enlil and, looking back on their destruction, they regret their decision and curse him for persuading them so. In short, the God of the biblical Flood account has everything under control, whereas Utnapishtim's gods are hopelessly confused (Austin Allen).

Assignments

- Warm-up: What do you say to someone who does not believe that there really was a global Flood?
- Students should complete Concept Builder 1-E.
- Essay is due. Students should take the chapter 1 test.

Compare and contrast the *Enuma Elish* and the biblical account of creation (Genesis 1).

	Creation	
	Enuma Elish	**Bible**
Setting	then from Apsu and Tiamat in the waters gods were created, in the waters silt precipitated, Lahmu and Lahumu, were named; they were not yet old not yet grown tall when Anshar and Kishar overtook them both, (i.e., born after) Before a world could be created, gods needed to be created.	1. In the beginning God created the heavens and the earth. 2 Now the earth was formless and empty, darkness was over the surface of the deep, and the Spirit of God was hovering over the waters. 3 And God said, "Let there be light," and there was light. 4 God saw that the light was good, and he separated the light from the darkness. 5 God called the light "day," and the darkness he called "night." And there was evening, and there was morning — the first day. God existed before time itself.
Characters		
Plot		
Diety(ies)		

www.sacred-texts.com/ane/enuma.htm

23

Chapter 2

Worldview Formation and Discernment

First Thoughts If you are a committed Christian believer, you will be challenged to analyze the worldviews of individuals and institutions around you. You are inextricably tied to your culture, but that does not mean you can't be in this culture but not of this culture. Throughout this course and your educational career you will be challenged to analyze the worldviews of many writers. You will be asked to articulate your own worldview and to defend it against all sorts of assaults. William Bradford, for instance, has a worldview that is radically different from many writers you have read and hopefully similar to yours. What is Bradford's worldview? It is obviously Christian theistic. For now, though, it is important that you pause and examine several worldviews that you will encounter in literature and the arts. You will then need to articulate your own worldview.

Chapter Learning Objectives In chapter 2 we will define worldview and write our own. We will use these exercises to prepare us to discern worldviews of world literature selections the rest of the year.

As a result of this chapter study you will be able to . . .

1. Compare the worldviews of each in the following passages.

2. Contrast C.S. Lewis' obvious Christian theistic worldview with the three others.

3. Write a worldview for yourself.

Weekly Essay Options: Begin on page 273 of the Teacher Guide.

Reading ahead: Book of Esther, author unknown; *Papyrus of Ani: Egyptian Book of the Dead* and *Hymn to Osiris Un-Nefer*, author unknown.

 History connections: *World History* chapter 2, "Foundations of Worldviews."

Background

Background What is a "worldview"? A worldview is a way that a person understands, relates to, and responds from a philosophical position that he embraces as his own. Worldview is a framework that ties everything together, that allows us to understand society, the world, and our place in it. A worldview helps us to make the critical decisions which will shape our future. A worldview colors all our decisions and all our artistic creations. In the first *Star Wars* movie (1977), for instance, Luke Skywalker clearly values a Judeo-Christian code of ethics. That does not mean that he is a believing Christian — indeed he is not — but he does uphold and fight for a moral world. Darth Vader, on the other hand, represents chaos and amoral behavior. He does whatever it takes to advance the emperor's agenda, regardless of who he hurts or what rule he breaks. It is important that you articulate your worldview now so that you will be ready to discern other worldviews later.

Assignments

- Warm-up: What is a worldview?
- Students should complete Concept Builder 2-A.
- Students should review the required reading(s) *before* the assigned chapter begins.
- Teachers may want to discuss assigned reading(s) with students.
- Teachers shall assign the required essay. The rest of the essays can be outlined, answered with shorter answers, discussed, or skipped.
- Students will review all readings for chapter 2.

In American culture the concept of "hero" has changed considerably over the last 80 years.

1940s classical/theism

John Wayne: Do the right thing the right way.

↓

1970s "nostalgic" theism

Star Wars: Do the right thing for the downtrodden.

↓

1980s "nostalgic" theism

Clint Eastwood: Do the right thing even if you have to do the wrong thing to get there.

↓

1990s absurdism

Toy Story character: Do the right thing the old-fashioned way — but toys can do it better.

↓

2000 existentialism/romanticism revivalism

Tom Cruise: Doing the right thing is what is right for me.

↓

How will the American hero evolve in the next 20 years?

Two Basic Worldviews

From our study of Greek history we know that there are basically two worldview roots: One originates from Aristotle and argues that the empirical world is primary. Thus, if one wants to advance knowledge one has to learn more about the world. Another root originates with Plato, who argues that the unseen world is primary. In Plato's case, that meant that if one wished to understand the world one studied the gods. In our case, we agree with Plato to the extent that we believe that God — who cannot be seen, measured — is in fact more real than the world.

Both Plato and Aristotle were impacted by Socrates. Socrates was one of the most influential but mysterious figures in Western philosophy. He wrote nothing, yet he had a profound influence on some-one who did: Plato. Plato carefully recorded most of his dialogues. Unlike earlier philosophers, Socrates' main concern was with ethics. There was nothing remotely pragmatic about Socrates, who was the consummate idealist. Until his day, philosophers invested most of their time explaining the natural world. In fact, the natural world often intruded into the abstract world of ideas and reality. Socrates kept both worlds completely separate. To Socrates, the natural laws governing the rotation of the earth were merely uninteresting speculation of no earthly good. Socrates was more interested in such meaty concepts as "virtue" and "justice." Taking issue with the Sophists, Socrates believed that ethics, specifically virtue, must be learned and practiced like any trade. One was not born virtuous; one developed virtue as he would a good habit. It could be practiced only by experts. There was, then, nothing pragmatic about the pursuit of virtue. It was systematic; it was intentional. Virtue was acquired and maintained by open and free dialogue. For the first time, the importance of human language was advanced by a philosopher

"Aristotle" by Francesco Hayez, 1811 (PD-Art).

(to reappear at the end of the 20th century in postmodern philosophy).

There was no more important philosopher in Western culture than Socrates' disciple, Plato. Plato, like Socrates, regarded ethics as the highest branch of knowledge. Plato stressed the intellectual basis of virtue, identifying virtue with wisdom. Plato believed that the world was made of *forms* (such as a rock) and *ideas* (such as virtue). The ability of human beings to appreciate forms made a person virtuous. Knowledge came from the gods; opinion was from man. Virtuous activity, then, was dependent upon knowledge of the forms.

To Plato, knowledge and virtue were inseparable. To Aristotle, they were unconnected. Aristotle was not on a search for absolute truth. He was not even certain it existed. Truth, beauty, and goodness were to be observed and quantified from human behavior and the senses, but they were not the legal tender of the land. Goodness in particular was not an absolute and in Aristotle's opinion it was much abused. Goodness was an average between two absolutes. Aristotle said that mankind should strike a balance between passion and temperance, between extremes of all sorts. He said that good people should seek the "Golden Mean," defined as a course of life that was never extreme. Finally, while Plato argued that reality lay in knowledge of the gods, Aristotle argued that reality lay in empirical, measurable knowledge. To Aristotle, reality was tied to purpose and to action. For these reasons, Aristotle, became known as the father of modern science. Aristotle's most enduring impact occurred in the area of metaphysics — philosophical speculation about the nature, substance, and structure of reality. It is not physics — concerned with the visible or natural world. Metaphysics is concerned with explaining the non-physical world. Aristotle then advanced the discussion about God, the human soul, and the nature of space and time. What makes this particularly interesting is Aristotle's penchant for delving into the metaphysical by talking about the gods in human terms. Aristotle said, "All men by nature desire to know" and it is by the senses that the gods were known — or not. Faith had nothing to do with it. In other words, Aristotle, for the first time, discussed the gods as if they were quantified entities. He spoke about them as if they were not present. The Hebrews had done this earlier (Genesis 3) but Aristotle was probably not aware of Moses' text. While some Christian thinkers such as Augustine and Aquinas employed Aristotelian logic in their discussions about God, they never speculated about His existence as Aristotle did. They only used Aristotle's techniques to understand more about Him.

Assignments

- Warm-up: Contrast the two basic worldviews that Aristotle and Plato champion.
- Students should complete Concept Builder 2-B.
- Students should review reading(s) from next chapter.
- Students should outline essays due at the end of the week.
- Per teacher instructions, students may answer orally, in a group setting, some of the essays that are not assigned as the formal essay.

Using the diagram below, show how you have matured as a person.

Being homeschooled

How you have matured as a person.

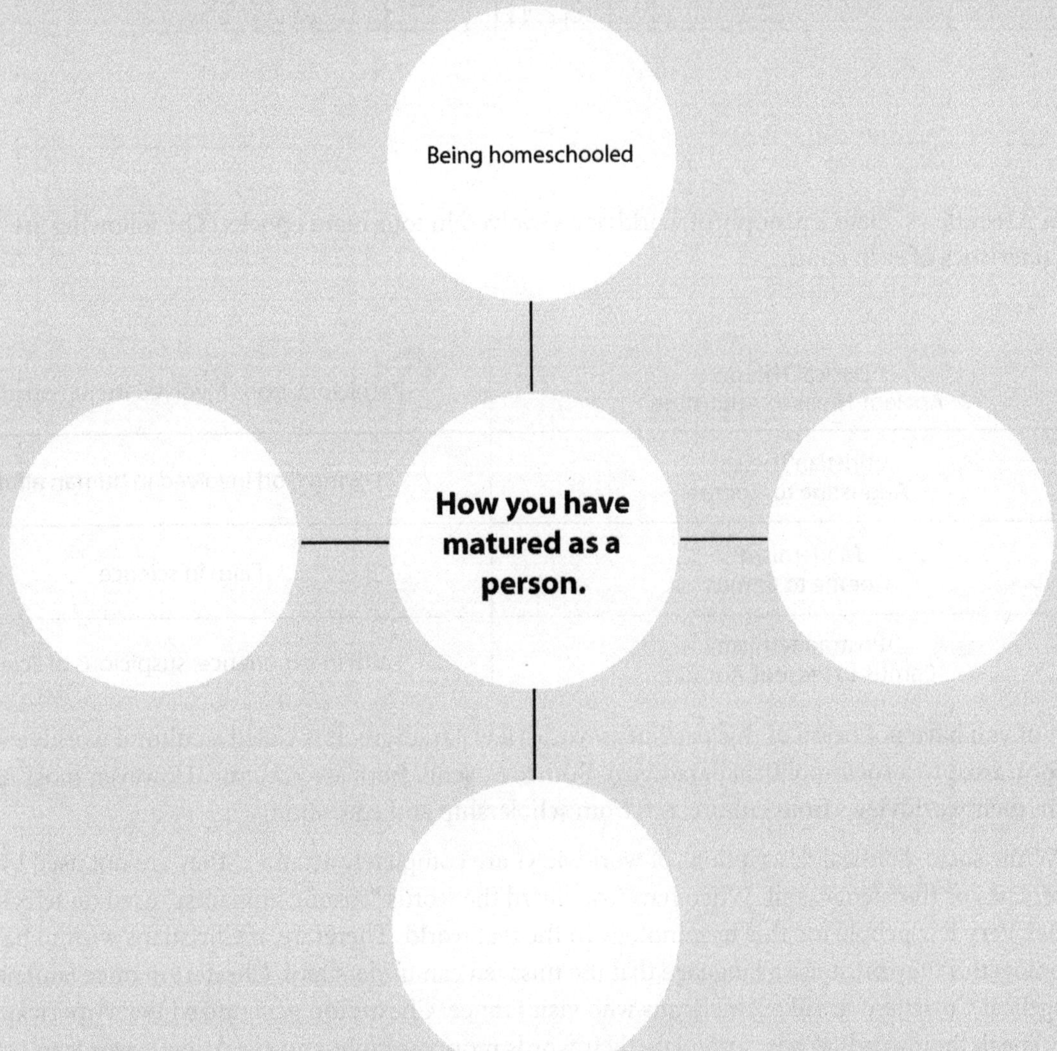

Four Main Epochs

From Aristotle vs. Plato a panoply of worldviews evolved in four main epochs. The following are characteristics of each epoch:

Classical Theism: Ancient Times to Augustine	Pernicious gods involved in human affairs
Christian Theism: Augustine to Goethe	Loving God involved in human affairs
Modernism: Goethe to Camus	Faith in science
Postmodernism: Camus to Present Authors	Faith in experience; suspicious of science

Most of you have not heard of this particular worldview paradigm. It is called a cultural worldview paradigm (as contrasted to a socio-political paradigm). Both are useful. Both are accurate. However, most Americans obtain their worldviews from culture, not from scholarship and education.

While socio-political descriptions of worldviews are completely accurate, they are not used by American universities or the media at all. When have you heard the words "cosmic humanist" used on television? In a movie? Very few people use this terminology in the real world. Therefore, if Christians wish to be involved in apologetics they must use a language that the unsaved can understand. Chesterton once lamented that evangelical Christians are like Americans who visit France. Chesterton generalized that Americans, by and large, speak their words slower, articulate their words more carefully, and speak fewer words to complete a thought. However, what they should do, Chesterton argues, is to speak French in France! If we believers want the world to hear us we need to speak their language.

Assignments

- Warm-up: Theism dominated most of world history. Why?
- Students should complete Concept Builder 2-C.
- Students should write rough draft of assigned essay.
- The teacher may correct rough draft.

What is the worldview of these artistic pieces? Match the appropriate letter with each picture.

1. ___		A. Romanticism: Celebrates nature and "natural things."
2. ___		B. Theism: Art implies that there is a higher power, usually an altruistic higher power.
3. ___		C. Existentialism: Celebrates feelings and thoughts. Abstract art based on real animals.
4. ___		D. Romanticism: Celebrates nature and "natural things."

All art is from www.clipart.com.

Seven Basic Worldviews

The four epochs manifested into the seven basic worldviews:

1. Theism: Christian theism advances a worldview that there is an omnipotent God who has authored an inspired, authoritative work called the Bible, upon whose precepts mankind should base its society.

2. Deism: Deism advances a worldview that accepts the notion that there is an authoritative, inspired source from which mankind should base its society (i.e., the Bible). Likewise, the deist is certain that there was once an omnipotent God. However, once the world was created, that same omnipotent God chose to absent himself from His creation. The world, then, is like a clock. It was once created by an intelligent process. However, now the Creator is absent, leaving mankind on its own to figure out how the clock works and go on living.

3. Romanticism: A natural companion to deism was rationalism. Rationalism (e.g., John Locke's philosophy) invited the deist to see mankind as a "chalkboard" on which was written experience that ultimately created a personality. Thus, rationalists/deists were fond of speaking of "unalienable right" or "common sense." The romantic (in America the romantic would be called "the transcendentalist") took issue with deism and theism. To the romantic, nature was god. Nature — an undefined indigenous, omnipotent presence — was very good. Original sin was man's separation from nature. In fact, the degree to which mankind returned to nature would determine his goodness and effectiveness. Thus, a man like Henry David Thoreau lived a year on Walden Pond so that he could find his God. In *The Deerslayer*, by James Fenimore Cooper, the protagonist is safe while he is on a lake separated from evil mankind. Only when he participates in human society is he in trouble. The romantic was naturally suspicious of theism because theism appeared to be dogmatic and close-minded. The romantics had confessions, but they had no dogma. Deism also bothered the romantics. Romanticism emphasized the subjective; deism emphasized the objective. In the romantic novel *Frankenstein*, the deist/rationalist Dr. Frankenstein creates a monster. Dr. Frankenstein, with disastrous results, turns his back on the subjective and tries to use science to create life.

4. Naturalism: Naturalism was inclined to agree with romanticism's criticism of theism and deism, but did not believe in a benevolent nature. In fact, nature, to the naturalist, was malevolent, mischievous, and unpredictable. Mankind, as it were, lost control of the universe and the person who had control did not really care much for his creation. Theism, of course, was absurd. How could any sane person who experienced World War I believe in a loving, living God? Deism was equally wrong.

God was not absent — He was present in an unpredictable, at times evil, way. Romanticism was on the right track, but terribly naive. God and His creation were certainly not "good" in any sense of the word. Nature was evil. Naturalism embraced a concept of fate similar to that held by the Greeks. In Homer's *The Iliad*, for instance, the characters were subject to uncontrolled fate and pernicious gods and goddesses who inflicted terrible and good things on mankind with no apparent design or reason. No, to the naturalist, God was at best absent or wimpish; at worst, He was malevolent.

5. Realism: Realism was philosophically akin to naturalism. In a sense, naturalism was a natural companion to realism. Realism was different from naturalism in degree, not in substance. Realism argued that if people were honest they would admit that God was not present at all. If there was anything worth embracing, it was reality. Realism advanced an in-your-face view of life. Realists prided themselves in "telling it like it is." They entered the cosmic arena and let the chips fall where they may. They shared the same criticisms of views that the naturalists held.

6. Absurdism: Absurdism certainly believed that realism was on track. Where realism erred, however, was its propensity to see meaning in life. Mind you, the meaning was tied to things one could see and feel — not in things that were abstract or immutable — but the realist still sought some meaning in this life. The absurdist abandoned all hope of finding meaning in life and embraced a sort of nihilism. The absurdist was convinced that everything was meaningless and absurd. The subjectivity of a romantic was appealing to the absurd. However, even that implied that something was transcendent — a desire — and the absurdist would have nothing to do with that. Billy Pilgrim, a protagonist in one of the absurdist Kurt Vonnegut Jr.'s novels, became "unhinged from time" and "wandered around in the cosmos." Things without meaning happened to him whose life had no meaning. Everything was absurd.

7. Existentialism: Existentialism stepped outside the debate of meaning altogether. Existentialists argued that the quest was futile. The only thing that mattered was subjective feeling. "Experience" was a god at whose feet the existentialist worshiped. Romanticism was on the right track in that it invited mankind to explore subjectivity. Where it erred was when it refused to give up the deity. Naturalism was an anomaly. It was too busy arguing with the cosmos to see that reality was in human desire not in providence. The degree to which mankind was to discover and experience these desires determined the degree to which people participated in the divine.

Assignments

- Warm-up: Compare naturalism to realism.
- Students should complete Concept Builder 2-D.
- Students will re-write corrected copies of essay due tomorrow.

What is the
priority of the
spiritual world?

+

What is the essen-
tial uniqueness of
mankind? → **My Worldview**

+

What is the
objective character
of truth and
goodness?

Student Essay

In 843 AD, a statement called the Synodikon was written, "As the prophets beheld, as the Apostles have taught . . . as the Church has received . . . as the teachers have dogmatized . . . as the Universe has agreed . . . as Grace has shown forth . . . as Truth has revealed . . . as falsehood has been dissolved . . . as Wisdom has presented . . . as Christ Awarded . . . thus we declare . . . thus we assert . . . thus we preach Christ our true God, and honor as Saints in words, in writings, in thoughts, in sacrifices, in churches, in Holy Icons; on the one hand worshipping and reverencing Christ as God and Lord; and on the other hand honoring as true servants of the same Lord of all and accordingly offering them veneration. This is the Faith of the Apostles, this is the Faith of the Fathers, this is the Faith of the Orthodox, this is the Faith which has established the Universe." This statement, which is still read during every Lent, is an ongoing call to all Orthodox Christians — a call to take the gift, orthodoxy, which they have been so unworthily bestowed with, and live the worldview of the church, to change and establish the universe. Not solely to believe in it, but to live it out, "from this day, from this hour, and from this minute" (St. Herman of Alaska).

One of the most important things that the church has given is to strive for obedience. One is offered the saint stories, and the traditions of holy obedience as real and tangible things he can learn and grow from. Also given us are the people around us that we must humble ourselves to obey, not out of some ridiculous compromise hoping one will get something in return, but out of pure love for them, and desire to obey. In the church, lay people are given spiritual fathers (priests) whom they are expected to obey. The priests are in obedience to their bishops, who are in obedience to God and the saints. Thus, the tradition and faith of the Apostles has survived these many centuries because of the faithful Orthodox and their pure obedience. Tito Collinder wrote in *The Way of the Ascetics*, "Obedience breaks down many barriers. You achieve freedom and peace as your heart practices non-resistance. You show obedience, and thorny hedges give way before you. Then love has open space in which to move about. By obedience you crush your pride, your desire to contradict, your self-wisdom and stubbornness that imprison you within a hard shell. Inside that shell you cannot meet the God of love and freedom." (Tito Collinder, *The Way of the Ascetics*, Crestwood, NY: St. Vladimirs Seminary, 1985). This is the obedience that one strives for.

Three of the most common "pillars" that orthodoxy gives to the church are prayer, fasting, and almsgiving. Archbishop Barlaam says about prayer, "Each of us, according to God's mercy, has or should have his own church — the heart; go in there and pray, as much as you have strength." (orthodoxinfo. com/praxis/pr_prayer.aspx). Prayer, for an Orthodox Christian, isn't something that is taken lightly; instead it is a beautiful mystery of the church, that when used in humility will sanctify and cause the church to grow.

Fasting is a very literal way of living the belief of the Orthodox. Going back to the Garden of Eden, one finds that the very first commandment God gave to Adam was to fast, "And the LORD God commanded the man, 'You are free to eat from any tree in the garden; but you must not eat from the tree of the knowledge of good and evil, for when you eat of it you will surely die' " (Gen. 2:16–17). St. Basil tells the church that, "Because we did not fast, we were chased out of Paradise; let us fast now, so that someday we return there." (www.orthodoxresearch institute.org/articles/liturgics/savich _meaning _of_fasting.htm). So one fasts, to overcome temptation, and to control himself.

The last of these three "pillars" is almsgiving. Almsgiving is important because it is a way to give of ourselves, in pure love to others. It is also important because that is how one loves and serves God. St. John Chrysostom says about almsgiving, "Do you wish to honor the Body of the Savior? Do not despise it when it is naked. Do not honor it in church with silk vestments while outside it is naked and numb with cold. He who said, 'This is my body,' and made it so by his word, is the same who said, 'You saw me hungry and you gave me no food. As you did it not to the least of these, you did it not to me.' Honor him then by sharing your property with the poor. For what God needs is not golden chalices but golden souls" (John Chrysostom, *On the Gospel of St. Matthew*, 50, iii, p. 58, 508; www.cornellocf. org/PrayerFastingAlmsgiving.dsp).

The life of an Orthodox Christian is lived out and made intimate with Christ by the seven sacraments. These sacraments allow him to search deep into his heart and find God. The seven sacraments of the Church are said to be, "the channels by which we receive the grace and blessings of the Holy Spirit" (www.copticchurch.net/topics/thecopticchurch/ sacraments/index.html). They are baptism, chrismation, the eucharist, confession, holy unction, marriage, and ordination. In baptism and chrismation, one is clothed with "a garment of light," and is given a guardian angel to walk with him throughout his life.

The high point of liturgy and in some senses the life of an Orthodox Christian is the eucharist. When one receives the eucharist, he comes to the altar, and face to face with God, receives Him into his very being. "The Holy Eucharist is called the 'sacrament of sacraments' in the Orthodox tradition. It is also called the 'sacrament of the Church.' The eucharist is the center of the Church's life. Everything in the Church leads to the Eucharist, and all things flow from it. It is the completion of all of the Church's sacraments — the source and the goal of all of the Church's doctrines and institutions" (oca.org/ orthodoxy/the-orthodox-faith/worship/the-sacraments/holy-eucharist). The eucharist is how the Orthodox Christian in fear and trembling, allows himself to be joined to Christ.

The sacraments of confession and holy unction are mysteries of healing, by which one finds himself spiritually renewed. These mysteries are so important because daily we find ourselves torn down by sin, and needing God's mercy, the fullness of which is found in confession. Bishop Job said about the sacrament of confession, "By our Baptism and Chrismation, we, the Church, are commanded to go out and to change the world in the same spirit as that of the Holy Apostles. . . . The transfiguration of the world is only possible through repentance, and repentance must begin within the Church" (www. orthodoxresearchinstitute.org/articles/liturgics/ job_confession.htm). This powerful statement goes back to the Synodikon, "the Faith which has established the universe."

Last Spring, on the first Sunday of Lent, as the church was commemorating the restoring of icons into the Orthodox Church in 843, the congregation had joy written all over their faces. As they recited in unison, "I believe in one God the father almighty, maker of heaven and earth . . ." and then powerfully proclaimed the Synodikon, it was plain that the church longed to answer the call to strive to live out with they believed, to be God's "golden souls." Assuredly they would fall, but even more undoubtedly they would find the strength to rise, repent, partake, and be joined to Christ continually through the grace's God had given to them. And through prayer and humility, they would stay on the narrow path that unfailingly has, is, and will, "establish the universe." (Anna Grace)

Assignments

- Warm-up: Compare this personal worldview, written by a student who offers her own personal religious views, to your worldview.

- Students should complete Concept Builder 2-E.

- Essay is due. Students should take the chapter 2 test.

Match the following quotes from *Star Wars* (6 movies) with worldviews. You will be using one answer twice.

____	**1**	"Follow your feelings, Luke, follow your feelings!" —Obi-Wan.
____	**2**	Anakin, in a vulnerable moment with Padme, says that he loves her. She says, "Jedi should not love anyone."
____	**3**	When Padme dies she says, "There is still good in Anakin."
____	**4**	"Kid, I've flown from one side of this galaxy to the other. I've seen a lot of strange stuff, but I've never seen anything to make me believe that there's one all-powerful Force controlling everything." —Han Solo
____	**5**	In *A New Hope*, Obi-Wan Kenobi describes the Force as "an energy field created by all living things. It surrounds and penetrates us. It binds the galaxy together." "A Jedi's strength flows from the Force," Yoda teaches.

A	Romanticism: To the romantic, nature was God.
B	Realism: Realism argued that if people were honest, they would admit that God was not present at all.
C	Existentialism: Existentialism stepped outside the debate of meaning altogether. Existentialists argued that the quest was futile. The only thing that mattered was subjective feeling.
D	Theism: Theism advances a worldview that there is a higher power upon whose precepts mankind should base its society.

Chapter 3

(3000 B.C.–300 B.C.)
Sumerian, Egyptian, and Hebrew Literature (Part 2)

First Thoughts Another Mesopotamian literary piece is the biblical Book of Esther. The authorship of Esther is unknown. It must have been written after the death of Ahasuerus (the Xerxes of the Greeks), which took place in 465 B.C. The writer was a contemporary with Mordecai and Esther and intimate with both. Hence, we may conclude that the book was written probably about 444 to 434 B.C., and that the author was one of the Jews of the Babylonian captivity. This book is more purely historical than any other book of Scripture, and it is remarkable that the name of God does not occur in it. Nonetheless, it is an incredibly powerful theocentric testimony to God's faithfulness.

Chapter Learning Objectives In chapter 3 we examine the biblical story of Esther and then we go almost to the other end of the spectrum: we study Egyptian literature.

As a result of this chapter study you will be able to . . .

1. Discuss the themes in Esther.

2. Contrast the way the Egyptians characterize their gods with the way the Hebrews characterize their God (i.e., the one true God!).

3. Discuss the different characters in Esther.

Weekly Essay Options: Begin on page 273 of the Teacher Guide.

Reading ahead: Book of Esther, author unknown; *Papyrus of Ani: Egyptian Book of the Dead* and *Hymn to Osiris Un-Nefer*, author unknown.

 History connections: *World History* chapter 3, "The Jewish Exile."

Handel

Esther

Esther is an oratorio (a musical composition for voices and instruments that has a religious theme, often telling a sacred story but not using costumes, scenery, or dramatic staging — Handel's "Messiah" is an example of this genre) by George Frideric Handel. The work was originally composed in about 1718, but was heavily revised into a full oratorio in 1732.

He heals the broken Hearted
He binds their wounds
He is Love

He finds those forgotten
Those have been abused
He is Love

He knows your name

[Chorus]

A father to the fatherless
A healer of the brokeness you make
Beauty from the ashes

A helper to the helpless
A fighter for the hopeless you Love
Those who are alone
Those who are alone
[echoes Those who are alone]

[Second Verse]
He comforts the lonely
He hears their Cry
He is Love

He holds the children
Through out the night
He is Love

He knows your name

[Chorus]

A father to the fatherless
A healer of the brokeness you make
Beauty from the ashes

A helper to the helpless
A fighter for the hopeless you love
Those who are alone

[Bridge]

Gives us your Heart Lord help us
Love the unseen
And give us your Eyes Lord help us
Love those in need

[Chorus]

You're a father of the fatherless
A healer of the brokeness you make
Beauty from the ashes

You're a helper to the helpless
A fighter for the hopeless you love
Those who are alone
Those who are alone

He knows your name
[Repeat 2x]

Assignments

- Warm-up: What are your favorite lines in this oratorio?

- Students should complete Concept Builder 3-A.

- Students should review the required reading(s) *before* the assigned chapter begins.

- Teachers may want to discuss assigned reading(s) with students.

- Teachers shall assign the required essay. The rest of the essays can be outlined, answered with shorter answers, discussed, or skipped.

- Students will review all readings for chapter 3.

Read this excerpt from the Book of Esther, and respond to the following:

This is what happened during the time of Xerxes, the Xerxes who ruled over 127 provinces stretching from India to Cush: At that time King Xerxes reigned from his royal throne in the citadel of Susa, and in the third year of his reign he gave a. banquet for all his nobles and officials. The military leaders of Persia and Media, the princes, and the nobles of the provinces were present.

For a full 180 days he displayed the vast wealth of his kingdom and the splendor and glory of his majesty. When these days were over, the king gave a banquet, lasting seven days, in the enclosed garden of the king's palace, for all the people from the least to the greatest, who were in the citadel of Susa. The garden had hangings of white and blue linen, fastened with cords of white linen and purple material to silver rings on marble pillars. There were couches of gold and silver on a mosaic pavement of porphyry, marble, mother-of-pearl and other costly stones. Wine was served in goblets of gold, each one different from the other, and the royal wine was abundant, in keeping with the king's liberality. By the king's command each guest was allowed to drink in his own way, for the king instructed all the wine stewards to serve each man what he wished.

Queen Vashti also gave a banquet for the women in the royal palace of King Xerxes.

On the seventh day, when King Xerxes was in high spirits from wine, he commanded the seven eunuchs who served him — Mehuman, Biztha, Harbona, Bigtha, Abagtha, Zethar and Carcas- to bring before him Queen Vashti, wearing her royal crown, in order to display her beauty to the people and nobles, for she was lovely to look at. But when the attendants delivered the king's command, Queen Vashti refused to come. Then the king became furious and burned with anger.

Since it was customary for the king to consult experts in matters of law and justice, he spoke with the wise men who understood the times and were closest to the king — Carshena, Shethar, Admatha, Tarshish, Meres, Marsena and Memucan, the seven nobles of Persia and Media who had special access to the king and were highest in the kingdom.

"According to law, what must be done to Queen Vashti?" he asked. "She has not obeyed the command of King Xerxes that the eunuchs have taken to her."

Then Memucan replied in the presence of the king and the nobles, "Queen Vashti has done wrong, not only against the king but also against all the nobles and the peoples of all the provinces of King Xerxes. For the queen's conduct will become known to all the women, and so they will despise their husbands and say, 'King Xerxes commanded Queen Vashti to be brought before him, but she would not come.' This very day the Persian and Median women of the nobility who have heard about the queen's conduct will respond to all the king's nobles in the same way. There will be no end of disrespect and discord.

"Therefore, if it pleases the king, let him issue a royal decree and let it be written in the laws of Persia and Media, which cannot be repealed, that Vashti is never again to enter the presence of King Xerxes. Also let the king give her royal position to someone else who is better than she. Then when the king's edict is proclaimed throughout all his vast realm, all the women will respect their husbands, from the least to the greatest." The king and his nobles were pleased with this advice, so the king did as Memucan proposed. He sent dispatches to all parts of the kingdom, to each province in its own script and to each people in its own language, proclaiming in each people's tongue that every man should be ruler over his own household.

Why did the author of Esther begin his story by introducing Xerxes?

Vashti is a perfect foil. Her only purpose is to develop King Xerxes. What is the author trying to tell us about King Xerxes?

Predict what will happen to Queen Vashti if she does not obey her husband.

The author is writing in omniscient narration — a narrative technique that allows the author to tell what all the characters are thinking. What advantages does this offer the author?

This first chapter advances the action and introduces most of the principal characters. Is it effective?

The Perfect Short Story

"For if you remain silent at this time, relief and deliverance for the Jews will arise from another place, but you and your father's family will perish. And who knows but that you have come to royal position for such a time as this?" (Esther 4:14). The Book of Esther is the quintessential short story. The setting is rich, the characters are few and powerful, the plot is quick and simple, and the theme is compelling.

First, the Book of Esther is set in the bustling capital of the Persian Empire, Susa. The King Ahasuerus has thrown a large party for his people. Taxes have been lifted, gifts have been given, wine flows without limit:

> There were white cotton curtains and violet hangings fastened with cords of fine linen and purple to silver rods and marble pillars, and also couches of gold and silver on a mosaic pavement of porphyry, marble, mother-of-pearl and precious stones. Drinks were served in golden vessels, vessels of different kinds, and the royal wine was lavished according to the bounty of the king. And drinking was according to this edict: "There is no compulsion." For the king had given orders to all the staff of his palace to do as each man desired (Esther 1:6–8; ESV).

The setting of the Book of Esther is one of luxury and wealth. The author of the Book of Esther lavishes description upon the reader, detailing all that was luxurious, unique, and rich. For Esther to be a successful short story, the reader must recognize that the setting is a vital catalyst for the story to occur — that it could not happen elsewhere. The reader obtains a vivid picture of life in Susa, creating the perfect backdrop for the story of a young Jewish girl,

taken from her humble home to stand before the king — and save a people.

Second, the main characters of the Book of Esther are few and powerful. First, there is the protagonist, Esther. "He was bringing up Hadassah, that is Esther, the daughter of his uncle, for she had neither father nor mother. The young woman had a beautiful figure and was lovely to look at, and when her father and her mother died, Mordecai took her as his own daughter" (Esther 2:7; ESV).

Next, there is her husband, Ahasuerus. Ahasuerus was a powerful king of the Persians, sometimes known as Xerxes the 1st. "Now in the days of Ahasuerus, the Ahasuerus who reigned from India to Ethiopia over 127 provinces, in those days when King Ahasuerus sat on his royal throne in Susa . . ." (Esther 1:1–2; ESV).

Third, there is Mordecai, Esther's uncle, a Godly Jew. "Now there was a Jew in Susa the citadel whose name was Mordecai, the son of Jair, son of Shimei, son of Kish, a Benjaminite, who had been carried away from Jerusalem among the captives carried away with Jeconiah king of Judah, whom Nebuchadnezzar king of Babylon had carried away" (Esther 2:5–6; ESV).

Finally, there is Haman, the villain: "After these things King Ahasuerus promoted Haman the Agagite, the son of Hammedatha, and advanced him and set his throne above all the officials who were with him" (Esther 3:1; ESV).

For the characters in a short story to be effective, they must be unique, and there must be a limited amount. The reader must be able to feel acquainted with all the characters — to understand them well enough to make the story successful. The characters in the Book of Esther are perfectly poised to carry out the book's powerful plot.

The Book of Esther has a simple plot, and compelling theme. The rising action starts when Esther is taken from her humble home in a province, and brought before the king. She marries him, and becomes a powerful queen. The climax occurs when Esther is informed of a plot by Haman to eradicate Mordecai and the Jews. She takes her life in her hands to stand before the king, who grants her mercy. The dénouement details how the king elevates Esther and Mordecai above all in the land, kills Haman, and saves the Jews. The action moves quickly in Esther, which is vital to the success of a short story. From the rising action to the dénoue-ment, the reader must be constantly wondering what will occur next.

Esther's theme is also compelling. It details courage at great risk of life. The theme of Esther is an inspiration to the reader, exhorting them to show courage in their day-to-day life. For a short story to be successful, it must have a compelling theme.

This theme must tie all the elements of the short story together — the setting, the characters, and the plot. It must be constantly demonstrated throughout all these elements. Esther shows courage in her setting by having the will to rise from her humble beginnings to queen of a large nation. Esther shows courage in the characterization by obeying her uncle and appealing to a temperamental king to save the nation from a cruel villain. Esther shows courage in the plot by taking action quickly to save her people. The Book of Esther truly is the quintessential short story. The setting is rich, the characters are few and powerful, the plot is quick and simple, and the theme is compelling (Alouette).

Assignments

- Warm-up: Why is this such a perfect short story?
- Students should complete Concept Builder 3-B.
- Students should review reading(s) from next chapter.
- Students should outline essays due at the end of the week.
- Per teacher instructions, students may answer orally, in a group setting, some of the essays that are not assigned as the formal essay.

Match the type of literature with the biblical example.

CONCEPT BUILDER 3-B
Types of Biblical Literature

Types of Literature		Biblical Example
1. ____	The song: Melodious verse meant to be sung.	A. Therefore, I urge you, brothers, in view of God's mercy, to offer your bodies as living sacrifices, holy and pleasing to God — this is your spiritual act of worship. Do not conform any longer to the pattern of this world, but be transformed by the renewing of your mind. Then you will be able to test and approve what God's will is — his good, pleasing and perfect will (Romans 12:1–2).
2. ____	Epistolary literature: A letter or epistle.	B. "When the princes in Israel take the lead, when the people willingly offer themselves — praise the LORD! "Hear this, you kings! Listen, you rulers! I will sing to the LORD, I will sing; I will make music to the LORD, the God of Israel. "O LORD, when you went out from Seir, when you marched from the land of Edom, the earth shook, the heavens poured, the clouds poured down water. The mountains quaked before the LORD, the One of Sinai, before the LORD, the God of Israel (Judges 5:2–5).
3. ____	The ode: An ode is a lyrical verse written in praise of someone or something which captures the poet's interest or serves as an inspiration for the ode.	C. I waited patiently for the LORD; he turned to me and heard my cry. He lifted me out of the slimy pit, out of the mud and mire; he set my feet on a rock and gave me a firm place to stand. He put a new song in my mouth, a hymn of praise to our God. Many will see and fear and put their trust in the LORD (Psalm 40:1–3).

Jewish Exile

In the Book of 2 Kings, Isaiah prophesied to Hezekiah near the end of his reign, "Hear the word of the LORD: The time will surely come when everything in your palace, and all that your fathers have stored up until this day, will be carried off to Babylon. Nothing will be left, says the LORD. And some of your descendants, your own flesh and blood, that will be born to you, will be taken away, and they will become eunuchs in the palace of the king of Babylon" (2 Kings 20:16–18). This prophecy was fulfilled in 597 B.C. when Nebuchadnezzar appeared before the walls of Jerusalem with his army for the purpose of punishing Josiah's son Jehoiakim because he had renounced his allegiance to Babylonia. After a short defense, Jehoiakim surrendered to the leaders of the Babylonian army, and Nebuchadnezzar ordered him, with the most distinguished men of the land and the most valuable treasures of the Temple and the palace, to be sent to Babylonia. The period of history that followed is known as the Babylonian Exile.

During the time of the exile, there were several prophets who ministered to the Jewish people. These were Daniel, Ezekiel, Jeremiah (who was in Egypt during the exile), and Ezra near the end of the exile. The Book of Daniel tells of the time during the exile. Stories in Daniel, like Daniel in the Lion's den and Shadrach, Meshach, and Abednego (the three men who survived the furnace), were meant to inspire the Jews to remain true to their faith.

For the Jewish people, life on the outside was not bad. They were permitted to "till the soil, to cultivate the family life, and, by thrift and diligence, to accumulate wealth. Perhaps, being permitted to administer their internal affairs through their elders, they were allowed the undisturbed exercise of their religion; and nowhere were there bloody persecutions heard" (www.Jewishencyclopedia.com). But figuratively speaking, they were imprisoned, and they knew it. The prophets during the exile wrote of the deep humiliation to which God had subjected His people by consigning them to ruin. They bewailed the circumstances that even the religious leaders, the priests, and the prophets themselves, had been delivered up to the profanation of a pagan people, instead of being permitted to serve the Lord in His holy Temple. They longed to return to their promised land. Psalm 137 speaks of their longing, "By the rivers of Babylon, we sat and wept when we remembered Zion" (Ps. 137:1).

But in 586 B.C. the hopes of the Jews were shattered when Nebuchadnezzar ordered the Temple, the royal palace, and all dwellings in the city of Jerusalem be set on fire, and the surviving inhabitants be taken captive to Babylon. They were then compelled to listen to the voice of the prophet Jeremiah: "Build houses and settle down; plant gardens and eat what they produce. Marry and have sons and daughters; find wives for your sons and give your daughters in marriage, so that they too may have sons and daughters. Increase in number there; do not decrease. Also seek the peace and prosperity of the city to which I have carried you into exile. Pray to the LORD for it, because if it prospers, you too will prosper" (Jer. 29:5–7). (Anna Grace)

Assignments

- Warm-up: When Nehemiah took his community home to Jerusalem, the majority of Jewish people opted to stay in Persia. Why?
- Students should complete Concept Builder 3-C.
- Students should write rough draft of assigned essay.
- The teacher may correct rough draft.

The epic is a long, narrative poem on a somber, important subject, related in a grandiose style where the hero/heroine project superhuman qualities to solve a great crisis. Match the following components of an epic with the following diagram.

A	Characterization	The heroes/heroines are figures of great national importance, usually extraordinary persons in their culture.
B	Setting	The setting is vast in scope. The characters are shaped by and shape the culture in which they live.
C	Plot	There is always a serious crisis that the heroes/heroines solve.
D	Tone	Supernatural forces interest themselves in the action and intervene at times.

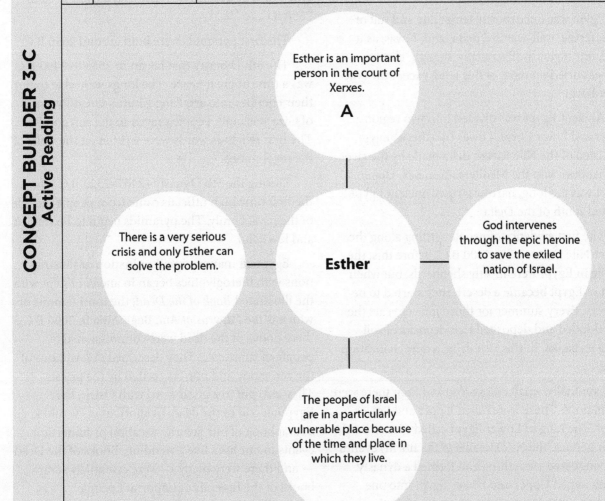

Esther is an important person in the court of Xerxes.
A

There is a very serious crisis and only Esther can solve the problem.

Esther

God intervenes through the epic heroine to save the exiled nation of Israel.

The people of Israel are in a particularly vulnerable place because of the time and place in which they live.

Egypt

Background Egypt is located at the crossroads of the African and Asian continents. Thus, from the beginning, it has important strategic importance to both continents. In ancient times, the boundaries of Egypt were the Mediterranean Sea to the north and Aswan to the south. Its eastern and western boundaries were deserts. The Nile River, the most important geographic feature in the area, runs the length of the country, flowing from south to north.

Egypt was once mostly temperate and full of large, fertile, well-watered delta land. It was, as it were, one big oasis. Eventually, though, climate changes dried up most of this land, except the Nile River basin.

Ancient Egypt was divided into two regions: upper and lower Egypt. Lower (northern) Egypt consisted of the Nile River's delta made by the river as it empties into the Mediterranean Sea. Upper Egypt was the long, narrow strip of ancient Egypt located south of the Delta.

The first evidence of people settling along the Lower Nile Delta was in 5000 B.C. Before this, the people in Egypt were mostly shepherds, but when most of Egypt became a desert, they started to be farmers. Every summer for thousands of years the Nile flooded and deposited rich deposits of soil along its banks. In this rich delta, a new civilization arose.

Eventually, small cities arose and then there were two nations. These were called Upper and Lower Egypt. The king of Lower Egypt called Menes (in the south because the Nile streams to the north) eventually conquered everything and formed a dynasty. Menes joined Upper and Lower Egypt into one kingdom with the capitol at Memphis. This was

around 3000 B.C. In this period, too, hieroglyphics — Egyptian writing — was invented and written on papyrus scrolls.

After much rivalry for the throne, Pharoah Hetepsekhemsy won. At this time the pharoahs disagreed over which god, Horus or Seth, was in power. This was finally settled when Khasekhemwy became ruler. He took both titles. Disorder erupted during the end of this dynasty. There was probably a civil war. The Second Dynasty lasted from 2770 to 2650 B.C.

The first pyramids were built around 2650 B.C.

The 4th Dynasty that began in 2550 to 2490 B.C. was a time of great peace. The kings were able to put their energies into art. King Khufu's Great Pyramid of Giza was built. People prayed to the sun god Ra. The first religious words were written on the walls of the royal tombs.

During the 5th Dynasty (2465–2323 B.C.), for the first time high officials came from people outside of the royal family. The pyramids begin to be smaller and less solid.

Egyptian manuscript illumination or illustrations with hieroglyphics began in ancient Egypt with the illustrated *Book of the Dead*, the most famous of which is the *Papyrus of Ani*. Beginning in 2000 B.C., these books of the dead were commissioned by people of substance. They described descriptions of the ceremony and prayers recited by the priests. They also put in a good word with Osiris, the Egyptian god of the dead. In short, as we would keep a scrapbook of our favorite vacation or important events in our lives like a wedding, Books of the Dead — and there were many — were essentially scrapbooks of the funerals of important people.

Assignments

- Warm-up: Why is Egypt a lot more than a bunch of pyramids and mummies?
- Students should complete Concept Builder 3-D.
- Students will re-write corrected copies of essay due tomorrow.

CONCEPT BUILDER 3-D
The Plot

Match the type of literature with the biblical example.

	Short Story Passage	Short Story
1. ___	Then Queen Esther answered, "If I have found favor with you, O king, and if it pleases your majesty, grant me my life — this is my petition. And spare my people — this is my request. For I and my people have been sold for destruction and slaughter and annihilation. If we had merely been sold as male and female slaves, I would have kept quiet, because no such distress would justify disturbing the king." King Xerxes asked Queen Esther, "Who is he? Where is the man who has dared to do such a thing?" Esther said, "The adversary and enemy is this vile Haman." Then Haman was terrified before the king and queen. The king got up in a rage, left his wine and went out into the palace garden. But Haman, realizing that the king had already decided his fate, stayed behind to beg Queen Esther for his life.	A. Inciting incident: where the conflict is first introduced.
2. ___	On the third day, Esther dressed up in her royal clothing and stood in the inner courtyard of the palace facing it. The king was sitting on his royal throne in the royal courtroom, facing its entrance. As soon as the king saw Queen Esther standing in the courtyard, she won his approval. The king extended the golden scepter in his hand toward Esther, and she approached and touched the tip of the scepter.	B. Rising action: plot events that increase the tension leading up to the climax.
3. ___	When Haman saw that Mordecai would not kneel down or pay him honor, he was enraged. Yet having learned who Mordecai's people were, he scorned the idea of killing only Mordecai. Instead Haman looked for a way to destroy all Mordecai's people, the Jews, through-out the whole kingdom of Xerxes.	C. Climax: turning point in the plot.
4. ___	Mordecai left the king's presence wearing royal garments of blue and white, a large crown of gold and a purple robe of fine linen. And the city of Susa held a joyous celebration. For the Jews it was a time of happiness and joy, gladness and honor. In every province and in every city, wherever the edict of the king went, there was joy and gladness among the Jews, with feasting and celebrating. And many people of other nationalities became Jews because fear of the Jews had seized them.	D. Conclusion (or denouement): falling action and resolution.

Papyrus of Ani: Egyptian Book of the Dead
Author Unknown

Translated by E.A. Wallis Budge (eawc.evansville.edu/anthology/ani.htm).

Hymn to Osiris

Homage to thee, Osiris, Lord of eternity, King of the Gods, whose names are manifold, whose forms are holy, thou being of hidden form in the temples, whose Ka is holy. Thou art the governor of Tattu (Busiris), and also the mighty one in Sekhem (Letopolis). Thou art the Lord to whom praises are ascribed in the nome of Ati, thou art the Prince of divine food in Anu. Thou art the Lord who is commemorated in Maati, the Hidden Soul, the Lord of Qerrt (Elephantine), the Ruler supreme in White Wall (Memphis). Thou art the Soul of Ra, his own body, and hast thy place of rest in Henensu (Herakleopolis). Thou art the beneficent one, and art praised in Nart. Thou makest thy soul to be raised up. Thou art the Lord of the Great House in Khemenu (Hermopolis). Thou art the mighty one of victories in Shas-hetep, the Lord of eternity, the Governor of Abydos. The path of his throne is in Ta-tcheser (a part of Abydos). Thy name is established in the mouths of men. Thou art the substance of Two Lands (Egypt). Thou art Tem, the feeder of Kau (Doubles), the Governor of the Companies of the gods. Thou art the beneficent Spirit among the spirits. The god of the Celestial Ocean (Nu) draweth from thee his waters. Thou sendest forth the north wind at eventide, and breath from thy nostrils to the satisfaction of thy heart. Thy heart reneweth its youth, thou producest the. . . . The stars in the celestial heights are obedient unto thee, and the great doors of the sky open themselves before thee. Thou art he to whom praises are ascribed in the southern heaven, and thanks are given for thee in the northern heaven. The imperishable stars are under thy supervision, and the stars which never set are thy thrones. Offerings appear before thee at the decree of Keb. The Companies of the Gods praise thee, and the gods of the Tuat (Other World) smell the earth in paying homage to thee. The uttermost parts of the earth bow before thee, and the limits of the skies entreat thee with supplications when they see thee. The holy ones are overcome before thee, and all Egypt offereth thanksgiving unto thee when it meeteth Thy Majesty. Thou art a shining Spirit-Body, the governor of Spirit-Bodies; permanent is thy rank, established is thy rule. Thou art the well-doing Sekhem (Power) of the Company of the Gods, gracious is thy face, and beloved by him that seeth it. Thy fear is set in all the lands by reason of thy perfect love, and they cry out to thy name making it the first of names, and all people make offerings to thee. Thou art the lord who art commemorated in heaven and upon earth. Many are the cries which are made to thee at the Uak festival, and with one heart and voice Egypt raiseth cries of joy to thee.

Thou art the Great Chief, the first among thy brethren, the Prince of the Company of the Gods, the stablisher of Right and Truth throughout the World, the Son who was set on the great throne of his father Keb. Thou art the beloved of thy mother Nut, the mighty one of valour, who overthrew the Sebau-fiend. Thou didst stand up and smite thine enemy, and set thy fear in thine adversary. Thou dost bring the boundaries of the mountains. Thy heart is fixed, thy legs are set firm. Thou art the heir of Keb and of the sovereignty of the Two Lands (Egypt). He (Keb) hath seen his splendours, he hath decreed for him the guidance of the world by thy hand as long as times endure. Thou hast made this earth with thy hand, and the waters, and the winds, and the vegetation, and all the cattle, and all the feathered fowl, and all the fish, and all the creeping things, and all the wild animals therof. The desert is the lawful possession of the son of Nut. The Two Lands (Egypt) are content to crown thee upon the throne of thy father, like Ra.

Thou rollest up into the horizon, thou hast set light over the darkness, thou sendest forth air from thy plumes, and thou floodest the Two Lands like the Disk at daybreak. Thy crown penetrateth the height of heaven, thou art the companion of the stars, and the guide of every god. Thou art beneficent in decree and speech, the favoured one of the Great Company of the Gods, and the beloved of the Little Company of the Gods.

His sister [Isis] hath protected him, and hath repulsed the fiends, and turned aside calamities (of evil). She uttered the spell with the magical power of her mouth. Her tongue was perfect, and it never halted at a word. Beneficent in command and word was Isis, the woman of magical spells, the advocate of her brother. She sought him untiringly, she wandered round and round about this earth in sorrow, and she alighted not without finding him. She made light with her feathers, she created air with her wings, and she uttered the death wail for her brother. She raised up the inactive members of whose heart was still, she drew from him his essence, she made an heir, she reared the child in loneliness, and the place where he was not known, and he grew in strength and stature, and his hand was mighty in the House of Keb. The Company of the Gods rejoiced, rejoiced, at the coming of Horus, the son of Osiris, whose heart was firm, the triumphant, the son of Isis, the heir of Osiris (www.touregypt.net/bod1.htm).

Hymn to Osiris Un-Nefer

A Hymn of Praise to Osiris Un-Nefer, the great god who dwelleth in Abtu, the king of eternity, the lord of everlastingness, who traverseth millions of years in his existence. Thou art the eldest son of the womb of Nut. Thou was begotten by Keb, the Erpat. Thou art the lord of the Urrt Crown. Thou art he whose White Crown is lofty. Thou art the King (Ati) of gods [and] men. Thou hast gained possession of the sceptre of rule, and the whip, and the rank and dignity of thy divine fathers. Thy heart is expanded with joy, O thou who art in the kingdom of the dead. Thy son Horus is firmly placed on thy throne. Thou hast ascended thy throne as the Lord of Tetu, and as the Heq who dwelleth in Abydos. Thou makest the Two Lands to flourish through Truth-speaking, in the presence of him who is the Lord to the Uttermost Limit. Thou drawest on that which hath not yet come into being in thy name of "Ta-her-sta-nef." Thou governest the Two Lands by Maat in thy name of "Seker." Thy power is wide-spread, thou art he of whom the fear is great in thy name of "Usar" (or "Asar"). Thy existence endureth for an infinite number of double henti periods in thy name of "Un-Nefer."

Homage to thee, King of Kings, and Lord of Lords, and Prince of Princes. Thou hast ruled the Two Lands from the womb of the goddess Nut. Thou hast governed the Lands of Akert. Thy members are of silver-gold, thy head is of lapis-lazuli, and the crown of thy head is of turquoise. Thou art An of millions of years. Thy body is all pervading, O Beautiful Face in Ta-tchesert. Grant thou to me glory in heaven, and power upon earth, and truth-speaking in the Divine Underworld, and [the power to] sail down the river to Tetu in the form of a living Ba-soul, and [the power to] sail up the river to Abydos in the form of a Benu bird, and [the power to] pass in through and to pass out from, without obstruction, the doors of the lords of the Tuat. Let there be given unto me bread-cakes in the House of Refreshing, and sepulchral offerings of cakes and ale, and propitiatory offerings in Anu, and a permanent homestead in Sekhet-Aaru, with wheat and barley therein- to the Double of the Osiris, the scribe Ani (www.touregypt.net/bod4.htm).

- Warm-up: Why do the Egyptians have such an obsession with death?
- Student should complete Concept Builder 3-E.
- Essay is due. Students should take the chapter 3 test.

CONCEPT BUILDER 3-E
Books of the Dead

Egyptian manuscript illumination or illustrations with hieroglyphics began in ancient Egypt with the illustrated book of the dead, the most famous of which is the *Papyrus of Ani* (www.thenazareneway.com/index_egyptain_book_dead.htm). Beginning in 2000 B.C. these books of the dead were commissioned by people of substance. They provided descriptions of the burial ceremony and prayers recited by the priests. They also put in a good word with Osiris, the Egyptian god of the dead. Just as we might keep a scrapbook of our favorite vacation or important events in our lives, books of the dead — and there were many — were essentially scrapbooks of the funerals of important people.
Read the following passage of adoration of the god Osiris from the *Book of the Dead*, and compare and contrast it with Psalm 8 from the Bible.

Adoration of Osiris Wen-Nefer, the great god in Abydos, king of eternity, lord of infinity, passing through millions of years as his lifetime, first son of the womb of Nut, begotten of Geb, chief, great lord of the Double Crown of Egypt, exalting the White Crown of the South. O prince of gods and men, you have received the crook and flail, and the office of the fathers, and your heart is glad in the Mountain [of Amentet]. Your son Horus is established on your throne, and you are crowned in Busiris as ruler in Abydos. You make the Two Lands to flourish by truth of voice in the presence of Neb-er-djer. He has drawn forth those who have not come into being in his name of "The Earth Is Drawn to Him;" he tows the Two Lands in truth in his name of "Seker." He is greatly powerful, great of fear in his name of "Osiris;" his existance is for 120 eternities in his name of "Wen-Nefer." Homage to you, king of kings, lord of lords, ruler of rulers, who has taken the Two Lands from the womb of Nut; he rules the lands of Igert. His limbs are silver; his head is lapis lazuli; the crown of his head is turquoise. Iwen of millions of years, wide of skin, beautiful of face in the Holy Land, you give glory in heaven, strength on earth, and truth of voice in the underworld, and the power to sail north to Busiris as a living soul, to sail south to Abydos as a phoenix, and to enter and exit without opposition at any door of the underworld. May bread be given to me in the House of Cool Water, and peace in Heliopolis, and an estate established in the the Field of Reeds with barley and wheat on it.

Psalm 8

O LORD, our Lord, how majestic is your name in all the earth! You have set your glory above the heavens. From the lips of children and infants you have ordained praise because of your enemies, to silence the foe and the avenger. When I consider your heavens, the work of your fingers, the moon and the stars, which you have set in place, what is man that you are mindful of him, the son of man that you care for him? You made him a little lower than the heavenly beings and crowned him with glory and honor.

You made him ruler over the works of your hands; you put everything under his feet: all flocks and herds, and the beasts of the field, the birds of the air, and the fish of the sea, all that swim the paths of the seas.

O LORD, our Lord, how majestic is your name in all the earth!

Comparison	The Book of the Dead	Psalm 8
Metaphors to describe the deity		
Man's relationship with the deity		

Chapter 4

(800 B.C.–300 B.C.):
Ancient Greece (Part 1)

First Thoughts Greece is the southernmost region on the European continent. Its mild, almost tropical climate attests to this fact. Greece is a land full of mountains, surrounded on all sides except the north by water, and populated with countless islands. The Aegean Sea and the many natural harbors along the coastlines allowed the Greeks to prosper in seafaring commerce and to develop an eclectic culture that drew contacts outside Greece. In other words, from the beginning, Greek culture and civilization had a cosmopolitan/international air. Greek culture, as we shall see, was ideally suited in this maritime setting, to spread throughout the Western world.

The Greek world encompassed many settlements around the Mediterranean and Black Seas and, during the height of the Alexandrian Empire, reaching as far east as India.

Chapter Learning Objectives In chapter 4 we read the same literature that the Apostle Paul read, that Robert E. Lee memorized. We will experience the timeless, epic classic, *The Iliad*.

As a result of this chapter study you will be able to . . .

1. Discuss the way Homer creates these characters: Achilleus, Agamemnon, Ajax, Diomedes, Odysseus, Hector, Helen, and Paris.

2. Give examples of how three motifs function throughout *The Iliad*.

3. Analyze how partisan Homer is.

4. Evaluate Helen's culpability in the Trojan Wars.

5. Analyze the values betrayed in this epic poem.

6. Discuss what role women play in *The Iliad*.

Weekly Essay Options: Begin on page 273 of the Teacher Guide.
Reading ahead: *The Odyssey*, Homer.

Greece

Background Never has a civilization been so influenced by its geography. From the beginning, the Greeks lived in independent communities isolated from one another by the landscape. Eventually these communities were organized into city-states. The rocky landscape obligated the Greeks to look beyond their borders to find lands where fertile soil was more abundant. They looked to the sea and its adjoining Mediterranean community to subsidize the paltry agrarian options open to them.

Their military was light years ahead of competitors. One reason that Greek armies were so successful is that their armies consisted of Hoplites. The Hoplites were the military elite, shock troops of the 7th century B.C. Hoplites were soldiers who worked together and formed a team, creating what was called a *phalanx*. Earlier, a looser and more individual battle style prevailed. This style of battle is described in *The Iliad*. The Hoplite was ineffective if he fought alone. He was armed in such a way that he could only fight effectively in formation, with his shield firmly fixed on his left to protect his own left side and his neighbor's right. That style of fighting was ideally suited for mountainous terrain.

All this required adequate training, commitment to the team, and larger numbers. The Hoplites were normally volunteers who could afford to fit themselves out with the appropriate armor and weapons. It was, then, so far as the term is applicable, an army of the wealthier middle class.

Thus the Hoplites developed into more than a military cadre: they became a social class. This caused the ruling nobles to lose some influence in the city-state. The citizen-soldier — the class which now provided the dominant force on the battlefield — was less easy to exclude from public life.

The ancient Greeks did not have a religion per se; they did not go to Sunday school and church like we do. They had no Ten Commandments or any other moral system, for that matter, to follow. Besides, hardly any self-respecting Greek really thought that mythological gods and goddesses were alive, at least not the way we think of our Judeo-Christian God. The Greek gods cared little, if they cared at all, for mankind. While it is true that Greek society had its gods, it did not place great importance on mystical beliefs. Indeed, what gods it did revere (not worship) were much different from the Christian God. In Christianity, man was made "in God's image." The Greek gods were made in the image of man. They were neither omnipotent nor omnipresent. One scholar, Edith Hamilton, stated, "Before Greece, all religion was magical." She further illustrated that mystical beliefs were based on fear of the unknown, whereas the Greeks "changed a world that was full of fear into a world full of beauty." Hamilton continued, "The Greeks were the first intellectuals. In a world where the irrational had played the chief role, they came forward as the protagonists of the mind" (Ibid). Thus, the Greeks introduced the idea that the universe was orderly, that man's senses were valid and, as a consequence, that man's proper purpose was to live his own life to the fullest. Man's chief end, however, was certainly not to please the gods. It was to enjoy the aesthetics (James Stobaugh, *Fire that Burns,* 2003).

Before 1200 B.C., the Mycenean Greeks lived in small tribal/family units. Some of these small tribes were sedentary and agricultural and some were certainly nomadic. All depended on subsistence crops and livestock for food. There was the beginning of small cities. However, for some reason, they abandoned their cities between 1200 and 1100 B.C. Many believe that an invasion of northern Greece by the Dorians had wiped out the Mycenean civilization.

Greek life flourished for the next 300 years. It was during this time that the Greeks created their religion, mythology, and the more elaborate city-state.

The largest of these city-states was the militaristic Sparta, which controlled more than 3,000 square miles of surrounding territory. The most famous of these city-states, which controlled most of the Mediterranean world, was the cultural apogee, Athens. There were others, but these two, by far, were the most famous and influential.

All the Greek city-states began as monarchies. However, by 800 B.C. most monarchies were replaced by representative democracies, the first of their kind. Homer lived and wrote in this transitional time. These were not democracies as we think of the term today — only propertied citizens could vote — but there was no autocracy like one would find in Babylon either.

When Homer wrote his epic narratives, there was as yet no military, political, or cultural center of the Greek world. This would change when Plato and Herodotus wrote their works.

Militaristic Sparta dominated more land mass than any other Greek city, but clearly Athens gained cultural hegemony.

It is hard to believe that so different a culture existed in a city-state only 100 miles away from Sparta. By 600 B.C., Athens was full of beautiful works of sculpture and architecture. This renaissance spread to the entire Mediterranean world and was to last until Sparta conquered it at the end of the Peloponnesian Wars in 404 B.C.

I first read Homer the way that he was meant to be read — in the middle of a hot southern Arkansas summer between baseball season and dove-hunting season. For a young boy whose life was significantly devoid of fecundity, Homer was the highlight of that summer. In the 14th summer of my life I fell in love with the drama and adventure so abundantly present in Homer's *The Iliad*. *The Iliad* remains one of the greatest literary works of Western literature. Almost 500 generations of young people have read Homer! It is a timeless image of how life unfolds for us all. Homer wrote about events that took place four or five hundred years before his own time, events already exaggerated by storytellers. However bold and courageous Achilleus and Hektor actually were, by Homer's time their reputations were legendary. For the Greeks, they were the George Washington and Benjamin Franklin of their nation.

Assignments

- Warm-up: "In its ultimate analysis, the balance between the particular and the general is that between the spirit and the mind. All that the Greeks achieved was stamped by that balance." — Edith Hamilton, *The Greek Way* (New York: W.W. Norton, 1993). Explain what Hamilton means.

- Students should complete Concept Builder 4-A.

- Students should review the required reading(s) before the assigned chapter begins.

- Teachers may want to discuss assigned reading(s) with students.

- Teachers shall assign the required essay. The rest of the essays can be outlined, answered with shorter answers, discussed, or skipped.

- Students will review all readings for chapter 4.

Read *The Iliad* (Book 22), "The Death of Hector" by Homer, and then answer the following questions.

1	What sort of man is Achilles? How does Homer develop him?
2	Why does Hector choose to fight Achilles?
3	What metaphor does Homer use to describe Achilles' pursuit of Hector? Why?
4	Clearly, Achilles is not a perfect hero. What flaws does Homer manifest with the fight with Hector?

The Demise of Achilles

This passage sets the scene for the demise of Achilles, one of the most tragic characters in *The Iliad*. The tragedy of Achilles is that he must play out the events he himself set in motion. Explain.

Thus then did they fight as it were a flaming fire. Meanwhile the fleet runner Antilochus, who had been sent as messenger, reached Achilles, and found him sitting by his tall ships and boding that which was indeed too surely true. "Alas," said he to himself in the heaviness of his heart, "why are the Achaeans again scouring the plain and flocking towards the ships? Heaven grant the gods be not now bringing that sorrow upon me of which my mother Thetis spoke, saying that while I was yet alive the bravest of the Myrmidons should fall before the Trojans, and see the light of the sun no longer. I fear the brave son of Menoetius has fallen through his own daring and yet I bade him return to the ships as soon as he had driven back those that were bringing fire against them, and not join battle with Hektor." As he was thus pondering, the son of Nestor came up to him and told his sad tale, weeping bitterly the while. "Alas," he cried, "son of noble Peleus, I bring you bad tidings, would indeed that they were untrue. Patroclus has fallen, and a fight is raging about his naked body — for Hektor holds his armour." A dark cloud of grief fell upon Achilles as he listened. He filled both hands with dust from off the ground, and poured it over his head, disfiguring his comely face, and letting the refuse settle over his shirt so fair and new. He flung himself down all huge and hugely at full length, and tore his hair with his hands. The bondswomen whom Achilles and Patroclus had taken captive screamed aloud for grief, beating their breasts, and with their limbs failing them for sorrow. Antilochus bent over him the while, weeping and holding both his hands as he lay groaning for he feared that he might plunge a knife into his own throat. Then Achilles gave a loud cry and his mother heard him as she was sitting in the depths of the sea by the old man her father, whereon she screamed, and all the goddesses daughters of Nereus that dwelt

Triumphant Achilles: Achilles dragging the dead body of Hector in front of the gates of Troy, by Franz Matsch 1892 (PD-US).

at the bottom of the sea, came gathering round her. There were Glauce, Thalia and Cymodoce, Nesaia, Speo, Thoe and dark-eyed Halie, Cymothoe, Actaea and Limnorea, Melite, Iaera, Amphithoe and Agave, Doto and Proto, Pherusa and Dynamene, Dexamene, Amphinome and Callianeira, Doris, Panope, and the famous sea-nymph Galatea, Nemertes, Apseudes and Callianassa. There were also Clymene, Ianeira and Ianassa, Maera, Oreithuia and Amatheia of the lovely locks, with other Nereids who dwell in the depths of the sea. The crystal cave was filled with their multitude and they all beat their breasts while Thetis led them in their lament (classics.mit.edu/Homer/iliad.html).

Assignments

- Warm-up: Achilles is full of hubris. What does that mean?
- Students should complete Concept Builder 4-B.
- Students should review reading(s) from the next chapter.
- Students should outline essay due at the end of the week
- Per teacher instructions, students may answer orally, in a group setting, some of the essays that are not assigned as formal essays. Students will review all readings for chapter 4.

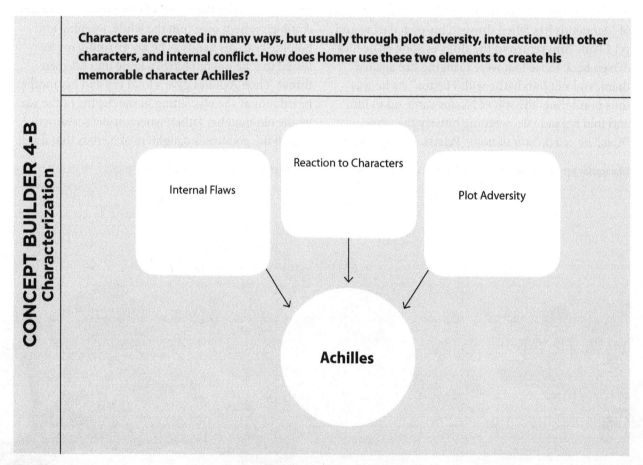

CONCEPT BUILDER 4-B
Characterization

Characters are created in many ways, but usually through plot adversity, interaction with other characters, and internal conflict. How does Homer use these two elements to create his memorable character Achilles?

Internal Flaws

Reaction to Characters

Plot Adversity

Achilles

The Shield of Achilles

When he had so said he left her and went to his bellows, turning them towards the fire and bidding them do their office. Twenty bellows blew upon the melting-pots, and they blew blasts of every kind, some fierce to help him when he had need of them, and others less strong as Vulcan willed it in the course of his work. He threw tough copper into the fire, and tin, with silver and gold; he set his great anvil on its block, and with one hand grasped his mighty hammer while he took the tongs in the other. First he shaped the shield so great and strong, adorning it all over and binding it round with a gleaming circuit in three layers; and the baldric was made of silver. He made the shield in five thicknesses, and with many a wonder did his cunning hand enrich it. He wrought the earth, the heavens, and the sea; the moon also at her full and the untiring sun, with all the signs that glorify the face of heaven- the Pleiads, the Hyads, huge Orion, and the Bear, which men also call the Wain and which turns round ever in one place, facing. Orion, and alone never dips into the stream of Oceanus. He wrought also two cities, fair to see and busy with the hum of men. In the one were weddings and wedding-feasts, and they were going about the city with brides whom they were escorting by torchlight from their chambers. Loud rose the cry of Hymen, and the youths danced to the music of flute and lyre, while the women stood each at her house door to see them. Meanwhile the people were gathered in assembly, for there was a quarrel, and two men were wrangling about the blood-money for a man who had been killed, the one saying before the people that he had paid damages in full, and the other that he had not been paid. Each was trying to make his own case good, and the people took sides, each man backing the side that he had taken; but the heralds kept them back, and the elders sat on their seats of stone in a solemn circle, holding the staves which the heralds had put into their hands. Then they rose and each in his turn gave judgement, and there were two talents laid down, to be given to him whose judgement should be deemed the fairest. About the other city there lay encamped two hosts in gleaming armour, and they were divided whether to sack it, or to spare it and accept the half of what it contained. But the men of the city would not yet consent, and armed themselves for a surprise; their wives and little children kept guard upon the walls, and with them were the men who were past fighting through age; but the others sallied forth with Mars and Pallas Minerva at their head — both of them wrought in gold and clad in golden raiment, great and fair with their armour as befitting gods, while they that followed were smaller. When they reached the place where they would lay their ambush, it was on a riverbed to which live stock of all kinds would come from far and near to water; here, then, they lay concealed, clad in full armour. Some way off them there were two scouts who were on the look-out for the coming of sheep or cattle, which presently came, followed by two shepherds who were playing on their pipes, and had not so much as a thought of danger. When those who were in ambush saw this, they cut off the flocks and herds and killed the shepherds. Meanwhile the besiegers, when they heard much noise among the cattle as they sat in council, sprang to their horses, and made with all speed towards them; when they reached them they set battle in array by the banks of the river, and the hosts aimed their bronze-shod spears at one another. With them were Strife and Riot, and fell Fate who was dragging three men after her, one with a fresh wound, and the other unwounded, while the third was dead, and she was dragging him along by his heel: and her robe was bedrabbled in men's blood. They went in and out with one another and fought as though they were living people haling away one another's dead. He wrought also a fair fallow field, large and thrice ploughed already. Many men were working at the plough within it, turning their oxen to and fro, furrow after furrow. Each time that they turned on reaching the headland a man would come up to them and give them a cup of wine, and they would go back to their furrows looking forward to the time when they should again reach the headland. The part that they had ploughed was dark behind them, so that the field, though it was of gold, still looked as if it were being ploughed- very curious to behold. He wrought also a field of harvest corn, and the reapers were reaping with sharp sickles in their hands. Swathe after swathe fell to the ground in a straight line behind them, and the binders bound them in bands of twisted straw. There were three binders, and behind them there were boys who gathered the cut corn in armfuls and kept on bringing them to be bound: among them all the owner of the land stood by in silence and was glad. The servants were getting a meal ready under an oak, for they had sacrificed a great ox, and were busy cutting him up, while the women were making a porridge of much white barley for the labourers' dinner. He wrought also a vineyard, golden and fair to see, and the vines were loaded with grapes. The bunches overhead were black, but the vines were trained on poles of silver. He ran a ditch of dark metal all round it, and fenced it with a fence of tin; there was only one path to it, and by this the vintagers went when they would gather the vintage. Youths and maidens all blithe and full of glee, carried the luscious fruit in plaited baskets; and with them there went a boy who made sweet music with his lyre, and sang the Linus-song with his clear boyish voice. He wrought also a herd of horned cattle. He made the cows of gold and tin, and they lowed as they came full speed out of the yards to go and feed among the waving reeds that grow by the banks of the river. Along with the cattle there went four shepherds, all of them in gold, and their nine fleet dogs went with them. Two terrible lions had fastened on a bellowing bull that was with the foremost cows, and bellow as he might they haled him, while the dogs and men gave chase: the lions tore through the bull's thick hide and were gorging on his blood and bowels, but the herdsmen were afraid to do anything, and only hounded on their dogs; the dogs dared not fasten on the lions but stood by barking and keeping out of harm's way. The god wrought also a pasture in a fair mountain dell, and large flock of sheep, with a homestead and huts, and sheltered sheepfolds. Furthermore he wrought a green, like that which Daedalus once made in Cnossus for lovely Ariadne. Hereon there danced youths and maidens whom all would woo, with their hands on one another's wrists. The maidens wore robes of light linen, and the youths well woven shirts that were slightly oiled. The girls were crowned with garlands, while the young men had daggers of gold that hung by silver baldrics; sometimes they would dance deftly in a ring with merry twinkling feet, as it were a potter sitting at his work and making trial of his wheel to see whether it will run, and sometimes they would go all in line with one another, and much people was gathered joyously about the green. There was a bard also to sing to them and play his lyre, while two tumblers went about performing in the midst of them when the man struck up with his tune. All round the outermost rim of the shield he set the mighty stream of the river Oceanus. Then when he had fashioned the shield so great and strong, he made a breastplate also that shone brighter than fire. He made helmet, close fitting to the brow, and richly worked, with a golden plume overhanging it; and he made greaves also of beaten tin. Lastly, when the famed lame god had made all the armour, he took it and set it before the mother of Achilles; whereon she darted like a falcon from the snowy summits of Olympus and bore away the gleaming armour from the house of Vulcan (Ibid).

- Warm-up: The following description of the shield of Achilles is probably the most famous section in the *The Iliad*. What is its literary purpose?

- Students should complete Concept Builder 4-C.

- Students should write rough drafts of assigned essay.

- The teacher may correct rough drafts.

- Per teacher instructions, students may answer orally, in a group setting, some of the essays that are not assigned as formal essays. Students will review all readings for chapter 4.

CONCEPT BUILDER 4-C
Epic Conventions

Homer established literary practices, rules, or devices that became commonplace in epic poetry written later. These rules or devices are now known as epic conventions.
Match the following epic conventions with textual examples from *The Iliad*.

A	A writer (e.g., Homer) requests divine help in composing his work.
B	Conflict in the heavenlies: God and goddesses fight over humans.
C	The epithet, a combination of a descriptive phrase and a noun.

___ **1**	Sing, O goddess, the anger of Achilles son of Peleus, that brought countless ills upon the Achaeans. Many a brave soul did it send hurrying down to Hades, and many a hero did it yield a prey to dogs and vultures, for so were the counsels of Zeus fulfilled from the day on which the son of Atreus, king of men, and great Achilles, first fell out with one another.
___ **2**	fleet-footed Achilles
___ **3**	Now when Morning, clad in her robe of saffron, had begun to suffuse light over the earth, Zeus called the gods in council on the topmost crest of serrated Olympus. Then he spoke and all the other gods gave ear. "Hear me," said he, "gods and goddesses, that I may speak even as I am minded. Let none of you neither goddess nor god try to cross me, but obey me every one of you that I may bring this matter to an end. If I see anyone acting apart and helping either Trojans or Danaans, he shall be beaten inordinately ere he come back again to Olympus; or I will hurl him down into dark Tartarus far into the deepest pit under the earth, where the gates are iron and the floor bronze, as far beneath Hades as heaven is high above the earth, that you may learn how much the mightiest I am among you. Try me and find out for yourselves. Hangs me a golden chain from heaven, and lay hold of it all of you, gods and goddesses together — tug as you will, you will not drag Zeus the supreme counsellor from heaven to earth; but were I to pull at it myself I should draw you up with earth and sea into the bargain, then would I bind the chain about some pinnacle of Olympus and leave you all dangling in the mid firmament. So far am I above all others either of gods or men."

Achilles' Shield

The famous ancient Greek playwright, Euripides, once stated, "The best and safest thing is to keep a balance in your life, acknowledge the great powers around us and in us. If you can do that, and live that way, you are really a wise man." In book 18 of *The Iliad*, Homer presents a new concept that is not necessarily visible in the rest of the epic poem: the balance of life. Through the artwork which Hephaestus engraves onto Achilles's shield, Homer portrays a series of contrasts which demonstrate nature's balance in four different ways.

Around the center of the shield are two illustrations, one of a city in a time of peace, and another in a time of war. "He wrought also two cities, fair to see and busy with the hum of men. In the one were weddings and wedding-feasts, and they were going about the city with brides whom they were escorting by torchlight from their chambers. . . . Meanwhile the people were gathered in assembly, for there was a quarrel, and two men were wrangling about the blood-money for a man who had been killed. . . . About the other city there lay encamped two hosts in gleaming armour." Of all the illustrations, these two provide the most obvious contrast: between peace and war. It is interesting to note, however, that because there is a trial in the peaceful city, Homer seems to imply that there is no absolute peace.

"He wrought also a fair fallow field, large and thrice ploughed already. . . . He wrought also a field of harvest corn, and the reapers were reaping with sharp sickles in their hands." These two scenes portray two opposite times of year: spring, and fall. The plowing season is presented in the first picture, and the harvesting season in the second. This is the second balance depicted on Achilles's shield.

"He wrought also a vineyard, golden and fair to see, and the vines were loaded with grapes. . . . Youths and maidens all blithe and full of glee, carried the luscious fruit in plaited baskets. . . . He wrought also a herd of horned cattle. . . . Two terrible lions had fastened on a bellowing bull . . . but the herdsmen were afraid to do anything." This pair of scenes provides another balance: between bliss and fear. The phrases "full of glee" and "afraid to do anything" contrast the situations perfectly.

A final contrast is between a mountain scene and a dance scene. "The god wrought also a pasture in a fair mountain dell, and a large flock of sheep, with a homestead and huts, and sheltered sheepfolds. Furthermore he wrought a green, like that which Daedalus once made in Cnossus for lovely Ariadne. Hereon there danced youths and maidens whom all would woo, with their hands on one another's wrists." Here, the comparison is between tranquillity and frivolity. The quietude of the peaceful mountain scene is easily seen in sharp contrast to the joviality of the dancing youths.

The various contrasts embossed on Achilles's shield provide an insight into how the ancient Greeks viewed the balances of life and nature. As the wise Israelite king, Solomon, once wrote, "There is an appointed time for everything. And there is a time for every event under heaven. . . . A time to plant and a time to uproot what is planted. . . . A time to weep and a time to laugh; a time to mourn and a time to dance. . . . A time for war and a time for peace" (Eccles. 3:1–8; KJV). (John Micah)

Assignments

- Warm-up: Offer at least one critical suggestion to this young author.
- Students should complete Concept Builder 4-D.
- Students will re-write corrected copy of essay due tomorrow.

CONCEPT BUILDER 4-D
Compare/Contrast

Compare and contrast the human characteristics of Hector and Achilles.

Human Characteristics	Hector	Achilles
Flaws	*Impetuous*	*Prideful and arrogant*
Strengths		
Personal Life		
Leadership Qualities		

Critics Corner

THE ILIAD: ON ACHILLES The Iliad traces almost clinically the stages of Achilles' development. More than tragedy, epic makes real use of time; whereas Oedipus, for instance, reveals himself before our eyes, Achilles creates himself in the course of the poem. He progresses from young hopefulness, cheerfully accepting the possibility of early death with glory, through various phases of disillusion, horror, and violence, to a final detachment which is godlike indeed. Tragedy, especially that of Sophocles, slowly uncovers a character which is complete from start to finish, but Achilles is actually not complete until the poem is complete. He is learning all the time.

— Cedric H. Whitman, *Homer and the Heroic Tradition*, 1958

THE ILIAD: ON SIMILES The similes have a double purpose: to crystallize, in a sphere close to the listener's own understanding, a sight or sound or a state of mind; and to give relief from the harshness and potential monotony of warfare by suddenly actualizing a quite different and often even peaceful, even domestic, scene. . . .

— G.S. Kirk, *The Songs of Homer*, 1962

THE ILIAD: ON HECTOR Hector is the pure patriot, who is fighting to save his city, not to defend his brother's guilt; he feels the sin of Paris as a stain upon his city's name, a fatal weakness in the Trojan cause. Thus he enters the poem with his nobility and purity of motive thrown into sharp relief against the background of guilt which spells Troy's inevitable destruction.

— E.T. Owen, *The Story of the "Iliad,"* 1966

THE ILIAD: ON NESTOR Nestor's constant claim is that he has lived a hero's life. Having already proved his worth in heroic encounters, he sets his life before the young heroes as paradigm. Now it is their turn to prove their characters. As paradigms, then, his stories are never told for their antiquarian interest but because they are his most persuasive form of rhetoric. . . . They reflect a pervasive need to justify an action in the present by an appeal to a past precedent.

— Norman Austin, "The Function of Digressions in the Iliad," in
John Wright, *Essays on the "Iliad,"* 1978

THE ILIAD: ON GREATNESS Achilles' greatness is a greatness of force and negation. He is different from other men by his greater capacity to deny, to refuse, to kill, and to face death. . . . Hector, by contrast, is a hero of illusions; he is finally trapped between a failed illusion and his own capacity for disillusionment. Hector is surely a figure less grand than Achilles, but it is Hector's story that gives Achilles' story meaning; Hector affirms all that Achilles denies.

— James Redfield, *Nature and Culture in The Iliad,* 1975

Assignments

- Warm-up: Do you agree with Redfield's unflattering assessment of Hector?
- Students should complete Concept Builder 4-E.
- Essays are due. Students should take the chapter 4 test.

Complete the chart.

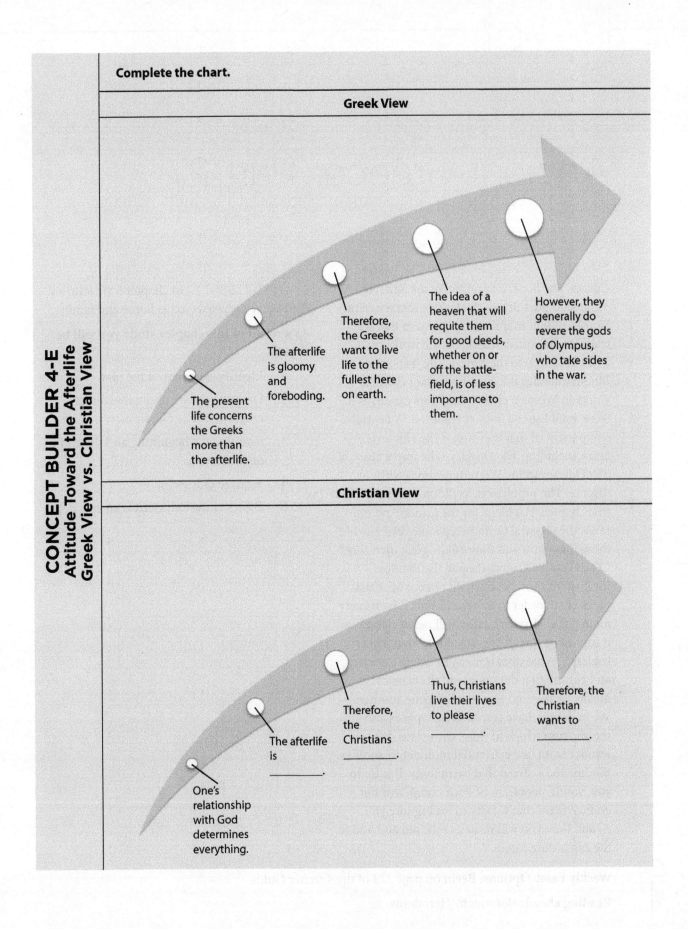

CONCEPT BUILDER 4-E
Attitude Toward the Afterlife
Greek View vs. Christian View

Greek View

The present life concerns the Greeks more than the afterlife.

The afterlife is gloomy and foreboding.

Therefore, the Greeks want to live life to the fullest here on earth.

The idea of a heaven that will requite them for good deeds, whether on or off the battle-field, is of less importance to them.

However, they generally do revere the gods of Olympus, who take sides in the war.

Christian View

One's relationship with God determines everything.

The afterlife is _____.

Therefore, the Christians _____.

Thus, Christians live their lives to please _____.

Therefore, the Christian wants to _____.

Chapter 5

(800 B.C.–300 B.C.)
Ancient Greece (Part 2)

First Thoughts In *The Western Canon: The Books and School of the Age* (New York: Harcourt Brace, 1994), Yale literary critic Harold Bloom examines the Western literary tradition by concentrating on the works of 26 authors central to the canon. The "canon" to Bloom includes the most important classical works in Western civilization. This canon, as it were, establishes a literary tradition. A central component of that tradition is the Homeric epics, including *The Odyssey*. The importance of *The Odyssey* to the Western canon is without dispute. The problem is, as Bloom laments in his first chapter, "An Elegy for the Canon," no one reads the classics! Or rather, people read any old thing they want and they call it "great literature." "The Western Canon, despite the limitless idealism of those who would open it up, exists precisely in order to impose limits . . . by its very nature, the Western Canon will never close, but it cannot be forced open by our current cheer-leaders." What does it mean to live in a society and culture that does not read the classics? It means we have no way to talk to one another. We no longer have common metaphors and motifs from which to share consensus. We wander from one existential moment to another. Bloom, and I, dread that eventuality. It is up to you, young people, to be such competent but godly writers that society cannot ignore you — and then you will resurrect the old and add to the expanding canon.

Chapter Learning Objectives In chapter 5 we journey with brave Odysseus to his home and family.

As a result of this chapter study you will be able to . . .

1. Identify each part of the plot.
2. Describe the writing style Homer employs in *The Odyssey*.
3. Examine the beginning and the ending of all sections.
4. Analyze Odysseus.
5. Discuss how Odysseus is an epic hero.

Weekly Essay Options: Begin on page 273 of the Teacher Guide.

Reading ahead: *Histories* by Herodotus.

Homer

Homer is the author of *The Iliad* and *The Odyssey*, and is celebrated as the most famous and best ancient Greek epic poet. These epics begin the Western canon of literature, and have had an enormous influence on all subsequent literature.

We don't know when Homer lived. Herodotus estimates that Homer lived 400 years before Herodotus' own time, which would place him at around 850 B.C., while other ancient sources claim that he lived much nearer to the Trojan War, in the early 12th century B.C.

Homer was a singer and poet. He probably recited his story to his children, grandchildren, and perhaps even the king. He probably couldn't read or write. *The Iliad* and *The Odyssey* were stories that were told and retold before they were written. Homer no doubt used familiar material that had been passed along through the ages by word of mouth, but he edited this material and embellished it. These two epic poems were probably written down by someone else around 750 B.C., 500 years after the fall of Troy.

Assignments

- Warm-up: Some scholars insist that Homer was a woman. Is that possible?
- Students should complete Concept Builder 5-A.
- Students should review the required reading(s) *before* the assigned chapter begins.
- Teachers may want to discuss assigned reading(s) with students.
- Teachers shall assign the required essay. The rest of the essays can be outlined, answered with shorter answers, discussed, or skipped.
- Students will review all readings for chapter 5.

Read *The Odyssey* (Book 1), by Homer, and then answer the following questions.

1	What is a muse?
2	*The Odyssey* is a frame story, or a story within a story. What are the two stories that emerge in this classic?
3	What is the dilemma Penelope faces?
4	Homer uses dialogue to develop his characters. How?
5	"Mother," answered Telemachus, "let the bard sing what he has a mind to; bards do not make the ills they sing of; it is Zeus, not they, who makes them, and who sends weal or woe upon mankind according to his own good pleasure." Based on this passage, what is Homer's worldview?

Plot

"Thus the story of the Odyssey may be stated briefly. A certain man is absent from home for many years; he is jealously watched by Poseidon, and left desolate. Meanwhile his home is in a wretched plight — suitors are wasting his substance and plotting against his son. At length, tempest-tost, he himself arrives; he makes certain persons acquainted with him; he attacks the suitors with his own hand and is himself preserved while he destroys them. This is the essence of the plot." This is how the famous Greek philosopher Aristotle summarizes *The Odyssey*, an epic poem commonly attributed to Homer. The plot of Homer's *The Odyssey* unfolds the story of Odysseus's adventures as he travels from Troy to Ithaca where he reclaims his property, his family, and his kingdom.

Odysseus Overcome by Demodocus' Song, by Francesco Hayez, 1813 (PD-Art).

As with most literature, *The Odyssey* begins with a short exposition that presents the setting for the rest of the plot. In Homer's poem there are two settings established in Book I. Odysseus mourns his marooned state on the island of Calypso, a fair nymph who seeks to convince Odysseus to marry her. Meanwhile, Telemachus, Odysseus's son who is still at home in Ithaca, attempts in vain to persuade his mother's many careless suitors to leave his house. Because of Odysseus's long absence, many consider him dead, and they therefore endeavor to convince Odysseus's wife, Penelope, to remarry, and Odysseus's son, Telemachus, to relinquish his authority over his father's kingdom to another man. These are the two settings provided in the exposition of *The Odyssey*.

By far the largest part of this epic poem is the rising action. This section covers from the second half of Book I all the way through Book XXI. The gods decide to release Odysseus from Calypso's island. Odysseus then constructs a rude vessel and voyages over stormy seas until he is cast ashore on the island of Phaeacia where he falls asleep in a bush. After traveling, Odysseus enters the palace of King Alcinous, who receives him hospitably and promises him a safe-conduct to his own country. Odysseus shares with his host the tale of his adventures from the battle of Troy to the land of the Lotus-Eaters, to the cave of the Cyclops, to the Island of the Winds, to the home of Circe, to the kingdom of the dead, to the cliff of the Sirens, to the lair of Scylla, to the island of the Sun, and to the residence of Calypso. As promised, the Phaecians return Odysseus to Ithaca. Odysseus, disguised by his patron goddess, Athena, as a beggar, enters his house where he is treated rudely by the suitors. After revealing himself to his son Telemachus, Odysseus constructs a plan to destroy the careless wooers. Penelope retrieves her husband's great bow and the quiver full of arrows, and Telemachus sets up a long row of axes in the floor, each with an opening in the blade. While the suitors attempt to string the bow, Odysseus quietly reveals himself to the drover and swineherd who promise to assist him. The three men return to the hall and find that no one is able to string the bow.

Then, by stringing the bow with ease and shooting the first arrow through the axes, Odysseus proves his identity to the suitors. This pivotal event, which occurs at the beginning of Book XXII, is the ultimate climax of Homer's epic poem. The purpose of the story line up to this point has been to reach this revelational moment. Odysseus's entire journey was an attempt to return home and reclaim his house and throne. Telemachus's struggles, similarly, were for the sole purpose of warding off the suitors. Now that Odysseus has revealed himself, the stage is set for a "happily ever after" ending.

The falling action is covered in the rest of Book XXII and Book XXIII, where Odysseus slays the suitors and then reveals himself to Penelope and confirms his true identity by expressing knowledge about his bed which only he and Penelope share. After this confirmation, Penelope is confident that Odysseus is who he claims to be, and the text reads, "So when the pair had joyed in happy love, they joyed in talking too, each one relating: she, the royal lady, what she endured at home . . . he, high-born Odysseus, what miseries he brought on other men and what he bore himself in anguish. . . ." (Homer, *The Odyssey*, "XXIII, The Recognition by Penelope," Mineola, NY: Dover Publications, 1999).

It appears that the story might end at this point. However, "Now a new plan the goddess formed, clear-eyed Athena." One loose end must still be tied up in the resolution in Book XXIV. After Odysseus slaughters the suitors, it is not long before all of Ithaca learns of the massacre. Odysseus therefore flees to the house of his father, Laertes. After discussing the matter thoroughly, Odysseus and Laertes, with the assistance of Odysseus's patron goddess, Athena, ward off the men and "then for all coming time betwixt the two a peace was made by Pallas Athena, daughter of aegis-bearing Zeus" (Ibid).

Aristotle once claimed that Homer "is of surpassing merit," (Ibid) and Homer and his works are named 35 times in Aristotle's Poetics and alluded to many other times. The context of the aforementioned quote is a chapter on plot, and indeed, "The transcendent excellence of Homer is manifest" (*Poetics*, "Aristotle," ch. 23, p. 71.) in that he holds the readers on the edges of their seats throughout his masterfully constructed plot. (John Micah)

Assignments

- Warm-up: Write a summary of the plot of *The Odyssey*. Next, write a précis of the book.
- Students should complete Concept Builder 5-B.
- Students should review reading(s) from next chapter.
- Students should outline essays due at the end of the week.
- Per teacher instructions, students may answer orally, in a group setting, some of the essays that are not assigned as the formal essay.

Odysseus is a man who indulges in his share of foolishness. He often is impulsive and vain — especially in the beginning of the *The Odyssey*. As the book progresses, however, Odysseus develops into a mature, disciplined man. Trace this development as it unfolds in *The Odyssey*. Match the developed character quality with the plot incident.

incident	Character Quality
1. ____ Odysseus describes how he visited the Island of the Winds and how Aeolus bottled up all the winds in a bag except the West Wind, which was to blow him home; how the sailors undid the bag to see what was in it and winds came out and blew them to the island of Circe the witch; how Circe turned the men into pigs, and how Odysseus made her turn them back into men. There they stayed for a year, then Circe let them go and they passed the land of eternal night.	A. Odysseus learns that maturity requires a person to patiently wait for things to happen and that giving into impulses will bring death.
2. ____ And visited the kingdom of the dead, where Odysseus talked with the souls of ancient heroes and women of old days, and Teiresias the seer told him how he would come to die in the end, and his mother's ghost was there and told him of his father.	B. Odysseus learns that he really loves and misses Penelope and his family and purposes to continue his journey home.
3. ____ After leaving the kingdom of the dead, he tells how he passed the isle of the Sirens with their beautiful song, which attracts all who hear it; how he plugged the men's ears with wax and made them tie him to the mast that he might hear the song himself, telling them to row away whatever he says or does. Thus they escaped this peril, and passed next between Scylla and Charybdis; they kept clear of Charybdis and her whirlpool, and rowed past Scylla's cave. Scylla is a monster with six heads at the end of six long necks and she caught up six men, one with each head, while the rest escaped. They reached the island of the Sun, and the men offended the Sun by killing his cattle; so when they sailed away Zeus struck the ship with a thunderbolt and all were drowned except Odysseus. That brings him to the shore of Phaeacia.	C. Odysseus learns that he is part of a larger story, a part of history. He realizes that he is insignificant in the face of the great thing that is happening over time. Odysseus accepts his place in the universe.

Dramatic Irony

Homer has set up a dramatic ironic situation, where we know something that Penelope doesn't — that Odysseus is alive.

"Mother," answered Telemachus, "let the bard sing what he has a mind to; bards do not make the ills they sing of; it is Jove, not they, who makes them, and who sends weal or woe upon mankind according to his own good pleasure. This fellow means no harm by singing the ill-fated return of the Danaans, for people always applaud the latest songs most warmly. Make up your mind to it and bear it; Ulysses is not the only man who never came back from Troy, but many another went down as well as he. Go, then, within the house and busy yourself with your daily duties, your loom, your distaff, and the ordering of your servants; for speech is man's matter, and mine above all others — for it is I who am master here."

She went wondering back into the house, and laid her son's saying in her heart. Then, going upstairs with her handmaids into her room, she mourned her dear husband till Minerva shed sweet sleep over her eyes. But the suitors were clamorous throughout the covered cloisters, and prayed each one that he might be her bed fellow.

Then Telemachus spoke, "Shameless," he cried, "and insolent suitors, let us feast at our pleasure now, and let there be no brawling, for it is a rare thing to hear a man with such a divine voice as Phemius has; but in the morning meet me in full assembly that I may give you formal notice to depart, and feast at one another's houses, turn and turn about, at your own cost. If on the other hand you choose to persist in spunging upon one man, heaven help me, but Jove shall reckon with you in full, and when you fall in my father's house there shall be no man to avenge you."

The suitors bit their lips as they heard him, and marvelled at the boldness of his speech. Then, Antinous, son of Eupeithes, said, "The gods seem to have given you lessons in bluster and tall talking; may Jove never grant you to be chief in Ithaca as your father was before you."

Telemachus answered, "Antinous, do not chide with me, but, god willing, I will be chief too if I can. Is this the worst fate you can think of for me? It is no bad thing to be a chief, for it brings both riches and honour. Still, now that Ulysses is dead there are many great men in Ithaca both old and young, and some other may take the lead among them; nevertheless I will be chief in my own house, and will rule those whom Ulysses has won for me."

Then Eurymachus, son of Polybus, answered, "It rests with heaven to decide who shall be chief among us, but you shall be master in your own house and over your own possessions; no one while there is a man in Ithaca shall do you violence nor rob you. And now, my good fellow, I want to know about this stranger. What country does he come from? Of what family is he, and where is his estate? Has he brought you news about the return of your father, or was he on business of his own? He seemed a well-to-do man, but he hurried off so suddenly that he was gone in a moment before we could get to know him."

"My father is dead and gone," answered Telemachus, "and even if some rumour reaches me I put no more faith in it now. My mother does indeed sometimes send for a soothsayer and question him, but I give his prophecyings no heed. As for the stranger, he was Mentes, son of Anchialus, chief of the Taphians, an old friend of my father's." But in his heart he knew that it had been the goddess.

The suitors then returned to their singing and dancing until the evening; but when night fell upon their pleasuring they went home to bed each in his own abode. Telemachus's room was high up in a tower that looked on to the outer court; hither, then, he hied, brooding and full of thought. A good old woman, Euryclea, daughter of Ops, the son of Pisenor, went before him with a couple of blazing torches. Laertes had bought her with his own money when she was quite young; he gave the worth of twenty oxen for her, and shewed as much respect to her in his household as he did to his own wedded wife, but he did not take her to his bed for he feared his wife's resentment. She it was who now lighted Telemachus to his room, and she loved him better than any of the other women in the house did, for she had nursed him when he was a baby. He opened the door of his bed room and sat down upon the bed; as he took off his shirt he gave it to the good old woman, who folded it tidily up, and hung it for him over a peg by his bed side, after which she went out, pulled the door to by a silver catch, and drew the bolt home by means of the strap. But Telemachus as he lay covered with a woollen fleece kept thinking all night through of his intended voyage of the counsel that Minerva had given him (Homer, *The Odyssey*, translated by Samuel Butler, Book I, http://classics. mit.edu/Homer/odyssey.1.i.html).

Assignments

- Warm-up: Give an example of dramatic irony from your life or another literary work.
- Students should complete Concept Builder 5-C.
- Students should write rough draft of assigned essay.
- The teacher may correct rough draft.

CONCEPT BUILDER 5-C Character Development: My Life		Relate several incidents in your life and how they developed your character. See sample below.	
		incident	**Character Quality**
	SAMPLE	I memorized all the books of the Bible.	This taught me that if I worked hard at a task that I would succeed.
	1.		
	2.		
	3.		

Critics Corner

When the heroes who fought at Troy are described in the Odyssey we are clearly back in the saga world. The description of Achilles' funeral, for example, in the twenty-fourth book was very likely a commonplace of high heroic epic. But the most conspicuous theme from saga is that of Return. Nestor and Menelaos between them describe the homecoming of several of the major figures from the Iliad. Clearly episodes relating the return of a hero were as common as the aristeiai describing their triumphs in battle. The story of homecoming had a name: nostos. The several nostoi are a leitmotiv throughout the Odyssey which is over-all a nostos, being the return of Odysseus. There is a hint in the Odyssey that epics of nostoi were currently fashionable. In describing the homecoming of Agamemnon the poet lingers over details that ordinarily an epic poet takes for granted. Indeed, the occasional remark on newness and originality suggest that the particular nostos of Odysseus, as our poet conceived it, was perhaps not merely fashionable, but almost novel.

— Charles Rowan Beye, *The "Iliad," The "Odyssey" and the Epic Tradition*, 1966

Book XIII of the Odyssey describes the return of Odysseus to Ithaca; Book XVII describes his return, in disguise, to his palace, and the subsequent books describe the events leading to his return to his wife, his marriage bed, and his royal throne. Return is a fact of the Odyssey, a structural element in the form of the poem, but the idea of return is more than just an event of mythology, or just a consequence of the Trojan War's being fought across the Ionian sea from mainland Greece. The idea of return as a life-giving process runs deep and strong in all primitive societies, and anthropologists have often noted how totally the lives of primitive peoples are polarized around the return of natural phenomena. The eternal cycles of night and day, winter and summer, birth and death, rise and fall, permeate their lives and shape their imaginations. To secure and celebrate the return of life is often the purpose of their rituals, and the returning god, hero, or king is a feature of their myths.

— Howard W. Clarke, *The Art of the "Odyssey,"* 1967

Before following Odysseus' travels and the further events in Ithaca, it will be useful to pause with the related questions of the method of characterization in the poem and its guiding theme. Neither question is easy, and the resonance of the myth to inwardlooking ages adds problems. Who shall catch the myriad overtones of the journey, the return, and what they jointly tell of human possibility? But a few points are clear. To Homer, unlike Dante, the journey and the return belong together. Dante's famous Ulysses of Inferno 26 is the endless quester. His unappeased Faustian search has no place for homecoming. Because of Homer the vast world and small Ithaca both claim part of Odysseus' mind, each describes him. Unlike the homestaying suitors, he partly belongs to the world. He is seen in its varied settings, responds to them singly and, in a more important sense, cumulatively, and becomes their pupil. But though he has lived with immortals and seen the dead, none of these holds him. He refuses Calypso's offer of agelessness and immortality for mortal Penelope in Ithaca. The questions of characterization and of theme belong together because, as a character, the hero becomes known by his situations. The adventures make him; he does not in a subjective sense make the adventures.

— M.I. Finley, *The World of Odysseus*, 1979

Such mixed motives may seem impure or ignoble to those who take their ideals from self-sacrificing patriotism, or from self-effacing saintliness, or from self-forgetting romanticism. But these are post-Homeric concepts. Within the context of the Heroic Age and perhaps of the Homeric Age, too, this identification of one's own best interests with the general welfare of one's kith, kin, and comrades, with one's philoi in fact, was a saving grace for both the individual and society. All the Homeric heroes are egotists; but Odysseus' egotism has sent its roots out more widely into his personal environment than that of Agamemnon, Achilles, or Ajax. One other aspect of Odysseus' Homeric character needs to be kept in mind at the last. In a way it is the most important of all for the development of the tradition. This is the fundamental ambiguity of his essential qualities. We have seen how prudence may decline towards timidity, tactfulness towards a blameworthy suppressio veri, serviceability towards servility, and so on. The ambiguity lies both in the qualities themselves and in the attitudes of others towards them. Throughout the later tradition this ambiguity in Odysseus' nature and in his reputation will vacillate between good and bad, between credit and infamy. Odysseus' personality and reputation at best are poised, as it were, on a narrow edge between Aristotelian faults of excess and deficiency. Poised between rashness and timorousness, he is prudently brave; poised between rudeness and obsequiousness he is "civilized"; poised between stupidity and overcleverness he, at his best, is wise.

—William B. Stanford, "The Untypical Hero," in George Steiner and Robert Fagles, eds., Homer, *A Collection of Critical Essays*, 1962

Assignments

- Warm-up: In what ways is Odysseus an untypical hero?
- Students should complete Concept Builder 5-D.
- Students will re-write corrected copies of essay due tomorrow.

CONCEPT BUILDER 5-D
Plot Structure

Many scholars argue that the ends and beginnings of units of Homeric narratives are often constructed as follows: there is a sequence of events, then some type of climax, then a sequence of events that in some way mirrors the first sequence, and then a climax which contrasts with (is dual with) the earlier climax. This structure is observable in narrative units of all sizes, from brief episodes to large sections of the epics. Evaluate this observation, supporting your answer with several excerpts from the text.
Match each plot structure with an event.

	Plot Structure	Event
1. ____	Odysseus resisted the song of the Sirens and sailed between the whirlpool and the cliff (first crisis).	A. A second climax which contrasts with (is dual with) the earlier climax .
2. ____	However, his men made the mistake of eating the forbidden cattle of the sun god, Helios.	B. The first sequence of events.
3. ____	So Zeus wrecked Odysseus' ship, drowning all his men (another crisis).	C. A sequence of events that in some way mirrors the first sequence
4. ____	Odysseus managed to survive Scylla and Charybdis again and washed up at Ogygia Island where he stayed eight years with Calypso.	D. The first climax

Epic Simile

An epic simile or extended simile, is a detailed comparison in the form of a simile that is many lines in length. In Book IV, Homer compares suitors to soft, weak fawns in a lion's den. The lion will return to devour them.

Then Medon said, "I wish, Madam, that this were all; but they are plotting something much more dreadful now — may heaven frustrate their design. They are going to try and murder Telemachus as he is coming home from Pylos and Lacedaemon, where he has been to get news of his father."

Then Penelope's heart sank within her, and for a long time she was speechless; her eyes filled with tears, and she could find no utterance. At last, however, she said, "Why did my son leave me? What business had he to go sailing off in ships that make long voyages over the ocean like sea-horses? Does he want to die without leaving any one behind him to keep up his name?"

"I do not know," answered Medon, "whether some god set him on to it, or whether he went on his own impulse to see if he could find out if his father was dead, or alive and on his way home."

Then he went downstairs again, leaving Penelope in an agony of grief. There were plenty of seats in the house, but she had no heart for sitting on any one of them; she could only fling herself on the floor of her own room and cry; whereon all the maids in the house, both old and young, gathered round her and began to cry too, till at last in a transport of sorrow she exclaimed,

"My dears, heaven has been pleased to try me with more affliction than any other woman of my age and country. First I lost my brave and lion-hearted husband, who had every good quality under heaven, and whose name was great over all Hellas and middle Argos, and now my darling son is at the

Odysseus's boat passing between the six-headed monster Scylla and the whirlpool Charybdis. Scylla has plucked five of Odysseus's men from the boat. Artist unknown, c.1560 (PD-Art).

mercy of the winds and waves, without my having heard one word about his leaving home. You hussies, there was not one of you would so much as think of giving me a call out of my bed, though you all of you very well knew when he was starting. If I had known he meant taking this voyage, he would have had to give it up, no matter how much he was bent upon it, or leave me a corpse behind him — one or other. Now, however, go some of you and call old Dolius, who was given me by my father on my marriage, and who is my gardener. Bid him go at once and tell everything to Laertes, who may be able to hit on some plan for enlisting public sympathy on our side, as against those who are trying to exterminate his own race and that of Ulysses."

Then the dear old nurse Euryclea said, "You may kill me, Madam, or let me live on in your house, whichever you please, but I will tell you the real truth. I knew all about it, and gave him everything he wanted in the way of bread and wine, but he made me take my solemn oath that I would not tell you anything for some ten or twelve days, unless you asked or happened to hear of his having gone, for he did not want you to spoil your beauty by crying. And now, Madam, wash your face, change your dress, and go upstairs with your maids to offer prayers to Minerva, daughter of Aegis-bearing Jove, for she can save him even though he be in the jaws of death. Do not trouble Laertes: he has trouble enough already. Besides, I cannot think that the gods hate die race of the race of the son of Arceisius so much, but there will be a son left to come up after him, and inherit both the house and the fair fields that lie far all round it."

With these words she made her mistress leave off crying, and dried the tears from her eyes. Penelope washed her face, changed her dress, and went upstairs with her maids. She then put some bruised barley into a basket and began praying to Minerva.

"Hear me," she cried, "Daughter of Aegis-bearing Jove, unweariable. If ever Ulysses while he was here burned you fat thigh bones of sheep or heifer, bear it in mind now as in my favour, and save my darling son from the villainy of the suitors."

She cried aloud as she spoke, and the goddess heard her prayer; meanwhile the suitors were clamorous throughout the covered cloister, and one of them said: "The queen is preparing for her marriage with one or other of us. Little does she dream that her son has now been doomed to die."

This was what they said, but they did not know what was going to happen. Then Antinous said, "Comrades, let there be no loud talking, lest some of it get carried inside. Let us be up and do that in silence, about which we are all of a mind."

He then chose twenty men, and they went down to their ship and to the sea side; they drew the vessel into the water and got her mast and sails inside her; they bound the oars to the thole-pins with twisted thongs of leather, all in due course, and spread the white sails aloft, while their fine servants brought them their armour. Then they made the ship fast a little way out, came on shore again, got their suppers, and waited till night should fall.

But Penelope lay in her own room upstairs unable to eat or drink, and wondering whether her brave son would escape, or be overpowered by the wicked suitors. Like a lioness caught in the toils with huntsmen hemming her in on every side she thought and thought till she sank into a slumber, and lay on her bed bereft of thought and motion.

Then Minerva bethought her of another matter, and made a vision in the likeness of Penelope's sister Iphthime daughter of Icarius who had married Eumelus and lived in Pherae. She told the vision to go to the house of Ulysses, and to make Penelope leave off crying, so it came into her room by the hole through which the thong went for pulling the door to, and hovered over her head, saying, "You are asleep, Penelope: the gods who live at ease will not suffer you to weep and be so sad. Your son has done them no wrong, so he will yet come back to you."

Penelope, who was sleeping sweetly at the gates of dreamland, answered, "Sister, why have you come here? You do not come very often, but I suppose that is because you live such a long way off. Am I, then, to leave off crying and refrain from all the sad thoughts that torture me? I, who have lost my brave and lion-hearted husband, who had every good quality under heaven, and whose name was great over all Hellas and middle Argos; and now my darling son has gone off on board of a ship — a foolish fellow who has never been used to roughing it, nor to going about among gatherings of men. I am even more anxious about him than about my husband; I am all in a tremble when I think of him, lest something should happen to him, either from the people among whom he has gone, or by sea, for he has many enemies who are plotting against him, and are bent on killing him before he can return home."

Then the vision said, "Take heart, and be not so much dismayed. There is one gone with him whom many a man would be glad enough to have stand by his side, I mean Minerva; it is she who has compassion upon you, and who has sent me to bear you this message."

"Then," said Penelope, "if you are a god or have been sent here by divine commission, tell me also about that other unhappy one — is he still alive, or is he already dead and in the house of Hades?"

And the vision said, "I shall not tell you for certain whether he is alive or dead, and there is no use in idle conversation."

Then it vanished through the thong-hole of the door and was dissipated into thin air; but Penelope rose from her sleep refreshed and comforted, so vivid had been her dream.

Meantime the suitors went on board and sailed their ways over the sea, intent on murdering Telemachus. Now there is a rocky islet called Asteris, of no great size, in mid channel between Ithaca and Samos, and there is a harbour on either side of it where a ship can lie. Here then the Achaeans placed themselves in ambush.

Assignments

- Warm-up: Write a 10 to 12-line epic simile of an event or person who is significant to you.
- Students should complete Concept Builder 5-E.
- Essay is due. Students should take the chapter 5 test.

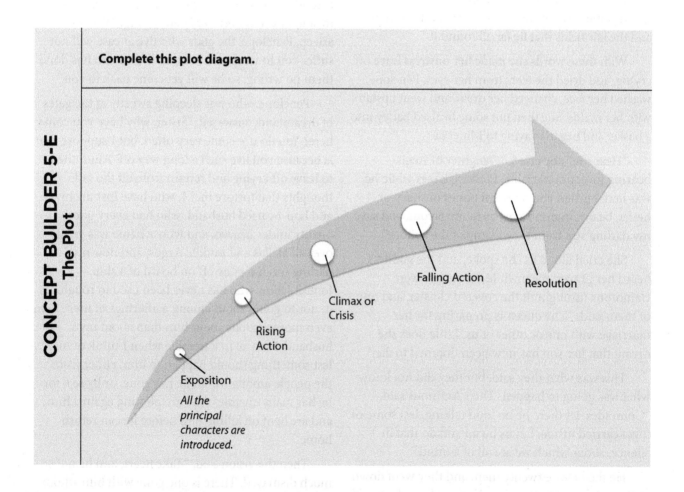

CONCEPT BUILDER 5-E
The Plot

Complete this plot diagram.

Exposition
All the principal characters are introduced.

Rising Action

Climax or Crisis

Falling Action

Resolution

(800 B.C.–300 B.C.):
Ancient Greece (Part 3)

First Thoughts Herodotus was born at Halicarnassus, on the southwest coast of Asia Minor, in the early part of the fifth century, B.C. Very little is known of his life. We know that he traveled a great deal and that he died in 424 B.C.

The story line of the history of Herodotus is the struggle between his community of Greeks and the barbarians, which he relates through the battle of Mycale in 479 B.C. He mainly gathered information from oral sources as he traveled through Asia Minor. He has wonderful digressions from time to time as he describes the country, the people, and their customs.

Notable among these descriptions is his account of Egypt. He tells of the strange ways of the crocodile and of that marvelous bird, the Phoenix; of the pyramids and the great labyrinth; and of Egypt's pharaohs and queens.

However, Herodotus is not merely a narrator of fantastic tales. He takes care to separate what he knows by his own observation, what he has merely inferred, and what he has been told. He is honest about acknowledging ignorance, and when versions differ, he gives both.

Chapter Learning Objectives In chapter 6 we explore the ancient world with the first historian.

As a result of this chapter study you will be able to . . .

1. Paraphrase Herodotus' version of the Trojan Wars.
2. Examine biblical parallels.
3. Evaluate Herodotus' philosophy of history.

Weekly Essay Options: Begin on page 273 of the Teacher Guide.

Reading ahead: "The Death of Socrates" by Plato.

History connections: *World History* chapter 6, "Greece."

Real Change

Herodotus was born at Halicarnassus, on the southwest coast of Asia Minor, in the early part of the fifth century B.C. Of his life we know almost nothing, except that he spent much of it traveling to collect the material for his writings, and that he finally settled down at Thurii in southern Italy where his great work was composed. He died in 424 B.C.

The subject of the history of Herodotus is the struggle between the Greeks and the barbarians, which he brings down to the battle of Mycale in 479 B.C. The work, as we have it, is divided into nine books, named after the nine Muses, but this division is probably due to the Alexandrine grammarians. He gathered his information mainly from oral sources as he traveled through Asia Minor, down into Egypt, round the Black Sea, and into various parts of Greece and the neighboring countries. The chronological narrative halts from time to time to give opportunity for descriptions of the country, the people, and their customs and previous history; and the political account is constantly varied by rare tales and wonders.

Among these descriptions of countries the most fascinating to the modern reader, as it was to the ancient, is his account of the marvels of the land of Egypt. From the priests at Memphis, Heliopolis, and the Egyptian Thebes he learned what he reports of the size of the country, the wonders of the Nile, the ceremonies of their religion, the sacredness of their animals. He tells also of the strange ways of the crocodile and of that marvelous bird, the phoenix; of dress and funerals and embalming; of the eating of lotos and papyrus; of the pyramids and the great labyrinth; of their kings and queens and courtesans.

Yet Herodotus is not a mere teller of strange tales. However credulous he may appear to a modern judgment, he takes care to keep separate what he knows by his own observation from what he has merely inferred and from what he has been told. He is candid about acknowledging ignorance, and when versions differ he gives both. Thus the modern scientific historian, with other means of corroboration, can sometimes learn from Herodotus more than Herodotus himself knew.

There is abundant evidence, too, that Herodotus had a philosophy of history. The unity which marks his work is due not only to the strong Greek national feeling running through it, the feeling that rises to a height in such passages as the descriptions of the battles of Marathon, Thermopylae, and Salamis, but also to his profound belief in fate and in nemesis. His belief in fate is due the frequent quoting of oracles and their fulfilment, the frequent references to things foreordained by providence. The working of nemesis he finds in the disasters that befall men and nations whose towering prosperity awakens the jealousy of the gods. The final overthrow of the Persians, which forms his main theme, is only one specially conspicuous example of the operation of this force from which human life can never free itself.

But, above all, he is the father of storytellers. "Herodotus is such simple and delightful reading,"

Statue of philosopher Herodotus in Vienna.

says Jevons; "he is so unaffected and entertaining, his story flows so naturally and with such ease that we have a difficulty in bearing in mind that, over and above the hard writing which goes to make easy reading there is a perpetual marvel in the work of Herodotus. It is the first artistic work in prose that Greek literature produced. This prose work, which for pure literary merit no subsequent work has surpassed, than which later generations, after using the pen for centuries, have produced no prose more easy or more readable, this was the first of histories and of literary prose" (Herodotus, *An Account of Egypt*, G.C. Macaulay, translator, www.gutenberg.org/files/2131/2131-h/2131-h.htm)

Assignments

- Warm-up: Compare Herodotus' *Histories* with 1 and 2 Kings.
- Students should complete Concept Builder 6-A.
- Students should review the required reading(s) *before* the assigned chapter begins.
- Teachers may want to discuss assigned reading(s) with students.
- Teachers shall assign the required essay. The rest of the essays can be outlined, answered with shorter answers, discussed, or skipped.
- Students will review all readings for chapter 6.

CONCEPT BUILDER 6-A Active Reading		Read *The Histories* (Book 1), by Herodotus, and then answer the following questions.
	1	Compare this history book to other history books you have read.
	2	Herodotus is writing a narrative history, or a history of stories. He tells one story after another. What problem might this pose for historians?
	3	Clearly, this is a history written in a way to put the Greeks in the best light. Offer two examples.

Herodotus in Egypt

Being set free after the reign of the priest of Hephaistos, the Egyptians, since they could not live any time without a king, set up over them twelve kings, having divided all Egypt into twelve parts. These made intermarriages with one another and reigned, making agreement that they would not put down one another by force, nor seek to get an advantage over one another, but would live in perfect friendship: and the reason why they made these agreements, guarding them very strongly from violation, was this, namely that an oracle had been given to them at first when they began to exercise their rule, that he of them who should pour a libation with a bronze cup in the temple of Hephaistos, should be king of all Egypt (for they used to assemble together in all the temples). Moreover they resolved to join all together and leave a memorial of themselves; and having so resolved they caused to be made a labyrinth, situated a little above the lake of Moiris and nearly opposite to that which is called the City of Crocodiles. This I saw myself, and I found it greater than words can say. For if one should put together and reckon up all the buildings and all the great works produced by Hellenes, they would prove to be inferior in labour and expense to this labyrinth, though it is true that both the temple at Ephesos and that at Samos are works worthy of note. The pyramids also were greater than words can say, and each one of them is equal to many works of the Hellenes, great as they may be; but the labyrinth surpasses even the pyramids. It has twelve courts covered in, with gates facing one another, six upon the North side and six upon the South, joining on one to another, and the same wall surrounds them all outside; and there are in it two kinds of chambers, the one kind below the ground and the other above upon these, three

thousand in number, of each kind fifteen hundred. The upper set of chambers we ourselves saw, going through them, and we tell of them having looked upon them with our own eyes; but the chambers under ground we heard about only; for the Egyptians who had charge of them were not willing on any account to show them, saying that here were the sepulchres of the kings who had first built this labyrinth and of the sacred crocodiles. Accordingly we speak of the chambers below by what we received from hearsay, while those above we saw ourselves and found them to be works of more than human greatness. For the passages through the chambers, and the goings this way and that way through the courts, which were admirably adorned, afforded endless matter for marvel, as we went through from a court to the chambers beyond it, and from the chambers to colonnades, and from the colonnades to other rooms, and then from the chambers again to other courts. Over the whole of these is a roof made of stone like the walls; and the walls are covered with figures carved upon them, each court being surrounded with pillars of white stone fitted together most perfectly; and at the end of the labyrinth, by the corner of it, there is a pyramid of forty fathoms, upon which large figures are carved, and to this there is a way made under ground.

Such is this labyrinth: but a cause for marvel even greater than this is afforded by the lake, which is called the lake of Moiris, along the side of which this labyrinth is built. The measure of its circuit is three thousand six hundred furlongs (being sixty schoines), and this is the same number of furlongs as the extent of Egypt itself along the sea. The lake lies extended lengthwise from North to South, and in depth where it is deepest it is fifty fathoms. That this lake is artificial and formed by digging is self-evident, for about in the middle of the lake stand two pyramids, each rising above the water to a height of fifty fathoms, the part which is built below the water being of just the same height; and upon each is placed a colossal statue of stone sitting upon a chair. Thus the pyramids are a hundred fathoms high; and these hundred fathoms are equal to a furlong of six hundred feet, the fathom being measured as six feet or four cubits, the feet being four palms each, and the cubits six. The water in the lake does not come from the place where it is, for the country there is very deficient in water, but it has been brought thither from the Nile by a canal; and for six months the water flows into the lake, and for six months out into the Nile again; and whenever it flows out, then for the six months it brings into the royal treasury a talent of silver a day from the fish which are caught, and twenty pounds when the water comes in. The natives of the place moreover said that this lake had an outlet under ground to the Syrtis which is in Libya, turning towards the interior of the continent upon the Western side and running along by the mountain which is above Memphis. Now since I did not see anywhere existing the earth dug out of this excavation (for that was a matter which drew my attention), I asked those who dwelt nearest to the lake where the earth was which had been dug out. These told me to what place it had been carried away; and I readily believed them, for I knew by report that a similar thing had been done at Nineveh, the city of the Assyrians. There certain thieves formed a design once to carry away the wealth of Sardanapallos son of Ninos, the king, which wealth was very great and was kept in treasure-houses under the earth. Accordingly they began from their own dwelling, and making estimate of their direction they dug under ground towards the king's palace; and the earth which was brought out of the excavation they used to carry away, when night came on, to the river Tigris which flows by the city of Nineveh, until at last they accomplished that which they desired. Similarly, as I heard, the digging of the lake in Egypt was effected, except that it was done not by night but during the day; for as they dug the Egyptians carried to the Nile the earth which was dug out; and the river, when it received it, would naturally bear it away and disperse it. Thus is this lake said to have been dug out.

Assignments

- Warm-up: Summarize Herodotus' description of the pyramids and how they were built.
- Students should complete Concept Builder 6-B.
- Students should review reading(s) from the next chapter.
- Students should outline essay due at the end of the week.
- Per teacher instructions, students may answer orally, in a group setting, some of the essays that are not assigned as formal essays.

Using the diagram below to show your history.

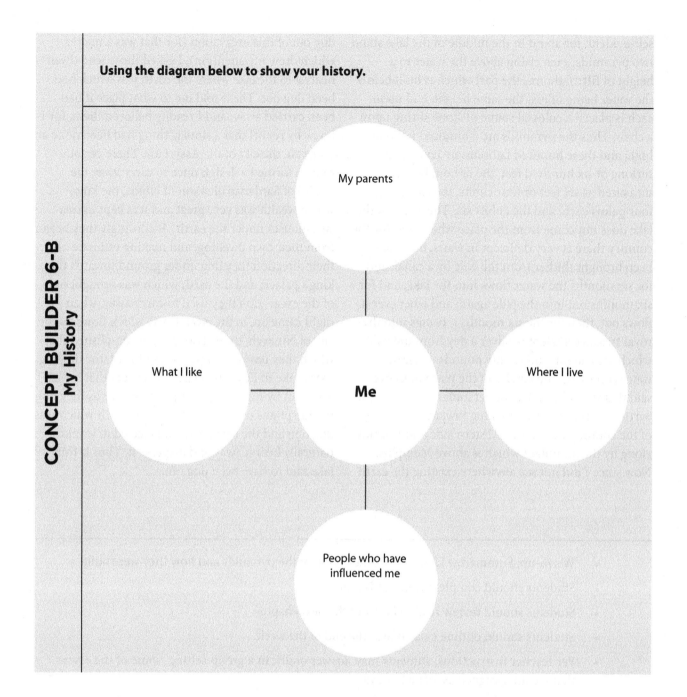

Biblical Parallels in *The Histories*

During the mid 4th century B.C., Herotodus, a Greek traveler, compiled his many journeys into one large volume, *The Histories*. In fact, his detailed, systematic, and accurate descriptions in this magnum opus earned him the title "Father of History." Herotodus' vivid depiction of Egypt in *The Histories* bears many resemblances to the biblical account of Egypt: the practice of foot washing is mentioned in both *The Histories* and the Bible, both describe the numerous canals in Egypt, and both reference the spices used in embalming.

Because of the prevalence of sandals (and unpaved streets) in ancient Egypt, one's feet would get filthy rather quickly. As part of their cleansing rituals, Egyptians washed their feet prior to meals. An Egyptian king's golden foot-pan is mentioned in Book II of *The Histories*, "Among his other splendour he had a golden foot-pan, in which his guests and himself were wont upon occasion to wash their feet." In the Bible, this Egyptian practice of foot washing is also found. When Joseph, the governor of Egypt, entertained his brothers, a foot-washing ceremony preceded the meal, "The steward took the men into Joseph's house, gave them water to wash their feet . . ." (Gen. 43:24). Before dining, Egyptians washed their feet — a practice referenced both in the Bible and in *The Histories*.

Another similarity between the biblical account of Egypt and *The Histories* is the mention of canals. To irrigate Egypt's crops in an arid climate, a large network of canals branched out from the Nile River. In book II of *The Histories*, Herotodus complains, "Though a flat country throughout its whole extent, it is now unfit for either horse or carriage, being cut up by the canals, which are extremely numerous and run in all directions." This extensive network of canals is also mentioned in Exodus 8:5, "Then the LORD said to Moses, 'Tell Aaron, "Stretch out your hand with your staff over the streams and canals and ponds, and make frogs come up on the land of Egypt!" ' " In this case, both the *The Histories* and the biblical account corroborate each other's mention of numerous canals.

Because of their complicated and lengthy embalming rituals, the Egyptians consumed spices rapidly. Herodotus mentions, in his description of the embalming rituals, "They fill the cavity with the purest bruised myrrh, with cassia, and every other sort of spicery except frankincense . . ." (Book II). The biblical account also mentions traders going to Egypt with the spices requisite for embalming: "They looked up and saw a caravan of Ishamaelites coming from Gilead. Their camels were loaded with spices, balm, and myrrh, and they were on their way to take them down to Egypt" (Gen. 37:25). Both the Bible and Herodotus record the Egyptian's need for large amounts of spices.

In Herodotus' tour de force *The Histories*, his description of the mysterious land of Egypt is remarkably similar to the account found in the Bible. Both mention the practice of washing one's feet prior to meals. The extensive network of canals, which Herodotus found to be inconvenient, is depicted in the Bible as well as in *The Histories*. Finally, both describe the need of the Egyptians for spices used in embalming. (Daniel)

Assignments

- Warm-up: List a few biblical parallels in *The Histories*.
- Students should complete Concept Builder 6-C.
- Students should write rough draft of assigned essay.
- The teacher may correct rough drafts.

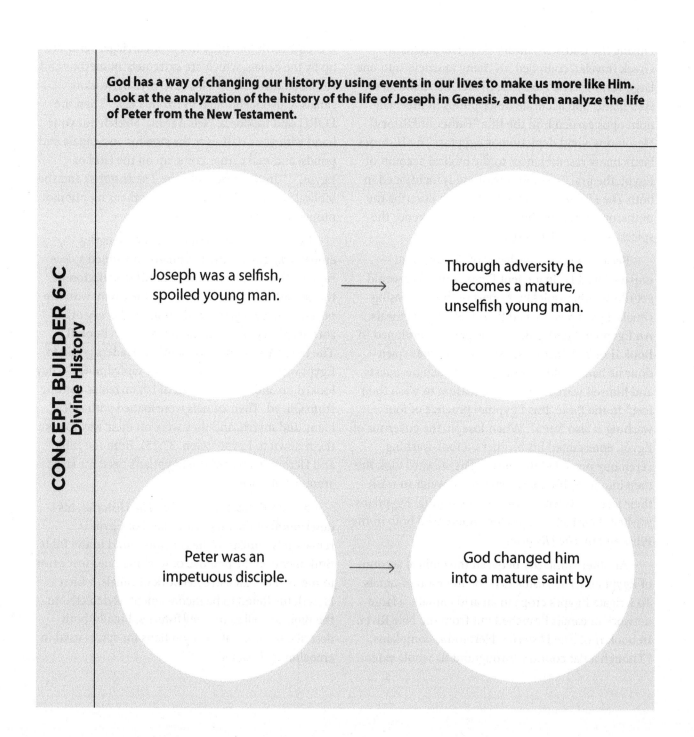

CONCEPT BUILDER 6-C
Divine History

God has a way of changing our history by using events in our lives to make us more like Him. Look at the analyzation of the history of the life of Joseph in Genesis, and then analyze the life of Peter from the New Testament.

Joseph was a selfish, spoiled young man. → Through adversity he becomes a mature, unselfish young man.

Peter was an impetuous disciple. → God changed him into a mature saint by

Herodotus' Philosophy of History

The Trojan War, the conquest of Babylon, the Persian conquest of Greece, and Greek navy battles are just a few of the many events listed in Herodotus' *The Histories*. Gathering his information about the history of each region he traveled to, Herodotus chose to discuss political rather than cultural events.

". . . if Helen had been at Troy, the inhabitants would, I think, haven given her up to the Greeks, whether Alexandra consented to it or no." One such political event recorded by Herodotus is the Trojan War. While the Trojan War did affect the culture of the Greeks, it was primarily a battle between two opposing generals and kings, rather than ideas.

During the second chapter of *The Histories*, Herodotus journeys to Egypt. "Now the Egyptians, before Psammetichos became king over them, supposed that they were the first of all men. . . ." This particular situation deals with the government of Egypt rather than the rituals or ceremonies performed in everyday life. But even though this is a political event, Herodotus gives some information about the culture of Egypt. "The priests of the gods in other lands wear long hair, but in Egypt they shave their heads. Among other men the custom is that in mourning those whom the matter concerns most nearly have their hair cut short, but the Egyptians, when deaths occur, let their hair grow long, both that on the head and that on the chin, having before been close shaven." Still, most of chapter two, titled, "Egypt: Geography, Customs, History, Tales," contains political events rather than cultural events.

All of chapter 7 contains information regarding the Persian conquest of Greece. The chapter is titled, "Xerxes' Expedition into Greece, Battle of Thermopylae." If one may recall, the battle of

Thermopylae was a famous battle in which 300 Spartan warriors fought against the vast Persian army at the Strait of Thermopylae. This is an event so important that several movies in modern times have been made retelling its events. Herodotus probably recognized the significance of such a battle and decided to record it, lest it be lost to future generations. While this event did have a substantial effect on the Greek culture, historians would classify it as a political event recording the battle between kings and armies not philosophers.

Another political event recorded by Herodotus is the conquest of Babylon. "After Babylon had been taken, the march of Dareios himself against the Scythians took place. . . ." As seen, this is another military and political event Herodotus chooses to include. And just as before, where a military conquest can alter the culture of a people, this military conquest is primarily a political event, a battle between two opposing armies.

Herodotus did not only record about two armies attacking two armies. He interjected the deity into the events. This was because, Herodotus, being Greek and assuming the gods were involved in daily human affairs, felt it was only normal to write of how the gods affected decisions. "However I heard from men of Kyrene, who told me that they had been to the Oracle of Ammon, and had spoken with Etearchos king of the Ammonians." Herodotus also discusses the gods giving happiness to humans. "But we must for everything examine the end and how it will turn out at the last, for to many God shows but a glimpse of happiness and then plucks them up by the roots and overturns them." From these quotes we see that Herodotus talks about how the gods are involved in human affairs.

Throughout *The Histories*, Herodotus chooses to record political events such as wars, men becoming kings, conquests of cities, and much more. While he does talk about some cultural things, such as the customs of priests in Egypt, his primary focus is on events dealing with kings and armies. In addition, Herodotus does not forget to interject how the gods play a large role in human affairs, mirroring the belief he was raised in. His choice to record such things makes *The Histories* probably the most important history book of ancient times. (Chris)

Assignments

- Warm-up: What is Herodotus' philosophy of history?
- Students should complete Concept Builder 6-D.
- Students will re-write corrected copies of essay due tomorrow.

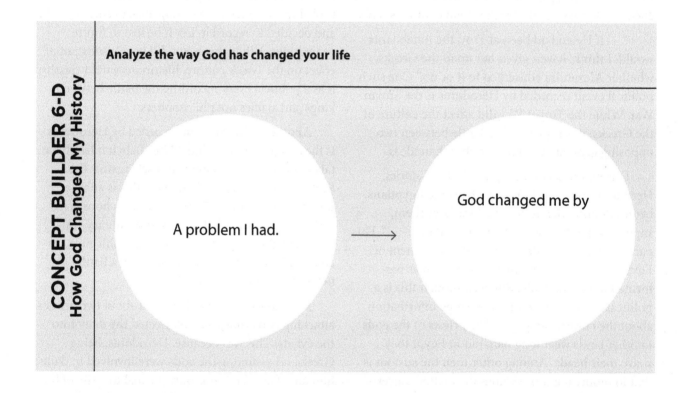

CONCEPT BUILDER 6-D
How God Changed My History

Analyze the way God has changed your life

A problem I had. → God changed me by

Father of History

"This is the showing forth of the inquiry of Herodotus of Halicarnassos so that neither the deeds of men may be forgotten by lapse of time, nor the works great and marvellous, which have been produced some by Hellenes and some by Barbarians, may lose their renown; and especially that the causes may be remembered for which these waged war with one another." (Herodotus, *Histories*, New York: Barnes & Noble, 2004, Book I, ch. 1, p. 3). Herodotus in *The Histories* created a type of literature that had not previously existed. This genre was dedicated to "historie," the Greek word from which the English word "history" is derived. It has been noted, however, that some information in *The Histories* is clearly exaggerated, such as the enumeration of Dareios' army in Book IV, chapter 87. Herodotus claims that Darieos led 700,000 soldiers, but armies were never this large in ancient times. This "fact" definitely does not appear to represent solid history. The reconciliation of Herodotus' purpose to "show forth (his) inquiry" with his occassional drift into inaccurate information may be found in his philosophy of history.

First, it is vital to recognize that, before Herodotus, there was no Greek word that was the literal equivalent of the English word "history." The Greek word "historie" translates most accurately as inquiry or research. When Herodotus' text reads, "This is the showing forth of the inquiry of Herodotus of Halicarnassos," "historie" is the word translated as inquiry. Therefore, a book of "historie" may be a book of scientific, mythological, geographical, cultural, or historical inquiries. Each of the five topics mentioned above is present in *The Histories*. When critics accuse Herodotus of allowing mythology to enter into his history, they are merely overlooking the multifaceted meaning of "historie."

However, "historie" is not the primary focus of *The Histories*. Herodotus' purpose for writing his book is often misunderstood because of its title. In modern English, "history" has come to mean, according to the *Oxford American Dictionary*, "the study of past events, particularly in human affairs." Therefore, when a modern reader undertakes a volume titled *The Histories*, "the study of past events" is what the title seems to imply. As has been seen, though, this is not the ancient idea of "historie," nor is it the purpose of Herodotus' work. Herodotus clearly states in the opening lines that his purpose is to preserve the memory of an important event in Greek culture, namely the Persian War. In a similar manner, Henry Wadsworth Longfellow, in his famous poem "The Midnight Ride of Paul Revere," writes, "Hardly a man is now alive/Who remembers that famous day and year," thus implying that his purpose in writing the poem is to preserve the memory of Revere's ride. Herodotus likewise states that he records the Graeco-Persian War "so that neither the deeds of men may be forgotten by lapse of time. . . ." Herodotus also intended to celebrate the glory of the Graeco-Persian War. ". . . nor the works great and marvellous . . . may lose their renown." In this sense, *The Histories* are akin to Homer's *The Iliad*, which focuses on the glory of war, even though these two works are starkly different in many other ways. Those who criticize Herodotus for not providing a focused historical text are mistaken about Herodotus' primary goal.

Another criticism that is commonly posed against *The Histories* is that Herodotus provides "excess" information that does not relate to the portion of history he focuses on. However, it is vital to understand the last clause of the first sentence of *The Histories*. Herodotus has listed two reasons for writing his book, and then concludes by stating his purpose: ". . . that the causes may be remembered for which these (Greeks and Persians) waged war with one another." Herodotus' focus is on the details of the Graeco-Persian War, but it is also on the causes of the Graeco-Persian War. Therefore, everything distantly related to this conflict is expedient to Herodotus' purpose. He presents scientific, cultural, and geographical information about many societies. Some critics have labeled these discussions as "digressions," but at this point one must remember that "historie" refers to inquiry not only about historical and mythological information, but about any topic, science, culture, and geography included. Herodotus presents many stories, such as the Trojan War, that are seemingly unrelated to the Graeco-Persian War. However, all of these events "set the stage" for the ultimate battle. For example, the Persian conquest of Egypt sheds some light on how

the Persians conquered powerful foreign empires. Therefore, discussions of Egypt and events which occurred on Egyptian soil are distantly related to the Graeco-Persian War and find an appropriate place in *The Histories*. Herodotus desired to know not only what happened, by why.

Even though many consider the inaccurate and "irrelevant" information in *The Histories* to be evidence of Herodotus' fallibility as a historian, it is equally, if not more related to Herodotus' philosophy of what *The Histories* should recount. Herodotus has been named "the father of lies," but this sprouts from a misunderstanding of Herodotus' purpose for writing and the meaning of the Greek word, "historie." With a clear understanding of Herodotus' philosophy of history, it is safe to assert that Herodotus was not "the father of lies," but truly "the father of history."

Assignments

- Warm-up: What is the primary purpose of Herodutus' works?
- Students should complete Concept Builder 6-E.
- Essays are due. Students should take the chapter 6 test.

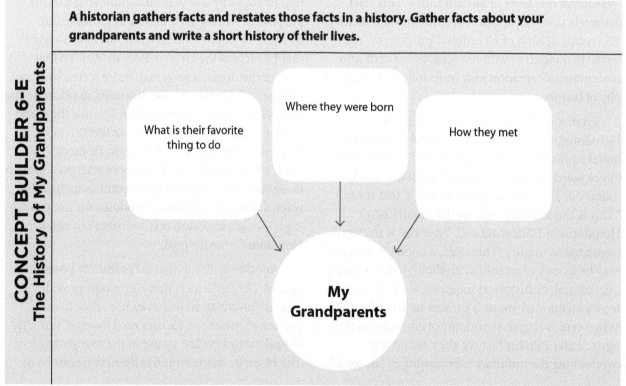

CONCEPT BUILDER 6-E
The History Of My Grandparents

A historian gathers facts and restates those facts in a history. Gather facts about your grandparents and write a short history of their lives.

What is their favorite thing to do

Where they were born

How they met

My Grandparents

Chapter 7

(800 B.C.–300 B.C.):
Ancient Greece (Part 4)

First Thoughts Plato (429–347 B.C.E.) is, by any reckoning, one of the most dazzling writers in the Western literary tradition and one of the most penetrating, wide-ranging, and influential authors in the history of philosophy. Charles Eliot, in the Harvard Classics, offers, "The philosophy of these dialogues has remained for over two thousand years one of the great intellectual influences of the civilized world; and they are as admirable from the point of view of literature as of philosophy. The style is not only beautiful in itself, but is adapted with great dramatic skill to the large variety of speakers; and the suggestion of situation and the drawing of character are the work of a great artist. The three dialogues here given are at once favorable examples of the literary skill of Plato and intimate pictures of the personality of his master" (www.bartleby.com/).

Objectives In this chapter we meet arguably the greatest philsosopher in world history. In the character of Socrates we are invited to examine the passion and struggle of choosing honor over everything else.

As a result of this chapter study you will be able to . . .

1. Examine Socrates' view of holiness.

2. Analyze the way Socrates prepares for death and why he does not escape.

3. Analyze the charge that Socrates corrupted the youth.

4. Analyze the meaning of impiety in Plato's writings.

5. Compare and contrast Socrates' view of the afterlife with 1 Corinthians 15 and other New Testament passages.

6. Socrates proclaims to his fellow Athenians that their obsession with wealth and the material world must never take precedence over the care of the soul. Compare this view with the Sermon on the Mount and other teachings by Jesus Christ (Matthew 5 and 6).

Chapter Learning

Weekly Essay Options: Begin on page 273 of the Teacher Guide.
Reading ahead: *The Republic* by Plato.

89

History connections: *World History* chapter 7, "Life in Athens: Part One."

The Death of Socrates

Background Ralph Waldo Emerson said, "Out of Plato come all things that are still written and debated among men of thought." Plato was born around the year 428 B.C. into a blue-blooded Athenian household. Plato's parents were Ariston and Perictone, his older brothers were Adeimantus and Glaucon, and his younger sister was Potone. What a mouthful! In keeping with his family heritage, Plato was destined for the political life. But the Peloponnesian War, which began a couple of years before he was born and continued until well after he was 20, led to the decline of the Athenian Empire. He barely had a city-state to govern! The war was followed by a reactionary period that led to the execution of Plato's mentor, Socrates. Together these events forever altered the course of Plato's life — the decline of Athenian hegemony and the execution of Socrates.

There was no more important philosopher in Western culture than Plato. Plato regarded ethics as the highest branch of knowledge. Plato stressed the intellectual basis of virtue, identifying virtue with wisdom. Plato believed that the world was made of *forms* (such as rocks) and *ideas* (such as virtue). The ability of human beings to appreciate forms made a person virtuous. Knowledge came from the gods; opinion was from man. Virtuous activity, then, was dependent upon knowledge of the forms (James Stobaugh, *A Fire that Burns but Does Not Consume* Hollsopple, PA: For Such a Time as This, 2003).

Assignments

- Warm-up: Central to Plato's thoughts was the notion that if people know the "good" they will do the good. Why is he wrong?

- Students should complete Concept Builder 7-A.

- Students should review the required reading(s) *before* the assigned chapter begins.

- Teachers may want to discuss assigned reading(s) with students.

- Teachers shall assign the required essay. The rest of the essays can be outlined, answered with shorter answers, discussed, or skipped.

- Students will review all readings for chapter 7.

Read this excerpt from "The Death of Socrates" (the ending of *Phaedo*) by Plato, and respond to the following:

CONCEPT BUILDER 7-A
Active Reading

Then Socrates turned to us, and added with a smile: "I cannot make Crito believe that I am the same Socrates who has been talking and conducting the argument; he fancies that I am the other Socrates whom he will soon see, a dead body — and he asks, How shall he bury me? And though I have spoken many words in the endeavor to show that when I have drunk the poison I shall leave you and go to the joys of the blessed — these words of mine, with which I was comforting you and myself, have had, as I perceive, no effect upon Crito. And therefore I want you to be surety for me to him how, as at the trial he was surety to the judges for me: but let the promise be of another sort; for he was surety for me to the judges that I would remain, and you must be my surety to him that I shall not remain, but go away and depart; and then he will suffer less at my death, and not be grieved when he sees my body being burned or buried. I would not have him sorrow at my hard lot, or say at the burial, Thus we lay out Socrates, or Thus we follow him to the grave or bury him; for false words are not only evil in themselves, but they infect the soul with evil. Be of good cheer then, my dear Crito, and say that you are burying my body only, and do with that whatever is usual, and what you think best."

When he had spoken these words, he arose and went into a chamber to bathe; Crito followed him and told us to wait. So we remained behind, talking and thinking of the subject of discourse, and also of the greatness of our sorrow; he was like a father of whom we were being bereaved, and we were about to pass the rest of our lives as orphans. When he had taken the bath his children were brought to him (he had two young sons and an elder one); and the women of his family also came, and he talked to them and gave them a few directions in the presence of Crito; then he dismissed them and returned to us.

Now the hour of sunset was near, for a good deal of time had passed while he was within. When he came out, he sat down with us again after his bath, but not much was said. Soon the jailer, who was the servant of the eleven, entered and stood by him, saying: "To you, Socrates, whom I know to be the noblest and gentlest and best of all who ever came to this place, I will not impute the angry feelings of other men, who rage and swear at me, when, in obedience to the authorities, I bid them drink the poison — indeed, I am sure that you will not be angry with me; for others, as you are aware, and not I, are to blame. And so fare you well, and try to bear lightly what must needs be — you know my errand." Then bursting into tears he turned away and went out.

This book is essentially one dialogue after another. What advantage does a dialogue style offer Plato?

"So we remained behind, talking and thinking of the subject of discourse, and also of the greatness of our sorrow; he was like a father of whom we were being bereaved, and we were about to pass the rest of our lives as orphans." Paraphrase this passage.

The Last Days of Socrates

The Last Days of Socrates contains four smaller books called, *Euthyphro*, *The Apology*, *Crito*, and *Phaedo*. Together they constitute some of the greatest Western literature. In these four books, the philosopher Plato, assuming the persona of Socrates, discusses most of the worldview issues relevant to man. He sets the agenda for philosophical discussion for three centuries. In *The Apology*, Socrates says, "The unexamined life is not worth living." In these four books, Plato examines life in great detail.

Socrates, the son of an Athenian sculptor, was born in 469 B.C. After giving up his father's occupation and serving as a soldier, Socrates devoted himself to being a philosopher. Like other philosophers, he did not give formal instruction but went about engaging people in conversation. He used rhetorical questions to entice his countrymen, and especially the young men, to think clearly and to act reasonably. It was natural that this should create enemies, and Socrates was finally accused of atheism and of corrupting the youth. His defense, as will be seen from *The Apology*, was conducted with his customary firm adherence to his convictions, and with entire fearlessness of consequences. He could, in all probability, have easily escaped the death sentence had he been willing to take a conciliatory tone, but he died (399 B.C.) a martyr to his unswerving devotion to truth. Socrates wrote nothing, and we learn what we know of his teachings chiefly from his disciples, Xenophon and Plato.

The story line of this philosophical book is therefore the death of Socrates. Socrates is on trial. During the trial he answers his accusers, "Despite what you've heard . . . I'm just a man who's aware of his ignorance . . . I'm like a gadfly who's always buzzing about, bothering horses and preventing them from becoming sluggish. . . . I buzz around town making sure no one thinks he knows something when he really doesn't!" Socrates is convicted by 30 votes. Athenian courts allow a convicted person to offer an alternative punishment to the one proposed by the court (i.e., death by hemlock poisoning). Socrates irritates the court by suggesting that he receive free meals for the rest of his life! The rest of the book is a series of dialogues with friends who visit him in jail.

Euthyphro, *Crito*, and *Phaedo* are full of dialogues in which there is an inquiry into a central problem. *Euthyphro* examines what human goodness is and how it can be recognized, *Crito* is concerned with legal authority, and *Phaedo* explores metaphysical themes. In *The Apology*, Socrates defends himself to the Athenian court of 502 of his peers.

Statue of Socrates (ancient Greek philosopher) in front of the Academy of Athens, Greece.

- Warm-up: How would you describe wisdom?

- Students should complete Concept Builder 7-B.

- Students should review reading(s) from the next chapter.

- Students should outline essay due at the end of the week.

- Per teacher instructions, students may answer orally, in a group setting, some of the essays that are not assigned as formal essays.

CONCEPT BUILDER 7-B
The Setting

The setting is where the story occurs.

Circle three places where Socrates might have worshipped his gods.

Check where Socrates would have been tried in court.

Box the place where he died.

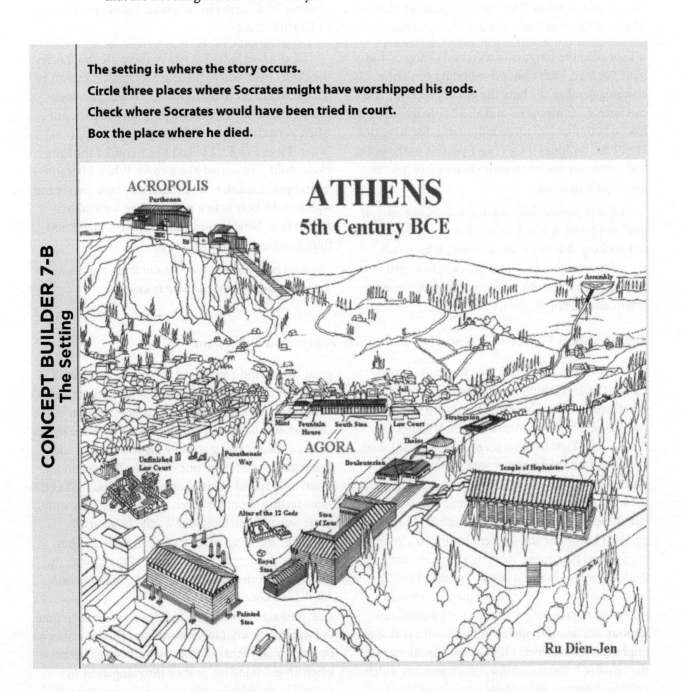

Plato and Paul

Paul is quite fond of Plato's teachings. Most Pharisees, including Paul, were philosophical followers of Plato. This is obvious in Paul's passage on the subject of love in 1 Corinthians 13:

If I speak in the tongues of men and of angels, but have not love, I am only a resounding gong or a clanging cymbal. If I have the gift of prophecy and can fathom all mysteries and all knowledge, and if I have a faith that can move mountains, but have not love, I am nothing. If I give all I possess to the poor and surrender my body to the flames, but have not love, I gain nothing.

Love is patient, love is kind. It does not envy, it does not boast, it is not proud. It is not rude, it is not self-seeking, it is not easily angered, it keeps no record of wrongs. Love does not delight in evil but rejoices with the truth. It always protects, always trusts, always hopes, always perseveres.

Love never fails. But where there are prophecies, they will cease; where there are tongues, they will be stilled; where there is knowledge, it will pass away. For we know in part and we prophesy in part, but when perfection comes, the imperfect disappears. When I was a child, I talked like a child, I thought like a child, I reasoned like a child. When I became a man, I put childish ways behind me. Now we see but a poor reflection as in a mirror; then we shall see face to face. Now I know in part; then I shall know fully, even as I am fully known.

And now these three remain: faith, hope and love. But the greatest of these is love.

The following is Plato's description of love in the preface to his book *Symposium*:

First Chaos came, and then broad-bosomed Earth, The everlasting seat of all that is, And Love. In other words, after Chaos, the Earth and Love, these two, came into being. Also Parmenides sings of Generation: First in the train of gods, he fashioned Love. And Acusilaus agrees with Hesiod. Thus numerous are the witnesses who acknowledge Love to be the eldest of the gods. And not only is he the eldest, he is also the source of the greatest benefits to us. For I know not any greater blessing to a young man who is beginning life than a virtuous lover, or to the lover than a beloved youth. For the principle which ought to be the guide of men who would nobly live at principle, I say, neither kindred, nor honour, nor wealth, nor any other motive is able to implant so well as love. Of what am I speaking? Of the sense of honour and dishonour, without which neither states nor individuals ever do any good or

great work. And I say that a lover who is detected in doing any dishonourable act, or submitting through cowardice when any dishonour is done to him by another, will be more pained at being detected by his beloved than at being seen by his father, or by his companions, or by any one else. The beloved too, when he is found in any disgraceful situation, has the same feeling about his lover. And if there were only some way of contriving that a state or an army should be made up of lovers and their loves, they would be the very best governors of their own city, abstaining from all dishonour, and emulating one another in honour; and when fighting at each other's side, although a mere handful, they would overcome the world. For what lover would not choose rather to be seen by all mankind than by his beloved, either when abandoning his post or throwing away his arms? He would be ready to die a thousand deaths rather than endure this. Or who would desert his beloved or fail him in the hour of danger? The veriest coward would become an inspired hero, equal to the bravest, at such a time; Love would inspire him. That courage which, as Homer says, the god breathes into the souls of some heroes, Love of his own nature infuses into the lover. Love will make men dare to die for their beloved-love alone; and women as well as men. Of this, Alcestis, the daughter of Pelias, is a monument to all Hellas; for she was willing to lay down her life on behalf of her husband, when no one else would, although he had a father and mother; but the tenderness of her love so far exceeded theirs, that she made them seem to be strangers in blood to their own son, and in name only related to him; and

St. Paul delivering the *Areopagus Sermon* in Athens by Raphael, 1515 (PD-Art).

so noble did this action of hers appear to the gods, as well as to men, that among the many who have done virtuously she is one of the very few to whom, in admiration of her noble action, they have granted the privilege of returning alive to earth; such exceeding honour is paid by the gods to the devotion and virtue of love. But Orpheus, the son of Oeagrus, the harper, they sent empty away, and presented to him an apparition only of her whom he sought, but herself they would not give up, because he showed no spirit; he was only a harp-player, and did not dare like Alcestis to die for love, but was contriving how he might enter Hades alive; moreover, they afterwards caused him to suffer death at the hands of women, as the punishment of his cowardliness.

Very different was the reward of the true love of Achilles towards his lover Patroclus — his lover and not his love (the notion that Patroclus was the beloved one is a foolish error into which Aeschylus has fallen, for Achilles was surely the fairer of the

two, fairer also than all the other heroes; and, as Homer informs us, he was still beardless, and younger far). And greatly as the gods honour the virtue of love, still the return of love on the part of the beloved to the lover is more admired and valued and rewarded by them, for the lover is more divine; because he is inspired by God. Now Achilles was quite aware, for he had been told by his mother, that he might avoid death and return home, and live to a good old age, if he abstained from slaying Hektor. Nevertheless he gave his life to revenge his friend, and dared to die, not only in his defence, but after he was dead. Wherefore the gods honoured him even above Alcestis, and sent him to the Islands of the Blest. These are my reasons for affirming that Love is the eldest and noblest and mightiest of the gods, and the chiefest author and giver of virtue in life, and of happiness after death (www.bartleby.com and www. textkit.com).

Assignments

- Warm-up: Compare and contrast the subject of love as presented by Plato and Paul.
- Students should complete Concept Builder 7-C.
- Students should write rough draft of assigned essay.
- The teacher may correct rough drafts.

Which artistic rendition seems more real to the actual event? Why?

Two versions of *The Death of Socrates*, the first by Daniel Chodowiecki, c.18th century, and the second by Jacques-Louis David, 1787 (PD-Art).

Despicable Sophists

In *Phaedo*, Socrates opposes the Sophists, arguing that there are absolute standards of right and wrong. He believes that once we understand what is truly good, we will act in accord with that knowledge. To Socrates, then, "The virtues are a kind of knowledge." He also firmly believes (as shown in the second passage) that the cosmos is grounded in goodness, that a good person will not suffer unduly, and that death is not something to be feared.

> Now as you see there has come upon me that which may be thought, and is generally believed to be, the last and worst evil. . . . I regard this as a proof that what has happened to me is a good, and that those of use who think that death is an evil are in error. . . . Let us reflect in another way, and we shall see that there is great reason to hope that death is a good, for one of two things: — either death is a state of nothingness and utter unconsciousness, or, as men say, there is a change and migration of the soul from this world to another. Now if you suppose that there is no consciousness, but a sleep like the sleep of him who is undisturbed even by the sight of dreams, death will be an unspeakable gain. . . . Now if death is like this, I say that to die is gain; for eternity is then only a single night. But if death is a journey to another place, and there, as men say, all the dead are, what good, O my friends and judges, can be greater than this? . . . Above all, I shall be able to continue my search into true and false knowledge; as in this world, so also in that; I shall find out who is wise, and who pretends to be wise, and is not. . . . The hour of departure has arrived, and we go our ways — I to die, and you to live. Which is better God only knows.

In what ways does this view violate Judeo-Christian views?

Assignments

- Warm-up: What is the form of function of the Socratic dialogues?
- Students should complete Concept Builder 7-D.
- Students will re-write corrected copies of essay due tomorrow.

One of the reasons that Socrates is not afraid of death is that he is going to hades (hell), a person and a place to the Greeks, which to Socrates, is not so bad a place. Going to hades (hell) is like falling asleep. However, this is not an accurate picture of hell. Draw a Christian view of hell.

Sappho

Background Sappho was the earliest known woman writer in Western literature. She lived on an island in the Aegean Sea during the seventh century B.C. Sappho was so highly regarded among Greek poets of her time that "Plato dubbed her the Tenth Muse." Even though only one of her poems and a few lines of others are extant — they were destroyed in the great fire that consumed the Alexandrian Library, she wrote "nine books of lyric poetry and influenced many later Greek poets . . . she created the verse form called Sapphics." We don't have much of her poetry left, and we know very little about her, but apparently she was not a lone female poet. She led a group of devoted female-student poets.

Tonight I've Watched	The night is now	Although they are
Tonight I've watched	Half-gone; youth	Only breath, words
The moon and then	goes; I am	which I command
The Pleiades	In bed alone.	are immortal.
go down.		

Constance Jones, editor, *1000 Things Everyone Should Know about Women's History* (New York: Doubleday, 1998), p. 173.

Assignments

- Warm-up: How do these short poem excerpts differ in form of function from other Greek writers (e.g., Plato, Homer, Aristotle)?

- Students should complete Concept Builder 7-E.

- Essays are due. Students should take the chapter 7 test.

Sappho and Alcaeus by Lawrence Alma-Tadema, 1881 (PD-Art).

The Greek poet Sappho wrote about ordinary, everyday subjects.

Tonight I've watched
The moon and then
The Pleiades
go down.

She writes about her feelings and her state of being.

The night is now
Half-gone; youth
goes; I am
In bed alone.

She writes pithy, wise sayings, or aphorisms.

Although they are
Only breath, words
which I command
are immortal. (*1000 Things*, 195)

Write a short poem about everyday subjects. For example:

This morning I got up from bed,
On the floor was my closed Bible.
Oh Bible, why didn't I read you last night?
I will today.

Now, write your own poem about an everyday subject:

Write a poem about your feelings:

Write a poem that offers wise counsel.

(800 B.C.–300 B.C.):
Ancient Greece (Part 5)

First Thoughts "What would a perfect society look like?" This is an age-old question asked again by Plato through the persona of Socrates. Socrates and his friends, while enjoying a lengthy dinner, discuss such weighty issues as the best government and the best society that there could be. As the night grows longer and the wine flasks are emptied, the speculation grows more fanciful and radical. Nonetheless, this great work gives great insight into the Greek worldview specifically and into Western political thought in general. According to Plato, an ideal state would consist of three classes. The benevolent philosopher-kings would exercise power in the service of justice, the soldiers would protect the state, and the civilian population would provide for the material needs of society.

Chapter Learning Objectives In chapter 8 we explore Plato's perfect society and weigh it against a Christian understanding of the same concept.

As a result of this chapter study you will be able to . . .

1. Discuss Plato's use of fictional dialogues with Socrates to present his views.

2. Identify Plato's influence in the 21st century.

3. Analyze Plato's rhetorical questions

4. Discuss a Christian perfect society.

5. Compare and contrast Plato's understanding of the soul with Paul's understanding of the soul.

6. Evaluate what will bring revival in America.

7. Analyze Plato's argument from analogy.

Weekly Essay Options: Begin on page 273 of the Teacher Guide.

Reading ahead: *The Poetics* by Aristotle.

 History connections: *World History* chapter 8, "Life in Athens: Part Two."

A Christian Angle on *The Republic*

Written in the 4th century B.C., Plato's *The Republic* is one of his best-known works, and one of the most important influences on modern philosophy. The main themes that are talked about in the book are the definition of justice, the just man, the just city, the theory of forms, the immortality of the soul, and many different poetic allegories. One of the most enduring allegories that Plato writes about is his allegory of the cave. In the allegory of the cave, Plato discusses the population chained and imprisoned at first, but eventually set free to see what life is really about. This in many ways parallels the cave of Hades in which mankind was chained and imprisoned until the Son of God came down and freed those who believed.

In Plato's cave it is very dark. The people are chained with very heavy chains. On the opposite wall there is what looks to them like shadows. This is all they can see and all they want to see. This symbolizes the ignorance of the people, in an ignorant world. The shadows on the wall symbolize the limitation of people's thinking, that that is all there is to life.

Before the incarnation, death, and Resurrection of Jesus Christ, everyone was chained with heavy chains and forced to live in the black cave of Hades. For the people in Hades, it was less of an illusion and more of a reality.

The shadows of demons in their cave were real and could not be pushed off as a dream or a misconception. But unlike Plato's cave dwellers, there were many who knew and had experienced the mercy of God, and bore their chains with patience and hope.

In the city Bethlehem near an old inn, there was another cave in which animals ate and slept in the darkness. But one night, this dark cave was lighted up by a huge star and Jesus, son of David, was born, wrapped in swaddling clothes and laid in a manger, illumining the cave and proclaiming that light had come and was overcoming the darkness. This was the light that the faithful in Hades had been waiting and hoping for.

Then the people in Plato's cave begin to question if this is all that there is to reality. If the dancing shadows on the wall are really what truth is. If they become released, they stand and begin to look around them. After a while they find an exit out of the cave, and they are thrown into the bright daylight. Some of the prisoners stay in the sunlight and learn what this truth and reality is. Others cannot handle the brightness and return to what feels safe and harmless to them.

Marble copy of the portrait of Plato made by Silanion, ca. 370 B.C. for the Academia in Athens, 1925 (CC BY 2.5).

"Into thy hands O lord I commend my spirit," As Jesus Christ spoke these words, He breathed His last breath and His soul departed from His body. His body was taken to rest in a tomb for three days, but His soul was very busy elsewhere. He traveled to the black cave of Hades to set free the captives, give light in the darkness, and to trample on death. For those who believed, He brought them with Him into his kingdom, and revealed hidden mysteries unto them. But to those who did not believe, He left in Hades because they could not see the truth and chose to return to what they knew.

For the man coming out of Plato's cave, he is enlightened, made wise, and comes to the fullness of knowledge and wisdom. What he knows and what he can tell and share with others will last him a lifetime. But for the righteous man coming out of the cave of Hades, he is humbled at the love that Christ shows to him, and he knows that he doesn't deserve it. But what he gains from his belief and humility is something that will go on forever — eternity with Christ in His Kingdom. (Anna Grace)

Assignments

- Warm-up: Why is "The Allegory of the Cave" a great story in a sermon? What text would the preacher use?

- Students should complete Concept Builder 8-A.

- Students should review the required reading(s) *before* the assigned chapter begins.

- Teachers may want to discuss assigned reading(s) with students.

- Teachers shall assign the required essay. The rest of the essays can be outlined, answered with shorter answers, discussed, or skipped.

- Students will review all readings for chapter 8.

Read this excerpt from *The Republic* (Book 1) by Plato, and respond to the following:

CONCEPT BUILDER 8-A
Active Reading

I went down yesterday to the Piraeus with Glaucon the son of Ariston, that I might offer up my prayers to the goddess (Bendis, the Thracian Artemis.); and also because I wanted to see in what manner they would celebrate the festival, which was a new thing. I was delighted with the procession of the inhabitants; but that of the Thracians was equally, if not more, beautiful. When we had finished our prayers and viewed the spectacle, we turned in the direction of the city; and at that instant Polemarchus the son of Cephalus chanced to catch sight of us from a distance as we were starting on our way home, and told his servant to run and bid us wait for him. The servant took hold of me by the cloak behind, and said: Polemarchus desires you to wait.

I turned round, and asked him where his master was.

There he is, said the youth, coming after you, if you will only wait.

Certainly we will, said Glaucon; and in a few minutes Polemarchus appeared, and with him Adeimantus, Glaucon's brother, Niceratus the son of Nicias, and several others who had been at the procession.

Polemarchus said to me: I perceive, Socrates, that you and your companion are already on your way to the city.

You are not far wrong, I said.

But do you see, he rejoined, how many we are?

Of course.

And are you stronger than all these? For if not, you will have to remain where you are.

May there not be the alternative, I said, that we may persuade you to let us go?

But can you persuade us, if we refuse to listen to you? he said.

Certainly not, replied Glaucon.

Then we are not going to listen; of that you may be assured.

Adeimantus added: Has no one told you of the torch-race on horseback in honor of the goddess which will take place in the evening?

With horses! I replied: That is a novelty. Will horsemen carry torches and pass them one to another during the race?

Yes, said Polemarchus, and not only so, but a festival will be celebrated at night, which you certainly ought to see. Let us rise soon after supper and see this festival; there will be a gathering of young men, and we will have a good talk. Stay then, and do not be perverse.

The text is written in first person by Plato who is speaking as Socrates. How does that work?

How would you describe Socrates? A mean old grouch? A joker? A friendly old man who is full of good questions?

104

Aristotle vs. Plato

All contemporary worldview discussions can be traced one way or another to Plato and Aristotle. Plato was the Pharisee of his day — the conservative, the one who believed that the gods were intimately involved with human beings. His *The Republic* was a perfect society based on the notion that mankind was creating a city based on the word of the gods. Cosmology, or the presence of supernatural being(s), in other words, was very important to Plato. Likewise, to the Pharisee, who believed strongly in the Resurrection, the supernatural was very involved in human life. To Plato, the gods defined reality.

Aristotle, on the other hand, in his important essay *The Poetics*, argued that the world was governed by impersonal laws. Aristotle argued that mankind defined who the gods were. As long as the gods were alive and well, they did not much concern themselves with the world. Therefore, mankind should be concerned about finding out about the world without worrying about the gods. This view was evident again in the Sadducees — who rejected the supernatural — and later in philosophers like David Hume. Discussing Hellenistic philosophy is for the reason of pointing out that the struggle over worldview is over 3,000 years old. It is the

Image of Plato and Aristotle cropped from the "School of Athens" by Stanza della Segnatura, 1509 (PD-Art).

struggle that Elijah joined when he fought King Ahab. King Ahab was a good Jew; the problem was, he did not live his life as if God were actually alive. Is God intentionally involved in the affairs of mankind or is He not? The answer to this question is more or less the battle that is raging on college campuses today.

Plato had a great influence upon Christianity. A Roman author named Plotinus (A.D. 204–270) combined Plato's philosophy with a heightened emphasis on personal relationship with God. His work deeply affected Augustine of Hippo. In Augustine, Plato's division of the world into the reality of True Being, as well as the separation of the soul from the body, were given Christian interpretations. In a sense, Augustine's "beatific vision of God" (Book IV, Ch. 16) is very similar to Plato's "gazing upon the forms." Paul, a student of Greek philosophy, was deeply affected by Plato. The Holy Spirit led Paul to write, "So we fix our eyes not on what is seen, but on what is unseen. For what is seen is temporary, but what is unseen is eternal" (2 Cor. 4:18).

- Warm-up: How did Platonic thought affect Christianity?

- Students should complete Concept Builder 8-B.

- Students should review reading(s) from the next chapter.

- Students should outline essay due at the end of the week.

- Per teacher instructions, students may answer orally, in a group setting, some of the essays that are not assigned as formal essays.

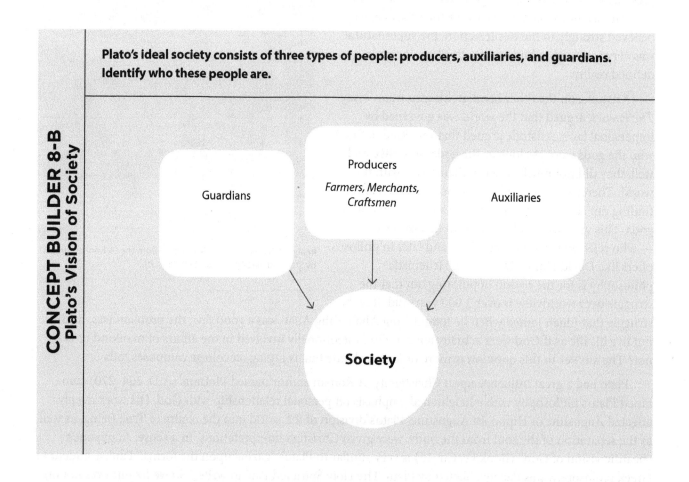

CONCEPT BUILDER 8-B
Plato's Vision of Society

Plato's ideal society consists of three types of people: producers, auxiliaries, and guardians. Identify who these people are.

Guardians

Producers
Farmers, Merchants, Craftsmen

Auxiliaries

Society

The Paradox: Philosophers Must Be Kings

But still I must say, Socrates, that if you are allowed to go on in this way you will entirely forget the other question which at the commencement of this discussion you thrust aside: Is such an order of things possible, and how, if at all? For I am quite ready to acknowledge that the plan which you propose, if only feasible, would do all sorts of good to the State. I will add, what you have omitted, that your citizens will be the bravest of warriors, and will never leave their ranks, for they will all know one another, and each will call the other father, brother, son; and if you suppose the women to join their armies, whether in the same rank or in the rear, either as a terror to the enemy, or as auxiliaries in case of need, I know that they will then be absolutely invincible; and there are many domestic advantages which might also be mentioned and which I also fully acknowledge: but, as I admit all these advantages and as many more as you please, if only this State of yours were to come into existence, we need say no more about them; assuming then the existence of the State, let us now turn to the question of possibility and ways and means — the rest may be left.

If I loiter for a moment, you instantly make a raid upon me, I said, and have no mercy; I have hardly escaped the first and second waves, and you seem not to be aware that you are now bringing upon me the third, which is the greatest and heaviest. When you have seen and heard the third wave, I think you be more considerate and will acknowledge that some fear and hesitation was natural respecting a proposal so extraordinary as that which I have now to state and investigate.

The more appeals of this sort that you make, he said, the more determined are we that you shall tell us how such a State is possible: speak out and at once.

Let me begin by reminding you that we found our way hither in the search after justice and injustice.

True, he replied; but what of that?

I was only going to ask whether, if we have discovered them, we are to require that the just man should in nothing fail of absolute justice; or may we be satisfied with an approximation, and the attainment in him of a higher degree of justice than is to be found in other men?

The approximation will be enough (www.classicreader.com/booktoc.php/sid.8/bookid.1788/ translation by Benjamin Jowett).

Assignments

- Warm-up: What is truth? What is beauty? What kind of society should we build?
- Students should complete Concept Builder 8-C.
- Students should write rough draft of assigned essay.
- The teacher or a peer evaluator may correct rough drafts.

Guardians, the rulers of the perfect state, are philosophers. Plato uses three analogies to illustrate his point. What do these analogies illustrate?

The Sun

The good is brighter than all other things.

The Line

The Cave

"The Allegory of the Cave" (Chapter XXV)

What does the cave symbolize to Plato? What other symbolic references does he make? What is the purpose of using a cave as a symbol? Use the portion provided below to assist you:

And now, I said, let me show in a figure how far our nature is enlightened or unenlightened: Behold! Human beings living in an underground den, which has a mouth open towards the light and reaching all along the den; here they have been from their childhood, and have their legs and necks chained so that they cannot move, and can only see before them, being prevented by the chains from turning round their heads. Above and behind them a fire is blazing at a distance, and between the fire and the prisoners there is a raised way; and you will see, if you look, a low wall built along the way, like the screen which marionette players have in front of them, over which they show the puppets.

I see.

And do you see, I said, men passing along the wall carrying all sorts of vessels, and statues and figures of animals made of wood and stone and various materials, which appear over the wall? Some of them are talking, others silent.

You have shown me a strange image, and they are strange prisoners.

Like ourselves, I replied; and they see only their own shadows, or the shadows of one another, which the fire throws on the opposite wall of the cave?

True, he said; how could they see anything but the shadows if they were never allowed to move their heads?

And of the objects which are being carried in like manner they would only see the shadows?

Plato's Allegory of the Cave by Jan Saenredam , 1604 (PD-Art).

Assignments

- Warm-up: Professor Cornford begins his translation of the *The Republic* with this statement: "The main question to be answered in the *The Republic* is what does Justice mean, and how can it be realized in human society?" What does the Bible say about justice?

- Students should complete Concept Builder 8-D.

- Students will re-write corrected copies of essay due tomorrow.

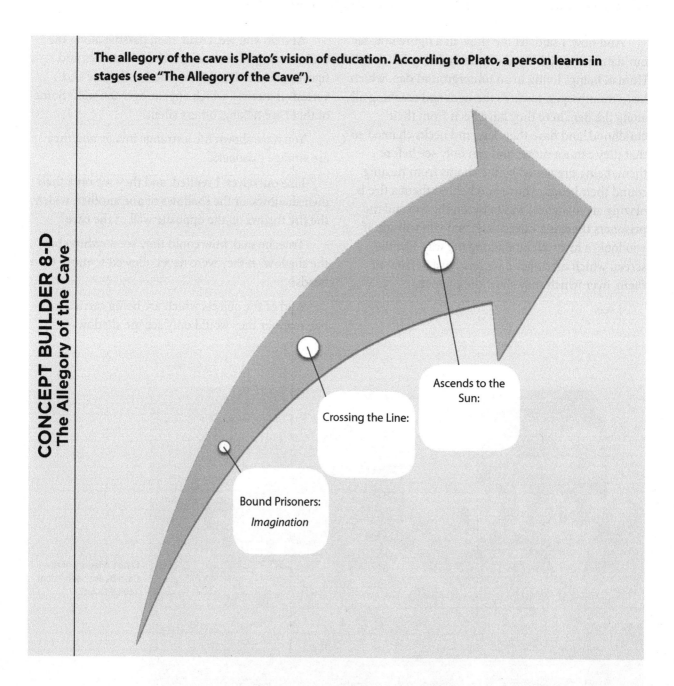

CONCEPT BUILDER 8-D
The Allegory of the Cave

The allegory of the cave is Plato's vision of education. According to Plato, a person learns in stages (see "The Allegory of the Cave").

Ascends to the Sun:

Crossing the Line:

Bound Prisoners:
Imagination

Critics Corner

Plato was a poet, with the desire to make every truth a visible image; and he was a statesman, with a passion for reformation. The two sides of his character were combined in his desire to create "the best state," in spirit at least, upon this foundation, and to set it up as a paradeigma before the eyes of mankind.

— Werner Jaeger, *Paideia*, 1943

Plato's modern readers, judging him by modern patterns of thought, used to spend much energy searching for his "system." But at last they became content to realize that — whether for artistic or for critical motives — he refrained from constructing a fixed body of doctrine like other philosophers. He wanted to show knowledge in process of becoming.

— Werner Jaeger, *Paideia*, 1943

The Allegory of the Cave may be viewed as a devastating criticism of our everyday lives as being in bondage to superficialities, to shadow rather than to substance. Truth is taken to be whatever is known by the senses. A good life is taken to be one in which we satisfy our desires. We are unaware that we are living with illusion, superficial knowledge. Our lives are dominated by the shadow-play on the walls of our caves made by newspaper headlines, by radio broadcasts, by the endlessly moving shadows on the television screen, by the echoing voices of opinion makers.

— T.Z. Lavine, *From Socrates to Sartre*, 1984

Unhappily, most historians of Plato's thought either glorify dialectic into something too rarefied to be anything actually practiced on a Monday morning; or they downgrade it into something too pettifogging to be permitted to blinker their seer. Yet for the understanding of Plato, as for the understanding of any other original philosopher, what is essential is the appreciation of the style and the structure of his heartfelt arguments.

— Gilbert Ryle, *Plato's Progress*, 1966

Philosophy is a rare plant, one which has flourished only in the West; it is perhaps the essence of that West. Its place is not simply assured everywhere and always as is the city's. The writings of Plato and a few others made it respectable. The Republic thus represents one of the most decisive moments of our history. In this work Socrates presents the grounds of his being brought to trial and shows why philosophy is always in danger and always needs a defense.

— Allan Bloom, *The Republic of Plato*, 1968

This choice between the philosophic and tyrannic lives explains the plot of The Republic. Socrates takes a young man [Glaucon] tempted by the tyrannic life and attempts to give him at least that modicum of awareness of philosophy which will cure him of the lust for tyranny. Any other exhortation would amount to empty moralism.

— Allan Bloom, *The Republic of Plato*, 1968

All critiques in this section are from http://www.pinkmonkey.com/booknotes/barrons/republc69.asp.

- Warm-up: The main question in the *The Republic* centers on what justice means and how can it be realized in human society. What does the Bible say about justice?

- Students should complete Concept Builder 8-E.

- Essays are due. Students should take the chapter 8 test.

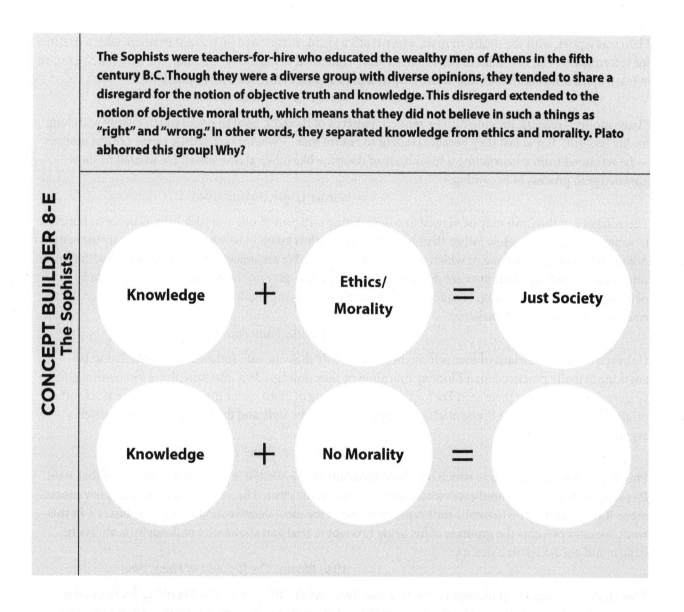

CONCEPT BUILDER 8-E
The Sophists

The Sophists were teachers-for-hire who educated the wealthy men of Athens in the fifth century B.C. Though they were a diverse group with diverse opinions, they tended to share a disregard for the notion of objective truth and knowledge. This disregard extended to the notion of objective moral truth, which means that they did not believe in such a things as "right" and "wrong." In other words, they separated knowledge from ethics and morality. Plato abhorred this group! Why?

Knowledge **+** Ethics/Morality **=** Just Society

Knowledge **+** No Morality **=**

Chapter 9

(800 B.C.–300 B.C.):
Ancient Greece (Part 6)

First Thoughts Aristotle (350 B.C. –?), a disciple of Plato, wrote what is essentially a modification, a taming down, of Plato's ideas. To Plato, knowledge and virtue were inseparable. To Aristotle, they were merely connected. Aristotle was not on a search for absolute truth; in fact, he was not certain it existed. Truth, beauty, and goodness were to be observed and quantified from human behavior and the senses. Goodness in particular was not an absolute. It was an average between two absolutes. Aristotle said that mankind should strike a balance between passion and temperance. He said that people should seek the "Golden Mean," defined as a course of life that was never extreme. Finally, Plato argued that reality lay in knowledge of the gods. Aristotle argued that truth lay in empirical, measurable knowledge. Aristotle, then, was the father of modern science (Stobaugh, *A Fire That Burns but Does Not Consume*, p. 23–27).

Having said that, *Rhetoric* and *The Poetics* are more handbooks of literary criticism than discussions of metaphysics. Most modern readers will be offended by Aristotle's autocratic tone. He is no reticent literary critic tiptoeing around his reader's literary feelings. He states succinctly what he believes good literature is.

Chapter Learning Objectives In chapter 9 we read two books that one wished that Plato, with his laudable views of "the form" wrote. Aristotle, the empiricist, the pragmatist, ruminates on the virtues of poetry and rhetoric.

As a result of this chapter study you will be able to . . .

1. Discuss Aristotle's views of poetry, tragedy, and the tragic hero.

2. Evaluate the dangers of Aristotlean thought.

3. Contrast views of Aristotle and Plato.

Weekly Essay Options: Begin on page 273 of the Teacher Guide.
Reading ahead: "Oedipus Rex" by Sophocles.

 History connections: *World History* chapter 9, "Greek Wars."

A Challenge from Plato

Gilbert Murray writes, "In the tenth book of *The Republic*, when Plato has completed his final burning denunciation of Poetry, the false Siren, the imitator of things which themselves are shadows, the ally of all that is low and weak in the soul against that which is high and strong, who makes us feed the things we ought to starve and serve the things we ought to rule, he ends with a touch of compunction: 'We will give her champions, not poets themselves but poet-lovers, an opportunity to make her defence in plain prose and show that she is not only sweet — as we well know — but also helpful to society and the life of man, and we will listen in a kindly spirit. For we shall be gainers, I take it, if this can be proved.' Aristotle certainly knew the passage, and it looks as if his treatise on poetry was an answer to Plato's challenge." (Aristotle, *On the Art of Poetry*, translated by Ingram Bywater, preface by Gilbert Murray, www.amazon.com/On-Art-Poetry-Aristotle/dp/1604444614).

From *The Republic*, Book X

In like manner the poet with his words and phrases may be said to lay on the colours of the several arts, himself understanding their nature only enough to imitate them; and other people, who are as ignorant as he is, and judge only from his words, imagine that if he speaks of cobbling, or of military tactics, or of anything else, in metre and harmony and rhythm, he speaks very well — such is the sweet influence which melody and rhythm by nature have. And I think that you must have observed again and again what a poor appearance the tales of poets make when stripped of the colours which music puts upon them, and recited in simple prose.

Yes, he said.

They are like faces which were never really beautiful, but only blooming; and now the bloom of youth has passed away from them?

Exactly.

Here is another point: The imitator or maker of the image knows nothing of true existence; he knows appearances only. Am I not right?

Yes.

Then let us have a clear understanding, and not be satisfied with half an explanation.

Proceed.

Of the painter we say that he will paint reins, and he will paint a bit?

Yes.

And the worker in leather and brass will make them?

Certainly.

But does the painter know the right form of the bit and reins? Nay, hardly even the workers in brass and leather who make them; only the horseman who knows how to use them — he knows their right form.

Most true.

And may we not say the same of all things?

What?

That there are three arts which are concerned with all things: one which uses, another which makes, a third which imitates them?

Yes.

And the excellence or beauty or truth of every structure, animate or inanimate, and of every action of man, is relative to the use for which nature or the artist has intended them.

True.

Then the user of them must have the greatest experience of them, and he must indicate to the maker the good or bad qualities which develop themselves in use; for example, the flute-player will tell the flute-maker which of his flutes is satisfactory to the performer; he will tell him how he ought to make them, and the other will attend to his instructions?

Of course.

The one knows and therefore speaks with authority about the goodness and badness of flutes, while the other, confiding in him, will do what he is told by him?

True.

www.gutenberg.org/files/1497/1497-h/1497-h.htm#2H_4_0013.

The instrument is the same, but about the excellence or badness of it the maker will only attain to a correct belief; and this he will gain from him who knows, by talking to him and being compelled to hear what he has to say, whereas the user will have knowledge?

True.

But will the imitator have either? Will he know from use whether or no his drawing is correct or beautiful? or will he have right opinion from being compelled to associate with another who knows and gives him instructions about what he should draw?

Neither.

Assignments

- Warm-up: Why were Plato and Aristotle mortal enemies?
- Students should complete Concept Builder 9-A.
- Students should review the required reading(s) *before* the assigned chapter begins.
- Teachers may want to discuss assigned reading(s) with students.
- Teachers shall assign the required essay. The rest of the essays can be outlined, answered with shorter answers, discussed, or skipped.
- Students will review all readings for chapter 9.

Read this excerpt from *The Poetics* (Book 5) by Aristotle, and respond to the following:

Plot: basic concepts
These principles being established, let us now discuss the proper structure of the plot, since this is the first and most important thing in tragedy.

Now, according to our definition tragedy is an imitation of an action that is complete, and whole, and of a certain magnitude; for there may be a whole that is wanting in magnitude. A whole is that which has a beginning, middle, and an end. A beginning is that which does not itself follow anything by causal necessity, but after which something naturally is or comes to be. An end, on the contrary, is that which itself naturally follows some other thing, either by necessity, or as a rule, but has nothing following it. A middle is that which follows something as some other thing follows it. A well constructed plot, therefore, must neither begin nor end at haphazard, but conform to these principles.

Again, a beautiful object, whether it be a living organism or any whole composed of parts, must not only have an orderly arrangement of parts, but must also be of a certain magnitude; for beauty depends on magnitude and order. Hence a very small animal organism cannot be beautiful; for the view of it is confused, the object being seen in an almost imperceptible moment of time. Nor, again, can one of vast size be beautiful; for as the eye cannot take it all in at once, the unity and sense of the whole is lost for the spectator; as for instance if there were one a thousand miles long. As, therefore, in the case of animate bodies and organisms a certain magnitude is necessary, and a magnitude which may be easily embraced in one view; so in the plot, a certain length is necessary, and a length which can be easily embraced by the memory. The limit of length in relation to dramatic competition and sensuous presentment is no part of artistic theory. For had it been the rule for a hundred tragedies to compete together, the performance would have been regulated by the water-clock — as indeed we are told was formerly done. But the limit as fixed by the nature of the drama itself is this: the greater the length, the more beautiful will the piece be by reason of its size, provided that the whole be perspicuous. And to define the matter roughly, we may say that the proper magnitude is comprised within such limits, that the sequence of events, according to the law of probability or necessity, will admit of a change from bad fortune to good, or from good fortune to bad.

What are three things a plot must have?

What is beauty?

www.poetryfoundation.org/bio/elizabeth-barrett-browning.

"Poetics"

"So in the arts . . . taken as a whole, the imitation is produced by rhythm, language, or 'harmony,' either singly or combined."

— Aristotle

Aristotle, in his *Poetics*, argues that poetry, or art, is representative of life. Plato, on the other hand, in his *Republic*, argues that art can go no further beyond what a man feels. Aristotle was a student of Plato, the great Grecian philosopher. Plato's name means broad — perhaps due to his large forehead, or his broad-minded philosophy. Cicero described Aristotle's writing style as "a river of gold." First, we will examine Aristotle's view of art, next, move on to Plato's view of art, and finally, compare and contrast the two.

Aristotle argues that art and poetry is representative of life, transcends feelings, and is an objective beautification of nature.

"The question may be raised whether the Epic or Tragic mode of imitation is the higher. If the more refined art is the higher, and the more refined in every case is that which appeals to the better sort of audience, the art which imitates anything and everything is manifestly most unrefined. . . . If, then, tragedy is superior to epic poetry in all these respects, and, moreover, fulfills its specific function better as an art — for each art ought to produce, not any chance   pleasure, but the pleasure proper to it, as already stated- it plainly follows that tragedy is the higher art, as attaining its end more perfectly."

In his discussion of art, poetry, and tragedy, Aristotle expounds on the theory that art is representative of life. It is an objective beautification of nature, the soul of a poet glorifying its inspiration. To Aristotle, art is better than its original subject — because it transcends feelings. Because of this, the reader feels that art is the highest or most important craft that can be obtained.

Plato, however, argues that art and poetry can go no further than what a man feels.

"But can you imagine, Glaucon, that if Homer had really been able to educate and improve man-kind — if he had possessed knowledge and not been a mere imitator. . . . Then must we not infer that all these poetical individuals, beginning with Homer, are only imitators; they copy images of virtue and the like, but the truth they never reach? The poet is like a painter who, as we have already observed, will make a likeness of a cobbler though he understands nothing of cobbling; and his picture is good enough for those who know no more than he does and judge only by colors and figures."

In his discussion of art, Plato argues that an artist is merely an imitator. He makes likenesses of which he understands nothing. To Plato, the artist can only manufacture a poor representation of the reality which the art represents, going no farther than what a man feels. Because of this, the reader is convinced that rhetoric and thought is more important, more lucid, than art.

Plato and Aristotle have very different views of art. Aristotle believes that art is representative of life — it transcends feelings. Plato believed that the artist is merely an imitator — his art can go no further than what the artist feels.

Although Aristotle and Plato were master and student, respectively, they had very different views on art. Plato believed it was a necessity that transcended belief. Plato believed that art was nothing more than a shadow of reality, and was unnecessary. (Alouette)

Assignments

- Warm-up: Aristotle argues that poetry is representative of life. Plato argues that poetry is imitative of life. Who is right?
- Students should complete Concept Builder 9-B.
- Students should review reading(s) from the next chapter.
- Students should outline essay due at the end of the week.
- Per teacher instructions, students may answer orally, in a group setting, some of the essays that are not assigned as formal essays.

CONCEPT BUILDER 9-B
Aristotle vs. Plato

All contemporary worldview discussions can be traced one way or another to Plato and Aristotle. Plato was the Pharisee of his day — the conservative, the one who believed that the gods were intimately involved with human beings. His "Republic" was a perfect society based on the notion that mankind was creating a city based on the word of the gods. Cosmology, or the presence of supernatural being(s), in other words, was very important to Plato. Likewise, to the Pharisee, who believed strongly in the Resurrection, the supernatural was very involved in human life. To Plato, the gods defined reality.

Aristotle, on the other hand, in his important essay "Poetics," argued that the world was governed by impersonal laws. Aristotle argued that mankind defined who the gods were. As long as the gods were alive and well, they did not much concern themselves with the world. Therefore, mankind should be concerned about finding out about his world without worrying about the gods. This view was evident again in the Sadducees — who rejected the supernatural — and later in philosophers like David Hume. Fill in the boxes below with occupations that would fit under each category.

Plato
- Pharisees
- Theologians

Aristotle
- Sadduccees
- Scientists

118

Rhetoric: Part One

Christof Rapp in *The Stanford Encyclopedia of Philosophy*, (Spring 2010 edition, Edward N. Zalta, editor, plato.stanford.edu/archives/spr2010/entries/aristotle-rhetoric/) argues that "Aristotle's *Rhetoric* has had an enormous influence on the development of the art of rhetoric. Not only authors writing in the peripatetic tradition, but also the famous Roman teachers of rhetoric, such as Cicero and Quintilian, frequently used elements stemming from the Aristotelian doctrine." The truth is, however, Aristotle's take on rhetoric is not always clear.

Rapp continues, "Nevertheless, these authors were interested neither in an authentic interpretation of the Aristotelian works nor in the philosophical sources and backgrounds of the vocabulary that Aristotle had introduced to rhetorical theory. Thus, for two millennia the interpretation of Aristotelian rhetoric has become a matter of the history of rhetoric, not of philosophy."

Frontispiece of Quintilian's *Institutio Oratoria* by F. Bleyswyk shows Quintilian teaching rhetorics, 1720 (PD-US).

Assignments

- Warm-up: Why do we usually study rhetoric in philosophy class and not in English class?
- Students should complete Concept Builder 9-C.
- Students should write rough draft of assigned essay.
- The teacher may correct rough drafts.

To Aristotle, rhetoric is defined as the faculty of observing in any given case the available means of persuasion. Discuss three ways that people use to persuade.

Logic

Rhetoric

Rhetoric: Part Two

While *Rhetoric* is not really a story from which one can discover and apply morals and lessons to real life, it does contain loads of information regarding Aristotle's views on rhetoric, persuasion through speaking; and poetry, persuasion by writing. What is Aristotle's definition of rhetoric, and how can it be used in daily life?

The great philosopher begins by arguing that rhetoric is the partner to logic. "Rhetoric is the counterpart of dialectic [or logic]. Both alike are concerned with such things as come, more or less, within the general ken of all men and belong to no definite science." As is seen, Aristotle, who would have used rhetoric repeatedly in his philosophical discussions, claims rhetoric is the partner to logic. It is not a particular science, unlike physics or biology, but instead deals with the arguments and thought processes we use in everyday life. Thus, while few may realize it, we all use rhetoric daily in conversations and decisions. "Accordingly all men make use, more or less, of both; for to a certain extent all men attempt to discuss statements and to maintain them, to defend themselves and to attack others." Here, Aristotle discusses how humans use it in real life.

Aristotle then goes on to give a more precise definition of rhetoric. "Rhetoric may be defined as the faculty of observing in any given case the available means of persuasion. This is not a function of any other art." This is a more specific definition that can be further understood by the reader. The audience now learns that rhetoric is not only used everyday by nearly everyone, but involves how humans learn to persuade in given situations. While it is not the art of persuasion, it is how we learn to persuade.

Aristotle then goes on to say rhetoric is not an exact science, but a skill that can be used everywhere. "Every other art can instruct or persuade about its own particular subject matter; for instance, medicine about what is healthy and unhealthy, geometry about the properties of magnitudes, arithmetic about numbers, and the same is true of the other arts and sciences. But rhetoric we look upon as the power of observing the means of persuasion on almost any subject presented to us; and that is why we say that, in its technical character, it is not concerned with any special or definite class of subjects." Once again, we see Aristotle discussing how rhetoric is a general science and not confined to any particular part of human life, but encompasses all aspects of life. While it does not seek to teach the audience about a certain topic, it does helps these other arts to persuade the audience.

Rhetoric then, in Aristotle's view, is a skill that can be used in daily life in a variety of situations whether it be science, math, or reading. Rhetoric is not the art of persuasion, but observing the means of persuasion. This is what makes it used by everyone in every aspect of life, regardless of if they recognize it or not. (Chris)

Assignments

- Warm-up: How does Aristotle define rhetoric?
- Students should complete Concept Builder 9-D.
- Students will re-write corrected copies of essay due tomorrow.

The tragic hero is greater than life but not necessarily perfect. The tragic hero inherently possesses a flaw that ultimately will destroy him. Oedipus, in Sophocles' "Oedipus Rex" is a perfect illustration of this tragic hero.

Who are two biblical tragic heroes?

Extraordinarily Gifted

Pride or Hubris: Internal Flaw

Auxiliaries

The Neutrality of Rhetoric

Aristotle believes that rhetoric is neutral and can be used by persons of virtuous or depraved character. This capacity can be used for good or bad purposes; it can cause great benefits as well as great harms. Aristotle himself regards his system of rhetoric as something having value, but the good purposes for which rhetoric is useful do not preclude the use of rhetoric for malfeasance. Aristotle, then, seeks to separate rhetoric from ethics. Aristotle does not hesitate to concede on the one hand that his art of rhetoric can be abused, but, in colloquial language, that is the way that the cookie crumbles. As Aristotle explains in *Nicomachean Ethics*, it is true of all goods, except virtue, that they can be misused. Besides, the risk of misuse is compensated by the benefits that can be accomplished by Aristotelian rhetoric (Ibid).

A page from Aristotle's *Nicomachean Ethics,* date unknown, (PD-Art).

Assignments

- Warm-up: Should aesthetic value be automous from both morality and politics? Should Christians read whatever they want as long as the literary work has artistic value?

- Students should complete Concept Builder 9-E.

- Essays are due. Students should take the chapter 9 test.

The chief end of man, to Aristotle, was to know. To Aristotle, the world would have existed even if mankind had not been created, but it would have not been known to exist — and this knowledge is the quintessential fact of the universe. What worldviews evolved from Aristotelian thought? Complete the following charts:

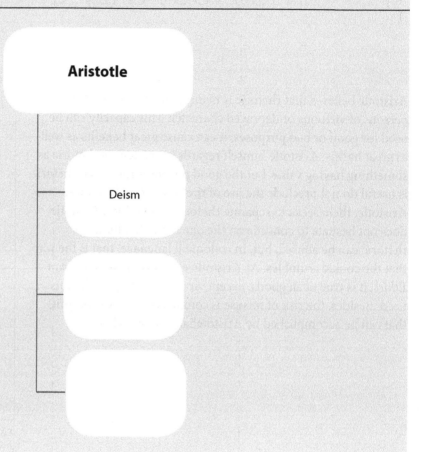

Aristotle

Deism

Chapter 10

(800 B.C.–300 B.C.):
Ancient Greece (Part 7)

First Thoughts Sophocles ranks among the very best playwrights in Western literature. And, from among his hundred or so plays, *Oedipus Rex* (or *The King*) is the best. What makes this play so powerful is its immutability — the struggles we see unfold are the same struggles we all experience. Sophocles was born in 496 B.C. and died in 406 B.C. (dates are approximate). Sophocles was one of the three great tragic dramatists of ancient Athens, the other two being Aeschylus and Euripides.

Chapter Learning Objectives In chapter 10 we study what Aristotle called the "perfect tragedy."

As a result of this chapter study you will be able to . . .

1. Analyze the plot of *Oedipus Rex*.
2. Compare the views of women with *Oedipus Rex* with those expressed in *The Republic*.
3. Contrast human free will and godly omniscience.
4. Analyze the theme of fate in *Oedipus Rex*.
5. Analyze Edith Hamilton's quote.

Weekly Essay Options: Begin on page 273 of the Teacher Guide.
Reading ahead: : *The Aeneid* by Virgil.

Oedipus Rex
Sophocles

The plot of *Oedipus Rex* is truly tragic. To Laius, King of Thebes, an oracle foretold that the child born to him by his queen Jocasta would slay his father Laius and wed his own mother. When in time a son was born, the infant's feet were riveted together and he was left to die on Mount Cithaeron. A shepherd found the infant and delivered him to another shepherd, who took him to his master, King Polybus of Corinth. Polybus adopted the boy and named him Oedipus. He grew up believing that he was indeed Ploybus' son. Later, doubting his parentage, Oedipus inquired of the Delphic god and heard himself identified as Laius' son. Therefore, he fled from what he thought was his father's house (but was really his adopted father's house) and in his flight he encountered and unwittingly killed his birth father, Laius. Arriving at Thebes, he answered the riddle of the Sphinx and the grateful Thebans made him king. Thus he reigned in the palace of Laius, and married the widowed queen who, unknown to Oedipus, was also his birth mother. After they had children a terrible plague fell upon the city. Again the oracle was consulted and it urged them to purge themselves of blood guilt. Oedipus denounced the crime of which he was unaware, and undertook to track out the criminal. Step by step it is brought home to Oedipus that he was the man. In the closing scene Jocasta killed herself and Oedipus blinded himself (Introduction by F. Storr, in a 1912 edition, public domain).

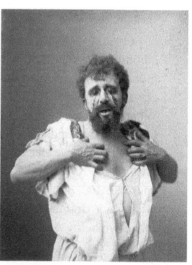

Louis Bouwmeester as Oedipus in a Dutch production of "Oedipus Rex," by Albert Greiner c.1896, (CC BY-SA 3.0).

Assignments

- Warm-up: Summarize the storyline of *Oedipus Rex*.
- Students should complete Concept Builder 10-A.
- Students review the required reading(s) *before* the assigned chapter begins.
- Teachers may want to discuss assigned reading(s) with students.
- Teachers shall assign the required essay. The rest of the essays can be outlined, answered with shorter answers, discussed, or skipped.
- Students will review all readings for chapter 10.

Read this excerpt from *Oedipus Rex* by Sophicles, and respond to the following:

Thebes. Before the Palace of Oedipus. Suppliants of all ages are seated round the altar at the palace doors, at their head a PRIEST OF ZEUS. To them enter OEDIPUS.

CONCEPT BUILDER 10-A
Active Reading

OEDIPUS
My children, latest born to Cadmus old,
Why sit ye here as suppliants, in your hands
Branches of olive filleted with wool?
What means this reek of incense everywhere,
And everywhere laments and litanies?
Children, it were not meet that I should learn
From others, and am hither come, myself,
I Oedipus, your world-renowned king.

PRIEST
Yea, Oedipus, my sovereign lord and king,
Thou seest how both extremes of age besiege
Thy palace altars--fledglings hardly winged,
And greybeards bowed with years, priests, as am I
Of Zeus, and these the flower of our youth.
Meanwhile, the common folk, with wreathed boughs
Crowd our two market-places, or before
Both shrines of Pallas congregate, or where
Ismenus gives his oracles by fire.
For, as thou seest thyself, our ship of State,
Sore buffeted, can no more lift her head,
Foundered beneath a weltering surge of blood.
A blight is on our harvest in the ear,
A blight upon the grazing flocks and herds,
A blight on wives in travail; and withal
Armed with his blazing torch the God of Plague
Hath swooped upon our city emptying
The house of Cadmus, and the murky realm
Of Pluto is full fed with groans and tears.
Therefore, O King, here at thy hearth we sit,
I and these children; not as deeming thee
A new divinity, but the first of men;
First in the common accidents of life,
And first in visitations of the Gods.
Art thou not he who coming to the town
Of Cadmus freed us from the tax we paid
To the fell songstress? Nor hadst thou received
Prompting from us or been by others schooled;
No, by a god inspired (so all men deem,
And testify) didst thou renew our life.
And now, O Oedipus, our peerless king,
All we thy votaries beseech thee, find
Some succor, whether by a voice from heaven
Whispered, or haply known by human wit.
Tried counselors, methinks, are aptest found
To furnish for the future pregnant rede.
Upraise, O chief of men, upraise our State!

Ho! aged sire, whose venerable locks
Proclaim thee spokesman of this company,
Explain your mood and purport. Is it dread
Of ill that moves you or a boon ye crave?
My zeal in your behalf ye cannot doubt;
Ruthless indeed were I and obdurate
If such petitioners as you I spurned.

Paraphrase this passage.

Look to thy laurels! for thy zeal of yore
Our country's savior thou art justly hailed:
O never may we thus record thy reign: —
"He raised us up only to cast us down."
Uplift us, build our city on a rock.
Thy happy star ascendant brought us luck,
O let it not decline! If thou wouldst rule
This land, as now thou reignest, better sure
To rule a peopled than a desert realm.
Nor battlements nor galleys aught avail,
If men to man and guards to guard them tail.

There is a "blight upon the grazing flocks and herds." It is caused, apparently, by some terrible "sin" in the kingdom. This scene is an example of dramatic irony. Dramatic irony is when the words and actions of the characters of a work of literature have a different meaning for the reader than they do for the characters. This is the result of the reader having a greater knowledge than the characters themselves. What is ironic about this scene?

Metaphors

Early in the play Oedipus approaches his friend Tiresias and says:

Teiresias, seer who comprehendest all,
Lore of the wise and hidden mysteries,
High things of heaven and low things of the earth,
Thou knowest, though thy blinded eyes see naught,
What plague infects our city; and we turn
To thee, O seer, our one defense and shield.
The purport of the answer that the God
Returned to us who sought his oracle,
The messengers have doubtless told thee how

One course alone could rid us of the pest,
To find the murderers of Laius,
And slay them or expel them from the land.
Therefore begrudging neither augury
Nor other divination that is thine,
O save thyself, thy country, and thy king,
Save all from this defilement of blood shed.
On thee we rest. This is man's highest end,
To others' service all his powers to lend.

In this figure of speech (a metaphor), Tiresias is compared with a shield.

Assignments

- Warm-up: Find other metaphors in *Oedipus Rex* and discuss why Sophocles used them.

- Students should complete Concept Builder 10-B.

- Students should review reading(s) from the next chapter.

- Students should outline essay due at the end of the week.

- Per teacher instructions, students may answer orally, in a group setting, some of the essays that are not assigned as formal essays.

The plot is central to the development of *Oedipus Rex.* **One act leads naturally to another until Sophocles' linked chain of events leads to a disastrous end.**

To Laius, king of Thebes, an oracle foretold that the child born to him by his queen Jocasta would slay his father Laius and wed his own mother.

When in time a son was born, the infant's feet were riveted together and he was left to die on Mount Cithaeron. A shepherd found the infant and delivered him to another shepherd, who took him to his master, King Polybus of Corinth. Polybus adopted the boy and named him Oedipus.

Aristotle and Sophocles

The greatest Greek tragedy of all time, in the opinion of Aristotle, was "Oedipus Rex." Aristotle loved the plot and chorus, the beautiful language, and the irony of the situations.

A perfect tragedy should imitate actions that excite pity and fear, and also effect the proper purgation of these emotions. The change of fortune presented should be that of a man who is not eminently good and just, yet whose misfortune is brought about not by vice or depravity, but by some error or frailty. He must be one who is highly renowned and prosperous — a personage like Oedipus, or other illustrious men of such families. The plot ought to be so constructed that, even without the aid of the eye, he who hears the tale told will thrill with horror and melt with pity at what takes place. This is the impression we should receive from hearing the story of Oedipus.

Assignments

- Warm-up: Why do we usually study rhetoric in philosophy class and not in English class?
- Students should complete Concept Builder 10-C.
- Students should write rough draft of assigned essay.
- The teacher may correct rough drafts.

A metaphor is the use of a dissimilar word or phrase to describe somebody or something.

"Teiresias, you who understand all things — those which can be taught and those which may not be mentioned, things in the heavens and things which walk the earth! You cannot see, but you understand the city's distress, the disease from which it is suffering. You, my lord, are our shield against it, our savior, the only one we have."

In this figure of speech (a metaphor), Tiresias is compared with a shield. Find other metaphors in *Oedipus Rex,* and discuss why Sophocles used them.

The gods will: Whirl upon Death, that all the Undying hate!/ Come with blinding torches, come in joy! In this case, the gods are given human characteristics (personification).

Metaphors

Sophocles, translated by Bernard Knox, "Oedipus the King" (New York: Washington Square Press, 1959), p. 19.

Critics Corner

Oedipus is man rather than an individual tragic hero. The play is characteristic of the Greek attitude towards men to see him not only as an individual but also as an individual in society, a political being as well as a private person.

— Bernard Knox, *Oedipus at Thebes*, 1957

The basic conflict in the play is most simply defined as one between man and god: The king's belief in reason and doing one's duty is smashed by a mysterious, immovable, supernatural force.

— Gilbert Norwood, *Greek Tragedy*, 1928

The gods of Sophocles are not like the God we are used to hearing about in the Bible. Our God rules absolutely, giving mercy and making judgment. The classical gods do not judge, they are merely forces of right or wrong. Judgment is the work of fate, and means simply to give a man his due.

— Tom Driver, *Oedipus the King*, 1961

. . . the proud tragic view of Sophocles sees in the fragility and inevitable defeat of human greatness the possibility of a purely human heroism to which the gods can never attain, for the condition of their existence is everlasting victory.

— Bernard Knox, *Oedipus at Thebes*, 1957

Each single incident in the play is the sort of thing that can and does happen. Sophocles does not blame these people; neither therefore must we; it is not a matter of guilt and punishment, but of how people can in fact be deceived.

— H.D.F. Kitto, *Greek Tragedy*, 1954

Oedipus'. . . humiliation is a lesson both to others and to him. Democritus' words, "The foolish learn modesty in misfortune," may be applied to Oedipus, who has indeed been foolish in his mistakes and illusions and has been taught modesty through suffering.

— C.M. Bowra, *Sophoclean Tragedy*, 1944

Sophocles' chorus is a character that takes an important role in the action of the play. The chorus may be described as a group personality, like an old Parliament. It has its own traditions, habits of thought and feeling.

— Francis Fergusson, *The Idea of a Theatre*, 1968

Sophocles plays continually on the opposition of light and darkness, sight and blindness. In the Teiresias scene, Oedipus is revealed as mentally blind to his real position and the dangers which surround him. It is the blind prophet who has true knowledge. At the end of the play, when Oedipus has found the truth, he destroys the sense organs which had led him into error. He is now blind, but sees truly.

— Peter Arnott, *Oedipus the King*, 1960

Assignments

- Warm-up: Why would one who believes in fate never quite feel in control of his or her life?
- Students should complete Concept Builder 10-D.
- Students will re-write corrected copies of essay due tomorrow.

CONCEPT BUILDER 10-D
Fate

A central theme of "Oedipus Rex" is fate. Fate is a view that a "nameless" and "malevolent" power is in control of the universe. Why is this view the opposite of the Christian view of providence?

Sophocles' View	Christian View
Malevolent god	Loving God
No purpose	Purposes of God
Fate	Providence

What biblical verses support the Christian view of providence (e.g., John 3:16)?

Student Essay

"You mock my blindness, do you? But I say that you, with both your eyes, are blind. . . . The double lash of your parents' curse will whip you out of this land some day, with only night upon your precious eyes. . . . No man that walks upon the earth shall be rooted out more horribly than you" (Sophocles, "Oedipus Rex," Orlando, FL: Harcourt Brace & Company, 1939, scene 1, p. 22–23). This prediction by the blind prophet Tiresias largely sums up the story of Sophocles' ancient Greek tragedy, "Oedipus Rex." As the quote implies, there is a sudden change of events in "Oedipus Rex" when the title character plummets from being king of Thebes to being a blind wandering beggar. In fact, "Oedipus Rex" is filled with this type of sudden change. Because of the many twists and turns in its plot, "Oedipus Rex" captivates its audiences and holds them on the edges of their seats.

The exposition of Sophocles' tragedy covers the prologue and is where the audience comes to understand the events immediately before the commencement of the play. A man named Oedipus has become king over Thebes because he answered the riddle of the Sphinx. The Sphinx was a horrible part-woman, part-lion, and part-bird monster who guarded the gates of Thebes and asked all travelers a riddle. (According to tradition, the riddle was, "What walks on four legs in the morning, two at mid-day, and three at night." The answer was, "A man crawls on all fours as a baby, walks on two in his prime age, and has a cane when he grows old.") If the traveler could not answer the question, the Sphinx would eat him. When Oedipus succeeded in answering the Sphinx's riddle, the Sphinx destroyed herself, and out of gratitude, the Thebans made Oedipus their new king. This is one of the sudden turns. Before answering the riddle, Oedipus was a mere traveler, but after his feat, he was a crowned king. It is in the exposition that the audience learns that the Thebans' last king, Laius, was killed by highwaymen at a crossroads. "A band of highwaymen attacked them, outnumbered them, and overwhelmed the King." (Ibid, p. 9). Finally, the exposition reveals that the god Apollo has placed a horrible plague over Thebes and that the only way to appease the god is to find the murderer of king Laius and either kill or banish him. "The herds are sick, children die unborn, and labor is vain. . . . (But) great afflictions will turn out well, if they are taken well . . . (Laius) was murdered, and Apollo commands us now to take revenge upon whoever killed him." In the exposition of Sophocles' play, the scene is set for the many sudden changes that follow.

The rising action of "Oedipus Rex" covers from scene I to the end of scene IV. Much of this section is spent recounting past events through flashbacks provided by several characters. In these flashbacks, the audience sees many of the twists and turns which are in "Oedipus Rex." In the scenes of the rising action, the play almost turns into a "who done it" mystery. The finger of guilt constantly changes direction. First, it seems to possibly point to Creon, but when Jocasta reveals an extra piece of information about Laius' murder, Oedipus then begins to worry that he himself might be the culprit. However, a messenger arrives with news that seemingly relieves Oedipus of the possibility of having murdered the king. Oedipus recounts a memory of having murdered a small band of men at a crossroads after they rudely pushed him out of their way. This seems parallel with the story of Laius' murder, but Jocasta, Oedipus' wife, points out that there was supposedly a band of highwaymen that attacked the king. As Oedipus says, "If there were several (marauders), clearly the guilt is not mine, I was alone" (Ibid, scene II, p. 44). Yet, as more and more pieces of information are revealed, the finger of guilt points more and more steadily at Oedipus. Finally, a conversation with a shepherd securely places the guilt on Oedipus himself.

The climax of "Oedipus Rex" is the last line of scene IV where Oedipus states, "I, Oedipus, Oedipus, damned in his birth, in his marriage damned, damned in the blood he shed with his own hand" (Ibid, scene IV, p. 64). This is when Oedipus finally realizes that there is no choice but to realize that he himself killed King Laius and has brought the plague on Thebes. The one man who escaped from Laius' murdered band of men says there was only one murderer. Jocasta says the king was killed at a crossroads, and Oedipus distinctly remembers killing a band of men at a similar location. Another messenger also says that, when Oedipus was a baby, he was given to the messenger by a shepherd. This causes Oedipus to realize that the man and woman who he thought were his mother and father are not his true parents. Oedipus then sends for the shepherd who gave the baby to the messenger. The conversation with this shepherd is the last nail in Oedipus' coffin. It reveals that Oedipus is the son of Laius and Jocasta. Laius had heard a prophecy that his son would kill Laius and marry Jocasta, so Laius tied his baby's feet together, and Jocasta gave the baby Oedipus to a shepherd to be killed. The shepherd could not bring himself to kill the baby and thus gave it to a messenger. At the climax of "Oedipus Rex," Oedipus knows that none but he is the guilty murderer. In this climax is yet another sudden twist in the plot. Oedipus quickly plummets from being highly esteemed by the Thebans to being one of their most despised criminals.

The falling action of "Oedipus Rex" covers the first part of the Exodos. In this part, Oedipus' realization becomes widely known. A messenger utters a line that is one of the "morals" of the whole play. "The greatest griefs are those we cause ourselves" (Ibid, exodos, p. 67). It is in the falling action that Jocasta murders herself, and Oedipus blinds himself. Even though none of this takes place on stage, the audience sees Oedipus walk back on stage with no eyes and hears him talk about seeing Jocasta

Oedipus at Colonus by Fulchran-Jean Harriet, 1798 (CC0 1.0).

dead. The falling action of "Oedipus Rex" is a time of utter grief and despair. Oedipus' world has fallen apart. Here is another twist. One minute, Oedipus is the beloved king of Thebes, and the next minute, he is the accursed exiled murderer of Laius. "God, God, is there a sorrow greater? Where shall I find harbor in this world? My voice is hurled far on a dark wind. What has God done to me?" (Ibid, exodos, p. 71.)

The final part, the resolution, covers the remainder of "Oedipus Rex." It is in this section that Oedipus exiles himself and begins to wander with his daughter Antigone. Creon becomes king of Thebes and the first signs of his arrogance, which is seen clearly in Antigone reveal themselves. Overall, the resolution provides a heartbreaking but satisfying ending to the play. Choragos best sums up the ending of the tragedy.

Men of Thebes, look upon Oedipus. This is the king who solved the famous riddle and towered up, most powerful of men. No mortal eyes but looked on him with envy, yet in the end ruin swept over him. Let every man in mankind's frailty consider his last day, and let none presume on his good fortune until he find life, at his death, a memory without pain (Ibid, exodos, p. 80–81).

From the intriguing exposition to the tragic resolution, Sophocles weaves together a riveting plot in "Oedipus Rex." Sophocles' famous tragedy is a tale of a man who plummeted from the highest possible position to the lowest. However, interestingly, as the story continues in "Oedipus at Colonus," it becomes evident that Oedipus is a wiser man now that he is ruler only over himself. Once Oedipus becomes blind, he can see with his mind's eye all the more clearly. In Sophocles' play, only the blind can truly see. As Tiresias, the blind seer, stated, "You mock my blindness, do you? But I say that you, with both your eyes, are blind. . . . The double lash of your parents' curse will whip you out of this land some day, with only night upon your precious eyes. . . . No man that walks upon the earth shall be rooted out more horribly than you" (Ibid, scene I, p. 22–23) (John Micah)

Assignments

- Warm-up: Tell about a tragic modern story (e.g., Anne Frank).
- Students should complete Concept Builder 10-E.
- Essays are due. Students should take the chapter 10 test.

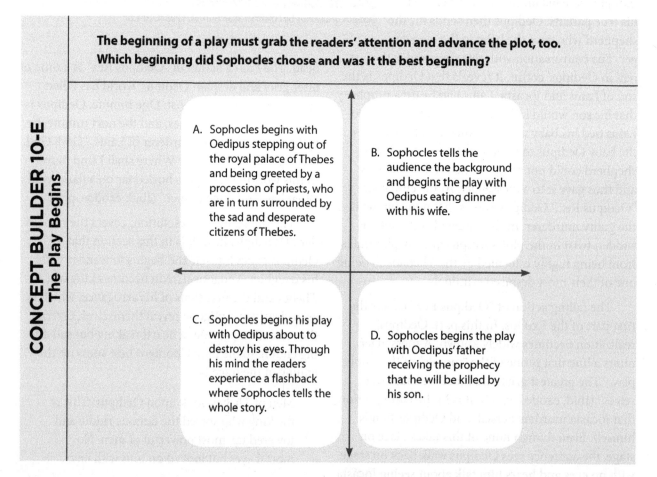

CONCEPT BUILDER 10-E
The Play Begins

The beginning of a play must grab the readers' attention and advance the plot, too. Which beginning did Sophocles choose and was it the best beginning?

A. Sophocles begins with Oedipus stepping out of the royal palace of Thebes and being greeted by a procession of priests, who are in turn surrounded by the sad and desperate citizens of Thebes.

B. Sophocles tells the audience the background and begins the play with Oedipus eating dinner with his wife.

C. Sophocles begins his play with Oedipus about to destroy his eyes. Through his mind the readers experience a flashback where Sophocles tells the whole story.

D. Sophocles begins the play with Oedipus' father receiving the prophecy that he will be killed by his son.

Chapter 11

(300 B.C.– A.D. 500):
Ancient Rome (Part 1)

First Thoughts

R.M. Ogilvie writes, "Aeneas is a hero in search of his soul. *The Aeneid* is very much a spiritual quest, which makes it unique in ancient literature. Only Virgil admits of the possibility that a character can change, grow and develop. Aeneas in the early books is unsure of himself, always seeking instructions from his father or from the gods before committing himself to any course of action. In the underworld he sees a panorama of the future history of Rome down to the time of Augustus, and that vision gives him the self-confidence to act on his own initiative" (*Cambridge History of Classical Literature*, histories.cambridge.org/extract?id=chol97 80521210430_CHOL9780521210430 A019&cited_by=1).

Chapter Learning Objectives

In chapter 11, journey with Aeneas to Rome and witness the founding of one the greatest civilizations in history.

As a result of this chapter study you will be able to . . .

1. Analyze the plot in *The Aeneid*.
2. Evaluate the importance of the setting.
3. Evaluate themes in *The Aeneid*.
4. Describe the gods and goddesses in *The Aeneid* and what character qualities they represent.
5. Contrast Virgil's view of fate with naturalism's view.
6. Contrast Aeneas with Homer's characters Achilles and Hector.
7. Analyze Aeneas' character.

Weekly Essay Options: Begin on page 273 of the Teacher Guide.

Reading ahead: *Meditations* by Marcus Aurelius.

History connections: *World History* chapter 11, "Roman History."

Roman History

Rome was one of the most important and influential city-states in world history. What Jerusalem was to the religious world, Rome was to the geo-political world. Legend said that in 753 B.C., twin boys Romulus and Remus were abandoned by the river Tiber to starve. A mother wolf cared for them until they were young adults. Years later, the Roman God of war Mars encouraged the boys to build a city where they had been found. The two boys built this city; however, they could not get along and ended up at war with each other. Romulus won the battle and the city became known as Rome. Today, historians and archaeologists agree that people started living in Rome long before the time of Romulus and Remus, but many people throughout Roman history continued to believe that this legend was true. Nonetheless, from this cryptic beginning the Roman civilization literally conquered the entire known world.

There is evidence, of course, that there were people in the Tiber River area long before the apocrypha stories about Romulus and Remus emerged. There were nomads in the Tiber River area that created sedentary villages around 800 B.C.

The history of Rome is marked by three epochs. In the first period, from 753–509 B.C., the city developed from a village to a city ruled by kings. Then the Romans expelled the kings and established the Roman Republic during the period from 509–27 B.C. It was much like the Greek Republic existing about the same time in Athens. The Republic collapsed and Rome was ruled by despotic, if at times benign, emperors from 27 B.C.– A.D. 476. It was during the last period that *The Aeneid* by Virgil, and *Meditations* by Marcus Aurelius, were written.

The Italian Peninsula provided the Romans with a secure base from which to expand over the Mediterranean and then European world. Italy was easy to defend and, with its numerous deep-water ports, was an ideal launching pad for expeditions into the interior Mediterranean world. Italy is a peninsula surrounded on three sides by the sea and protected to the north by the Alps mountain range. The climate is not bad either. The climate is generally temperate, although summers are hot in the south.

From the beginning, there were Italian competitors to Roman hegemony. At the beginning of Roman history, somewhat south and north of Rome, Etruscans had a vigorous civilization. Nonetheless, by A.D. 80 the Etruscans were conquered and absorbed into the expanding Roman city-state.

From the beginning of Roman history, the family lay at the center of all personal and social relations in Rome and even influenced public and political activities. Romans valued stable family life and passed laws to reward families led by two parents. At the same time, religion — which until the

The Tiber valley seen from Citerna (Umbria) by Pilou 08, 2007 (CC BY-SA 3.0).

middle of the first millennium A.D. was a form of polytheism — was the most important element that shaped early Roman life. Religion and stable families remained closely connected as the twin pillars of Roman society, especially for the five centuries of the Roman Republic. Later in Roman history, some Romans looked back to these early institutions for the salvation of the Roman Empire. These values are expressed in both the writings of Virgil and Marcus Aurelius.

Assignments

- Warm-up: Why was Rome the perfect place for Virgil to be born?
- Students should complete Concept Builder 11-A.
- Students should review the required reading(s) *before* the assigned chapter begins.
- Teachers may want to discuss assigned reading(s) with students.
- Teachers shall assign the required essay. The rest of the essays can be outlined, answered with shorter answers, discussed, or skipped.
- Students will review all readings for chapter 11.

Read this excerpt from *The Aeneid* (Book 1) by Virgil, and respond to the following:

Arms, and the man I sing, who, forc'd by fate,
And haughty Juno's unrelenting hate,
Expell'd and exil'd, left the Trojan shore.
Long labors, both by sea and land, he bore,
And in the doubtful war, before he won
The Latian realm, and built the destin'd town;
His banish'd gods restor'd to rites divine,
And settled sure succession in his line,
From whence the race of Alban fathers come,
And the long glories of majestic Rome.

Against the Tiber's mouth, but far away,
An ancient town was seated on the sea;
A Tyrian colony; the people made
Stout for the war, and studious of their trade:
Carthage the name; belov'd by Juno more
Than her own Argos, or the Samian shore.
Here stood her chariot; here, if Heav'n were kind,
The seat of awful empire she design'd.
Yet she had heard an ancient rumor fly,
(Long cited by the people of the sky,)
That times to come should see the Trojan race
Her Carthage ruin, and her tow'rs deface;
Nor thus confin'd, the yoke of sov'reign sway
Should on the necks of all the nations lay.
She ponder'd this, and fear'd it was in fate;
Nor could forget the war she wag'd of late
For conqu'ring Greece against the Trojan state.
Besides, long causes working in her mind,
And secret seeds of envy, lay behind;
Deep graven in her heart the doom remain'd
Of partial Paris, and her form disdain'd;
The grace bestow'd on ravish'd Ganymed,
Electra's glories, and her injur'd bed.
Each was a cause alone; and all combin'd
To kindle vengeance in her haughty mind.
For this, far distant from the Latian coast
She drove the remnants of the Trojan host;
And sev'n long years th' unhappy wand'ring train
Were toss'd by storms, and scatter'd thro' the main.
Such time, such toil, requir'd the Roman name,
Such length of labor for so vast a frame.

Arms, and the man I sing, who, forc'd by fate,
And haughty Juno's unrelenting hate . . .

Paraphrase this passage.

What is the motif of this epic narrative?

Virgil

Virgil was born in a rural town north of Rome and grew up in the most prosperous era of Roman hegemony. Emperor Augustus was reigning and he heralded unprecedented prosperity and peace for the Roman Empire. Virgil became one of the most famous poets in Roman history. His most famous work was *The Aeneid*. Virgil worked on *The Aeneid* for 11 years. This epic poem reflects his great skill and care in writing and his tremendous knowledge of Greek literature, which he had studied ever since he was a boy.

Since Virgil's birth in 70 B.C. there had been discord approaching anarchy in Rome. He and many other young men of his generation were totally fed up with Roman politics. Virgil stayed in Naples and spent these years studying philosophy and writing poetry about the joys of country living. Then in 31 B.C., something happened that completely changed Virgil's feelings about Rome and about what he wanted to write. The Emperor Augustus finally managed to end the civil wars that had plagued the city for so long and restored order and peace. For the first time in his life, Virgil had hope for the future of his country, and he felt deep gratitude and admiration for Augustus, the man who had made it all possible. Virgil was inspired to write his great epic poem, *The Aeneid*, to celebrate Roman and Emperor Augustus' achievement.

Virgil Reading *The Aeneid* to Augustus, Octavia, and Livia by Jean-Baptiste Wicar, c.1790 (PD-Art)

- Warm-up: Discuss the political situation in Rome when *The Aeneid* was written. In what ways was Virgil's epic a political poem about Rome?

- Students should complete Concept Builder 11-B.

- Students should review reading(s) from the next chapter.

- Students should outline essay due at the end of the week.

- Per teacher instructions, students may answer orally, in a group setting, some of the essays that are not assigned as formal essays.

CONCEPT BUILDER 11-B
Legend

A legend is a narrative of human actions that are perceived both by teller and listeners to take place within human history and to possess certain qualities that give the narrative credibility. Most modern readers would agree that *The Aeneid* includes some exaggeration and even untrue facts; however, to Virgil's audience, it was the absolute truth. Recall other legends that you have heard that may or may not be true.

George Washington cuts down a cherry tree and admits he did it. "I cannot tell a lie."	King Arthur becomes king by pulling a sword from a stone.
A legend from *The Aeneid*	A legend from my family history.

Perspectives: *The Aeneid*

Generations have wept at the injustices suffered by Queen Dido! "For what more miserable than a miserable being who commiserates not himself; weeping the death of Dido for love to Aeneas . . ." Augustine, Confessions, Book I. "On Dido in her desolation now/ Terror grew at her fate. She prayed for death,/ Being heartsick at the mere sight of heaven" Virgil, *The Aeneid*, Book IV, Lines 623–624."

The Aeneid

The wretched queen, pursued by cruel fate,
Begins at length the light of heav'n to hate,
And loathes to live. Then dire portents she sees,
To hasten on the death her soul decrees:
Strange to relate! for when, before the shrine,
She pours in sacrifice the purple wine,
The purple wine is turn'd to putrid blood,
And the white offer'd milk converts to mud.
This dire presage, to her alone reveal'd,
From all, and ev'n her sister, she conceal'd.
A marble temple stood within the grove,
Sacred to death, and to her murther'd love;
That honor'd chapel she had hung around
With snowy fleeces, and with garlands crown'd:
Oft, when she visited this lonely dome,
Strange voices issued from her husband's tomb;
She thought she heard him summon her away,
Invite her to his grave, and chide her stay.
Hourly 't is heard, when with a boding note
The solitary screech owl strains her throat,
And, on a chimney's top, or turret's height,
With songs obscene disturbs the silence of the night.
Besides, old prophecies augment her fears;
And stern Aeneas in her dreams appears,
Disdainful as by day: she seems, alone,
To wander in her sleep, thro' ways unknown,
Guideless and dark; or, in a desart plain,
To seek her subjects, and to seek in vain:
Like Pentheus, when, distracted with his fear,
He saw two suns, and double Thebes, appear;
Or mad Orestes, when his mother's ghost

Full in his face infernal torches toss'd,
And shook her snaky locks: he shuns the sight,
Flies o'er the stage, surpris'd with mortal fright;
The Furies guard the door and intercept his flight.

Now, sinking underneath a load of grief,
From death alone she seeks her last relief;
The time and means resolv'd within her breast,
She to her mournful sister thus address'd
(Dissembling hope, her cloudy front she clears,
And a false vigor in her eyes appears):
"Rejoice!" she said. "Instructed from above,
My lover I shall gain, or lose my love.
Nigh rising Atlas, next the falling sun,
Long tracts of Ethiopian climates run:
There a Massylian priestess I have found,
Honor'd for age, for magic arts renown'd:
Th' Hesperian temple was her trusted care;
'T was she supplied the wakeful dragon's fare.
She poppy seeds in honey taught to steep,
Reclaim'd his rage, and sooth'd him into sleep.
She watch'd the golden fruit; her charms unbind
The chains of love, or fix them on the mind:
She stops the torrents, leaves the channel dry,
Repels the stars, and backward bears the sky.
The yawning earth rebellows to her call,
Pale ghosts ascend, and mountain ashes fall.
Witness, ye gods, and thou my better part,
How loth I am to try this impious art!
Within the secret court, with silent care,
Erect a lofty pile, expos'd in air:

Hang on the topmost part the Trojan vest,
Spoils, arms, and presents, of my faithless guest.
Next, under these, the bridal bed be plac'd,
Where I my ruin in his arms embrac'd:
All relics of the wretch are doom'd to fire;
For so the priestess and her charms require."

Thus far she said, and farther speech forbears;
A mortal paleness in her face appears:
Yet the mistrustless Anna could not find
The secret fun'ral in these rites design'd;
Nor thought so dire a rage possess'd her mind.
Unknowing of a train conceal'd so well,
She fear'd no worse than when Sichaeus fell;
Therefore obeys. The fatal pile they rear,
Within the secret court, expos'd in air.
The cloven holms and pines are heap'd on high,
And garlands on the hollow spaces lie.
Sad cypress, vervain, yew, compose the wreath,
And ev'ry baleful green denoting death.
The queen, determin'd to the fatal deed,
The spoils and sword he left, in order spread,
And the man's image on the nuptial bed.

And now (the sacred altars plac'd around)
The priestess enters, with her hair unbound,
And thrice invokes the pow'rs below the ground.
Night, Erebus, and Chaos she proclaims,
And threefold Hecate, with her hundred names,
And three Dianas: next, she sprinkles round
With feign'd Avernian drops the hallow'd ground;
Culls hoary simples, found by Phoebe's light,
With brazen sickles reap'd at noon of night;
Then mixes baleful juices in the bowl,
And cuts the forehead of a newborn foal,
Robbing the mother's love. The destin'd queen
Observes, assisting at the rites obscene;
A leaven'd cake in her devoted hands
She holds, and next the highest altar stands:
One tender foot was shod, her other bare;
Girt was her gather'd gown, and loose her hair.
Thus dress'd, she summon'd, with her dying breath,
The heav'ns and planets conscious of her death,
And ev'ry pow'r, if any rules above,
Who minds, or who revenges, injur'd love.
"'T was dead of night, when weary bodies close
Their eyes in balmy sleep and soft repose:
The winds no longer whisper thro' the woods,

Aeneas' Flight from Troy by Federico Barocci, 1598 (PD-Art).

Nor murm'ring tides disturb the gentle floods.
The stars in silent order mov'd around;
And Peace, with downy wings, was brooding on the
ground
The flocks and herds, and party-color'd fowl,
Which haunt the woods, or swim the weedy pool,
Stretch'd on the quiet earth, securely lay,
Forgetting the past labors of the day.
All else of nature's common gift partake:
Unhappy Dido was alone awake.
Nor sleep nor ease the furious queen can find;
Sleep fled her eyes, as quiet fled her mind.
Despair, and rage, and love divide her heart;
Despair and rage had some, but love the greater part.

Then thus she said within her secret mind:
"What shall I do? what succor can I find?
Become a suppliant to Hyarba's pride,
And take my turn, to court and be denied?
Shall I with this ungrateful Trojan go,
Forsake an empire, and attend a foe?
Himself I refug'd, and his train reliev'd-
'T is true- but am I sure to be receiv'd?
Can gratitude in Trojan souls have place!
Laomedon still lives in all his race!
Then, shall I seek alone the churlish crew,
Or with my fleet their flying sails pursue?
What force have I but those whom scarce before
I drew reluctant from their native shore?
Will they again embark at my desire,
Once more sustain the seas, and quit their second
Tyre?
Rather with steel thy guilty breast invade,

And take the fortune thou thyself hast made.
Your pity, sister, first seduc'd my mind,
Or seconded too well what I design'd.
These dear-bought pleasures had I never known,
Had I continued free, and still my own;
Avoiding love, I had not found despair,
But shar'd with salvage beasts the common air.
Like them, a lonely life I might have led,
Not mourn'd the living, nor disturb'd the dead."
These thoughts she brooded in her anxious breast.
On board, the Trojan found more easy rest.
Resolv'd to sail, in sleep he pass'd the night;
And order'd all things for his early flight.

To whom once more the winged god appears;
His former youthful mien and shape he wears,
And with this new alarm invades his ears:
"Sleep'st thou, O goddess-born! and canst thou drown
Thy needful cares, so near a hostile town,
Beset with foes; nor hear'st the western gales
Invite thy passage, and inspire thy sails?
She harbors in her heart a furious hate,
And thou shalt find the dire effects too late;
Fix'd on revenge, and obstinate to die.
Haste swiftly hence, while thou hast pow'r to fly.
The sea with ships will soon be cover'd o'er,
And blazing firebrands kindle all the shore.
Prevent her rage, while night obscures the skies,
And sail before the purple morn arise.
Who knows what hazards thy delay may bring?
Woman's a various and a changeful thing."
Thus Hermes in the dream; then took his flight
Aloft in air unseen, and mix'd with night.
Twice warn'd by the celestial messenger,
The pious prince arose with hasty fear;
Then rous'd his drowsy train without delay:
"Haste to your banks; your crooked anchors weigh,
And spread your flying sails, and stand to sea.
A god commands: he stood before my sight,
And urg'd us once again to speedy flight.
O sacred pow'r, what pow'r soe'er thou art,
To thy blest orders I resign my heart.
Lead thou the way; protect thy Trojan bands,
And prosper the design thy will commands."
He said: and, drawing forth his flaming sword,
His thund'ring arm divides the many-twisted cord.
An emulating zeal inspires his train:

They run; they snatch; they rush into the main.
With headlong haste they leave the desert shores,
And brush the liquid seas with lab'ring oars.

Aurora now had left her saffron bed,
And beams of early light the heav'ns o'erspread,
When, from a tow'r, the queen, with wakeful eyes,
Saw day point upward from the rosy skies.
She look'd to seaward; but the sea was void,
And scarce in ken the sailing ships descried.
Stung with despite, and furious with despair,
She struck her trembling breast, and tore her hair.
"And shall th' ungrateful traitor go," she said,
"My land forsaken, and my love betray'd?
Shall we not arm? not rush from ev'ry street,
To follow, sink, and burn his perjur'd fleet?
Haste, haul my galleys out! pursue the foe!
Bring flaming brands! set sail, and swiftly row!
What have I said? where am I? Fury turns
My brain; and my distemper'd bosom burns.
Then, when I gave my person and my throne,
This hate, this rage, had been more timely shown.
See now the promis'd faith, the vaunted name,
The pious man, who, rushing thro' the flame,
Preserv'd his gods, and to the Phrygian shore
The burthen of his feeble father bore!
I should have torn him piecemeal; strow'd in floods
His scatter'd limbs, or left expos'd in woods;
Destroy'd his friends and son; and, from the fire,
Have set the reeking boy before the sire.
Events are doubtful, which on battles wait:
Yet where's the doubt, to souls secure of fate?
My Tyrians, at their injur'd queen's command,
Had toss'd their fires amid the Trojan band;
At once extinguish'd all the faithless name;
And I myself, in vengeance of my shame,
Had fall'n upon the pile, to mend the fun'ral flame.
Thou Sun, who view'st at once the world below;
Thou Juno, guardian of the nuptial vow;
Thou Hecate hearken from thy dark abodes!
Ye Furies, fiends, and violated gods,
All pow'rs invok'd with Dido's dying breath,
Attend her curses and avenge her death!
If so the Fates ordain, Jove commands,
Th' ungrateful wretch should find the Latian lands,
Yet let a race untam'd, and haughty foes,
His peaceful entrance with dire arms oppose:
Oppress'd with numbers in th' unequal field,

His men discourag'd, and himself expell'd,
Let him for succor sue from place to place,
Torn from his subjects, and his son's embrace.
First, let him see his friends in battle slain,
And their untimely fate lament in vain;
And when, at length, the cruel war shall cease,
On hard conditions may he buy his peace:
Nor let him then enjoy supreme command;
But fall, untimely, by some hostile hand,
And lie unburied on the barren sand!
These are my pray'rs, and this my dying will;
And you, my Tyrians, ev'ry curse fulfil.
Perpetual hate and mortal wars proclaim,
Against the prince, the people, and the name.
These grateful off'rings on my grave bestow;
Nor league, nor love, the hostile nations know!
Now, and from hence, in ev'ry future age,
When rage excites your arms, and strength supplies
the rage

Rise some avenger of our Libyan blood,
With fire and sword pursue the perjur'd brood;
Our arms, our seas, our shores, oppos'd to theirs;
And the same hate descend on all our heirs!"

This said, within her anxious mind she weighs
The means of cutting short her odious days.
Then to Sichaeus' nurse she briefly said
(For, when she left her country, hers was dead):
"Go, Barce, call my sister. Let her care
The solemn rites of sacrifice prepare;
The sheep, and all th' atoning off'rings bring,
Sprinkling her body from the crystal spring
With living drops; then let her come, and thou
With sacred fillets bind thy hoary brow.
Thus will I pay my vows to Stygian Jove,
And end the cares of my disastrous love;
Then cast the Trojan image on the fire,
And, as that burns, my passions shall expire."

Assignments

- Warm-up: Have you experienced great disappointment? How did you react?
- Students should complete Concept Builder 11-C.
- Students should write rough draft of assigned essay.
- The teacher may correct rough drafts.

CONCEPT BUILDER 11-C The Climax	*The Aeneid,* like Homer's *The Odyssey,* describes a quest, a journey. Identify the climax. The crisis or climax is the moment or event in the plot in which the conflict is most directly addressed: the main character "wins" or "loses"; the secret is revealed. After the climax, the falling action occurs.	
	Rising Action	
	Climax	
	Falling Action	

Roman Contemporary

The Greek Epictetus was born at Hierapolis in Phrygia (close to Turkey), probably about the middle of the first century A.D. His early history is unknown until we find him in Rome, the slave of Epaphroditus, a freedman living during the reign of Emperor Nero. Epictetus was a main authority on Stoic morals. The points on which he laid chief stress were the importance of cultivating complete independence of external circumstances, the realization that man can find happiness only by accepting his lot in life, and the duty of reverencing common sense. Epictetus, like Socrates and Jesus Christ, did not write any books. The following, and all the sayings of Epictetus, were recorded by his disciples. Epictetus exhibits the idea that people are created in the image of the gods, and in that sense partner with the gods to rule the earth. "Are we not in a manner kinsman of the Gods, and have we not come from them?" He also has a rudimentary understanding of heaven. He even invited his audience to a theological position that states that the gods determine one's fate. "Let us show them that they have power over none." On the other hand, there is no notion that the gods have the best interest of mankind in mind, nor is there any statement about the love that the gods might have toward mankind.

I do not think that an old fellow like me need have been sitting here to try and prevent your entertaining abject notions of yourselves, and talking of yourselves in an abject and ignoble way: but to prevent there being by chance among you any such young men as, after recognizing their kindred to the Gods, and their bondage in these chains of the body and its manifold necessities, should desire to cast them off as burdens too grievous to be borne, and depart to their true kindred. This is the struggle in which your Master and Teacher, were he worthy of the name, should be engaged. You would come to me and say: "Epictetus, we can no longer endure being chained to this wretched body, giving it food and drink and rest and purification; aye, and for its sake forced to be subservient to this man and that." Are not these things indifferent and nothing to us? Is it not true that death is no evil? Are we not in a manner kinsmen of the gods, and have we not come from them? Let us depart thither, whence we came: let us be freed from these chains that confine and press us down. Here are thieves and robbers and tribunals: and they that are called tyrants, who deem that they have after a fashion power over us, because of the miserable body and what appertains to it. Let us show them that they have power over none (Epictetus, The golden sayings of Epictetus, with the Hymn of Cleanthes; translated and arranged by Hastings Crossley in www.bartleby.com).

Assignments

- Warm-up: Find Christian principles in this passage.
- Students should complete Concept Builder 11-D.
- Students will re-write corrected copies of essay due tomorrow.

The setting is the place and time of the story, including the historical period, social milieu of the characters, geographical location, and descriptions of indoor and outdoor locales. Why is the setting so important to *The Aeneid*?

Setting

The Historical Period	Social Milieu of the Characters (the internal temperament and agendas of each character)	Geographical Location
Importance	Importance	Importance

Critics Corner

Unlike Homer's heroes, the figure of Aeneas simultaneously comprises past, present, and future. . . . In The Aeneid we see for the first time the tragedy of man suffering from historical fate. The hero is never allowed to belong completely to the moment. If and when, as in Carthage, he seems to be caught up in the moment, a god reminds him of his duty.

— Viktor Poschl, *The Art of Vergil*, 1962

The real subject of *The Aeneid* is not Aeneas . . . it is Rome and the glories of her empire, seen as the roman-ticist sees the great past. The first title given it was *The Deeds of the Roman People*. Aeneas is important because he carries Rome's destiny; he is to be her founder by the high decrees of fate.

— Edith Hamilton, *The Roman Way*, 1960

Virgil owed his immediate acceptance as the prince of Latin poets, and still owes his place among the supreme poets of the world, not merely to his insight into the life of man and nature, his majesty and tender-ness, and the melodious perfection of his verse. Over and above all these, he was the interpreter, we may even call him the creator, of a great national ideal. That ideal was at once political, social and religious. The supremacy of Rome took in his hands the aspect of an ordinance of Providence, towards which an previous history had been leading up under divine guidance. It meant the establishment of an empire to which no limit of time or space was set, and in which the human race would find ordered peace, settled government, material prosperity, the reign of law and the commonwealth of freedom.

— J.W. Mackail, *Virgil and His Meaning to the World of Today*, 1963

Each detail of *The Aeneid* is drenched with symbolism and . . . it must be read at several levels. But the symbolism of the sum is simple. An inevitable civil war — all the participants were Italians, all ancestors of the Romans — had happily come to its period. All had fought well and, according to their best fights, justly. All bitterness and all passion was now laid at rest, and all could now join hands as comrades and together walk to meet the shining future.

— Moses Hadas, *A History of Latin Literature*, 1952

The struggle and final victory of order — this subduing of the demonic which is the basic theme of the poem, appears and reappears in many variations. The demonic appears in history as civil or foreign war, in the soul as passion, and in nature as death and destruction. Jupiter, Aeneas, and Augustus are its conquerors, while Juno, Dido, Turnus, and Antony are its conquered representatives. The contrast between Jupiter's powerful composure and Juno's confused passion reappears in the contrast between Aeneas and Dido and between Aeneas and Turnus.

— Viktor Poschl, *The Art of Vergil*, 1962

Vergil, I think, has caught a truth in this representation of angry, murderous Aeneas. Killing Turnus is a victory for the cause, but not for Aeneas. In this final struggle . . . Aeneas can only be the loser. Triumphant he should never be; angry, I feel that I understand him better. It is his final assertion against (enslavement to?) the destiny that has almost dehumanized him, the final proof by Vergil that "pius Aeneas" (pious Aeneas) is not passive, but more tragic than Dido and Turnus together.

— William S. Anderson, *The Art of The Aeneid*, 1969

Assignments

- Warm-up: Do you agree with Edith Hamilton that the real subject of *The Aeneid* is not Aeneas, but the glory of Rome?

- Students should complete Concept Builder 11-E.

- Essays are due. Students should take the chapter 11 test.

CONCEPT BUILDER 11-E **The Theme**	The theme is the one-sentence major purpose of a literary piece, rarely stated but implied. The theme is not a moral that is a statement of the author's didactic purpose of his literary piece. What are at least three themes of *The Aeneid*? Explain your answer.	
	Themes	
	The Aeneid is a national epic. In that sense, it is a story of heroes struggling to create a new nation.	

Chapter 12

(300 B.C.– A.D. 500):
Ancient Rome (Part 2)

First Thoughts Marcus Aurelius (full name Marcus Aelius Aurelius Antoninus) (A.D. 121–180) was a Roman emperor (A.D. 161–180) and Stoic philosopher. Stoicism became the most influential school of the Greco-Roman world, represented by Roman slave Epictetus and the Roman emperor Marcus Aurelius. The Stoics taught that one can achieve happiness only by rejecting material comforts and by dedicating oneself to a life of reason and virtue. Human reason was also considered part of the divine Logos, and therefore immortal. They also taught that each person was part of God and that all people form a universal family. Stoicism celebrated the human spirit, disciplined and controlled. It became the measuring rod against which all social and religious institutions were measured.

Marcus Aurelius became emperor in 161, and throughout his reign he was engaged in defensive wars on the northern and eastern frontiers of the empire. He greatly enlarged the Roman Empire and is generally considered to be one of the finest post-Augustinian emperors. As a philosopher he is remembered for his *Meditations*.

Chapter Learning Objectives In chapter 12 we will examine the winsome champion of Stoicism and we will wonder, again, why Aurelius chose to persecute Christians.

As a result of this chapter study you will be able to . . .

1. Analyze the two types of writing of Marcus Aurelius.

2. Define Stoicism and compare this philosophy to truth found in Scripture.

3. Discuss Aurelius' view of the gods' impact on mankind.

4. Evaluate why Aurelius persecuted Christians.

Weekly Essay Options: Begin on page 273 of the Teacher Guide.

Reading ahead: The Sermon on the Mount, *The Didache* (Lesson 14), writings by Clement and Justin Martyr, *The Martyrdom of Polycarp* (Lesson 15), Author Unknown.

151

 History connections: *World History* chapter 12, "Roman Life."

Marcus Aurelius

The following is from the introduction in an amended edition of Casaubon's translation of *Meditations* by Marcus Aurelius (www.gutenberg.org/files/2680/2680-h/2680-h.htm#2H_INTR).

MARCUS AURELIUS ANTONINUS was born on April 26, A.D. 121. His real name was M. Annius Verus, and he was sprung of a noble family which claimed descent from Numa, second King of Rome. Thus the most religious of emperors came of the blood of the most pious of early kings. His father, Annius Verus, had held high office in Rome, and his grandfather, of the same name, had been thrice Consul. Both his parents died young, but Marcus held them in loving remembrance. On his father's death Marcus was adopted by his grandfather, the consular Annius Verus, and there was deep love between these two. On the very first page of his book Marcus gratefully declares how of his grandfather he had learned to be gentle and meek, and to refrain from all anger and passion. The Emperor Hadrian divined the fine character of the lad, whom he used to call not Verus but Verissimus, more Truthful than his own name. He advanced Marcus to equestrian rank when six years of age, and at the age of eight made him a member of the ancient Salian priesthood. The boy's aunt, Annia Galeria Faustina, was married to Antoninus Pius, afterwards emperor. Hence it came about that Antoninus, having no son, adopted Marcus, changing his name to that which he is known by, and betrothed him to his daughter Faustina. His education was conducted with all care. The ablest teachers were engaged for him, and he was trained in the strict doctrine of the Stoic philosophy, which was his great delight. He was taught to dress plainly and to live simply, to avoid all softness and luxury. His body was trained to hardihood by wrestling, hunting, and outdoor games; and though his constitution was weak, he showed great personal courage to encounter the fiercest boars. At the same time he was kept from the extravagancies of his day. The great excitement in Rome was the strife of the Factions, as they were called, in the circus. The racing drivers used to adopt one of four colours — red, blue, white, or green — and their partisans showed an eagerness in supporting them which nothing could surpass. Riot and corruption went in the train of the racing chariots; and from all these things Marcus held severely aloof.

In 140 Marcus was raised to the consulship, and in 145 his betrothal was consummated by marriage. Two years later Faustina brought him a daughter; and soon after the tribunate and other imperial honours were conferred upon him.

Antoninus Pius died in 161, and Marcus assumed the imperial state. He at once associated with himself L. Ceionius Commodus, whom Antoninus had adopted as a younger son at the same time with Marcus, giving him the name of Lucius Aurelius Verus. Henceforth the two are colleagues in the empire, the junior being trained as it were to succeed. No sooner was Marcus settled upon the throne than wars broke out on all sides. In the east, Vologeses III. of Parthia began a long-meditated revolt by destroying a whole Roman

Marble bust of the roman emperor Marcus Aurelius.

Legion and invading Syria (162). Verus was sent off in hot haste to quell this rising; and he fulfilled his trust by plunging into drunkenness and debauchery, while the war was left to his officers. Soon after Marcus had to face a more serious danger at home in the coalition of several powerful tribes on the northern frontier. Chief among those were the Marcomanni or Marchmen, the Quadi (mentioned in this book), the Sarmatians, the Catti, the Jazyges. In Rome itself there was pestilence and starvation, the one brought from the east by Verus's legions, the other caused by floods which had destroyed vast quantities of grain. After all had been done possible to allay famine and to supply pressing needs — Marcus being forced even to sell the imperial jewels to find money — both emperors set forth to a struggle which was to continue more or less during the rest of Marcus's reign. During these wars, in 169, Verus died. We have no means of following the campaigns in detail; but thus much is certain, that in the end the Romans succeeded in crushing the barbarian tribes, and effecting a settlement which made the empire more secure. Marcus was himself commander-in-chief, and victory was due no less to his own ability than to his wisdom in choice of lieutenants, shown conspicuously in the case of Pertinax. There were several important battles fought in these campaigns; and one of them has become celebrated for the legend of the Thundering Legion. In a battle against the Quadi in 174, the day seemed to be going in favour of the foe, when on a sudden arose a great storm of thunder and rain the lightning struck the barbarians with terror, and they turned to rout. In later days this storm was said to have been sent in answer to the prayers of a legion which contained many Christians, and the name Thundering Legion should be given to it on this account. The title of Thundering Legion is known at an earlier date, so this part of the story at least cannot be true; but the aid of the storm is acknowledged by one of the scenes carved on Antonine's Column at Rome, which commemorates these wars.

The settlement made after these troubles might have been more satisfactory but for an unexpected rising in the east. Avidius Cassius, an able captain who had won renown in the Parthian wars, was at this time chief governor of the eastern provinces. By whatever means induced, he had conceived the project of proclaiming himself emperor as soon as Marcus, who was then in feeble health, should die; and a report having been conveyed to him that Marcus was dead, Cassius did as he had planned. Marcus, on hearing the news, immediately patched up a peace and returned home to meet this new peril. The emperors great grief was that he must needs engage in the horrors of civil strife. He praised the qualities of Cassius, and expressed a heartfelt wish that Cassius might not be driven to do himself a hurt before he should have the opportunity to grant a free pardon. But before he could come to the east news had come to Cassius that the emperor still lived; his followers fell away from him, and he was assassinated. Marcus now went to the east, and while there the murderers brought the head of Cassius to him; but the emperor indignantly refused their gift, nor would he admit the men to his presence.

On this journey his wife, Faustina, died. At his return the emperor celebrated a triumph (176). Immediately afterwards he repaired to Germany, and took up once more the burden of war. His operations were followed by complete success; but the troubles of late years had been too much for his constitution, at no time robust, and on March 17, 180, he died in Pannonia.

The good emperor was not spared domestic troubles. Faustina had borne him several children, of whom he was passionately fond. Their innocent faces may still be seen in many a sculpture gallery, recalling with odd effect the dreamy countenance of their father. But they died one by one, and when Marcus came to his own end only one of his sons still lived — the weak and worthless Commodus. On his father's death Commodus, who succeeded him, undid the work of many campaigns by a hasty and unwise peace; and his reign of twelve years proved him to be a ferocious and bloodthirsty tyrant. Scandal has made free with the name of Faustina herself, who is accused not only of unfaithfulness, but of intriguing with Cassius and egging him on to his fatal rebellion, it must be admitted that these charges rest on no sure evidence; and the emperor, at all events, loved her dearly, nor ever felt the slightest qualm of suspicion.

- Warm-up: Was Marcus Aurelius a good emperor?

- Students should complete Concept Builder 12-A.

- Students should review the required reading(s) *before* the assigned chapter begins.

- Teachers may want to discuss assigned reading(s) with students.

- Teachers shall assign the required essay. The rest of the essays can be outlined, answered with shorter answers, discussed, or skipped.

- Students will review all readings for chapter 12.

CONCEPT BUILDER 12-A
Active Reading

Read this excerpt from *Meditations* (Book 1) by Marcus Aurelius, and respond to the following:

To the gods I am indebted for having good grandfathers, good parents, a good sister, good teachers, good associates, good kinsmen and friends, nearly everything good. Further, I owe it to the gods that I was not hurried into any offence against any of them, though I had a disposition which, if opportunity had offered, might have led me to do something of this kind; but, through their favor, there never was such a concurrence of circumstances as put me to the trial. Further, I am thankful to the gods that I made the right choices as a youth; that I was subjected to a ruler and a father who was able to take away all pride from me, and to bring me to the knowledge that it is possible for a man to live in a palace without wanting either guards or embroidered dresses, or torches and statues, and such-like show; but that it is in such a man's power to bring himself very near to the fashion of a private person, without being for this reason either meaner in thought, or more remiss in action, with respect to the things which must be done for the public interest in a manner that befits a ruler. I thank the gods for giving me such a brother, who was able by his moral character to rouse me to vigilance over myself, and who, at the same time, pleased me by his respect and affection; that my children have not been stupid nor deformed in body; that I did not make more proficiency in rhetoric, poetry, and the other studies, in which I should perhaps have been completely engaged, if I had seen that I was making progress in them; that I made haste to place those who brought me up in the station of honor, which they seemed to desire, without putting them off with hope of my doing it sometime after.

What are three things for which Aurelius is thankful?

1.

2.

3.

What are three things for which you are thankful?

1.

2.

3.

Stoicism

The following is from the introduction in an amended edition of Casaubon's translation of *Meditations* by Marcus Aurelius (Ibid).

As a soldier we have seen that Marcus was both capable and successful; as an administrator he was prudent and conscientious. Although steeped in the teachings of philosophy, he did not attempt to remodel the world on any preconceived plan. He trod the path beaten by his predecessors, seeking only to do his duty as well as he could, and to keep out corruption. He did some unwise things, it is true. To create a compeer in empire, as he did with Verus, was a dangerous innovation which could only succeed if one of the two effaced himself; and under Diocletian this very precedent caused the Roman Empire to split into halves. He erred in his civil administration by too much centralising. But the strong point of his reign was the administration of justice. Marcus sought by-laws to protect the weak, to make the lot of the slaves less hard, to stand in place of father to the fatherless. Charitable foundations were endowed for rearing and educating poor children. The provinces were protected against oppression, and public help was given to cities or districts which might be visited by calamity. The great blot on his name, and one hard indeed to explain, is his treatment of the Christians. In his reign Justin at Rome became a martyr to his faith, and Polycarp at Smyrna, and we know of many outbreaks of fanaticism in the provinces which caused the death of the faithful. It is no excuse to plead that he knew nothing about the atrocities done in his name: it was his duty to know, and if he did not he would have been the first to confess that he had failed in his duty. But from his own tone in speaking of the Christians it is clear he knew them only from calumny; and we hear of no measures taken even to secure that they should have a fair hearing. In this respect Trajan was better than he.

To a thoughtful mind such a religion as that of Rome would give small satisfaction. Its legends were often childish or impossible; its teaching had little to do with morality. The Roman religion was in fact of the nature of a bargain: men paid certain sacrifices and rites, and the gods granted their favour, irrespective of right or wrong. In this case all devout souls were thrown back upon philosophy, as they had been, though to a less extent, in Greece. There were under the early empire two rival schools which practically divided the field between them, Stoicism and Epicureanism. The ideal set before each was nominally much the same. The Stoics aspired to the repression of all emotion, and the Epicureans to freedom from all disturbance; yet in the upshot the one has become a synonym of stubborn endurance, the other for unbridled licence. With Epicureanism we have nothing to do now; but it will be worth while to sketch the history and tenets of the Stoic sect. Zeno, the founder of Stoicism, was born in Cyprus at some date unknown, but his life may be said roughly to be between the years 350 and 250 B.C. Cyprus has been from time immemorial a meeting-place

Herma of Zeno of Citium. Photo by user: shakko, 2008 (CC BY-SA 3.0).

155

of the East and West, and although we cannot grant any importance to a possible strain of Phoenician blood in him (for the Phoenicians were no philosophers), yet it is quite likely that through Asia Minor he may have come in touch with the Far East. He studied under the cynic Crates, but he did not neglect other philosophical systems. After many years' study he opened his own school in a colonnade in Athens called the Painted Porch, or Stoa, which gave the Stoics their name. Next to Zeno, the School of the Porch owes most to Chrysippus (280—207 B.C.), who organised Stoicism into a system. Of him it was said, "But for Chrysippus, there had been no Porch."

The Stoics regarded speculation as a means to an end and that end was, as Zeno put it, to live consistently omologonuenws zhn or as it was later explained, to live in conformity with nature. This conforming of the life to nature was the Stoic idea of Virtue.

This dictum might easily be taken to mean that virtue consists in yielding to each natural impulse; but that was very far from the Stoic meaning. In order to live in accord with nature, it is necessary to know what nature is; and to this end a threefold division of philosophy is made — into Physics, dealing with the universe and its laws, the problems of divine government and teleology; Logic, which trains the mind to discern true from false; and Ethics, which applies the knowledge thus gained and tested to practical life. The Stoic system of physics was materialism with an infusion of pantheism. In contradiction to Plato's view that the Ideas, or Prototypes, of phenomena alone really exist, the Stoics held that material objects alone existed; but immanent in the material universe was a spiritual force which acted through them, manifesting itself under many forms, as fire, aether, spirit, soul, reason, the ruling principle.

The universe, then, is God, of whom the popular gods are manifestations; while legends and myths are allegorical. The soul of man is thus an emanation from the godhead, into whom it will eventually be re-absorbed. The divine ruling principle makes all things work together for good, but for the good of the whole. The highest good of man is consciously to work with God for the common good, and this is the sense in which the Stoic tried to live in accord with nature. In the individual it is virtue alone which enables him to do this; as Providence rules the universe, so virtue in the soul must rule man.

In Logic, the Stoic system is noteworthy for their theory as to the test of truth, the Criterion. They compared the new-born soul to a sheet of paper ready for writing. Upon this the senses write their impressions, fantasias and by experience of a number of these the soul unconsciously conceives general notions koinai eunoiai or anticipations. prolhyeis When the impression was such as to be irresistible it was called (katalnptikh fantasia) one that holds fast, or as they explained it, one proceeding from truth. Ideas and inferences artificially produced by deduction or the like were tested by this "holding perception." Of the Ethical application I have already spoken. The highest good was the virtuous life. Virtue alone is happiness, and vice is unhappiness. Carrying this theory to its extreme, the Stoic said that there could be no gradations between virtue and vice, though of course each has its special manifestations. Moreover, nothing is good but virtue, and nothing but vice is bad. Those outside things which are commonly called good or bad, such as health and sickness, wealth and poverty, pleasure and pain, are to him indifferent adiofora. All these things are merely the sphere in which virtue may act. The ideal Wise Man is sufficient unto himself in all things, autarkhs and knowing these truths, he will be happy even when stretched upon the rack. It is probable that no Stoic claimed for himself that he was this Wise Man, but that each strove after it as an ideal much as the Christian strives after a likeness to Christ. The exaggeration in this statement was, however, so obvious, that the later Stoics were driven to make a further subdivision of things indifferent into what is preferable (prohgmena) and what is undesirable. They also held that for him who had not attained to the perfect wisdom, certain actions were proper. (kaqhkonta) These were neither virtuous nor vicious, but, like the indifferent things, held a middle place. Two points in the Stoic system deserve special mention. One is a careful distinction between things which are in our power and things which are not. Desire and dislike, opinion and affection, are within the power of the will; whereas health, wealth, honour, and other such are generally not so. The Stoic was called upon to control his desires and affections, and to guide his opinion; to bring his whole being under the sway of the will or leading principle, just as the universe is guided and governed by divine Providence. This is a special application of the favourite Greek virtue of moderation, (swfrosuum) and has also its parallel in Christian ethics. The second point is a strong insistence on the unity of the universe, and on man's duty as part of a great whole. Public spirit was the most splendid political virtue of the ancient world, and it is here made cosmopolitan. It is again instructive to note that Christian sages insisted on the same thing. Christians are taught that they are members of a worldwide brotherhood, where is neither Greek nor Hebrew, bond nor free and that they live their lives as fellow-workers with God.

Such is the system which underlies the Meditations of Marcus Aurelius. Some knowledge of it is necessary to the right understanding of the book, but for us the chief interest lies elsewhere. We do not come to Marcus Aurelius for a treatise on Stoicism. He is no head of a school to lay down a body of doctrine for students; he does not even contemplate that others should read what he writes. His philosophy is not an eager intellectual inquiry, but more what we should call religious feeling. The uncompromising stiffness of Zeno or Chrysippus is softened and transformed by passing through a nature reverent and tolerant, gentle and free from guile; the grim resignation which made life possible to the Stoic sage becomes in him almost a mood of aspiration. His book records the innermost thoughts of his heart, set down to ease it, with such moral maxims and reflections as may help him to bear the burden of duty and the countless annoyances of a busy life.

It is instructive to compare the Meditations with another famous book, The Imitation of Christ. There is the same ideal of self-control in both. It should be a man's task, says the Imitation, "to overcome himself, and every day to be stronger than himself." "In withstanding of the passions standeth very peace of heart." "Let us set the axe to the root, that we being purged of our passions may have a peaceable mind." To this end there must be continual self-examination. "If thou may not continually gather thyself together, namely sometimes do it, at least once a day, the morning or the evening. In the morning purpose, in the evening discuss the manner, what thou hast been this day, in word, work, and thought." But while the Roman's temper is a modest self-reliance, the Christian aims at a more passive mood, humbleness and meekness, and reliance on the presence and personal friendship of God. The Roman scrutinises his faults with severity, but without the self-contempt which makes the Christian 'vile in his own sight." The Christian, like the Roman, bids "study to withdraw thine heart from the love of things visible"; but it is not the busy life of duty he has in mind so much as the contempt of all worldly things, and the "cutting away of all lower delectations." Both rate men's praise or blame at their real worthlessness; "Let not thy peace," says the Christian, "be in the mouths of men." But it is to God's censure the Christian appeals, the Roman to his own soul. The petty annoyances of injustice or unkindness are looked on by each with the same magnanimity. "Why doth a little thing said or done against thee make thee sorry? It is no new thing; it is not the first, nor shall it be the last, if thou live long. At best suffer patiently, if thou canst not suffer joyously." The Christian should sorrow more for other men's malice than for our own wrongs; but the Roman is inclined to wash his hands of the offender. "Study to be patient in suffering and bearing other men's defaults and all manner infirmities," says the Christian; but the Roman would never have thought to add, "If all men were perfect, what had we then to suffer of other men for God?" The virtue of suffering in itself is an idea which does not meet us in the Meditations. Both alike realise that man is one of a great community. "No man is sufficient to himself," says the Christian; "we must bear together, help together, comfort together." But while he sees a chief importance in zeal, in exalted emotion that is, and avoidance of lukewarmness, the Roman thought mainly of the duty to be done as well as might be, and less of the feeling which should go with the doing of it. To the saint as to the emperor, the world is a poor thing at best. "Verily it is a misery to live upon the earth," says the Christian; few and evil are the days of man's life, which passeth away suddenly as a shadow.

But there is one great difference between the two books we are considering. The Imitation is addressed to others, the Meditations by the writer to himself. We learn nothing from the Imitation of the author's own life, except in so far as he may be assumed to have practised his own preachings; the Meditations reflect mood by mood the mind of him who wrote them. In their intimacy and frankness lies their great charm. These notes are not sermons; they are not even confessions. There is always an air of self-consciousness in confessions; in such revelations there is always a danger of unctuousness or of vulgarity for the best of men. St. Augus-tine is not always clear of offence, and John Bunyan himself exaggerates venial peccadilloes into heinous sins. But Marcus Aurelius is neither vulgar nor unctuous; he extenuates nothing, but nothing sets down in malice. He never poses before an audience; he may not be profound, he is always sincere. And it is a lofty and serene soul which is here disclosed before us. Vulgar vices seem to have no temptation for him; this is not one tied and bound with chains which he strives to break. The faults he detects in himself are often such as most men would have no eyes to see. To serve the divine spirit which is implanted within him, a man must "keep himself pure from all violent passion and evil affection, from all rashness and vanity, and from all manner of discontent, either in regard of the gods or men": or, as he says elsewhere, "unspotted by pleasure, undaunted by pain." Unwavering courtesy and consideration are his aims. "Whatsoever any man either doth or saith, thou must be good;" "doth any man offend? It is against himself that he doth offend: why should it trouble thee?" The offender needs pity, not wrath; those who must needs be corrected, should be treated with tact and gentleness; and one must be always ready to learn better. "The best kind of revenge is, not to become like unto them." There are so many hints of offence forgiven, that we may believe the notes followed sharp on the facts. Perhaps he has fallen short of his aim, and thus seeks to call his principles to mind, and to strengthen himself for the future. That these sayings are not mere talk is plain from the story of Avidius Cassius, who would have usurped his imperial throne. Thus the emperor faithfully carries out his own principle, that evil must be overcome with good. For each fault in others, Nature (says he) has given us a counteracting virtue; "as, for example, against the unthankful, it hath given goodness and meekness, as an antidote."

One so gentle towards a foe was sure to be a good friend; and indeed his pages are full of generous gratitude to those who had served him. In his First Book he sets down to account all the debts due to his kinsfolk and teachers. To his grandfather he owed his own gentle spirit, to his father shamefastness and courage; he learnt of his mother to be religious and bountiful and single-minded. Rusticus did not work in vain, if he showed his pupil that his life needed amending. Apollonius taught him simplicity, reasonableness, gratitude, a love of true liberty. So the list runs on; every one he had dealings with seems to have given him something good, a sure proof of the goodness of his nature, which thought no evil.

If his was that honest and true heart which is the Christian ideal, this is the more wonderful in that he lacked the faith which makes Christians strong. He could say, it is true, "either there is a God, and then all is well; or if all things go by chance and fortune, yet mayest thou use thine own providence in those things that concern thee properly; and then art thou well." Or again, "We must needs grant that there is a nature that doth govern the universe." But his own part in the scheme of things is so small, that he does not hope for any personal happiness beyond what a serene soul may win in this mortal life. "O my soul, the time I trust will be, when thou shalt be good, simple, more open and visible, than that body by which it is enclosed;" but this is said of the calm contentment with human lot which he hopes to attain, not of a time when the trammels of the body shall be cast off. For the rest, the world and its fame and wealth, "all is vanity." The gods may perhaps have a particular care for him, but their especial care is for the universe at large: thus much should suffice. His gods are better than the Stoic gods, who sit aloof from all human things, untroubled and uncaring, but his personal hope is hardly stronger. On this point he says little, though there are many allusions to death as the natural end; doubtless he expected his soul one day to be absorbed into the universal soul, since nothing comes out of nothing, and nothing can be annihilated. His mood is one of strenuous weariness; he does his duty as a good soldier, waiting for the sound of the trumpet which shall sound the retreat; he has not that cheerful confidence which led Socrates through a life no less noble, to a death which was to bring him into the company of gods he had worshipped and men whom he had revered.

But although Marcus Aurelius may have held intellectually that his soul was destined to be absorbed, and to lose consciousness of itself, there were times when he felt, as all who hold it must sometimes feel, how unsatisfying is such a creed. Then he gropes blindly after something less empty and vain. "Thou hast taken ship," he says, "thou hast sailed, thou art come to land, go out, if to another life, there also shalt thou find gods, who are every-where." There is more in this than the assumption of a rival theory for argument's sake. If worldly things be but as a dream, the thought is not far off that there may be an awakening to what is real. When he speaks of death as a necessary change, and points out that nothing useful and profitable can be brought about without change, did he perhaps think of the change in a corn of wheat, which is not quickened except it die? Nature's marvellous power of recreat-ing out of Corruption is surely not confined to bodily things. Many of his thoughts sound like far-off echoes of St. Paul; and it is strange indeed that this most Christian of emperors has nothing good to say of the Christians. To him they are only sectaries violently and passionately set upon opposition.

Profound as philosophy these Meditations certainly are not; but Marcus Aurelius was too sincere not to see the essence of such things as came within his experience. Ancient religions were for the most part concerned with outward things. Do the necessary rites, and you propitiate the gods; and these rites were often trivial, sometimes violated right feeling or even morality. Even when the gods stood on the side of righteousness, they were con-cerned with the act more than with the intent. But Marcus Aurelius knows that what the heart is full of, the man will do. "Such as thy thoughts and ordinary cogitations are," he says, "such will thy mind be in time." And every page of the book shows us that he knew thought was sure to issue in act. He drills his

soul, as it were, in right principles, that when the time comes, it may be guided by them. To wait until the emergency is to be too late. He sees also the true essence of happiness. "If happiness did consist in pleasure, how came notorious robbers, impure abominable livers, parricides, and tyrants, in so large a measure to have their part of pleasures?" He who had all the world's pleasures at command can write thus "A happy lot and portion is, good inclinations of the soul, good desires, good actions."

By the irony of fate this man, so gentle and good, so desirous of quiet joys and a mind free from care, was set at the head of the Roman Empire when great dangers threatened from east and west. For several years he himself commanded his armies in chief. In camp before the Quadi he dates the first book of his Meditations, and shows how he could retire within himself amid the coarse clangour of arms. The pomps and glories which he despised were all his; what to most men is an ambition or a dream, to him was a round of weary tasks which nothing but the stern sense of duty could carry him through. And he did his work well. His wars were slow and tedious, but successful. With a statesman's wisdom he foresaw the danger to Rome of the barbarian hordes from the north, and took measures to meet it. As it was, his settlement gave two centuries of respite to the Roman Empire; had he fulfilled the plan of pushing the imperial frontiers to the Elbe, which seems to have been in his mind, much more might have been accomplished. But death cut short his designs.

Truly a rare opportunity was given to Marcus Aurelius of showing what the mind can do in despite of circumstances. Most peaceful of warriors, a magnificent monarch whose ideal was quiet happi-ness in home life, bent to obscurity yet born to greatness, the loving father of children who died young or turned out hateful, his life was one para-dox. That nothing might lack, it was in camp before the face of the enemy that he passed away and went to his own place.

Assignments

- Warm-up: Why was Stoicism so popular to Christians?

- Students should complete Concept Builder 12-B.

- Students should review reading(s) from the next chapter.

- Students should outline essay due at the end of the week.

- Per teacher instructions, students may answer orally, in a group setting, some of the essays that are not assigned as formal essays.

Compare the writings of Marcus Aurelius and Romans 8 written by the Apostle Paul.

Marcus Aurelius	Christianity
Get rid of the judgment, get rid of the "I am hurt," you are rid of the hurt itself.	Romans 8:35: Who shall separate us from the love of Christ? Shall trouble or hardship or persecution or famine or nakedness or danger or sword?
How ridiculous and how strange to be surprised at anything which happens in life!	
Or is it your reputation that's bothering you? But look at how soon we're all forgotten. The abyss of endless time that swallows it all. The emptiness of those applauding hands.	
Don't worry. Be happy.	

Student Essay: Stoicism

Beginning around the third century B.C. Zeno founded a school in Athens to teach stoicism. Stoicism then continued until about A.D. 529 with its peak being in Rome during the first few centuries of the Common Era. Stoicism started as a philosophy that was taught throughout Greece and Rome, but as stoics define it, philosophy is an exercise and a way of life, and so stoicism for them became a religion.

One of the biggest things that stoics believe and teach is that emotions are wrong. Envy, fear, passionate love of anything, arose from false judgments making a person weaker instead of stronger. Staying away from these taught self-control and an indifference to pain or pleasure while promoting a firm detachment from all of the wrong emotions. This allowed stoics to be clear thinking, level headed and unbiased. Marcus Aurelius author of *Meditations* and a strong stoic during the second century in Rome wrote, "If you work at that which is before you, following right reason seriously, vigorously, calmly, without allowing anything else to distract you, but keeping your divine part pure, as if you were bound to give it back immediately; if you hold to this, expecting nothing, but satisfied to live now according to nature, speaking heroic truth in every word which you utter, you will live happy. And there is no man able to prevent this." The common belief of the Stoics was that by denouncing these emotions and becoming independent, a man would be live his life in virtue and be happy.

The stoics believed in what they called the Logos, and they held this "Logos" as the active principle of all reality. Robert S. Brumbaugh wrote about this belief, "The Logos is conceived as a rational divine power that orders and directs the universe; it is identified with God, nature, and fate. The Logos is present everywhere and seems to be understood as both a divine mind and at least a semi physical force, acting through space and time. Within the cosmic order determined by the Logos are individual centers of potentiality, vitality, and growth. These are "seeds" of the Logos. Through the faculty of reason, all human beings share in the divine reason." Stoic philosophers stressed the rule to follow where reason (the Logos) leads.

Following and living by reason (the Logos), was so important for the stoics, because it not only helped them to have a happy life, but it also was the goal of life so that their souls, "transmuted and diffused, assuming a fiery nature by being received into the Seminal Reason of the Universe" (Marcus Aurelius). Once in the universe, the Stoics believe that all things revolved and kept working together in an ongoing circle. "The universe itself is god and the universal outpouring of its soul; it is this same world's guiding principle, operating in mind and reason, together with the common nature of things and the totality which embraces all existence; then the foreordained might and necessity of the future; then fire and the principle of aether; then those elements whose natural state is one of flux and transition, such as water, earth, and air; then the sun, the moon, the stars; and the universal existence in which all things are contained" (Chrysippus).

Although stoicism only lasted a couple of centuries, it had a huge effect on many of the writings of the early Church throughout the world. While it lasted, those who were Stoics were strong and held to what they believed without shaking. As Lucius Annaeus Seneca wrote, "It is the power of the mind to be unconquerable." (Anna Grace)

- Warm-up: What is the thesis of this essay?
- Students should complete Concept Builder 12-C.
- Students should write rough draft of assigned essay.
- The teacher may correct rough drafts.

CONCEPT BUILDER 12-C
Aphorisms

An aphorism is an original thought written in a short and memorable form. An example of an aphorism from Marcus Aurelius is "Be content with what you are, and wish not change; nor dread your last day, nor long for it." What do these contemporary aphorisms mean? Are they true?

Aphorism	Meaning	Is It true?
Be faithful in the little things and greater things will come your way.		
Fish or cut bait.		
You can have it your way!		
Seize the day!		
Live and let live.		

Persecuted Christians

During his reign Rome was visited by a severe pestilence, and this, with reverses suffered by his armies, threw the populace into a panic, and led them to demand the sacrifice of the Christians, whom they regarded as having brought down the anger of the gods. Aurelius seems to have shared the panic; and his record it stained by his sanction of a cruel persecution. This incident in the career of the last, and one of the loftiest, of the pagan moralists may be regarded as symbolic of the dying effort of heathenism to check the advancing tide of Christianity.

The "Meditations" picture with faithfulness the mind and character of this noblest of the Emperors. Simple in style and sincere in tone, they record for all time the height reached by pagan aspiration in its effort to solve the problem of conduct; and the essential agreement of his practice with his teaching proved that "Even in a palace life may be led well" (Marcus Aurelius Antoninus (121–180), *The Meditations of Marcus Aurelius*, The Harvard Classics, 1909–1914, www.bartleby.com/2/3/1001.html).

Assignments

- Warm-up: Even though Marcus Aurelius was an intelligent, benevolent man, he blamed the Christians for Roman woes. Why? Could the same thing happen today?

- Students should complete Concept Builder 12-D.

- Students will re-write corrected copies of essay due tomorrow.

Marcus Aurelius wrote *Meditations* in Greek at his base in Sirmium in modern-day Serbia and also while positioned at Aquincum on campaign in Pannonia in modern-day Hungary. Photo by Ian Pitchford, 2006 (CC BY-SA 3.0).

Describe characteristics of Aurelius' father.

In my father I observed mildness of temper, and unchangeable resolution in the things which he had determined after due deliberation; and no vainglory in those things which men call honors; and a love of labour and perseverance; and a readiness to listen to those who had anything to propose for the common weal; and undeviating firmness in giving to every man according to his deserts; and a knowledge derived from experience of the occasions for vigorous action and for remission.

Mildness of temper

Marcus Aurelius' Father

Different Styles in *Meditations*

"Accustom thyself to attend carefully to what is said by another, and as much as it is possible, be in the speaker's mind. . . . What kind of people are those whom men wish to please, and for what objects, and by what kinds of acts?" (*Meditations*, p. 50) In this quote from *Meditations*, Marcus Aurelius writes as if he was talking to the audiences, at some times, and sometimes as if he was talking to himself. These two types of writing change the reader from receiving Marcus' advice, to sometimes observing Marcus reflect on his experiences.

"Repentance is a kind of self-reproof for having neglected something useful. . . ." (*Meditations*, p. 63) At some points, the book has a preacher-like feeling as Marcus tells the reader how to act and what to do in life. This is possibly why the book is entitled Meditations as Marcus related his thoughts to the reader. "Whatever man thou meetest with, immediately say to thyself: What opinions has this man about good and bad." (*Meditations*, p. 63) Here, Marcus gives the reader ideas and suggestions of what to say in areas such as meeting people. These parts of the story are like a guidebook for life, telling the reader how to live and how to behave around others. For passages in which Marcus writes like this, the reader receives Marcus' advice, such as an audience receives the advice of the preacher.

But in other parts of *Mediations*, Marcus reflects on his past experiences, and he is almost talking to himself. "From my Grandfather Verus [I learned] good morals and the government of my temper." (*Mediations*, p. 1) *Meditations* opens with Marcus reflecting on everything he learned from various figures in his life, including his grandparents, parents, tutors, governors, and many other people. This is a reflection on what he has learned over the years. This is one way Marcus talks to himself. In some later areas, Marcus asks himself rhetorical questions to recall what he has done. "Have I done something for the general interest? Well, then, I have had my reward." (*Meditations*, p. 93) At these points, the readers can see Marcus' answers, and then can ask themselves these questions. This is another example of Marcus talking to himself, with the reader simply being an outside observer, watching Marcus ask and answer questions, while reflecting on his past experiences.

What effect does this have on the reader? As Marcus rotates between advising the reader and reflecting on himself, the reader changes roles. With the repeating changes of where the words are directed, the reader switches between receiving Marcus' advice and observing Marcus' reflections. The reader, at some points, is being advised in how to live, and then can stop momentarily, watching Marcus think about his experiences.

As Marcus changes how he writes, the readers' role changes. Sometimes the readers are the audience to Marcus' preaching while sometimes they are simply sitting back and watching Marcus focus on himself. This creates intervals in the book where the reader listens then watches, and then listens and watches. (Chris)

Assignments

- Warm-up: How convincing is Aurelius?
- Students should complete Concept Builder 12-E.
- Essays are due. Students should take the chapter 12 test.

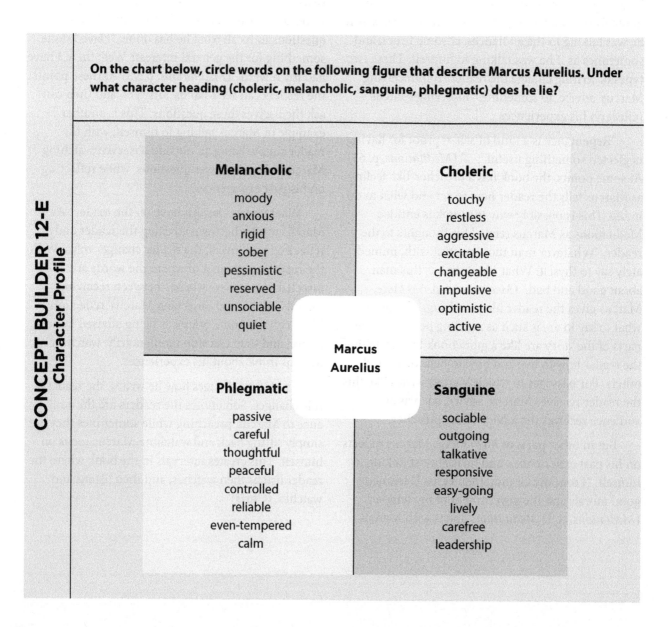

On the chart below, circle words on the following figure that describe Marcus Aurelius. Under what character heading (choleric, melancholic, sanguine, phlegmatic) does he lie?

CONCEPT BUILDER 12-E
Character Profile

Melancholic

moody
anxious
rigid
sober
pessimistic
reserved
unsociable
quiet

Choleric

touchy
restless
aggressive
excitable
changeable
impulsive
optimistic
active

Marcus Aurelius

Phlegmatic

passive
careful
thoughtful
peaceful
controlled
reliable
even-tempered
calm

Sanguine

sociable
outgoing
talkative
responsive
easy-going
lively
carefree
leadership

(A.D. 30–500):
Early Church History (Part 1)

First Thoughts In the first five years after the death and Resurrection of the Lord Jesus Christ, the Church He founded became the majority religion of the greatest empire the world has ever known. This cultural revolution was started by a man (wholly man and wholly God) with a three-year ministry, who wrote nothing, who created no organization, who owned no property.

Chapter Learning Objectives In chapter 13 we examine the most important corpus of writing in world history: the Bible and other sacred writing.

As a result of this chapter study you will be able to . . .

1. Discuss the form and style of the Sermon on the Mount.

2. Analyze the authorship of the Book of Matthew.

3. Based on these teachings, speculate upon what life was like for the early Christian.

4. Women in particular flocked to the Christian faith. Using the Didache as evidence, speculate on why that was so.

5. Compare the Sermon on the Mount with "On the Liberty of Thought and Discussion" by John Stuart Mills.

Weekly Essay Options: Begin on page 273 of the Teacher Guide.

Reading ahead: Writings by Clement and Justin Martyr, *The Martyrdom of Polycarp*, Author Unknown.

167

The Early Church

At first, the early group, called "followers of Jesus Bar Joseph," was only a sect of Judaism. They observed strict Judaic customs, including dietary customs. These rituals were to change quickly.

For one thing, Emperor Nero instituted a persecution against Christians. Many Jews, however, were persecuted by mistake. Jewish people, therefore, enthusiastically sought to differentiate themselves from the Christians.

An important source of the alienation of Christianity from its Jewish roots was the change in the membership of the Church that took place by the end of the second century when Christians with Gentile backgrounds began to outnumber Jewish Christians. The early Church decided not to make new converts become "Jewish" before they were Christian. Clearly, the work of the Apostle Paul was influential in this regard.

The Pharisee Paul, who also studied Plato, was the one who formulated, in his many letters to several early Christian congregations, much of the theology of the early Church.

Within 30 years after Christ died, the sect was called "Christian," and within four short centuries, without any army, navy, or air force, they had conquered the known world. While Rome was conquered by the barbarians, the Christians "conquered" the barbarians. That is, the Christians captured the hearts and souls of the barbarians. Today, there are two billion Christians.

One should not suppose that Judaism was the only source from which Christian converts were drawn. During the infancy days of the Church, there were at least five primary religious beliefs competing for the souls of people. First, of course, was the polytheistic religion of Rome focused upon the gods associated with the forces of nature. This religion was mostly a superstitious one with virtually no temples and no ethical teachings. By the time of Pentecost, the emphasis upon these gods had already begun to decline.

The mystery religions were a greater threat. These mystery religions invited converts both to be in relationship with deities and to use this relationship to gain power. These religions taught that the entire world was inhabited by good spirits and evil spirits, both of which could be persuaded by rituals and formulas to perform certain acts of power.

There were other worldviews/religions competing for the hearts of men. The more educated in the Roman Empire were being influenced by the major philosophical teachings of that era. For instance, according to the teaching of Plato, the physical world was merely an imperfect copy of a spiritual world that consisted of divine thoughts and ideas (called forms). Through knowledge, a person would strive to be more and more like the forms or spiritual types of his physical surroundings. Salvation, then, was nothing more than bringing down to earth the spirit of God.

Saint Paul arrested. Artist unknown, c.1900 (PD-US).

Assignments

- Warm-up: Why did Christianity grow so quickly?

- Students should complete Concept Builder 13-A.

- Students should review the required reading(s) *before* the assigned chapter begins.

- Teachers may want to discuss assigned reading(s) with students.

- Teachers shall assign the required essay. The rest of the essays can be outlined, answered with shorter answers, discussed, or skipped.

- Students will review all readings for chapter 13.

Read Matthew 5:1–31 (The Sermon on the Mount), and respond to the following:

When He saw the crowds, He went up on the mountain, and after He sat down, His disciples came to Him. Then He began to teach them, saying: "The poor in spirit are blessed, for the kingdom of heaven is theirs. Those who mourn are blessed, for they will be comforted. The gentle are blessed, for they will inherit the earth. Those who hunger and thirst for righteousness are blessed, for they will be filled. The merciful are blessed, for they will be shown mercy. The pure in heart are blessed, for they will see God. The peacemakers are blessed, for they will be called sons of God. Those who are persecuted for righteousness are blessed, for the kingdom of heaven is theirs.

"You are blessed when they insult and persecute you and falsely say every kind of evil against you because of Me. Be glad and rejoice, because your reward is great in heaven. For that is how they persecuted the prophets who were before you.

"You are the salt of the earth. But if the salt should lose its taste, how can it be made salty? It's no longer good for anything but to be thrown out and trampled on by men.

"You are the light of the world. A city situated on a hill cannot be hidden. No one lights a lamp and puts it under a basket, but rather on a lampstand, and it gives light for all who are in the house. In the same way, let your light shine before men, so that they may see your good works and give glory to your Father in heaven. Don't assume that I came to destroy the Law or the Prophets. I did not come to destroy but to fulfill. For I assure you: Until heaven and earth pass away, not the smallest letter or one stroke of a letter will pass from the law until all things are accomplished. Therefore, whoever breaks one of the least of these commandments and teaches people to do so will be called least in the kingdom of heaven. But whoever practices and teaches these commands will be called great in the kingdom of heaven. For I tell you, unless your righteousness surpasses that of the scribes and Pharisees, you will never enter the kingdom of heaven.

"You have heard that it was said to our ancestors, Do not murder, and whoever murders will be subject to judgment. But I tell you, everyone who is angry with his brother will be subject to judgment. And whoever says to his brother, 'Fool!' will be subject to the Sanhedrin. But whoever says, 'You moron!' will be subject to hellfire. So if you are offering your gift on the altar, and there you remember that your brother has something against you, leave your gift there in front of the altar. First go and be reconciled with your brother, and then come and offer your gift. . . .

"Do not commit adultery. But I tell you, everyone who looks at a woman to lust for her has already committed adultery with her in his heart. If your right eye causes you to sin, gouge it out and throw it away. For it is better that you lose one of the parts of your body than for your whole body to be thrown into hell. And if your right hand causes you to sin, cut it off and throw it away. For it is better that you lose one of the parts of your body than for your whole body to go into hell!

"It was also said, Whoever divorces his wife must give her a written notice of divorce."

Where is the setting of the Sermon on the Mount?

Is this significant?

Who is He addressing?

Is this significant?

What is so radical about these teachings?

What does Jesus mean when He says, "If your right eye causes you to sin, gouge it out and throw it away."

Gnosticism

By far the greatest threat to Christianity was gnosticism. Gnosticism was popular among the followers of Plato. Salvation came through the knowledge of the spirit world and denial of the material. As it is today, gnosticism was practiced among intellectual centers (e.g., universities) of the Empire.

Beginning in Jerusalem, ultimately Christianity fought these cultural and worldview battles and won. Jerusalem was the center of Christianity, until its destruction by Roman armies in A.D. 70, but from this center Christianity spread to other cities and towns in Palestine and beyond.

One place in particular was Antioch. Perhaps the most successful Christian church, Antioch sent out more missionaries than any other early church. Interracial, full of rich and poor, Antioch was a palatable alternative to the corruption that had become part of the early Roman Empire period.

Christian teaching was particularly radical. Paul wrote that there was neither Jew nor Greek in Christ Jesus (Gal. 3:28). Paul emphasized that three major first-century social distinctions no longer mattered in Christ: ethnicity, socioeconomic status, and gender. Paul stressed, "You are one in Christ Jesus.

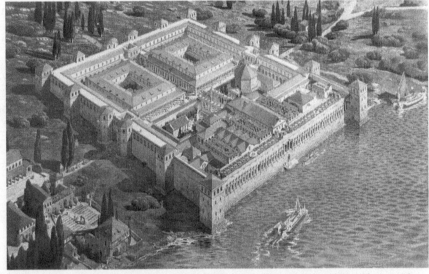

Reconstruction of Diocletian's palace in Split/Spalato by the architect Ernest Hébrard. Photograph from E. Hébrard and J. Zeiller, *Spalato, le Palais de Dioclétien*, Paris, 1912 (PD-US).

. . ." The first century Church struggled with many problems. For instance, Hellenist widows, traditionally neglected by the Jews, were now being neglected by Hebrew Christians (Acts 6:1).

Paul not only wrote extensively to the churches about the faith, he made four missionary journeys. Perhaps more than any man, Paul did much to advance the cause of the Gospel.

As a Jewish sect, the primitive Christian church shared the status of Judaism in the Roman Empire and enjoyed the fruits of Roman toleration. However, Emperor Nero in A.D. 68 singled out Christians as an enemy. The grounds for hostility to the Christians were not always the same, and often opposition and persecution were localized. The loyalty of

Marble head of Nero Claudius Caesar Augustus Germanicus.

171

Christians to "Jesus as Lord," however, was irreconcilable with the worship of the Roman emperor as lord, and such emperors as Trajan, Claudius, and Marcus Aurelius, who were emperors during social stress and conflict, saw the Christians as a great threat. However, it was not until the fourth century that Christianity had grown so much that it had to be eradicated. Or at least that is what Emperor Diocletian felt. He tried but failed.

Assignments

- Warm-up: What is Gnosticism, and why was it such a great threat to Christians?
- Students should complete Concept Builder 13-B.
- Students should review reading(s) from the next chapter.
- Students should outline essay due at the end of the week.
- Per teacher instructions, students may answer orally, in a group setting, some of the essays that are not assigned as formal essays.

<table>
<tr><td rowspan="4">CONCEPT BUILDER 13-B
Early Church History: The Christian Life</td><td colspan="2">The Didache is a book full of instructions for the early church. Based on The Didache, speculate upon what life was like for the early Christian.</td></tr>
<tr><td>Church Life</td><td>There were no church buildings at the time The Didache was written (at the end of the first century). Believers worshiped and fellowshipped together in homes.</td></tr>
<tr><td>Occupations</td><td></td></tr>
<tr><td>Family Life</td><td></td></tr>
</table>

Monasticism

An early and strong movement was monasticism. Renunciation of the world, or monasticism, had in fact nourished the growth of Christianity from the start, and by A.D. 300, people who wished an ascetic life had many exemplars from which to choose. As young people had in the past pursued wisdom by going to the philosopher, so now Christian youth sought out Christian ascetics under whom they might learn the new Christian philosophy. In Egypt, the church leader Origen taught new converts about Christianity and encouraged them with his ascetic lifestyle, including sleeping on the floor, fasting, and abstaining completely from all alcohol.

From the beginning, the Roman authorities perceived Christians as a threat. This was primarily because Christians (like Jews) refused to worship any other God. However, the Christians, unlike other religions, also refused to serve in the army. While they did not openly subvert the civil authorities, Christians did not enthusiastically embrace public office either. All these things, and others, conspired to unleash a series of persecutions. These continued off and on until Emperor Constantine gave the Christian faith "most favored status."

Most readers are familiar with the secret meetings in the catacombs, or tombs underneath Rome. Roman authorities were naturally reluctant to search for or to persecute Christians who were hiding in the creepy catacombs. Thus, the very thing that represented death to others represented life to the Christians.

This persecution ended with the reign of Constantine. One of the most influential acts of Constantine the Great was his decision in 330 to move the capital of the empire from Rome to the city of Byzantium at the eastern end of the Mediterranean Sea. The new capital, named Constantinople, was also the home base of a new Christian church. While Western Christianity became increasingly centralized around the pope (Bishop of Rome), eastern city fellowships — Constantinople, Jerusalem, Antioch, and Alexandria — developed separately from one another. So while worship practices evolved along similar lines, church government and minor doctrines evolved much differently.

Assignments

- Warm-up: What commands of the Lord are the most difficult to obey? Write an argumentative essay.
- Students should complete Concept Builder 13-C.
- Students should write rough draft of assigned essay.
- The teacher may correct rough drafts.

Create a "didache" for your home.

Object or Task	Rule
Television watching	*No television watching on school nights.*
Chores	
Soccer practice	
Attending youth group	
Spending the night with friends	
Curfew	

The Sermon on the Mount

Background The Sermon on the Mount is a series of aphorisms (truths). They are spoken by Jesus Christ in the early part of His ministry. They capture some of the most profound truth of the New Testament. The following is Matthew 5 (HCSB):

When He saw the crowds, He went up on the mountain, and after He sat down, His disciples came to Him. Then He began to teach them, saying:

"The poor in spirit are blessed, for the kingdom of heaven is theirs. Those who mourn are blessed, for they will be comforted. The gentle are blessed, for they will inherit the earth. Those who hunger and thirst for righteousness are blessed, for they will be filled. The merciful are blessed,

The Sermon On the Mount by Carl Heinrich Bloch. Date unknown (PD-Art).

for they will be shown mercy. The pure in heart are blessed, for they will see God. The peacemakers are blessed, for they will be called sons of God. Those who are persecuted for righteousness are blessed, for the kingdom of heaven is theirs.

"You are blessed when they insult and persecute you and falsely say every kind of evil against you because of Me. Be glad and rejoice, because your reward is great in heaven. For that is how they persecuted the prophets who were before you.

"You are the salt of the earth. But if the salt should lose its taste, how can it be made salty? It's no longer good for anything but to be thrown out and trampled on by men.

"You are the light of the world. A city situated on a hill cannot be hidden. No one lights a lamp and puts it under a basket, but rather on a lampstand, and it gives light for all who are in the house. In the same way, let your light shine before men, so that they may see your good works and give glory to your Father in heaven.

"Don't assume that I came to destroy the Law or the Prophets. I did not come to destroy but to fulfill.

For I assure you: Until heaven and earth pass away, not the smallest letter or one stroke of a letter will pass from the law until all things are accomplished. Therefore, whoever breaks one of the least of these commands and teaches people to do so will be called least in the kingdom of heaven. But whoever practices and teaches these commands will be called great in the kingdom of heaven. For I tell you, unless your righteousness surpasses that of the scribes and Pharisees, you will never enter the kingdom of heaven.

"You have heard that it was said to our ancestors, Do not murder, and whoever murders will be subject to judgment. But I tell you, everyone who is angry with his brother will be subject to judgment. And whoever says to his brother, 'Fool!' will be subject to the Sanhedrin. But whoever says, 'You moron!' will be subject to hellfire. So if you are offering your gift on the altar, and there you remember that your brother has something against you, leave your gift there in front of the altar. First go and be reconciled with your brother, and then come and offer your gift. Reach a settlement quickly with your adversary while you're on the way with him, or your adversary will hand you over to the judge, the judge to the officer, and you will be thrown into prison. I assure you: You will never get out of there until you have paid the last penny!

"You have heard that it was said, Do not commit adultery. But I tell you, everyone who looks at a woman to lust for her has already committed adultery with her in his heart. If your right eye causes you to sin, gouge it out and throw it away. For it is better that you lose one of the parts of your body than for your whole body to be thrown into hell. And if your right hand causes you to sin, cut it off and throw it away. For it is better that you lose one of the parts of your body than for your whole body to go into hell!

"It was also said, Whoever divorces his wife must give her a written notice of divorce. But I tell you, everyone who divorces his wife, except in a case of sexual immorality, causes her to commit adultery. And whoever marries a divorced woman commits adultery.

"Again, you have heard that it was said to our ancestors, You must not break your oath, but you must keep your oaths to the Lord. But I tell you, don't take an oath at all: either by heaven, because it is God's throne; or by the earth, because it is His footstool; or by Jerusalem, because it is the city of the great King. Neither should you swear by your head, because you cannot make a single hair white or black. But let your word 'yes' be 'yes,' and your 'no' be 'no.' Anything more than this is from the evil one.

"You have heard that it was said, An eye for an eye and a tooth for a tooth. But I tell you, don't resist an evildoer. On the contrary, if anyone slaps you on your right cheek, turn the other to him also. As for the one who wants to sue you and take away your shirt, let him have your coat as well. And if anyone forces you to go one mile, go with him two. Give to the one who asks you, and don't turn away from the one who wants to borrow from you.

"You have heard that it was said, Love your neighbor and hate your enemy. But I tell you, love your enemies and pray for those who persecute you, so that you may be sons of your Father in heaven. For He causes His sun to rise on the evil and the good, and sends rain on the righteous and the unrighteous. For if you love those who love you, what reward will you have? Don't even the tax collectors do the same? And if you greet only your brothers, what are you doing out of the ordinary? Don't even the Gentiles do the same? Be perfect, therefore, as your heavenly Father is perfect."

Assignments

- Warm-up: What figures of speech are used in Matthew 5? Discuss how Jesus uses these figures of speech to make His point.

- Students should complete Concept Builder 13-D.

- Students will re-write corrected copies of essay due tomorrow.

The Didache begins, "There are two ways, one of life and one of death, and there is a great difference between the two ways." This statement, and the whole document, is a dialectic. Dialectic is a method of argument, which has been central to both Eastern and Western philosophy since ancient times. The word "dialectic" originates in ancient Greece, and was made popular by Plato's Socratic dialogues. Dialectic is based on a dialogue between two or more people who hold different ideas and wish to persuade each other. It can also be, as in *The Didache*, an exploration of two viewpoints, or lifestyles, and, in the process, both alternatives are evaluated. Discuss the two ways of *The Didache*.

The Way of Life	The Way of Death
First of all, thou shalt love the God that made thee; secondly, thy neighbour as thyself.	*Living life selfishly will lead to heartache and unproductive living.*
And all things whatsoever thou wouldest not have befall thyself neither do thou unto another.	
Abstain thou from fleshly and bodily lusts.	
To every man that asketh of thee give, and ask not back.	
My child, flee from every evil and everything that resembleth it.	

www.earlychristianwritings.com/text/didache-roberts.html.

The Didache

Background Another famous didache was written soon after Matthew wrote his Gospel. Rediscovered in a Constantinople monastery in 1873, *The Didache*, or *The Teaching*, may be the earliest piece of Christian literature outside the New Testament. *The Didache* gives practical instruction on Christian living. *The Didache* (*The Teaching*) is one of the most fascinating yet perplexing documents to emerge from the early Church. It is composed of two parts: (1) instruction about the "Two Ways" and (2) a manual of church order and practice. The "Two Ways" material is a summary of the Christian life, probably used to instruct those who were preparing for baptism and church membership.

1:1 There are two ways, one of life and one of death, and there is a great difference between the two ways.

1:2 The way of life is this.

1:3 First of all, thou shalt love the God that made thee;

1:4 secondly, thy neighbour as thyself.

1:5 And all things whatsoever thou wouldest not have befal thyself neither do thou unto another.

1:6 Now of these words the doctrine is this.

1:7 Bless them that curse you, and pray for your enemies and fast for them that persecute you;

1:8 for what thank is it, if ye love them that love you? Do not even the Gentiles the same? But do ye love them that hate you, and ye shall not have an enemy.

1:9 Abstain thou from fleshly and bodily lusts.

1:10 If any man give thee a blow on thy right cheek, turn to him the other also, and thou shalt be perfect;

1:11 if a man impress thee to go with him, one mile, go with him twain;

1:12 if a man take away thy cloak, give him thy coat also;

1:13 if a man take away from thee that which is thine own, ask it not back, for neither art thou able.

1:14 To every man that asketh of thee give, and ask not back;

1:15 for the Father desireth that gifts be given to all from His own bounties.

1:16 Blessed is he that giveth according to the commandment;

1:17 for he is guiltless.

1:18 Woe to him that receiveth;

1:19 for, if a man receiveth having need, he is guiltless;

1:20 but he that hath no need shall give satisfaction why and wherefore he received;

1:21 and being put in confinement he shall be examined concerning the deeds that he hath done, and he shall not come out thence until he hath given back the last farthing.

1:22 Yea, as touching this also it is said;

1:23 Let thine alms sweat into thine hands, until thou shalt have learnt to whom to give.

2:1 And this is the second commandment of the teaching.

2:2 Thou shalt do no murder, thou shalt not commit adultery, thou shalt not corrupt boys, thou shalt not commit fornication, thou shalt not steal, thou shalt not deal in magic, thou shalt do no sorcery, thou shalt not murder a child by abortion nor kill them when born, thou shalt not covet thy neighbour's goods, thou shalt not perjure thyself, thou shalt not bear false witness, thou shalt not speak evil, thou shalt not cherish a grudge, thou shalt not be double-minded nor double-tongued;

2:3 for the double tongue is a snare of death.

2:4 Thy word shall not be false or empty, but fulfilled by action.

2:5 Thou shalt not be avaricious nor a plunderer nor a hypocrite nor ill-tempered nor proud.

2:6 Thou shalt not entertain an evil design against thy neighbour.

2:7 Thou shalt not hate any man, but some thou shalt reprove, and for others thou shalt pray, and others thou shalt love more than thy life.

3:1 My child, flee from every evil and everything that resembleth it.

3:2 Be not angry, for anger leadeth to murder, nor jealous nor contentious nor wrathful;

3:3 for of all these things murders are engendered.

3:4 My child, be not lustful, for lust leadeth to fornication, neither foul-speaking neither with uplifted eyes;

3:5 for of all these things adulteries are engendered.

3:6 My child, be no dealer in omens, since it leads to idolatry, nor an enchanter nor an astrologer nor a magician, neither be willing to look at them;

3:7 for from all these things idolatry is engendered.

3:8 My child, be not a liar, since lying leads to theft, neither avaricious neither vainglorious;

3:9 for from all these things thefts are engendered.

3:10 My child, be not a murmurer, since it leadeth to blasphemy, neither self-willed neither a thinker of evil thoughts;

3:11 for from all these things blasphemies are engendered.

3:12 But be meek, since the meek shall inherit the earth.

3:13 Be long-suffering and pitiful and guileless and quiet and kindly and always fearing the words which thou hast heard.

3:14 Thou shalt not exalt thyself, neither shalt thou admit boldness into thy soul.

3:15 Thy soul shall not cleave together with the lofty, but with the righteous and humble shalt thou walk.

3:16 The accidents that befal thee thou shalt receive as good, knowing that nothing is done without God.

4:1 My child, thou shalt remember him that speaketh unto thee the word of God night and day, and shalt honour him as the Lord;

4:2 for whencesoever the Lordship speaketh, there is the Lord.

4:3 Moreover thou shalt seek out day by day the persons of the saints, that thou mayest find rest in their words.

4:4 Thou shalt not make a schism, but thou shalt pacify them that contend;

4:5 thou shalt judge righteously, thou shalt not make a difference in a person to reprove him for transgressions.

4:6 Thou shalt not doubt whether a thing shall be or not be.

4:7 Be not thou found holding out thy hands to receive, but drawing them in as to giving.

4:8 If thou hast ought passing through thy hands, thou shalt give a ransom for thy sins.

4:9 Thou shalt not hesitate to give, neither shalt thou murmur when giving;

4:10 for thou shalt know who is the good paymaster of thy reward.

4:11 Thou shalt not turn away from him that is in want, but shalt make thy brother partaker in all things, and shalt not say that anything is thine own.

4:12 For if ye are fellow_partakers in that which is imperishable, how much rather in the things which are perishable? Thou shalt not withhold thy hand from thy son or from thy daughter, but from their youth thou shalt teach them the fear of God.

4:13 Thou shalt not command thy bondservant or thine handmaid in thy bitterness, who trust in the same God as thyself, lest haply they should cease to fear the God who is over both of you;

4:14 for He cometh, not to call men with respect of persons, but He cometh to those whom the Spirit hath prepared.

4:15 But ye, servants, shall be subject unto your masters, as to a type of God, in shame and fear.

4:16 Thou shalt hate all hypocrisy, and everything that is not pleasing to the Lord.

4:17 Thou shalt never forsake the commandments of the Lord;

4:18 but shalt keep those things which thou hast received, neither adding to them nor taking away from them.

4:19 In church thou shalt confess thy transgressions, and shalt not betake thyself to prayer with an evil conscience.

4:20 This is the way of life.

5:1 But the way of death is this.

5:2 First of all, it is evil and full of a curse murders, adulteries, lusts, fornications, thefts, idolatries, magical arts, witchcrafts, plunderings, false witness-ings, hypocrisies, doubleness of heart, treachery, pride, malice, stubbornness, covetousness, foul-speaking, jealousy, boldness, exaltation, boastfulness;

5:3 persecutors of good men, hating truth, loving a lie, not perceiving the reward of righteousness, not cleaving to the good nor to righteous judgment, wakeful not for that which is good but for that which is evil;

5:4 from whom gentleness and forbearance stand aloof;

5:5 loving vain things, pursuing a recompense, not pitying the poor man, not toiling for him that is oppressed with toil, not recognizing Him that made them, murderers of children, corrupters of the creatures of God, turning away from him that is in want, oppressing him that is afflicted, advocates of the wealthy, unjust judges of the poor, altogether sinful.

5:6 May ye be delivered, my children, from all these things.

6:1 See lest any man lead you astray from this way of righteousness, for he teacheth thee apart from God.

6:2 For if thou art able to bear the whole yoke of the Lord, thou shalt be perfect;

6:3 but if thou art not able, do that which thou art able.

6:4 But concerning eating, bear that which thou art able;

6:5 yet abstain by all means from meat sacrificed to idols;

6:6 for it is the worship of dead gods.

7:1 But concerning baptism, thus shall ye baptize.

7:2 Having first recited all these things, baptize in the name of the Father and of the Son and of the Holy Spirit in living (running) water.

7:3 But if thou hast not living water, then baptize in other water;

7:4 and if thou art not able in cold, then in warm.

7:5 But if thou hast neither, then pour water on the head thrice in the name of the Father and of the Son and of the Holy Spirit.

7:6 But before the baptism let him that baptizeth and him that is baptized fast, and any others also who are able;

7:7 and thou shalt order him that is baptized to fast a day or two before.

8:1 And let not your fastings be with the hypocrites, for they fast on the second and the fifth day of the week;

8:2 but do ye keep your fast on the fourth and on the preparation (the sixth) day.

8:3 Neither pray ye as the hypocrites, but as the Lord commanded in His Gospel, thus pray ye.

8:4 Our Father, which art in heaven, hallowed be Thy name;

8:5 Thy kingdom come;

8:6 Thy will be done, as in heaven, so also on earth;

8:7 give us this day our daily bread;

8:8 and forgive us our debt, as we also forgive our debtors;

8:9 and lead us not into temptation, but deliver us from the evil one;

8:10 for Thine is the power and the glory for ever and ever.

8:11 Three times in the day pray ye so.

9:1 But as touching the eucharistic thanksgiving give ye thanks thus.

9:2 First, as regards the cup:

9:3 We give Thee thanks, O our Father, for the holy vine of Thy son David, which Thou madest known unto us through Thy Son Jesus;

9:4 Thine is the glory for ever and ever.

9:5 Then as regards the broken bread:

9:6 We give Thee thanks, O our Father, for the life and knowledge which Thou didst make known unto us through Thy Son Jesus;

9:7 Thine is the glory for ever and ever.

9:8 As this broken bread was scattered upon the mountains and being gathered together became one, so may Thy Church be gathered together from the ends of the earth into Thy kingdom;

9:9 for Thine is the glory and the power through Jesus Christ for ever and ever.

9:10 But let no one eat or drink of this eucharistic thanksgiving, but they that have been baptized into the name of the Lord;

9:11 for concerning this also the Lord hath said:

9:12 Give not that which is holy to the dogs.

10:1 And after ye are satisfied thus give ye thanks:

10:2 We give Thee thanks, Holy Father, for Thy holy name, which Thou hast made to tabernacle in our hearts, and for the knowledge and faith and immortality, which Thou hast made known unto us through Thy Son Jesus;

10:3 Thine is the glory for ever and ever.

10:4 Thou, Almighty Master, didst create all things for Thy name's sake, and didst give food and drink unto men for enjoyment, that they might render thanks to Thee;

10:5 but didst bestow upon us spiritual food and drink and eternal life through Thy Son.

Illustration of Revelation 22:17 (King James' Version), to which the prayer in Didache 10 bears some similarity, from page 366 of the 1880 omnibus printing of *The Sunday at Home* by Joseph Marin Kronheims, 1880 (PD-US).

10:6 Before all things we give Thee thanks that Thou art powerful;

10:7 Thine is the glory for ever and ever.

10:8 Remember, Lord, Thy Church to deliver it from all evil and to perfect it in Thy love;

10:9 and gather it together from the four winds—even the Church which has been sanctified—into Thy kingdom which Thou hast prepared for it;

10:10 for Thine is the power and the glory for ever and ever.

10:11 May grace come and may this world pass away.

10:12 Hosanna to the God of David.

10:13 If any man is holy, let him come;

10:14 if any man is not, let him repent. Maranatha. Amen.

10:15 But permit the prophets to offer thanksgiving as much as they desire.

11:1 Whosoever therefore shall come and teach you all these things that have been said before, receive him;

11:2 but if the teacher himself be perverted and teach a different doctrine to the destruction thereof, hear him not;

11:3 but if to the increase of righteousness and the knowledge of the Lord, receive him as the Lord.

11:4 But concerning the apostles and prophets, so do ye according to the ordinance of the Gospel.

11:5 Let every apostle, when he cometh to you, be received as the Lord;

11:6 but he shall not abide more than a single day, or if there be need,

11:7 but if he abide three days, he is a false prophet.

11:8 And when he departeth let the apostle receive nothing save bread, until he findeth shelter;

11:9 but if he ask money, he is a false prophet.

11:10 And any prophet speaking in the Spirit ye shall not try neither discern;

11:11 for every sin shall be forgiven, but this sin shall not be forgiven.

11:12 Yet not every one that speaketh in the Spirit is a prophet, but only if he have the ways of the Lord.

11:13 From his ways therefore the false prophet and the prophet shall be recognized.

11:14 And no prophet when he ordereth a table in the Spirit shall eat of it;

11:15 otherwise he is a false prophet.

11:16 And every prophet teaching the truth, if he doeth not what he teacheth, is a false prophet.

11:17 And every prophet approved and found true, if he doeth ought as an outward mystery typical of the Church, and yet teacheth you not to do all that he himself doeth, shall not be judged before you;

11:18 he hath his judgment in the presence of God;

11:19 for in like manner also did the prophets of old time.

11:20 And whosoever shall say in the Spirit, Give me silver or anything else, ye shall not listen to him;

11:21 but if he tell you to give on behalf of others that are in want, let no man judge him.

12:1 But let every one that cometh in the name of the Lord be received;

12:2 and then when ye have tested him ye shall know him, for ye shall have understanding on the right hand and on the left.

12:3 If the comer is a traveller, assist him, so far as ye are able;

12:4 but he shall not stay with you more than two or three days, if it be necessary.

12:5 But if he wishes to settle with you, being a craftsman, let him work for and eat his bread.

12:6 But if he has no craft, according to your wisdom provide how he shall live as a Christian among you, but not in idleness.

12:7 If he will not do this, he is trafficking upon Christ.

12:8 Beware of such men.

13:1 But every true prophet desiring to settle among you is worthy.

13:2 In like manner a true teacher is also worthy, like the workman.

13:3 Every first fruit then of the produce of the wine-vat and of the threshing-floor, of thy oxen and of thy sheep, thou shalt take and give as the first fruit to the prophets;

13:4 for they are your chief_priests.

13:5 But if ye have not a prophet, give them to the poor.

13:6 If thou makest bread, take the first fruit and give according to the commandment.

13:7 In like manner, when thou openest a jar of wine or of oil, take the first fruit and give to the prophets;

13:8 yea and of money and raiment and every possession take the first fruit, as shall seem good to thee, and give according to the commandment.

14:1 And on the Lord's own day gather yourselves together and break bread and give thanks, first confessing your transgressions, that your sacrifice may be pure.

14:2 And let no man, having his dispute with his -fellow, join your assembly until they have been reconciled, that your sacrifice may not be defiled;

14:3 for this sacrifice it is that was spoken of by the Lord;

14:4 In every place and at every time offer Me a pure sacrifice;

14:5 for I am a great king, saith the Lord and My name is wonderful among the nations.

15:1 Appoint for yourselves therefore bishops and deacons worthy of the Lord, men who are meek and not lovers of money, and true and approved;

15:2 for unto you they also perform the service of the prophets and teachers.

15:3 Therefore despise them not;

15:4 for they are your honourable men along with the prophets and teachers.

15:5 And reprove one another, not in anger but in peace, as ye find in the Gospel;

15:6 and let no one speak to any that has gone wrong towards his neighbour, neither let him hear a word from you, until he repent.

15:7 But your prayers and your almsgivings and all your deeds so do ye as ye find it in the Gospel of our Lord.

16:1 Be watchful for your life;

16:2 let your lamps not be quenched and your loins not ungirded, but be ye ready;

16:3 for ye know not the hour in which our Lord cometh.

16:4 And ye shall gather yourselves together frequently, seeking what is fitting for your souls;

www.spurgeon.org/~phil/didache.htm

16:5 for the whole time of your faith shall not profit you, if ye be not perfected at the last season.

16:6 For in the last days the false prophets and corrupters shall be multiplied, and the sheep shall be turned into wolves, and love shall be turned into hate.

16:7 For as lawlessness increaseth, they shall hate one another and shall persecute and betray.

16:8 And then the world-deceiver shall appear as a son of God;

16:9 and shall work signs and wonders, and the earth shall be delivered into his hands;

16:10 and he shall do unholy things, which have never been since the world began.

16:11 Then all created mankind shall come to the fire of testing, and many shall be offended and perish;

16:12 but they that endure in their faith shall be saved by the Curse Himself.

16:13 And then shall the signs of the truth appear;

16:14 first a sign of a rift in the heaven, then a sign of a voice of a trumpet, and thirdly a resurrection of the dead;

16:15 yet not of all, but as it was said:

16:16 The Lord shall come and all His saints with Him.

16:17 Then shall the world see the Lord coming upon the clouds of heaven.

Assignments

- Warm-up: Read carefully the *The Didache*. Compare and contrast it with the Bible.

- Students should complete Concept Builder 13-E.

- Essays are due. Students should take the chapter 13 test.

CONCEPT BUILDER 13-E

The Teachings of the New Testament

The teachings of the New Testament profoundly impacted the first century church and continue to impact the world today. Note the specific principles, providing a definition, in your own words, and how Christians can demonstrate this in their lives.

Principle	Definition in Your Own Words	Daily Demonstration
Love		
Mercy		
Forgiveness		

www.earlychristianwritings.com/celsus.html

(A.D. 30-500):
Early Church History (Part 2)

First Thoughts In the midst of chaos and despair, the early Church was hopeful. We cannot live without hope. Walter Bruggemann, in his book *Hope within History* (Atlanta, GA: J. Knox Press, 1987), explores the meaning of apocalyptic hope in history. Using Jeremiah as background, Bruggemann argues that the true history makers are not those whom we expect — politicians, doctors, and lawyers. Real history makers, he argues, are those who can invest in a dream. In spite of pretty bleak conditions — Jeremiah's nation was about to be conquered and taken into captivity — Jeremiah was able to still have great hope. He had apocalyptic (i.e., based in history) hope. He understood who really had power — those who had hope in spite of the circumstances they faced. God told Jeremiah to buy a piece of land. He did. Even though Jeremiah was never to enjoy this land, never to really own it, he invested in it anyway. Apocalyptic hope causes us to invest in dreams we may never see consummated. People with apocalyptic hope, assert the sovereign and omnipotent will of God in all circumstances, no matter how bad things may be. They "have a bold conviction about alternative possibilities which go under the name of hope . . . they see clearly that things are deeply wrong, but they still have hope." Modern,

existential hope of men like Viktor E. Frankl pales in the light of the apocalyptic hope of a committed Christian. "Was Du erlebt, kann keine Macht der Welt Dir rauben" (What you have experienced, no power on earth can take from you), Frankl writes (Viktor Frankl, *Man's Search for Meaning* (New York: Pocket Books, 1963), p. 131).

Chapter Learning Objectives In chapter 14 we are reminded again that price that countless martyrs paid on our behalf.

As a result of this chapter study you will be able to . . .

1. Agree or disagree with Justin Martyr's views of civil disobedience.

2. Imagine that you are one of those opposing Christianity in Justin Martyr's day. Write a two-page rebuttal to Martyr's arguments. Make your essay as persuasive as you can using various references from the text.

3. Martyrdom literature has a certain "form" or style format in almost every piece. Identify the pattern advanced by the Polycarp martyrdom material.

Weekly Essay Options: Begin on page 273 of the Teacher Guide.
Reading ahead: *Confessions* by Augustine.

Clement of Rome

Background Clement of Rome (A.D. 30–100) was a bishop, or overseer, of Rome. Clement led his flock through severe persecution under the Emperor Domitian. When prosperity returned, he was saddened to hear of quarrels breaking out in the well-established Corinthian Church.

Let our whole body, then, be preserved in, Christ Jesus; and let every one be subject to his neighbour, according to the special gift bestowed upon him. Let the strong not despise the weak, and let the weak show respect unto the strong. Let the rich man provide for the wants of the poor; and let the poor man bless God, because He hath given him one by whom his need may be supplied. Let the wise man display his wisdom, not by [mere] words, but through good deeds. Let the humble not bear testimony to himself, but leave witness to be borne to him by another. Let him that is pure in the flesh not grow proud of it, and boast, knowing that it was another who bestowed on him the gift of continence. Let us consider, then, brethren, of what matter we were made, — who and what manner of beings we came into the world, as it were out of a sepulchre, and from utter darkness. He who made us and fashioned us, having prepared His bountiful gifts for us before we were born, introduced us into His world. Since, therefore, we receive all these things from Him, we ought for everything to give Him thanks; to whom be glory for ever and ever. Amen.

Saint Clement by Giovanni Battista Tiepolo, c1730 (PD-US).

CHAPTER XXXIX — THERE IS NO REASON FOR SELF-CONCEIT.

Foolish and inconsiderate men, who have neither wisdom nor instruction, mock and deride us, being eager to exalt themselves in their own conceits. For what can a mortal man do? or what strength is there in one made out of the dust? For it is written, "There was no shape before mine eyes, only I heard a sound, and a voice [saying], What then? Shall a man be pure before the Lord? or shall such an one be [counted] blameless in his deeds, seeing He does not confide in His servants, and has charged even His angels with perversity? The heaven is not clean in His sight: how much less they that dwell in houses of clay, of which also we ourselves were made! He smote them as a moth; and from morning even until evening they endure not. Because they could furnish no assistance to themselves, they perished. He breathed upon them, and they died, because they had no wisdom. But call now, if any one will answer thee, or if thou wilt look to any of the holy angels; for wrath destroys the foolish man, and envy killeth him that is in error. I have seen the foolish taking root, but their habitation was presently consumed. Let their sons be far from safety; let them be despised before the gates of those less than themselves, and there shall be none to deliver. For what was prepared for them, the righteous shall eat; and they shall not be delivered from evil."

CHAPTER XL — LET US PRESERVE IN THE CHURCH THE ORDER APPOINTED BY GOD.

These things therefore being manifest to us, and since we look into the depths of the divine knowledge, it behoves us to do all things in [their proper] order, which the Lord has commanded us to perform at stated times. He has enjoined offerings [to be presented] and service to be performed [to Him], and that not thoughtlessly or irregularly, but at the appointed times and hours. Where and by whom He desires these things to be done, He Himself has fixed by His own supreme will, in order that all things being piously done according to His good pleasure, may be acceptable unto Him. Those, therefore, who present their offerings at the appointed times, are accepted and blessed; for inasmuch as they follow the laws of the Lord, they sin not. For his own peculiar services are assigned to the high priest, and their own proper place is prescribed to the priests, and their own special ministrations devolve on the Levites. The layman is bound by the laws that pertain to laymen.

CHAPTER XLI — CONTINUATION OF THE SAME SUBJECT.

Let every one of you, brethren, give thanks to God in his own order, living in all good conscience, with becoming gravity, and not going beyond the rule of the ministry prescribed to him. Not in every place, brethren, are the daily sacrifices offered, or the peace-offerings, or the sin-offerings and the trespass-offerings, but in Jerusalem only. And even there they are not offered in any place, but only at the altar before the temple, that which is offered being first carefully examined by the high priest and the ministers already mentioned. Those, therefore, who do anything beyond that which is agreeable to His will, are punished with death. Ye see, brethren, that the greater the knowledge that has been vouchsafed to us, the greater also is the danger to which we are exposed.

Assignments

- Warm-up: Write a précis of the piece by Clement.
- Students should complete Concept Builder 14-A.
- Students should review the required reading(s) *before* the assigned chapter begins.
- Teachers may want to discuss assigned reading(s) with students.
- Teachers shall assign the required essay. The rest of the essays can be outlined, answered with shorter answers, discussed, or skipped.
- Students will review all readings for chapter 14.

This literary piece is a didactic sermon. In other words, Clement is using his personal reflections to teach his community something. Read this letter from Clement of Rome (Pope Clement I), and respond to the following questions:

Let our whole body, then, be preserved in, Christ Jesus; and let every one be subject to his neighbour, according to the special gift bestowed upon him. Let the strong not despise the weak, and let the weak show respect unto the strong. Let the rich man provide for the wants of the poor; and let the poor man bless God, because He hath given him one by whom his need may be supplied. Let the wise man display his wisdom, not by [mere] words, but through good deeds. Let the humble not bear testimony to himself, but leave witness to be borne to him by another. Let him that is pure in the flesh not grow proud of it, and boast, knowing that it was another who bestowed on him the gift of continence. Let us consider, then, brethren, of what matter we were made, — who and what manner of beings we came into the world, as it were out of a sepulchre, and from utter darkness. He who made us and fashioned us, having prepared His bountiful gifts for us before we were born, introduced us into His world. Since, therefore, we receive all these things from Him, we ought for everything to give Him thanks; to whom be glory forever and ever. Amen.

CHAPTER XXXIX — THERE IS NO REASON FOR SELF-CONCEIT.
Foolish and inconsiderate men, who have neither wisdom nor instruction, mock and deride us, being eager to exalt themselves in their own conceits. For what can a mortal man do? or what strength is there in one made out of the dust? For it is written, "There was no shape before mine eyes, only I heard a sound, and a voice [saying], What then? Shall a man be pure before the Lord? or shall such an one be [counted] blameless in his deeds, seeing He does not confide in His servants, and has charged even His angels with perversity? The heaven is not clean in His sight: how much less they that dwell in houses of clay, of which also we ourselves were made! He smote them as a moth; and from morning even until evening they endure not. Because they could furnish no assistance to themselves, they perished. He breathed upon them, and they died, because they had no wisdom. But call now, if any one will answer thee, or if thou wilt look to any of the holy angels; for wrath destroys the foolish man, and envy killeth him that is in error. I have seen the foolish taking root, but their habitation was presently consumed. Let their sons be far from safety; let them be despised before the gates of those less than themselves, and there shall be none to deliver. For what was prepared for them, the righteous shall eat; and they shall not be delivered from evil."

CHAPTER XL — LET US PRESERVE IN THE CHURCH THE ORDER APPOINTED BY GOD.
These things therefore being manifest to us, and since we look into the depths of the divine knowledge, it behoves us to do all things in [their proper] order, which the Lord has commanded us to perform at stated times. He has enjoined offerings [to be presented] and service to be performed [to Him], and that not thoughtlessly or irregularly, but at the appointed times and hours. Where and by whom He desires these things to be done, He Himself has fixed by His own supreme will, in order that all things being piously done according to His good pleasure, may be acceptable unto Him.

What is Clement teaching?

What problem can you infer is occurring in the Church?

Justin Martyr

Background The word apology is perhaps most often used today in regard to regret for failure or wrongdoing. It does not have the same meaning in the first century A.D. Take time now to look up in your dictionary the words apologetics, apologist, apologize, and apology to find out how they relate to literature and to theology. Then, read the following passage from Justin Martyr.

JUSTIN MARTYR — THE FIRST APOLOGY OF JUSTIN

CHAPTER I — ADDRESS.

To the Emperor Titus Aelius Adrianus Antoninus Pius Augustus Caesar, and to his son Verissimus the Philosopher, and to Lucius the Philosopher, the natural son of Caesar, and the adopted son of Pius, a lover of learning, and to the sacred Senate, with the whole People of the Romans, I, Justin, the son of Priscus and grandson of Bacchius, natives of Flavia Neapolis in Palestine, present this address and petition in behalf of those of all nations who are unjustly hated and wantonly abused, myself being one of them.

CHAPTER II — JUSTICE DEMANDED.

Reason directs those who are truly pious and philosophical to honour and love only what is true, declining to follow traditional opinions, if these be worthless. For not only does sound reason direct us to refuse the guidance of those who did or taught anything wrong, but it is incumbent on the lover of truth, by all means, and if death be threatened, even before his own life, to choose to do and say what is right. Do you, then, since ye are called pious and philosophers, guardians of justice and lovers of learning, give good heed, and hearken to my address; and if ye are indeed such, it will be manifested. For we have come, not to flatter you by this writing, nor please you by our address, but to beg that you pass judgment, after an accurate and searching investigation, not flattered by prejudice or by a desire of pleasing superstitious men, nor induced by irrational impulse or evil rumours which have long been prevalent, to give a decision which will prove to be against yourselves. For as for us, we reckon that no evil can be done us, unless we be convicted as evil-doers or be proved to be wicked men; and you, you can kill, but not hurt us.

CHAPTER III — CLAIM OF JUDICIAL INVESTIGATION.

But lest any one think that this is an unreasonable and reckless utterance, we demand that the charges against the Christians be investigated, and that, if these be substantiated, they be punished as they deserve; [or rather, indeed, we ourselves will punish them.] But if no one can convict us of anything, true reason forbids you, for the sake of a wicked rumor, to wrong blameless men, and indeed rather yourselves, who think fit to direct affairs, not by judgment, but by passion. And every sober-minded person will declare this to be the only fair and equitable adjustment, namely, that the subjects render an unexceptional account of their own life and doctrine; and that, on the other hand, the rulers should give their decision in obedience, not to violence and tyranny, but to piety and philosophy. For thus would both rulers and ruled reap benefit. For even one of the ancients somewhere said, "Unless both rulers and ruled philosophize, it is impossible to make states blessed." It is our task, therefore, to afford to all an opportunity of inspecting our life and teachings, lest, on account of those who are accustomed to be ignorant of our affairs, we should incur the penalty due to them for mental blindness; and it is your business, when you hear us, to be found, as reason demands, good judges. For if, when ye have learned the truth, you do not what is just, you will be before God without excuse.

CHAPTER IV — CHRISTIANS UNJUSTLY CONDEMNED FOR THEIR MERE NAME.

By the mere application of a name, nothing is decided, either good or evil, apart from the actions implied in the name; and indeed, so far at least as one may judge from the name we are accused of, we are most excellent people. But as we do not think it just to beg to be acquitted on account of the name, if we be convicted as evildoers, so, on the other hand, if we be found to have committed no offence, either in the matter of thus naming ourselves, or of our conduct as citizens, it is your part very earnestly to guard against incurring just punishment, by unjustly punishing those who are not convicted. For from a name neither praise nor punishment could reasonably spring, unless something excellent or base in action be proved. And those among yourselves who are accused you do not punish before they are convicted; but in our case you receive the name as proof against us, and this although, so far as the name goes, you ought rather to punish our accusers. For we are accused of being Christians, and to hate what is excellent Christian is unjust. Again, if any of the accused deny the name, and say that he is not a Christian, you acquit him, as having no evidence against him as a wrong-doer; but if any one acknowledge that he is a Christian, you punish him on account of this acknowledgment. Justice requires that you inquire into the life both of him who confesses and of him who denies, that by his deeds it may be apparent what kind of man each is. For as some who have been taught by the Master, Christ, not to deny Him, give encouragement to others when they are put to the question, so in all probability do those who lead wicked lives give occasion to those who, without consideration, take upon them to accuse all the Christians of impiety and wickedness. And this also is not right. For of philosophy, too, some assume the name and the garb who do nothing worthy of their profession; and you are well aware, that those of the ancients whose opinions and teachings were quite diverse, are yet all called by the one name of philosophers. And of these some taught atheism; and the poets who have flourished among you raise a laugh out of the uncleanness of Jupiter with his own children. And those who now adopt such instruction are not restrained by you; but, on the contrary, you bestow prizes and honors upon those who euphoniously insult the gods.

CHAPTER V — CHRISTIANS CHARGED WITH ATHEISM.

Why, then, should this be? In our case, who pledge ourselves to do no wickedness, nor to hold these atheistic opinions, you do not examine the charges made against us; but, yielding to unreasoning passion, and to the instigation of evil demons, you punish us without consideration or judgment. For the truth shall be spoken; since of old these evil demons, effecting apparitions of themselves, both defiled women and corrupted boys, and showed such fearful sights to men, that those who did not use their reason in judging of the actions that were done, were struck with terror; and being carried away by fear, and not knowing that these were demons, they called them gods, and gave to each the name which each of the demons chose for himself. And when Socrates endeavoured, by true reason and examination, to bring these things to light, and deliver men from the demons, then the demons themselves, by means of men who rejoiced in iniquity, compassed his death, as an atheist and a profane person, on the charge that "he was introducing new divinities;" and in our case they display a similar activity. For not only among the Greeks did reason (Logos) prevail to condemn these things through Socrates, but also among the Barbarians were they condemned by Reason (or the Word, the Logos) Himself, who took shape, and became man, and was called Jesus Christ; and in obedience to Him, we not only deny that they who did such things as these are gods, but assert that they are wicked and impious demons, whose actions will not bear comparison with those even of men desirous of virtue.

CHAPTER VI — CHARGE OF ATHEISM REFUTED.

Hence are we called atheists. And we confess that we are atheists, so far as gods of this sort are concerned, but not with respect to the most true God, the Father of righteousness and temperance and the other virtues, who is free from all impurity. But both Him, and the Son who came forth from Him and taught us these things, and the host of the other good angels who follow and are made like to Him, and the prophetic Spirit, we worship and adore, knowing them in reason and truth, and declaring without grudging to every one who wishes to learn, as we have been taught.

CHAPTER VII — EACH CHRISTIAN MUST BE TRIED BY HIS OWN LIFE.

But some one will say, Some have ere now been arrested and convicted as evil-doers. For you condemn many, many a time, after inquiring into the life of each of the accused severally, but not on account of those of whom we have been speaking. And this we acknowledge, that as among the Greeks those who teach such theories as please themselves are all called by the one name "Philosopher," though their doctrines be diverse, so also among the Barbarians this name on which accusations are accumulated is the common property of those who are and those who seem wise. For all are called Christians. Wherefore we demand that the deeds of all those who are accused to you be judged, in order that each one who is convicted may be punished as an evil-doer, and not as a Christian; and if it is clear that any one is blameless, that he may be acquitted, since by the mere fact of his being a Christian he does no wrong. For we will not require that you punish our accusers; they being sufficiently punished by their present wickedness and ignorance of what is right.

CHAPTER VIII — CHRISTIANS CONFESS THEIR FAITH IN GOD.

And reckon ye that it is for your sakes we have been saying these things; for it is in our power, when we are examined, to deny that we are Christians; but we would not live by telling a lie. For, impelled by the desire of the eternal and pure life, we seek the abode that is with God, the Father and Creator of all, and hasten to confess our faith, persuaded and convinced as we are that they who have proved to God by their works that they followed Him, and loved to abide with Him where there is no sin to cause disturbance, can obtain these things. This, then, to speak shortly, is what we expect and have learned from Christ, and teach. And Plato, in like manner, used to say that Rhadamanthus and Minos would punish the wicked who came before them; and we say that the same thing will be done, but at the hand of Christ, and upon the wicked in the same bodies united again to their spirits which are now to undergo everlasting punishment; and not only, as Plato said, for a period of a thousand years. And if any one say that this is incredible or impossible, this error of ours is one which concerns ourselves only, and no other person, so long as you cannot convict us of doing any harm.

CHAPTER IX — FOLLY OF IDOL, WORSHIP.

And neither do we honour with many sacrifices and garlands of flowers such deities as men have formed and set in shrines and called gods; since we see that these are soulless and dead, and have not the form of God for we do not consider that God has such a form as some say that they imitate to His honour, but have the names and forms of those wicked demons which have appeared. For why need we tell you who already know, into what forms the craftsmen, carving and cutting, casting and hammering, fashion the materials? And often out of vessels of dishonour, by merely changing the form, and making an image of the requisite shape, they make what they call a god; which we consider not only senseless, but to be even insulting to God, who, having ineffable glory and form, thus gets His name attached to things that are corruptible, and require constant service. And that the artificers of these are both intemperate, and, not to enter into particulars, are practised in every vice, you very well know; even their own girls who work along with them they corrupt. What infatuation! that dissolute men should be said to fashion and make gods for your worship, and that you should appoint such men the guardians of the temples where they are enshrined; not recognizing that it is unlawful even to think or say that men are the guardians of gods.

CHAPTER X — HOW GOD IS TO BE SERVED.

But we have received by tradition that God does not need the material offerings which men can give, seeing, indeed, that He Himself is the provider of all things. And we have been taught, and are convinced, and do believe, that He accepts those only who imitate the excellences which reside in Him, temperance, and justice, and philanthropy, and as many virtues as are peculiar to a God who is called by no proper name. And we have been taught that He in the beginning did of His goodness, for man's sake, create all things out of unformed matter; and if men by their works show themselves worthy of this His design, they are deemed worthy, and so we have received — of reigning in company with Him, being delivered from corruption and suffering. For as in the beginning He created us when we were not, so do we consider that, in like manner, those who choose what is pleasing to Him are, on account of their choice, deemed worthy of incorruption and of fellowship with Him. For the coming into being at first was not in our own power; and in order that we may follow those things which please Him, choosing them by means of the rational faculties He has Himself endowed us with, He both persuades us and leads us to faith. And we think it for the advantage of all men that they are not restrained from learning these things, but are even urged thereto. For the restraint which human laws could not effect, the Word, inasmuch as He is divine, would have effected, had not the wicked demons, taking as their ally the lust of wickedness which is in every man, and which draws variously to all manner of vice, scattered many false and profane accusations, none of which attach to us.

CHAPTER XI — WHAT KINGDOM CHRISTIANS LOOK FOR.

And when you hear that we look for a kingdom, you suppose, without making any inquiry, that we speak of a human kingdom; whereas we speak of that which is with God, as appears also from the confession of their faith made by those who are charged with being Christians, though they know that death is the punishment awarded to him who so confesses. For if we looked for a human kingdom, we should also deny our Christ, that we might not be slain; and we should strive to escape detection, that we might obtain what we expect. But since our thoughts are not fixed on the present, we are not concerned when men cut us off; since also death is a debt which must at all events be paid.

CHAPTER XII — CHRISTIANS LIVE AS UNDER GOD'S EYE.

And more than all other men are we your helpers and allies in promoting peace, seeing that we hold this view, that it is alike impossible for the wicked, the covetous, the conspirator, and for the virtuous, to escape the notice of God, and that each man goes to everlasting punishment or salvation according to the value of his actions. For if all men knew this, no one would choose wickedness even for a little, knowing that he goes to the everlasting punishment of fire; but would by all means restrain himself, and adorn himself with virtue, that he might obtain the good gifts of God, and escape the punishments. For those who, on account of the laws and punishments you impose, endeavour to escape detection when they offend and they offend, too, under the impression that it is quite possible to escape your detection, since you are but men), those persons, if they learned and were convinced that nothing, whether actually done or only intended, can escape the knowledge of God, would by all means live decently on account of the penalties threatened, as even you yourselves will admit. But you seem to fear lest all men become righteous, and you no longer have any to punish. Such would be the concern of public executioners, but not of good princes. But, as we before said, we are persuaded that these things are prompted by evil spirits, who demand sacrifices and service even from those who live unreasonably; but as for you, we presume that you who aim at [a reputation for] piety and philosophy will do nothing unreasonable. But if you also, like the foolish, prefer custom to truth, do what you have power to do. But just so much power have rulers who esteem opinion more than truth, as robbers have in a desert. And that you will not succeed is declared by the Word, than whom, after God who begat Him, we know there is no ruler more kingly and just. For as all shrink from succeeding to the poverty or sufferings or obscurity of their fathers, so whatever the Word forbids us to choose, the sensible man will not choose. That all these things should come to pass, I say, our Teacher foretold, He who is both Son and Apostle of God the Father of all and the Ruler, Jesus Christ; from whom also we have the name of Christians. Whence we become more assured of all the things He taught us, since whatever He beforehand foretold should come to pass, is seen in fact coming to pass; and this is the work of God, to tell of a thing before it happens, and as it was foretold so to show it happening. It were possible to pause here and add no more, reckoning that we demand what is just and true; but because we are well aware that it is not easy suddenly to change a mind possessed by ignorance, we intend to add a few things, for the sake of persuading those who love the truth, knowing that it is not impossible to put ignorance to flight by presenting the truth.

CHAPTER XIII — CHRISTIANS SERVE GOD RATIONALLY.

What sober-minded man, then, will not acknowledge that we are not atheists, worshipping as we do the Maker of this universe, and declaring, as we have been taught, that He has no need of streams of blood and libations and incense; whom we praise to the utmost of our power by the exercise of prayer and thanksgiving for all things wherewith we are supplied, as we have been taught that the only honour that is worthy of Him is not to consume by fire what He has brought into being for our sustenance, but to use it for ourselves and those who need, and with gratitude to Him to offer thanks by invocations and hymns for our creation, and for all the means of health, and for the various qualities of the different kinds of things, and for the changes of the seasons; and to present before Him petitions for our existing again in incorruption through faith in Him. Our teacher of these things is Jesus Christ, who also was born for this purpose, and was crucified under Pontius Pilate, procurator of Judaea, in the times of Tiberius Caesar; and that we reasonably worship Him, having learned that He is the Son of the true God Himself, and holding Him in the second place, and the prophetic Spirit in the third, we will prove. For they proclaim our madness to consist in this, that we give to a crucified man a place second to the unchangeable and eternal God, the Creator of all; for they do not discern the mystery that is herein, to which, as we make it plain to you, we pray you to give heed.

CHAPTER XIV — THE DEMONS MISREPRESENT CHRISTIAN DOCTRINE.

For we forewarn you to be on your guard, lest those demons whom we have been accusing should deceive you, and quite divert you from reading and understanding what we say. For they strive to hold you their slaves and servants; and sometimes by appearances in dreams, and sometimes by magical impositions, they subdue all who make no strong opposing effort for their own salvation. And thus do we also, since our persuasion by the Word, stand aloof from them (i.e., the demons), and follow the only unbegotten God through His Son — we who formerly delighted in fornication, but now embrace chastity alone; we who formerly used magical arts, dedicate ourselves to the good and unbegotten God; we who valued above all things the acquisition of wealth and possessions, now bring what we have into a common stock, and communicate to every one in need; we who hated and destroyed one another, and on account of their different manners would not live with men of a different tribe, now, since the coming of Christ, live familiarly with them, and pray for our enemies, and endeavour to persuade those who hate us unjustly to live comformably to the good precepts of Christ, to the end that they may become par-takers with us of the same joyful hope of a reward from God the ruler of all. But lest we should seem to be reasoning sophistically, we consider it right, before giving you the promised explanation, to cite a few precepts given by Christ Himself. And be it yours, as powerful rulers, to inquire whether we have been taught and do teach these things truly. Brief and concise utterances fell from Him, for He was no sophist, but His word was the power of God.

CHAPTER XV — WHAT CHRIST HIMSELF TAUGHT.

Concerning chastity, He uttered such sentiments as these: "Whosoever looketh upon a woman to lust after her, hath committed adultery with her already in his heart before God." And, "If thy right eye offend thee, cut it out; for it is better for thee to enter into the kingdom of heaven with one eye, than, having two eyes, to be cast into everlasting fire." And, "Whosoever shall many her that is divorced from another husband, committeth adultery." And, "There are some who have been made eunuchs of men, and some who were born eunuchs, and some who have made themselves eunuchs for the kingdom of heaven's sake; but all cannot receive this saying." So that all who, by human law, are twice married, are in the eye of our Master sinners, and those who look upon a woman to lust after her. For not only he who in act commits adultery is rejected by Him, but also he who desires to commit adultery: since not only our works, but also our thoughts, are open before God. And many, both men and women, who have been Christ's disciples from childhood, remain pure at the age of sixty or seventy years; and I boast that I could produce such from every race of men. For what shall I say, too, of the countless multitude of those who have reformed intemperate habits, and learned these things? For Christ called not the just nor the chaste to repentance, but the ungodly, and the licentious, and the unjust; His words being, "I came not to call the righteous, but sinners to repentance." For the heavenly Father desires rather the repentance than the punishment of the sinner. And of our love to all, He taught thus: "If ye love them that love you, what new thing do ye? for even fornicators do this. But I say unto you, Pray for your enemies, and love them that hate you, and bless them that curse you, and pray for them that despite-fully use you." And that we should communicate to the needy, and do nothing for glory, He said, "Give to him that asketh, and from him that would borrow turn not away; for if ye lend to them of whom ye hope to receive, what new thing do ye? even the publicans do this. Lay not up for yourselves treasure upon earth, where moth and rust doth corrupt, and where robbers break through; but lay up for your-selves treasure in heaven, where neither moth nor rust doth corrupt. For what is a man profited, if he shall gain the whole world, and lose his own soul? or what shall a man give in exchange for it? Lay up treasure, therefore, in heaven, where neither moth nor rust doth corrupt." And, "Be ye kind and merci-ful, as your Father also is kind and merciful, and maketh His sun to rise on sinners, and the righteous, and the wicked. Take no thought what ye shall eat, or what ye shall put on: are ye not better than the birds and the beasts? And God feedeth them. Take no thought, therefore, what ye shall eat, or what ye shall put on; for your heavenly Father knoweth that ye have need of these things. But seek ye the kingdom of heaven, and all these things shall be added unto you. For where his treasure is, there also is the mind of a man." And, "Do not these things to be seen of men; otherwise ye have no reward from your Father which is in heaven."

CHAPTER XVI — CONCERNING PATIENCE AND SWEARING.

And concerning our being patient of injuries, and ready to serve all, and free from anger, this is what He said: "To him that smiteth thee on the one cheek, offer also the other; and him that taketh away thy cloak or coat, forbid not. And whosoever shall be angry, is in danger of the fire. And every one that compelleth thee to go with him a mile, follow him two. And let your good works shine before men, that they, seeing them, may glorify your Father which is in heaven." For we ought not to strive; neither has He desired us to be imitators of wicked men, but He has exhorted us to lead all men, by patience and gentleness, from shame and the love of evil. And this indeed is proved in the case of many who once were of your way of thinking, but have changed their violent and tyrannical disposition, being overcome either by the constancy which they have witnessed in their neighbours' lives, or by the extraordinary forbearance they have observed in their fellow-travellers when defrauded, or by the honesty of those with whom they have transacted business.

And with regard to our not swearing at all, and always speaking the truth, He enjoined as follows: "Swear not at all; but let your yea be yea, and your nay, nay; for whatsoever is more than these cometh of evil." And that we ought to worship God alone, He thus persuaded us: "The greatest commandment is, Thou shalt worship the Lord thy God, and Him only shall thou serve, with all thy heart, and with all thy strength, the Lord God that made thee." And when a certain man came to Him and said, "Good Master," He answered and said, "There is none good but God only, who made all things." And let those who are not found living as He taught, be understood to be no Christians, even though they profess with the lip the precepts of Christ; for not those who make profession, but those who do the works, shall be saved, according to His word: "Not every one who saith to Me, Lord, Lord, shall enter into the kingdom of heaven, but he that doeth the will of My Father which is in heaven. For whosoever heareth Me, and doeth My sayings, heareth Him that sent Me. And many will say unto Me, Lord, Lord, have we not eaten and drunk in Thy name, and done wonders? And then will I say unto them, Depart from Me, ye workers of iniquity. Then shall there be wailing and gnashing of teeth, when the righteous shall shine as the sun, and the wicked are sent into everlasting fire. For many shall come in My name, clothed outwardly in sheep's clothing, but inwardly being ravening wolves. By their works ye shall know them. And every tree that bringeth not forth good fruit, is hewn down and cast into the fire."And as to those who are not living pursuant to these His teachings, and are Christians only in name, we demand that all such be punished by you.

CHAPTER XVII — CHRIST TAUGHT CIVIL OBEDIENCE.

And everywhere we, more readily than all men, endeavour to pay to those appointed by you the taxes both ordinary and extraordinary as we have been taught by Him; for at that time some came to Him and asked Him, if one ought to pay tribute to Caesar; and He answered, "Tell Me, whose image does the coin bear?" And they said, "Caesar's." And again He answered them, "Render therefore to Caesar the things that are Caesar's, and to God the things that are God's." Whence to God alone we render worship, but in other things we gladly serve you, acknowledging you as kings and rulers of men, and praying that with your kingly power you be found to possess also sound judgment. But if you pay no regard to our prayers and frank explanations, we shall suffer no loss, since we believe or rather, indeed, are persuaded that every man will suffer punishment in eternal fire according to the merit of his deed, and will render account according to the power he has received from God, as Christ intimated when He said, "To whom God has given more, of him shall more be required" (www.earlychristianwritings.com/text/justinmartyr-firstapology.html).

Assignments

- Warm-up: Theology originally was written to persuade the outside world to convert to Christ. Today it seems most Christians simply talk to other Christians! Write your own apologetic of the faith being careful to identify deceptions of our age.

- Students should complete Concept Builder 14-B.

- Students should review reading(s) from the next chapter.

- Students should outline essay due at the end of the week.

- Per teacher instructions, students may answer orally, in a group setting, some of the essays that are not assigned as formal essays.

<table>
<tr><td rowspan="4">CONCEPT BUILDER 14-B
Sitz Im Leben</td><td colspan="2">Sitz im Leben is a German phrase that means "setting in life." What is the Sitz im Leben of the following texts?</td></tr>
<tr><td>Text</td><td>Sitz Im Leben</td></tr>
<tr><td>Letters from Clement</td><td></td></tr>
<tr><td>Writings by Justin Martyr</td><td></td></tr>
<tr><td colspan="0">The Encyclical Epistle of the Church at Smyrna Concerning the Martyrdom of Polycarp</td><td></td></tr>
</table>

Apologetics

Today, more than ever, Christians are called to write apologetic literature. The first three hundred years of Church history were also the age of apologists, and these apologists engaged in warfare on two fronts. First, there was the allure of pagan society. Because of its strict moral code, the Church was popularly suspected of sheltering all sorts of immoralities and thus of threatening the established order. At the same time, the pagan world sought to draw Christians away from the faith by offering all sorts of enticement. The greatest enticement was intellectual. The Christian faith was accused of being anti-intellectual and old-fashioned (even when it was only a few decades old!). The Platonist thinker Celsus, who followed the religiously inclined form of Platonism that flourished from the third century B.C. to the third century A.D., were only two among many "cultured despisers." Celsus was the Carl Sagan of his age. But, second, orthodoxy had to take issue with distorting tendencies within, whether these took the form of Gnosticism or of other heresies, such as the so-called semi-Gnostic Marcion's rejection of the Old Testament revelation or the claim of the ecstatic prophet from Phrygia, Montanus, to be the vehicle of a new outpouring of the Holy Spirit. Christianity had also to define exactly where it stood in relation to Hellenistic culture. Hellenistic culture was as ubiquitous in its day as American culture is today. Likewise, the greatest threat today is a form of Gnosticism that worships knowledge over everything. It is interesting to note, for instance, that the most prominent feature of the University of Pittsburgh (Pennsylvania) is aptly named "the Cathedral of Learning!" We worship at our Gnostic shrines (i.e., the university) all over our country. The most famous apologist, however, was Justin (later called Justin Martyr), who converted to Christianity after he tried various philosophical schools, paid lengthy visits to Rome, and was martyred there (165). Justin's two *Apologies* are skillful presentations of the Christian case to the pagan critics; and his *Dialogue with Trypho* is an elaborate defense of Christianity against Judaism. In a real sense, the first two generations of apologists were the first Christian theologians. Theology originally was written to persuade the outside world to convert to Christ. Today it seems most Christians talk only with other Christians!

Assignments

- Warm-up: How might the world be impacted by Christians who defend their faith?
- Students should complete Concept Builder 14-C.
- Students should write rough draft of assigned essay.
- The teacher or a peer evaluator may correct rough drafts.

There were known to be ten waves of persecutions under the Roman emperors. Whole families died for their faith in horrible ways. Drowning, burning parts of the body, being torn in pieces, burnings at the stake, and being beheaded were commonplace. It is said for several weeks the countryside was lit up by Christians who were torched. But with all this being done, the Church increased. Martyrdom literature follows a certain pattern. Find examples from Polycarp's martyrdom that fit that pattern.

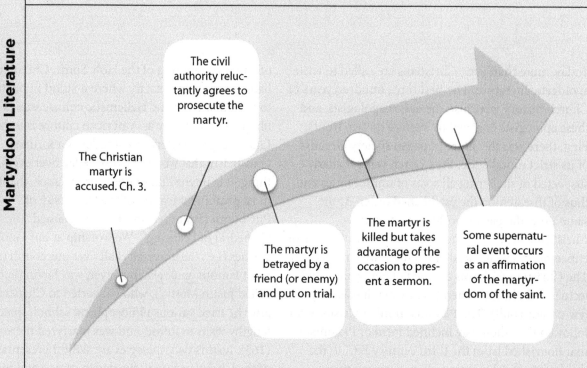

The civil authority reluctantly agrees to prosecute the martyr.

The Christian martyr is accused. Ch. 3.

The martyr is betrayed by a friend (or enemy) and put on trial.

The martyr is killed but takes advantage of the occasion to present a sermon.

Some supernatural event occurs as an affirmation of the martyrdom of the saint.

Polycarp

Background *The Encyclical Epistle of the Church at Smyrna Concerning the Martyrdom of the Holy Polycarp* is one of the most powerful pieces of Church history that exists today. Polycarp was martyred in the middle of the third century (www.newadvent.org/fathers/0102.htm).

The Church of God which sojourns at Smyrna, to the Church of God sojourning in Philomelium, and to all the congregations of the Holy and Catholic Church in every place: Mercy, peace, and love from God the Father, and our Lord Jesus Christ, be multiplied.

CHAPTER I — SUBJECT OF WHICH WE WRITE.

We have written to you, brethren, as to what relates to the martyrs, and especially to the blessed Polycarp, who put an end to the persecution, having, as it were, set a seal upon it by his martyrdom. For almost all the events that happened previously [to this one], took place that the Lord might show us from above a martyrdom becoming the Gospel. For he waited to be delivered up, even as the Lord had done, that we also might become his followers, while we look not merely at what concerns ourselves but have regard also to our neighbours. For it is the part of a true and well-founded love, not only to wish one's self to be saved, but also all the brethren.

CHAPTER II — THE WONDERFUL CONSTANCY OF THE MARTYRS.

All the martyrdoms, then, were blessed and noble which took place according to the will of God. For it becomes us who profess greater piety than others, to ascribe the authority over all things to God. And truly, who can fail to admire their nobleness of mind, and their patience, with that love towards their Lord which they displayed? — who, when they were so torn with scourges, that the frame of their bodies, even to the very inward veins and arteries, was laid open, still patiently endured, while even those that stood by pitied and bewailed them. But they reached such a pitch of magnanimity, that not one of them let a sigh or a groan escape them; thus proving to us all that those holy martyrs of Christ, at the very time when they suffered such torments, were absent from the body, or rather, that the Lord then stood by them, and communed with them. And, looking to the grace of Christ, they despised all the torments of this world, redeeming themselves from eternal punishment by [the suffering of] a single hour. For this reason the fire of their savage executioners appeared cool to them. For they kept before their view escape from that fire which is eternal and never shall be quenched, and looked forward with the eyes of their heart to those good things which are laid up for such as endure; things "which ear hath not heard, nor eye seen, neither have entered into the heart of man," but were revealed by the Lord to them, inasmuch as they were no longer men, but had already become angels. And, in like manner, those who were condemned to the wild beasts endured dreadful tortures, being stretched out upon beds full of spikes, and subjected to various other kinds of torments, in order that, if it were possible, the tyrant might, by their lingering tortures, lead them to a denial [of Christ].

CHAPTER III — THE CONSTANCY OF GERMANICUS. THE DEATH OF POLYCARP IS DEMANDED.

For the devil did indeed invent many things against them; but thanks be to God, he could not prevail over all. For the most noble Germanicus strengthened the timidity of others by his own patience, and fought heroically with the wild beasts. For, when the proconsul sought to persuade him, and urged him to take pity upon his age, he attracted the wild beast towards himself, and provoked it, being desirous to escape all the more quickly from an unrighteous and impious world. But upon this the whole multitude, marvelling at the nobility of mind displayed by the devout and godly race of Christians, cried out, "Away with the Atheists; let Polycarp be sought out !"

CHAPTER IV — QUINTUS THE APOSTATE.

Now one named Quintus, a Phrygian, who was but lately come from Phrygia, when he saw the wild beasts, became afraid. This was the man who forced himself and some others to come forward voluntarily [for trial]. Him the proconsul, after many entreaties, persuaded to swear and to offer sacrifice. Wherefore, brethren, we do not commend those who give themselves up [to suffering], seeing the Gospel does not teach so to do.

CHAPTER V — THE DEPARTURE AND VISION OF POLYCARP.

But the most admirable Polycarp, when he first heard [that he was sought for], was in no measure disturbed, but resolved to continue in the city. However, in deference to the wish of many, he was persuaded to leave it. He departed, therefore, to a country house not far distant from the city. There he stayed with a few [friends], engaged in nothing else night and day than praying for all men, and for the Churches throughout the world, according to his usual custom. And while he was praying, a vision presented itself to him three days before he was taken; and, behold, the pillow under his head seemed to him on fire. Upon this, turning to those that were with him, he said to them prophetically, "I must be burnt alive."

CHAPTER VI — POLYCARP IS BETRAYED BY A SERVANT.

And when those who sought for him were at hand, he departed to another dwelling, whither his pursuers immediately came after him. And when they found him not, they seized upon two youths [that were there], one of whom, being subjected to torture, confessed. It was thus impossible that he should continue hid, since those that betrayed him were of his own household. The Irenarch then whose office is the same as that of the Cleronomus, by name Herod, hastened to bring him into the stadium. [This all happened] that he might fulfil his special lot, being made a partaker of Christ, and that they who betrayed him might undergo the punishment of Judas himself.

CHAPTER VII — POLYCARP IS FOUND BY HIS PURSUERS.

His pursuers then, along with horsemen, and taking the youth with them, went forth at supper-time on the day of the preparation with their usual weapons, as if going out against a robber. And being come about evening [to the place where he was], they found him lying down in the upper room of a certain little house, from which he might have escaped into another place; but he refused, saying, "The will of God be done." So when he heard that they were come, he went down and spake with them. And as those that were present marvelled at his age and constancy, some of them said. "Was so much effort made to capture such a venerable man?" Immediately then, in that very hour, he ordered that something to eat and drink should be set before them, as much indeed as they cared for, while he besought them to allow him an hour to pray without disturbance. And on their giving him leave, he stood and prayed, being full of the grace of God, so that he could not cease for two full hours, to the astonishment of them that heard him, insomuch that many began to repent that they had come forth against so godly and venerable an old man.

CHAPTER VIII — POLYCARP IS BROUGHT INTO THE CITY.

Now, as soon as he had ceased praying, having made mention of all that had at any time come in contact with him, both small and great, illustrious and obscure, as well as the whole Catholic Church throughout the world, the time of his departure having arrived, they set him upon an ass, and conducted him into the city, the day being that of the great Sabbath. And the Irenarch Herod, accompanied by his father Nicetes both riding in a chariot, met him, and taking him up into the chariot, they seated themselves beside him, and endeavoured to persuade him, saying, "What harm is there in saying, Lord Caesar, and in sacrificing, with the other ceremonies observed on such occasions, and so make sure of safety?" But he at first gave them no answer; and when they continued to urge him, he said, "I shall not do as you advise me." So they, having no hope of persuading him, began to speak bitter words unto him, and cast him with violence out of the chariot, insomuch that, in getting down from the carriage, he dislocated his leg [by the fall]. But without being disturbed, and as if suffering nothing, he went eagerly forward with all haste, and was conducted to the stadium, where the tumult was so great, that there was no possibility of being heard.

CHAPTER IX — POLYCARP REFUSES TO REVILE CHRIST.

Now, as Polycarp was entering into the stadium, there came to him a voice from heaven, saying, "Be strong, and show thyself a man, O Polycarp!" No one saw who it was that spoke to him; but those of our brethren who were present heard the voice. And as he was brought forward, the tumult became great when they heard that Polycarp was taken. And when he came near, the proconsul asked him whether he was Polycarp. On his confessing that he was, [the proconsul] sought to persuade him to deny [Christ], saying, "Have respect to thy old age," and other similar things, according to their custom, [such as], "Swear by the fortune of Caesar; repent, and say, "Away with the Atheists." But Polycarp, gazing with a stern countenance on all the multitude of the wicked heathen then in the stadium, and waving his hand towards them, while with groans he looked up to heaven, said, "Away with the Atheists." Then, the proconsul urging him, and saying, "Swear, and I will set thee at liberty, reproach Christ;" Polycarp declared, "Eighty and six years have I served Him, and He never did me any injury: how then can I blaspheme my King and my Saviour?"

CHAPTER X — POLYCARP CONFESSES HIMSELF A CHRISTIAN.

And when the proconsul yet again pressed him, and said, "Swear by the fortune of Caesar," he answered, "Since thou art vainly urgent that, as thou sayest, I should swear by the fortune of Caesar, and pretendest not to know who and what I am, hear me declare with boldness, I am a Christian. And if you wish to learn what the doctrines of Christianity are, appoint me a day, and thou shalt hear them." The proconsul replied, "Persuade the people." But Polycarp said, "To thee I have thought it right to offer an account [of my faith]; for we are taught to give all due honour which entails no injury upon ourselves to the powers and authorities which are ordained of God. But as for these, I do not deem them worthy of receiving any account from me."

CHAPTER XI — NO THREATS HAVE ANY EFFECT ON POLYCARP.

The proconsul then said to him, "I have wild beasts at hand; to these will I cast thee, except thou repent." But he answered, "Call them then, for we are not accustomed to repent of what is good in order to

201

adopt that which is evil; and it is well for me to be changed from what is evil to what is righteous." But again the proconsul said to him, "I will cause thee to be consumed by fire, seeing thou despisest the wild beasts, if thou wilt not repent." But Polycarp said, "Thou threatenest me with fire which burneth for an hour, and after a little is extinguished, but art ignorant of the fire of the coming judgment and of eternal punishment, reserved for the ungodly. But why tarriest thou? Bring forth what thou wilt."

CHAPTER XII — POLYCARP IS SENTENCED TO BE BURNED.

While he spoke these and many other like things, he was filled with confidence and joy, and his countenance was full of grace, so that not merely did it not fall as if troubled by the things said to him, but, on the contrary, the proconsul was astonished, and sent his herald to proclaim in the midst of the stadium thrice, "Polycarp has confessed that he is a Christian." This proclamation having been made by the herald, the whole multitude both of the heathen and Jews, who dwelt at Smyrna, cried out with uncontrollable fury, and in a loud voice, "This is the teacher of Asia, the father of the Christians, and the overthrower of our gods, he who has been teaching many not to sacrifice, or to worship the gods." Speaking thus, they cried out, and besought Philip the Asiarch to let loose a lion upon Polycarp. But Philip answered that it was not lawful for him to do so, seeing the shows of wild beasts were already finished. Then it seemed good to them to cry out with one consent, that Polycarp should be burnt alive. For thus it behooved the vision which was revealed to him in regard to his pillow to be fulfilled, when, seeing it on fire as he was praying, he turned about and said prophetically to the faithful that were with him, "I must be burnt alive."

CHAPTER XIII — THE FUNERAL PILE IS ERECTED,

This, then, was carried into effect with greater speed than it was spoken, the multitudes immediately gathering together wood and fagots out of the shops and baths; the Jews especially, according to custom, eagerly assisting them in it. And when the funeral pile was ready, Polycarp, laying aside all his garments, and loosing his girdle, sought also to take off his sandals, — a thing he was not accustomed to do, inasmuch as every one of the faithful was always eager who should first touch his skin. For, on account of his holy life, he was, even before his martyrdom, adorned with every kind of good. Immediately then they surrounded him with those substances which had been prepared for the funeral pile. But when they were about also to fix him with nails, he said, "Leave me as I am; for He that giveth me strength to endure the fire, will also enable me, without your securing me by nails, to remain without moving in the pile."

CHAPTER XIV — THE PRAYER OF POLYCARP.

They did not nail him then, but simply bound him. And he, placing his hands behind him, and being bound like a distinguished ram [taken] out of a great flock for sacrifice, and prepared to be an acceptable burnt-offering unto God, looked up to heaven, and said, "O Lord God Almighty, the Father of thy beloved and blessed Son Jesus Christ, by whom we have received the knowledge of Thee, the God of angels and powers, and of every creature, and of the whole race of the righteous who live before thee, I give Thee thanks that Thou hast counted me, worthy of this day and this hour, that I should have a part in the number of Thy martyrs, in the cup of thy Christ, to the resurrection of eternal life, both of soul and body, through the incorruption [imparted] by the Holy Ghost. Among whom may I be accepted this day before Thee as a fat and acceptable sacrifice, according as Thou, the ever-truthful God, hast fore-ordained, hast revealed beforehand to me, and now hast fulfilled. Wherefore also I praise Thee for all things, I bless Thee, I glorify Thee, along with the everlasting and heavenly Jesus Christ, Thy beloved Son, with whom, to Thee, and the Holy Ghost, be glory both now and to all coming ages. Amen."

CHAPTER XV — POLYCARP IS NOT INJURED BY THE FIRE.

When he had pronounced this amen, and so finished his prayer, those who were appointed for the purpose kindled the fire. And as the flame blazed forth in great fury, we, to whom it was given to witness it, beheld a great miracle, and have been preserved that we might report to others what then took place. For the fire, shaping itself into the form of an arch, like the sail of a ship when filled with the wind, encompassed as by a circle the body of the martyr. And he appeared within not like flesh which is burnt, but as bread that is baked, or as gold and silver glowing in a furnace. Moreover, we perceived such a sweet odour [coming from the pile], as if frankincense or some such precious spices had been smoking there.

CHAPTER XVI — POLYCARP IS PIERCED BY A DAGGER.

At length, when those wicked men perceived that his body could not be consumed by the fire, they commanded an executioner to go near and pierce him through with a dagger. And on his doing this, there came forth a dove, and a great quantity of blood, so that the fire was extinguished; and all the people wondered that there should be such a difference between the unbelievers and the elect, of whom this most admirable Polycarp was one, having in our own times been an apostolic and prophetic teacher, and bishop of the Catholic Church which is in Smyrna. For every word that went out of his mouth either has been or shall yet be accomplished.

CHAPTER XVII — THE CHRISTIANS ARE REFUSED POLYCARP'S BODY.

But when the adversary of the race of the righteous, the envious, malicious, and wicked one, perceived the impressive nature of his martyrdom, and [considered] the blameless life he had led from the beginning, and how he was now crowned with the wreath of immortality, having beyond dispute received his reward, he did his utmost that not the least memorial of him should be taken away by us, although many desired to do this, and to become possessors of his holy flesh. For this end he suggested it to Nicetes, the father of Herod and brother of Alce, to go and entreat the governor not to give up his body to be buried, "lest," said he, "forsaking Him that was crucified, they begin to worship this one." This he said at the suggestion and urgent persuasion of the Jews, who also watched us, as we sought to take him out of the fire, being ignorant of this, that it is neither possible for us ever to forsake Christ, who suffered for the salvation of such as shall be saved throughout the whole world the blameless one for sinners, nor to worship any other. For Him indeed, as being the Son of God, we adore; but the martyrs, as disciples and followers of the Lord, we worthily love on account of their extraordinary affection towards their own King and Master, of whom may we also be made companions and fellow disciples!

CHAPTER XVIII — THE BODY OF POLYCARP IS BURNED.

The centurion then, seeing the strife excited by the Jews, placed the body in the midst of the fire, and consumed it. Accordingly, we afterwards took up his bones, as being more precious than the most exquisite jewels, and more purified than gold, and deposited them in a fitting place, whither, being gathered together, as opportunity is allowed us, with joy and rejoicing, the Lord shall grant us to celebrate the anniversary of his martyrdom, both in memory of those who have already finished their course, and for the exercising and preparation of those yet to walk in their steps.

CHAPTER XIX — PRAISE OF THE MARTYR POLYCARP.

This, then, is the account of the blessed Polycarp, who, being the twelfth that was martyred in Smyrna reckoning those also of Philadelphia, yet occupies a place of his own in the memory of all men, insomuch that he is everywhere spoken of by the heathen themselves. He was not merely an illustrious teacher, but also a pre-eminent martyr, whose martyrdom all desire to imitate, as having been altogether consistent with the Gospel of Christ. For, having through patience overcome the unjust governor, and thus acquired the crown of immortality, he now, with the apostles and all the righteous [in heaven], rejoicingly glorifies God, even the Father, and blesses our Lord Jesus Christ, the Saviour of our souls, the Governor of our bodies, and the Shepherd of the Catholic Church throughout the world.

CHAPTER XX — THIS EPISTLE IS TO BE TRANSMITTED TO THE BRETHREN.

Since, then, ye requested that we would at large make you acquainted with what really took place, we have for the present sent you this summary account through our brother Marcus. When, therefore, ye have yourselves read this Epistle, be pleased to send it to the brethren at a greater distance, that they also may glorify the Lord, who makes such choice of His own servants. To Him who is able to bring us all by His grace and goodness into his everlasting kingdom, through His only-begotten Son Jesus Christ, to Him be glory, and honour, and power, and majesty, for ever. Amen. Salute all the saints. They that are with us salute you, and Evarestus, who wrote this Epistle, with all his house.

CHAPTER XXI — THE DATE OF THE MARTYRDOM.

Now, the blessed Polycarp suffered martyrdom on the second day of the month Xanthicus just begun, the seventh day before the Kalends of May, on the great Sabbath, at the eighth hour. He was taken by Herod, Philip the Trallian being high priest, Statius Quadratus being proconsul, but Jesus Christ being King for ever, to whom be glory, honour, majesty, and an everlasting throne, from generation to generation. Amen.

CHAPTER XXII — SALUTATION.

We wish you, brethren, all happiness, while you walk according to the doctrine of the Gospel of Jesus Christ; with whom be glory to God the Father and the Holy Spirit, for the salvation of His holy elect, after whose example the blessed Polycarp suffered, following in whose steins may we too be found in the kingdom of Jesus Christ!

These things Caius transcribed from the copy of Irenaeus (who was a disciple of Polycarp), having himself been intimate with Irenaeus. And I Socrates transcribed them at Corinth from the copy of Caius. Grace be with you all.

Assignments

- Warm-up: Are there modern martyrs?
- Students should complete Concept Builder 14-D.
- Students will re-write corrected copies of essay due tomorrow.

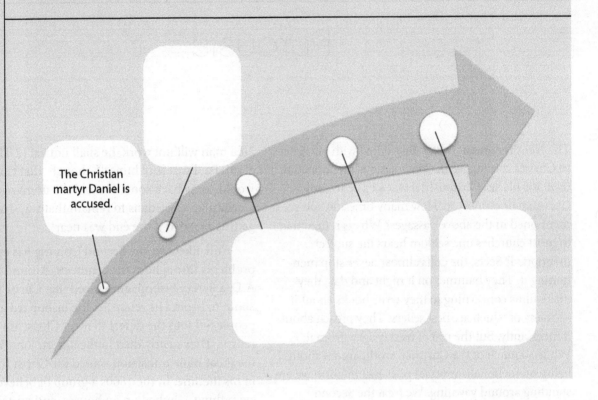

CONCEPT BUILDER 14-D
Martyrdom Literature Application

Apply the same form to a biblical character (e.g., Daniel).

The Christian martyr Daniel is accused.

Parousia

The New Testament is literally riddled with references to Christ's coming again. The matter is mentioned in over 300 places. Obviously, it was a basic to early Christian doctrine, too. How many times do you see it mentioned in the above passages? Why is it then that in most churches one seldom hears the subject mentioned? Sects, the cults almost never stop mentioning it. They hammer on it night and day; they make films concerning it; they write books about it — many of which are best sellers. They preach about it incessantly. But the rest of us stay away from it. While so much of the Christian world argues about being premellinialism verses post-mellinialism we are standing around yawning. We treat the Second Coming as though it were only for the religious fanatics who knock on doors. What bothers us about the Second Coming of Christ? It bothers us because it seems so weird. The Parousia cannot be quantified, commercialized, explained or predicted. Kurt Vonnegut Jr. — not exactly a paradigm of the faith I know!!! — says that his fiction is so accurate that it is non-fiction. In a way he is right. The truth can be so bizarre, so true, that it becomes threatening and seems like it is untrue. I think that is why many of my colleagues and many of my congregation find eschatological talk to be on one hand irrelevant and, on the other, sensationalistic. We are in good company. The doctrine of the Second Coming has proved to be embarrassing and troublesome to various groups of Christians throughout history.

Take the Apostle Paul, for instance. Many of the Christians in Thessalonica believed that Christ was going to come and wrap everything up any time now, so they quit their jobs and were just sitting around waiting for the day. Paul had to write to them: "We hear that some among you are idle. They are not busy; they are busybodies " (2 Thess. 3:11).

"If a man will not work, he shall not eat (2 Thess. 3:10). Paul was sure himself, though, that Christ would come back soon. He told the unmarried Corinthian Christians to remain that way. No use getting married if the end was near!

And, likewise, the Second Coming has created problems throughout the centuries. Around 200 A.D. a Syrian bishop announced that Christ was about to begin His reign. So, the bishop led all of his people out into the desert to meet Christ at His return. They nearly died in the desert. John Wycliffe, the great Bible translator, waited for Christ to return in his lifetime. In the 1800s a group of believers sold everything, climbed up on houses, and waited for the Lord. Finally, they sheepishly came down (after many weeks). Setting dates for the return of Christ has been especially embarrassing. The Adventist leaders in the last century calculated 1843. When that proved to be wrong, they tried 1844. The Jehovah Witnesses thought it would be 1914. Indeed, hardly a year goes by that someone, often in California, "the land of fruit and nuts," does not predict the Second Coming. Hal Lindsay, author of *The Late Great Planet Earth*, was sure that the end would occur in 1988.

What is truly amazing, though, is that the Bible is very clear on this point. Very plainly Jesus says, "No one knows about that day or hour, not even the angels in heaven, nor the Son, but only the Father" (Mark 13:32). Someone might well ask, "Well, given Paul's error and the embarrassment of wrong-guessing all through the centuries, and considering all the excesses, why not forget the whole thing?" And that is pretty much what we have done. But it was not always so. But the question arises; Is it fair for us to dismiss casually a theme that pulsates so insistently through the whole of the New Testament? And again, do we not find it slipping into our worship services even when we try to ignore it? We repeat the Apostles' Creed, for example, and there read that Christ "sitteth as the right hand of God the Father almighty from thence he shall come to judge the quick and the dead." We sing a hymn such as "How Great Thou Art" and there it is: "When Christ shall come with a shout of acclamation and take me home, what joy shall fill my heart." So, while we can ignore the concept of the Second Coming, we cannot escape it. What then can be said? Will Christ come again as both the New Testament and the Creeds tell us? No doubt on this point — Christ will return. The New Testament looks forward quite realistically to an end time, to a consummation of history, to a time when everything shall be wrapped up. The New Testament sees Christ coming at the end of history to gather his own and to vindicate them before everyone. The New Testament looks confidently forward to the time when the "kingdom of the world has become the kingdom of our Lord and of his Christ, and he will reign for ever and ever" (Rev. 11:15).

"So who cares?" you may still ask. What difference does it make? I asked myself this. While I was a pastor in a New Jersey church, occasionally I would escape to a Jersey diner and eat lunch. I loved to go around 2:30 when the crowds had left and the waitresses were standing around gossiping. I surreptitiously carried a notebook with me so that I could garnish some sermon illustrations from the ever-loquacious waitresses. I learned more about human nature in one afternoon at Windsor Diner than all my courses at Princeton. A Jersey diner is somewhere between an ostentatious trailer and your proverbial greasy spoon. The Jersey diner is truly a slice of Americana — where the "youse guys" and "Couffee" runs freely. Built in only a couple of days in my former hometown, Middlesex, New Jersey, these diners have been able to withstand the onslaught of McDonalds and Burger Kings. Besides having the best cheesecake on the East Coast, the diner is the best place for a pastor to keep in touch with his world. When I was tired of all the pedantic gobbledygoop that the modern pastorate demanded, I escaped to Windsor Diner. As I ate my underdone, greasy, overpriced cheeseburger, I eavesdropped on two waitresses at the end of the counter. I love to eat lunch at the counter with the postman and the truck driver. Who knows, maybe someone will mistake me for a workingman!

"Can you believe it," one fat little waitress mused, "The blankety-blank guy let his daughter die in a fire." The waitress was referring to a sensationalistic story about a father who chained his daughter to her room so that she would not "fall into immorality." Too bad she burned to death in fire when he was away! This little waitress ended with a statement that was uncharacteristic fare for a mid-afternoon lunch in central New Jersey. "I just hope that I die soon so that I will not have to suffer much more."

We all want to shout, like that waitress, "Come quickly, Lord Jesus! My world is too crazy and I am hurting too much!" But, the message of the Second Coming and the First Coming (Christmas), for that matter, is that no matter what happens on earth, it is all going to end in victory for Christ and those who belong to him. Period. The hope of the Second Coming is that, beyond all our doubts, he is after all Lord of all, the King of kings. The doctrine of the Second Coming reminds us always to look to the future, but not to forget the past. We are a pilgrim people on the move. Our faces are forever set toward the future. As we resolutely and confidently move forward, we should keep glancing back over our shoulders to see from where we have come. We keep remembering and hoping, but it is hope that gives us light for the journey into the unknown. We still look for the coming of Christ. It reminds us that our lives are intertwined with the misery we see around us, but that we are forever faced to the future. Someday, we will face our returning Lord. He will consummate history, offer some explanation, justification, for all this heartbreak we experience and see around us. The Second Coming promises a clarity that we do not now experience.

The world does not give us this hope nor can it take it away. "No, in all these things we are more than conquerors" Paul writes (Romans 8:37). I remember a duck-hunting trip almost 15 years ago when I nearly lost all hope. As most serious duck hunters, Dad and I entered a swamp named appropriately Devil's Den, long before daylight. As usual, within an hour or two Dad and I were hopelessly lost. I began to worry. Not that I did not trust my father, but I was old enough to understand that Arkansas swamps held all kinds of dangerous surprises for lost daddies and little boys. But, even worse, I sensed worry in my father's voice, too. Finally, though, we paused and Dad calmly said, "Never mind Jim. It will be dawn soon. We'll get our bearings from the sun." Sure enough, the dawn came and we were able to escape Devil's Den. Even now after all these years, after I watched my dad go to be with our Lord, I have never forgotten Dad's voice, "Never mind, Jim, the dawn will come soon." That is the true meaning of the Parousia. In the face of inevitable nuclear holocaust, impenetrable loneliness, when we are lost and confused, God says to us in a clear voice, "The dawn is coming." As Millard Erickson cautions us, we must keep perspective (Millard J. Erickson, *Christian Theology*, Grand Rapids, MI: Baker Books, 1985, p. 1135). But we must also keep the Parousia uppermost in our minds and hearts. I sincerely believe, in the days ahead, that we will need more than the wimpish God of so much of our theology. We need the God who does not change, whose will is irrevocable.

Maranatha! Christ will come back to see that history ends the way God intends it. When it appears that the world is going to hell in a handbasket, we are tempted to be distressed and overwhelmed by the realities of the present. But we must not forget this message: Christ is here, now, living and loving us through hard times. But, we must never forget, especially when our present situations cause us to gasp for air, He is coming back, the dawn is coming. Maranatha! Come quickly Lord Jesus!

Assignments

- Warm-up: Reflect on the meaning of the Parousia (Second Coming of Jesus Christ) to your life.
- Students should complete Concept Builder 14-E.
- Essays are due. Students should take the chapter 14 test.

CONCEPT BUILDER 14-E
Theme: The Promise is in Danger

In martyrdom literature, there is great fear that the hero(ine) will die and that the promise is in jeopardy. Polycarp, for instance, does indeed die, but the cause of Christ is advanced. The reader, however, does not know the outcome and there is fear that the faith will be compromised — either by Polycarp recanting his faith or by the death of Polycarp himself. Of course, neither outcome occurs. What dangers to the promise occur in the following biblical stories?

Story	Danger to the Promise
The story of Abraham sacrificing Isaac.	*The reader supposes that the promise will end with the death of Isaac. God of course intervenes and Abraham does not sacrifice Isaac.*
Joseph may languish in prison forever.	
The people of Israel are in bondage in Egypt.	
Daniel is in danger of dying for his faith.	
It appears that the nation of Israel is doomed until God intervenes through Esther.	
The death of Christ seems to end all hope that He is the Messiah.	

(A.D. 30–500):
Early Church History (Part 3)

First Thoughts Augustinus, bishop of Hippo in Roman Africa from 396 to 430, and the dominant personality of the Western Church of his time, is generally recognized as having been the greatest thinker of Church history. As one theologian explained, "His mind was the crucible in which the religion of the New Testament was most completely fused with the Platonic tradition of Greek philosophy; and it was also the means by which the product of this fusion was transmitted to the Christendoms of medieval Roman Catholicism and Renaissance Protestantism" (Encyclopedia Britannica, "Augustine," introduction, www.astrologos.su/Int_Ast_Community/Personalities/A_R/Augustin_Saint.htm). All this would have been true even if Augustine had never written the famous *Confessions*, in which at the age of about 45 he told the story of his own life. Homeschooled in the Christian faith by his mother, Monica, he nonetheless rejected the Christian faith until he was much older. After Augustine received Christ, God used the theologian's keen mind and interest in philosophy to propel the Christian faith forward into the Middle Ages.

Chapter Learning Objectives In chapter 15 we discuss one of the most influential literary works in world history: Augustine's *Confessions*.

As a result of this chapter study you will be able to . . .

1. Discuss the narrative technique of *Confessions* and decide whether or not you think it works.

2. Compare and contrast this piece to an epic narrative (e.g., *The Aeneid* by Virgil).

3. Discuss in some detail Augustine's conversion.

4. Augustine's *Confession* is a testimony to a mother's faith. "And thou sentest Thine hand from above, and drewest my soul out of that profound darkness, my mother . . ." (Book III). Give examples from Scripture of other great mothers.

5. One criticism of *Confessions* is that Augustine's ending is anti-climatic, even superfluous. In other words, some critics claim that he does not know how to end his autobiography. Agree or disagree.

Weekly Essay Options: Begin on page 273 of the Teacher Guide.
Reading ahead: Japanese Ancient Literature: Poems by Ono no Komachi, Kakinomoto Hitomaro, and Minamoto no Toshiyori.

History connections: *World History* chapter 15, "Christianity Spreads."

Man and God

Great are you, O Lord, and exceedingly worthy of praise; your power is immense, and your wisdom beyond reckoning. And so we men, who are a due part of your creation, long to praise you — we also carry our mortality about with us, carry the evidence of our sin and with it the proof that you thwart the proud. You arouse us so that praising you may bring us joy, because you have made us and drawn us to yourself, and our heart is unquiet until it rests in you.

Grant me to know and understand, Lord, which comes first. To call upon you or to praise you? To know you or to call upon you? Must we know you before we can call upon you? Anyone who invokes what is still unknown may be making a mistake. Or should you be invoked first, so that we may then come to know you? But how can people call upon someone in whom they do not yet believe? And how can they believe without a preacher?

But scripture tells us that those who seek the Lord will praise him, for as they seek they find him, and on finding him they will praise him. Let me seek you then, Lord, even while I am calling upon you, and call upon you even as I believe in you; for to us you have indeed been preached. My faith calls upon you, Lord, this faith which is your gift to me, which you have breathed into me through the humanity of your Son and the ministry of your preacher.

How shall I call upon my God, my God and my Lord, when by the very act of calling upon him I would be calling him into myself? Is there any place within me into which my God might come? How should the God who made heaven and earth come into me? Is there any room in me for you, Lord, my God? Even heaven and earth, which you have made and in which you have made me – can even they contain you? Since nothing that exists would exist

Praying Hands by Albrecht Dürer, date unknown (PD-Art).

without you, does it follow that whatever exists does in some way contain you?

But if this is so, how can I, who am one of these existing things, ask you to come into me, when I would not exist at all unless you were already in me? Not yet am I in hell, after all but even if I were, you would be there too; for if I descend into the underworld, you are there. No, my God, I would not exist, I would not be at all, if you were not in me. Or should I say, rather, that I should not exist if I were not in you, from whom are all things, through whom are all things, in whom are all things? Yes, Lord, that is the truth, that is indeed the truth. To what place can I invite you, then, since I am in you? Or where could you come from, in order to come into me? To what place outside heaven and earth could I travel, so that my God could come to me there, the God who said, I fill heaven and earth?

Who will grant it to me to find peace in you? Who will grant me this grace, that you should come into my heart and inebriate it, enabling me to forget the evils that beset me and embrace you, my only good? What are you to me? Have mercy on me, so that I may tell. What indeed am I to you, that you should command me to love you, and grow angry with me if I do not, and threaten me with enormous woes? Is not the failure to love you woe enough in itself?

Alas for me! Through your own merciful dealings with me, O Lord my God, tell me what you are to me. Say to my soul, I am your salvation. Say it so that I can hear it. My heart is listening, Lord; open the ears of my heart and say to my soul, I am your salvation. Let me run towards this voice and seize hold of you. Do not hide your face from me: let me die so that I may see it, for not to see it would be death to me indeed (*The Confessions of Saint Augustine*, www.gutenberg.org/cache/epub/3296/pg3296.html).

Assignments

- Warm-up: What is necessary for mankind to have peace?
- Students should complete Concept Builder 15-A.
- Students should review the required reading(s) *before* the assigned chapter begins.
- Teachers may want to discuss assigned reading(s) with students.
- Teachers shall assign the required essay. The rest of the essays can be outlined, answered with shorter answers, discussed, or skipped.
- Students will review all readings for chapter 15.

Read *Confessions* by Augustine, and respond to the following:

Great art Thou, O Lord, and greatly to be praised; great is Thy power, and Thy wisdom infinite. And Thee would man praise; man, but a particle of Thy creation; man, that bears about him his mortality, the witness of his sin, the witness that Thou resistest the proud: yet would man praise Thee; he, but a particle of Thy creation. Thou awakest us to delight in Thy praise; for Thou madest us for Thyself, and our heart is restless, until it repose in Thee. Grant me, Lord, to know and understand which is first, to call on Thee or to praise Thee? and, again, to know Thee or to call on Thee? for who can call on Thee, not knowing Thee? for he that knoweth Thee not, may call on Thee as other than Thou art. Or, is it rather, that we call on Thee that we may know Thee? but how shall they call on Him in whom they have not believed? or how shall they believe without a preacher? and they that seek the Lord shall praise Him: for they that seek shall find Him, and they that find shall praise Him. I will seek Thee, Lord, by calling on Thee; and will call on Thee, believing in Thee; for to us hast Thou been preached. My faith, Lord, shall call on Thee, which Thou hast given me, wherewith Thou hast inspired me, through the Incarnation of Thy Son, through the ministry of the Preacher.

And how shall I call upon my God, my God and Lord, since, when I call for Him, I shall be calling Him to myself? and what room is there within me, whither my God can come into me? whither can God come into me, God who made heaven and earth? is there, indeed, O Lord my God, aught in me that can contain Thee? do then heaven and earth, which Thou hast made, and wherein Thou hast made me, contain Thee? or, because nothing which exists could exist without Thee, doth therefore whatever exists contain Thee? Since, then, I too exist, why do I seek that Thou shouldest enter into me, who were not, wert Thou not in me? Why? because I am not gone down in hell, and yet Thou art there also. For if I go down into hell, Thou art there. I could not be then, O my God, could not be at all, wert Thou not in me; or, rather, unless I were in Thee, of whom are all things, by whom are all things, in whom are all things? Even so, Lord, even so. Whither do I call Thee, since I am in Thee? or whence canst Thou enter into me? for whither can I go beyond heaven and earth, that thence my God should come into me, who hath said, I fill the heaven and the earth.

Why would Augustine choose to tell his life story in the form of a prayer?

What does Augustine mean when he says, "And how shall I call upon my God, my God and Lord, since, when I call for Him, I shall be calling Him to myself"?

Augustine's *Confessions* vs. Virgil's *Aeneid*

A man is called by his God to make a long and tedious journey that will eventually bring him to his ultimate home. This extremely generic and highly oversimplified skeleton describes the plot of a handful of books. This summary draws an extremely interesting and very surprising connection between two books in particular, Virgil's *The Aeneid* and Augustine's *Confessions*. Even though these two famous works seem entirely different on the surface, there are several striking similarities between them.

The first similarity between the two books is that of the protagonist's calling. In *The Aeneid*, Aeneas' dead wife comes to him as a spirit and instructs him in what he must do after fleeing his burning home-town of Troy. "High Olympus will(s) it. Long exile must be your lot, the vast expanse of sea be ploughed; and you shall see the Hesperian land, where Lydian Tiber flows with gentle course between the fertile fields where heroes dwell. Prosperity, a kingdom, and a spouse of royal rank are there obtained for you." As the spirit of Creusa, Aeneas' wife, states, the gods have called Aeneas to marry again and found a great city, Rome. Aeneas was called by the gods to begin his journey. In the *Confessions*, Augustine, too, felt called by his God. "I call upon you, Lord, in my faith which you have given me, which you have inspired in me through the humanity of your son, and through the ministry of your preacher." The phrase, "my faith which *you have* given me," shows that Augustine clearly felt that it was only because of God that he was able to undertake the amazing journey that eventually led him to become one of the greatest Christian leaders who ever lived.

Aeneas and Augustine start at the same point, but do their journeys actually remain parallel past the beginning? In *The Aeneid*, Aeneas faces many obstacles as he travels along what proves to be an extremely tedious journey. Aeneas faces Cyclops, Harpies, evil spirits, and many other difficulties as he makes his way to his destination. On the other hand, as one wrote, "The *Confessions* are a history of the young Augustine's fierce struggle to overcome his profligate ways and achieve a life of spiritual grace." Much of this second book is a story of Augustine's wearisome journey from an "unsaved" immoral life to a "redeemed" Christian life. Like Aeneas, Augustine faced many impediments along his spiritual journey, two of the largest being peer pressure and the teachings of Manichaeism. Aeneas' and Augustine's journeys are indeed similar.

Finally, Aeneas' and Augustine's goals are parallel. Aeneas wishes to arrive at his ultimate home. To Aeneas, this ultimate home is the future location of Rome. Because he was called by the gods to found a great city, Aeneas' journey eventually leads him to where this great city should be founded. Augustine, too, wishes to arrive at his ultimate home. The primary difference between the two goals, however, lies in the two protagonists' views of "home." Whereas, to Aeneas, it is merely an earthly location, to Augustine, the ultimate dwelling place is in heaven. Augustine's whole life looks forward to this end goal. As Dr. Noble wrote, "He (Augustine) regarded salvation as the goal of life" (Dr. Thomas F.X. Noble, *Western Civilization: Beyond Boundaries*).

Webster's 1828 Dictionary defines salvation as, "The redemption of man from the bondage of sin and liability to eternal death, and the conferring on him everlasting happiness." Therefore, Augustine's goal was, indirectly heaven, which, to a Christian, is attained at death.

Aeneas' and Augustine's journeys presented in *The Aeneid* and *Confessions,* respectively, are surprisingly parallel from beginning to end. Don Williams Jr. once stated, "The road of life twists and turns and no two directions are ever the same." However, the twists and turns of the road of life ultimately directed two travelers — one down a physical road and one down a spiritual road, in the same direction. In the case of Aeneas and Augustine, "two directions (were) ever the same" (thinkexist.com/quotation/the-road-of-life-twists-and-turns-and-no-two/763577.html). (John Micah)

Assignments

- Warm-up: What is the major thesis of this essay?

- Students should complete Concept Builder 15-B.

- Students should review reading(s) from the next chapter.

- Students should outline essay due at the end of the week.

- Per teacher instructions, students may answer orally, in a group setting, some of the essays that are not assigned as formal essays.

CONCEPT BUILDER 15-B
Style

Style is the distinctive, special way that an author writes his particular literary piece. Style refers not to what is said but how it is said. Among the many things that contribute to style are vocabulary, sentence structure, tone, figurative language, and dialogue. Identify the style of Augustine's *Confessions*.

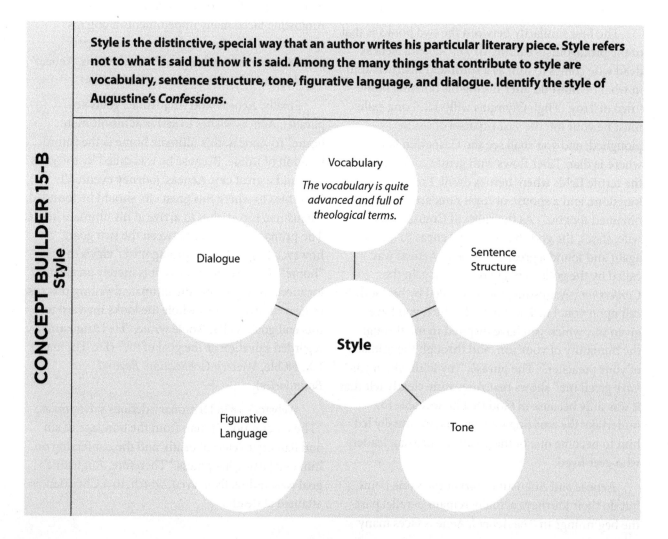

Vocabulary
The vocabulary is quite advanced and full of theological terms.

Sentence Structure

Dialogue

Style

Figurative Language

Tone

How We Can Know God

Excerpts from Book X

Having in the former books spoken of himself before his receiving the grace of baptism, in this Augustine confesses what he then was. But first, he enquires by what faculty we can know God at all, whence he enlarges on the mysterious character of the memory, wherein God, being made known, dwells, but which could not discover Him. Then he examines his own trials under the triple division of temptation, "lust of the flesh, lust of the eyes, and pride"; what Christian continency prescribes as to each. On Christ the Only Mediator, who heals and will heal all infirmities.

Let me know Thee, O Lord, who knowest me: let me know Thee, as I am known. Power of my soul, enter into it, and fit it for Thee, that Thou mayest have and hold it without spot or wrinkle. This is my hope, therefore do I speak; and in this hope do I rejoice, when I rejoice healthfully. Other things of this life are the less to be sorrowed for, the more they are sorrowed for; and the more to be sorrowed for, the less men sorrow for them. For behold, Thou lovest the truth, and he that doth it, cometh to the light. This would I do in my heart before Thee in confession: and in my writing, before many witnesses.

And from Thee, O Lord, unto whose eyes the abyss of man's conscience is naked, what could be hidden in me though I would not confess it? For I should hide Thee from me, not me from Thee. But now, for that my groaning is witness, that I am displeased with myself, Thou shinest out, and art pleasing, and beloved, and longed for; that I may be ashamed of myself, and renounce myself, and choose Thee, and neither please Thee nor myself, but in Thee. To Thee therefore, O Lord, am I open, whatever I am; and with what fruit I confess unto Thee, I have said. Nor do I it with words and sounds of the flesh, but with the words of my soul, and the cry of the thought which Thy ear knoweth. For when I am evil, then to confess to Thee is nothing else than to be displeased with myself; but when holy, nothing else than not to ascribe it to myself: because Thou, O Lord, blessest the godly, but first Thou justifieth him when ungodly. My confession then, O my God, in Thy sight, is made silently, and not silently. For in sound, it is silent; in affection, it cries aloud. For neither do I utter any thing right unto men, which Thou hast not before heard from me; nor dost Thou hear any such thing from me, which Thou hast not first said unto me.

What then have I to do with men, that they should hear my confessions — as if they could heal all my infirmities — a race, curious to know the lives of others, slothful to amend their own? Why seek they to hear from me what I am; who will not hear from Thee what themselves are? And how know they, when from myself they hear of myself, whether I say true; seeing no man knows what is in man, but the spirit of man which is in him? But if they hear from Thee of themselves, they cannot say, "The Lord lieth." For what is it to hear from Thee of themselves, but to know themselves? and who knoweth and saith, "It is false," unless himself lieth? But because charity believeth all things (that is, among those whom knitting unto itself it maketh one), I also, O Lord, will in such wise confess unto Thee, that men may hear, to whom I cannot demonstrate whether I confess truly; yet they believe me, whose ears charity openeth unto me.

But do Thou, my inmost Physician, make plain unto me what fruit I may reap by doing it. For the confessions of my past sins, which Thou hast forgiven and covered, that Thou mightest bless me in Thee, changing my soul by Faith and Thy Sacrament, when read and heard, stir up the heart, that it sleep not in despair and say "I cannot," but awake in the love of Thy mercy and the sweetness of Thy grace, whereby whoso is weak, is strong, when by it he became conscious of his own weakness. And the good delight to hear of the past evils of such as are now freed from them, not because they are evils, but because they have been and are not. With what fruit then, O Lord my God, to Whom my conscience daily confesseth, trusting more in the hope of Thy mercy than in her own innocency, with what fruit, I pray, do I by this book confess to men also in Thy presence what I now am, not what I have been? For that other fruit I have seen and spoken of. But what I now am, at the very time of making these confessions, divers desire to know, who have or have not known me, who have heard from me or of me; but their ear is not at my heart where I am, whatever I am. They wish then to hear me confess what I am within; whither neither their eye, nor ear, nor understanding can reach; they wish it, as ready to believe- but will they know? For charity, whereby they are good, telleth them that in my confessions I lie not; and she in them, believeth me.

But for what fruit would they hear this? Do they desire to joy with me, when they hear how near, by Thy gift, I approach unto Thee? and to pray for me, when they shall hear how much I am held back by my own weight? To such will I discover myself For it is no mean fruit, O Lord my God, that by many thanks should be given to Thee on our behalf, and Thou be by many entreated for us. Let the brotherly mind love in me what Thou teachest is to be loved, and lament in me what Thou teachest is to be lamented. Let a brotherly, not a stranger, mind, not that of the strange children, whose mouth talketh of vanity, and their right hand is a right hand of iniquity, but that brotherly mind which when it approveth, rejoiceth for me, and when it disapproveth me, is sorry for me; because whether it approveth or disapproveth, it loveth me. To such will I discover myself: they will breathe freely at my good deeds, sigh for my ill. My good deeds are Thine appointments, and Thy gifts; my evil ones are my offences, and Thy judgments. Let them breathe

freely at the one, sigh at the other; and let hymns and weeping go up into Thy sight, out of the hearts of my brethren, Thy censers. And do Thou, O Lord, be pleased with the incense of Thy holy temple, have mercy upon me according to Thy great mercy for Thine own name's sake; and no ways forsaking what Thou hast begun, perfect my imperfections.

This is the fruit of my confessions of what I am, not of what I have been, to confess this, not before Thee only, in a secret exultation with trembling, and a secret sorrow with hope; but in the ears also of the believing sons of men, sharers of my joy, and partners in my mortality, my fellow-citizens, and fellow-pilgrims, who are gone before, or are to follow on, companions of my way. These are Thy servants, my brethren, whom Thou willest to be Thy sons; my masters, whom Thou commandest me to serve, if I would live with Thee, of Thee. But this Thy Word were little did it only command by speaking, and not go before in performing. This then I do in deed and word, this I do under Thy wings; in over great peril, were not my soul subdued unto Thee under Thy wings, and my infirmity known unto Thee. I am a little one, but my Father ever liveth, and my Guardian is sufficient for me. For He is the same who begat me, and defends me: and Thou Thyself art all my good; Thou, Almighty, Who are with me, yea, before I am with Thee. To such then whom Thou commandest me to serve will I discover, not what I have been, but what I now am and what I yet am. But neither do I judge myself. Thus therefore I would be heard.

For Thou, Lord, dost judge me: because, although no man knoweth the things of a man, but the spirit of a man which is in him, yet is there something of man, which neither the spirit of man that is in him, itself knoweth. But Thou, Lord, knowest all of him, Who hast made him. Yet I, though in Thy sight I despise myself, and account myself dust and ashes; yet know I something of Thee, which I know not of myself. And truly, now we see through a glass darkly, not face to face as yet. So long therefore as I be absent from Thee, I am more present with myself than with Thee; and yet know I Thee that Thou art in no ways passible; but I, what temptations I can resist, what I cannot, I know not. And there is hope, because Thou art faithful, Who wilt not suffer us to be tempted above that we are able; but wilt with the temptation also make a way to escape, that we may be able to bear it. I will confess then what I know of myself, I will confess also what I know not of myself. And that because what I do know of myself, I know by Thy shining upon me; and what I know not of myself, so long know I not it, until my darkness be made as the noon-day in Thy countenance.

Not with doubting, but with assured consciousness, do I love Thee, Lord. Thou hast stricken my heart with Thy word, and I loved Thee. Yea also heaven, and earth, and all that therein is, behold, on every side they bid me love Thee; nor cease to say so unto all, that they may be without excuse. But more deeply wilt Thou have mercy on whom Thou wilt have mercy, and wilt have compassion on whom Thou hast had compassion: else in deaf ears do the heaven and the earth speak Thy praises. But what do I love, when I love Thee? not beauty of bodies, nor the fair harmony of time, nor the brightness of the light, so gladsome to our eyes, nor sweet melodies of varied songs, nor the fragrant smell of flowers, and ointments, and spices, not manna and honey, not limbs acceptable to embracements of flesh. None of these I love, when I love my God; and yet I love a kind of light, and melody, and fragrance, and meat, and embracement when I love my God, the light, melody, fragrance, meat, embracement of my inner man: where there shineth unto my soul what space cannot contain, and there soundeth what time beareth not away, and there smelleth what breathing disperseth not, and there tasteth what eating diminisheth not, and there clingeth what satiety divorceth not. This is it which I love when I love my God.

Assignments

- Warm-up: How can we know God?
- Students should complete Concept Builder 15-C.
- Students should write rough draft of assigned essay.
- The teacher may correct rough drafts.

CONCEPT BUILDER 15-C
Style: Prayer Form

In *Confessions* Augustine writes in a prayer form. In other words, he follows the same pattern. From Book I, give examples of how this form is exhibited.

The passage begins with adoration and praise of God.

Great art Thou, O Lord, and greatly to be praised; great is Thy power, and Thy wisdom infinite.

↓

Next, is a delineation of the awesome power of God.

↓

Mankind's relative insignificance in relation to God's importance.

↓

Mankind is empowered by relationship with God.

Augustine's Legacy

Augustine remains a central figure both in Christianity and in the history of Western thought. Heavily influenced by Plato, Augustine was an important part of the reintroduction of Greek thought and its entrance into the Christian, and subsequently the European, intellectual tradition. In a sense, Augustine was the first Renaissance man. Also important was his early and influential writing on the human will, which is a core topic in psychology and ethics, and one which became a focus for later philosophers such as Schopenhauer and Nietzsche, writers like John Milton, and psychologists such as Sigmund Freud and Carl Jung. Only Plato has had more impact on western thought.

Gerald Bonner writes, "It is largely due to Augustine's influence that Western Christianity subscribes to the doctrine of original sin, and the Roman Catholic Church holds that baptisms and ordinations done outside of the Roman Catholic Church can be valid (the Roman Catholic Church recognizes ordinations done in Eastern Orthodox and Oriental Orthodox churches, but not in Protestant churches, and recognizes baptisms done in nearly all Christian churches). Catholic theologians generally subscribe to Augustine's belief that God exists outside of time in the 'eternal present,' with time existing only within the created universe" (Gerald Bonner, *St. Augustine of Hippo: Life and Controversies*, 3rd edition (Norwich, UK: Canterbury Press 2002). In that sense, Augustine deeply influenced John Calvin.

The Consecration of Saint Augustine by Jaume Huguet, c.1466 (PD-Art).

Augustine's writings were at the heart of Reinhold Niebuhr's theory of just war.

Thomas Aquinas took much from Augustine while creating his own unique view of Greek and Christian thought.

Assignments

- Warm-up: What legacy does Augustine have?
- Students should complete Concept Builder 15-D.
- Students will re-write corrected copies of essay due tomorrow.

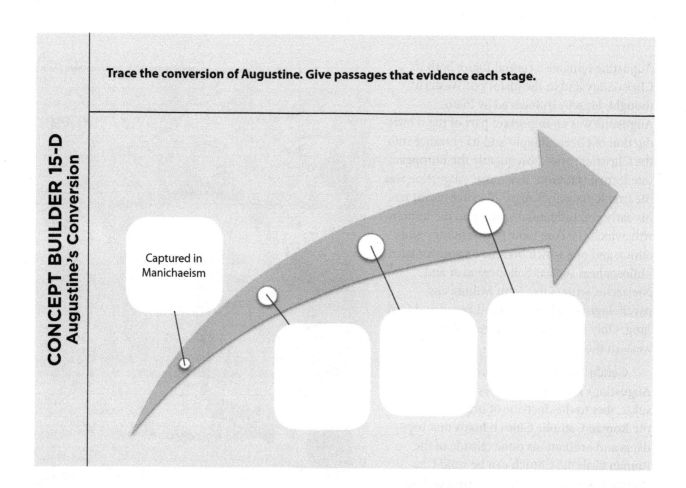

CONCEPT BUILDER 15-D
Augustine's Conversion

Trace the conversion of Augustine. Give passages that evidence each stage.

Captured in Manichaeism

Augustine's Challenge for Today

Born in A.D. 354, St. Augustine the Blessed was a Latin-speaking theologian and philosopher whose writings were very influential in the development of Christianity. One of his major works is his book *The City of God*. In this book he challenges Christians to be the salt and light in a world that is becoming increasingly dark. Today the age-old question still begs for an answer, "How can one be salt and light? How can one change the world? What can one do?"

The desert father, St. John the Dwarf, once prayed for "strength to continue the fight." The fight that he was talking about was the spiritual warfare "For we do not wrestle against flesh and blood, but against principalities, against powers, against the rulers of the darkness of this age, against spiritual hosts of wickedness in the heavenly places" (Eph. 6:12, NKJV). This strength, the strength needed to fight the good fight, pray, fast, take up our crosses, and follow, is not a strength that the world is familiar with. This strength comes through submission, a dying to our own will. The witness of one who has died to the world, and is strong to continue in the fight, is a powerful light. The Monk Evagrius said, "Charity and meekness strengthen the soul. Repentance and humility establish it." (www.ortho-dox.net/gleanings/love.html).

Submission does not come naturally, and pride gets in the way. The opposite of pride, however, is humility, this and repentance are our greatest assets in overcoming our own will and being able to submit. St. Isaac of Syria said, "This life has been given to you for repentance. Do not waste it on vain pursuits" (orthodoxinfo.com/praxis/pr_prayer.aspx).

Here, St. Isaac is urging one to give up pride and to repent and become humble. In St. Augustine's *The City of God*, he writes, "God is always trying to give good things to us, but our hands are too full to receive them" (www.goodreads.com/quotes/75226). This is proclaiming that unless we put aside our vain pursuits, unless God is made above all in one's life, than we are incapable of receiving the grace He longs to give us . . . the grace that comes through repentance and humility.

The repentant man; the submissive man; the humble man . . . these are the attributes that will change the world. As one of the desert fathers said, "The goal of human freedom is not in freedom itself, nor is it in man, but in God. By giving man freedom, God has yielded to man a piece of His divine authority, but with the intention that man himself would voluntarily bring it as a sacrifice to God, as a most perfect offering" (orthodoxwayoflife.blogspot.com/2010/01/what-is-freedom_25.html). One cannot change the world in some huge majestic way, but in one person.

When St. Augustine wrote his book *The City of God*, he was challenged to be a clear light. Today it is much the same, but one is reminded that St. Augustine's life itself as witness of being salt and light; his strong character no longer asking the question, "How can one change the world?" The question that now pleads for an answer is, "Who will be *this* change? Will I?" (Anna Grace)

Assignments

- Warm-up: What does the author mean by this: "Who will be this change? Will I?"
- Students should complete Concept Builder 15-E.
- Essays are due. Students should take the chapter 15 test.

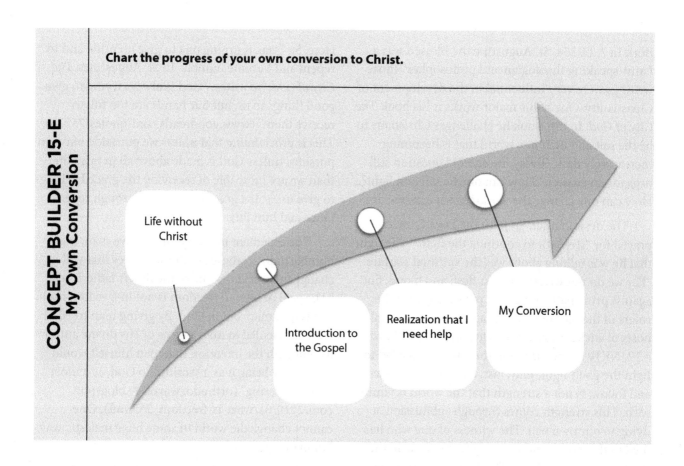

CONCEPT BUILDER 15-E
My Own Conversion

Chart the progress of your own conversion to Christ.

Life without Christ

Introduction to the Gospel

Realization that I need help

My Conversion

Chapter 16

(500 B.C.–A.D. 100):
Japanese Literature

First Thoughts

Japanese literature is one of the oldest and richest national literatures. It may seem strange to Western literary tastes, but that in no way denigrates the literature. Japanese is new, refreshing and offers Western readers many important insights into this Far Eastern culture. Indigenous Japanese literature, such as the haiku verse, has had a substantial impact on literature in many parts of the world.

Chapter Learning Objectives

In chapter 16 we explore Japanese poetry and its impact on Japanese society and the world.

As a result of this chapter study you will be able to . . .

1. All of the above Japanese poets were never merely observers of a scene but were participants in it and through their participation drew their readers into the events described in their poems. Evaluate this statement.

2. Hitomaro's "I Love Her Like the Leaves" has naturalistic tendencies. Explain.

3. Japanese women produced more art than their Western counterparts. Why?

4. Read and compare *The Pillow Book* by Sei Shonagan, and *The Tales of Genji* by Murasaki Shikibu.

Weekly Essay Options: Begin on page 273 of the Teacher Guide.

Reading ahead: *The Bhagavad-Gîtâ*, author unknown, *Panchatantra*, attributed to Bidpai.

223

Japanese Literature

Background Japanese literature in particular is indebted to Chinese influences. Chinese literature was introduced to Japan sometime in the third century A.D. Nevertheless, during the ancient period, at least, literature evolved with a particularly unique flavor.

A consistent theme in Japanese literature over the centuries has been the tension within a very severe caste system. Japanese literature is also very sensitive to the place of nature in life. In that sense, Japanese literature would fall into the romantic worldview category. Finally, Japanese literature manifests an uncharacteristically large number of female writers as compared to other cultures.

Scholars customarily divide the general history of Japan into periods based on such changes in governmental institutions as the Heian period (794–1185), the Muromachi period (1333–1603), and the Tokugawa period (1603–1868). The literary history of Japan can be broken down according to these same periods. The major dividing line between the traditional and modern periods of the country is the Meiji Restoration of 1868, which also signaled a new era of modernization and contact with the West.

Very early in its existence, Japanese literature exhibited several nuances. The development of the *waka* in Japanese literature was as radical an event as the development of the sonnet or iambic pentameter rhyme in Western literature.

Originally, *waka* were composed to celebrate victories in battle or for religious reasons, and this tradition of poetry for public occasions carried through to the first great age of written waka in the seventh and eighth centuries, with highly wrought *nagauta* "long poems," consisting of alternating "lines" of five and seven syllables, being composed for performance on public occasions at the imperial court. At the same time, *tanka* "short poems," consisting of five "lines" in the pattern of 5-7-5-7-7

Kinkaku at Kinkakuji (Rokuonji), a Buddhist temple in Kyoto, Japan. Photographer and date unknown (PD-US).

syllables, became a useful shorthand for private communication between friends and lovers, and the ability to compose a tanka on a given topic became an essential skill for any gentleman or lady at court. While young men today would send flowers as a token of affection for a young lady, in 11th-century Japan, young men would send a *tanka*. Over time, the *tanka* became a preferred manifestation of the Japanese poetry genre.

Finally, the initial 5-7-5 of a *tanka* became a poetic form on its own, the *haiku*, and great poets came to be found among the samurai warriors and the townsfolk of early modern Japan.

Assignments

- Warm-up: Give an example of romanticism from Japanese poetry.

- Students should complete Concept Builder 16-A.

- Students should review the required reading(s) *before* the assigned chapter begins.

- Teachers may want to discuss assigned reading(s) with students.

- Teachers shall assign the required essay. The rest of the essays can be outlined, answered with shorter answers, discussed, or skipped.

- Students will review all readings for chapter 16.

CONCEPT BUILDER 16-A
Active Reading

Read "I Loved Her Like the Leaves" by Hitomaro, and respond to the following:

I loved her like the leaves,
The lush leaves of spring
That weighed the branches of the willows
Standing on the jutting bank
Where we two walked together.
While she was of this world.
My life was built on her;
But man cannot flout
The laws of this world.
To the wide fields where the heat haze shimmers,
Hidden in a white cloud,
White as white mulberry scarf,
She soared like the morning bird
Hidden in a white cloud,
White as white mulberry scarf,
She soared like the morning bird
Hidden from our world like the setting sun.
The child she left as token
Whimpers, begs for food; but always
Finding nothing that I might give,
Like birds that gather rice-heads in their beaks,
I pick him up and clasp him in my arms.
By the pillows where we lay,
My wife and I, as one,
The daylight I pass lonely till the dusk,
The black night I lie sighting till the dawn,
I grieve, yet know no remedy:
I pine, yet have no way to meet her.
The one I love, men say,
Is in the hills of Hagai,
So I labour my way there,
Smashing rock-roots in my path,
Yet get no joy from it.
For, as I knew her in this world,
I find no the dimmest trace.

A simile is a comparison with the words "like" or "as." What is the simile?

What is the tone of this poem? How do you know?

Identify other similes.

Who is the speaker, and what relationship does he have to the deceased?

www.humanistictexts.org/hitomaro.htm.

Ono no Komachi

Nothing is known about Ono no Komachi except that she belonged to a literary family, was perhaps an attendant to Emperor Nimmei (d. 850), and exchanged poems with some of the major male poets of the mid-800s. Ono no Komachi wrote *tanka* poems (Geoffrey Bownas and Anthony Thwaite, translators, *The Penguin Book of Japanese Verse*, New York: Penguin Books, 1964, p. 84–85).

The luster of the flowers
Has faded and passed,
While on idle things
I have spent my body
In the world's long rains.

How helpless my heart!
Were the stream to tempt,
My body, like a reed
Severed at the roots,
Would drift along, I think.

Assignments

- Warm-up: Write a tanka poem.

- Students should complete Concept Builder 16-B.

- Students should review reading(s) from the next chapter.

- Students should outline essay due at the end of the week.

- Per teacher instructions, students may answer orally, in a group setting, some of the essays that are not assigned as formal essays.

CONCEPT BUILDER 16-B The Japanese Haiku	The Japanese haiku is a three-lined poem that is divided into lines by syllable count. The syllabic pattern is 5-7-5.
	Winter-evening snow . . . **The uncompleted bridge is all** **An arch of whiteness.** **Basho**
	Also, every haiku has a reference to nature. Write two haikus.
	Haikus 1 Haikus 2

www.haikupoetshut.com/basho1.html.

Kakinomoto no Hitomaro

Background Much of what is known about Hitomaro has been gleaned from his poems. From his poems we learn that Hitomaro was a middle-ranking government official and served as court poet to at least three sovereigns: Emperor Temmu (r. 673–686), Empress Jitô (690–697) and Emperor Mommu (697–707). Many of his poems were written for public occasions. Other poems were written on occasions in his life when he was particularly moved — like the death of his wife (Ibid., p. 24–26).

In Praise of Empress Jito

Our great Empress
Who rules in tranquility,
True god of true god,
Has done a divine thing.
Deep in the valley
Of Yoshino's foaming torrents
She builds high
Her tall palace.

She climbs and looks
Across her lands:
The mountain folds,
Like green walls,
As offerings
From their deity,
When spring comes
Bring cherry garlands:
When autumn begins
They bring crimson leaves.
The river spirit too
Makes gift of sacred food:
In the upper shoals
He sets the cormorants,
In the lower shallows
He spreads small nets.
Mountain and river too
Come near and serve
This godlike land.

Kakinomoto no Hitomaro by Utagawa Kuniyoshi, c.1844 (PD-Art).

227

I Loved Her Like the Leaves

I loved her like the leaves,
The lush leaves of spring
That weighed the branches of the willows
Standing on the jutting bank
Where we two walked together.
While she was of this world.
My life was built on her;
But man cannot flout
The laws of this world.
To the wide fields where the heat haze shimmers,
Hidden in a white cloud,
White as white mulberry scarf,
She soared like the morning bird
Hidden in a white cloud,
White as white mulberry scarf,
She soared like the morning bird
Hidden from our world like the setting sun.
The child she left as token
Whimpers, begs for food; but always
Finding nothing that I might give,
Like birds that gather rice-heads in their beaks,
I pick him up and clasp him in my arms.
By the pillows where we lay,
My wife and I, as one,
The daylight I pass lonely till the dusk,
The black night I lie sighting till the dawn,
I grieve, yet know no remedy:
I pine, yet have no way to meet her.
The one I love, men say,

Kakinomoto no Hitomaro by Kikuchi Yosai, date unknown (PD-Japan-oldphoto).

Is in the hills of Hagai,
So I labour my way there,
Smashing rock-roots in my path,
Yet get no joy from it.
For, as I knew her in this world,
I find no the dimmest trace.

Ibid., p. 25–26.

Assignments

- Warm-up: Was Hitomaro writing this poem for the public? How do you know?
- Students should complete Concept Builder 16-C.
- Students should write rough draft of assigned essay.
- The teacher may correct rough drafts.

Japanese poets often described, in great detail, an object or event. Their images and thoughts were connected. Compose a poem with a sequence of associated thoughts. You must begin and end with an image of the same object. (See example below.)

Oh, so small, but you make my world so large.

Distant, muffled sounds become sharp, clear resonance.

My little hearing aids.

You save my life — I hear the angry bus, I hear the vengeful train.

My little hearing aids.

Minamoto no Toshiyori

Background Minamoto no Toshiyori (most scholars call him Shunrai) (1055?–1129?) was born in Kyûshû, Japan, while his father, Minamoto no Tsunenobu, was governor. This provincial, backwater upbringing may be one of the reasons that he failed to find favor in the court of Emperor Horikawa (1079–1107; 1086–1107).

Shunrai was an innovator in waka composition. The word *waka* is made up of two parts: *wa* meaning "Japanese" and *ka* meaning "poem" or "song." Today, the type of *waka* best known outside of Japan is probably the *haiku*, a sequence of three "lines" of five, seven, and five syllables and describing an aspect of nature. *Haiku* are now written in many languages other than Japanese, and widely in Japan itself. They are, however, a relatively late form of *waka*, beginning to be written in the 17th century, by which time the Japanese had already been writing poetry for a thousand years.

Shunrai, the master of the waka, had several disputes with the arch-conservative Fujiwara. The Fujiwara family was a noble family that controlled the Japanese emperors and dominated the imperial court from the 9th to the 12th century. The Fujiwara period, however, was marked by a great flowering of literature and the arts, and Shunrai was one of the most important of these artists. Unfortunately, though, Shunrai failed to win favor with the Fujiwara clan and found himself a pariah in 11th century Japanese society. This perspective is reflected in his poetry. Nonetheless, Shunrai's skill could not be ignored, and he was eventually rewarded by Emperor Horikawa with the commission to produce an anthology from which many of the following poems come.

The wind howling through the pines —
The forlorn feeling of autumn;
Women fulling cloth
In a hamlet by the Tama River.
(Ibid., p. 87).

It was not for this
I prayed at the holy shrines.
That she would become
As pitiless and as cold
As the storm on Hase's Hills.
(www.geocities.com/jisei/ogura3.h).

Assignments

- Warm-up: Write a haiku poem.
- Students should complete Concept Builder 16-D.
- Students will re-write corrected copies of essay due tomorrow.

Japanese poets struggled to describe things that they could not explain in prose. Describe the following creature and give it a name, any name, even a nonsensical one.

CONCEPT BUILDER 16-D
Description

Japanese Authors

Murasakai Shikubu

Background Murasaki Shikubu was a contemporary of Izumi Shikibu (but was unrelated). They were employed by the same empress and apparently did not like each other very much. Nonetheless, they were enormously gifted writers. Both women kept diaries of their time in court. Murasaki Shikubu also wrote the famous novel *Tales of Genji* in 1002 — about 600 years before Europeans were to write a novel!

Diary Entry (A.D. 1007–1010) As the autumn season approaches, the tree-tops near the pond, the bushes near the stream, are dyed in varying tints whose colors grow deeper in the mellow light of evening. The murmuring sound of waters mingles all the night through with the never-ceasing recitation of sutras which appeal more to one's heart as the breezes grow cooler.

Izumi Shikibu

Background Izumi Shikibu (974?–1034?) was perhaps the greatest poet of Japanese literature. Like so much ancient Japanese poetry written by women, Shikibu's poetry was both religious and practical. "Although the wind/blows terribly here,/ the moonlight also leaks/between the roof planks/of this ruined house" evidences that Shikibu espoused the Buddhist optimism — the moonlight leaks through the roof along with rain — but also laments that she has to live in a ruined house (www.digital.library.upenn.edu/women/omori/court/murasaki.html).

The cuckoo sings on the same branch

With voice unchanged,

That you shall know.

The night passes,

We dream no faintest dreams —

There is no night for that.

Sei Shonagon

Background Another contemporary of Izumi Shikibu and Murasaki Shikibu was Sei Shonagon. She was the author of the entertaining *Pillow Book* written a few years before *The Tales of Genji*. The *Pillow Book* is a sort of "Spoon River Anthology" of the tenth century Heian royal court. It is a witty collection of colorful characters and incidents in this important period of Japanese history. Sei Shonagon invented the "zuihitsu" form of writing, which was a sort of collection of observations made by a single author. The American author Mark Twain made this literary style famous several centuries later (e.g., *Innocents Abroad*). Students are urged to read *Pillow Book*.

Assignments

- Warm-up: Write a poem that explores an unspoken feeling, such as joy, loneliness, or love.

- Students should complete Concept Builder 16-E.

- Essays are due. Students should take the chapter 16 test.

CONCEPT BUILDER 16-E
Descriptive Poetry vs. Art

Write a poem about and then draw a picture of an elephant lying down. Entitle each artistic rendition "An Elegant Repose."

A poem:

An Elegant Repose

A picture:

233

Chapter 17

(1400 B.C.-A.D. 1900)
Indian Literature

First Thoughts In India and other East Asian countries, religion and culture — especially literature — are more intertwined than they are in the West. Therefore, if one is to study East Asian literature, one is obligated to read religious texts.

During the centuries in which Buddhism was establishing itself in the east of India, religious changes were occurring in the west that produced Hinduism, which is the dominant religion in India today. The main ancient sources of information with regard to these Hindu beliefs and practices are the two great epics, the *Ramyana* and the *Mahabhrata*. The former is based on legend and ascribed to one man, Valmki. The latter is a composite production, begun probably as early as the fourth or fifth century B.C. and completed by the end of A.D. 500. *The Bhagavad-Gîtâ* is merely an episode in the *Mahabhrata*. The poem is a dialogue between Prince Arjuna, the brother of King Yudhisthira, and Vishnu, the Supreme God, incarnated as Krishna, and wearing the disguise of a charioteer. The conversation takes place in a war-chariot, stationed between the armies of the Kauravas and Pndavas, who are about to engage in battle.

To the Western reader, much of the discussion seems disjointed and illogical. To East Asians these words are sacred and pregnant with spirituality. To insist upon logic and sequence would be sacrilegious.

Chapter Learning Objectives In chapter 17 we examine South Asian literature and we are amazed — perhaps inspired — at the religious fervency exhibited by Hindu authors.

As a result of this chapter study you will be able to . . .

1. Based on *The Bhagavad-Gîtâ*, describe the panoply of gods presented. Which ones exhibit Judeo-Christian characteristics?

2. Discuss the moral imperatives advanced in each fable in *Panchatantra*.

3. Create a fable to illustrate a biblical truth.

234

Weekly Essay Options: Begin on page 273 of the Teacher Guide.

Reading ahead: *The Rubaiyat* by Omar Kyayyam, the Koran.

 History connections: *World History* chapter 17, "Indian (South Asian) History."

The Bhagavad-Gîtâ

When he beheld the host of Pandavas
Raja Duryôdhana to Drona drew,
And spake these words: "Ah, Guru! see this line,
How vast it is of Pandu fighting-men,
Embattled by the son of Drupada,
Thy scholar in the war! Therein stand ranked
Chiefs like Arjuna, like to Bhîma chiefs,
Benders of bows; Virâta, Yuyudhân,
Drupada, eminent upon his car,
Dhrishtaket, Chekitân, Kasi's stout lord,
Purujit, Kuntibhôj, and Saivya,
With Yudhâmanyu, and Uttamauj
Subhadra's child; and Drupadi's; — all famed!
All mounted on their shining chariots!
On our side, too, — thou best of Brahmans! see
Excellent chiefs, commanders of my line,
Whose names I joy to count: thyself the first,
Then Bhishma, Karna, Kripa fierce in fight,
Vikarna, Aswatthâman; next to these
Strong Saumadatti, with full many more
Valiant and tried, ready this day to die
For me their king, each with his weapon grasped,
Each skilful in the field. Weakest — meseems —
Our battle shows where Bhishma holds command,
And Bhima, fronting him, something too strong!
Have care our captains nigh to Bhishma's ranks
Prepare what help they may! Now, blow my shell!"
Then, at the signal of the aged king,
With blare to wake the blood, rolling around
Like to a lion's roar, the trumpeter
Blew the great Conch; and, at the noise of it,
Trumpets and drums, cymbals and gongs and horns
Burst into sudden clamor; as the blasts
Of loosened tempest, such the tumult seemed!
Then might be seen, upon their car of gold
Yoked with white steeds, blowing their battle-shells,
Krishna the God, Arjuna at his side:

Krishna, with knotted locks, blew his great conch
Carved of the "Gaint's bone;" Arjuna blew
Indra's loud gift; Bhima the terrible —
Wolf-bellied Bhima — blew a long reed-conch;
And Yudhisthira, Kunti's blameless son,
Winded a mighty shell, "Victory's Voice";
And Nakula blew shrill upon his conch
Named the "Sweet-sounding," Sahadev on his
Called "Gem-bedecked," and Kasi's Prince on his.
Sikhandi on his car, Dhrishtadyumn,
Virâta, Sâtyaki the Unsubdued,
Drupada, with his sons, (O Lord of Earth!)
Long-armed Subhadra's children, all blew loud
So that the clangor shook their foemen's hearts,
With quaking earth and thundering heav'n.
Then 'twas —
Beholding Dhritirashtra's battle set,
Weapons unsheathing, bows drawn forth, the war
Instant to break — Arjun, whose ensign-badge
Was Hanuman the monkey, spake this thing
To Krishna the Divine, his charioteer:
"Drive, Dauntless One! to yonder open ground
Betwixt the armies; I would see more nigh
These who will fight with us, those we must slay
To-day, in war's arbitrament; for, sure,
On bloodshed all are bent who throng this plain,
Obeying Dhritirashtra's sinful son."

Thus, by Arjuna prayed (O Bharata!)
Between the hosts that heavenly Charioteer
Drove the bright car, reining its milk-white steeds
Where Bhishma led, and Drona, and their Lords.
"See!" spake he to Arjuna, "where they stand,
Thy kindred of the Kurus:" and the Prince
Marked on each hand the kinsmen of his house,
Grandsires and sires, uncles and brothers and sons,
Cousins and sons-in-law and nephews, mixed

With friends and honored elders; some this side,
Some that side ranged: and, seeing those opposed,
Such kith grown enemies — Arjuna's heart
Melted with pity, while he uttered this:

Krishna! as I behold, come here to shed
Their common blood, yon concourse of our kin,
My members fail, my tongue dries in my mouth,
A shudder thrills my body, and my hair
Bristles with horror; from my weak hand slips
Gandîv, the goodly bow; a fever burns
My skin to parching; hardly may I stand;
The life within me seems to swim and faint;
Nothing do I foresee save woe and wail!
It is not good, O Keshav! nought of good
Can spring from mutual slaughter! Lo, I hate
Triumph and domination, wealth and ease,
Thus sadly won! Aho! what victory
Can bring delight, Govinda! what rich spoils
Could profit; what rule recompense; what span
Of life itself seem sweet, bought with such blood?
Seeing that these stand here, ready to die,
For whose sake life was fair, and pleasure pleased,
And power grew precious: — grandsires, sires, and
sons.
Brothers, and fathers-in-law, and sons-in-law,
Elders and friends! Shall I deal death on these
Even though they seek to slay us? Not one blow,
O Madhusudan! will I strike to gain
The rule of all Three Worlds; then, how much less
To seize an earthly kingdom! Killing these
Must breed but anguish, Krishna! If they be

Guilty, we shall grow guilty by their deaths;
Their sins will light on us, if we shall slay
Those sons of Dhritirashtra, and our kin;
What peace could come of that, O Madhava?
For if indeed, blinded by lust and wrath,
These cannot see, or will not see, the sin
Of kingly lines o'erthrown and kinsmen slain,
How should not we, who see, shun such a crime —
We who perceive the guilt and feel the shame —
Oh, thou Delight of Men, Janârdana?
By overthrow of houses perisheth
Their sweet continuous household piety,
And — rites neglected, piety extinct —
Enters impiety upon that home;
Its women grow unwomaned, whence there spring
Mad passions, and the mingling-up of castes,
Sending a Hell-ward road that family,
And whoso wrought its doom by wicked wrath.
Nay, and the souls of honored ancestors
Fall from their place of peace, being bereft
Of funeral-cakes and the wan death-water.
So teach our holy hymns. Thus, if we slay
Kinsfolk and friends for love of earthly power,
Ahovat! what an evil fault it were!
Better I deem it, if my kinsmen strike,
To face them weaponless, and bare my breast
To shaft and spear, than answer blow with blow.

So speaking, in the face of those two hosts,
Arjuna sank upon his chariot-seat,
And let fall bow and arrows, sick at heart.

Assignments

- Warm-up: Contrast a Hindu hero with a Christian one.
- Students should complete Concept Builder 17-A.
- Students should review the required reading(s) *before* the assigned chapter begins.
- Teachers may want to discuss assigned reading(s) with students.
- Teachers shall assign the required essay. The rest of the essays can be outlined, answered with shorter answers, discussed, or skipped.
- Students will review all readings for chapter 17.

The poem is a dialogue between Prince Arjuna, the brother of King Yudhisthira, and Vishnu, the Supreme God, incarnated as Krishna, and wearing the disguise of a charioteer. The conversation takes place in a war-chariot, stationed between the armies of the Kauravas and Pndavas, who are about to engage in battle. Read this excerpt from *The Bhagavad-Gîtâ* and respond to the following:

When he beheld the host of Pandavas
Raja Duryôdhana to Drona drew,
And spake these words: "Ah, Guru! see this line,
How vast it is of Pandu fighting-men,
Embattled by the son of Drupada,
Thy scholar in the war! Therein stand ranked
Chiefs like Arjuna, like to Bhîma chiefs,
Benders of bows; Virâta, Yuyudhân,
Drupada, eminent upon his car,
Dhrishtaket, Chekitân, Kasi's stout lord,
Purujit, Kuntibhôj, and Saivya,
With Yudhâmanyu, and Uttamauj
Subhadra's child; and Drupadi's; — all famed!
All mounted on their shining chariots!
On our side, too, — thou best of Brahmans! see
Excellent chiefs, commanders of my line,
Whose names I joy to count: thyself the first,
Then Bhishma, Karna, Kripa fierce in fight,
Vikarna, Aswatthâman; next to these
Strong Saumadatti, with full many more
Valiant and tried, ready this day to die
For me their king, each with his weapon grasped,
Each skilful in the field. Weakest — meseems —
Our battle shows where Bhishma holds command,
And Bhima, fronting him, something too strong!
Have care our captains nigh to Bhishma's ranks
Prepare what help they may! Now, blow my shell!"
Then, at the signal of the aged king,
With blare to wake the blood, rolling around
Like to a lion's roar, the trumpeter
Blew the great Conch; and, at the noise of it,
Trumpets and drums, cymbals and gongs and horns
Burst into sudden clamor; as the blasts
Of loosened tempest, such the tumult seemed!
Then might be seen, upon their car of gold
Yoked with white steeds, blowing their battle-shells,
Krishna the God, Arjuna at his side:
Krishna, with knotted locks, blew his great conch
Carved of the "Gaint's bone;" Arjuna blew

Alliteration is the repetition of consonant sounds. Find two examples.

The author compares the sound of the conch shell to what?

237

Panchatantra
Bidpai

Background One of India's most influential contributions to world literature, the *Panchatantra* consists of five books of animal fables that were compiled, in their current form, between the third and fifth centuries A.D. . . . . The tales' self-proclaimed purpose is to educate the sons of royalty.

Although the original author's or compiler's name is unknown, an Arabic translation from about A.D. 750 attributes the *Panchatantra* to a Hindu wise man called Bidpai.

These fables, some of which were beast fables, greatly influenced European fable writers (perhaps even Geoffrey Chaucer).

The Foolish Friend

A king, while visiting his wives' apartments, took a monkey from a neighboring stable for a pet. He kept him constantly close at hand for his amusement, for as it is said, parrots, partridges, doves, rams, monkeys, and such creatures are a king's natural companions.

It goes without saying that the monkey, fed on the various dishes that the king gave him, grew large and was given respect by all who surrounded the king. Indeed, the king, due to his love and exceeding trust of the monkey, even gave him a sword to carry.

In the vicinity of the palace the king had a grove artfully planted with many trees of various sorts. Early in the springtime the king noticed how beautiful the grove was. Its blossoms exuded a magnificent fragrance, while swarms of bees sang praise to the god of love. Thus overcome by love, he entered the grove with his favorite wife. He ordered all his servants to wait for him at the entrance.

After having pleasantly strolled through and observing the grove, he grew tired and said to his monkey, "I want to sleep a little while in this arbor of flowers. Take care that nothing disturbs me!" Having said this, the king fell asleep.

Presently a bee, pursuing the aroma of the flowers, betel, and musk, flew up and lit on his head. Seeing this, the monkey thought angrily, "What is this? Am I to allow this common creature to bite the king before my very eyes?"

With that he proceeded to drive it away. However, in spite of the monkey's defense, the bee approached the king again and again. Finally, blinded by anger, the monkey drew his sword and struck down the bee with a single blow. However, the same blow also split the king's head.

The queen, who was sleeping next to the king jumped up in terror. Seeing the crime, she said, "Oh, oh, you foolish monkey! What have you done to the king who placed such trust in you?"

The monkey explained how it had happened, but thereafter he was shunned and scorned by everyone. Thus it is said, "Do not choose a fool for a friend, for the king was killed by a monkey."

And I say, "It is better to have a clever enemy than a foolish friend" (www.pitt.edu/~dash/panchatantra.html).

Assignments

- Warm-up: Compare a fable from the *Panchatantra* with a fable from *The Canterbury Tales*.

- Students should complete Concept Builder 17-B.

- Students should review reading(s) from next chapter.

- Students should outline essays due at the end of the week.

- Per teacher instructions, students may answer orally, in a group setting, some of the essays that are not assigned as the formal essay.

CONCEPT BUILDER 17-B
Heroes

So far we have met several different heroes. Compare three of them: Achilles, Oedipus, and Arjuna. When you finish, compare these heroes to a family member.

Hero	Views Toward the Gods	Personal Flaws	Personal Strengths
Achilles	Basically is unimpressed with the gods and makes no effort to please them.	Prideful to a fault.	Very brave and strong.
Oedipus			
Arjuna			
A Family Member			

Fables of India

The Gold-Giving Snake

In a certain place there lived a Brahman by the name of Haridatta. He tilled the soil, but his time in the field brought him no harvest. Then one day, as the hottest hours were just over, tormented by the heat, he lay down in the shade of a tree in the middle of his field for a sleep. He saw a frightful snake, decorated with a large hood, crawl from an anthill a little way off, and thought to himself, "This is surely the goddess of the field, and I have not once paid her homage. That is why the field remains barren. I must bring her an offering." After thus thinking it over, he got some milk, poured it into a basin, then went to the anthill, and said, "Oh, protector of this field, for a long time I did not know that you live here. For this reason I have not yet brought you an offering. Please forgive me!"

Having said this, he set forth the milk, and went home. The next day he returned to see what had happened, and he found a dinar in the basin. And thus it continued day by day. He brought the snake milk, and always found a dinar there the next morning.

One day the Brahman asked his son to take the milk to the anthill, and he himself went into the village. The son brought the milk, set it there, and returned home. When he came back the next day and found a dinar, he said to himself, "This anthill must be full of gold dinars. I will kill the snake and take them all at once!"

Having decided this, the Brahman's son returned the next day with the milk and a club. As he gave the milk to the snake, he struck her on the head with the club. The snake, as fate willed it, escaped with her life. Filled with rage, she bit the boy with her sharp, poisoned teeth, and the boy fell dead at once. His people built a funeral pyre not far from the field and cremated him.

Two days later his father returned. When he discovered under what circumstances his son had died, he said that justice had prevailed. The next morning, he once again took milk, went to the anthill, and praised the snake with a loud voice. A good while later the snake appeared in the entrance to the anthill, and said, "You come here from greed, letting even your grief for your son pass by. From now on friendship between you and me will no longer be possible. Your son, in his youthful lack of understanding, struck me. I bit him. How can I forget the club's blow? How can you forget the pain and sorrow for your son?" After saying this she gave him a costly pearl for a pearl chain, said, "Do not come back," and disappeared into her cave.

The Brahman took the pearl, cursed his son's lack of understanding, and returned home.

The Brahman's Wife and the Mongoose

In a certain city there lived a Brahman by the name of Devasarman. His wife gave birth to a son, and then to a mongoose. Full of love for her children, she cared for the mongoose like a son, nursing him at her breast, rubbing him with salve, and so forth. However, she did not trust him, thinking that in keeping with the evil nature of his species he might harm her son.

As is rightly said: "A son will bring joy to his parents' heart, even if he is uneducated, bad, malformed, foolish, and sinful." And as also is said: "Sandalwood salve cools and soothes, but a son's embrace far excels sandalwood salve. The relationship with one's son is more important than that with a best friend, a good father, or any other person."

One day, after nicely tucking the boy into his bed, she took the water pitcher and said to her husband, "Listen, master, I am going to the pond to fetch water. You must protect our son from the mongoose."

After she departed, the Brahman went off somewhere to collect alms, leaving the house empty. In the meantime a black snake crept out of its hole and — as fate would have it — approached the boy's bed. However, the mongoose confronted this, his natural enemy, and fearing that it might kill his brother, the mongoose attacked the wicked snake, tore it to bits, and threw the pieces far and wide.

Proud of his valor and his face covered with blood, the mongoose approached the mother to tell her what had happened.

However, the mother, seeing his blood-spattered face and sensing his excitement, feared, "without doubt this evildoer has devoured our son." Driven by anger and without further investigation she threw the water-filled pitcher at the mongoose, killing him instantly.

Paying no further attention to the mongoose, she rushed into the house where she found the boy still asleep. Near the bed she saw a large black snake, torn to bits. Then her heart was overcome with sorrow because of the thoughtless murder of her praiseworthy son, the mongoose, and she beat herself on the head, the breast, and her other body parts.

While this was happening the Brahman returned home with alms from wherever he had been begging.

"See there!" she cried, overcome with grief for her son, the mongoose. "Oh, you greedy one! Because you let greed rule you instead of doing what I told you to, you now must taste the fruit of your own tree of sin, the pain of your son's death" (www.pitt.edu/~dash/type0178a.html).

Assignments

- Warm-up: What lesson or moral is being advanced in these fables?
- Students should complete Concept Builder 17-C.
- Students should write rough draft of assigned essay.
- The teacher may correct rough draft.

Compare Hindu gods/goddesses to the Judeo-Christian God.

Vishnu (Krishna)

Hanuman
(Monkey Deity)

Judeo-Christian God

Vishnu
(Madhava)

Shiva
(Not mentioned in
the poem)

Judeo-Christian God

Hindu gods

Characteristic #1

Characteristic #1

Characteristic #2

Characteristic #2

Mahadeviyakka

Background Mahadeviyakka lived in the 19th century A.D. and was a devoted Hindu. She was also an accomplished poet.

Other Men

Other men are thorn

Under the smooth leaf.

I cannot touch them,

Go near them, nor trust them,

Nor speak to them confidences.

Mother,

Because they all have thorns

In their chests,

I cannot take

Any man in my arms but my lord

White as jasmine.

(www.loyno.edu/~wessing/docs/deviyakkaMira.html).

It Was Like a Stream

It was like a stream

Running into the dry bed

Of a lake.

Like rain

Pouring on plants

Parched to sticks.

It was like this world's pleasure

And the way to the other,

Both

Walking toward me.

Seeing the feet of the master,

O Lord white as jasmine,

I was made

Worthwhile.

(poetry-chaikhana.com/M/MahadeviAkka/Itwaslikeast.htm).

Assignments

- Warm-up: Evidence the religious aspect of Mahadeviyakka's poetry.
- Students should complete Concept Builder 17-D.
- Students will re-write corrected copies of essay due tomorrow.

Discuss the moral imperatives advanced in each fable in *The Panchatantra* (an ancient Indian inter-related collection of animal fables in verse and prose).

The Foolish Friend

Moral Imperative

The Gold-Giving Snake

Moral Imperative

The Brahman's Wife and the Mongoose

Moral Imperative

Mirabai

Background Perhaps the most referenced woman in Indian history is Mirabai (A.D. 1498–1546). Mirabai was a Brahmin aristocrat, which means that she was in the highest-educated class.

Oh Friends on This Path

Oh friends on this Path,

My eyes are no longer my eyes.

A sweetness has entered through them,

Has pierced through to my heart.

For how long did I stand in the house of this body

And stare at the road?

My beloved is a steeped herb, he has cured me for life.

Mira belongs to Giridhara [place of worship or the gods themselves],

The One who lifts all,

And everyone says she is mad.

(peacefulrivers.homestead.com/.SeptOctNovDec08archive.html).

This Bundle of Suffering

Having taken up this bundle of suffering, this body,

How can I throw it away?

It belongs to Ranchodrai Sheth...

Meera's lord is Giridhar Naagar;

I am longing to reach the ultimate,

How can I throw It away?

(exoticindia.com./product/HC40/aff10150).

Assignments

- Warm-up: Can you discern any difference between poetry written by men and poetry written by women?
- Students should complete Concept Builder 17-E.
- Essay is due. Students should take the chapter 17 test.

A fable is a short story that uses animals to illustrate a moral point. Outline (do not write) a fable.

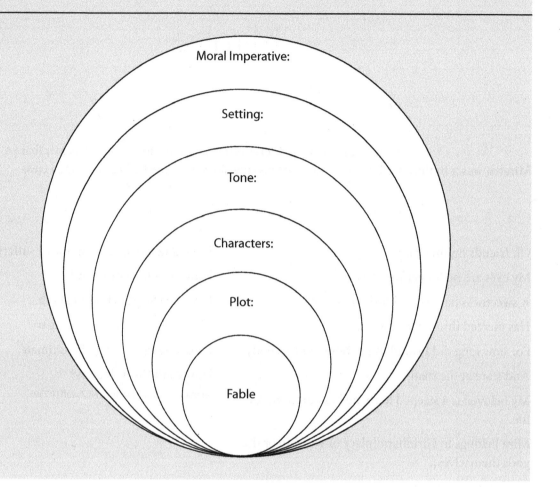

Moral Imperative:

Setting:

Tone:

Characters:

Plot:

Fable

Chapter 18

(A.D. 600–1400):
Persian and Arabic Literature

First Thoughts Omar Khayyam was a Persian author of one of the world's best-known works of poetry. He was born in Iran. As astronomer to the royal court, he was engaged with several other scientists to reform the calendar; their work resulted in the adoption of a new era, called the Jalalian or the Seljuk. As a writer on algebra, geometry, and related subjects, Omar was one of the most notable mathematicians of his time. However, he is most famous as the author of the *Rubáiyát*. The *Rubáiyát* includes 1,000+ line stanzas of wise sayings (Omar Khayyam, *Rubaiyat*, translated by Edward Fitzgerald (New York: Quality Paperback Book Club, 1996).

Chapter Learning Objectives In chapter 18 we examine the most exotic and, to many, the most enigmatic of Eastern literature, the Persian corpus, including Omar Khayyam.

As a result of this chapter study you will be able to . . .

1. Analyze the iconoclastic aspects of Omar Khayyam's *Rubaiyat*.

2. Contrast the earlier passage in the Koran with two biblical entries.

Weekly Essay Options: Begin on page 273 of the Teacher Guide.

Reading ahead: Poems by T'ao Ch'ien and *The Sayings of Confucius* by Confucius.

247

Rubaiyat
Omar Khayyam

I

WAKE! For the Sun behind yon Eastern height
Has chased the Session of the Stars from Night;
And to the field of Heav'n ascending, strikes
The Sulta´n's Turret with a Shaft of Light.

II

Before the phantom of False morning died,
Methought a Voice within the Tavern cried,
"When all the Temple is prepared within,
Why lags the drowsy Worshipper outside?"

III

And, as the Cock crew, those who stood before
The Tavern shouted — "Open then the Door!
You know how little while we have to stay,
And, once departed, may return no more."

IV

Now the New Year reviving old Desires,
The thoughtful Soul to Solitude retires,
Where the WHITE HAND OF MOSES on the Bough
Puts out, and Jesus from the Ground suspires.

V

Iram indeed is gone with all his Rose,
And Jamshy'd's Sev'n-ring'd Cup where no one knows;
But still a Ruby gushes from the Vine,
And many a Garden by the Water blows.

VI

And David's lips are lockt; but in divine
High-piping Pe'hlevi, with "Wine! Wine! Wine!
Red Wine!" — the Nightingale cries to the Rose
That sallow cheek of hers to incarnadine.

VII

Come, fill the Cup, and in the fire of Spring
Your Winter-garment of Repentance fling:
The Bird of Time has but a little way
To flutter — and the Bird is on the Wing.

VIII

Whether at Naisha'pu'r or Babylon,
Whether the Cup with sweet or bitter run,
The Wine of Life keeps oozing drop by drop,
The Leaves of Life keep falling one by one.

IX

Morning a thousand Roses brings, you say;
Yes, but where leaves the Rose of Yesterday?
And this first Summer month that brings the Rose
Shall take Jamshy'd and Kaikoba'd away.

X

Well, let it take them! What have we to do
With Kaikoba'd the Great, or Kaikhosru'?
Let Rustum cry "To Battle!" as he likes,
Or Ha´tim Tai "To supper!"—heed not you.

XI

With me along the strip of Herbage strown
That just divides the desert from the sown,
Where name of Slave and Sulta'n is forgot —
And Peace to Ma'hmu'd on his golden Throne!

XII

Here with a little Bread beneath the Bough,
A Flask of Wine, a Book of Verse — and Thou
Beside me singing in the Wilderness —
Oh, Wilderness were Paradise enow!

XIII

Some for the Glories of This World; and some
Sigh for the Prophet's Paradise to come;
Ah, take the Cash, and let the Promise go,
Nor heed the music of a distant Drum!

XIV

Were it not Folly, Spider-like to spin
The Thread of present Life away to win —
What? for ourselves, who know not if we shall
Breathe out the very Breath we now breathe in!

XV

Look to the blowing Rose about us — "Lo,
Laughing," she says, "into the world I blow,
At once the silken tassel of my Purse
Tear, and its Treasure on the Garden throw."

XVI

For those who husbanded the Golden grain,
And those who flung it to the winds like Rain,
Alike to no such aureate Earth are turn'd
As, buried once, Men want dug up again.

XVII

The Worldly Hope men set their Hearts upon
Turns Ashes — or it prospers; and anon,
Like Snow upon the Desert's dusty Face,
Lighting a little hour or two — was gone.

XVIII

Think, in this batter'd Caravanserai
Whose Portals are alternate Night and Day,
How Sulta'n after Sulta'n with his Pomp
Abode his destined Hour, and went his way.

XIX

They say the Lion and the Lizard keep
The Courts where Jamshy'd gloried and drank deep:
And Bahra'm, that great Hunter — the Wild Ass
Stamps o'er his Head, but cannot break his Sleep.

XX

The Palace that to Heav'n his pillars threw,
And Kings the forehead on his threshold drew —
I saw the solitary Ringdove there,
And "Coo, coo, coo," she cried; and "Coo, coo, coo."

XXI

Ah, my Belove'd, fill the Cup that clears
TO-DAY of past Regret and Future Fears:
To-morrow! — Why, To-morrow I may be
Myself with Yesterday's Sev'n thousand Years.

XXII

For some we loved, the loveliest and the best
That from his Vintage rolling Time has prest,
Have drunk their Cup a Round or two before,
And one by one crept silently to rest.

XXIII

And we, that now make merry in the Room
They left, and Summer dresses in new bloom,
Ourselves must we beneath the Couch of Earth
Descend — ourselves to make a Couch — for
whom?

XXIV

I sometimes think that never blows so red
The Rose as where some buried Cæsar bled;
That every Hyacinth the Garden wears
Dropt in her Lap from some once lovely Head.

XXV

And this delightful Herb whose living Green
Fledges the River's Lip on which we lean —
Ah, lean upon it lightly! for who knows
From what once lovely Lip it springs unseen!

XXVI

Ah, make the most of what we yet may spend,
Before we too into the Dust descend;
Dust into Dust, and under Dust to lie
Sans Wine, sans Song, sans Singer, and — sans End!

XXVII

Alike for those who for TO-DAY prepare,
And those that after some TO-MORROW stare,
A Muezzi´n from the Tower of Darkness cries,
"Fools! your Reward is neither Here nor There!"

XXVIII

Another Voice, when I am sleeping, cries,
"The Flower should open with the Morning skies."
And a retreating Whisper, as I wake —
"The Flower that once has blown for ever dies."

XXIX

Why, all the Saints and Sages who discuss'd
Of the Two Worlds so learnedly are thrust
Like foolish Prophets forth; their Words to Scorn
Are scatter'd, and their Mouths are stopt with Dust.

XXX

Myself when young did eagerly frequent
Doctor and Saint, and heard great argument
About it and about: but evermore
Came out by the same door as in I went.

XXXI

With them the seed of Wisdom did I sow,
And with my own hand wrought to make it grow;
And this was all the Harvest that I reap'd —
"I came like Water, and like Wind I go."

XXXII

Into this Universe, and Why not knowing
Nor Whence, like Water willy-nilly flowing;
And out of it, as Wind along the Waste,
I know not Whither, willy-nilly blowing.

XXXIII

What, without asking, hither hurried Whence?
And, without asking, Whither hurried hence!
Ah, contrite Heav'n endowed us with the Vine
To drug the memory of that insolence!

XXXIV

Up from Earth's Centre through the Seventh Gate
I rose, and on the Throne of Saturn sate;
And many Knots unravel'd by the Road;
But not the Master-knot of Human Fate.

XXXV

There was the Door to which I found no Key:
There was the Veil through which I could not see:
Some little talk awhile of ME and THEE
There was — and then no more of THEE and ME.

XXXVI

Earth could not answer; nor the Seas that mourn
In flowing Purple, of their Lord forlorn;
Nor Heaven, with those eternal Signs reveal'd
And hidden by the sleeve of Night and Morn.

XXXVII

Then of the THEE IN ME who works behind
The Veil of Universe I cried to find
A Lamp to guide me through the Darkness; and
Something then said — "An Understanding blind."

XXXVIII

Then to the Lip of this poor earthen Urn
I lean'd, the secret Well of Life to learn:
And Lip to Lip it murmur'd — "While you live,
Drink! — for, once dead, you never shall return."

XXXIX

I think the Vessel, that with fugitive
Articulation answer'd, once did live,
And drink; and that impassive Lip I kiss'd,
How many Kisses might it take — and give!

XL

For I remember stopping by the way
To watch a Potter thumping his wet Clay:
And with its all-obliterated Tongue
It murmur'd — "Gently, Brother, gently, pray!"

XLI

For has not such a Story from of Old
Down Man's successive generations roll'd
Of such a clod of saturated Earth
Cast by the Maker into Human mould?

XLII

And not a drop that from our Cups we throw
On the parcht herbage, but may steal below
To quench the fire of Anguish in some Eye
There hidden — far beneath, and long ago.

XLIII

As then the Tulip for her wonted sup
Of Heavenly Vintage lifts her chalice up,
Do you, twin offspring of the soil, till Heav'n
To Earth invert you like an empty Cup.

XLIV

Do you, within your little hour of Grace,
The waving Cypress in your Arms enlace,
Before the Mother back into her arms
Fold, and dissolve you in a last embrace.

XLV

And if the Cup you drink, the Lip you press,
End in what All begins and ends in — Yes;
Imagine then you are what heretofore
You were — hereafter you shall not be less.

XLVI

So when at last the Angel of the Drink
Of Darkness finds you by the river-brink,
And, proffering his Cup, invites your Soul
Forth to your Lips to quaff it — do not shrink.

XLVII

And fear not lest Existence closing your
Account, should lose, or know the type no more;
The Eternal Sa'kì from that Bowl has pour'd
Millions of Bubbles like us, and will pour.

XLVIII

When You and I behind the Veil are past,
Oh, but the long long while the World shall last,
Which of our Coming and Departure heeds
As much as Ocean of a pebble-cast.

XLIX

One Moment in Annihilation's Waste,
One Moment, of the Well of Life to taste —
The Stars are setting, and the Caravan
Draws to the Dawn of Nothing — Oh make haste.

L

Would you that spangle of Existence spend
About THE SECRET — quick about it, Friend!
A Hair, they say, divides the False and True —
And upon what, prithee, does Life depend?

LI

A Hair, they say, divides the False and True;
Yes; and a single Alif were the clue —
Could you but find it — to the Treasure-house,
And peradventure to THE MASTER too;

LII

Whose secret Presence, through Creation's veins
Running, Quicksilver-like eludes your pains;
Taking all shapes from Ma'h to Ma'hi; and
They change and perish all — but He remains;

LIII

A moment guess'd — then back behind the Fold
Immerst of Darkness round the Drama roll'd
Which, for the Pastime of Eternity,
He does Himself contrive, enact, behold.

LIV

But it in vain, down on the stubborn floor
Of Earth, and up to Heav'n's unopening Door,
You gaze TO-DAY, while You are YOU — how then
TO-MORROW, You when shall be You no more?

LV

Oh, plagued no more with Human or Divine,
To-morrow's tangle to itself resign,
And lose your fingers in the tresses of
The Cypress-slender Minister of Wine.

LVI

Waste not your Hour, nor in the vain pursuit
Of This and That endeavour and dispute;
Better be merry with the fruitful Grape
Than sadden after none, or bitter, Fruit.

LVII

You know, my Friends, how bravely in my House
For a new Marriage I did make Carouse;
Divorced old barren Reason from my Bed,
And took the Daughter of the Vine to Spouse.

LVIII

For "IS" and "IS-NOT" though with Rule and Line
And "UP-AND-DOWN" by Logic I define,
Of all that one should care to fathom, I
Was never deep in anything but — Wine.

LIX

Ah, but my Computations, People say,
Have squared the Year to human compass, eh?
If so, by striking from the Calendar
Unborn To-morrow, and dead Yesterday.

LX

And lately, by the Tavern Door agape,
Came shining through the Dusk an Angel Shape
Bearing a Vessel on his Shoulder; and
He bid me taste of it; and 'twas — the Grape!

LXI

The Grape that can with Logic absolute
The Two-and-Seventy jarring Sects confute:
The sovereign Alchemist that in a trice
Life's leaden metal into Gold transmute:

LXII

The mighty Mahmu'd, Allah-breathing Lord,
That all the misbelieving and black Horde
Of Fears and Sorrows that infest the Soul
Scatters before him with his whirlwind Sword.

LXIII

Why, be this Juice the growth of God, who dare
Blaspheme the twisted tendril as a Snare?
A Blessing, we should use it, should we not?
And if a Curse — why, then, Who set it there?

LXIV

I must abjure the Balm of Life, I must,
Scared by some After-reckoning ta'en on trust,
Or lured with Hope of some Diviner Drink,
When the frail Cup is crumbled into Dust!

LXV

If but the Vine and Love-abjuring Band
Are in the Prophet's Paradise to stand,
Alack, I doubt the Prophet's Paradise
Were empty as the hollow of one's Hand.

LXVI

Oh threats of Hell and Hopes of Paradise!
One thing at least is certain — This Life flies;
One thing is certain and the rest is Lies;
The Flower that once is blown for ever dies.

LXVII

Strange, is it not? that of the myriads who
Before us pass'd the door of Darkness through,
Not one returns to tell us of the Road,
Which to discover we must travel too.

LXVIII

The Revelations of Devout and Learn'd
Who rose before us, and as Prophets burn'd,
Are all but Stories, which, awoke from Sleep
They told their fellows, and to Sleep return'd.

LXIX

Why, if the Soul can fling the Dust aside,
And naked on the Air of Heaven ride,
Is't not a Shame — is't not a Shame for him
So long in this Clay Suburb to abide?

LXX

But that is but a Tent wherein may rest
A Sultan to the realm of Death addrest;
The Sulta'n rises, and the dark Ferra'sh
Strikes, and prepares it for another Guest.

LXXI

I sent my Soul through the Invisible,
Some letter of that After-life to spell:
And after many days my Soul return'd,
And said, "Behold, Myself am Heav'n and Hell:"

LXXII

Heav'n but the Vision of fulfill'd Desire,
And Hell the Shadow of a Soul on fire,
Cast on the Darkness into which Ourselves,
So late emerged from, shall so soon expire.

LXXIII

We are no other than a moving row
Of visionary Shapes that come and go
Round with this Sun-illumin'd Lantern held
In Midnight by the Master of the Show;

LXXIV

Impotent Pieces of the Game He plays
Upon this Chequer-board of Nights and Days;
Hither and thither moves, and checks, and slays,
And one by one back in the Closet lays.

LXXV

The Ball no question makes of Ayes and Noes,
But Right or Left as strikes the Player goes;
And He that toss'd you down into the Field,
He knows about it all — HE knows — HE knows!

LXXVI

The Moving Finger writes; and, having writ,
Moves on: nor all your Piety nor Wit
Shall lure it back to cancel half a Line,
Nor all your Tears wash out a Word of it.

LXXVII

For let Philosopher and Doctor preach
Of what they will, and what they will not — each
Is but one Link in an eternal Chain
That none can slip, nor break, nor over-reach.

LXXVIII

And that inverted Bowl we call The Sky,
Whereunder crawling coop'd we live and die,
Lift not your hands to It for help — for It
As impotently rolls as you or I.

LXXIX

With Earth's first Clay They did the Last Man knead,
And there of the Last Harvest sow'd the Seed:
And the first Morning of Creation wrote
What the Last Dawn of Reckoning shall read.

LXXX

YESTERDAY This Day's Madness did prepare;
TO-MORROW'S Silence, Triumph, or Despair:
Drink! for you know not whence you came, nor why:
Drink! for you know not why you go, nor where.

LXXXI

I tell you this — When, started from the Goal,
Over the flaming shoulders of the Foal
Of Heav'n Parwi´n and Mushtari they flung,
In my predestined Plot of Dust and Soul.

LXXXII

The Vine had struck a fibre: which about
If clings my being — let the Dervish flout;
Of my Base metal may be filed a Key,
That shall unlock the Door he howls without.

LXXXIII

And this I know: whether the one True Light
Kindle to Love, or Wrath-consume me quite,
One Flash of It within the Tavern caught
Better than in the Temple lost outright.

LXXXIV

What! out of senseless Nothing to provoke
A conscious Something to resent the yoke
Of unpermitted Pleasure, under pain
Of Everlasting Penalties, if broke!

LXXXV

What! from his helpless Creature be repaid
Pure Gold for what he lent us dross-allay'd
Sue for a Debt we never did contract,
And cannot answer — Oh the sorry trade!

LXXXVI

Nay, but, for terror of his wrathful Face,
I swear I will not call Injustice Grace;
Not one Good Fellow of the Tavern but
Would kick so poor a Coward from the place.

LXXXVII

Oh Thou, who didst with pitfall and with gin
Beset the Road I was to wander in,
Thou wilt not with Predestined Evil round
Enmesh, and then impute my Fall to Sin!

LXXXVIII

Oh, Thou, who Man of baser Earth didst make,
And ev'n with Paradise devise the Snake:
For all the Sin the Face of wretched Man
Is black with — Man's Forgiveness give — and take!

LXXXIX

As under cover of departing Day
Slunk hunger-stricken Ramaza'n away,
Once more within the Potter's house alone
I stood, surrounded by the Shapes of Clay.

XC

And once again there gather'd a scarce heard
Whisper among them; as it were, the stirr'd
Ashes of some all but extinguisht Tongue,
Which mine ear kindled into living Word.

XCI

Said one among them — "Surely not in vain
My substance from the common Earth was ta'en
That he who subtly wrought me into Shape
Should stamp me back to shapeless Earth again?"

XCII

Another said — "Why, ne'er a peevish Boy
Would break the Cup from which he drank in Joy;
Shall He that of His own free Fancy made
The Vessel, in an after-rage destroy!"

XCIII

None answer'd this; but after silence spake
Some Vessel of a more ungainly Make;
"They sneer at me for leaning all awry:
What! did the Hand then of the Potter shake?"

XCIV

Thus with the Dead as with the Living, What?
And Why? so ready, but the Wherefore not,
One on a sudden peevishly exclaim'd,
"Which is the Potter, pray, and which the Pot?"

XCV

Said one — "Folks of a surly Master tell,
And daub his Visage with the Smoke of Hell;
They talk of some sharp Trial of us — Pish!
He's a Good Fellow, and 'twill all be well."

XCVI

"Well," said another, "Whoso will, let try,
My Clay with long Oblivion is gone dry:
But fill me with the old familiar Juice,
Methinks I might recover by and by."

XCVII

So while the Vessels one by one were speaking,
One spied the little Crescent all were seeking:
And then they jogg'd each other, "Brother! Brother!
Now for the Porter's shoulder-knot a-creaking!"

XCVIII

Ah, with the Grape my fading Life provide,
And wash my Body whence the Life has died,
And lay me, shrouded in the living Leaf,
By some not unfrequented Garden-side.

XCIX

Whither resorting from the vernal Heat
Shall Old Acquaintance Old Acquaintance greet,
Under the Branch that leans above the Wall
To shed his Blossom over head and feet.

C

Then ev'n my buried Ashes such a snare
Of Vintage shall fling up into the Air
As not a True-believer passing by
But shall be overtaken unaware.

CI

Indeed the Idols I have loved so long
Have done my credit in Men's eyes much wrong:
Have drown'd my Glory in a shallow Cup
And sold my Reputation for a Song.

CII

Indeed, indeed, Repentance oft before
I swore — but was I sober when I swore?
And then and then came Spring, and Rose-in-hand
My thread-bare Penitence apieces tore.

CIII

And much as Wine has play'd the Infidel,
And robb'd me of my Robe of Honour — Well,
I often wonder what the Vintners buy
One half so precious as the ware they sell.

CIV

Yet Ah, that Spring should vanish with the Rose!
That Youth's sweet-scented manuscript should close!
The Nightingale that in the branches sang,
Ah whence, and whither flown again, who knows!

CV

Would but the Desert of the Fountain yield
One glimpse — if dimly, yet indeed, reveal'd,
Toward which the fainting Traveller might spring,
As springs the trampled herbage of the field!

CVI

Oh if the World were but to re-create,
That we might catch ere closed the Book of Fate,
And make The Writer on a fairer leaf
Inscribe our names, or quite obliterate!

CVII

Better, oh better, cancel from the Scroll
Of Universe one luckless Human Soul,
Than drop by drop enlarge the Flood that rolls
Hoarser with Anguish as the Ages roll.

CVIII

Ah Love! could you and I with Fate conspire
To grasp this sorry Scheme of Things entire,
Would not we shatter it to bits — and then
Re-mould it nearer to the Heart's Desire!

CIX

But see! The rising Moon of Heav'n again

Looks for us, Sweet-heart, through the quivering
Plane:

How oft hereafter rising will she look

Among those leaves — for one of us in vain!

CX

And when Yourself with silver Foot shall pass

Among the Guests Star-scatter'd on the Grass,

And in your joyous errand reach the spot

Where I made One — turn down an empty Glass!

Assignments

- Warm-up: What is the rhyme scheme of the first 12 lines this poem?

- Student should complete Concept Builder 18-A.

- Students should review the required reading(s) *before* the assigned chapter begins.

- Teachers may want to discuss assigned reading(s) with students.

- Teachers shall assign the required essay. The rest of the essays can be outlined, answered with shorter answers, discussed, or skipped.

- Students will review all readings for chapter 18.

CONCEPT BUILDER 18-A
Active Reading

Read this excerpt from *Rubaiyat* by Omar Khayam and respond to the following:

I
WAKE! For the Sun behind yon Eastern height
Has chased the Session of the Stars from Night;
And to the field of Heav'n ascending, strikes
The Sulta'n's Turret with a Shaft of Light.

II
Before the phantom of False morning died,
Methought a Voice within the Tavern cried,
"When all the Temple is prepared within,
Why lags the drowsy Worshipper outside?"

III
And, as the Cock crew, those who stood before
The Tavern shouted — "Open then the Door!
You know how little while we have to stay,
And, once departed, may return no more."

VII
Come, fill the Cup, and in the fire of Spring
Your Winter-garment of Repentance fling:
The Bird of Time has but a little way
To flutter — and the Bird is on the Wing.

This is a special metaphor called personification (when an inanimate object is described as if it is a person). Identify at least two examples of personification.

A rhyme scheme is the pattern of rhyme between lines of a poem or song. One uses letters to indicate which lines rhyme. What is the rhyme scheme of each of these stanzas?

The Koran

Background The following chapter is from the Qur'ân or Koran, in which are collected Mohammed's revelations (www.bartleby.com/45/5/101.html).

In the name of the merciful and compassionate God.

Read, in the name of thy Lord!

Who created man from congealed blood!

Read, for thy Lord is most generous!

Who taught the pen!

Taught man what he did not know!

Nay, verily, man is indeed outrageous at seeing himself get rich!

Verily, unto thy Lord is the return!

Common calligraphic representation of Muhammad's name (CC BY-SA 3.0).

Hast thou considered him who forbids a servant when he prays ?

Hast thou considered if he were in guidance or bade piety?

Hast thou considered if he said it was a lie, and turned his back?

Did he not know that God can see?

Nay, surely, if he do not desist we will drag him by the forelock! — the lying sinful forelock! So let him call his counsel: we will call the guards of hell!

Nay, obey him not, but adore and draw nigh!

Assignments

- Warm-up: Should a Christian read the Koran? Why or why not?
- Students should complete Concept Builder 18-B.
- Students should review reading(s) from the next chapter.
- Students should outline essay due at the end of the week.
- Per teacher instructions, students may answer orally, in a group setting, some of the essays that are not assigned as formal essays.

Given these passages, compare and contrast the Islamic view of Allah and the Judeo-Christian view of God.

The Koran	Psalm 23
In the name of the merciful and compassionate God. Read, in the name of thy Lord! Who created man from congealed blood! Read, for thy Lord is most generous! Who taught the pen! Taught man what he did not know! Nay, verily, man is indeed outrageous at seeing himself get rich! Verily, unto thy Lord is the return! Hast thou considered him who forbids a servant when he prays ? Hast thou considered if he were in guidance or bade piety? Hast thou considered if he said it was a lie, and turned his back? Did he not know that God can see? Nay, surely, if he do not desist we will drag him by the forelock! — the lying sinful forelock! So let him call his counsel: we will call the guards of hell! Nay, obey him not, but adore and draw nigh!	The Lord is my shepherd; there is nothing I lack. He lets me lie down in green pastures; He leads me beside quiet waters. He renews my life; He leads me along the right paths for His name's sake. Even when I go through the darkest valley, I fear no danger, for You are with me; Your rod and Your staff — they comfort me. You prepare a table before me in the presence of my enemies; You anoint my head with oil; my cup overflows. Only goodness and faithful love will pursue me all the days of my life, and I will dwell in house of the Lord as long as I live.

Subject	View of God	View of Man
Islam		
	Textual Evidence:	Textual Evidence:
Christianity/Judaism		
	Textual Evidence:	Textual Evidence:

Rabi'a

Background Rabi'a al-Adawiyya (born around A.D. 717) is a major saint of Islam. She was a fervent follower of Islam and was purported to perform several miracles (sufism.org/lineage/sufism/writings-on-sufism/doorkeeper-of-the-heart-versions-of-rabia-by-charles-upton-excerpt-2).

In Love

In love, nothing exists between breast and breast,

Speech is born out of longing.

True description from the real taste.

The one who tastes, knows;

The one who explains, lies.

How can you describe the true form of something

In whose presence you are blotted out?

And in whose being you still exist?

And who lives as a sign for your journey?

Doorkeeper of the Heart

(Excerpt)

My hope in my heart is the rarest treasure

Your name on my tongue is the sweetest word

My choicest hours

Are the hours I spend with you.

O Allah, I cannot live in this world

Without remembering you,

How can I endure the next world

Without seeing your face?

I am a stranger in your country

And lonely among your worshippers:

This is the subtance of my complaint.

Al-Masjid al-Nabawi (the Mosque of the Prophet) in Medina, Saudi Arabia, with the Green Dome built over Muhammad's tomb in the center. Photo by Ahmed Medineli, 2004 (PD-US).

- Warm-up: Contrast this poetry to Christian poetry and song lyrics of equal intensity.
- Students should complete Concept Builder 18-C.
- Students should write rough draft of assigned essay.
- The teacher may correct rough drafts.

Omar Khayyam did not believe in the seminal Islamic belief of the resurrection of the body after death, and he suggested that drinking wine was better than worrying about religious theories and dogmas. In an instance that must have been particularly enraging for orthodox Muslims, he upturned the argument for future rewards in paradise by thinking it through to its logical end:

They promise there will be Paradise and the houri-eyed,
Where clear wine and honey will flow:
Should we prefer wine and a lover, what's the harm?
Are not these the final recompense?

Find one other example where Khayyam offered unorthodox notions.

Kassiane

Background Kassiane (A.D. 810–867) was a Byzantine aristocratic Christian born in Constantinople. Kassiane wrote about 50 hymns (30 are used in the Eastern Orthodox Church).

Hymn

The angel Gabriel

Was sent from heaven by God

To an undefiled virgin,

To a city of Galilee, Nazareth,

To announce to her the strange manner of her conception.

The bodiless servant was sent

To the living city and the spiritual gate

To make know the descent of the master's presence.

The heavenly soldier was sent

To the spotless palace of glory

To prepare the everlasting dwelling for the creator.

And coming before her he proclaimed:

"Hail, fiery throne

more glorious by far than the fourfold-form living beings.

Hail, heavenly royal seat,

Hail, unhewn mountain,

Most honored vessel.

For in you has come to dwell bodily

The fullness of the Godhead,

By the good will of the everlasting Father

And with the joint cooperation of the Holy Spirit.

Hail, you who are favored

The Lord is with you."

Most Impartial Judge

Most impartial judge

When you weigh

Our deeds,

Don't judge with reason,

But let your goodness prevail;

And add weight to the scale, Lord,

When the evil deeds tip it the other way.

We pray, O Deliverer,

That you mix the terrible cup

Of unmixed drink in your hand

With gentleness,

And save those of your servants

Whom you have already taken from the earth,

From this sediment, and place them

In the land of the meek, Merciful One,

To praise and bless you forever.

Assignments

- Warm-up: Research the Eastern Orthodox Church and compare it to the Roman Catholic Church.

- Students should complete Concept Builder 18-D.

- Students will re-write corrected copies of essay due tomorrow.

CONCEPT BUILDER 18-D
Tone and Mood

The tone or mood of a poem is the way authors feel about their subjects. In this poem the author begins with a complimentary tone and ends with a satirical tone.

**The golden hair that Gulla wears
Is hers: who would have thought it?
She swears 'tis hers, and true she wears,
For I know where she bought it.**

Use textual examples from "In Love" and "Doorkeeper of the Heart" by Rabi'a to illustrate how the poet creates a mood and tone toward her subject.

Tone/Mood	Texual Passage
Reverence	
Affection	
Fear	

Omar Khayyam: Non-Conformist

"Indeed the Idols I have loved so long/ Have done my credit in Men's eyes much wrong/ Have drown'd my Glory in a shallow Cup/ And sold my Reputation for a Song." The Persian poet Omar Khayyam, author of the *Rubaiyat*, often expressed unorthodox views regarding morality. A blithe iconoclast, Khayyam flouts Islamic cultural and religious norms in his poetry as he writes about the afterlife, morality, and love.

First, Khayyam writes about the afterlife in a non-conformist manner. The promised Islamic paradise is detailed in the Qur'ans' Surah 78:31-34:

Verily, for the Muttaqûan (holy), there will be a success (Paradise); Gardens and grapeyards; and young maidens of equal age; and a full cup (of wine).

Khayyam prefers to think through the implications of the Qur'ans' statement:

They promise there will be Paradise and the houri-eyed/ Where clear wine and honey will flow/ Should we prefer wine and a lover, what's the harm? Are not these the final recompense? (*Rubaiyat* 88)

In a rhetorical statement that necessarily must have infuriated the orthodox Muslim ideal, Khayyam wonders why carnal pleasures should not be enjoyed on earth as well as in paradise. The Muslim reader considered the pleasures of paradise

A Ruby kindles in the vine from *The Rubaiyat of Omar Khayyam* by Adelaide Hanscom, 1905 (PD-US).

reserved for the holy on earth, not the sinful. Contrastingly, Khayyam suggests if these pleasures were commanded in Paradise, why would they be sinful on earth? One can imagine Khayyam — with deceptively upturned eyes and ambrosial voice — imploring the reader to not delay "celestial" pleasures in an earthly realm.

Next, Khayyam writes about morality and love in a non-conformist manner.

Oh, plagued no more with Human or Divine/ Tommorow's tangle to itself resign/ and lose your fingers in the tresses of/ The Cypress-slender Minister of Wine…Another said/ Why, ne'er a peevish Boy/ Would break the Cup from which he drank in Joy/ Shall He that of His own free Fancy made/ The Vessel, in an after-rage destroy! (*Rubaiyat* 55, 92)

Omar Khayyam contradicts popular Islamic culture by extolling the pleasures of life without any "payment." Intrinsic to the Muslim identity was the idea that salvation must be earned by good deeds, or meeting the five pillars of Islam. Khayyam questions the very need for any sort of morality.

Omar Khayyam, Persian poet, iconoclast, and author of the Rubaiyat expressed a nontraditional view of Islamic culture by flouting their ideas of the afterlife, love, and morality. (Alouette)

- Warm-up: How would you describe a non-conformist?
- Students should complete Concept Builder 18-E.
- Essays are due. Students should take the chapter 18 test.

CONCEPT BUILDER 18-E
Attributes of God

The Byzantine poet Kassiane in his poems "Hymn" and "Most Impartial Judge" highlights several attributes of God. What are they?

Attributes	Texual Passage
God does miracles	*For in you has come to dwell bodily/The fullness of the Godhead.*
God is full of good will toward His people	
God is a fair, impartial judge	
God is merciful	
God is a deliverer	

Chapter 19

(1400 B.C.–A.D. 1890):
Chinese Literature

First Thoughts Chinese literature is one of the oldest forms of literature that exists in world cultures. Two distinct traditions exist in Chinese literature: the literary traditions and the colloquial, often oral traditions. The latter can be traced back more than a thousand years before Christ and has existed in one form or another continuously until modern times. This form of literature — colloquial — appears normally in folk ballads written in everyday language. Folk literature was long considered beneath the upper classes, who more or less determined the standards of literary taste. Highly stylized writings set the standards for the orthodox literary tradition that began about the same time as colloquial literary appeared. However, not until the 20th century did colloquial literature gain the support of the intellectual class.

Chinese literature may be divided into three major historical periods that roughly correspond to those of Western literary history: the classical period, the medieval period, and the modern period. This survey course, unfortunately, will only be able to look at a few classical offerings.

Chapter Learning Objectives In chapter 19 we examine Chinese poetry and philosophy.

As a result of this chapter study you will be able to . . .

1. Evaluate Confucius' thought.

2. Contrast Buddhism and Christianity.

3. Discuss if there are any contemporary equivalents to Confucius.

Weekly Essay Options: Begin on page 273 of the Teacher Guide.

Reading ahead: *Divine Comedy* (The Inferno Only) by Dante Alighieri.

 History connections: *World History* chapter 19, "Chinese History."

T'ao Ch'ien

Background T'ao Ch'ien (365–427), was the first writer to make poetry his natural voice and so stands at the head of the Chinese colloquial tradition. A recluse farmer with a rich philosophical depth, T'ao's main themes concerned Buddhism. Buddhism was founded in northeastern India and based on the teachings of Siddhartha Gautama, who is known as the Buddha, or Enlightened One (www.poemhunter.com/tao-chien/biography).

After the Ancients

Spring's second moon brings timely rain,
thunder rumbles in the East.
Insects stir from secret places.
Grasses, trees, and brush spread green.
Wing! Wings everywhere! The new come swallows,
pairs and pairs within my home
find last year's nests still here
and come, together, to rest, again.

Since you and I were parted, I have
watched the garden gate pile up in leaves.My heart's
no rolling stone.
And yours?

Without all that Racket

I live in town without all that racket
horses and carts stir up, and you wonder

how that could be. Wherever the mind
dwells apart is itself a distant place.

Picking chrysanthemums at my east fence,
far off, I see South Mountain:

mountain air lovely at dusk, birds in flight
returning home. All this means something,

something absolute. Whenever I start
explaining it, I've forgotten the words.

The Tale of the Peach-Blossom Land. Photo by Rolf Müller, 2005 (CC BY-SA 3.0).

Assignments

- Warm-up: What type of metaphor does T'ao Ch'ien prefer?

- Students should complete Concept Builder 19-A.

- Students should review the required reading(s) *before* the assigned chapter begins.

- Teachers may want to discuss assigned reading(s) with students.

- Teachers shall assign the required essay. The rest of the essays can be outlined, answered with shorter answers, discussed, or skipped.

- Students will review all readings for chapter 19.

CONCEPT BUILDER 19-A
Active Reading

Read the poems of T'ao Ch'ien and respond to the following:

After the Ancients

Spring's second moon brings timely rain,
thunder rumbles in the East.
Insects stir from secret places.
Grasses, trees, and brush spread green.
Wing! Wings everywhere! The new come swallows,
pairs and pairs within my home
find last year's nests still here
and come, together, to rest, again.

Since you and I were parted, I have
watched the garden gate pile up in leaves.
My heart's no rolling stone.
And yours?

Without All That Racket

I live in town without all that racket
horses and carts stir up, and you wonder
how that could be. Wherever the mind
dwells apart is itself a distant place.

Picking chrysanthemums at my east fence,
far off, I see South Mountain:
mountain air lovely at dusk, birds in flight
returning home. All this means something,
something absolute. Whenever I start
explaining it, I've forgotten the words.

What is the poet describing?

List several specific images he uses.

The descriptions that the poet uses in the first stanza is merely preparation for the main theme of the poem. What is the theme?

Describe the narrator of "Without all that Racket."

www.poetryintranslation.com/PITBR/Chinese/AllwaterTaoChien.htm.

Peach Blossom Spring

During the reign-period T'ai yuan [376–397] of the Chin dynasty there lived in Wu-ling a certain fisherman. One day, as he followed the course of a stream, he became unconscious of the distance be had travelled. All at once he came upon a grove of blossoming peach trees which lined either bank for hundreds of paces. No tree of any other kind stood amongst them, but there were fragrant flowers, delicate and lovely to the eye, and the air was filled with drifting peachbloom.

The fisherman, marvelling, passed on to discover where the grove would end. It ended at a spring; and then there came a hill. In the side of the hill was a small opening which seemed to promise a gleam of light. The fisherman left his boat and entered the opening. It was almost too cramped at first to afford him passage; but when he had taken a few dozen steps he emerged into the open light of day. He faced a spread of level land. Imposing buildings stood among rich fields and pleasant ponds all set with mulberry and willow. Linking paths led everywhere, and the fowls and dogs of one farm could be heard from the next. People were coming and going and working in the fields. Both the men and the women dressed in exactly the same manner as people outside; white-haired elders and tufted children alike were cheerful and contented.

Some, noticing the fisherman, started in great surprise and asked him where he had come from. He told them his story. They then invited him to their home, where they set out wine and killed chickens for a feast. When news of his coining spread through the village everyone came in to question him. For their part they told how their forefathers, fleeing from the troubles of the age of Ch'in, had come with their wives and neighbours to this isolated place, never to leave it. From that time on they had been cut off from the outside world. They asked what age was this: they had never even heard of the Han, let alone its successors the Wei and the Chin. The fisherman answered each of their questions in full, and they sighed and wondered at what he had to tell. The rest all invited him to their homes in turn, and in each house food and wine were set before him. It was only after a stay of several days that he took his leave.

"Do Dot speak of us to the people outside," they said. But when he had regained his boat and was retracing his original route, he marked it at point after point; and on reaching the prefecture he sought audience of the prefect and told him of all these things. The prefect immediately despatched officers to go back with the fisherman. He hunted for the marks he had made, but grew confused and never found the way again.

The learned and virtuous hermit Liu Tzu-chi heard the story and went off elated to find the place. But he had no success, and died at length of a sickness. Since that time there have been no further "seekers of the ford (www.artsci.wustl.edu/~rhegel/EAS224%20Page/images/web%20material/tao_chien.htm).

Assignments

- Warm-up: Why is T'ao Ch'ien called the "colloquial poet"?
- Students should complete Concept Builder 19-B.
- Students should review reading(s) from the next chapter.
- Students should outline essay due at the end of the week.
- Per teacher instructions, students may answer orally, in a group setting, some of the essays that are not assigned as formal essays.

CONCEPT BUILDER 19-B
Imagery in Chinese Poetry

Imagery is figurative language, especially metaphors and similes, used in poetry, plays, and other literary works. Find examples of imagery in poems by Wang Wei.

Poem	Poem
Deer Forest Hermitage Through the deep wood, the slanting sunlight Casts motley patterns on the jade-green mosses. No glimpse of man in this lonely mountain, Yet faint voices drift in the air.	*The central image is a forest in early evening, with the "slanting sunlight." In the background the reader sees "no glimpse of man in this lonely mountain" but hears "faint voices drift in the air." The reader sees and feels the loneliness that the poet is portraying.*
Magnolia Hermitage The autumn hills hoard scarlet from the setting sun. Flying birds chase their mates. Now and then patches of blue sky break clear — Tonight the evening mists find nowhere to gather.	
On Parting with Spring Day after day we can't help growing older. Year after year spring can't help seeming younger. Come let's enjoy our winecup today, Not pity the flowers fallen!	

www.chinese-poems.com/wang.html.

LESSON 3

Wang Wei and Pan Zhao

Wang Wei (699–759) was a very gifted man in many areas. Musician, poet, painter, he excelled in everything he pursued. In many ways his poems seem to be landscape paintings (All poems are from www.darsie.net/library/wangwei.html).

Deer Forest Hermitage

Through the deep wood, the slanting sunlight
Casts motley patterns on the jade-green mosses.
No glimpse of man in this lonely mountain,
Yet faint voices drift in the air.

Magnolia Hermitage

The autumn hills hoard scarlet from the setting sun.
Flying birds chase their mates.
Now and then patches of blue sky break clear —
Tonight the evening mists find nowhere to gather.

On Parting with Spring

Day after day we can't help growing older.
Year after year spring can't help seeming younger.
Come let's enjoy our winecup today,
Not pity the flowers fallen!

Landscapes in the Manner of Old Masters (Wang Wei) by Dong Qichang, 1621 (PD-Art).

Pan Zhao (A.D. 48–117) was the only woman to hold the post of official historian in ancient China. She was a great historian and accomplished poet, whose attention to details was quite advanced for her time.

Needle and Thread

Tempered, annealed, the hard essence of autumn metals

Finely forged, subtle, yet perdurable and straight,

By nature penetrating deep yet advancing by inches
To span all things yet stitch them up together,

Only needle-and-thread's delicate footsteps
Are truly broad-ranging yet without beginning!

"Withdrawing elegantly" to mend a loose thread,
and restore to white silk a lamb's-down purity. . . .

How can those who count pennies calculate their worth?
They may carve monuments yet lack all understanding.

sybilarchibald.com/blog/category/pan-zhao/.

Assignments

- Warm-up: In what way are Wang Wei's poems landscape poems?
- Students should complete Concept Builder 19-C.
- Students should write rough draft of assigned essay.
- The teacher or a peer evaluator may correct rough drafts.

CONCEPT BUILDER 19-C Imagery	Imagery is figurative language, especially metaphors and similes, used in poetry, plays, and other literary works. Find examples of imagery in poems by Wang Wei.	
	Object	**Imagery Poem**
	Peach	*Round and smooth* *My peach is true.* *It is fuzzy and smooth.* *Like a lazy afternoon at the pool.* *No waves. No schedule. No obligations.* *Round and smooth, my peach.*
	Dandelion	
	Anger	

Li Po

Background Li Po (701–762) was probably the greatest Chinese poet of pre-modern times. He was quite a man — over 8 feet tall; he was China's poet laureate in one of the greatest cultural renaissances of its history.

Drinking Alone with the Moon

From a pot of wine among the flowers

I drank alone. There was no one with me

Till raising my cup, I asked the bright moon

To bring me my shadow and make us three.

Alas, the moon was unable to drink

And my shadow tagged me vacantly;

But still for a while I had these friends

To cheer me through the end of spring.

I sang. The moon encouraged me.

I danced. My shadow tumbled after.

As long as I knew, we were born companions.

And then I was drunk and we lost one another.

Shall goodwill ever be secure?

I watch the long road of the river of stars.

www.topchinatravel.com/china-guide/literature-of-the-tang-dynasty.htm.

Assignments

- Warm-up: Why is Li Po drinking alone with the moon?
- Students should complete Concept Builder 19-D.
- Students will re-write corrected copies of essay due tomorrow.

CONCEPT BUILDER 19-D Epigrams	Confucius normally wrote in epigrams, or tersely phrased statements of a truth or opinion. Offer a few epigrams and discuss what they mean.	
	Epigram	**Meaning**
	Whatever you sow, that will you reap.	*One's actions will have a consequence.*
	Aim for nothing and you will always reach it.	
	Treat others as you would have them treat you.	
	Unforgiveness is like holding a rattlesnake by the tail.	
	A thousand-mile journey begins with a single step.	

The Sayings of Confucius
Confucius

Background Confucius was born in a distinguished family in China 551 B.C. The name Confucius is the Latin form of the Chinese characters, K 'ung Foo-tsze, meaning, "The master, K 'ung." His father was governor of a province, but not a man of great wealth. Confucius himself entered government service but enjoyed teaching more. He became a public teacher and soon attracted numerous disciples. At this time in China, as in Greece, wise people attracted disciples who literally made it a vocation to listen and to record sayings of wise people. When Confucius was nearly 50, in the year 500 B.C., he again took public office. In spite of some success, he lost the support of his emperor in 496 B.C., and until his death in 478 B.C., he wandered from state to state, sometimes well-treated, sometimes enduring severe hardships. After his death, his wisdom was universally recognized and, in Chinese religion that worshiped wisdom more than a deity, he was venerated. Sacrifices were offered to him, temples were built in his honor, and a cult which has lasted almost 2,000 years was established. *The Sayings of Confucius* were probably compiled by Confucius' disciples.

- Warm-up: It is one thing to venerate Confucius as a wise man. It is quite another thing to call him "god." The latter is quite dangerous. Explain.

- Students should complete Concept Builder 19-E.

- Essays are due. Students should take the chapter 19 test.

CONCEPT BUILDER 19-E
Archetype

Given these passages, compare and contrast the Islamic view of Allah and the Judeo-Christian view of God.

Drinking Alone with the Moon	Mr. Flood's Party
From a pot of wine among the flowers I drank alone. There was no one with me Till raising my cup, I asked the bright moon To bring me my shadow and make us three. Alas, the moon was unable to drink And my shadow tagged me vacantly; But still for a while I had these friends To cheer me through the end of spring. I sang. The moon encouraged me. I danced. My shadow tumbled after. As long as I knew, we were born companions. And then I was drunk and we lost one another. Shall goodwill ever be secure? I watch the long road of the river of stars.	Old Eben Flood, climbing alone one night Over the hill between the town below And the forsaken upland hermitage That held as much as he should ever know On earth again of home, paused warily. The road was his with not a native near; And Eben, having leisure, said aloud, For no man else in Tilbury Town to hear: "Well, Mr. Flood, we have the harvest moon Again, and we may not have many more; The bird is on the wing, the poet says, And you and I have said it here before. Drink to the bird." He raised up to the light The jug that he had gone so far to fill, And answered huskily: "Well, Mr. Flood, Since you propose it, I believe I will." Alone, as if enduring to the end A valiant armor of scarred hopes outworn, He stood there in the middle of the road Like Roland's ghost winding a silent horn. Below him, in the town among the trees, Where friends of other days had honored him, A phantom salutation of the dead Rang thinly till old Eben's eyes were dim. . .

http://clatterymachinery.wordpress.com/2007/01/26/li-bai-drinking-alone-with-the-moon-his-shadow-32-translators/.
http://www.bartleby.com/233/802.html.

Chapter 20

(A.D. 500–1500):
Middle Ages (Part 1)

First Thoughts Dante Alighieri lived during the end of the Middle Ages. When we think of the Middle Ages we think of knights in shining armor, Robin Hood, dragons, lavish banquets, kings, queens, wandering minstrels, and magnificent sword fights. The fact is, though, life in the Middle Ages was anything but glamorous. Life generally was harsh, tentative, and downright dangerous. People did not live very long and those who made it to "old" age usually died before age 40. In the midst of this anachronism emerged some of the best literature in world history.

Chapter Learning Objectives In chapter 20 we analyze *The Divine Comedy* and enter the mind of medieval man.

As a result of this chapter study you will be able to . . .

1. Discuss the narrative technique Dante employs.

2. Analyze Dante's journey.

3. Evaluate when violence in literary works is necessary and unnecessary.

Weekly Essay Options: Begin on page 273 of the Teacher Guide.
Reading ahead: *Poem of the Cid,* Author Unknown (Lesson 22).

Middle Ages

Background The Middle Ages, or the Dark Ages, stretched roughly from the close of the Roman Empire (A.D. 476) to the 15th century (A.D. 1500). The Middle Ages began with the collapse of the Roman Empire and, although Roman culture continued to predominate for a while, it was soon replaced by feudalism.

Feudalism was a system of life where there was strict adherence to status, to station, and to position. In this feudal system, the king — who was on top of the status pyramid — awarded land grants to his most important nobles, his barons, and his bishops, in return for their loyalty and support. At the bottom of the status pyramid were the very poor people or peasants, also called serfs. In exchange for living and working on his land the owner of the manor offered his peasants protection. And they were "his" peasants. Everything they owned — their food, homes, and animals — all belonged to the lord of the manor. These peasants were not free people. They could not live where they wished nor perform any job they wished. Most were glad to do it. The fact is, as I stated, things were pretty dangerous for peasants. No one wanted to live away from the manor.

Normally, the peasants farmed part time and worked at a trade. They gave a portion of their earnings to the lord of the manor as a form of rent. These manors were isolated, with occasional visits from peddlers, pilgrims on their way to the Crusades, or soldiers from other fiefdoms.

Nobles, however, were not such docile subjects. Nobles divided their land among the lesser nobility, who became their vassals. Many of these vassals became so powerful that the kings had difficulty controlling them. In 1215, the English barons formed an alliance that forced King John to sign the Magna Carta. While it gave no rights to ordinary people, the Magna Carta limited the king's powers of taxation and required trials before punishment. It was the first time that an English monarch came under the control of the law and was the precedent for later constitutions.

On the feudal manors, however, the lord was master. The lords, working with the local priest, acted as judge in carrying out the laws of the manor.

It was particularly tough to be a woman in this world. Women mostly performed household tasks such as cooking and sewing. Some, however, especially serf women, also hunted for food and fought beside their husbands if their home was attacked. There were also some rare instances where medieval women were blacksmiths, merchants, and apothecaries (pharmacists). Some women were like witches, capable of sorcery and healing. Others became nuns and devoted their lives to God and spiritual matters. Famous women of the Middle Ages included Joan of Arc, who led Franch troops against an English invasion. She was an exception, though.

The Catholic Church was the only church in Europe during the Middle Ages. Therefore, church leaders played leading roles in government and in everyday life. The bishop was an advisor to kings. The village priest was a central part of peasant life. The priest was doctor and teacher. He was counselor and pastor.

As the population of Europe expanded, the little round-arched roof churches that had been built in the Roman style became too small. As a result, huge cathedrals were built. Monasticism expanded and increased. It was a safe place for people and a place that also allowed persons to fervently seek the Lord. Monasteries in the Middle Ages were based initially on the rules set down by St. Benedict in the 6th century. Later, the Order of St. Francis, the Society of

Jesus, and the Cistercian Society emerged. The monks took vows of poverty, chastity, and obedience to their leaders. They were required to perform manual labor and were forbidden to own property or to leave the monastery. Monasteries and nunneries were safe havens for pilgrims and other travelers.

Monks typically worshiped in the monastery chapel eight times a day. In a ritual that involved chanting, singing, and reciting prayers from the divine offices and from the service for Mass, the first office, "Matins," began at 2 a.m. and the next seven followed at regular intervals, culminating in "Vespers" in the evening and "Compline" before the monks retired at night. Between prayers, the monks read or copied religious texts and music. This was an important practice that enabled the Scriptures to be preserved accurately over a century. Monks were often well-educated and devoted their lives to writing and learning. The 7th-century Venerable Bede, for instance, an English Benedictine monk, wrote a history of England entitled *An Ecclesiastical History of the English People*.

Pilgrimages were an important part of religious life in the Middle Ages. Many people took journeys to visit holy shrines such as the Church of St. James in Spain, the Canterbury Cathedral in England, and, of course, sites in Jerusalem and Rome. Chaucer's *Canterbury Tales* is a series of stories told by 30 pilgrims as they traveled to Canterbury.

Homes — even beautiful castles — were not really very comfortable in the Middle Ages. Most medieval homes were cold, damp, and dark. Sometimes it was warmer and lighter outside the home than inside. For security purposes, windows, when they were present, were very small openings with wooden shutters that were closed at night or in bad weather. Besides, most medieval persons thought that it was unhealthy to breathe too much fresh air. Peasant families ate, slept, and spent time together in very small quarters, rarely more than one or two rooms. The houses had thatched roofs and were easily destroyed.

Castles were more elaborate than the peasants' homes, but they were still dark and dreary inside. Tapestries were hung on the stone walls, providing not only decoration but also an extra layer of warmth. The stones in castles stayed cold most of the winter, and once they were hot in the summer, stayed oppressively hot most of the summer. Only the very wealthy could afford panes of glass; sometimes only churches and royal residences had glass windows. Most used cheesecloth to keep out the bugs.

Nonetheless, populations of medieval towns and cities increased significantly. Great plagues broke out several times during this century with devastating results. The Plague or Black Death was an outbreak of bubonic plague that struck Europe and the Mediterranean area from 1347 through 1351. These plagues had been preceded by a cycle of ancient plagues between the 6th and 8th centuries A.D.

Europeans, thanks to Marco Polo, knew a great deal about China, but were unable to do much about it until they were able technologically, through their advanced sailing ships, to reach the Far East.

Wars were common. The Crusades against the Muslim Turks was fought for three centuries, and the Hundred Years' War in which England fought against France lasted from 1337 to 1453. In the early Middle Ages, the fully armored knight ruled much of the battlefield. He scorned the foot soldiers, who were usually just peasants, forced to fight by their lords. But by the 15th century the knight was fast becoming obsolete and ordinary soldiers were becoming more important. Technological advances — like the crossbow — made orthodox warfare obsolete. Lords started employing mercenary soldiers, who hired themselves out to the lord who offered the most money.

Dante Alighieri wrote as the Middle Ages was ending and the Renaissance was beginning. The Italian nationalism was emerging as a potent force in the European landscape.

- Warm-up: Some Protestants are critical of Dante's theology, but Dante merely expressed the orthodox views of his generation. Describe one.

- Students should complete Concept Builder 20-A.

- Students should review the required reading(s) *before* the assigned chapter begins.

- Teachers may want to discuss assigned reading(s) with students.

- Teachers shall assign the required essay. The rest of the essays can be outlined, answered with shorter answers, discussed, or skipped.

- Students will review all readings for chapter 20.

CONCEPT BUILDER 20-A
Active Reading

Read this excerpt from Dante's *Inferno* (Canto 1), and respond to the following:

The writer, having lost his way in a gloomy forest, and being hindered by
certain wild beasts from ascending a mountain, is met by Virgil, who promises
to show him the punishments of Hell, and afterward of Purgatory; and that he
shall then be conducted by Beatrice into Paradise. He follows the Roman poet.

Midway the path of life that men pursue
I found me in a darkling wood astray,
For the direct way had been lost to view.
Ah me, how hard a thing it is to say
What was this thorny wildwood intricate
Whose memory renews the first dismay!
Scarcely in death is bitterness more great:
But as concerns the good discovered there
The other things I saw will I relate.

In the midway of this our mortal life,
I found me in a gloomy wood, astray
Gone from the path direct: and e'en to tell,
It were no easy task, how savage wild
That forest, how robust and rough its growth,
Which to remember only, my dismay
Renews, in bitterness not far from death.
Yet, to discourse of what there good befel,
All else will I relate discover'd there.

How first I enter'd it I scarce can say,
Such sleepy dulness in that instant weigh'd
My senses down, when the true path I left;
But when a mountain's foot I reach'd, where closed
The valley that had pierced my heart with dread,
I look'd aloft, and saw his shoulders broad
Already vested with that planet's beam,
Who leads all wanderers safe through every way.

What is the central motif or theme of Canto I?

This epic poem employs first-person narration. What advantage does first-person narration offer Dante?

The Divine Comedy: Inferno
Dante Alighieri

Background Dante Alighieri (1265–1321) is Italy's greatest poet and also one of the most important writers in western European literature. He is best known for his monumental epic poem *La Commedia* later named *La Divina Commedia* (*The Divine Comedy*). Dante is one of the truly seminal writers of the Middle Ages. Besides, this great work of medieval literature is a profound Christian vision of the human condition and is edifying for all Christians to read. On the surface, Dante draws on his own experience of exile from his native city of Florence. In other words, in one sense *The Divine Comedy* is autobiographical. Dante was involved in Italian politics that deeply affected his vision. In another sense, however, *The Divine Comedy* is a Christian narrative on human life — birth to death and beyond. *The Divine Comedy* is an allegory (symbolic story), taking the form of a journey through hell, purgatory, and paradise. Also, by choosing to write his poem in Italian rather than in Latin, Dante decisively influenced the course of literary development. He was writing — believe it or not — a book for the common man.

Dante's Italian is considered not a particularly difficult read. So not only did he lend a voice to the emerging lay culture (i.e., common people) of his own country, thanks to Dante, the Italian language replaced Latin as the literary language in western Europe for several centuries. Italy was not even a nation, much less a paradigm of literary prominence. Dante brought Italy recognition and helped advance nationalistic causes. Dante also reintroduced the classics into Western literature. For his own purposes he drew on such writers as Virgil, Cicero, and Boethius (household names during the Middle Ages). While Augustine, a millennium earlier, had promoted the classics, during the medieval period most Christian writers had abandoned the classics. Dante had a firm grasp of Christianity and the classics. Later writers, such as John Milton, copied Dante's approach.

The famous poet Dante Alighieri's statue in Piazza Santa Croce in Florence, Italy.

- Warm-up: Who would be a contemporary equivalent to Dante?

- Students should complete Concept Builder 20-B.

- Students should review reading(s) from the next chapter.

- Students should outline essay due at the end of the week.

- Per teacher instructions, students may answer orally, in a group setting, some of the essays that are not assigned as formal essays.

CONCEPT BUILDER 20-B
Different Views of Hell

Several hundred years after Dante wrote *The Divine Comedy,* a German poet, Goethe, presents a much different view of hell. In this version of hell, Faust, who has sold his soul to the devil, escapes eternal damnation by "repenting of his bad choices on the way to hell." In French writer Jean Paul Sartre's play *No Exit,* three damned souls are brought to the same room in hell by a mysterious valet. They had all expected to burn for eternity, but instead find a plain room furnished comfortably. Then, for all of eternity, through conversation, they make each other miserable. Sartre concludes, "Hell is other people." It is not necessary for you to read Sartre or Goethe to answer this question. Merely, based on the above descriptions, analyze each view.

Contrast this contemporary view of hell with Dante's view of hell.

Component of Hell	Dante	Goethe	Sartre
God's participation	*God loves the world so much He sent His only begotten Son. If people accept that Savior as Lord of their lives, they will avoid hell.*	*Human behavior is secondary to human intention.*	*God is basically absent from Sartre's understanding of hell.*
Man's participation			
Notion of judgment			
Longevity of punishment			

Style

Inferno contains some very graphic — at times so powerful that it almost seems obscene — language. However, the poem is epic, moral, and grand, and is about Dante's interpretation of God and His purposes. Why does Dante do this?

Canto III

Through me the way is to the city dolent;
Through me the way is to eternal dole;
Through me the way among the people lost.

Justice incited my sublime Creator;
Created me divine Omnipotence,
The highest Wisdom and the primal Love.

Before me there were no created things,
Only eterne, and I eternal last.
All hope abandon, ye who enter in!"

These words in sombre colour I beheld
Written upon the summit of a gate;
Whence I: "Their sense is, Master, hard to me!"

And he to me, as one experienced:
"Here all suspicion needs must be abandoned,
All cowardice must needs be here extinct.

We to the place have come, where I have told thee
Thou shalt behold the people dolorous
Who have foregone the good of intellect."

And after he had laid his hand on mine
With joyful mien, whence I was comforted,
He led me in among the secret things.

There sighs, complaints, and ululations loud
Resounded through the air without a star,
Whence I, at the beginning, wept thereat.

Languages diverse, horrible dialects,
Accents of anger, words of agony,
And voices high and hoarse, with sound of hands,

Made up a tumult that goes whirling on
For ever in that air for ever black,
Even as the sand doth, when the whirlwind breathes.

And I, who had my head with horror bound,
Said: "Master, what is this which now I hear?
What folk is this, which seems by pain so vanquished?"

And he to me: "This miserable mode
Maintain the melancholy souls of those
Who lived withouten infamy or praise.

Commingled are they with that caitiff choir
Of Angels, who have not rebellious been,
Nor faithful were to God, but were for self.

The heavens expelled them, not to be less fair;
Nor them the nethermore abyss receives,
For glory none the damned would have from them."

And I: "O Master, what so grievous is
To these, that maketh them lament so sore?"
He answered: " I will tell thee very briefly.

These have no longer any hope of death;
And this blind life of theirs is so debased,
They envious are of every other fate.

No fame of them the world permits to be;
Misericord and Justice both disdain them.
Let us not speak of them, but look, and pass."

And I, who looked again, beheld a banner,
Which, whirling round, ran on so rapidly,
That of all pause it seemed to me indignant;
And after it there came so long a train
Of people, that I ne'er would have believed
That ever Death so many had undone.

When some among them I had recognised.
I looked, and I beheld the shade of him
Who made through cowardice the great refusal.

Forthwith I comprehended, and was certain,
That this the sect was of the caitiff wretches
Hateful to God and to his enemies.

These miscreants, who never were alive,
Were naked, and were stung exceedingly
By gadflies and by hornets that were there.

These did their faces irrigate with blood,
Which, with their tears commingled, at their feet
By the disgusting worms was gathered up.
And when to gazing farther I betook me.
People I saw on a great river's bank;
Whence said I: " Master, now vouchsafe to me,

That I may know who these are, and what law
Makes them appear so ready to pass over,
As I discern athwart the dusky light."

And he to me: "These things shall all be known
To thee, as soon as we our footsteps stay
Upon the dismal shore of Acheron."

Then with mine eyes ashamed and downward cast,
Fearing my words might irksome be to him,
From speech refrained I till we reached the river.

And lo! towards us coming in a boat
An old man, hoary with the hair of eld,
Crying: " Woe unto you, ye souls depraved

Hope nevermore to look upon the heavens;
I come to lead you to the other shore,
To the eternal shades in heat and frost.

And thou, that yonder standest, living soul,
Withdraw thee from these people, who are dead-
But when he saw that I did not withdraw,

"He said: "By other ways, by other ports
Thou to the shore shalt come, not here, for, passage;
A lighter vessel needs must carry thee."
And unto him the Guide: "Vex thee not, Charon;
It is so willed there where is power to do
That which is willed; and farther question not.
Thereat were quieted the fleecy cheeks
Of him the ferryman of the livid fen,
Who round about his eyes had wheels of flame.

But all those souls who weary were and naked
Their colour changed and gnashed their teeth
together,
As soon as they had heard those cruel words.

God they blasphemed and their progenitors,
The human race, the place, the time, the seed
Of their engendering and of their birth!

Thereafter all together they drew back,
Bitterly weeping, to the accursed shore,
Which waiteth every man who fears not God.

Charon the demon, with the eyes of glede,
Beckoning to them, collects them all together,
Beats with his oar whoever lags behind.

As in the autumn-time the leaves fall off,
First one and then another, till the branch
Unto the earth surrenders all its spoils;
In similar wise the evil seed of Adam

Throw themselves from that margin one by one,
At signals, as a bird unto its lure.

So they depart across the dusky wave,
And ere upon the other side they land,
Again on this side a new troop assembles.

"My son,"the courteous Master said to me,
"All those who perish in the wrath of God
Here meet together out of every land;

And ready are they to pass o'er the river,
Because celestial Justice spurs them on,
So that their fear is turned into desire.

This way there never passes a good soul;
And hence if Charon doth complain of thee
Well mayst thou know now what his speech
imports."

This being finished, all the dusk champaign
Trembled so violently, that of that terror
The recollection bathes me still with sweat.

The land of tears gave forth a blast of wind,
And fulminated a vermilion light,
'Which overmastered in me every sense,

And as a man whom sleep hath seized I fell.

Assignments

- Warm-up: From your reading of Canto III, identify some of this graphic imagery and explain how it enhances the effect of Dante's work.

- Students should complete Concept Builder 20-C.

- Students should write rough draft of assigned essay.

- The teacher may correct rough drafts.

CONCEPT BUILDER 20-C
Allegory

An allegory is a work in which the characters and events are to be understood as representing other things and symbol. There is allegory in *The Divine Comedy*. What does each character represent?

Character	Allegory
Virgil	*Reason*
Beatrice	
Francesca	
Farinata	

Critics Corner

***Divine Comedy: The Inferno:* On Beatrice** She is an invention, but an archtypal one, appealing to the deepest emotions, which was not only to be the focus of Dante's own religious idealism but was also, in a less calculable way, to affect ideas of the relationship between art, religion, saintliness and womanhood permanently. Though made so early in his career she is in a sense Dante's most original and profound creation.

— George Holmes, *Dante*, 1980

***Divine Comedy: The Inferno:* The Inexhaustibility Of Dante** The supreme art of poetry is not to assert meaning but to release it by the juxtaposition of poetic elements. Form, in its interrelations, is the most striking element. Because in any extended poetic structure these juxtapositions when looked at from different points of vantage, that release of meaning is subject to endless meaningful reinterpretation. The inexhaustibility of *The Divine Comedy* is a consequence of this structural quality. It is for that reason that no one can ever finish reading it. There will always be a new way of viewing the elements. But if no man can finish the poem, any man can begin it and be the richer for having begun. The present imperfect gloss — skimming though it be — is really about all one needs to start with. And having started, all he needs is to pay attention. The poem itself is the rest of the way, and the way is marked.

— John Ciardi, "How to Read Dante," 1961

***Divine Comedy: The Inferno:* Dante's Allegory** The greatest mistake consists in measuring Dante's allegory on the same terms as all other allegories: that is, as an idea which is dressed up, a concept in figurative terms. It is precisely the contrary. Dante moves from earth to heaven, from human to divine. . . . He refuses to make of his figures merely the symbols of ideas, as if they had no reality in themselves. But for him, form has a reality precisely because it is a symbol; thus, inasmuch as it signifies something, it is such as it is; and art is the portrayal of this something, by which every form lives in its allegorical essence, not as a garment but rather in its authentic reality. It is not Grace which becomes Beatrice; it is Beatrice who lives in her essential form of divine Grace. It is clear that we have here an absolute reversal of the concept of allegory. Whoever does not understand this cannot understand Dante.

— Luigi Pirandello, *Dante: A Collection of Critical Essays*, 1965.

***Divine Comedy: The Inferno:* Dante's Language**
If we start from his predecessors, Dante's language is a well-nigh incomprehensible miracle. There were great poets among them. But, compared with theirs, his style is so immeasurably richer in directness, vigor, and subtlety, he knows and uses such an immeasurably greater stock of forms, he expresses the most varied phenomena and subjects with such an immeasurably superior assurance and firmness, that we come to the conclusion that this man used his language to discover the world anew.

— Erich Auerbach, *Mimesis*, 1953

Divine Comedy: The Inferno: **The Journey** If this journey to God begins in the figure of an Exodus, and then leaves that figure, to return to it after a long descent through Hell, the reason for this is clearly a matter worthy of attention. What we have here, in its simplest statement, is a first attempt to climb that fails, then a long descent that returns the wayfarer to a second attempt that succeeds. Can this configuration of event in the journey beyond be pointing to the truth that it is necessary for us to descend that we may ascend (this being, in the moral allegory, our journey)?

— Charles Singleton, *Dante: A Collection of Critical Essays*, 1965.

Assignments

- Warm-up: Which critic do you find most persuasive?
- Students should complete Concept Builder 20-D.
- Students will re-write corrected copies of essay due tomorrow.

CONCEPT BUILDER 20-D
Dante's Nine Levels of Hell

Label Dante's nine levels of hell.

Purgatory

Allegory in *The Divine Comedy*

Written during the 14th century, *The Divine Comedy* is an allegory capturing at the time the largely believed medieval concept of hell. It represents the soul's journey toward God, with the first book, *The Inferno*, describing Dante's journey through the nine circles of hell, symbolizing his recognition and rejection of sin. In the very last circle, Dante illustrates treachery, treachery against man, and the ultimate sin, personal treachery against God. It is here in the very center of hell that Dante depicts Satan, and the tortures he must endure. In psalm 139:7 David writes, "Where can I go from your Spirit? Where can I flee from your presence?" Did Dante portray God's love even in the very center of hell?

In Revelation 12:7–12, the story of the fall of Satan is told, "And war broke out in heaven: Michael and his angels fought with the dragon; and the dragon and his angels fought, but they did not prevail, nor was a place found for them in heaven any longer. So the great dragon was cast out, that serpent of old, called the Devil and Satan, who deceives the whole world; he was cast to the earth, and his angels were cast out with him. Then I heard a loud voice saying in heaven, 'Now salvation, and strength, and the kingdom of our God, and the power of His Christ have come, for the accuser of our brethren, who accused them before our God day and night, has been cast down. And they overcame him by the blood of the Lamb and by the word of their testimony, and they did not love their lives to the death. Therefore rejoice, O heavens, and you who dwell in them! Woe to the inhabitants of the earth and the sea! For the devil has come down to you, having great wrath, because he knows that he has a short time' " (NKJV). In *The Inferno* Dante shows this great wrath of Satan as he describes "the emperor of the despondent kingdom." He is portrayed as a terrible giant beast with three faces, one black, one red, and one yellow. He is waist deep, stuck in ice, but is ever beating six scaly wings to try and escape, while his six eyes are gushing with tears. He is "raising his brows against his Maker," and, "with gnashing teeth tearing to bits a sinner." This depiction of Satan on the outside seems completely void of any love.

But if one searches deeper, one finds that love does not always mean happiness. A 7th-century ascetic monk, St. Isaac of Syria, wrote about heaven and hell, "Those who find themselves in hell will be chastised by the scourge of love. How cruel and bitter this torment of love will be! For those who understand that they have sinned against love, undergo no greater suffering than those produced by the most fearful tortures. The sorrow which takes hold of the heart, which has sinned against love, is more piercing than any other pain. It is not right to say that the sinners in hell are deprived of the love of God. . . . But love acts in two ways, as suffering of the reproved, and as joy in the blessed!" (St. Isaac of Syria, *Mystic Treatises*, www.abovetopsecret.com/forum/thread871912/pg1).

In the rest of Psalm 139, David concludes, "Where can I go from Your Spirit? Or where can I flee from Your presence? If I ascend into heaven, You are there; if I make my bed in hell, behold, You are there. If I take the wings of the morning, and dwell in the uttermost parts of the sea, even there Your hand shall lead me, and Your right hand shall hold me" (Ps. 139:7–10). Even in the very center of hell, at the place completely void of hope, the love of God is as strong as ever tormenting those who rejected it, and those who refused to repent, the ultimate object of this love: Satan. (Anna Grace)

Assignments

- Warm-up: What does the author say about Psalm 139?

- Students should complete Concept Builder 20-E.

- Essays are due. Students should take the chapter 20 test.

CONCEPT BUILDER 20-E
Form

The form of a literary work is the internal and external structure that an author employs to communicate his topic.

Match each form with the label.

1. ____	The Comedy	A. A long narrative poem of grand scale involving superhuman heroes upon whom the nation or even the world depends. Usually is written in elevated or very formal language in the middle of the action.
2. ____	The Epic	B. The hero wants something and certain people and/or elements are stopping him from getting it. The obstacles to a hero's goals make up the action; overcoming the obstacles is the resolution. Dante's attempt to get to heaven, to Beatrice, and to God is successful.
3. ____	The Quest	C. The hero becomes separated from the people and/or the place of his birth, becomes aware of a need or a problem, takes a dangerous journey to an unknown place to win either a prize or knowledge to help him resolve the problem, and returns to save the people.

Chapter 21

(A.D. 500–1500):
Middle Ages (Part 2)

First Thoughts Literary critic Erich Auerbach writes, "*The Comedy*, among other things, is a didactic poem of encyclopedic dimensions, in which the physico-cosmological, the ethical, the historical political order of the universe is collectively presented; it is, further, a literary work which imitates reality and in which all imaginable spheres of reality appear: past and present, sublime grandeur and vile vulgarity, history and legend, tragic and comic occurrences, man and nature; finally, it is the story of Dante's — i.e., one single individual's — life and salvation, and thus a figure of the story of mankind's salvation in general."

Chapter Learning Objectives In chapter 21 we analyze *The Divine Comedy* and enter the mind of medieval man.

As a result of this chapter study you will be able to . . .

1. Write a definition paragraph on what hell is to Dante. Compare this view of hell to contemporary understandings of hell (e.g., *No Exit* by Jean-Paul Sartre).

2. Contrast Dante's cosmology with Scripture.

3. Evaluate the prayer lives of Hildegard von Bingen and Catherine of Siena.

4. Give examples of polarity in Dante's writing.

5. Explain why New Age mystics find Hildegard von Bingen and Catherine of Siena so appealing.

Weekly Essay Options: Begin on page 273 of the Teacher Guide.

Reading ahead: *Poem of the Cid*, Author Unknown, "May Heaven Serve as Plate for the Engraving" and "Yet if, for Singing your Praise" by Sor Juana Ines de la Cruz.

History connections: *World History* chapter 21, "The Crusades."

Styles and Symbols

Continuing his thoughts on Dante's *Divine Comedy*, Erich Auerbach states: "Its dramatis personae included figures from antique mythology, often (but not always) in the guise of fantastic demons; allegorical personifications and symbolic animals stemming from late antiquity and the Middle Ages; bearers of specific significations chosen from among the angels, the saints, and the blessed in the hierarchy of Christianity; Apollo, Lucifer and Christ, Fortuna and Lady Poverty, Medusa as an emblem of the deeper circles of Hell, and Cato of Utica as the guardian of Purgatory. Yet, in respect to an attempt at the elevated style, all these things are not so new and problematic as is Dante's undisguised incursions into the realm of real life neither selected nor preordained by aesthetic criteria. And, indeed, it is this contact with real life which is responsible for all the verbal forms whose directness and rigor — almost unknown in the elevated style — offended classicistic taste" (Erich Auerbach, *Mimesis*, Princeton, NJ: Princeton University Press, 1953).

Dante gazes at Mount Purgatory by Agnolo Bronzino, c.1530 (PD-US).

Assignments

- Warm-up: What is your favorite symbol; an element or image that conveys meaning to you?
- Students should complete Concept Builder 21-A.
- Students should review the required reading(s) *before* the assigned chapter begins.
- Teachers may want to discuss assigned reading(s) with students.
- Teachers shall assign the required essay. The rest of the essays can be outlined, answered with shorter answers, discussed, or skipped.
- Students will review all readings for chapter 21.

One feature of Dante's vision of the universe is the concept of polarities: the universe is two extreme opposites, between which people were pulled (Barron's Notes, unpublished Aol.com).

Match the polarities.

1. ___	Plato vs. Augustine	A. There was a power struggle between the Church and state.
2. ___	The pope vs. the German emperor.	B. There was a struggle for intellectual authority between theology (the study of religion and the Bible) and philosophy (which included science and mathematics).
3. ___	Sin vs. the image of God	C. Man was considered to fall halfway between the animals and the angels, and was therefore torn between the brutish and the angelic sides of his nature.
4. ___	Allegory vs. symbolism	D. Dante also felt that writing should reflect a balance between the ideas and the realities of a man's life, so we see him moving between two different aesthetic approaches in his poetry: personal realism and symbolism in allegory.

Dante's Hell

For Dante, both the physical and the spiritual worlds were set up as a hierarchy, leading up to God. Everything began with God and existed in layers radiating outward from Him. This was a typical Medieval Christian perspective. The story line of the *Inferno, Book I* of *The Divine Comedy* is Dante's journey through hell. (It should be noted that this journey is Dante's rendition of hell—not a biblical account.)

He starts at the top of hell—purgatory—and walks through to the bottom. In effect, Dante journeys deeper into hell and, at the same time, deeper into levels of sin. Dante places himself in the story, an effective narrative technique for the storyline. At the same time, Dante meets several guides who lead him through his rendition of hell.

Satan is trapped in the frozen central zone in the Ninth Circle of Hell, Canto 34 by Gustave Doré, c.1861 (PD-Art).

Assignments

- Warm-up: Draw your own version of hell.
- Students should complete Concept Builder 21-B.
- Students should review reading(s) from the next chapter.
- Students should outline essay due at the end of the week.
- Per teacher instructions, students may answer orally, in a group setting, some of the essays that are not assigned as formal essays.

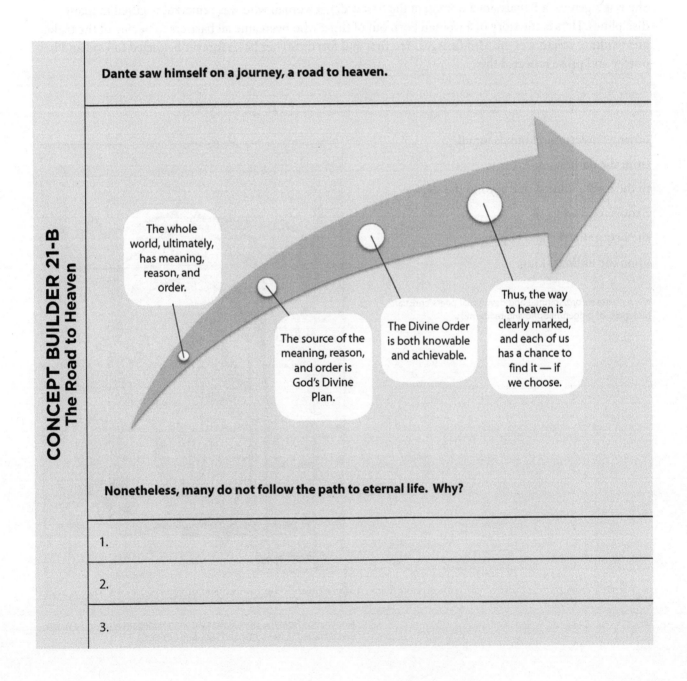

CONCEPT BUILDER 21-B
The Road to Heaven

Dante saw himself on a journey, a road to heaven.

The whole world, ultimately, has meaning, reason, and order.

The source of the meaning, reason, and order is God's Divine Plan.

The Divine Order is both knowable and achievable.

Thus, the way to heaven is clearly marked, and each of us has a chance to find it — if we choose.

Nonetheless, many do not follow the path to eternal life. Why?

1.

2.

3.

Hildegard von Bingen

Background Hildegard von Bingen (1098–1179) was an extraordinary woman in many ways. She was a genius, a Renaissance woman of the first order, a woman who was remarkably gifted in many disciplines. Hers is the story of a woman born out of time, who overcame all barriers to be one of the truly great culture creators of the Middle Ages. Yet, first and foremost, her heart forever belonged to God and her poetry and prose reflected this.

Loving Tenderness Abounds

Loving tenderness abounds for all

from the darkest

to the most eminent one beyond the stars.

Exquisitely loving all

she bequeaths the kiss of peace

upon the ultimate king.

www.poetseers.org/spiritual-and-devotional-poets/christian/
hildegard-of-bingen/hildp/loving-tenderness/.

Illumination from the Liber Scivias showing Hildegard receiving a vision and dictating to her scribe and secretary (PD-OLD).

Assignments

- Warm-up: Describe a godly person who inspires you by his/her prayer life.

- Students should complete Concept Builder 21-C.

- Students should write rough draft of assigned essay.

- The teacher may correct rough drafts.

CONCEPT BUILDER 21-C

Dante's Satan

In Dante's *Inferno*, Satan is portrayed as a giant beast, frozen mid-breast in ice at the center of hell. Satan has three heads, and affixed under each chin are pairs of bat-like wings. As Satan beats his wings, he creates a cold wind that continues to freeze the ice surrounding him, and the other sinners in the Ninth Circle. The winds he creates are felt throughout the other circles of hell. Each of his three mouths chew on Judas, Brutus, and Cassius. Draw a picture of Dante's Satan.

Catherine of Siena

Saint Catherine of Siena (1347–1380), Dominican nun, was a gifted, pious woman who was also a poet and prose writer. Remarkably, she was probably learning-disabled, suffering from dysgraphia. She learned to read at an early age but could not write until she was an adult. This challenge did not deter her walk with the Lord — she was a very devoted Christian noted for her gift of contemplation and her devotion to the poor.

A Treatise of Prayer

When the soul has passed through the doctrine of Christ crucified, with true love of virtue and hatred of vice, and has arrived at the house of self-knowledge and entered therein, she remains, with her door barred, in watching and constant prayer, separated entirely from the consolations of the world. Why does she thus shut herself in? She does so from fear, knowing her own imperfections, and also from the desire, which she has, of arriving at pure and generous love. And because she sees and knows well that in no other way can she arrive thereat, she waits, with a lively faith for My arrival, through increase of grace in her. How is a lively faith to be recognized? By perseverance in virtue, and by the fact that the soul never turns back for anything, whatever it be, nor rises from holy prayer, for any reason except (note well) for obedience for charity's sake. For no other reason ought she to leave off prayer, for, during the time ordained for prayer, the Devil is wont to arrive in the soul, causing much more conflict and trouble than when the soul is not occupied in prayer. This he does in order that holy prayer may become tedious to the soul, tempting her often with these words, "This prayer avails you nothing, for you need attend to nothing except your vocal prayers." He acts thus in order that, becoming wearied and confused in mind, she may abandon the exercise of prayer, which is a weapon with which the soul can defend herself from every adversary, if grasped with the hand of love, by the arm of free choice in the light of the Holy Faith (www.ccel.org/ccel/catherine/dialog.iv.iv.i.html).

Assignments

- Warm-up: Describe your prayer life.
- Students should complete Concept Builder 21-D.
- Students will re-write corrected copies of essay due tomorrow.

Dante writes an entire literary piece that assumes a certain biblical knowledge base. Dante assumes his readers bring certain presumptions to their reading of his *Inferno*. Assuming an audience has certain knowledge is a form of allusion. This often happens in literature. Langston Hughes' "I, Too, Sing America," refers to another poem, written 50 years before, "I Hear America Singing," by Walt Whitman. Compare these two poems.

I, Too, Sing America	I Hear America Singing
I, too, sing America. I am the darker brother. They send me to eat in the kitchen When company comes, But I laugh, And eat well, And grow strong. Tomorrow, I'll be at the table When company comes. Nobody'll dare Say to me, "Eat in the kitchen," Then. Besides, They'll see how beautiful I am And be ashamed — I, too, am America.	I hear America singing, the varied carols I hear; Those of mechanics — each one singing his, as it should be, blithe and strong; The carpenter singing his, as he measures his plank or beam, The mason singing his, as he makes ready for work, or leaves off work; The boatman singing what belongs to him in his boat — the deckhand singing on the steamboat deck; The shoemaker singing as he sits on his bench — the hatter singing as he stands; The wood-cutter's song — the ploughboy's, on his way in the morning, or at the noon intermission, or at sundown; The delicious singing of the mother — or of the young wife at work — or of the girl sewing or washing — Each singing what belongs to her, and to none else; The day what belongs to the day — At night, the party of young fellows, robust, friendly, Singing, with open mouths, their strong melodious songs

	Hughes	Whitman
Title		
Form		
Topic		
Mood		
Repetition		

Dante's World

As seen in Dante's *Inferno*, a common medieval belief stated that the physical and spiritual words were set up in layers with God in the center. Essentially, everything circled around God and extended outward in layers. However, the Bible never mentions different layers but instead mentions three distinct worlds.

"In the beginning God created the heavens and the earth. . . . Then God said, 'Let there be a firmament in the midst of the waters, and let it divide the waters from the waters.' Thus God made the firmament, and divided the waters which were under the firmament from the waters which were above the firmament; and it was so. And God called the firmament Heaven" (Gen. 1:1–8; NKJV). As we see in Genesis chapter 1, God created heaven and the earth. These are two distinct places, separated from each other. Heaven is a perfect world with no death or suffering, while earth is a sinful place. In addition, there is a third world, called hell. "Let death seize them; Let them go down alive into hell, for wickedness is in their dwellings and among them" (Ps. 55:15; NKJV). In addition to perfect heaven and sinful earth, there is an evil place called hell, where non-Christians are eternally punished. It is a world of eternal suffering and pain. These worlds are not set up in layers, but are three distinct, separate worlds.

Dante believes in these three worlds but believes they radiate outward from God. This is especially seen in *Inferno*. "Thus I descended out of the first circle down to the second" (*Inferno* 25). Dante views hell as various circles spreading out from Satan. "In the third circle am I of the rain eternal, malicious, and cold, and heavy" (*Inferno* 31). As Dante passes through each circle, he comes closer to Satan, and the center of hell. "Thus we descended into the fourth chain" (*Inferno* 35). In each circle, different sins are punished. For example, gluttonous sinners are punished in the third circle by fiery hail and rain. But in the tenth circle, forgers are punished by being unable to discern anything. The circles radiate out from Satan. However, in the *Inferno*, Dante is traveling from the outer circles toward Satan. Thus, as he enters each new circle, the sins and their respective punishments grow increasingly evil and severe.

While heaven, earth, and hell are different worlds, and separated from each other, they are not made up of layers. "The wicked shall be turned into hell, and all the nations that forget God" (Ps. 9:17; NKJV). Psalm 9:17 speaks of hell. It says the wicked shall be punished in hell. But it does not speak of various layers throughout hell, or different layers for different punishments. "Hell and Destruction are before the LORD" (Prov. 15:11; NKJV). There are no layers or circles. God can see everything in hell from heaven. "And being in torments in Hades, he lifted up his eyes and saw Abraham afar off and Lazarus in his bosom. Then he cried and said, 'Father Abraham have mercy on me, and send Lazarus that he may dip the tip of his finger in water and cool my tongue; for I am tormented in this flame" (Luke 16:23–24; NKJV). In fact, those in heaven can see the people in hell, and vice-versa. There are no layers radiating from God. He, in heaven, can see hell and earth. The only "layers" are between the three different worlds.

Unlike the common medieval belief, the Bible does not mention anything about circles or layers radiating out from God. Instead, there are three worlds which are separated from each other. Heaven, earth, and hell are not made up of layers, but are all one place. In fact, those in heaven can see the suffering in hell, and those in hell can see the perfection of heaven. (Chris)

Assignments

- Warm-up: Summarize this essay in 50 words.

- Students should complete Concept Builder 21-E.

- Essays are due. Students should take the chapter 21 test.

Historically, Virgil was a Roman poet who created a mythological beginning for the Roman Empire in his poem, *The Aeneid*. The hero of the poem, Aeneas, was a Trojan who survived the final sacking of Troy in the Trojan War by escaping with his father, his son, and some loyal men. They set off in ships to found a new Troy, which became Rome. The expedition was, like Dante's own "journey" in the comedy, divinely inspired and aided (by Virgil's pagan gods). But Dante felt there was even more significance than that to Virgil's theme. The Roman Empire not only spread peace and stability; it was eventually responsible for the spread of Christianity. Although it was not biblical, Dante probably saw *The Aeneid* as a very important myth for Christians. She is an invention, but an archetypal one, appealing to the deepest emotions, which was not only to be the focus of Dante's own religious idealism but was also, in a less calculable way, to affect ideas of the relationship between art, religion, saintliness, and womanhood permanently. Though made so early in his career, she is in a sense Dante's most original and profound creation. Dante Alighieri (1265–1321) was born in Florence, Italy, where he also spent much of his life. In 1274, at the age of nine, he was introduced to Beatrice Portinari; they met again nine years later, and Dante was profoundly affected by her beauty and grace. When she died in 1290, Dante was inspired to commemorate her in several works. What does each guide represent?

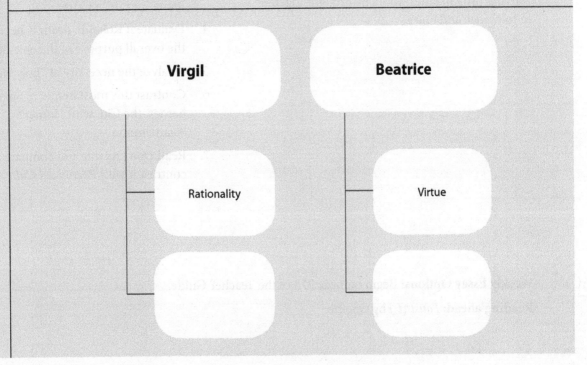

Virgil

Beatrice

Rationality

Virtue

Chapter 22

(A.D. 500–1500)
Middle Ages (Part 3)

First Thoughts The *Poema del Cid* (*Hero's Song*) was written by an unknown Castilian Spaniard around A.D. 1140. It is the only great medieval epic surviving in its original form and is considered Spain's great national epic. It tells the exploits of Rodrigo Diaz de Bivar, who was named the Cid (hero) by both his followers and his enemies. Invincible in battle, the Cid checked and then drove out the Moors (Islamic peoples) who invaded Spanish shores. The Cid embodied the best of Spanish culture: valor, self-control, dignity, piety, patriotism, magnanimity, and honor. He was a man of relatively humble origins; he triumphed over the Moors and the arrogant members of the Spanish nobility by force and by law. In advance of his time, the Cid conceived of a nation where warring principalities would be brought together in tolerance and unity.

Chapter Learning Objectives In chapter 22 we march with El Cid to defeat the Saracens, and, we die with Roland, fighting the same enemy. We glorify the Lord with a brilliant, but conflicted nun in old Mexico.

As a result of this chapter study you will be able to . . .

1. Identify the structure *Poema del Cid* (*Song of the Cid*) employs.

2. State the purposes of the villains Fernando Gonzalez and Gonzlo Ansurez.

3. Identify the themes of "Yet if, for Singing your Praise" and "May Heaven Serve as Plate for the Engraving" by Sor Juana Inéz de la Cruz.

4. Evaluate if Roland's death is necessary to the overall purpose of the epic poem.

5. Analyze the necessity of "holy wars."

6. Contrast this most heroic of Spanish heroes, the Cid, with Homer's Agamemnon.

7. Read *Don Quixote* and compare and contrast it with *Poema del Cid*.

Weekly Essay Options: Begin on page 273 of the Teacher Guide.

Reading ahead: *Faust (I)* by Goethe.

 History connections: *World History* chapter 22, "Age of Discovery."

Poema del Cid
Author Unknown

Background Nations have been around for a very long time, though they take different shapes at different points in history. What is a nation? Benedict Anderson, in Imagined Communities, defines a nation as "an imagined political community — and imagined as both inherently limited and sovereign. It is imagined because the members of even the smallest nation will never know most of their fellow-members, meet them, or even hear of them, yet in the minds of each lives the image of their communion." (Benedict Anderson, *Imagined Communities: Reflections on the Origin and Spread of Nationalism*, revised edition. London and New York: Verso, 1991, p. 5; www.nationalismproject.org/what/anderson.htm). Millions of strangers rally around a flag, an idea, a charismatic leader.

Adrian Hastings, in *The Construction of Nationhood*, examines this concept. For the development of nationhood from many different cultures and ethnicities, by far the most important factor is that of an extensively used vernacular literature. A long struggle against an external threat may also have a unifying, significant effect as is evidenced in France at the end of the 18th century. An ethnicity is a group of people with a shared cultural identity and spoken language. Ethnic groups can exist in one nation, but somehow they must find a way to unify. Outside threats and a common language all conspire to make a people unite as a nation.

Hastings writes, "A nation is a far more self-conscious community than an ethnic group. Formed from one or more ethnicities, and normally identified by a literature of its own, [a nation] possesses or claims the right to political identity and autonomy as a people, together with the control of specific territory, comparable to that of biblical Israel and of other independent entities in a world thought of as one of nation-states."

Often a nation is formed by geographical barriers as the Pyrenees Mountains separate France from Spain and as the Atlantic Ocean separates England from everyone else.

Professor Hastings concludes, "A nation-state is a state which identifies itself in terms of one specific nation whose people are not seen simply as 'subjects' of the sovereign but as a horizontally bonded society to whom the state in a sense belongs. There is thus an identity of character between state and people. In some way the state's sovereignty is inherent within the people, expressive of its historic identity. In it, ideally, there is a basic equivalence between the borders and character of the political unit upon the one hand and a self-conscious cultural community on the other. In most cases this is a dream as much as a reality. Most nation-states in fact include groups of people who do not belong to its core culture or feel themselves to be part of a nation so defined. Nevertheless almost all modern states act on the bland assumption that they are nation-states" (Adrian Hastings, *The Construction of*

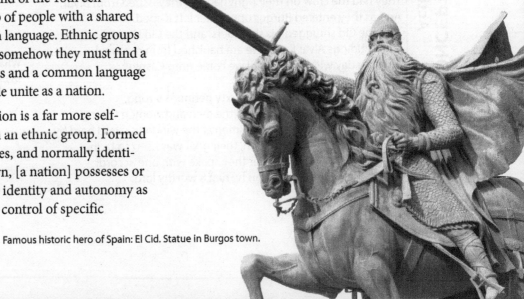

Famous historic hero of Spain: El Cid. Statue in Burgos town.

Nationhood: Ethnicity, Religion and Nationalism (Cambridge and New York: Cambridge University Press, 1997), p. 2–5, www.nationalismproject.org/what/hastings.htm).

The Bible provides the original model of the nation. The nation of Israel was a people of destiny in a geographical area serving the same God.

In summary, most nations develop on the basis of common ties of religion and language. Spain was developing as a country when the *Poem of the Cid* was written.

Assignments

- Warm-up: What role does valor and honor play in *Poema del Cid*?
- Students should complete Concept Builder 22-A.
- Students should review the required reading(s) *before* the assigned chapter begins.
- Teachers may want to discuss assigned reading(s) with students.
- Teachers shall assign the required essay. The rest of the essays can be outlined, answered with shorter answers, discussed, or skipped.
- Students will review all readings for chapter 22.

CONCEPT BUILDER 22-A
Active Reading

Read this excerpt from *The Lay of the Cid* (Canto 1) "The Banishment of the Cid," and respond to the following:

He turned and looked upon them, and he wept very sore
As he saw the yawning gateway and the hasps wrenched off the door,
And the pegs whereon no mantle nor coat of vair there hung.
There perched no moulting goshawk, and there no falc on swung.
My lord the Cid sighed deeply such grief was in his heart
And he spake well and wisely: "Oh Thou, in Heaven that art
Our Father and our Master, now I give thanks to Thee.
Of their wickedness my foemen have done this thing to me."

Then they shook out the bridle rein further to ride afar.
They had the crow on their right hand as they issued from Bivar;
And as they entered Burgos upon their left it sped.
And the Cid shrugged his shoulders, and the Cid shook his head:
"Good tidings Alvar Fanez We are banished from our weal,
But on a day with honor shall we come unto Castile."

Roy Diaz entered Burgos with sixty pennons strong,
And forth to look upon him did the men and women throng.
And with their wives the townsmen at the windows stood hard by,
And they wept in lamentation, their grief was risen so high.
As with one mouth, together they spake with one accord:
"God, what a noble vassal, an he had a worthy lord.

In his moment of grief, to whom does the Cid turn?

Why is the Cid still hopeful?

What is the purpose of the townsmen?

Sor Juana Inéz de la Cruz

Background Juana Inéz de la Cruz was born on November 12, 1651, in Mexico, then called New Spain, in a small town not far from Mexico City. Learning to read before she was 3 years old, she displayed from her earliest childhood an extraordinary passion for knowledge. By the time she was 19 she devoted her great gifts to the glory of God and entered a monastery. She died when she was 46. The following are two poems translated by Alan Trueblood. More poems may be obtained from *A Sor Juana Anthology*, with both Spanish and English versions (*A Sor Juana Anthology*, translated by Alan S. Trueblood (Cambridge, MA and London: Harvard University Press, 1988), p. 29, 49–51).

Yet if, for Singing Your Praise

Yet if, for singing your praise

no power on earth will do

if your feather-pen alone

is worthy to celebrate you,

why should I make the attempt,

why throw to the winds all caution,

especially when feathers are known

to have written their lessons in water!

So I'll leave it up to your praise

to drink to its own health,

since whoever is his own model

has no other rule than self.

May Heaven Serve as Plate for the Engraving

May Heaven serve as plate for the engraving

portraying, Lysis, your angelic figure;

may the sun turn its beams into quills,

may all the stars compose their syllables.

Your skein of locks is as a prison-house,

a Cretan labyrinth that twists and curls

in webbings of golden Ophirs,

in Tibbars of fair prison-cells.

Your cheeks are April's lecture halls,

with classic lessons to impart to May:

recipes for making jasmine snowy,

formulas for redness in the rose.

In your mouth Aurora's chill tears

are kept in a many-scented vase;

its rubric is written in carmine,

its clause penned in coral and pearl.

Assignments

- Warm-up: Write a poem glorifying God.

- Students should complete Concept Builder 22-B.

- Students should review reading(s) from next chapter.

- Students should outline essays due at the end of the week.

- Per teacher instructions, students may answer orally, in a group setting, some of the essays that are not assigned as the formal essay.

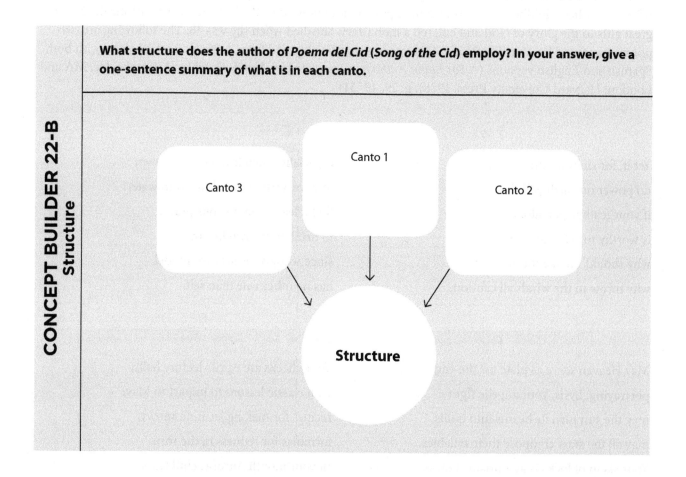

CONCEPT BUILDER 22-B
Structure

What structure does the author of *Poema del Cid* (*Song of the Cid*) employ? In your answer, give a one-sentence summary of what is in each canto.

Canto 1

Canto 3

Canto 2

Structure

The Song of Roland
Turoldus (?)

Background There is a growing consensus that an obscure 11th-century monk named Turoldus copied or even wrote *The Song of Roland*. The oldest surviving manuscript, the Oxford Digby 23, is signed "Turoldus" and is written in Anglo-Norman, a language predominant in England following the Norman invasion from France in 1066. Since almost no one in 11th-century France knew how to write, this document must have been written by a monk or some other clergy person. If Turoldus wrote this tale, he still probably acted chiefly as a recorder. The epic was no doubt popular in oral French folklore and used in celebrations long before Turoldus put it into writing. The legend, existing from the time of Charlemagne (died 814), was probably put into poetic form by a single individual.

The great medieval French epic poem *The Song of Roland* is as significant to the French as the Anglo-Saxon *Beowulf* is to the English and as the *Poema del Cid* is to the Spanish. Charlemagne's nephew, the warrior Roland, fights bravely to his death in a legendary battle — one of the most memorable in Western literature — rivaled only by the great fight scenes in Homer's *Iliad*. Against the backdrop of the struggle between Christianity and Islam, *The Song of Roland* remains a vivid portrayal of knightly chivalry and adventure.

Song of Roland (Charlemagne grieving the death of brave Roland and his knights):

LXVI

High are the peaks, the valleys shadowful,
Swarthy the rocks, the narrows wonderful.
Franks passed that day all very sorrowful,
Fifteen leagues round the rumour of them grew.
When they were come, and Terra Major knew,
Saw Gascony their land and their seigneur's,
Remembering their fiefs and their honours,
Their little maids, their gentle wives and true;
There was not one that shed not tears for rue.
Beyond the rest Charles was of anguish full,
In Spanish Pass he'd left his dear nephew;
Pity him seized; he could but weep for rue.

www.gutenberg.org/cache/epub/391/pq391.html.

Eight phases of *The Song of Roland* in one picture. Located at St. Petersburg. artist and date unknown (PD-Art).

- Warm-up: How does Oliver function in this poem?
- Students should complete Concept Builder 22-C.
- Students should write rough draft of assigned essay.
- The teacher may correct rough draft.

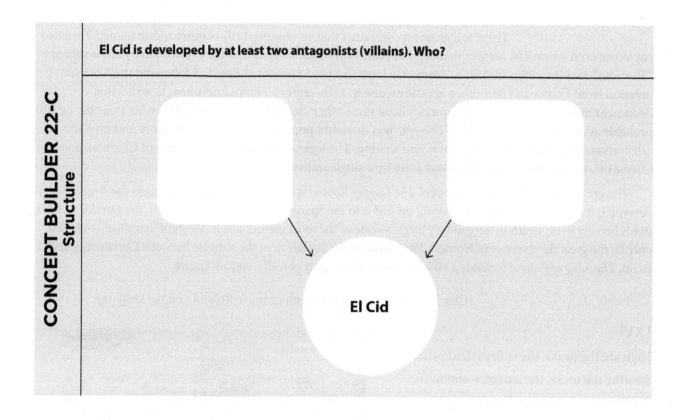

CONCEPT BUILDER 22-C
Structure

El Cid is developed by at least two antagonists (villains). Who?

El Cid

Sor Juana Ines de la Cruzs

As a prolific female poet living in the 17th century, Sor Juana Inés de la Cruzs received a deluge of often misogynistic criticism from her contemporaries. In an attempt to separate herself from her gender and dedicate her life to intellectual pursuits, Sor Juana entered a convent and took a vow of celibacy. However, this attempt was futile: the comments and criticism continued. An unidentified but indignant Peruvian poet went so far as to send Sor Juana a few clay pots, accompanied by a crude suggestion to change her gender. Sor Juana's response, "Respond-iendo a un caballero del Peru" (Poem 48), feigns speechlessness. In fact, she uses indifference to make it clear that she will not reply on his terms. Instead of replying on his terms, Sor Juana uses the rhetoric of praise to devalue his work.

Sor Juana begins her response by claiming that words fail her — or rather, that they fail the Muses (the "nueve hermanas"). Since Greek times, the Muses have been the traditional deities of inspiration for male poets. By pointing out this tradition, Sor Juana is also cleverly showing that poetry, at least in the 17th century, is bound up with assumptions about gender: women cannot have knowledge and write poetry, they can only be objects of poetic discourse. She continues praising the Peruvian poet's work:

> Yet if, for singing your praise
> no power on earth will do
> if your feather-pen alone
> is worthy to celebrate you,
> why should I make the attempt,
> why throw to the winds all caution,

especially when feathers are known
to have written their lessons in water!

Here, Sor Juana sardonically laments her own inability to appreciate his work — and even his criticism. As a woman, Sor Juana is unable to even appreciate his poetry (much less be an author her-self). If she is not able to appreciate his poetry, then Sor Juana is not able to appreciate his criticism or reply on his terms.

The most devastating part of Sor Juana's reply; however, is in the second stanza, where she contem-plates the implications of his works surpassing excellence:

> So I'll leave it up to your praise
> to drink to its own health,
> since whoever is his own model
> has no other rule than self.

Here, Sor Juana uses the rhetoric of praise to depreciate his poetry: she argues that his work is of such surpassing excellence that only he could possibly appreciate it. If only he can appreciate his poetry, then it does not have much value at all. If his poetry does not have value, then who is he to offer criticism?

In her response to the Peruvian poet's criticism, Sor Juana uses indifference and praise to deflate his poetry. By praising his poetry, Sor Juana distance herself from his work — and also from his criticism. Furthermore, she argues that his poetry is of such surpassing value that no one (much less herself) can appreciate it — effectively stripping it of all its merit. (Daniel)

Assignments

- Warm-up: Was de la Cruz a feminist or an intensely religious poet or both?
- Students should complete Concept Builder 22-D.
- Students will re-write corrected copies of essay due tomorrow.

El Cid is an epic hero.

Unusual circumstances surround the hero's birth

After the final task is successfully accomplished, the hero returns home, a leader of his people

Epic Hero

The hero encounters women as temptresses who threaten his completion of the journey

At the end of the journey, the hero must complete a final task alone

In what way is Samson an epic hero, too?

Samson is born under unique, extraordinary conditions.

Samson

Epic Hero

Student Essay

The Song of Roland

In the *Epic of Gilgamesh*, Gilgamesh safely arrives at the place where one may find the secret to immortality, but returns home empty-handed, forced to acknowledge that his death is inevitable and will not be avoided. In Homer's *Iliad*, Achilles leads the Achaeans to push back their enemies, the Trojans, only to be killed in a peaceful lull by a poisoned arrow shot at his heel. Similarly, in *The Song of Roland*, Roland leads his army to victory over the Spanish, only to himself die shortly afterward. In all of these works, the hero accomplishes a great part of his mission, but then dies before he can either complete it or reap the rewards of his toil. Why would an author allow the primary hero of a work to die before he could fully complete his mission? In the anonymously written *The Song of Roland*, Roland's death was a necessary evil to complete the author's intent to espouse certain values in his work.

The idea of pride before a fall is clearly espoused in *The Song of Roland*. Roland has been appointed as commander of the rear guard of Charlemagne's army, a division which ensures that no enemies attempt to attack while the army is passing through a narrow mountain pass. However, when all of Charlemagne's Frankish army has passed through, Roland and his companion, Olivier, discover that the Spanish have laid a trap to attack the rear guard by itself. Olivier immediately implores Roland to blow his horn to summon Charlemagne and save them from disaster. However, Roland, in his pride, refuses, insisting that the action would bring shame upon him and his descendants. Even once they are in the middle of the battle and the odds are clearly against the Franks, Roland will not blow on his horn. It is not until almost the entire Frankish rear guard has been killed that Roland finally consents to blow his horn, but by this time, it is too late. Were Roland to have

recovered from his wounds and seen France again in good health, the fall would not have been complete, and the theme of pride before a fall would not have been fully developed.

Another theme in *The Song of Roland* is the danger of treachery. After hearing proposed terms of peace from Marsilla, king of Spain, Charlemagne decides to accept the agreement, and sends Ganelon, one of his knights, to act as his official messenger. Ganelon is enraged at being chosen for this task, so he is easily bought over by Marsilla once he has entered the king of Spain's court. Ganelon betrays Charlemagne's plans and agrees to set up a way for Marsilla to overcome the best division of Charlemagne's army. When Ganelon returns to Charlemagne, the Frank king does not suspect him enough to ignore his advice to have Roland, Olivier, and a noble division of the army act as the rear guard. Ganelon's treachery causes this division of the army to be entirely annihilated, and the fact that Roland himself was killed greatly increases the impact of the author's treatment of the theme of the danger of treachery.

The author of *The Song of Roland* clearly believed that victory always comes at a cost, and he wove this theme into his work. For example, in the last battle of this poem, Charlemagne's ultimate victory over the Spanish comes at the expense of many of his own soldiers. The battle between the Spanish army and the Frankish rear guard does end in a victory for the Franks, even though the victory is by a very small margin. This victory comes at the cost of literally every Frank soldier in the rear guard. Roland, being Charlemagne's favorite general, was very close to the Frankish king. Thus, Roland's death adds immeasurably to the cost of the victory of the Frankish rear guard over the Spanish army. The cost of this victory is much higher because Roland dies.

309

The death of Roland was absolutely necessary to the purpose of *The Song of Roland*. If Roland had not died, then his fall would not have been complete, and the theme of pride before a fall would not have been fully developed. If Roland had not died, then Ganelon's treacherous maneuvers would not have achieved their purpose, and the theme of the danger of treachery would not have been brought to its climax. If Roland had not died, then the greatest soldier in the rear guard would have survived, and the cost of victory would not have been nearly as high. Roland's death is indeed a catastrophic event. *The Song of Roland* is filled with words of great praise for the noble general. "By Count Roland's valor, King Charles his realm has won. And Roland will win the world for him from here to the rising sun." (Anonymous, *The Song of Roland* (Mineola, NY: Dover Publications, 2002), "XXXI.") However, this cataclysm was essential to the poem's purpose. It was the death of a hero; a necessary evil. (John Micah)

Assignments

- Warm-up: Why must Roland die?
- Student should complete Concept Builder 22-E.
- Essay is due. Students should take the chapter 22 test.

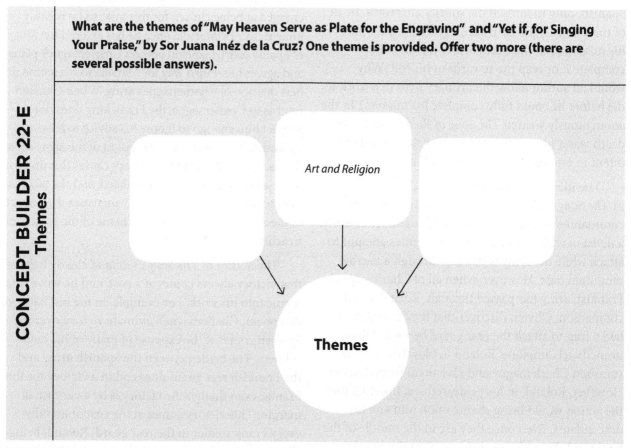

CONCEPT BUILDER 22-E
Themes

What are the themes of "May Heaven Serve as Plate for the Engraving" and "Yet if, for Singing Your Praise," by Sor Juana Inéz de la Cruz? One theme is provided. Offer two more (there are several possible answers).

Art and Religion

Themes

http://www.latin-american.cam.ac.uk/SorJuana/SorJuana4.htm/.
http://www.latin-american.cam.ac.uk/SorJuana/SorJuana3.htm.

Chapter 23

(1800–1890):
Romanticism (Part 1)

First Thoughts Faust is a very learned professor who is dissatisfied with human knowledge, which by its nature is limited. Using magic, he conjures up the Earth Spirit in his darkened study. Regarding himself as more than mortal, he tries to claim the Earth Spirit as a colleague, but the Spirit rejects him scornfully and disappears. Despairing, Faust contemplates suicide. He is saved by the sound of the bells welcoming Easter morning. He and his research assistant, Wagner, go out into the sunlight and enjoy the greetings of the crowd, which remembers the medical attention given to the people by Faust and his father. Faust is still depressed, denying the value of medicine and feeling torn between the two souls in him, one longing for earthly pleasures, the other seeking the highest spiritual knowledge. A dog follows Faust and Wagner home. The dog, of course, is Mephistopheles! The overall theme of this work is the struggle mankind undertakes to overcome evil and to discriminate between good and evil.

Chapter Learning Objectives In chapter 23 we examine the disturbing vision of life that is German romanticism.

As a result of this chapter study you will be able to . . .

1. Discuss in detail the characters whom Goethe introduces in his work.

2. Two disturbing themes of Goethe's *Faust* are that salvation comes intuitively in the natural world and that God is, after all, a weak reflection of the deity. Discuss how Goethe develops these themes and why they are biblically inaccurate.

3. Write a report on the rise of romanticism and its effect on Western literature.

Weekly Essay Options: Begin on page 273 of the Teacher Guide.

Reading ahead: *Faust (II)* by Goethe.

311

Johann Wolfgang von Goethe

Johann Wolfgang von Goethe was born in Frankfurt, Germany, into an upper middle-class family. His father, Johann, withdrew from public life and homeschooled his children. Goethe's six-volume autobiography, *Memoirs of Goethe*, recalls his home life as a chaotic experience with which some homeschool families may identify, but it may have been stimulating nourishment for his brilliant mind. At 16, the immature but brilliant Goethe began his studies at the University of Leipzig, the Berkeley university of his day — a university to which scores of radicals flocked. Later, after graduation, Goethe practiced law with his father and wrote two popular works. During a two-year sojourn in Italy, Goethe recognized that he was an artist and resolved to devote the rest of his life to writing.

Johann Wolfgang von Goethe at age 79, by Joseph Karl Stieler, 1828 (PD-Art).

Assignments

- Warm-up: Discuss the impact of Goethe's early life on his later romanticism.
- Students should complete Concept Builder 23-A.
- Students should review the required reading(s) *before* the assigned chapter begins.
- Teachers may want to discuss assigned reading(s) with students.
- Teachers shall assign the required essay. The rest of the essays can be outlined, answered with shorter answers, discussed, or skipped.
- Students will review all readings for chapter 23.

Read this excerpt from *Faust* (part 1) by Goethe, and respond to the following:

I've studied now Philosophy
And Jurisprudence, Medicine, —
And even, alas! Theology, —
From end to end, with labor keen;
And here, poor fool! with all my lore
I stand, no wiser than before:
I'm Magister — yea, Doctor — hight,
And straight or cross-wise, wrong or right,
These ten years long, with many woes,
I've led my scholars by the nose, —
And see, that nothing can be known!
That knowledge cuts me to the bone.
I'm cleverer, true, than those fops of teachers,
Doctors and Magisters, Scribes and Preachers;
Neither scruples nor doubts come now to smite me,
Nor Hell nor Devil can longer affright me.

For this, all pleasure am I foregoing;
I do not pretend to aught worth knowing,
I do not pretend I could be a teacher
To help or convert a fellow-creature.
Then, too, I've neither lands nor gold,
Nor the world's least pomp or honor hold —
No dog would endure such a curst existence!
Wherefore, from Magic I seek assistance,
That many a secret perchance I reach
Through spirit-power and spirit-speech,
And thus the bitter task forego
Of saying the things I do not know, —
That I may detect the inmost force
Which binds the world, and guides its course;
Its germs, productive powers explore,
And rummage in empty words no more!

O full and splendid Moon, whom I
Have, from this desk, seen climb the sky
So many a midnight, — would thy glow
For the last time beheld my woe!
Ever thine eye, most mournful friend,
O'er books and papers saw me bend;
But would that I, on mountains grand,
Amid thy blessed light could stand,
With spirits through mountain-caverns hover,
Float in thy twilight the meadows over,
And, freed from the fumes of lore that swathe me,
To health in thy dewy fountains bathe me!

What are the academic disciplines that have failed Faust?

What does this statement mean?

Apparently Dr. Faust has abandoned Judeo-Christian morality as a legitimate frame of reference. Explain.

Ah, me! this dungeon still I see.
This drear, accursed masonry,
Where even the welcome daylight strains
But duskly through the painted panes.
Hemmed in by many a toppling heap
Of books worm-eaten, gray with dust,
Which to the vaulted ceiling creep,

Against the smoky paper thrust, —
With glasses, boxes, round me stacked,
And instruments together hurled,
Ancestral lumber, stuffed and packed —
Such is my world: and what a world!

And do I ask, wherefore my heart
Falters, oppressed with unknown needs?
Why some inexplicable smart
All movement of my life impedes?
Alas! in living Nature's stead,
Where God His human creature set,
In smoke and mould the fleshless dead
And bones of beasts surround me yet!

Fly! Up, and seek the broad, free land!
And this one Book of Mystery
From Nostradamus' very hand,
Is't not sufficient company?
When I the starry courses know...

Where, then, will Faust find his fulfillment?

The Faust Legend

The Faust legend was a popular legend at the end of the 18th century (www.pitt.edu/~dash/faust.html). Johann Faustus was born of God-fearing parents in Roda in the province of Weimar. Although he acted absent-minded and foolish, at an early age he proved himself a scholar and a committed Christian. His interests, though, did not merely lie in theology. He mastered not only the Holy Scriptures, but also the sciences of medicine, mathematics, astrology, and sorcery. These pursuits aroused in him a desire to commune with the devil, so — having made the necessary evil preparations — he went one night to a crossroads in the Spesser Forest near Wittenberg and summoned the devil. Feigning anger at having been summoned against his will, the devil arrived in the midst of a great storm. After the winds and lightning had subsided, the devil asked Dr. Faustus to reveal his will, to which the scholar replied that he was willing to enter into a pact. The devil, for his part, would agree: (1) to serve Dr. Faustus for as long as he should live, (2) to provide Dr. Faustus with whatever information he might request, and (3) never to utter an untruth to Dr. Faustus. The devil agreed to these particulars, on the condition that Dr. Faustus would promise: (1) at the expiration of 24 years to surrender his body and soul to the devil, (2) to confirm the pact with a signature written in his own blood, and (3) to renounce his Christian faith. Faust agreed and sold his soul to the devil. He definitely lived to regret his decision. Twenty-four years later the devil came for Faust and Faust suffered in hell forever.

His hero does not sell his soul to the devil — he makes a bet with him, and the devil, Mephistopheles, loses. Faust does not disobey God's commands, as he does in the legend.

Assignments

- Warm-up: Goethe's God has complete confidence in Faust's good sense and gives His permission for Mephistopheles to tempt Faust in order to keep Faust on his toes. Goethe obviously did not write a Christian cautionary tale. What, then, is it?
- Students should complete Concept Builder 23-B.
- Students should review reading(s) from the next chapter.
- Students should outline essay due at the end of the week.
- Per teacher instructions, students may answer orally, in a group setting, some of the essays that are not assigned as formal essays.

Romanticism, the worldview, captured a generation of Western thinkers, authors, and artists. These included Emerson, Thoreau, Wordsworth, Beethoven, and, of course, Goethe. Find examples of romanticism in *Faust*.

CHARACTERISTIC	EXAMPLE FROM FAUST
The **Imagination** was elevated to a position as the supreme faculty of the mind. This contrasted distinctly with the traditional arguments for the supremacy of reason. The romantics tended to define and to present the imagination as our ultimate "shaping" or creative power, the approximate human equivalent of the creative powers of nature or even deity. It is dynamic, an active rather than passive power, with many functions. Imagination is the primary faculty for creating all art.	Early in the poem, Faust rejects theology, education, and other objective evidences of reality. He embraces the imagination as the primary faculty for creating all art. O full and splendid Moon, whom I Have, from this desk, seen climb the sky So many a midnight, — would thy glow For the last time beheld my woe! Ever thine eye, most mournful friend, O'er books and papers saw me bend; But would that I, on mountains grand, Amid thy blessed light could stand, With spirits through mountain-caverns hover, Float in thy twilight the meadows over, And, freed from the fumes of lore that swathe me, To health in thy dewy fountains bathe me!
Nature meant many things to the romantics. It was often presented as itself a work of art, constructed by a divine imagination, in emblematic language. Romantic nature poetry is essentially a poetry of meditation.	
Symbolism and myth were given great prominence in the romantic conception of art. In the romantic view, symbols were the human aesthetic correlatives of nature's emblematic language. They were valued too because they could simultaneously suggest many things, and were thus thought superior to the one-to-one communications of allegory (as one finds in Dante's *The Divine Comedy*).	
Intuition and subjectivity: The imagination was accompanied by greater emphasis on the importance of intuition, instincts, and feelings, and romantics generally called for greater attention to the emotions as a necessary supplement to purely logical reason.	
Individualism: The Romantic Hero The romantics asserted the importance of the individual, the unique, even the eccentric.	

315

Romanticism

Elements of Romanticism Worldview	Frontier is a vast expanse representing freedom, innocence, and opportunity
Writing Techniques	1. Appeals to imagination; use of the "willing suspension of disbelief" 2. Stress on emotion and imagination rather than reason; optimism, geniality 3. Subjective in form and meaning 4. Prefers the remote setting in time and space 5. Prefers exotic and improbable plots 6. Prefers aberrant characterization 7. Form rises out of content, non-formal 8. Prefers individualized, subjective writing

Assignments

- Warm-up: The music of Beethoven sought to capture the humanism of Goethe. Listen to Beethoven's *Fifth Symphony*, explore the life and work of Beethoven, and analyze his music in light of the contemporary Goethe's works. What vision are they advancing?

- Students should complete Concept Builder 23-C.

- Students should write rough draft of assigned essay.

- The teacher may correct rough drafts.

A cautionary tale is a warning to its hearer of a danger. There are three essential parts to a cautionary tale, though they can be introduced in a large variety of ways. First, there is a warning; some act is said to be dangerous. Then, the protagonist ignores the warning and performs the forbidden act. Finally, the violator comes to an unpleasant fate. This pattern, however, is broken in Goethe's *Faust*. How?

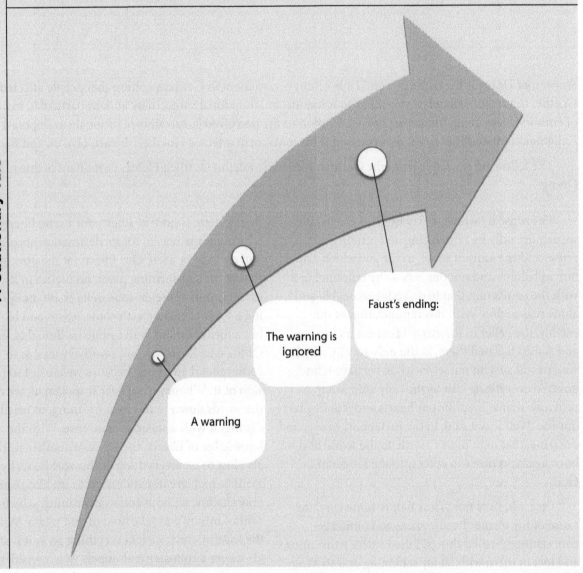

A warning

The warning is ignored

Faust's ending:

Sturm und Drang

Sturm und Drang is the name of a late 18th-century movement in German culture that deeply affected Goethe. In this movement, very similar to romanticism, individual subjectivity and, in particular, extremes of emotion were given free expression in reaction to the perceived constraints of rationalism imposed by the Enlightenment and Protestant Reformation. This movement affected Goethe, Mozart, Hydan, and Bach.

The following is a quote from the German romantic, Johann Gottlieb Fichte, proponent of Sturm and Drang:

The sense by which we lay hold on eternal life we acquire only by renouncing and offering up sense, and the aims of sense, to the law which claims our will alone, and not our acts — by renouncing it with the conviction that to do so is reasonable and alone reasonable. With this renunciation of the earthly, the belief in the eternal first enters our soul and stands isolated there, as the only stay by which we can still sustain ourselves when we have relinquished everything else, as the only animating principle that still uplifts our hearts and still inspires our life. Well was it said, in the metaphors of a sacred doctrine, that man must first die to the world and be born again, in order to enter into the kingdom of God.

I see, oh, I see now, clear before mine eyes, the cause of my former heedlessness and blindness concerning spiritual things! Filled with earthly aims, and lost in them with all my scheming and striving; put in motion and impelled only by the idea of a result, which is to be actualized without us, by the desire of such a result and pleasure in it — insensible and dead to the pure impulse of that Reason which gives the law to itself, which sets before us a purely spiritual aim, the immortal Psyche remains chained to the earth; her wings are bound. Our philosophy becomes the history of our own heart and life. As we find ourselves, so we imagine man in general and his destination. Never impelled by any other motive than the desire of that which can be realized in this world, there is no true liberty for us, no liberty which has the reason for its destination absolutely and entirely in itself. Our liberty, at the utmost, is that of the self-forming plant, no higher in its essence, only more curious in its result, not producing a form of matter with roots, leaves and blossoms, but a form of mind with impulses, thoughts, actions. Of the true liberty we are positively unable to comprehend anything, because we are not in possession of it. Whenever we hear it spoken of, we draw the words down to our own meaning, or briefly dismiss it with a sneer, as nonsense. With the knowledge of liberty, the sense of another world is also lost to us. Everything of this sort floats by like words which are not addressed to us; like an ash-gray shadow without color or meaning, which we cannot by any end take hold of and retain. Without the least interest, we let everything go as it is stated. Or if ever a robuster zeal impels us to consider it seriously, we see clearly and can demonstrate that all those ideas are untenable, hollow visions, which a man of sense casts from him. And, according to the premises from which we set out and which are taken from our own innermost experience, we are quite right, and are alike unanswerable and unteachable, so long as we remain what we are. The excellent doctrines which are current among the people, fortified with special authority, concerning freedom, duty and eternal life, change themselves for us into grotesque fables, like those of Tartarus and the

Elysian fields, although we do not disclose the true opinion of our hearts, because we think it more advisable to keep the people in outward decency by means of these images. Or if we are less reflective, and ourselves fettered by the bands of authority, then we sink, ourselves, to the true plebeian level, by believing that which, so understood, would be foolish fable; and by finding, in those purely spiritual indications, nothing but the promise of a continuance, to all eternity, of the same miserable existence which we lead here below.

To say all in a word: Only through a radical reformation of my will does a new light arise upon my being and destination. Without this, however much I may reflect, and however distinguished my mental endowments, there is nothing but darkness in me and around me. The reformation of the heart alone conducts to true wisdom. So then, let my whole life be directed unrestrainedly toward this one end! (Johann Gottlieb Fichte, *The Destiny of Man*, adapted from the translation by Frederic H. Hedge, Book III: Faith; www.gutenberg.org/cache/epub/12888/pg12888.html.)

Assignments

- Warm-up: Subjectivity is well and good, but what happens when one builds an ethical system on feelings and subjectivity?
- Students should complete Concept Builder 23-D.
- Students will re-write corrected copies of essay due tomorrow.

CONCEPT BUILDER 23-D
Epic Hero

Discuss the following foils in *Faust* and show how Goethe uses them to develop his main character.

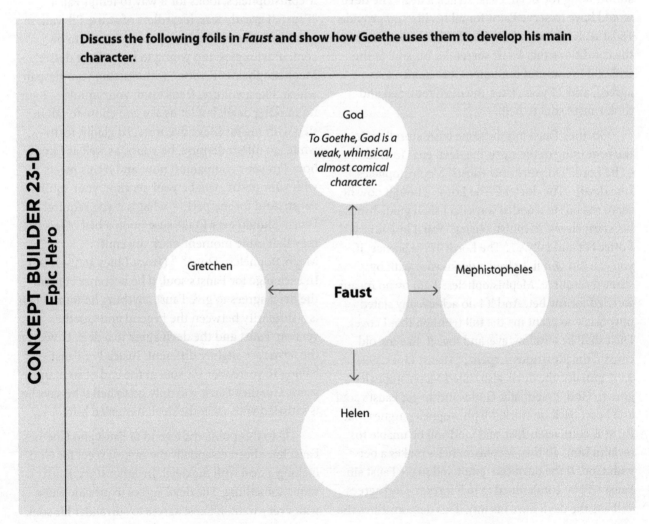

God

To Goethe, God is a weak, whimsical, almost comical character.

Gretchen

Faust

Mephistopheles

Helen

Student Essay:
The Faust Legend

At the end of the 1700s, the legend of Johann Faust was very popular in Europe. Goethe's *Faust* closely resembles this story, with a few differences. While the legend is like a warning to readers against making deals with the devil, Goethe's story is not. Instead, Goethe's work has a romantic twist.

Goethe's *Faust* is based on the legend of Johann Faust, a magician. Through his various pursuits, his spirit developed a want to speak with the devil. After summoning the devil, Faust struck a deal. The devil would have to serve Faust for all his life and provide Faust with whatever he wanted. The devil agreed, on the conditions that Faust surrender his soul at the end of 24 years and renounce Christianity. Faust agreed, and 24 years later, the devil returned and took Faust's soul to hell.

Goethe's Faust has the same basic storyline. In the beginning of the story, the devil goes to God. "The Lord: 'Do you know Faust?' Mephistopheles [the devil]: 'The doctor?' The Lord: 'Though now he serve me but in clouded ways, so I shall guide him so his spirit clears.' Mephistopheles: 'You'll lose him yet! I offer bet and tally. . . .' The Lord: 'Have licence, if you can but win it, to lead it down your path by shrewd resource.' Mephistopheles: 'I am by no means worried for my bet. And if I do achieve my stated purpose, you grant me the full triumph that I covet. Dust shall he swallow, aye, and love it, like my old cousin, the illustrious serpent.' " (Faust Lines 299–335) Initially, the devil, also called Mephistopheles , goes to God. Essentially, God wants to get Faust's soul and heart back on track. Mephistopheles argues that Faust is completely lost, and God will be unable to reclaim him. To this, Mephistopheles makes a bet with God. If the devil can tempt and make Faust sin, Faust will be condemned to hell forever. God agrees and lets the devil have his way. This demonstrates the first difference between Goethe and the legend of Faust. Being a naturalist, Goethe believed God was either uninterested in man, or just mean. This deal between the devil and God demonstrates this concept. The typical reader probably asks himself, Why would God do such a thing? On the contrary, the average reader of the legend of Faust would probably just blame Faust's outcome on man's stupidity.

After making the deal with God, Mephistopheles, looks for a way to tempt Faust. "Faust: 'I greatly fear, regardless of attire, I'll walk in pain the narrow earthly way. I am too old to be content with play, too young to be without desire.' Mephistopheles: 'Be done with nursing your despair, which, like a vulture, feeds upon your mind . . . I am no ranking devil; but let us say you chose to fall in step with me for life's adventure, I'd gladly, forthwhile, go into indenture, be yours, as well as I know how. I'm your companion now, and if this meets with your desire, will be your servitor, your squire.' Faust: 'And for my part — what is it you require?' Faust: 'Should ever I take ease upon a bed of leisure, may that same moment mark my end!' Mephistopheles: 'Done!' " (*Faust* Lines 1635–1697) In exchange for Faust's soul, if he becomes content, the devil agrees to give Faust anything he wants. This is a similarity between the Legend and Goethe's version. Faust and the devil agree to a deal. However, the terms are slightly different. Instead of Faust having to surrender his soul at the end of so many years, Goethe's Faust will only go to hell if he says he is satisfied with what the devil has given him.

Up to this point, the legend of Faust and Goethe's Faust have been essentially the same, except for God making a deal with the devil. In either story, Faust wants something. The devil agrees to provide Faust with every want, if Faust agrees to surrender his soul.

At the end of Goethe's Faust, Faust survives. "No joy could sate him, no delight but cloyed, for changing shapes, he lusted to the last; the final moment, worthless, stale, and void." (*Faust* Lines 11586–11589) In the end, the devil loses his bet. Faust, being human, never becomes fully satisfied. The devil attends to Faust's every need, want or desire, but still, Faust never says he is totally content with what he has. He always wants something more.

This is where the legend of Faust and Goethe's *Faust* really differ. Essentially, the Legend of Faust warns the reader about making deals with the devil or becoming involved with sin and things of the devil, since in the end, one will go to hell. In this way, it is a Christian cautionary tale. However, Goethe does not write like this. His Faust makes a different deal with the devil with different conditions. And in the end, Faust goes to heaven. Goethe's message essentially argues that even though one may commune with the devil, or make deals and bets

with evil spirits, you can still go to heaven. Faust makes a deal with the devil, one of the worst things a person could do, according to standards during Goethe's time, yet still is saved by God. Ultimately, *Faust* says man can do anything he wants on earth, but as long as he is never fully satisfied, he can go to heaven. In this way, the legend of Faust and Goethe's Faust have two very different meanings.

Johann Goethe does not write a Christian cautionary tale at all. In fact, he does not warn the reader against anything. Instead, it seems he is actually encouraging the reader to partake in evil, since you will still go to heaven in the end. Faust speaks with and makes a bet with the devil, yet somehow manages to make it to heaven. This concept resembles Goethe's naturalistic worldview that says there is no good or evil, just whatever man wants. This allows Faust to do whatever he wants, even make deals with evil spirits, but still go to heaven. (Chris)

Assignments

- Warm-up: What temptations do you see leading people away from God?
- Students should complete Concept Builder 23-E.
- Essays are due. Students should take the chapter 23 test.

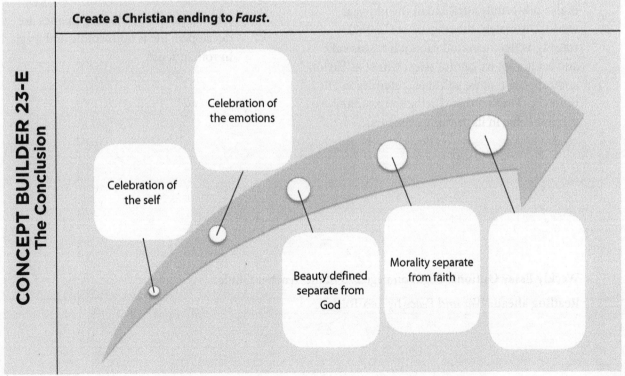

CONCEPT BUILDER 23-E
The Conclusion

Create a Christian ending to *Faust*.

- Celebration of the emotions
- Celebration of the self
- Beauty defined separate from God
- Morality separate from faith

Chapter 24

(1800–1890)

Romanticism (Part 2)

First Thoughts Where is Dante when we need him? *Faust* is indeed a tragedy, but neither Goethe or Faust know it. The tragedy is that this romantic tale lacks a tragic ending. We Christians earnestly, fervently hope that it does. The notion that there is no moral universe with no consequences, no cause and effect, invites inevitable chaos and nihilism that is so much a part of our postmodern world. Faust's yearning for experience and knowledge created a type for the modern (1900–1990) and postmodern (1990–present) ages still known as the Faustian hero, though in reality Goethe's Faust is more a villain than a hero; and the purported villain — Mephistopheles — is one of the most likable characters in the play. His yearnings draw him toward the heavens, yet he is also powerfully attracted to the physical world. Ultimately, the tragedy of Goethe's tragedy, is that mankind cannot have his cake and eat it, too: we cannot reject Christ as Savior and suppose that we will spend eternity in His presence. The fact that Goethe thinks otherwise is remarkable in its presumptuousness.

Objectives In chapter 24 we continue to analyze this most seminal of 19th-century works, when the German romantic Goethe resurrected the recalcitrant Faust as an enlightened intellectual rather than an unrepentant sinner.

As a result of this chapter study you will be able to . . .

1. Write an analysis of the plot and identify the climax of *Faust*.

2. Rosetti is poking fun at a famous American romantic poem. What poem is it and how does she attack its central theme?

3. Compare and contrast *Faust* with the Book of Job.

4. Discuss how the following themes are developed: life is both comic and tragic in romanticism.

Chapter Learning

Weekly Essay Options: Begin on page 273 of the Teacher Guide.

Reading ahead: *War and Peace* by Leo Tolstoy.

Student Essay

Goethe's *Faust* is the story of a man who, dissatisfied even after having reached the bounds of human greatness, seeks fulfillment through dark spiritual means. To this purpose, he makes a pact with the devil Mephistopheles, rendering him Faust's servant until Faust's first moment of satisfaction, whence the roles will be reversed eternally. In order then to fulfill his side of the bargain and raise Faust to the pinnacle of human happiness, Mephistopheles introduces him to a beautiful young maiden named Gretchen, with whom Faust falls madly in love. Each of these three characters is a vital and detailed piece of Goethe's cautionary tale about the dangers of boredom, seduction, and even love.

Goethe's *Faust* is a caution to the bored. Faust has tried everything: philosophy, law, medicine, theology, you name it. He pursues ever study he undertakes zealously, tears it apart, examines its contents, and puts it back together. Nevertheless, even after he has acquired every ounce of knowledge which the human brain can possess, he finds himself void of purpose, dissatisfied, and incredibly bored. "Mephistopheles: 'The ferment in him drives him on and on, and yet he half-knows that he's mad. He demands the fairest stars from heaven and every deepest lust from earth. The nearest and the farthest leave his churning heart dissatisfied.' "

Idle hands are the devil's handiwork. Soon Faust resorts to seeking a different kind of fulfillment: that of black magic. "Faust: 'Spirits, now you hover close to me; if you hear me, answer me!' (He opens the book and sees the sign of the macrocosm) 'Ha! A rush of bliss flows suddenly through all my senses!' " First, the doctor summons the earth spirit and addresses him as an equal, but the spirit denies their equality. With his second spirit, Mephistopheles, however, he settles for a bargain. "Mephistopheles: 'I pledge myself to serve you here and now; the slightest hint will put me at your beck and call, and if beyond we meet again, you shall do the same for me.' Faust: 'If ever I should tell the moment: Oh, stay! You are so beautiful! Then you may cast me into chains, then I shall smile upon perdition.' " Without so much as a second thought, Faust enters into this deal, essentially selling his soul to the devil in exchange for a moment of thrill. This, because he was bored.

Mephistopheles is a seducer. Faust even is aware of this fact, but doesn't care. "Faust: 'If you ever lure me with your lying flatteries . . . if you bamboozle me with pleasure, then let this be my final day.' " Mephistopheles' goal is to lure Faust away even from what vague progress he is making toward God and into the pits of hell. He even goes so far as to make a bet with God over Faust's soul. "Mephistopheles: 'What will you bet? You'll lose him in the end, if you'll just give me your permission to lead him gently down my street.' " In order to secure Faust's soul, he offers the bored doctor the use of all of his satanic powers, that he might at last achieve fulfillment. Thus, Mephistopheles is a representation of all kinds of temptation that promise happiness, but ultimately lead to damnation.

Finally, Gretchen is a caution to the lovers. She is a classic Juliet. She is a godly young woman, an obedient daughter, and an overall good person. She has a bright future, but then she falls in love. When Faust first tells her he loves her, she falls head over heels. Suddenly, she becomes dissatisfied with a life without him. "Gretchen: 'My peace is gone, my heart is sore; I'll find it never and nevermore. My heart is yearning to be at his side, to clasp and enfold him and hold him tight. To love and to kiss, to murmur and sigh, and under his kiss to melt and to die!' "

It is unwise to commit one's love to one who has entered a pact with the devil. Faust, whom she loves devoutly to her death, is her undoing, just as Romeo was the undoing of Juliet. In order that she and Faust might sleep together, she gives her mother a sleeping potion, but accidentally overdoses her and kills her. Next, she kills their baby in order that they might be more free to run away together. "Gretchen: 'I killed my mother, drowned my child; was it not a gift for you and me?' " She is executed for her crimes. Thus, Gretchen is a caution to all of those who love blindly; they often fall.

While the entirety of Goethe's Faust is romantic in tone and substance, an "everything will be okay" sort of story, it is more of a cautionary tale. Faust is a caution to those with idle hands who end up becoming the devil's handiwork; Mephistopheles is a caution to those who are seduced and are led into evil; and Gretchen is a caution to the blind lovers who, seeing nothing clearly but the lone star of their love, fall into darkness. (Austin)

Assignments

- Warm-up: What was the thesis of this essay?
- Students should complete Concept Builder 24-A.
- Students should review the required reading(s) *before* the assigned chapter begins.
- Teachers may want to discuss assigned reading(s) with students.
- Teachers shall assign the required essay. The rest of the essays can be outlined, answered with shorter answers, discussed, or skipped.
- Students will review all readings for chapter 24.

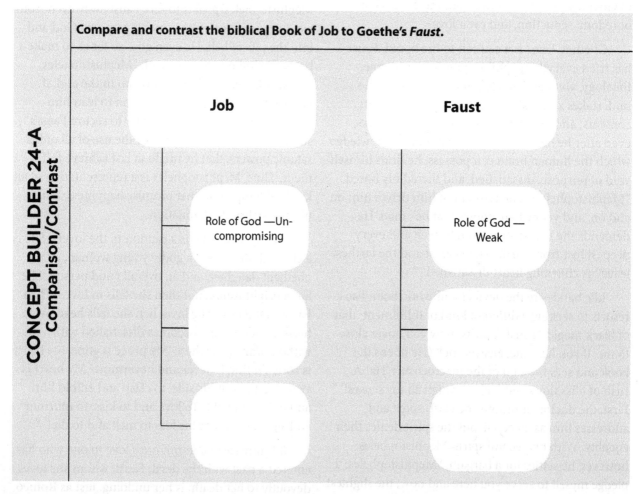

CONCEPT BUILDER 24-A
Comparison/Contrast

Compare and contrast the biblical Book of Job to Goethe's *Faust*.

Job

Faust

Role of God —Uncompromising

Role of God —Weak

Poetry
Goethe

The Muses' Son

THROUGH field and wood to stray,
And pipe my tuneful lay, —
'Tis thus my days are pass'd;
And all keep tune with me,
And move in harmony,
And so on, to the last.

To wait I scarce have power
The garden's earliest flower,
The tree's first bloom in Spring;
They hail my joyous strain, —
When Winter comes again,
Of that sweet dream I sing.

My song sounds far and near,
O'er ice it echoes clear,
Then Winter blossoms bright;

And when his blossoms fly,
Fresh raptures meet mine eye,
Upon the well-till'd height.
When 'neath the linden tree,
Young folks I chance to see,
I set them moving soon;

His nose the dull lad curls,
The formal maiden whirls,
Obedient to my tune.
Wings to the feet ye lend,
O'er hill and vale ye send
The lover far from home;

When shall I, on your breast,.
Ye kindly muses, rest,
And cease at length to roam?

The Poems of Goethe, translated in the original meters by Edgar Alfred Bowring, www.gutenberg.org/cache/epub/1287/pg1287.html.

Assignments

- Warm-up: What evidences of romanticism do you see in Goethe's poetry?
- Students should complete Concept Builder 24-B.
- Students should review reading(s) from next chapter.
- Students should outline essays due at the end of the week.
- Per teacher instructions, students may answer orally, in a group setting, some of the essays that are not assigned as the formal essay.

A theme is a precise statement of the meaning of a literary work. There are at least three themes in *Faust*. Discuss how they are developed.

Fate

Themes

Volition

Justice

Student Essay:
Plot Analysis of *Faust*

Faust, by Johann Wolfgang von Goethe, is a book about a man named Faust who makes a bet with the devil. There are many diverse characters and characteristics portrayed in this book.

Starting at the very beginning of the book, in the "Prologue in Heaven," readers meet the antagonist of *Faust*, Mephistopheles. Mephistopheles is the devil. "I'd give myself over to the devil, if I were not he himself" (2709–2810; Promenade). Mephistopheles is sly and cunning. He describes himself as Evil. "And thus what you call havoc, deadly sin, or briefly stated: Evil, that is my proper element" (1342–1344; Faust's Study). Not only does he describe himself as evil, others describe him as evil. Though Mephistopheles can change himself so that he does not look like the devil, the aura of his evilness follows him wherever he goes. "That person whom you have with you — I hate him from the bottom of my soul; nothing has in all my days wounded me as deeply in my heart as that repulsive person's horrid face" (3472–3476; Martha's Garden). Mephistopheles is the antagonist because he tries to tempt Faust. He was given permission by God to tempt Faust to keep him on his toes.

Immediately following the introduction of Mephistopheles, Goethe presents God. However, this is not the same God that Christians believe. This God is portrayed in a romantic view. Because he believes that Faust needs some tempting every now and then, he lets the devil tempt Faust. "I'm therefore pleased to give him a companion who must goad and prod and be a devil" (342–343; Prologue in Heaven). God in this story in a foil who helps develop the protagonist.

The protagonist Faust is heavily reliant on his intuition and knowledge. He knows a lot about religion, but he does not truly believe. "When you say it so, it seems all right, and yet there's something wrong; you have no proper Christian faith" (3466–3468; Martha's Garden). Faust shows the best and the worst in man. He shows the best because he has great knowledge and intuition. He uses that to get him through life. However, he also knows how man is characterized with greed. Because Mephistopheles is his servant-companion, Faust makes sure he gets the most out of Mephistopheles. "I'll be brief and to the point: unless that sweet and youthful blood lies in my arms this very evening, by midnight you and I part company" (2635–2638; A Street).

The "sweet and youthful blood" Faust is referring to is Margaret. She is another one of the foils in Faust. She is the one Faust loves. She is the one that he would do anything for. Faust describes her as "so proper and so virtuous, and yet a little snippy too. The red of her lips, the light of her face, will forever be in my mind! The way she shyly drops her eyes is stamped profoundly in my heart. How pert and curt she was with me — a sheer delight, an ecstasy" (2611–2617; A Street). Though Faust believes she is so pretty and great, Margaret characterizes her as nothing more than poor, ". . . and we stay poor forever" (2804; Promenade). Mephistopheles uses Margaret to tempt Faust. (Hannah)

Assignments

- Warm-up: What is the climax in *Faust*?
- Students should complete Concept Builder 24-C.
- Students should write rough draft of assigned essay.
- The teacher may correct rough draft.

CONCEPT BUILDER 24-C
Plot

Analyze the plot.

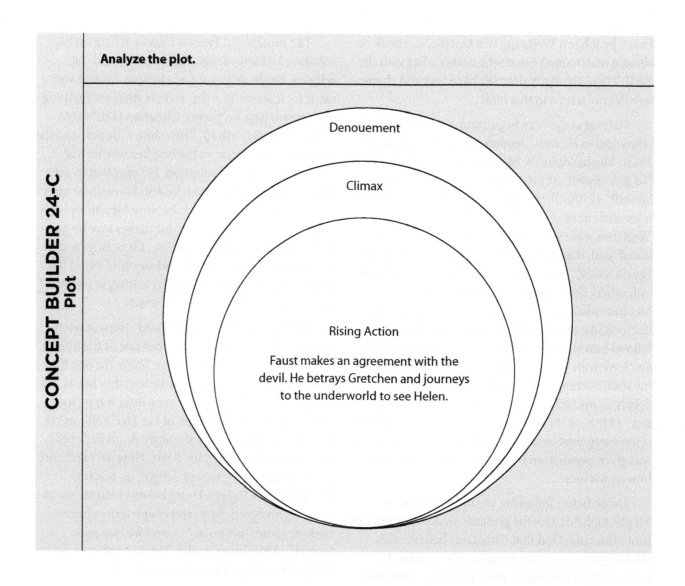

Denouement

Climax

Rising Action

Faust makes an agreement with the
devil. He betrays Gretchen and journeys
to the underworld to see Helen.

Student Essay:
Faust & Job

Although they were written hundreds, even thousands of years apart, *Faust*, by Johann Goethe, and the Biblical Book of Job record the accounts of two men being tempted by Satan. Seeking to test and strengthen his followers' faith, God allows Satan to tempt Faust and Job.

Since both Job and Faust are tempted, the two stories have some things in common. "The Lord: 'Do you know Faust?' Mephistopheles [the Devil]: 'The doctor?' The Lord: 'Though now he serve me but in clouded ways, so I shall guide him so his spirit clears.' Mephistopheles: 'You'll lose him yet! I offer bet and tally. . . .' The Lord: 'Have license, if you can but win it, to lead it down your path by shrewd resource.' Mephistopheles: 'I am by no means worried for my bet. And if I do achieve my stated purpose, you grant me the full triumph that I covet. Dust shall he swallow, aye, and love it, like my old cousin, the illustrious serpent' (Faust Lines 299–335). In Faust, God sees Faust rebelling. In an effort to bring Faust back, God allows the devil to try to entice Faust. Of course, Satan feels confident he can destroy Faust. In fact, he is so confident that he strikes a deal with God, betting that he can lead Faust astray.

Poster for Goethe's *Faust* by Richard Roland Holst, 1918 (PD-Art).

Job, on the contrary, is very faithful. "There was a man in the land of Uz, whose name was Job; and that man was blameless and upright, and one who feared God and shunned evil" (Job 1:1; NKJV). The only reason the devil makes a deal with God is to try and get Job to curse God. "So Satan answered the LORD and said, 'Does Job fear God for nothing? Have You not made a hedge around him, around his household, and around all that he has on every side? You have blessed the work of his hands, and his possessions have increased in the land. But now, stretch out Your hand and touch all that he has, and he will surely curse You to Your face!' " (Job 1:9–11; NKJV). Job is the most righteous man in the land, and Satan wishes to destroy him. Once again, Satan, just as in Faust, uses this opportunity to try to deceive and lead a faithful man astray.

Just as Satan's motives for tempting both men are very similar, so are the methods used. "Faust: 'And for my part-what is it you require?' Faust: 'Should ever I take ease upon a bed of leisure, may that same moment mark my end!' Mephistopheles: 'Done!' " (Faust Lines 1635–1697). Satan tempts Faust by giving him anything and everything he can possibly want, such as knowledge, experience, or material goods. On the contrary, Job is tempted by losing everything he has, as seen above, when Satan asks God for permission to tempt Job. Job's children die, he loses his house, herds of animals, servants, possessions and even his health. In fact, at one point, Job is told by his three "friends" and wife to curse God.

With all the pressure and the constantly worsening situation, Job never cursed God. "After this Job live one hundred and forty years, and saw his children and grandchildren for four generations. So Job died, old and full of days" (Job 42:16–17; NKJV). Despite all the troubles and tribulations, Job never cursed or blamed God for his situation. Job never did what Satan wanted him to, and Satan lost his bet with God.

"No joy could sate him, no delight but cloyed, for changing shapes, he lusted to the last; the final moment, worthless, stale, and void" (Faust Lines 11586–11589). In Faust's case, he never was totally satisfied with his life. Satan had provided knowledge to Faust, and guided him through life, but Faust was never totally satisfied. Since Faust had agreed to go to hell if he was ever satisfied, in his deal with the devil, the devil lost. Instead of being condemned to hell, Faust's soul ascended to heaven.

Through Job's torment, his friends constantly talk with him. As he is sitting in the dust and destruction of all he owned, his friends try to convince him to curse God. "Then Bildad the Shuhite answered and said: 'How long will you speak these things, and the words of your mouth be like a strong wind? Does God subvert judgment? Or does the Almighty pervert justice? If your sons have sinned against Him, He has cast them away for their transgression. If you would earnestly seek God and make your supplication to the Almighty . . .'" (Job 8:1–5; NKJV). Here, Job's "friend" Bildad urges Job to repent and curse Job since Job must have sinned to bring this destruction upon him. Job is able to stand up against this constant urging by his friends, and he refuses to curse God. On the contrary, Faust never is tempted by friends to tempt God. In fact, Faust goes through life with very few friends, if any at all. And his friends never mention anything about repenting or cursing God.

Even though Job and Faust were written probably thousands of years apart, they share the same basic story line. Both men are tempted by Satan, with God's permission. However, Satan's strategies differ. Satan takes everything away from Job while attempting to give Faust everything he desires. And Job has an added temptation. His three closest "friends" tempt him to curse God. But Faust does not have any friends trying to tempt him. Overall, while tempted by the same person, Job and Faust face different challenges. (Chris)

Assignments

- Warm-up: How do you prepare your heart and mind to overcome temptation?
- Students should complete Concept Builder 24-D.
- Students will re-write corrected copies of essay due tomorrow.

The Faustian spirit refers to the restless striving for knowledge and power. It cannot stop. It is human to strive ever upward and, unfortunately, often to make mistakes in the process. The problem is, Faust goes too far. One cannot find ultimate fulfillment in human action, however laudable. Something else must happen. Contrast this with the Christian view of salvation.

The Faustian life: one strives for meaning. In the "struggle" there is salvation.

Christian salvation

_____

Christina Georgina Rosetti

Background Christina Rosetti (1830–1894) was one of the most gifted and certainly most modern poets in substance and style of the Victorian age. An English woma Rosetti nevertheless defied all literary conventions embraced by the Victorian Age. For one thing, she poked fun at the romantics. She was neither a Mary Shelley nor a Charlotte Brontë. She was a unique person in life and in her writing.

Where Are the Songs I Used to Know

Where are the songs I used to know,

Where are the notes I used to sing?

I have forgotten everything

I used to know so long ago.

poetry.poetryx.com/poems/6862/.

There is a Budding Morrow in the Midnight

Wintry boughs against a wintry sky;

Yet the sky is partly blue

And the clouds are partly bright.

Who can tell but sap is mounting high

Out of sight,

Ready to burst through?

Winter is the mother-nurse of Spring,

Lovely for her daughter's sake.

Not unlovely for her own;

For a future buds in everything

Grown or blown

Or about to break.

www.readbookonline.net/readOnLine/15949/

Assignments

- Warm-up: What is modern about Rosetti's writings?
- Students should complete Concept Builder 24-E.
- Essay is due. Students should take the chapter 24 test.

Christina Rosetti (1830–1894) was one of the most gifted and certainly most modern poets in substance and style of the Victorian Age. An English woman, Rosetti nevertheless defied all literary conventions embraced by the Victorian Age. For one thing, she poked fun at the romantics (e.g., Goethe). Below is a poem by Rosetti where she is poking fun at Edgar Allan Poe's "The Raven." Draw lines between the similar sections.

The Raven (excerpts)	There Is a Budding Morrow in the Midnight
Once upon a midnight dreary, while I pondered weak and weary, Over many a quaint and curious volume of forgotten lore, While I nodded, nearly napping, suddenly there came a tapping, As of some one gently rapping, rapping at my chamber door. "'Tis some visitor," I muttered, "tapping at my chamber door — Only this, and nothing more."	A robin said A rosebush said Never stir Never stir Half Moon Ocean Springtime came Red Robin built And thrilled Rose Moon Ocean Thirsted Evermore.
"Prophet!" said I, "thing of evil! — prophet still, if bird or devil! It shall clasp a sainted maiden whom the angels named Lenore	
Clasp a rare and radiant maiden, whom the angels named Lenore?" Quoth the raven, "Nevermore."	It came to pass Upon that day When May was young Ah pleasant May!
"Be that word our sign of parting, bird or fiend!" I shrieked upstarting — "Get thee back into the tempest and the Night's Plutonian shore! Leave no black plume as a token of that lie thy soul hath spoken! Leave my loneliness unbroken! — quit the bust above my door! Take thy beak from out my heart, and take thy form from off my door!" Quoth the raven, "Nevermore."	All Sweet things pass away Leave me cold And old and gray Alas! You love me better cold Like frozen pyramids of old Unyieldingly?
And the raven, never flitting, still is sitting, still is sitting On the pallid bust of Pallas just above my chamber door; And his eyes have all the seeming of a demon's that is dreaming, And the lamp-light o'er him streaming throws his shadow on the floor; And my soul from out that shadow that lies floating on the floor Shall be lifted — nevermore!	

http://www.poetry-archive.com/r/rossetti_christina.html.
www.poestories.com.

Chapter 25

(1800–1890)
Realism (Part 1)

First Thoughts Count Leo (Lev) Nikolayevich Tolstoy was born to an aristocratic Russian family on September 9, 1828. At the age of 23, Tolstoy joined the Russian Army and fought in the Crimean War. Tolstoy returned to his family's estate in 1861 and married in 1862. He devoted the next 15 years to managing the estate and writing his two major works, *War and Peace* (1865) and *Anna Karenina* (1875). During his later years, Tolstoy grew increasingly disenchanted with the teachings of the Russian Orthodox Church and gradually formulated for himself a new Christian ideal, the central creed of which involved non-resistance to evil. His new faith was a sort of Pentecostal Holiness. Many think that it was during this period in Tolstoy's life that he committed his life to Christ. He continued to write voluminously, including the novella *The Death of Ivan Ilyich* (1886) and the novels *The Kreutzer Sonata* (1891) and *Resurrection* (1899). In 1910, still unable to reconcile his life as an aristocrat with the simpler existence he craved, he abandoned his estate. He soon fell ill and was found dead on a cot in a railway station. He was buried on his estate at Yasnaya Pulyana.

Chapter Learning Objectives In chapter 25 we will analyze perhaps the great novel of all time: *War and Peace* by Leo Tolstoy.

As a result of this chapter study you will be able to . . .

1. Discuss distinctive elements and decide how *War and Peace* measures up in each category.

2. Describe how the following characters change: Prince Andrew, Pierre, Natasha, and Nicholas.

3. Analyze the modern literary techniques developed by the Russian poet Tsvetaeva.

4. Discuss biblical parallels (e.g., the Prodigal Son).

5. Explore the history surrounding Napoleon's invasion of Russia and compare and contrast British, American, and Russian impressions of this important era.

6. Evaluate if Leo Tolstoy was a born-again Christian or not.

Weekly Essay Options: Begin on page 273 of the Teacher Guide.

Reading ahead: *Crime and Punishment* by Fyodor Dostoevsky.

 History connections: *World History* chapter 25, "The French Revolution."

War and Peace
Leo Tolstoy

I must admit, I cannot pretend any objectivity about *War and Peace*. It is my favorite novel! Perhaps it is the measure of my own "geekiness" that I would prefer a 1,000+ Russian novel over all other literary fiction, but even a cursory examination of this classic will explain why I feel this way.

War and Peace was first published in 1869 and is really historical fiction. It recounts in great detail one of the greatest victories in Russian history: the defeat of Napoleon. Readers observe the war through the eyes of five Russian aristocratic families.

Some scholars feel that both Pierre and Prince Andrew represent Leo Tolstoy himself. If that is so, then Prince Andrew's spiritual journey represents Tolstoy's own journey. As Prince Andrew struggles with his war wound, he says, "There is nothing certain, nothing at all except the unimportance of everything I understand, and the greatness of something incomprehensible but all-important" (Book 3, chapter 13).

Tolstoy dressed in peasant clothing by Ilya Repin, 1901 (PD-Art).

Assignments

- Warm-up: Discuss Prince Andrew's spiritual journey in *War and Peace* and speculate as to whether or not he ever commits his life to Jesus Christ.

- Student should complete Concept Builder 25-A.

- Students should review the required reading(s) *before* the assigned chapter begins.

- Teachers may want to discuss assigned reading(s) with students.

- Teachers shall assign the required essay. The rest of the essays can be outlined, answered with shorter answers, discussed, or skipped.

- Students will review all readings for chapter 25.

Read this excerpt from Leo Tolstoy's *War and Peace*, and respond to the following:

"Well, Prince, so Genoa and Lucca are now just family estates of the Bonapartes. But I warn you, if you don't tell me that this means war, if you still try to defend the infamies and horrors perpetrated by that Antichrist — I really believe he is Antichrist — I will have nothing more to do with you and you are no longer my friend, no longer my 'faithful slave,' as you call yourself! But how do you do? I see I have frightened you — sit down and tell me all the news." It was in July 1805, and the speaker was the well-known Anna Pavlovna Scherer, maid of honor and favorite of the Empress Marya Fedorovna. With these words she greeted Prince Vasili Kuragin, a man of high rank and importance, who was the first to arrive at her reception. Anna Pavlovna had had a cough for some days. She was, as she said, suffering from la grippe; grippe being then a new word in St. Petersburg, used only by the elite.

All her invitations without exception, written in French, and delivered by a scarlet-liveried footman that morning, ran as follows: "If you have nothing better to do, Count (or Prince), and if the prospect of spending an evening with a poor invalid is not too terrible, I shall be very charmed to see you tonight between 7 and 10 — Annette Scherer."

"Heavens! What a virulent attack!" replied the prince, not in the least disconcerted by this reception. He had just entered, wearing an embroidered court uniform, knee breeches, and shoes, and had stars on his breast and a serene expression on his flat face. He spoke in that refined French in which our grandfathers not only spoke but thought, and with the gentle, patronizing intonation natural to a man of importance who had grown old in society and at court. He went up to Anna Pavlovna, kissed her hand, presenting to her his bald, scented, and shining head, and complacently seated himself on the sofa.

"First of all, dear friend, tell me how you are. Set your friend's mind at rest," said he without altering his tone, beneath the politeness and affected sympathy of which indifference and even irony could be discerned.

"Can one be well while suffering morally? Can one be calm in times like these if one has any feeling?" said Anna Pavlovna. "You are staying the whole evening, I hope?"

"And the fete at the English ambassador's? Today is Wednesday. I must put in an appearance there," said the prince. "My daughter is coming for me to take me there."

Tolstoy uses dialogue to develop characters. How?

Tolstoy is poking fun at the wealthy of St. Petersburg. How?

What sort of person is Anna Pavlovna?

Anarchy

Pierre Joseph Proudhon, a contemporary of Leo Tolstoy, was the first philosopher to advance a philosophy called *anarchy*. Proudhon became what Tolstoy would have become without the intervention of the Lord Jesus Christ.

Anarchists argued that all structure — social, political, and religious — was an impediment to the development of the human spirit and identity. This was the precursor of later existentialist views of philosophers such as Jean Paul Sartre. His views were the antithesis of orthodox Christianity. "Man is by nature a sinner," Proudhon admitted, "that is to say not essentially a wrongdoer but rather wrongly made, and his destiny is perpetually to re-create his idea in himself" (Michael Ossar, *Anarchism in the Dramas of Ernst Toller*, New York: State University of New York Press, 1980, p. 32).

As the reader can see, this is one of the earliest attacks on the Christian concept of sin, and therefore redemption and responsibility. It was a link to the nihilism later developed by Sigmund Freud and other humanist thinkers. Proudhon was the worst of both worlds. On one hand, he rejected the optimism of the Enlightenment but, on the other hand, was unwilling to accept the pessimism of naturalism. He invited the world to chaos.

The following is an excerpt from Proudhon's *The Evolution of Capitalism*:

"Before entering upon the subject-matter of these new memoirs, I must explain an hypothesis which will undoubtedly seem strange, but in the absence of which it is impossible for me to proceed intelligibly: I mean the hypothesis of a God. To suppose God, it will be said, is to deny him" (Joseph-Pierre Proudhon, The Evolution of Capitalism, introduction, www.gutenberg.org/cache/epub/444/pg444.html).

Assignments

- Warm-up: In what ways does anarchy violate Scripture?
- Students should complete Concept Builder 25-B.
- Students should review reading(s) from next chapter.
- Students should outline essays due at the end of the week.
- Per teacher instructions, students may answer orally, in a group setting, some of the essays that are not assigned as the formal essay.

Describe how the following characters change: Prince Andrew, Pierre, Natasha, and Nicholas.

Prince Andrew

Narcissist

Selfish & Forgiving

Pierre

Awkward

Natasha

Spoiled

Nicholas

Shy

How have my family members changed?

Myself

My mother

My father

A sibling

The Death of Ivan Ilych
Leo Tolstoy

During an interval in the Melvinski trial in the large building of the Law Courts the members and public prosecutor met in Ivan Egorovich Shebek's private room, where the conversation turned on the celebrated Krasovski case. Fedor Vasilievich warmly maintained that it was not subject to their jurisdiction, Ivan Egorovich maintained the contrary, while Peter Ivanovich, not having entered into the discussion at the start, took no part in it but looked through the Gazette which had just been handed in.

"Gentlemen," he said, "Ivan Ilych has died!"

"You don't say so!"

"Here, read it yourself," replied Peter Ivanovich, handing Fedor Vasilievich the paper still damp from the press. Surrounded by a black border were the words: "Praskovya Fedorovna Golovina, with profound sorrow, informs relatives and friends of the demise of her beloved husband Ivan Ilych Golovin, Member of the Court of Justice, which occurred on February the 4th of this year 1882. The funeral will take place on Friday at one o'clock in the afternoon."

Ivan Ilych had been a colleague of the gentlemen present and was liked by them all. He had been ill for some weeks with an illness said to be incurable. His post had been kept open for him, but there had been conjectures that in case of his death Alexeev might receive his appointment, and that either Vinnikov or Shtabel would succeed Alexeev. So on receiving the news of Ivan Ilych's death the first thought of each of the gentlemen in that private room was of the changes and promotions it might occasion among themselves or their acquaintances.

"I shall be sure to get Shtabel's place or Vinnikov's," thought Fedor Vasilievich. "I was promised that long ago, and the promotion means an extra eight hundred rubles a year for me besides the allowance."

"Now I must apply for my brother-in-law's transfer from Kaluga," thought Peter Ivanovich.

"My wife will be very glad, and then she won't be able to say that I never do anything for her relations."

"I thought he would never leave his bed again," said Peter Ivanovich aloud. "It's very sad."

"But what really was the matter with him?"

"The doctors couldn't say — at least they could, but each of them said something different. When last I saw him I thought he was getting better."

"And I haven't been to see him since the holidays. I always meant to go."

"Had he any property?"

"I think his wife had a little — but something quite trifling."

"We shall have to go to see her, but they live so terribly far away."

"Far away from you, you mean. Everything's far away from your place."

"You see, he never can forgive my living on the other side of the river," said Peter Ivanovich, smiling at Shebek. Then, still talking of the distances between different parts of the city, they returned to the Court.

Besides considerations as to the possible transfers and promotions likely to result from Ivan Ilych's death, the mere fact of the death of a near acquaintance aroused, as usual, in all who heard of it the complacent feeling that, "it is he who is dead and not I."

Each one thought or felt, "Well, he's dead but I'm alive!" But the more intimate of Ivan Ilych's acquaintances, his so-called friends, could not help thinking also that they would now have to fulfill the very tiresome demands of propriety by attending the funeral service and paying a visit of condolence to the widow.

Fedor Vasilievich and Peter Ivanovich had been his nearest acquaintances. Peter Ivanovich had studied law with Ivan Ilych and had considered himself to be under obligations to him.

Having told his wife at dinner-time of Ivan Ilych's death, and of his conjecture that it might be possible to get her brother transferred to their circuit, Peter Ivanovich sacrificed his usual nap, put on his evening clothes and drove to Ivan Ilych's house.

At the entrance stood a carriage and two cabs. Leaning against the wall in the hall downstairs near the cloakstand was a coffin-lid covered with cloth of gold, ornamented with gold cord and tassels, that had been polished up with metal powder. Two ladies in black were taking off their fur cloaks. Peter Ivanovich recognized one of them as Ivan Ilych's sister, but the other was a stranger to him. His colleague Schwartz was just coming downstairs, but on seeing Peter Ivanovich enter he stopped and winked at him, as if to say: "Ivan Ilych has made a mess of things — not like you and me."

Schwartz's face with his Piccadilly whiskers, and his slim figure in evening dress, had as usual an air of elegant solemnity which contrasted with the playfulness of his character and had a special piquancy here, or so it seemed to Peter Ivanovich.

Peter Ivanovich allowed the ladies to precede him and slowly followed them upstairs. Schwartz did not come down but remained where he was, and Peter Ivanovich understood that he wanted to arrange where they should play bridge that evening. The ladies went upstairs to the widow's room, and Schwartz with seriously compressed lips but a playful look in his eyes, indicated by a twist of his eyebrows the room to the right where the body lay.

Peter Ivanovich, like everyone else on such occasions, entered feeling uncertain what he would have to do. All he knew was that at such times it is always safe to cross oneself. But he was not quite sure whether one should make obeisances while doing so. He therefore adopted a middle course. On entering the room he began crossing himself and made a slight movement resembling a bow. At the same time, as far as the motion of his head and arm allowed, he surveyed the room. Two young men — apparently nephews, one of whom was a high-school pupil — were leaving the room, crossing themselves as they did so. An old woman was standing motionless, and a lady with strangely arched eyebrows was saying something to her in a whisper. A vigorous, resolute Church Reader, in a frock-coat, was reading something in a loud voice with an expression that precluded any contradiction. The butler's assistant, Gerasim, stepping lightly in front of Peter Ivanovich, was strewing something on the floor. Noticing this, Peter Ivanovich was immediately aware of a faint odour of a decomposing body.

The last time he had called on Ivan Ilych, Peter Ivanovich had seen Gerasim in the study. Ivan Ilych had been particularly fond of him and he was performing the duty of a sick nurse.

Peter Ivanovich continued to make the sign of the cross slightly inclining his head in an intermediate direction between the coffin, the Reader, and the icons on the table in a corner of the room. Afterwards, when it seemed to him that this movement of his arm in crossing himself had gone on too long, he stopped and began to look at the corpse.

The dead man lay, as dead men always lie, in a specially heavy way, his rigid limbs sunk in the soft cushions of the coffin, with the head forever bowed on the pillow. His yellow waxen brow with bald patches over his sunken temples was thrust up in the way peculiar to the dead, the protruding nose seeming to press on the upper lip. He was much changed and grown even thinner since Peter Ivanovich had last seen him, but, as is always the case with the dead, his face was handsomer and above all more dignified than when he was alive. The expression on the face said that what was necessary had been accomplished, and accomplished rightly. Besides this there was in that expression a reproach and a warning to the living. This warning seemed to Peter Ivanovich out of place, or at least not applicable to him. He felt a certain discomfort and so he hurriedly crossed himself once more and turned and went out of the door — too hurriedly and too regardless of propriety, as he himself was aware.

Schwartz was waiting for him in the adjoining room with legs spread wide apart and both hands toying with his top-hat behind his back. The mere sight of that playful, well-groomed, and elegant figure refreshed Peter Ivanovich. He felt that Schwartz was above all these happenings and would not surrender to any depressing influences. His very look said that this incident of a church service for Ivan Ilych could not be a sufficient reason for infringing the order of the session — in other words, that it would certainly not prevent his unwrapping a new pack of cards and shuffling them that evening while a footman placed fresh candles on the table: in fact, that there was no reason for supposing that this incident would hinder their spending the evening agreeably. Indeed he said this in a whisper as Peter Ivanovich passed him, proposing that they should meet for a game at Fedor Vasilievich's. But apparently Peter Ivanovich was not destined to play bridge that evening. Praskovya Fedorovna (a short, fat woman who despite all efforts to the contrary had continued to broaden steadily from her shoulders downwards and who had the same extraordinarily arched eyebrows as the lady who had been standing by the coffin), dressed all in black, her head covered with lace, came out of her own room with some other ladies, conducted them to the room where the dead body lay, and said: "The service will begin immediately. Please go in."

Schwartz, making an indefinite bow, stood still, evidently neither accepting nor declining this invitation. Praskovya Fedorovna recognizing Peter Ivanovich, sighed, went close up to him, took his hand, and said: "I know you were a true friend to Ivan Ilych. . . ." and looked at him awaiting some suitable response. And Peter Ivanovich knew that, just as it had been the right thing to cross himself in that room, so what he had to do here was to press her hand, sigh, and say,

"Believe me. . . ." So he did all this and as he did it felt that the desired result had been achieved: that both he and she were touched.

"Come with me. I want to speak to you before it begins," said the widow. "Give me your arm."

Peter Ivanovich gave her his arm and they went to the inner rooms, passing Schwartz who winked at Peter Ivanovich compassionately.

"That does for our bridge! Don't object if we find another player. Perhaps you can cut in when you do escape," said his playful look.

Peter Ivanovich sighed still more deeply and despondently, and Praskovya Fedorovna pressed his arm gratefully. When they reached the drawing-room, upholstered in pink cretonne and lighted by a dim lamp, they sat down at the table — she on a sofa and Peter Ivanovich on a low pouffe, the springs of which yielded spasmodically under his weight. Praskovya Fedorovna had been on the point of warning him to take another seat, but felt that such a warning was out of keeping with her present condition and so changed her mind. As he sat down on the pouffe Peter Ivanovich recalled how Ivan Ilych had arranged this room and had consulted him regarding this pink cretonne with green leaves. The whole room was full of furniture and knick-knacks, and on her way to the sofa the lace of the widow's black shawl caught on the edge of the table. Peter Ivanovich rose to detach it, and the springs of the pouffe, relieved of his weight, rose also and gave him a push. The widow began detaching her shawl herself, and Peter Ivanovich again sat down, suppressing the rebellious springs of the pouffe under him. But the widow had not quite freed herself and Peter Ivanovich got up again, and again the pouffe rebelled and even creaked. When this was all over she took out a clean cambric handkerchief and began to weep. The episode with the shawl and the struggle with the pouffe had cooled Peter Ivanovich's emotions and he sat there with a sullen look on his face. This awkward situation was interrupted by Sokolov, Ivan Ilych's butler, who came to report that the plot in the cemetery that Praskovya Fedorovna had chosen would cost two hundred rubles. She stopped weeping and, looking at Peter Ivanovich with the air of a victim, remarked in French that it was very hard for her. Peter Ivanovich made a silent gesture signifying his full conviction that it must indeed be so.

"Please smoke," she said in a magnanimous yet crushed voice, and turned to discuss with Sokolov the price of the plot for the grave.

Peter Ivanovich while lighting his cigarette heard her inquiring very circumstantially into the prices of different plots in the cemetery and finally decide which she would take. When that was done she gave instructions about engaging the choir. Sokolov then left the room.

"I look after everything myself," she told Peter Ivanovich, shifting the albums that lay on the table; and noticing that the table was endangered by his cigarette-ash, she immediately passed him an ash-tray, saying as she did so: "I consider it an affectation to say that my grief prevents my attending to practical affairs. On the contrary, if anything can — I won't say console me, but — distract me, it is seeing to everything concerning him." She again took out her handkerchief as if preparing to cry, but suddenly, as if mastering her feeling, she shook herself and began to speak calmly. "But there is something I want to talk to you about."

Peter Ivanovich bowed, keeping control of the springs of the pouffe, which immediately began quivering under him.

"He suffered terribly the last few days."

"Did he?" said Peter Ivanovich.

"Oh, terribly! He screamed unceasingly, not for minutes but for hours. For the last three days he screamed incessantly. It was unendurable. I cannot understand how I bore it; you could hear him three rooms off. Oh, what I have suffered!"

"Is it possible that he was conscious all that time?" asked Peter Ivanovich.

"Yes," she whispered. "To the last moment. He took leave of us a quarter of an hour before he died, and asked us to take Vasya away."

The thought of the suffering of this man he had known so intimately, first as a merry little boy, then as a schoolmate, and later as a grown-up colleague, suddenly struck Peter Ivanovich with horror, despite an unpleasant consciousness of his own and this woman's dissimulation. He again saw that brow, and that nose pressing down on the lip, and felt afraid for himself.

"Three days of frightful suffering and the death! Why, that might suddenly, at any time, happen to me," he thought, and for a moment felt terrified. But — he did not himself know how — the customary reflection at once occurred to him that this had happened to Ivan Ilych and not to him, and that it

should not and could not happen to him, and that to think that it could would be yielding to depression which he ought not to do, as Schwartz's expression plainly showed. After which reflection Peter Ivanovich felt reassured, and began to ask with interest about the details of Ivan Ilych's death, as though death was an accident natural to Ivan Ilych but certainly not to himself.

After many details of the really dreadful physical sufferings Ivan Ilych had endured (which details he learnt only from the effect those sufferings had produced on Praskovya Fedorovna's nerves) the widow apparently found it necessary to get to business.

"Oh, Peter Ivanovich, how hard it is! How terribly, terribly hard!" and she again began to weep.

Peter Ivanovich sighed and waited for her to finish blowing her nose. When she had done so he said, "Believe me. . . ." and she again began talking and brought out what was evidently her chief concern with him — namely, to question him as to how she could obtain a grant of money from the government on the occasion of her husband's death. She made it appear that she was asking Peter Ivanovich's advice about her pension, but he soon saw that she already knew about that to the minutest detail, more even than he did himself. She knew how much could be got out of the government in consequence of her husband's death, but wanted to find out whether she could not possibly extract something more. Peter Ivanovich tried to think of some means of doing so, but after reflecting for a while and, out of propriety, condemning the government for its niggardliness, he said he thought that nothing more could be got. Then she sighed and evidently began to devise means of getting rid of her visitor. Noticing this, he put out his cigarette, rose, pressed her hand, and went out into the anteroom.

In the dining-room where the clock stood that Ivan Ilych had liked so much and had bought at an antique shop, Peter Ivanovich met a priest and a few acquaintances who had come to attend the service, and he recognized Ivan Ilych's daughter, a handsome young woman. She was in black and her slim figure appeared slimmer than ever. She had a gloomy, determined, almost angry expression, and bowed to Peter Ivanovich as though he were in some way to blame. Behind her, with the same offended look, stood a wealthy young man, an examining magistrate, whom Peter Ivanovich also knew and who was her fiance, as he had heard. He bowed mournfully to them and was about to pass into the death-chamber, when from under the stairs appeared the figure of Ivan Ilych's schoolboy son, who was extremely like his father. He seemed a little Ivan Ilych, such as Peter Ivanovich remembered when they studied law together. His tear-stained eyes had in them the look that is seen in the eyes of boys of thirteen or fourteen who are not pure-minded. When he saw Peter Ivanovich he scowled morosely and shamefacedly. Peter Ivanovich nodded to him and entered the death-chamber. The service began: candles, groans, incense, tears, and sobs. Peter Ivanovich stood looking gloomily down at his feet. He did not look once at the dead man, did not yield to any depressing influence, and was one of the first to leave the room. There was no one in the anteroom, but Gerasim darted out of the dead man's room, rummaged with his strong hands among the fur coats to find Peter Ivanovich's and helped him on with it.

"Well, friend Gerasim," said Peter Ivanovich, so as to say something. "It's a sad affair, isn't it?"

"It's God's will. We shall all come to it some day," said Gerasim, displaying his teeth — the even white teeth of a healthy peasant — and, like a man in the thick of urgent work, he briskly opened the front door, called the coachman, helped Peter Ivanovich into the sledge, and sprang back to the porch as if in readiness for what he had to do next.

Peter Ivanovich found the fresh air particularly pleasant after the smell of incense, the dead body, and carbolic acid.

"Where to sir?" asked the coachman.

"It's not too late even now . . . I'll call round on Fedor Vasilievich."

He accordingly drove there and found them just finishing the first rubber, so that it was quite convenient for him to cut in.

Ivan Ilych's life had been most simple and most ordinary and therefore most terrible.

He had been a member of the Court of Justice, and died at the age of forty-five. His father had been an official who after serving in various ministries and departments in Petersburg had made the sort of career which brings men to positions from which by reason of their long service they cannot be dismissed, though they are obviously unfit to hold any responsible position, and for whom therefore posts are specially created, which though fictitious carry salaries of from six to ten thousand rubles that are not fictitious, and in receipt of which they live on to a great age.

Such was the Privy Councillor and superfluous member of various superfluous institutions, Ilya Epimovich Golovin.

He had three sons, of whom Ivan Ilych was the second. The eldest son was following in his father's footsteps only in another department, and was already approaching that stage in the service at which a similar sinecure would be reached. The third son was a failure. He had ruined his prospects in a number of positions and was now serving in the railway department. His father and brothers, and still more their wives, not merely disliked meeting him, but avoided remembering his existence unless compelled to do so. His sister had married Baron Greff, a Petersburg official of her father's type. Ivan Ilych was neither as cold and formal as his elder brother nor as wild as the younger, but was a happy mean between them — an intelligent, polished, lively, and agreeable man. He had studied with his younger brother at the School of Law, but the latter had failed to complete the course and was expelled when he was in the fifth class. Ivan Ilych finished the course well. Even when he was at the School of Law he was just what he remained for the rest of his life: a capable, cheerful, good-natured, and sociable man, though strict in the fulfillment of what he considered to be his duty: and he considered his duty to be what was so considered by those in authority. Neither as a boy nor as a man was he a toady, but from early youth was by nature attracted to people of high station as a fly is drawn to the light, assimilating their ways and views of life and establishing friendly relations with them. All the enthusiasms of childhood and youth passed without leaving much trace on him; he succumbed to sensuality, to vanity, and latterly among the highest classes to liberalism, but always within limits which his instinct unfailingly indicated to him as correct.

At school he had done things which had formerly seemed to him very horrid and made him feel disgusted with himself when he did them; but when later on he saw that such actions were done by people of good position and that they did not regard them as wrong, he was able not exactly to regard them as right, but to forget about them entirely or not be at all troubled at remembering them. Having graduated from the School of Law and qualified for the tenth rank of the civil service, and having received money from his father for his equipment, Ivan Ilych ordered himself clothes at Scharmer's, the fashionable tailor, hung a medallion inscribed respice, on his watch-chain, took leave of his professor and the prince who was patron of the school, had a farewell dinner with his comrades at Donon's first-class restaurant, and with his new and fashionable portmanteau, linen, clothes, shaving and other toilet appliances, and a travelling rug, all purchased at the best shops, he set off for one of the provinces where through his father's influence, he had been attached to the governor as an official for special service.

In the province Ivan Ilych soon arranged as easy and agreeable a position for himself as he had had at the School of Law. He performed his official task, made his career, and at the same time amused himself pleasantly and decorously. Occasionally he paid official visits to country districts where he behaved with dignity both to his superiors and inferiors, and performed the duties entrusted to him, which related chiefly to the sectarians, with an exactness and incorruptible honesty of which he could not but feel proud.

In official matters, despite his youth and taste for frivolous gaiety, he was exceedingly reserved, punctilious, and even severe; but in society he was often amusing and witty, and always good-natured, correct in his manner, and bon enfant, as the governor and his wife — with whom he was like one of the family — used to say of him.

In the province he had an affair with a lady who made advances to the elegant young lawyer, and there was also a milliner; and there were carousals with aides-de-camp who visited the district, and after-supper visits to a certain outlying street of doubtful reputation; and there was too some obsequiousness to his chief and even to his chief's wife,

but all this was done with such a tone of good breeding that no hard names could be applied to it. It was all done with clean hands, in clean linen, with French phrases, and above all among people of the best society and consequently with the approval of people of rank.

So Ivan Ilych served for five years and then came a change in his official life. The new and reformed judicial institutions were introduced, and new men were needed. Ivan Ilych became such a new man. He was offered the post of examining magistrate, and he accepted it though the post was in another province and obliged him to give up the connections he had formed and to make new ones. His friends met to give him a send-off; they had a group photograph taken and presented him with a silver cigarette-case, and he set off to his new post.

As examining magistrate Ivan Ilych was just as comme il faut and decorous a man, inspiring general respect and capable of separating his official duties from his private life, as he had been when acting as an official on special service. His duties now as examining magistrate were far more interesting and attractive than before. In his former position it had been pleasant to wear an undress uniform made by Scharmer, and to pass through the crowd of petitioners and officials who were timorously awaiting an audience with the governor, and who envied him as with free and easy gait he went straight into his chief's private room to have a cup of tea and a cigarette with him. But not many people had then been directly dependent on him — only police officials and the sectarians when he went on special missions — and he liked to treat them politely, almost as comrades, as if he were letting them feel that he who had the power to crush them was treating them in this simple, friendly way. There were then but few such people. But now, as an examining magistrate, Ivan Ilych felt that everyone without exception, even the most important and self-satisfied, was in his power, and that he need only write a few words on a sheet of paper with a certain heading, and this or that important, self-satisfied person would be brought before him in the role of an accused person or a witness, and if he did not choose to allow him to sit down, would have to stand before him and answer his questions. Ivan Ilych never abused his power; he tried on the contrary to soften its expression, but the consciousness of it and the possibility of softening its effect, supplied the chief interest and attraction of his office. In his work itself, especially in his examinations, he very soon acquired a method of eliminating all considerations irrelevant to the legal aspect of the case, and reducing even the most complicated case to a form in which it would be presented on paper only in its externals, completely excluding his personal opinion of the matter, while above all observing every prescribed formality. The work was new and Ivan Ilych was one of the first men to apply the new Code of 1864.

On taking up the post of examining magistrate in a new town, he made new acquaintances and connections, placed himself on a new footing and assumed a somewhat different tone. He took up an attitude of rather dignified aloofness towards the provincial authorities, but picked out the best circle of legal gentlemen and wealthy gentry living in the town and assumed a tone of slight dissatisfaction with the government, of moderate liberalism, and of enlightened citizenship. At the same time, without at all altering the elegance of his toilet, he ceased shaving his chin and allowed his beard to grow as it pleased.

Ivan Ilych settled down very pleasantly in this new town. The society there, which inclined towards opposition to the governor was friendly, his salary was larger, and he began to play vint [a form of bridge], which he found added not a little to the pleasure of life, for he had a capacity for cards, played good-humouredly, and calculated rapidly and astutely, so that he usually won.

After living there for two years he met his future wife, Praskovya Fedorovna Mikhel, who was the most attractive, clever, and brilliant girl of the set in which he moved, and among other amusements and relaxations from his labours as examining magistrate, Ivan Ilych established light and playful relations with her.

While he had been an official on special service he had been accustomed to dance, but now as an examining magistrate it was exceptional for him to do so. If he danced now, he did it as if to show that though he served under the reformed order of things, and had reached the fifth official rank, yet when it came to dancing he could do it better than most people. So at the end of an evening he sometimes danced with Praskovya Fedorovna, and it was chiefly during these dances that he captivated her. She fell in love with him. Ivan Ilych had at first no definite intention of marrying, but when the girl fell in love with him he said to himself: "Really, why shouldn't I marry?"

Praskovya Fedorovna came of a good family, was not bad looking, and had some little property. Ivan Ilych might have aspired to a more brilliant match, but even this was good. He had his salary, and she, he hoped, would have an equal income. She was well connected, and was a sweet, pretty, and thoroughly correct young woman. To say that Ivan Ilych married because he fell in love with Praskovya Fedorovna and found that she sympathized with his views of life would be as incorrect as to say that he married because his social circle approved of the match. He was swayed by both these considerations: the marriage gave him personal satisfaction, and at the same time it was considered the right thing by the most highly placed of his associates. So Ivan Ilych got married.

The preparations for marriage and the beginning of married life, with its conjugal caresses, the new furniture, new crockery, and new linen, were very pleasant until his wife became pregnant — so that Ivan Ilych had begun to think that marriage would not impair the easy, agreeable, gay and always decorous character of his life, approved of by society and regarded by himself as natural, but would even improve it. But from the first months of his wife's pregnancy, something new, unpleasant, depressing, and unseemly, and from which there was no way of escape, unexpectedly showed itself.

His wife, without any reason, de gaiete de coeur, as Ivan Ilych expressed it to himself — began to disturb the pleasure and propriety of their life. She began to be jealous without any cause, expected him to devote his whole attention to her, found fault with everything, and made coarse and ill-mannered scenes.

At first Ivan Ilych hoped to escape from the unpleasantness of this state of affairs by the same easy and decorous relation to life that had served him heretofore: he tried to ignore his wife's disagreeable moods, continued to live in his usual easy and pleasant way, invited friends to his house for a game of cards, and also tried going out to his club or spending his evenings with friends. But one day his wife began upbraiding him so vigorously, using such coarse words, and continued to abuse him every time he did not fulfill her demands, so resolutely and with such evident determination not to give way till he submitted — that is, till he stayed at home and was bored just as she was — that he became alarmed. He now realized that matrimony — at any rate with Praskovya Fedorovna — was not always conducive to the pleasures and amenities of life, but on the contrary often infringed both comfort and propriety, and that he must therefore entrench himself against such infringement. And Ivan Ilych began to seek for means of doing so. His official duties were the one thing that imposed upon Praskovya Fedorovna, and by means of his official work and the duties attached to it he began struggling with his wife to secure his own independence.

With the birth of their child, the attempts to feed it and the various failures in doing so, and with the real and imaginary illnesses of mother and child, in which Ivan Ilych's sympathy was demanded but about which he understood nothing, the need of securing for himself an existence outside his family life became still more imperative.

As his wife grew more irritable and exacting and Ivan Ilych transferred the center of gravity of his life more and more to his official work, so did he grow to like his work better and became more ambitious than before.

Very soon, within a year of his wedding, Ivan Ilych had realized that marriage, though it may add some comforts to life, is in fact a very intricate and difficult affair towards which in order to perform one's duty, that is, to lead a decorous life approved of by society, one must adopt a definite attitude just as towards one's official duties.

And Ivan Ilych evolved such an attitude towards married life. He only required of it those conveniences — dinner at home, housewife, and bed — which it could give him, and above all that propriety of external forms required by public opinion. For the rest he looked for lighthearted pleasure and propriety, and was very thankful when he found them, but if he met with antagonism and querulousness he at once retired into his separate fenced-off world of official duties, where he found satisfaction.

Ivan Ilych was esteemed a good official, and after three years was made Assistant Public Prosecutor. His new duties, their importance, the possibility of indicting and imprisoning anyone he chose, the publicity his speeches received, and the success he had in all these things, made his work still more attractive.

More children came. His wife became more and more querulous and ill-tempered, but the attitude Ivan Ilych had adopted towards his home life rendered him almost impervious to her grumbling.

After seven years' service in that town he was transferred to another province as Public Prosecutor. They moved, but were short of money and his wife did not like the place they moved to. Though the salary was higher the cost of living was greater, besides which two of their children died and family life became still more unpleasant for him.

Praskovya Fedorovna blamed her husband for every inconvenience they encountered in their new home. Most of the conversations between husband and wife, especially as to the children's education, led to topics which recalled former disputes, and these disputes were apt to flare up again at any moment. There remained only those rare periods of amorousness which still came to them at times but did not last long. These were islets at which they anchored for a while and then again set out upon that ocean of veiled hostility which showed itself in their aloofness from one another. This aloofness might have grieved Ivan Ilych had he considered that it ought not to exist, but he now regarded the position as normal, and even made it the goal at which he aimed in family life. His aim was to free himself more and more from those unpleasantnesses and to give them a semblance of harmlessness and propriety. He attained this by spending less and less time with his family, and when obliged to be at home he tried to safeguard his position by the presence of outsiders. The chief thing however was that he had his official duties. The whole interest of his life now centered in the official world and that interest absorbed him. The consciousness of his power, being able to ruin anybody he wished to ruin, the importance, even the external dignity of his entry into court, or meetings with his subordinates, his success with superiors and inferiors, and above all his masterly handling of cases, of which he was conscious — all this gave him pleasure and filled his life, together with chats with his colleagues, dinners, and bridge. So that on the whole Ivan Ilych's life continued to flow as he considered it should do — pleasantly and properly.

So things continued for another seven years. His eldest daughter was already sixteen, another child had died, and only one son was left, a schoolboy and a subject of dissension. Ivan Ilych wanted to put him in the School of Law, but to spite him Praskovya Fedorovna entered him at the High School. The daughter had been educated at home and had turned out well: the boy did not learn badly either.

So Ivan Ilych lived for seventeen years after his marriage. He was already a Public Prosecutor of long standing, and had declined several proposed transfers while awaiting a more desirable post, when an unanticipated and unpleasant occurrence quite upset the peaceful course of his life. He was expecting to be offered the post of presiding judge in a University town, but Happe somehow came to the front and obtained the appointment instead. Ivan Ilych became irritable, reproached Happe, and quarrelled both with him and with his immediate superiors — who became colder to him and again passed him over when other appointments were made.

This was in 1880, the hardest year of Ivan Ilych's life. It was then that it became evident on the one hand that his salary was insufficient for them to live on, and on the other that he had been forgotten, and not only this, but that what was for him the greatest and most cruel injustice appeared to others a quite ordinary occurrence. Even his father did not consider it his duty to help him. Ivan Ilych felt himself abandoned by everyone, and that they regarded his position with a salary of 3,500 rubles as quite normal and even fortunate. He alone knew that with the consciousness of the injustices done him, with his wife's incessant nagging, and with the debts he had contracted by living beyond his means, his position was far from normal.

In order to save money that summer he obtained leave of absence and went with his wife to live in the country at her brother's place.

In the country, without his work, he experienced ennui for the first time in his life, and not only ennui but intolerable depression, and he decided that it was impossible to go on living like that, and that it was necessary to take energetic measures.

Having passed a sleepless night pacing up and down the veranda, he decided to go to Petersburg and bestir himself, in order to punish those who had failed to appreciate him and to get transferred to another ministry.

Next day, despite many protests from his wife and her brother, he started for Petersburg with the sole object of obtaining a post with a salary of five thousand rubles a year. He was no longer bent on any particular department, or tendency, or kind of activity. All he now wanted was an appointment to another post with a salary of five thousand rubles, either in the administration, in the banks, with the railways, in one of the Empress Marya's Institutions, or even in the customs — but it had to carry with it a salary of five thousand rubles and be in a ministry other than that in which they had failed to appreciate him.

And this quest of Ivan Ilych's was crowned with remarkable and unexpected success. At Kursk an acquaintance of his, F. I. Ilyin, got into the first-class carriage, sat down beside Ivan Ilych, and told him of a telegram just received by the governor of Kursk announcing that a change was about to take place in the ministry: Peter Ivanovich was to be superseded by Ivan Semonovich.

The proposed change, apart from its significance for Russia, had a special significance for Ivan Ilych, because by bringing forward a new man, Peter Petrovich, and consequently his friend Zachar Ivanovich, it was highly favourable for Ivan Ilych, since Sachar Ivanovich was a friend and colleague of his.

In Moscow this news was confirmed, and on reaching Petersburg Ivan Ilych found Zachar Ivanovich and received a definite promise of an appointment in his former Department of Justice.

A week later he telegraphed to his wife: "Zachar in Miller's place. I shall receive appointment on presentation of report."

Thanks to this change of personnel, Ivan Ilych had unexpectedly obtained an appointment in his former ministry which placed him two states above his former colleagues besides giving him five thousand rubles salary and three thousand five hundred rubles for expenses connected with his removal. All his ill humour towards his former enemies and the whole department vanished, and Ivan Ilych was completely happy.

He returned to the country more cheerful and contented than he had been for a long time. Praskovya Fedorovna also cheered up and a truce was arranged between them. Ivan Ilych told of how he had been feted by everybody in Petersburg, how all those who had been his enemies were put to shame and now fawned on him, how envious they were of his appointment, and how much everybody in Petersburg had liked him.

Praskovya Fedorovna listened to all this and appeared to believe it. She did not contradict anything, but only made plans for their life in the town to which they were going. Ivan Ilych saw with delight that these plans were his plans, that he and his wife agreed, and that, after a stumble, his life was regaining its due and natural character of pleasant lightheartedness and decorum.

Ivan Ilych had come back for a short time only, for he had to take up his new duties on the 10th of September. Moreover, he needed time to settle into the new place, to move all his belongings from the province, and to buy and order many additional things: in a word, to make such arrangements as he had resolved on, which were almost exactly what Praskovya Fedorovna too had decided on.

Now that everything had happened so fortunately, and that he and his wife were at one in their aims and moreover saw so little of one another, they got on together better than they had done since the first years of marriage. Ivan Ilych had thought of taking his family away with him at once, but the insistence of his wife's brother and her sister-in-law, who had suddenly become particularly amiable and friendly to him and his family, induced him to depart alone.

So he departed, and the cheerful state of mind induced by his success and by the harmony between his wife and himself, the one intensifying the other, did not leave him. He found a delightful house, just the thing both he and his wife had dreamt of. Spacious, lofty reception rooms in the old style, a convenient and dignified study, rooms for his wife and daughter, a study for his son — it might have been specially built for them. Ivan Ilych himself superintended the arrangements, chose the wallpapers, supplemented the furniture (preferably with antiques which he considered particularly comme il faut), and supervised the upholstering. Everything progressed and progressed and approached the ideal he had set himself: even when things were only half completed they exceeded his expectations. He saw what a refined and elegant character, free from vulgarity, it would all have when it was ready. On falling asleep he pictured to himself how the reception room would look. Looking at the yet unfinished drawing room he could see the fireplace, the screen, the what-not, the little chairs dotted here and there, the dishes and plates on the walls, and the bronzes, as they would be when everything was in place. He was pleased by the thought of how his wife and daughter, who shared his taste in this matter, would be impressed by it. They were certainly not expecting as much. He had been particularly successful in finding, and buying cheaply, antiques which gave a particularly aristocratic character to the whole place. But in his letters he intentionally understated everything in order to be able to surprise them. All this so absorbed him that his new duties — though he liked his official work — interested him less than he had expected. Sometimes he even had moments of absent-mindedness during the court sessions and would consider whether he should have straight or curved cornices for his curtains. He was so interested in it all that he often did things himself, rearranging the furniture, or rehanging the curtains. Once when mounting a step-ladder to show the upholsterer, who did not understand, how he wanted the hangings draped, he made a false step and slipped, but being a strong and agile man he clung on and only knocked his side against the knob of the window frame. The bruised place was painful but the pain soon passed, and he felt particularly bright and well just then. He wrote: "I feel fifteen years younger." He thought he would have everything ready by September, but it dragged on till mid-October. But the result was charming not only in his eyes but to everyone who saw it.

In reality it was just what is usually seen in the houses of people of moderate means who want to appear rich, and therefore succeed only in resembling others like themselves: there are damasks, dark wood, plants, rugs, and dull and polished bronzes — all the things people of a certain class have in order to resemble other people of that class. His house was so like the others that it would never have been noticed, but to him it all seemed to be quite exceptional. He was very happy when he met his family at the station and brought them to the newly furnished house all lit up, where a footman in a white tie opened the door into the hall decorated with plants, and when they went on into the drawing-room and the study uttering exclamations of delight. He conducted them everywhere, drank in their praises eagerly, and beamed with pleasure. At tea that evening, when Praskovya Fedorovna among other things asked him about his fall, he laughed, and showed them how he had gone flying and had frightened the upholsterer.

"It's a good thing I'm a bit of an athlete. Another man might have been killed, but I merely knocked myself, just here; it hurts when it's touched, but it's passing off already — it's only a bruise."

So they began living in their new home — in which, as always happens, when they got thoroughly settled in they found they were just one room short — and with the increased income, which as always was just a little (some five hundred rubles) too little, but it was all very nice.

Things went particularly well at first, before everything was finally arranged and while something had still to be done: this thing bought, that thing ordered, another thing moved, and something else adjusted. Though there were some disputes between husband and wife, they were both so well satisfied and had so much to do that it all passed off without any serious quarrels. When nothing was left to arrange it became rather dull and something seemed to be lacking, but they were then making acquaintances, forming habits, and life was growing fuller.

Ivan Ilych spent his mornings at the law court and came home to dinner, and at first he was generally in a good humour, though he occasionally became irritable just on account of his house. (Every spot on the tablecloth or the upholstery, and every broken window-blind string, irritated him. He had devoted so much trouble to arranging it all that every disturbance of it distressed him.) But on the whole his life ran its course as he believed life should do: easily, pleasantly, and decorously.

He got up at nine, drank his coffee, read the paper, and then put on his undress uniform and went to the law courts. There the harness in which he worked had already been stretched to fit him and he donned it without a hitch: petitioners, inquiries at the chancery, the chancery itself, and the sittings public and administrative. In all this the thing was to exclude everything fresh and vital, which always disturbs the regular course of official business, and to admit only official relations with people, and then only on official grounds. A man would come, for instance, wanting some information. Ivan Ilych, as one in whose sphere the matter did not lie, would have nothing to do with him: but if the man had some business with him in his official capacity, something that could be expressed on officially stamped paper, he would do everything, positively everything he could within the limits of such relations, and in doing so would maintain the semblance of friendly human relations, that is, would observe the courtesies of life. As soon as the official relations ended, so did everything else. Ivan Ilych possessed this capacity to separate his real life from the official side of affairs and not mix the two, in the highest degree, and by long practice and natural aptitude had brought it to such a pitch that sometimes, in the manner of a virtuoso, he would even allow himself to let the human and official relations mingle. He let himself do this just because he felt that he could at any time he chose resume the strictly official attitude again and drop the human relation. And he did it all easily, pleasantly, correctly, and even artistically. In the intervals between the sessions he smoked, drank tea, chatted a little about politics, a little about general topics, a little about cards, but most of all about official appointments. Tired, but with the feelings of a virtuoso — one of the first violins who has played his part in an orchestra with precision — he would return home to find that his wife and daughter had been out paying calls, or had a visitor, and that his son had been to school, had done his homework with his tutor, and was surely learning what is taught at High Schools. Everything was as it should be. After dinner, if they had no visitors, Ivan Ilych sometimes read a book that was being much discussed at the time, and in the evening settled down to work, that is, read official papers, compared the depositions of witnesses, and noted paragraphs of the Code applying to them. This was neither dull nor amusing. It was dull when he might have been playing bridge, but if no bridge was available it was at any rate better than doing nothing or sitting with his wife. Ivan Ilych's chief pleasure was giving little dinners to which he invited men and women of good social position, and just as his drawing-room resembled all other drawing-rooms so did his enjoyable little parties resemble all other such parties.

Once they even gave a dance. Ivan Ilych enjoyed it and everything went off well, except that it led to a violent quarrel with his wife about the cakes and sweets. Praskovya Fedorovna had made her own plans, but Ivan Ilych insisted on getting everything from an expensive confectioner and ordered too many cakes, and the quarrel occurred because some of those cakes were left over and the confectioner's bill came to forty-five rubles. It was a great and disagreeable quarrel. Praskovya Fedorovna called him "a fool and an imbecile," and he clutched at his head and made angry allusions to divorce.

But the dance itself had been enjoyable. The best people were there, and Ivan Ilych had danced with Princess Trufonova, a sister of the distinguished founder of the Society "Bear My Burden."

The pleasures connected with his work were pleasures of ambition; his social pleasures were those of vanity; but Ivan Ilych's greatest pleasure was playing bridge. He acknowledged that whatever disagreeable incident happened in his life, the pleasure that beamed like a ray of light above everything else was to sit down to bridge with good players, not noisy partners, and of course to four-handed bridge (with five players it was annoying to have to stand out, though one pretended not to mind), to play a clever and serious game (when the cards allowed it) and then to have supper and drink a glass of wine. After a game of bridge, especially if he had won a little (to win a large sum was

unpleasant), Ivan Ilych went to bed in a specially good humour.

So they lived. They formed a circle of acquaintances among the best people and were visited by people of importance and by young folk. In their views as to their acquaintances, husband, wife, and daughter were entirely agreed, and tacitly and unanimously kept at arm's length and shook off the various shabby friends and relations who, with much show of affection, gushed into the drawing-room with its Japanese plates on the walls. Soon these shabby friends ceased to obtrude themselves and only the best people remained in the Golovins' set.

Young men made up to Lisa, and Petrishchev, an examining magistrate and Dmitri Ivanovich Petrishchev's son and sole heir, began to be so attentive to her that Ivan Ilych had already spoken to Praskovya Fedorovna about it, and considered whether they should not arrange a party for them, or get up some private theatricals.

So they lived, and all went well, without change, and life flowed pleasantly.

They were all in good health. It could not be called ill health if Ivan Ilych sometimes said that he had a queer taste in his mouth and felt some discomfort in his left side.

But this discomfort increased and, though not exactly painful, grew into a sense of pressure in his side accompanied by ill humour. And his irritability became worse and worse and began to mar the agreeable, easy, and correct life that had established itself in the Golovin family. Quarrels between husband and wife became more and more frequent, and soon the ease and amenity disappeared and even the decorum was barely maintained. Scenes again became frequent, and very few of those islets remained on which husband and wife could meet without an explosion. Praskovya Fedorovna now had good reason to say that her husband's temper was trying. With characteristic exaggeration she said he had always had a dreadful temper, and that it had needed all her good nature to put up with it for twenty years. It was true that now the quarrels were started by him. His bursts of temper always came just before dinner, often just as he began to eat his soup. Sometimes he noticed that a plate or dish was chipped, or the food was not right, or his son put his elbow on the table, or his daughter's hair was not done as he liked it, and for all this he blamed Praskovya Fedorovna. At first she retorted and said disagreeable things to him, but once or twice he fell into such a rage at the beginning of dinner that she realized it was due to some physical derangement brought on by taking food, and so she restrained herself and did not answer, but only hurried to get the dinner over. She regarded this self-restraint as highly praiseworthy. Having come to the conclusion that her husband had a dreadful temper and made her life miserable, she began to feel sorry for herself, and the more she pitied herself the more she hated her husband. She began to wish he would die; yet she did not want him to die because then his salary would cease. And this irritated her against him still more. She considered herself dreadfully unhappy just because not even his death could save her, and though she concealed her exasperation, that hidden exasperation of hers increased his irritation also.

After one scene in which Ivan Ilych had been particularly unfair and after which he had said in explanation that he certainly was irritable but that it was due to his not being well, she said that he if was ill it should be attended to, and insisted on his going to see a celebrated doctor.

He went. Everything took place as he had expected and as it always does. There was the usual waiting and the important air assumed by the doctor, with which he was so familiar (resembling that which he himself assumed in court), and the sounding and listening, and the questions which called for answers that were foregone conclusions and were evidently unnecessary, and the look of importance which implied that "if only you put yourself in our hands we will arrange everything — we know indubitably how it has to be done, always in the same way for everybody alike." It was all just as it was in the law courts. The doctor put on just the same air towards him as he himself put on towards an accused person.

The doctor said that so-and-so indicated that there was so-and-so inside the patient, but if the investigation of so-and-so did not confirm this, then he must assume that and that. If he assumed that and that, then . . . and so on. To Ivan Ilych only one question was important: was his case serious or not?

But the doctor ignored that inappropriate question. From his point of view it was not the one under consideration, the real question was to decide between a floating kidney, chronic catarrh, or appendicitis. It was not a question the doctor solved brilliantly, as it seemed to Ivan Ilych, in favour of the appendix, with the reservation that should an examination of the urine give fresh indications the matter would be reconsidered. All this was just what Ivan Ilych had himself brilliantly accomplished a thousand times in dealing with men on trial. The doctor summed up just as brilliantly, looking over his spectacles triumphantly and even gaily at the accused. From the doctor's summing up Ivan Ilych concluded that things were bad, but that for the doctor, and perhaps for everybody else, it was a matter of indifference, though for him it was bad. And this conclusion struck him painfully, arousing in him a great feeling of pity for himself and of bitterness towards the doctor's indifference to a matter of such importance.

He said nothing of this, but rose, placed the doctor's fee on the table, and remarked with a sigh: "We sick people probably often put inappropriate questions. But tell me, in general, is this complaint dangerous, or not?"

The doctor looked at him sternly over his spectacles with one eye, as if to say: "Prisoner, if you will not keep to the questions put to you, I shall be obliged to have you removed from the court."

"I have already told you what I consider necessary and proper. The analysis may show something more." And the doctor bowed.

Ivan Ilych went out slowly, seated himself disconsolately in his sledge, and drove home. All the way home he was going over what the doctor had said, trying to translate those complicated, obscure, scientific phrases into plain language and find in them an answer to the question: "Is my condition bad? Is it very bad? Or is there as yet nothing much wrong?" And it seemed to him that the meaning of what the doctor had said was that it was very bad. Everything in the streets seemed depressing. The cabmen, the houses, the passers-by, and the shops, were dismal. His ache, this dull gnawing ache that never ceased for a moment, seemed to have acquired a new and more serious significance from the doctor's dubious remarks. Ivan Ilych now watched it with a new and oppressive feeling.

He reached home and began to tell his wife about it. She listened, but in the middle of his account his daughter came in with her hat on, ready to go out with her mother. She sat down reluctantly to listen to this tedious story, but could not stand it long, and her mother too did not hear him to the end.

"Well, I am very glad," she said. "Mind now to take your medicine regularly. Give me the prescription and I'll send Gerasim to the chemist's." And she went to get ready to go out.

While she was in the room Ivan Ilych had hardly taken time to breathe, but he sighed deeply when she left it.

"Well," he thought, "perhaps it isn't so bad after all."

He began taking his medicine and following the doctor's directions, which had been altered after the examination of the urine. But then it happened that there was a contradiction between the indications drawn from the examination of the urine and the symptoms that showed themselves. It turned out that what was happening differed from what the doctor had told him, and that he had either forgotten or blundered, or hidden something from him. He could not, however, be blamed for that, and Ivan Ilych still obeyed his orders implicitly and at first derived some comfort from doing so.

From the time of his visit to the doctor, Ivan Ilych's chief occupation was the exact fulfillment of the doctor's instructions regarding hygiene and the taking of medicine, and the observation of his pain and his excretions. His chief interest came to be people's ailments and people's health. When sickness, deaths, or recoveries were mentioned in his presence, especially when the illness resembled his own, he listened with agitation which he tried to hide, asked questions, and applied what he heard to his own case.

The pain did not grow less, but Ivan Ilych made efforts to force himself to think that he was better. And he could do this so long as nothing agitated him. But as soon as he had any unpleasantness with his wife, any lack of success in his official work, or held bad cards at bridge, he was at once acutely

sensible of his disease. He had formerly borne such mischances, hoping soon to adjust what was wrong, to master it and attain success, or make a grand slam. But now every mischance upset him and plunged him into despair. He would say to himself: "There now, just as I was beginning to get better and the medicine had begun to take effect, comes this accursed misfortune, or unpleasantness." And he was furious with the mishap, or with the people who were causing the unpleasantness and killing him, for he felt that this fury was killing him but he could not restrain it. One would have thought that it should have been clear to him that this exasperation with circumstances and people aggravated his illness, and that he ought therefore to ignore unpleasant occurrences. But he drew the very opposite conclusion: he said that he needed peace, and he watched for everything that might disturb it and became irritable at the slightest infringement of it. His condition was rendered worse by the fact that he read medical books and consulted doctors. The progress of his disease was so gradual that he could deceive himself when comparing one day with another — the difference was so slight. But when he consulted the doctors it seemed to him that he was getting worse, and even very rapidly. Yet despite this he was continually consulting them.

That month he went to see another celebrity, who told him almost the same as the first had done but put his questions rather differently, and the interview with this celebrity only increased Ivan Ilych's doubts and fears. A friend of a friend of his, a very good doctor, diagnosed his illness again quite differently from the others, and though he predicted recovery, his questions and suppositions bewildered Ivan Ilych still more and increased his doubts. A homeopathist diagnosed the disease in yet another way, and prescribed medicine which Ivan Ilych took secretly for a week. But after a week, not feeling any improvement and having lost confidence both in the former doctor's treatment and in this one's, he became still more despondent. One day a lady acquaintance mentioned a cure effected by a wonder-working icon. Ivan Ilych caught himself listening attentively and beginning to believe that it had occurred. This incident alarmed him. "Has my mind really weakened to such an extent?" he asked himself. "Nonsense! It's all rubbish. I mustn't give way to nervous fears but having chosen a doctor must keep strictly to his treatment. That is what I will do. Now it's all settled. I won't think about it, but will follow the treatment seriously till summer, and then we shall see. From now there must be no more of this wavering!" This was easy to say but impossible to carry out. The pain in his side oppressed him and seemed to grow worse and more incessant, while the taste in his mouth grew stranger and stranger. It seemed to him that his breath had a disgusting smell, and he was conscious of a loss of appetite and strength. There was no deceiving himself: something terrible, new, and more important than anything before in his life, was taking place within him of which he alone was aware. Those about him did not understand or would not understand it, but thought everything in the world was going on as usual. That tormented Ivan Ilych more than anything. He saw that his household, especially his wife and daughter who were in a perfect whirl of visiting, did not understand anything of it and were annoyed that he was so depressed and so exacting, as if he were to blame for it. Though they tried to disguise it he saw that he was an obstacle in their path, and that his wife had adopted a definite line in regard to his illness and kept to it regardless of anything he said or did. Her attitude was this: "You know," she would say to her friends, "Ivan Ilych can't do as other people do, and keep to the treatment prescribed for him. One day he'll take his drops and keep strictly to his diet and go to bed in good time, but the next day unless I watch him he'll suddenly forget his medicine, eat sturgeon — which is forbidden — and sit up playing cards till one o'clock in the morning."

"Oh, come, when was that?" Ivan Ilych would ask in vexation. "Only once at Peter Ivanovich's."

"And yesterday with Shebek."

"Well, even if I hadn't stayed up, this pain would have kept me awake."

"Be that as it may you'll never get well like that, but will always make us wretched."

Praskovya Fedorovna's attitude to Ivan Ilych's illness, as she expressed it both to others and to him, was that it was his own fault and was another of the annoyances he caused her. Ivan Ilych felt that this opinion escaped her involuntarily — but that did not make it easier for him.

At the law courts too, Ivan Ilych noticed, or thought he noticed, a strange attitude towards himself. It sometimes seemed to him that people were watching him inquisitively as a man whose place might soon be vacant. Then again, his friends would suddenly begin to chaff him in a friendly way about his low spirits, as if the awful, horrible, and unheard-of thing that was going on within him, incessantly gnawing at him and irresistibly drawing him away, was a very agreeable subject for jests. Schwartz in particular irritated him by his jocularity, vivacity, and savoir-faire, which reminded him of what he himself had been ten years ago.

Friends came to make up a set and they sat down to cards. They dealt, bending the new cards to soften them, and he sorted the diamonds in his hand and found he had seven. His partner said "No trumps" and supported him with two diamonds. What more could be wished for? It ought to be jolly and lively. They would make a grand slam. But suddenly Ivan Ilych was conscious of that gnawing pain, that taste in his mouth, and it seemed ridiculous that in such circumstances he should be pleased to make a grand slam.

He looked at his partner Mikhail Mikhaylovich, who rapped the table with his strong hand and instead of snatching up the tricks pushed the cards courteously and indulgently towards Ivan Ilych that he might have the pleasure of gathering them up without the trouble of stretching out his hand for them. "Does he think I am too weak to stretch out my arm?" thought Ivan Ilych, and forgetting what he was doing he over-trumped his partner, missing the grand slam by three tricks. And what was most awful of all was that he saw how upset Mikhail Mikhaylovich was about it but did not himself care. And it was dreadful to realize why he did not care.

They all saw that he was suffering, and said: "We can stop if you are tired. Take a rest." Lie down? No, he was not at all tired, and he finished the rubber. All were gloomy and silent. Ivan Ilych felt that he had diffused this gloom over them and could not dispel it. They had supper and went away, and Ivan Ilych was left alone with the consciousness that his life was poisoned and was poisoning the lives of others, and that this poison did not weaken but penetrated more and more deeply into his whole being.

With this consciousness, and with physical pain besides the terror, he must go to bed, often to lie awake the greater part of the night. Next morning he had to get up again, dress, go to the law courts, speak, and write; or if he did not go out, spend at home those twenty-four hours a day each of which was a torture. And he had to live thus all alone on the brink of an abyss, with no one who understood or pitied him.

So one month passed and then another. Just before the New Year his brother-in-law came to town and stayed at their house. Ivan Ilych was at the law courts and Praskovya Fedorovna had gone shopping. When Ivan Ilych came home and entered his study he found his brother-in-law there — a healthy, florid man — unpacking his portmanteau himself. He raised his head on hearing Ivan Ilych's footsteps and looked up at him for a moment without a word. That stare told Ivan Ilych everything. His brother-in-law opened his mouth to utter an exclamation of surprise but checked himself, and that action confirmed it all.

"I have changed, eh?"

"Yes, there is a change."

And after that, try as he would to get his brother-in-law to return to the subject of his looks, the latter would say nothing about it. Praskovya Fedorovna came home and her brother went out to her. Ivan Ilych locked the door and began to examine himself in the glass, first full face, then in profile. He took up a portrait of himself taken with his wife, and compared it with what he saw in the glass. The change in him was immense. Then he bared his arms to the elbow, looked at them, drew the sleeves down again, sat down on an ottoman, and grew blacker than night.

"No, no, this won't do!" he said to himself, and jumped up, went to the table, took up some law papers and began to read them, but could not continue. He unlocked the door and went into the reception-room. The door leading to the drawing-room was shut. He approached it on tiptoe and listened.

"No, you are exaggerating!" Praskovya Fedorovna was saying.

"Exaggerating! Don't you see it? Why, he's a dead man! Look at his eyes — there's no life in them. But what is it that is wrong with him?"

"No one knows. Nikolaevich said something, but I don't know what. And Leshchetitsky said quite the contrary. . . ."

Ivan Ilych walked away, went to his own room, lay down, and began musing; "The kidney, a floating kidney." He recalled all the doctors had told him of how it detached itself and swayed about. And by an effort of imagination he tried to catch that kidney and arrest it and support it. So little was needed for this, it seemed to him. "No, I'll go to see Peter Ivanovich again." [That was the friend whose friend was a doctor.] He rang, ordered the carriage, and got ready to go.

"Where are you going, Ivan?" asked his wife with a specially sad and exceptionally kind look.

This exceptionally kind look irritated him. He looked morosely at her.

"I must go to see Peter Ivanovich."

He went to see Peter Ivanovich, and together they went to see his friend, the doctor. He was in, and Ivan Ilych had a long talk with him.

Reviewing the anatomical and physiological details of what in the doctor's opinion was going on inside him, he understood it all.

There was something, a small thing, in the vermiform appendix. It might all come right. Only stimulate the energy of one organ and check the activity of another, then absorption would take place and everything would come right. He got home rather late for dinner, ate his dinner, and conversed cheerfully, but could not for a long time bring himself to go back to work in his room. At last, however, he went to his study and did what was necessary, but the consciousness that he had put something aside — an important, intimate matter which he would revert to when his work was done — never left him. When he had finished his work he remembered that this intimate matter was the thought of his vermiform appendix. But he did not give himself up to it, and went to the drawing-room for tea. There were callers there, including the examining magistrate who was a desirable match for his daughter, and they were conversing, playing the piano, and singing. Ivan Ilych, as Praskovya Fedorovna remarked, spent that evening more cheerfully than usual, but he never for a moment forgot that he had postponed the important matter of the appendix. At eleven o'clock he said goodnight and went to his bedroom. Since his illness he had slept alone in a small room next to his study. He undressed and took up a novel by Zola, but instead of reading it he fell into thought, and in his imagination that desired improvement in the vermiform appendix occurred. There were the absorption and evacuation and the re-establishment of normal activity. "Yes, that's it!" he said to himself. "One need only assist nature, that's all." He remembered his medicine, rose, took it, and lay down on his back watching for the beneficent action of the medicine and for it to lessen the pain. "I need only take it regularly and avoid all injurious influences. I am already feeling better, much better." He began touching his side: it was not painful to the touch. "There, I really don't feel it. It's much better already." He put out the light and turned on his side. "The appendix is getting better, absorption is occurring." Suddenly he felt the old, familiar, dull, gnawing pain, stubborn and serious. There was the same familiar loathsome taste in his mouth. His heart sank and he felt dazed. "My God! My God!" he muttered.

"Again, again! And it will never cease." And suddenly the matter presented itself in a quite different aspect. "Vermiform appendix! Kidney!" he said to himself. "It's not a question of appendix or kidney, but of life and . . . death. Yes, life was there and now it is going, going and I cannot stop it. Yes. Why deceive myself? Isn't it obvious to everyone but me that I'm dying, and that it's only a question of weeks, days . . . it may happen this moment. There was light and now there is darkness. I was here and now I'm going there! Where?" A chill came over him, his breathing ceased, and he felt only the throbbing of his heart.

"When I am not, what will there be? There will be nothing. Then where shall I be when I am no more? Can this be dying? No, I don't want to!" He jumped up and tried to light the candle, felt for it with trembling hands, dropped candle and candlestick on the floor, and fell back on his pillow.

"What's the use? It makes no difference," he said to himself, staring with wide-open eyes into the darkness. "Death. Yes, death. And none of them

knows or wishes to know it, and they have no pity for me. Now they are playing." (He heard through the door the distant sound of a song and its accompaniment.) "It's all the same to them, but they will die too! Fools! I first, and they later, but it will be the same for them. And now they are merry . . . the beasts!"

Anger choked him and he was agonizingly, unbearably miserable. "It is impossible that all men have been doomed to suffer this awful horror!" He raised himself.

"Something must be wrong. I must calm myself — must think it all over from the beginning." And he again began thinking. "Yes, the beginning of my illness: I knocked my side, but I was still quite well that day and the next. It hurt a little, then rather more. I saw the doctors, then followed despondency and anguish, more doctors, and I drew nearer to the abyss. My strength grew less and I kept coming nearer and nearer, and now I have wasted away and there is no light in my eyes. I think of the appendix — but this is death! I think of mending the appendix, and all the while here is death! Can it really be death?" Again terror seized him and he gasped for breath. He leant down and began feeling for the matches, pressing with his elbow on the stand beside the bed. It was in his way and hurt him, he grew furious with it, pressed on it still harder, and upset it. Breathless and in despair he fell on his back, expecting death to come immediately.

Meanwhile the visitors were leaving. Praskovya Fedorovna was seeing them off. She heard something fall and came in.

"What has happened?"

"Nothing. I knocked it over accidentally."

She went out and returned with a candle. He lay there panting heavily, like a man who has run a thousand yards, and stared upwards at her with a fixed look.

"What is it, Ivan?"

"No . . . no . . . thing. I upset it." ("Why speak of it? She won't understand," he thought.)

And in truth she did not understand. She picked up the stand, lit his candle, and hurried away to see another visitor off. When she came back he still lay on his back, looking upwards.

"What is it? Do you feel worse?"

"Yes."

She shook her head and sat down.

"Do you know, Ivan, I think we must ask Leshchetitsky to come and see you here."

This meant calling in the famous specialist, regardless of expense. He smiled malignantly and said "No." She remained a little longer and then went up to him and kissed his forehead.

While she was kissing him he hated her from the bottom of his soul and with difficulty refrained from pushing her away.

"Good night. Please God you'll sleep."

"Yes."

Ivan Ilych saw that he was dying, and he was in continual despair.

In the depth of his heart he knew he was dying, but not only was he not accustomed to the thought, he simply did not and could not grasp it.

The syllogism he had learnt from Kiesewetter's Logic: "Caius is a man, men are mortal, therefore Caius is mortal," had always seemed to him correct as applied to Caius, but certainly not as applied to himself. That Caius — man in the abstract — was mortal, was perfectly correct, but he was not Caius, not an abstract man, but a creature quite, quite separate from all others. He had been little Vanya, with a mamma and a papa, with Mitya and Volodya, with the toys, a coachman and a nurse, afterwards with Katenka and with all the joys, griefs, and delights of childhood, boyhood, and youth. What did Caius know of the smell of that striped leather ball Vanya had been so fond of? Had Caius kissed his mother's hand like that, and did the silk of her dress rustle so for Caius? Had he rioted like that at school when the pastry was bad? Had Caius been in love like that? Could Caius preside at a session as he did? "Caius really was mortal, and it was right for him to die; but for me, little Vanya, Ivan Ilych, with all my thoughts and emotions, it's altogether a different matter. It cannot be that I ought to die. That would be too terrible."

Such was his feeling.

"If I had to die like Caius I would have known it was so. An inner voice would have told me so, but there was nothing of the sort in me and I and all my friends felt that our case was quite different from that of Caius. and now here it is!" he said to himself. "It can't be. It's impossible! But here it is. How is this? How is one to understand it?"

He could not understand it, and tried to drive this false, incorrect, morbid thought away and to replace it by other proper and healthy thoughts. But that thought, and not the thought only but the reality itself, seemed to come and confront him.

And to replace that thought he called up a succession of others, hoping to find in them some support. He tried to get back into the former current of thoughts that had once screened the thought of death from him. But strange to say, all that had formerly shut off, hidden, and destroyed his consciousness of death, no longer had that effect. Ivan Ilych now spent most of his time in attempting to re-establish that old current. He would say to himself: "I will take up my duties again — after all I used to live by them." And banishing all doubts he would go to the law courts, enter into conversation with his colleagues, and sit carelessly as was his wont, scanning the crowd with a thoughtful look and leaning both his emaciated arms on the arms of his oak chair; bending over as usual to a colleague and drawing his papers nearer he would interchange whispers with him, and then suddenly raising his eyes and sitting erect would pronounce certain words and open the proceedings. But suddenly in the midst of those proceedings the pain in his side, regardless of the stage the proceedings had reached, would begin its own gnawing work. Ivan Ilych would turn his attention to it and try to drive the thought of it away, but without success. It would come and stand before him and look at him, and he would be petrified and the light would die out of his eyes, and he would again begin asking himself whether it alone was true. And his colleagues and subordinates would see with surprise and distress that he, the brilliant and subtle judge, was becoming confused and making mistakes. He would shake himself, try to pull himself together, manage somehow to bring the sitting to a close, and return home with the sorrowful consciousness that his judicial labours could not as formerly hide from him what he wanted them to hide, and could not deliver him from it. And what was worst of all was that it drew his attention to itself not in order to make him take some action but only that he should look at it, look it straight in the face: look at it and without doing anything, suffer inexpressibly.

And to save himself from this condition Ivan Ilych looked for consolations — new screens — and new screens were found and for a while seemed to save him, but then they immediately fell to pieces or rather became transparent, as if it penetrated them and nothing could veil it.

In these latter days he would go into the drawing-room he had arranged — that drawing-room where he had fallen and for the sake of which (how bitterly ridiculous it seemed) he had sacrificed his life — for he knew that his illness originated with that knock. He would enter and see that something had scratched the polished table. He would look for the cause of this and find that it was the bronze ornamentation of an album, that had got bent. He would take up the expensive album which he had lovingly arranged, and feel vexed with his daughter and her friends for their untidiness — for the album was torn here and there and some of the photographs turned upside down. He would put it carefully in order and bend the ornamentation back into position. Then it would occur to him to place all those things in another corner of the room, near the plants. He would call the footman, but his daughter or wife would come to help him. They would not agree, and his wife would contradict him, and he would dispute and grow angry. But that was all right, for then he did not think about It. It was invisible.

But then, when he was moving something himself, his wife would say: "Let the servants do it. You will hurt yourself again." And suddenly It would flash through the screen and he would see it. It was just a flash, and he hoped it would disappear, but he would involuntarily pay attention to his side. "It sits there as before, gnawing just the same!" And he could no longer forget It, but could distinctly see it looking at him from behind the flowers. "What is it all for?"

"It really is so! I lost my life over that curtain as I might have done when storming a fort. Is that

possible? How terrible and how stupid. It can't be true! It can't, but it is."

He would go to his study, lie down, and again be alone with it: face to face with it. And nothing could be done with it except to look at it and shudder.

How it happened it is impossible to say because it came about step by step, unnoticed, but in the third month of Ivan Ilych's illness, his wife, his daughter, his son, his acquaintances, the doctors, the servants, and above all he himself, were aware that the whole interest he had for other people was whether he would soon vacate his place, and at last release the living from the discomfort caused by his presence and be himself released from his sufferings.

He slept less and less. He was given opium and hypodermic injections of morphine, but this did not relieve him. The dull depression he experienced in a somnolent condition at first gave him a little relief, but only as something new, afterwards it became as distressing as the pain itself or even more so.

Special foods were prepared for him by the doctors' orders, but all those foods became increasingly distasteful and disgusting to him.

For his excretions also special arrangements had to be made, and this was a torment to him every time — a torment from the uncleanliness, the unseemliness, and the smell, and from knowing that another person had to take part in it.

But just through his most unpleasant matter, Ivan Ilych obtained comfort. Gerasim, the butler's young assistant, always came in to carry the things out. Gerasim was a clean, fresh peasant lad, grown stout on town food and always cheerful and bright. At first the sight of him, in his clean Russian peasant costume, engaged on that disgusting task embarrassed Ivan Ilych.

Once when he got up from the commode too weak to draw up his trousers, he dropped into a soft armchair and looked with horror at his bare, enfeebled thighs with the muscles so sharply marked on them.

Gerasim with a firm light tread, his heavy boots emitting a pleasant smell of tar and fresh winter air, came in wearing a clean Hessian apron, the sleeves of his print shirt tucked up over his strong bare young arms; and refraining from looking at his sick master out of consideration for his feelings, and restraining the joy of life that beamed from his face, he went up to the commode.

"Gerasim!" said Ivan Ilych in a weak voice.

"Gerasim started, evidently afraid he might have committed some blunder, and with a rapid movement turned his fresh, kind, simple young face which just showed the first downy signs of a beard.

"Yes, sir?"

"That must be very unpleasant for you. You must forgive me. I am helpless."

"Oh, why, sir," and Gerasim's eyes beamed and he showed his glistening white teeth, "what's a little trouble? It's a case of illness with you, sir."

And his deft strong hands did their accustomed task, and he went out of the room stepping lightly. Five minutes later he as lightly returned.

Ivan Ilych was still sitting in the same position in the armchair.

"Gerasim," he said when the latter had replaced the freshly-washed utensil. "Please come here and help me." Gerasim went up to him. "Lift me up. It is hard for me to get up, and I have sent Dmitri away."

Gerasim went up to him, grasped his master with his strong arms deftly but gently, in the same way that he stepped — lifted him, supported him with one hand, and with the other drew up his trousers and would have set him down again, but Ivan Ilych asked to be led to the sofa. Gerasim, without an effort and without apparent pressure, led him, almost lifting him, to the sofa and placed him on it.

"Thank you. How easily and well you do it all!"

Gerasim smiled again and turned to leave the room. But Ivan Ilych felt his presence such a comfort that he did not want to let him go.

"One thing more, please move up that chair. No, the other one — under my feet. It is easier for me when my feet are raised."

Gerasim brought the chair, set it down gently in place, and raised Ivan Ilych's legs on it. It seemed to Ivan Ilych that he felt better while Gerasim was holding up his legs.

"It's better when my legs are higher," he said. "Place that cushion under them."

Gerasim did so. He again lifted the legs and placed them, and again Ivan Ilych felt better while Gerasim held his legs. When he set them down Ivan Ilych fancied he felt worse.

"Gerasim," he said. "Are you busy now?"

"Not at all, sir," said Gerasim, who had learnt from the townsfolk how to speak to gentlefolk.

"What have you still to do?"

"What have I to do? I've done everything except chopping the logs for tomorrow."

"Then hold my legs up a bit higher, can you?"

"Of course I can. Why not?" and Gerasim raised his master's legs higher and Ivan Ilych thought that in that position he did not feel any pain at all.

"And how about the logs?"

"Don't trouble about that, sir. There's plenty of time."

Ivan Ilych told Gerasim to sit down and hold his legs, and began to talk to him. And strange to say it seemed to him that he felt better while Gerasim held his legs up.

After that Ivan Ilych would sometimes call Gerasim and get him to hold his legs on his shoulders, and he liked talking to him. Gerasim did it all easily, willingly, simply, and with a good nature that touched Ivan Ilych. Health, strength, and vitality in other people were offensive to him, but Gerasim's strength and vitality did not mortify but soothed him.

What tormented Ivan Ilych most was the deception, the lie, which for some reason they all accepted, that he was not dying but was simply ill, and that he only need keep quiet and undergo a treatment and then something very good would result. He however knew that do what they would nothing would come of it, only still more agonizing suffering and death. This deception tortured him — their not wishing to admit what they all knew and what he knew, but wanting to lie to him concerning his terrible condition, and wishing and forcing him to participate in that lie. Those lies — lies enacted over him on the eve of his death and destined to degrade this awful, solemn act to the level of their visitings, their curtains, their sturgeon for dinner — were a terrible agony for Ivan Ilych. And strangely enough, many times when they were going through their antics over him he had been within a hair-breadth of calling out to them: "Stop lying! You know and I know that I am dying. Then at least stop lying about it!" But he had never had the spirit to do it. The awful, terrible act of his dying was, he could see, reduced by those about him to the level of a casual, unpleasant, and almost indecorous incident (as if someone entered a drawing room defusing an unpleasant odour) and this was done by that very decorum which he had served all his life long. He saw that no one felt for him, because no one even wished to grasp his position. Only Gerasim recognized it and pitied him. And so Ivan Ilych felt at ease only with him. He felt comforted when Gerasim supported his legs (sometimes all night long) and refused to go to bed, saying: "Don't you worry, Ivan Ilych. I'll get sleep enough later on," or when he suddenly became familiar and exclaimed: "If you weren't sick it would be another matter, but as it is, why should I grudge a little trouble?" Gerasim alone did not lie; everything showed that he alone understood the facts of the case and did not consider it necessary to disguise them, but simply felt sorry for his emaciated and enfeebled master. Once when Ivan Ilych was sending him away he even said straight out: "We shall all of us die, so why should I grudge a little trouble?" — expressing the fact that he did not think his work burdensome, because he was doing it for a dying man and hoped someone would do the same for him when his time came.

Apart from this lying, or because of it, what most tormented Ivan Ilych was that no one pitied him as he wished to be pitied. At certain moments after prolonged suffering he wished most of all (though he would have been ashamed to confess it) for someone to pity him as a sick child is pitied. He longed to be petted and comforted. He knew he was an important functionary, that he had a beard turning grey, and that therefore what he longed for was impossible, but still he longed for it. And in Gerasim's attitude towards him there was something akin to what he wished for, and so that attitude comforted him. Ivan Ilych wanted to weep, wanted to be petted and cried over, and then his colleague Shebek would come, and instead of weeping and being petted, Ivan Ilych would assume a serious, severe, and profound air, and by force of habit would express his opinion on a decision of the Court of Cessation and would stubbornly insist on that view. This falsity around him and within him did more than anything else to poison his last days.

It was morning. He knew it was morning because Gerasim had gone, and Peter the footman had come and put out the candles, drawn back one of the curtains, and begun quietly to tidy up. Whether it was morning or evening, Friday or Sunday, made no difference, it was all just the same: the gnawing, unmitigated, agonizing pain, never ceasing for an instant, the consciousness of life inexorably waning but not yet extinguished, the approach of that ever dreaded and hateful Death which was the only reality, and always the same falsity. What were days, weeks, hours, in such a case?

"Will you have some tea, sir?"

"He wants things to be regular, and wishes the gentlefolk to drink tea in the morning," thought ivan Ilych, and only said "No."

"Wouldn't you like to move onto the sofa, sir?"

"He wants to tidy up the room, and I'm in the way. I am uncleanliness and disorder," he thought, and said only:

"No, leave me alone."

The man went on bustling about. Ivan Ilych stretched out his hand. Peter came up, ready to help.

"What is it, sir?"

"My watch."

Peter took the watch which was close at hand and gave it to his master.

"Half-past eight. Are they up?"

"No sir, except Vladimir Ivanovich" (the son) "who has gone to school. Praskovya Fedorovna ordered me to wake her if you asked for her. Shall I do so?"

"No, there's no need to." "Perhaps I'd better have some tea," he thought, and added aloud: "Yes, bring me some tea."

Peter went to the door, but Ivan Ilych dreaded being left alone. "How can I keep him here? Oh yes, my medicine." "Peter, give me my medicine." "Why not? Perhaps it may still do some good." He took a spoonful and swallowed it. "No, it won't help. It's all tomfoolery, all deception," he decided as soon as he became aware of the familiar, sickly, hopeless taste. "No, I can't believe in it any longer. But the pain, why this pain? If it would only cease just for a moment!" And he moaned. Peter turned towards him. "It's all right. Go and fetch me some tea."

Peter went out. Left alone Ivan Ilych groaned not so much with pain, terrible though that was, as from mental anguish. Always and for ever the same, always these endless days and nights. If only it would come quicker! If only what would come quicker? Death, darkness? No, no! anything rather than death!

When Peter returned with the tea on a tray, Ivan Ilych stared at him for a time in perplexity, not realizing who and what he was. Peter was disconcerted by that look and his embarrassment brought Ivan Ilych to himself.

"Oh, tea! All right, put it down. Only help me to wash and put on a clean shirt."

And Ivan Ilych began to wash. With pauses for rest, he washed his hands and then his face, cleaned his teeth, brushed his hair, looked in the glass. He was terrified by what he saw, especially by the limp way in which his hair clung to his pallid forehead.

While his shirt was being changed he knew that he would be still more frightened at the sight of his body, so he avoided looking at it. Finally he was ready. He drew on a dressing-gown, wrapped himself in a plaid blanket, and sat down in the armchair to take his tea. For a moment he felt refreshed, but as soon as he began to drink the tea he was again aware of the same taste, and the pain also returned. He finished it with an effort, and then lay down stretching out his legs, and dismissed Peter.

Always the same. Now a spark of hope flashes up, then a sea of despair rages, and always pain; always pain, always despair, and always the same. When alone he had a dreadful and distressing desire to call someone, but he knew beforehand that with others present it would be still worse. "Another dose of morphine — to lose consciousness. I will tell him, the doctor, that he must think of something else. It's impossible, impossible, to go on like this."

An hour and another pass like that. But now there is a ring at the door bell. Perhaps it's the doctor? It is. He comes in fresh, hearty, plump, and cheerful, with that look on his face that seems to say: "There now, you're in a panic about something, but we'll arrange it all for you directly!" The doctor knows this expression is out of place here, but he has put it on once for all and can't take it off — like a man who has put on a frock-coat in the morning to pay a round of calls.

The doctor rubs his hands vigorously and reassuringly.

"Brr! How cold it is! There's such a sharp frost; just let me warm myself!" he says, as if it were only a matter of waiting till he was warm, and then he would put everything right.

"Well now, how are you?"

Ivan Ilych feels that the doctor would like to say: "Well, how are our affairs?" but that even he feels that this would not do, and says instead: "What sort of a night have you had?"

Ivan Ilych looks at him as much as to say: "Are you really never ashamed of lying?" But the doctor does not wish to understand this question, and Ivan Ilych says: "Just as terrible as ever. The pain never leaves me and never subsides. If only something. . . ."

"Yes, you sick people are always like that. . . . There, now I think I am warm enough. Even Praskovya Fedorovna, who is so particular, could find no fault with my temperature. Well, now I can say good-morning," and the doctor presses his patient's hand.

Then dropping his former playfulness, he begins with a most serious face to examine the patient, feeling his pulse and taking his temperature, and then begins the sounding and auscultation.

Ivan Ilych knows quite well and definitely that all this is nonsense and pure deception, but when the doctor, getting down on his knee, leans over him, putting his ear first higher then lower, and performs various gymnastic movements over him with a significant expression on his face, Ivan Ilych submits to it all as he used to submit to the speeches of the lawyers, though he knew very well that they were all lying and why they were lying.

The doctor, kneeling on the sofa, is still sounding him when Praskovya Fedorovna's silk dress rustles at the door and she is heard scolding Peter for not having let her know of the doctor's arrival.

She comes in, kisses her husband, and at once proceeds to prove that she has been up a long time already, and only owing to a misunderstanding failed to be there when the doctor arrived.

Ivan Ilych looks at her, scans her all over, sets against her the whiteness and plumpness and cleanness of her hands and neck, the gloss of her hair, and the sparkle of her vivacious eyes. He hates her with his whole soul. And the thrill of hatred he feels for her makes him suffer from her touch.

Her attitude towards him and his diseases is still the same. Just as the doctor had adopted a certain relation to his patient which he could not abandon, so had she formed one towards him — that he was not doing something he ought to do and was himself to blame, and that she reproached him lovingly for this — and she could not now change that attitude.

"You see he doesn't listen to me and doesn't take his medicine at the proper time. And above all he lies in a position that is no doubt bad for him — with his legs up."

She described how he made Gerasim hold his legs up.

The doctor smiled with a contemptuous affability that said: "What's to be done? These sick people do have foolish fancies of that kind, but we must forgive them."

When the examination was over the doctor looked at his watch, and then Praskovya Fedorovna announced to Ivan Ilych that it was of course as he pleased, but she had sent today for a celebrated specialist who would examine him and have a consultation with Michael Danilovich (their regular doctor).

"Please don't raise any objections. I am doing this for my own sake," she said ironically, letting it be felt that she was doing it all for his sake and only said this to leave him no right to refuse. He remained silent, knitting his brows. He felt that he was surrounded and involved in a mesh of falsity that it was hard to unravel anything.

Everything she did for him was entirely for her own sake, and she told him she was doing for herself what she actually was doing for herself, as if that was so incredible that he must understand the opposite.

At half-past eleven the celebrated specialist arrived. Again the sounding began and the significant conversations in his presence and in another room, about the kidneys and the appendix, and the questions and answers, with such an air of importance that again, instead of the real question of life and death which now alone confronted him, the question arose of the kidney and appendix which were not behaving as they ought to and would now be attached by Michael Danilovich and the specialist and forced to amend their ways.

The celebrated specialist took leave of him with a serious though not hopeless look, and in reply to the timid question Ivan Ilych, with eyes glistening with fear and hope, put to him as to whether there was a chance of recovery, said that he could not vouch for it but there was a possibility. The look of hope with which Ivan Ilych watched the doctor out was so pathetic that Praskovya Fedorovna, seeing it, even wept as she left the room to hand the doctor his fee.

The gleam of hope kindled by the doctor's encouragement did not last long. The same room, the same pictures, curtains, wall-paper, medicine bottles, were all there, and the same aching suffering body, and Ivan Ilych began to moan. They gave him a subcutaneous injection and he sank into oblivion.

It was twilight when he came to. They brought him his dinner and he swallowed some beef tea with difficulty, and then everything was the same again and night was coming on.

After dinner, at seven o'clock, Praskovya Fedorovna came into the room in evening dress, her full bosom pushed up by her corset, and with traces of powder on her face. She had reminded him in the morning that they were going to the theatre. Sarah Bernhardt was visiting the town and they had a box, which he had insisted on their taking. Now he had forgotten about it and her toilet offended him, but he concealed his vexation when he remembered that he had himself insisted on their securing a box and going because it would be an instructive and aesthetic pleasure for the children.

Praskovya Fedorovna came in, self-satisfied but yet with a rather guilty air. She sat down and asked how he was, but, as he saw, only for the sake of asking and not in order to learn about it, knowing that there was nothing to learn — and then went on to what she really wanted to say: that she would not on any account have gone but that the box had been taken and Helen and their daughter were going, as well as Petrishchev (the examining magistrate, their daughter's fiancé) and that it was out of the question to let them go alone; but that she would have much preferred to sit with him for a while; and he must be sure to follow the doctor's orders while she was away.

"Oh, and Fedor Petrovich" (the fiancé) "would like to come in. May he? And Lisa?"

"All right."

Their daughter came in in full evening dress, her fresh young flesh exposed (making a show of that very flesh which in his own case caused so much suffering), strong, healthy, evidently in love, and impatient with illness, suffering, and death, because they interfered with her happiness.

Fedor Petrovich came in too, in evening dress, his hair curled à la Capoul, a tight stiff collar round his long sinewy neck, an enormous white shirt-front and narrow black trousers tightly stretched over his strong thighs. He had one white glove tightly drawn on, and was holding his opera hat in his hand.

Following him the schoolboy crept in unnoticed, in a new uniform, poor little fellow, and wearing gloves. Terribly dark shadows showed under his eyes, the meaning of which Ivan Ilych knew well.

His son had always seemed pathetic to him, and now it was dreadful to see the boy's frightened look of pity. It seemed to Ivan Ilych that Vasya was the only one besides Gerasim who understood and pitied him.

They all sat down and again asked how he was. A silence followed. Lisa asked her mother about the opera glasses, and there was an altercation between mother and daughter as to who had taken them and where they had been put. This occasioned some unpleasantness.

Fedor Petrovich inquired of Ivan Ilych whether he had ever seen Sarah Bernhardt. Ivan Ilych did not at first catch the question, but then replied: "No, have you seen her before?"

"Yes, in Adrienne Lecouvreur."

Praskovya Fedorovna mentioned some roles in which Sarah Bernhardt was particularly good. Her daughter disagreed. Conversation sprang up as to the elegance and realism of her acting — the sort of conversation that is always repeated and is always the same.

In the midst of the conversation Fedor Petrovich glanced at Ivan Ilych and became silent. The others also looked at him and grew silent. Ivan Ilych was staring with glittering eyes straight before him, evidently indignant with them. This had to be rectified, but it was impossible to do so. The silence had to be broken, but for a time no one dared to break it and they all became afraid that the conventional deception would suddenly become obvious and the truth become plain to all. Lisa was the first to pluck up courage and break that silence, but by trying to hide what everybody was feeling, she betrayed it.

"Well, if we are going it's time to start," she said, looking at her watch, a present from her father, and with a faint and significant smile at Fedor Petrovich relating to something known only to them. She got up with a rustle of her dress.

They all rose, said good-night, and went away.

When they had gone it seemed to Ivan Ilych that he felt better; the falsity had gone with them. But the pain remained — that same pain and that same fear that made everything monotonously alike, nothing harder and nothing easier. Everything was worse.

Again minute followed minute and hour followed hour. Everything remained the same and there was no cessation. And the inevitable end of it all became more and more terrible.

"Yes, send Gerasim here," he replied to a question Peter asked.

His wife returned late at night. She came in on tiptoe, but he heard her, opened his eyes, and made haste to close them again. She wished to send Gerasim away and to sit with him herself, but he opened his eyes and said: "No, go away."

"Are you in great pain?"

"Always the same."

"Take some opium."

He agreed and took some. She went away.

Till about three in the morning he was in a state of stupefied misery. It seemed to him that he and his pain were being thrust into a narrow, deep black sack, but though they were pushed further and further in they could not be pushed to the bottom. And this, terrible enough in itself, was accompanied by suffering. He was frightened yet wanted to fall through the sack, he struggled but yet co-operated. And suddenly he broke through, fell, and regained consciousness. Gerasim was sitting at the foot of the bed dozing quietly and patiently, while he himself lay with his emaciated stockinged legs resting on Gerasim's shoulders; the same shaded candle was there and the same unceasing pain.

"Go away, Gerasim," he whispered.

"It's all right, sir. I'll stay a while."

"No. Go away."

He removed his legs from Gerasim's shoulders, turned sideways onto his arm, and felt sorry for himself. He only waited till Gerasim had gone into the next room and then restrained himself no longer but wept like a child. He wept on account of his helplessness, his terrible loneliness, the cruelty of man, the cruelty of God, and the absence of God.

"Why hast Thou done all this? Why hast Thou brought me here? Why, why dost Thou torment me so terribly?"

He did not expect an answer and yet wept because there was no answer and could be none. The pain again grew more acute, but he did not stir and did not call. He said to himself: "Go on! Strike me! But what is it for? What have I done to Thee? What is it for?"

Then he grew quiet and not only ceased weeping but even held his breath and became all attention. It was as though he were listening not to an audible voice but to the voice of his soul, to the current of thoughts arising within him.

"What is it you want?" was the first clear conception capable of expression in words that he heard.

"What do you want? What do you want?" he repeated to himself.

"What do I want? To live and not to suffer," he answered.

And again he listened with such concentrated attention that even his pain did not distract him.

"To live? How?" asked his inner voice.

"Why, to live as I used to — well and pleasantly."

"As you lived before, well and pleasantly?" the voice repeated.

And in imagination he began to recall the best moments of his pleasant life. But strange to say none of those best moments of his pleasant life now seemed at all what they had then seemed — none of them except the first recollections of childhood. There, in childhood, there had been something really pleasant with which it would be possible to live if it could return. But the child who had experienced that happiness existed no longer, it was like a reminiscence of somebody else.

As soon as the period began which had produced the present Ivan Ilych, all that had then seemed joys now melted before his sight and turned into something trivial and often nasty.

And the further he departed from childhood and the nearer he came to the present the more worthless and doubtful were the joys. This began with the School of Law. A little that was really good was still found there — there was light-heartedness, friendship, and hope. But in the upper classes there had already been fewer of such good moments. Then during the first years of his official career, when he was in the service of the governor, some pleasant moments again occurred: they were the memories of love for a woman. Then all became confused and there was still less of what was good; later on again there was still less that was good, and the further he went the less there was. His marriage, a mere accident, then the disenchantment that followed it, his wife's bad breath and the sensuality and hypocrisy:

then that deadly official life and those preoccupations about money, a year of it, and two, and ten, and twenty, and always the same thing. And the longer it lasted the more deadly it became. "It is as if I had been going downhill while I imagined I was going up. And that is really what it was. I was going up in public opinion, but to the same extent life was ebbing away from me. And now it is all done and there is only death.

"Then what does it mean? Why? It can't be that life is so senseless and horrible. But if it really has been so horrible and senseless, why must I die and die in agony? There is something wrong!

"Maybe I did not live as I ought to have done," it suddenly occurred to him. "But how could that be, when I did everything properly?" he replied, and immediately dismissed from his mind this, the sole solution of all the riddles of life and death, as something quite impossible.

"Then what do you want now? To live? Live how? Live as you lived in the law courts when the usher proclaimed 'The judge is coming!' The judge is coming, the judge!" he repeated to himself. "Here he is, the judge. But I am not guilty!" he exclaimed angrily. "What is it for?" And he ceased crying, but turning his face to the wall continued to ponder on the same question: Why, and for what purpose, is there all this horror? But however much he pondered he found no answer. And whenever the thought occurred to him, as it often did, that it all resulted from his not having lived as he ought to have done, he at once recalled the correctness of his whole life and dismissed so strange an idea.

Another fortnight passed. Ivan Ilych now no longer left his sofa. He would not lie in bed but lay on the sofa, facing the wall nearly all the time. He suffered ever the same unceasing agonies and in his loneliness pondered always on the same insoluble question: "What is this? Can it be that it is Death?" And the inner voice answered: "Yes, it is Death."

"Why these sufferings?" And the voice answered, "For no reason — they just are so." Beyond and besides this there was nothing.

From the very beginning of his illness, ever since he had first been to see the doctor, Ivan Ilych's life had been divided between two contrary and alternating moods: now it was despair and the expectation of this uncomprehended and terrible death, and now hope and an intently interested observation of the functioning of his organs. Now before his eyes there was only a kidney or an intestine that temporarily evaded its duty, and now only that incomprehensible and dreadful death from which it was impossible to escape.

These two states of mind had alternated from the very beginning of his illness, but the further it progressed the more doubtful and fantastic became the conception of the kidney, and the more real the sense of impending death.

He had but to call to mind what he had been three months before and what he was now, to call to mind with what regularity he had been going downhill, for every possibility of hope to be shattered.

Latterly during the loneliness in which he found himself as he lay facing the back of the sofa, a loneliness in the midst of a populous town and surrounded by numerous acquaintances and relations but that yet could not have been more complete anywhere — either at the bottom of the sea or under the earth — during that terrible loneliness Ivan Ilych had lived only in memories of the past. Pictures of his past rose before him one after another. They always began with what was nearest in time and then went back to what was most remote — to his childhood — and rested there. If he thought of the stewed prunes that had been offered him that day, his mind went back to the raw shrivelled French plums of his childhood, their peculiar flavour and the flow of saliva when he sucked their stones, and along with the memory of that taste came a whole series of memories of those days: his nurse, his brother, and their toys. "No, I mustn't think of that. . . . It is too painful," Ivan Ilych said to himself, and brought himself back to the present — to the button on the back of the sofa and the creases in its morocco. "Morocco is expensive, but it does not wear well: there had been a quarrel about it. It was a different kind of quarrel and a different kind of morocco that time when we tore father's portfolio and were punished, and mamma brought us some tarts...." And again his thoughts dwelt on his childhood, and again it was painful and he tried to banish them and fix his mind on something else.

Then again together with that chain of memories another series passed through his mind — of how his illness had progressed and grown worse. There also the further back he looked the more life there had been. There had been more of what was good in life and more of life itself. The two merged together. "Just as the pain went on getting worse and worse, so my life grew worse and worse," he thought. "There is one bright spot there at the back, at the beginning of life, and afterwards all becomes blacker and blacker and proceeds more and more rapidly — in inverse ratio to the square of the distance from death," thought Ivan Ilych. And the example of a stone falling downwards with increasing velocity entered his mind. Life, a series of increasing sufferings, flies further and further towards its end — the most terrible suffering. "I am flying...." He shuddered, shifted himself, and tried to resist, but was already aware that resistance was impossible, and again with eyes weary of gazing but unable to cease seeing what was before them, he stared at the back of the sofa and waited — awaiting that dreadful fall and shock and destruction.

"Resistance is impossible!" he said to himself. "If I could only understand what it is all for! But that too is impossible. An explanation would be possible if it could be said that I have not lived as I ought to. But it is impossible to say that," and he remembered all the legality, correctitude, and propriety of his life. "That at any rate can certainly not be admitted," he thought, and his lips smiled ironically as if someone could see that smile and be taken in by it. "There is no explanation! Agony, death. . . . What for?"

Another two weeks went by in this way and during that fortnight an event occurred that Ivan Ilych and his wife had desired. Petrishchev formally proposed. It happened in the evening. The next day Praskovya Fedorovna came into her husband's room considering how best to inform him of it, but that very night there had been a fresh change for the worse in his condition. She found him still lying on the sofa but in a different position. He lay on his back, groaning and staring fixedly straight in front of him.

She began to remind him of his medicines, but he turned his eyes towards her with such a look that she did not finish what she was saying; so great an animosity, to her in particular, did that look express.

"For Christ's sake let me die in peace!" he said.

She would have gone away, but just then their daughter came in and went up to say good morning. He looked at her as he had done at his wife, and in reply to her inquiry about his health said dryly that he would soon free them all of himself. They were both silent and after sitting with him for a while went away.

"Is it our fault?" Lisa said to her mother. "It's as if we were to blame! I am sorry for papa, but why should we be tortured?"

The doctor came at his usual time. Ivan Ilych answered "Yes" and "No," never taking his angry eyes from him, and at last said: "You know you can do nothing for me, so leave me alone."

"We can ease your sufferings."

"You can't even do that. Let me be."

The doctor went into the drawing room and told Praskovya Fedorovna that the case was very serious and that the only resource left was opium to allay her husband's sufferings, which must be terrible.

It was true, as the doctor said, that Ivan Ilych's physical sufferings were terrible, but worse than the physical sufferings were his mental sufferings which were his chief torture.

His mental sufferings were due to the fact that that night, as he looked at Gerasim's sleepy, good-natured face with its prominent cheek-bones, the question suddenly occurred to him: "What if my whole life has been wrong?"

It occurred to him that what had appeared perfectly impossible before, namely that he had not spent his life as he should have done, might after all be true. It occurred to him that his scarcely perceptible attempts to struggle against what was considered good by the most highly placed people, those scarcely noticeable impulses which he had immediately suppressed, might have been the real thing, and all the rest false. And his professional duties and the whole arrangement of his life and of his family, and all his social and official interests, might all have been false. He tried to defend all those things to himself and suddenly felt the weakness of what he was defending. There was nothing to defend. "But if that is so," he said to himself, "and I am leaving this life with the consciousness that I have lost all that was given me and it is impossible to rectify it — what then?"

He lay on his back and began to pass his life in review in quite a new way. In the morning when he saw first his footman, then his wife, then his daughter, and then the doctor, their every word and movement confirmed to him the awful truth that had been revealed to him during the night. In them he saw himself — all that for which he had lived — and saw clearly that it was not real at all, but a terrible and huge deception which had hidden both life and death. This consciousness intensified his physical suffering tenfold. He groaned and tossed about, and pulled at his clothing which choked and stifled him. And he hated them on that account.

He was given a large dose of opium and became unconscious, but at noon his sufferings began again. He drove everybody away and tossed from side to side.

His wife came to him and said:

"Ivan, my dear, do this for me. It can't do any harm and often helps. Healthy people often do it."

He opened his eyes wide.

"What? Take communion? Why? It's unnecessary! However. . . ."

She began to cry.

"Yes, do, my dear. I'll send for our priest. He is such a nice man."

"All right. Very well," he muttered.

When the priest came and heard his confession, Ivan Ilych was softened and seemed to feel a relief from his doubts and consequently from his sufferings, and for a moment there came a ray of hope. He again began to think of the vermiform appendix and the possibility of correcting it. He received the sacrament with tears in his eyes.

When they laid him down again afterwards he felt a moment's ease, and the hope that he might live awoke in him again. He began to think of the operation that had been suggested to him. "To live! I want to live!" he said to himself.

His wife came in to congratulate him after his communion, and when uttering the usual conventional words she added: "You feel better, don't you?"

Without looking at her he said "Yes."

Her dress, her figure, the expression of her face, the tone of her voice, all revealed the same thing. "This is wrong, it is not as it should be. All you have lived for and still live for is falsehood and deception, hiding life and death from you." And as soon as he admitted that thought, his hatred and his agonizing physical suffering again sprang up, and with that suffering a consciousness of the unavoidable, approaching end. And to this was added a new sensation of grinding shooting pain and a feeling of suffocation.

The expression of his face when he uttered that "Yes" was dreadful. Having uttered it, he looked her straight in the eyes, turned on his face with a rapidity extraordinary in his weak state and shouted: "Go away! Go away and leave me alone!"

From that moment the screaming began that continued for three days, and was so terrible that one could not hear it through two closed doors without horror. At the moment he answered his wife he realized that he was lost, that there was no return, that the end had come, the very end, and his doubts were still unsolved and remained doubts. "Oh! Oh! Oh!" he cried in various intonations. He had begun by screaming "I won't!" and continued screaming on the letter "O."

For three whole days, during which time did not exist for him, he struggled in that black sack into which he was being thrust by an invisible, resistless force. He struggled as a man condemned to death struggles in the hands of the executioner, knowing that he cannot save himself. And every moment he felt that despite all his efforts he was drawing nearer and nearer to what terrified him. He felt that his agony was due to his being thrust into that black hole and still more to his not being able to get right into it. He was hindered from getting into it by his conviction that his life had been a good one. That very justification of his life held him fast and prevented his moving forward, and it caused him most torment of all.

Suddenly some force struck him in the chest and side, making it still harder to breathe, and he fell through the hole and there at the bottom was a light. What had happened to him was like the sensation one sometimes experiences in a railway carriage when one thinks one is going backwards while one is really going forwards and suddenly becomes aware of the real direction.

"Yes, it was not the right thing," he said to himself, "but that's no matter. It can be done. But what is the right thing? he asked himself, and suddenly grew quiet.

This occurred at the end of the third day, two hours before his death. Just then his schoolboy son had crept softly in and gone up to the bedside. The dying man was still screaming desperately and waving his arms. His hand fell on the boy's head, and the boy caught it, pressed it to his lips, and began to cry.

At that very moment Ivan Ilych fell through and caught sight of the light, and it was revealed to him that though his life had not been what it should have been, this could still be rectified. He asked himself, "What is the right thing?" and grew still, listening. Then he felt that someone was kissing his hand. He opened his eyes, looked at his son, and felt sorry for him. His wife came up to him and he glanced at her. She was gazing at him open-mouthed, with undried tears on her nose and cheek and a despairing look on her face. He felt sorry for her too.

"Yes, I am making them wretched," he thought. "They are sorry, but it will be better for them when I die." He wished to say this but had not the strength to utter it. "Besides, why speak? I must act," he thought. With a look at his wife he indicated his son and said: "Take him away . . . sorry for him . . . sorry for you too. . . ." He tried to add, "Forgive me," but said "Forego" and waved his hand, knowing that He whose understanding mattered would understand.

And suddenly it grew clear to him that what had been oppressing him and would not leave him was all dropping away at once from two sides, from ten sides, and from all sides. He was sorry for them, he must act so as not to hurt them: release them and free himself from these sufferings. "How good and how simple!" he thought. "And the pain?" he asked himself. "What has become of it? Where are you, pain?"

He turned his attention to it.

"Yes, here it is. Well, what of it? Let the pain be."

"And death . . . where is it?"

He sought his former accustomed fear of death and did not find it. "Where is it? What death?" There was no fear because there was no death.

In place of death there was light.

"So that's what it is!" he suddenly exclaimed aloud. "What joy!"

To him all this happened in a single instant, and the meaning of that instant did not change. For those present his agony continued for another two hours. Something rattled in his throat, his emaciated body twitched, then the gasping and rattle became less and less frequent.

"It is finished!" said someone near him.

He heard these words and repeated them in his soul.

"Death is finished," he said to himself. "It is no more!"

He drew in a breath, stopped in the midst of a sigh, stretched out, and died (www.classicallibrary. org/tolstoy/ivan/index.htm).

Assignments

- Warm-up: What vision of life and death does Tolstoy present in the following short story?
- Students should complete Concept Builder 25-C.
- Students should write rough draft of assigned essay.
- The teacher may correct rough draft.

Theme

A central theme of *War and Peace* is the forgiveness that Prince Andrew expresses to Natasha. Yet this hardly compensates for the heartache that Natasha brings on her family and friends. Discuss biblical parallels (e.g., the prodigal son).

Natasha

Prodigal

Makes bad choices.

Marina Ivanova Tsvetaeva

Marina Ivanova Tsvetaeva (1892–1941) was a Russian poet who wrote at the end of the Tolstoy era. In a significant way, she introduced modern poetry (i.e., free verse, realistic metaphors) into Russian society.

What Shall I Do

What shall I do?

Singer and first-born

In a world where the deepest black is grey,

www.kirjasto.sci.fi/tsveta.htm.

And inspiration is kept in a thermos?

With all this immensity

In a measured world?

Assignments

- Warm-up: Tsvetaeva found herself in a world that did not appreciate poetry (e.g., Bolshevik Russia). How do you suppose this affected Tsvetaeva and her desire to write?

- Students should complete Concept Builder 25-D.

- Students will re-write corrected copies of essay due tomorrow.

CONCEPT BUILDER 25-D
Christian Theism

Leo Tolstoy advances a Christian theistic vision. A Christian theist argues that the Bible is the only reliable and inerrant revelation of who God is and how mankind should relate to this God. In that sense, Christian theism insists that salvation for mankind must come through a faithful and sincere commitment to Jesus Christ as Lord and Savior. In Goethe's *Faust* the main character is saved via a more existential experience. Compare and contrast the worldviews of Tolstoy and Goethe.

Student Essay

Written by Leo Tolstoy around 1869, *War and Peace* is one of the finest literary works of all time. Beautifully woven into 19th-century Russia and the French invasion, Tolstoy composes the stories of the lives of five aristocratic families and their contact with each other. One of these families is the Rostov family, and it is here that the author creates one of the most beautiful, feeling, and true characters: Countess Natasha. As the novel progresses and Natasha grows, she experiences much spiritual development, which ultimately leads her to peace.

In the beginning of the novel, Natasha is introduced as a 13-year-old girl, "She was not pretty, her mouth was too big, but she was full of life, and with her childish uncovered shoulders and her bodice slipping down from all that running, her curly black hair tossed back, her slender bare arms and little legs in lace trimmed drawers and open slippers on her feet, she was at that charming age when the girl is no longer a child, and the child is not yet a young girl." Natasha is blunt, and completely void of any self-consciousness. She demonstrates this when without any hesitation she kisses her childhood sweetheart Boris and makes him promise to marry her in four years.

As the book continues, Natasha begins to experience herself as unintentionally captivating others in a way she never imagined. Prince Andrew Bolkonsky, the widower of Princess Lise, falls in love with her at the sound of her voice, recognizing in her, "a strange and special new world, brimful of unknown joys." It was not long before they became engaged, but because of Andrew's father's disagreement they decided to wait a year until getting married. The love Natasha felt for him was real and she felt herself unworthy of him, "What does he see in me? What does he want when he stares like that?

What if I haven't got what he's looking for? Above all, she loved to watch him laugh. He seldom laughed, but when he did so with complete abandon, she always felt closer to him."

But the year of waiting was hard, in fact it was too hard for the girl who loved to be admired, and she soon found herself as the accidental captivator of Anatole Kuragin. Anatole was a flirt and "had driven all of the Moscow ladies crazy." Also, not known to most, he was married. From the moment that he saw her, Anatole wanted to have her and began to seduce her. At first Natasha felt as if something was wrong, but she enjoyed the attention, and soon found herself giving it back to him. "She looked him straight in the eyes. One glance at him, standing so close, with all that self-assurance and the warmth of his sweet smile, and she was lost. She stared into his eyes, and her smile was the mirror image of his. And again she sensed with horror there was no barrier between the two of them." The next week, she wrote to Andrew, telling him that she was breaking off the engagement, and made plans to elope with Anatole. Learning of her secret plans, Natasha's cousin Sonya, kept Natasha from eloping, creating instead a depressed Natasha who had no hope left of life or love.

For weeks, Natasha didn't know what to do with herself; she was deathly ill, and refused to sing. But it was Pierre, an old family friend, who brought hope back into her life again. "No one could have been gentler, more caring, and yet more serious minded than Pierre in his dealings with her. " Another thing which gave her new hope was the fasting and preparation she did for a week in order to receive Holy Communion. "She crossed herself, bowed low, and when she didn't understand she simply yeilded in disgust to a sense of her own vileness and prayed for forgiveness, total forgiveness, and mercy, "she was overwhelmed by a new sense of humility before the sublime mystery as she gazed up at the black face of the blessed virgin lit up by candles." When Sunday finally came and Natasha received communion she experienced a peace of mind that she had not had for many months.

Ultimately Natasha found peace. After finding Prince Andrew, and begging his forgiveness on his death bed, the repentant girl found love once more and married Pierre. Society's reaction to her marriage was how much she had changed. To them it was a negative change, because she rarely went into society, and didn't care about adorning herself, but cared rather for her family. But for Natasha, Tolstoy closes with his most magnificent character having found the peace she had always sought. (Anna Grace)

Assignments

- Warm-up: What is the thesis of this essay?
- Students should complete Concept Builder 25-E.
- Essay is due. Students should take the chapter 25 test.

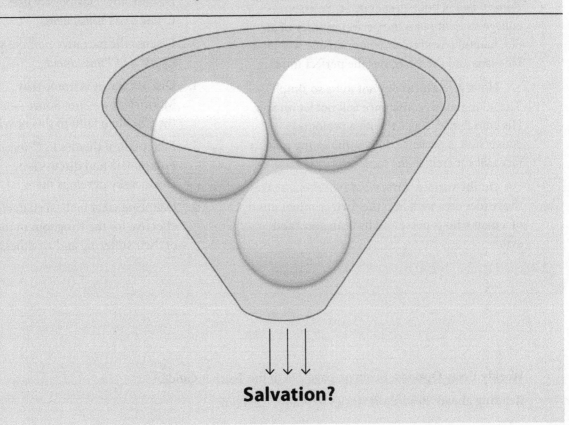

CONCEPT BUILDER 25-E
Prince Andrew's Spiritual Journey

Some scholars feel that both Pierre and Prince Andrew represent Leo Tolstoy himself. If that is so, then Prince Andrew's spiritual journey represents Tolstoy's own journey. As Prince Andrew struggles with his war wound, he says, "There is nothing certain, nothing at all except the unimportance of everything I understand, and the greatness of something incomprehensible but all-important" (Book Three, chapter 13). What is Prince Andrew's spiritual journey in *War and Peace*? There are several acceptable answers. Does he ever commit his life to Jesus Christ?

Salvation?

Chapter 26

(1800–1890)

Realism (Part 2)

First Thoughts Fyodor Dostoevsky was a brilliant 19th-century Russian novelist. Rejecting the impulses of romanticism and naturalism, Dostoevsky tenaciously held to a theistic worldview. As the protagonist Raskolnikov discovers, no one is above the law of God. Man may escape man's law, but he cannot escape God's law. Dostoevsky is one of the most personable writers who ever lived. He invites the reader into the most personal and empathic parts of our existence.

In Fyodor Dostoevsky's *Crime and Punishment*, a poor, desperate St. Petersburg college student plans the perfect murder of an old, hateful pawnbroker whom no one will miss. He plans and then executes the perfect murder.

However, it turns out not to be so simple. The young man's conscience will not let him go. His conscience, coupled with a profound conversion experience, forces this young man to face evil squarely in the face.

On the surface, *Crime and Punishment* takes the reader on a path into the dark criminal mind of a man who is possessed by both good and evil.

Chapter Learning Objectives In chapter 26 we will analyze one of the first truly psychological novels. We will watch Raskolnikov's struggle through naturalism into Christian theism and we will be grateful for the breakthrough!

As a result of this chapter study you will be able to . . .

1. Discuss how Dostoevsky develops him and how he shows Raskolnikov growth as a character.

2. Discuss how Dostoevsky uses dreams in *Crime and Punishment*.

3. Discuss the narrative point of view in *Crime and Punishment*.

4. Discuss why it is ironic that Marmeladov — not Sonya — introduces the Christian faith to this novel.

5. Find biblical themes in *Crime and Punishment* and discuss how Dostoevsky develops them.

6. Delineate what biblical characters were effective for the Kingdom in the midst of their suffering and weakness.

Weekly Essay Options: Begin on page 273 of the Teacher Guide.

Reading ahead: Read short stories by Anton Chekhov.

 History connections: *World History* chapter 26, "Nationalism."

Crime and Punishment
Fyodor Dostoevsky

Background Fyodor Mikhilovich Dostoevsky was born in 1821 in Moscow. His first novel, *Poor Folk*, brought him instant success, but his writing career was cut short due to an arrest for alleged subversion against Tsar Nicholas I in 1849. His prison experiences, coupled with his conversion to Christianity, formed the basis for his great novels. Finally, his marriage to another strong believer, Anna Snitkina, provided him with a platform to write some of the best literature in the world. Following a period of backsliding brought about by his compulsive gambling, Dostoevsky manifested an unparalleled writing spree. In a few short years he wrote the masterpieces *Crime and Punishment, The Idiot, The Possessed,* and *The Brothers Karamazov.*

Portrait of Fedor Dostoyevsky
by Vasily Perov, 1872 (PD-Art).

Assignments

- Warm-up: Compare and contrast the events as they unfold in *Crime and Punishment* with Dostoevsky's own life.

- Students should complete Concept Builder 26-A.

- Students should review the required reading(s) *before* the assigned chapter begins.

- Teachers may want to discuss assigned reading(s) with students.

- Teachers shall assign the required essay. The rest of the essays can be outlined, answered with shorter answers, discussed, or skipped.

- Students will review all readings for chapter 26.

Read this excerpt from Fyodor Dostoevsky's *Crime and Punishment*, and respond to the following:

On an exceptionally hot evening early in July a young man came out of the garret in which he lodged in S. Place and walked slowly, as though in hesitation, towards K. bridge.

He had successfully avoided meeting his landlady on the staircase. His garret was under the roof of a high, five-storied house and was more like a cupboard than a room. The landlady who provided him with garret, dinners, and attendance, lived on the floor below, and every time he went out he was obliged to pass her kitchen, the door of which invariably stood open. And each time he passed, the young man had a sick, frightened feeling, which made him scowl and feel ashamed. He was hopelessly in debt to his landlady, and was afraid of meeting her.

This was not because he was cowardly and abject, quite the contrary; but for some time past he had been in an overstrained irritable condition, verging on hypochondria. He had become so completely absorbed in himself, and isolated from his fellows that he dreaded meeting, not only his landlady, but anyone at all. He was crushed by poverty, but the anxieties of his position had of late ceased to weigh upon him. He had given up attending to matters of practical importance; he had lost all desire to do so. Nothing that any landlady could do had a real terror for him. But to be stopped on the stairs, to be forced to listen to her trivial, irrelevant gossip, to pestering demands for payment, threats and complaints, and to rack his brains for excuses, to prevaricate, to lie — no, rather than that, he would creep down the stairs like a cat and slip out unseen.

This evening, however, on coming out into the street, he became acutely aware of his fears.

"I want to attempt a thing like that and am frightened by these trifles," he thought, with an odd smile. "Hm . . . yes, all is in a man's hands and he lets it all slip from cowardice, that's an axiom. It would be interesting to know what it is men are most afraid of. Taking a new step, uttering a new word is what they fear most. . . . But I am talking too much. It's because I chatter that I do nothing. Or perhaps it is that I chatter because I do nothing. I've learned to chatter this last month, lying for days together in my den thinking . . . of Jack the Giant-killer. Why am I going there now? Am I capable of that? Is that serious? It is not serious at all. It's simply a fantasy to amuse myself; a plaything! Yes, maybe it is a plaything."

The heat in the street was terrible: and the airlessness, the bustle and the plaster, scaffolding, bricks, and dust all about him, and that special Petersburg stench, so familiar to all who are unable to get out of town in summer — all worked painfully upon the young man's already overwrought nerves. The insufferable stench from the pot-houses, which are particularly numerous in that part of the town, and the drunken men whom he met continually, although it was a working day, completed the revolting misery of the picture. An expression of the profoundest disgust gleamed for a moment in the young man's refined face. He was, by the way, exceptionally hand-some, above the average in height, slim, well-built, with beautiful dark eyes and dark brown hair. Soon he sank into deep thought, or more accurately speaking into a complete blankness of mind; he walked along not observing what was about him and not caring to observe it.

The author avoids telling the reader the name of his protagonist until well into the story. Why?

The author employs limited omniscient narration where he tells the story from one perspective. What advantages and disadvantages does this offer the author?

What is the setting, and does that have an important impact on the plot?

Friedrich Nietzsche

At the same time Dostoevsky was writing *Crime and Punishment*, the prophetic atheist Friedrich Nietzsche was writing his very disturbing alternative vision of free will. Nietzsche coined the phrase "God is dead." He said that the only reality was a world of life and death, conflict and change, creation and destruction. For centuries, religious ideas gave meaning to life in the Western world, but in the late 19th century they were collapsing. This presented humanity with a grave crisis of nihilism and despair.

Nietzsche took the hopeless vision of naturalism and Social Darwinism to its natural conclusion. Nietzsche saw that a world where only power prevailed, a world without Christianity, would inevitably lead to totalitarianism and destruction. He predicted in the late 19th century that inevitably Western culture would create an Adolf Hitler or Joseph Stalin in the early part of the 20th century. The basic character of life in this world was the "will to power." Nietzsche admired those who were strong enough to face this reality: for they alone could live joyfully. This "modern superman" lived without God and without any hope of salvation. Nietzsche was basically a naturalist. Man is fundamentally only an animal who has developed in an unusual way. The "will to power" brought about new forms of competition and superiority, and could lead to a "superman" humanity.

When we hear the ancient bells growling on a Sunday morning we ask ourselves: Is it really possible! This, for a Jew, crucified two thousand years ago, who said he was God's son? The proof of such a claim is lacking. Certainly the Christian religion is an antiquity projected into our times from remote prehistory; and the fact that the claim is believed — whereas one is otherwise so strict in examining pretensions — is perhaps the most ancient piece of this heritage. A god who begets children with a mortal woman; a sage who bids men work no more, have no more courts, but look for the signs of the impending end of the world; a justice that accepts the innocent as a vicarious sacrifice; someone who orders his disciples to drink his blood; prayers for miraculous interventions; sins perpetrated against a god, atoned for by a god; fear of a beyond to which death is the portal; the form of the cross as a symbol in a time that no longer knows the function and ignominy of the cross — how ghoulishly all this touches us, as if from the tomb of a primeval past! Can one believe that such things are still believed? (*Human, all too Human*) (www.theperspectivesofnietzsche.com/nietzsche/nchrist.html).

Assignments

- Warm-up: Respond to Nietzsche's view of Christianity as presented in *Human, all too Human*.
- Students should complete Concept Builder 26-B.
- Students should review reading(s) from next chapter.
- Students should outline essays due at the end of the week.
- Per teacher instructions, students may answer orally, in a group setting, some of the essays that are not assigned as the formal essay.

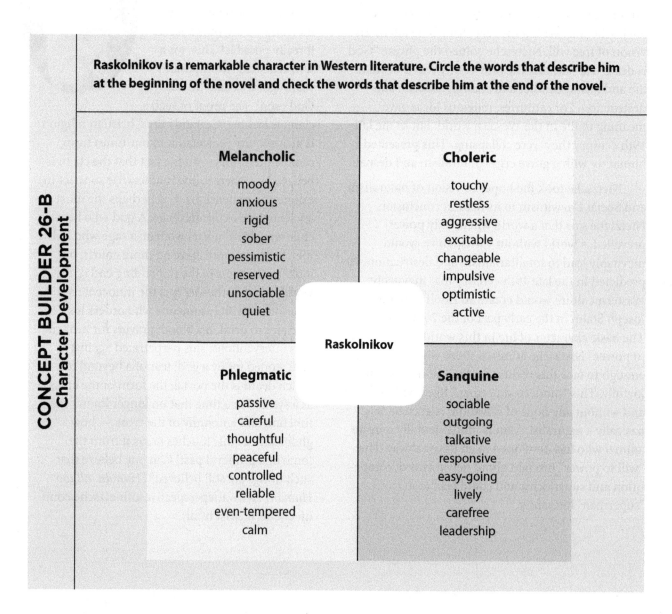

CONCEPT BUILDER 26-B
Character Development

Raskolnikov is a remarkable character in Western literature. Circle the words that describe him at the beginning of the novel and check the words that describe him at the end of the novel.

Melancholic

moody
anxious
rigid
sober
pessimistic
reserved
unsociable
quiet

Choleric

touchy
restless
aggressive
excitable
changeable
impulsive
optimistic
active

Raskolnikov

Phlegmatic

passive
careful
thoughtful
peaceful
controlled
reliable
even-tempered
calm

Sanquine

sociable
outgoing
talkative
responsive
easy-going
lively
carefree
leadership

Norton and Gretton, Writing Incredibly Short Plays, Poems, Stories.

Hegel's Superman

Raskolnikov is a choleric, unbalanced protagonist. He feels unhappy and anxious and he is moved by what he perceives to be an invisible power, or what German philosopher Georg Wilhelm Hegel calls "the will," to kill the pawnbroker. Leading up to the murder, he feels simultaneously the desire to kill and the fear of retribution. This sets up what Hegel calls a "dialectic." During this time, Raskolnikov undergoes similar trials and negative life experiences as a "superman" from Hegel's *History of Philosophy.* Furthermore, the force that Raskolnikov believes guided him to commit the crime resembles that sense of spirit that Hegel argued moved men to act. All this "tension" will remain unresolved until Raskolnikov meets Sonya's God of the Old and the New Testament!

J. Loewenberg, in his book *The Life of Georg Wilhelm Friedrich Hegel,* (www.gutenberg.org/files/12351/12351.txt) writes:

The task of Hegel's whole philosophy consists in showing, by means of one uniform principle, that the world manifests everywhere a genuine evolution. Unlike the participants in the biological "struggle for existence," the struggling beings of Hegel's universe never end in slaying, but in reconciliation. Their very struggle gives birth to a new being which includes them, and this being is "higher" in the scale of existence, because it represents the preservation of two mutually opposed beings. Only where conflicts are adjusted, oppositions overcome, negations removed, is there advance, in Hegel's sense; and only where there is a passage from the positive through its challenging negative to a higher form inclusive of both is there a case of real development.

The ordinary process of learning by experience illustrates somewhat Hegel's meaning. An individual finds himself, for instance, in the presence of a wholly new situation that elicits an immediate, definite reaction. In his ignorance, he chooses the wrong mode of behavior. As a consequence, trouble ensues; feelings are hurt, pride is wounded, motives are misconstrued. Embittered and disappointed with himself, he experiences great mental sorrow. But he soon learns to see the situation in its true light; he condemns his deed and offers to make amends. And after the wounds begin to heal again, the inner struggles experienced commence to assume a positive worth. They have led him to a deeper insight into his own motives, to a better self-comprehension. And he finally comes forth from the whole affair enriched and enlightened. Now in this formal example, to which any content may be supplied, three phases can be distinguished. First, we have the person as he meant to be in the presence of the new situation, unaware of trouble. Then, his wrong reaction engendered a hostile element. He was at war with himself; he was not what he meant to be. And finally, he returned to himself richer and wiser, including within himself the negative experience as a valuable asset in the advance of his development.

This process of falling away from oneself, of facing oneself as an enemy whom one reconciles to and includes in one's larger self, is certainly a familiar process. It is a process just like this that develops one's personality. However the self may be defined metaphysically, it is for every self-conscious individual a never-ceasing battle with conflicting motives and antagonistic desires — a never-ending cycle of endeavor, failure, and success through the very agency of failure.

- Warm-up: Dostoevsky attacks the Hegelian idea of a superman. Give a report on the philosopher Hegel and tell why Dostoevsky finds Hegel's views so objectionable.

- Students should complete Concept Builder 26-C.

- Students should write rough draft of assigned essay.

- The teacher or a peer evaluator may correct rough draft.

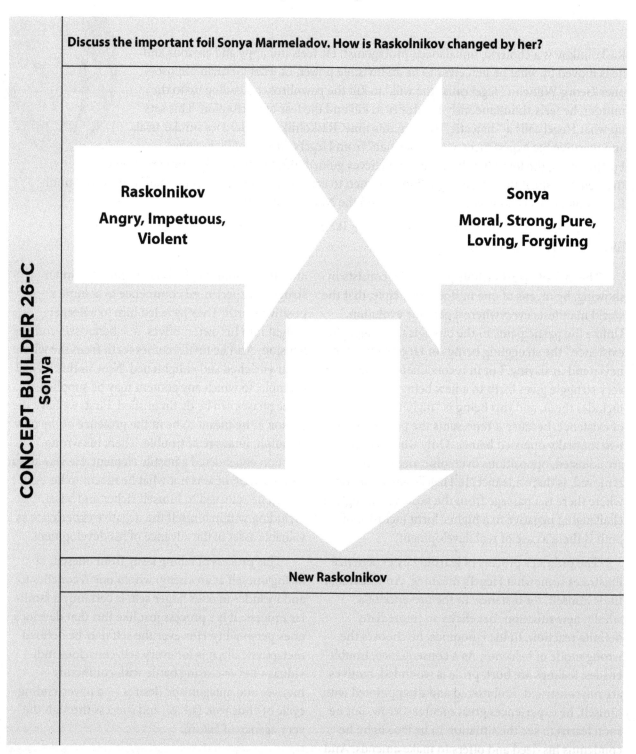

CONCEPT BUILDER 26-C
Sonya

Discuss the important foil Sonya Marmeladov. How is Raskolnikov changed by her?

Raskolnikov

Angry, Impetuous, Violent

Sonya

Moral, Strong, Pure, Loving, Forgiving

New Raskolnikov

Student Essay:
Dostoevsky and Hegel

Called "the stepfather of Karl Marx," G.W.F. Hegel (1770–1831) created a system of philosophical thought that came to dominate "at least the first half of the nineteenth century." Serving as the foundation of Hegel's philosophy was the idea that, through a process of evolution, human thought could through itself reach the elusive ideal of absolute truth. The Russian writer Fyodor Dostoevsky, however, found this idea objectionable. In his seminal novel *Crime and Punishment*, Dostoevsky forcefully showed that human thought is incapable of reaching absolute truth without the moral guidance provided in the Scriptures.

In his writings, G.W.F. Hegel made an important distinction from the thought of his contemporary, Immanuel Kant. Unlike Kant, Hegel seperated the ideas of human understanding and Reason — that is, Reason with a capital "R." According to Hegel, Reason was a lofty idea similar to a Platonic form which was the essence of pure thought, knowledge, or absolute truth. Understanding, on the other hand, could be defined as mere human thought. Via a tension of ideas, now known as "Hegel's Dialectic," it was possible for human understanding to evolve upward toward Reason. In Hegel's dialectic, a plausible starting point, or thesis, naturally draws to itself an opposite truth statement, or antithesis. Of course, the thesis and antithesis are in competition and cannot coexist. Therefore, the discerning philosopher's duty is to combine the best parts of both thesis and antithesis into a new starting point, the synthesis. This synthesis inevitably attracts a new antithesis, and the whole process begins anew. Through this procedure, Hegel believed that human thought could come ever closer to Reason by the continual refining of ideas using his dialectic. In other words, by understanding — human thought — alone, absolute truth could be obtained.

In *Crime and Punishment*, Dostoevsky demonstrated the disastrous consequences of relying on human reason alone to reach absolute truth. Raskolinkov, the protagonist, used Hegel's dialectic to develop a philosophy where a worthy, noble, man had the freedom to rise above the law to accomplish his means. Naturally, Raskolnikov deemed himself to be both worthy and noble. To put his philosophy to the test, Raskolnikov decided to murder an old pawnbroker near his flat. Sonya, one of Raskolnikov's foils, later lamented the foolishness of such a decision — and, by extension, Hegel's dialectic:

> "But how will you go on living? What will you live for?" cried Sonya, "how is it possible now? Why, how can you talk to your mother? (Oh, what will become of them now?) But what am I saying? You have abandoned your mother and your sister already. He has abandoned them already! Oh, God!" she cried, "why, he knows it all himself. How, how can he live by himself! What will become of you now?"

Without a moral compass, Raskolnikov created a philosophy that led him to disaster: the penal servitude was bad enough, but the metaphysical suffering and guilt was worse. Hegel's dialectic led Raskolnikov into error. He had not, as he hoped, transcended ordinary men and proved himself to be noble and worthy.

Even though Hegel's atheistic worldview assumed that human understanding could reach truth without a morality, Dostoevesky showed this prediction to be inaccurate. In a world that operates on theistic principles, Hegel's atheistic philosophy and the practical desicions which flowed from it could not operate unimpeded. With Crime and Punishment, Dostoevsky demonstrated the foolishness of imposing Hegel's atheistic values and philosophy on a moral world. (Daniel)

Assignments

- Warm-up: Contrast the relationship of Svidrigailov/Dunya and Raskolnikov/Sonya.

- Students should complete Concept Builder 26-D.

- Students will re-write corrected copies of essay due tomorrow.

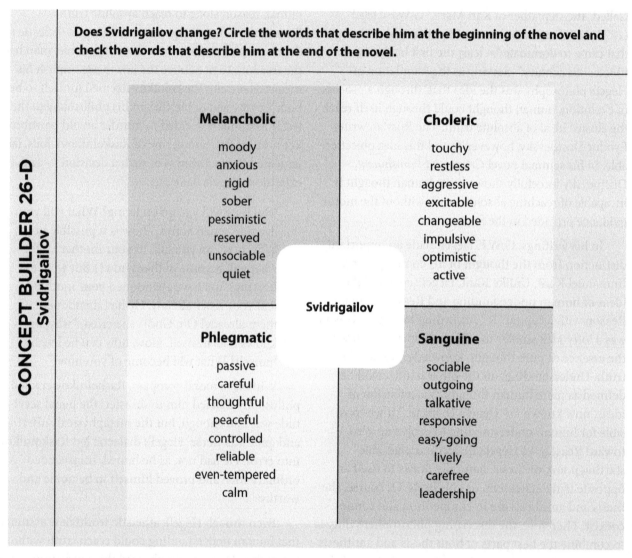

CONCEPT BUILDER 26-D
Svidrigailov

Does Svidrigailov change? Circle the words that describe him at the beginning of the novel and check the words that describe him at the end of the novel.

Melancholic

moody
anxious
rigid
sober
pessimistic
reserved
unsociable
quiet

Choleric

touchy
restless
aggressive
excitable
changeable
impulsive
optimistic
active

Svidrigailov

Phlegmatic

passive
careful
thoughtful
peaceful
controlled
reliable
even-tempered
calm

Sanguine

sociable
outgoing
talkative
responsive
easy-going
lively
carefree
leadership

Norton and Gretton, *Writing Incredibly Short Plays, Poems, Stories.*

Student Essay:

Sonya

Written around 1866, *Crime and Punishment* is one of the most famous works in Russian Literature. It tells the story of a poor ex-student Raskolnikov in St. Petersburg who murders a pawnbroker for her money. Justifying this act in his head beforehand, he is shocked when his conscience will not let him go, and he is forced to face the evil he committed. In all of the many characters that Dostoevsky brings into contact with Raskolnikov, Sonya and the role that she plays is the most influential on Raskolnikov.

Dostoevsky introduces Sonya in his novel through her father and gambler Marmelodov. Marmelodov tells Raskolnikov twice that Sonya is a prostitute and that "she lives by her yellow card." At the time, this meant that she was a registered prostitute and a "yellow card" would keep her from having any other less lowly job or way of earning money. On the surface this is what Sonya appears to be: a timid, shy, easily embarrassed prostitute.

But deeper down, she is a compassionate, extremely devout Christian, making the sacrifice of prostituting herself for the sake of her family to support them, because her father is unable to control his drinking habit. It is not what she wishes to do, but it is a selflessness that she endures for the sake of her family.

This strong character of Sonya is the one that plays a crucial role in the turning around of Raskolnikov's life. When Raskolnikov first meets Sonya, he bows to her and kisses her feet saying, "I did not bow down to you, I bowed down to all the suffering of humanity." At first Raskolnikov seems to think that he is somehow better than her, and urges her to flee with him and her younger siblings. But as

time progresses, he learns that Sonya is not a prostitute of her own will, and he begins to trust her. Sonya, on the other hand, when she first meets Raskolnikov is somewhat frightened of the half-delirious man stooping to kiss her feet, but soon in her compassion and understanding she begins to sense his suffering and care deeply for him.

Through this mutual trust, Raskolnikov is driven to confess his crime to none other than Sonya. In utter dismay and unable to avoid the truth any longer, Raskolnikov admits his guilt, "I wanted to murder, for my own satisfaction. . . . At that moment I did not care a damn whether I would spend the rest of my life like a spider catching them all in my web and sucking the living juices out of them." It is here that Sonya plays the vital part in the novel. Non-judgmental, but fearful for his soul, she entreats him earnestly, "Go at once, this very minute, stand at the cross-roads, bow down, first kiss the earth which you have defiled, and then bow down to all the world and say to all men aloud, 'I am a murderer!' Then God will send you life again. Will you go, will you go?"

After Raskolnikov confesses his crime, the strong, undaunted character of Sonya continued to shine through as she followed him to his punishment of exile in Siberia for seven years. Because of her and the encouragement that she offered to Raskolnikov, the story in Siberia became a new story, "the story of the gradual renewal of a man, the story of his gradual regeneration, of his passing from one world into another, of his initiation into a new unknown life." That was the strength of the devout prostitute. (Daniel)

- Warm-up: Discuss the important foil Sonya Marmeladov. Why is Raskolnikov attracted to her?
- Students should complete Concept Builder 26-E.
- Essay is due. Students should take the chapter 26 test.

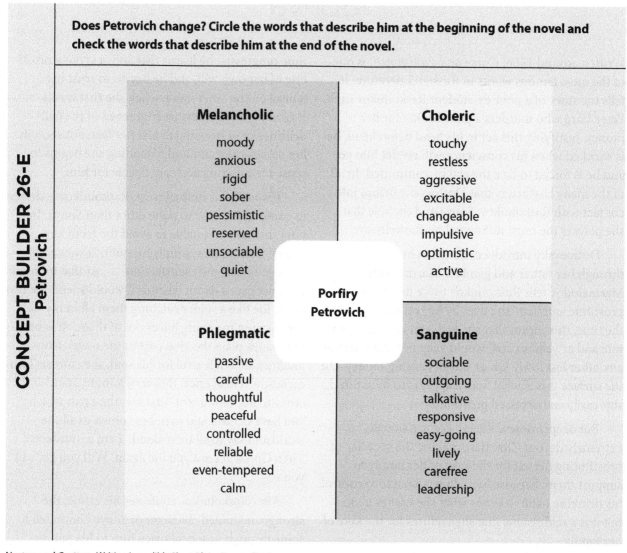

CONCEPT BUILDER 26-E
Petrovich

Does Petrovich change? Circle the words that describe him at the beginning of the novel and check the words that describe him at the end of the novel.

Melancholic

moody
anxious
rigid
sober
pessimistic
reserved
unsociable
quiet

Choleric

touchy
restless
aggressive
excitable
changeable
impulsive
optimistic
active

Porfiry Petrovich

Phlegmatic

passive
careful
thoughtful
peaceful
controlled
reliable
even-tempered
calm

Sanguine

sociable
outgoing
talkative
responsive
easy-going
lively
carefree
leadership

Norton and Gretton, *Writing Incredibly Short Plays, Poems, Stories.*

(1800–1890):
Realism (Part 3)

First Thoughts Anton Pavlovich Chekhov (1860–1904) was a Russian physician and a writer of short stories and plays. Only the American Edgar Allan Poe could rival Chekhov's ability to write short stories. We will be reading some of his best. At the same time, Chekhov was a great playwright. Most of his great plays are still performed, such as "The Sea Gull" (1896), "The Three Sisters" (1901), and "The Cherry Orchard" (1904). Chekhov died July 2, 1904, in Germany, of pulmonary tuberculosis. The great Russian writer Vladimir Nabokov wrote, "What really attracted the Russian reader was that in Chekhov's heroes he recognized . . . the Russian idealist . . . a man who combined the deepest human decency of which man is capable with an almost ridiculous inability to put his ideals and principles into action; a man devoted to moral beauty, the welfare of his people, the welfare of the universe, but unable in his private life to do anything useful; frittering away his provincial existence in a haze of utopian dreams; knowing exactly what is good, what is worthwhile living for, but at the same time sinking lower and lower in the mud of a humdrum existence, unhappy in love, hopelessly inefficient in everything — a good man who cannot make good. This is the character that passes — in the guise of a doctor, a student, a village teacher, many other professional people — all through Chekhov's stories" (Vladimir Nabokov, "Vladimir Nabokov on Chekhov," *Atlantic Magazine,* August 1981).

Chapter Learning Objectives

In chapter 27 we will study two short stories by arguably the best Russian short story writer, Anton Chekhov.

As a result of this chapter study you will be able to . . .

1. Read the following short stories very carefully and complete a short story checkup (appendices) after each story.

2. Read and complete a checkup sheet (appendices) on one of Chekhov's plays.

Weekly Essay Options: Begin on page 273 of the Teacher Guide.

Reading ahead: "A Doll's House" by Henrik Ibsen.

383

"Easter Eve"
Anton Chekhov

I was standing on the bank of the River Goltva, waiting for the ferry-boat from the other side. At ordinary times the Goltva is a humble stream of moderate size, silent and pensive, gently glimmering from behind thick reeds; but now a regular lake lay stretched out before me. The waters of spring, running riot, had overflowed both banks and flooded both sides of the river for a long distance, submerging vegetable gardens, hayfields and marshes, so that it was no unusual thing to meet poplars and bushes sticking out above the surface of the water and looking in the darkness like grim solitary crags.

The weather seemed to me magnificent. It was dark, yet I could see the trees, the water and the people. . . . The world was lighted by the stars, which were scattered thickly all over the sky. I don't remember ever seeing so many stars. Literally one could not have put a finger in between them. There were some as big as a goose's egg, others tiny as hempseed. . . . They had come out for the festival procession, every one of them, little and big, washed, renewed and joyful, and everyone of them was softly twinkling its beams. The sky was reflected in the water; the stars were bathing in its dark depths and trembling with the quivering eddies. The air was warm and still. . . . Here and there, far away on the further bank in the impenetrable darkness, several bright red lights were gleaming. . . .

A couple of paces from me I saw the dark silhouette of a peasant in a high hat, with a thick knotted stick in his hand.

"How long the ferry-boat is in coming!" I said.

"It is time it was here," the silhouette answered.

"You are waiting for the ferry-boat, too?"

"No I am not," yawned the peasant. "I am waiting for the illumination. I should have gone, but to tell you the truth, I haven't the five kopecks for the ferry,"

"I'll give you the five kopecks."

"No; I humbly thank you. . . . With that five kopecks put up a candle for me over there in the monastery. . . . That will be more interesting, and I will stand here. What can it mean, no ferry-boat, as though it had sunk in the water!"

The peasant went up to the water's edge, took the rope in his hands, and shouted; "Ieronim! Ieron-im!"

As though in answer to his shout, the slow peal of a great bell floated across from the further bank. The note was deep and low, as from the thickest string of a double bass; it seemed as though the darkness itself had hoarsely uttered it. At once there was the sound of a cannon shot. It rolled away in the darkness and ended somewhere in the far distance behind me. The peasant took off his hat and crossed himself.

"Christ is risen," he said.

Before the vibrations of the first peal of the bell had time to die away in the air a second sounded, after it at once a third, and the darkness was filled with an unbroken quivering clamour. Near the red lights fresh lights flashed, and all began moving together and twinkling restlessly.

"Ieron-im!" we heard a hollow prolonged shout.

"They are shouting from the other bank," said the peasant, "so there is no ferry there either. Our Ieronim has gone to sleep."

The lights and the velvety chimes of the bell drew one towards them. . . . I was already beginning to lose patience and grow anxious, but behold at last, staring into the dark distance, I saw the outline of something very much like a gibbet. It was the long-expected ferry. It moved towards us with such deliberation that if it had not been that its lines grew gradually more definite, one might have supposed that it was standing still or moving to the other bank.

"Make haste! Ieronim!" shouted my peasant. "The gentleman's tired of waiting!"

The ferry crawled to the bank, gave a lurch and stopped with a creak. A tall man in a monk's cassock and a conical cap stood on it, holding the rope.

"Why have you been so long?" I asked jumping upon the ferry.

"Forgive me, for Christ's sake," Ieronim answered gently. "Is there no one else?"

"No one. . . ."

Ieronim took hold of the rope in both hands, bent himself to the figure of a mark of interrogation, and gasped. The ferry-boat creaked and gave a lurch. The outline of the peasant in the high hat began slowly retreating from me — so the ferry was moving off. Ieronim soon drew himself up and began working with one hand only. We were silent, gazing towards the bank to which we were floating. There the illumination for which the peasant was waiting had begun. At the water's edge barrels of tar were flaring like huge camp fires. Their reflections, crimson as the rising moon, crept to meet us in long broad streaks. The burning barrels lighted up their own smoke and the long shadows of men flitting about the fire; but further to one side and behind them from where the velvety chime floated there was still the same unbroken black gloom. All at once, cleaving the darkness, a rocket zigzagged in a golden ribbon up the sky; it described an arc and, as though broken to pieces against the sky, was scattered crackling into sparks. There was a roar from the bank like a far-away hurrah.

"How beautiful!" I said.

"Beautiful beyond words!" sighed Ieronim. "Such a night, sir! Another time one would pay no attention to the fireworks, but to-day one rejoices in every vanity. Where do you come from?"

I told him where I came from.

"To be sure . . . a joyful day to-day. . . ." Ieronim went on in a weak sighing tenor like the voice of a convalescent. "The sky is rejoicing and the earth and what is under the earth. All the creatures are keeping holiday. Only tell me kind sir, why, even in the time of great rejoicing, a man cannot forget his sorrows?"

I fancied that this unexpected question was to draw me into one of those endless religious conversations which bored and idle monks are so fond of. I was not disposed to talk much, and so I only asked: "What sorrows have you, father?"

"As a rule only the same as all men, kind sir, but to-day a special sorrow has happened in the monastery: at mass, during the reading of the Bible, the monk and deacon Nikolay died."

"Well, it's God's will!" I said, falling into the monastic tone. "We must all die. To my mind, you ought to rejoice indeed. . . . They say if anyone dies at Easter he goes straight to the kingdom of heaven."

"That's true."

We sank into silence. The figure of the peasant in the high hat melted into the lines of the bank. The tar barrels were flaring up more and more.

"The Holy Scripture points clearly to the vanity of sorrow and so does reflection," said Ieronim, breaking the silence, "but why does the heart grieve and refuse to listen to reason? Why does one want to weep bitterly?"

Ieronim shrugged his shoulders, turned to me and said quickly: "If I died, or anyone else, it would not be worth notice perhaps; but, you see, Nikolay is dead! No one else but Nikolay! Indeed, it's hard to believe that he is no more! I stand here on my ferry-boat and every minute I keep fancying that he will lift up his voice from the bank. He always used to come to the bank and call to me that I might not be afraid on the ferry. He used to get up from his bed at night on purpose for that. He was a kind soul. My God! how kindly and gracious! Many a mother is not so good to her child as Nikolay was to me! Lord, save his soul!"

Ieronim took hold of the rope, but turned to me again at once.

"And such a lofty intelligence, your honour," he said in a vibrating voice. "Such a sweet and harmonious tongue! Just as they will sing immediately at early matins: 'Oh lovely! oh sweet is Thy Voice!' Besides all other human qualities, he had, too, an extraordinary gift!"

"What gift?" I asked.

The monk scrutinized me, and as though he had convinced himself that he could trust me with a secret, he laughed good-humouredly.

"He had a gift for writing hymns of praise," he said. "It was a marvel, sir; you couldn't call it anything else! You would be amazed if I tell you about it. Our Father Archimandrite comes from Moscow, the Father Sub-Prior studied at the Kazan academy, we have wise monks and elders, but, would you believe it, no one could write them; while Nikolay, a simple monk, a deacon, had not studied anywhere, and had not even any outer appearance of it, but he wrote them! A marvel! A real marvel!" Ieronim clasped his hands and, completely forgetting the rope, went on eagerly:

"The Father Sub-Prior has great difficulty in composing sermons; when he wrote the history of the monastery he worried all the brotherhood and drove a dozen times to town, while Nikolay wrote canticles! Hymns of praise! That's a very different thing from a sermon or a history!"

"Is it difficult to write them?" I asked.

"There's great difficulty!" Ieronim wagged his head. "You can do nothing by wisdom and holiness if God has not given you the gift. The monks who Don't understand argue that you only need to know the life of the saint for whom you are writing the hymn, and to make it harmonize with the other hymns of praise. But that's a mistake, sir. Of course, anyone who writes canticles must know the life of the saint to perfection, to the least trivial detail. To be sure, one must make them harmonize with the other canticles and know where to begin and what to write about. To give you an instance, the first response begins everywhere with 'the chosen' or 'the elect.' . . . The first line must always begin with the 'angel.' In the canticle of praise to Jesus the Most Sweet, if you are interested in the subject, it begins like this: 'Of angels Creator and Lord of all powers!' In the canticle to the Holy Mother of God:

'Of angels the foremost sent down from on high,' to Nikolay, the Wonder-worker — 'An angel in semblance, though in substance a man,' and so on. Everywhere you begin with the angel. Of course, it would be impossible without making them harmonize, but the lives of the saints and conformity with the others is not what matters; what matters is the beauty and sweetness of it. Everything must be harmonious, brief and complete. There must be in every line softness, graciousness and tenderness; not one word should be harsh or rough or unsuitable. It must be written so that the worshipper may rejoice at heart and weep, while his mind is stirred and he is thrown into a tremor. In the canticle to the Holy Mother are the words: 'Rejoice, O Thou too high for human thought to reach! Rejoice, O Thou too deep for angels' eyes to fathom!' In another place in the same canticle: 'Rejoice, O tree that bearest the fair fruit of light that is the food of the faithful! Rejoice, O tree of gracious spreading shade, under which there is shelter for multitudes!' "

Ieronim hid his face in his hands, as though frightened at something or overcome with shame, and shook his head.

"Tree that bearest the fair fruit of light . . . tree of gracious spreading shade. . . ." he muttered. "To think that a man should find words like those! Such a power is a gift from God! For brevity he packs many thoughts into one phrase, and how smooth and complete it all is! Light-radiating torch to all that be . . .' comes in the canticle to Jesus the Most Sweet. 'Light-radiating!' There is no such word in conversation or in books, but you see he invented it, he found it in his mind! Apart from the smoothness and grandeur of language, sir, every line must be beautified in every way, there must be flowers and lightning and wind and sun and all the objects of the visible world. And every exclamation ought to be put so as to be smooth and easy for the ear. 'Rejoice, thou flower of heavenly growth!' comes in the hymn to Nikolay the Wonder-worker. It's not simply 'heavenly flower,' but 'flower of heavenly growth.' It's smoother so and sweet to the ear. That was just as Nikolay wrote it! Exactly like that! I can't tell you how he used to write!"

"Well, in that case it is a pity he is dead," I said, "but let us get on, father, or we shall be late."

Ieronim started and ran to the rope; they were beginning to peal all the bells. Probably the procession was already going on near the monastery, for all the dark space behind the tar barrels was now dotted with moving lights.

"Did Nikolay print his hymns?" I asked Ieronim.

"How could he print them?" he sighed. "And indeed, it would be strange to print them. What would be the object? No one in the monastery takes any interest in them. They Don't like them. They knew Nikolay wrote them, but they let it pass unnoticed. No one esteems new writings nowadays, sir!"

"Were they prejudiced against him?"

"Yes, indeed. If Nikolay had been an elder perhaps the brethren would have been interested, but he wasn't forty, you know. There were some who laughed and even thought his writing a sin."

"What did he write them for?"

"Chiefly for his own comfort. Of all the brotherhood, I was the only one who read his hymns. I used to go to him in secret, that no one else might know of it, and he was glad that I took an interest in them. He would embrace me, stroke my head, speak to me in caressing words as to a little child. He would shut his cell, make me sit down beside him, and begin to read. . . ."

Ieronim left the rope and came up to me.

"We were dear friends in a way," he whispered, looking at me with shining eyes. "Where he went I would go. If I were not there he would miss me. And he cared more for me than for anyone, and all because I used to weep over his hymns. It makes me sad to remember. Now I feel just like an orphan or a widow. You know, in our monastery they are all good people, kind and pious, but . . . there is no one with softness and refinement, they are just like peasants. They all speak loudly, and tramp heavily when they walk; they are noisy, they clear their throats, but Nikolay always talked softly, caressingly, and if he noticed that anyone was asleep or praying he would slip by like a fly or a gnat. His face was tender, compassionate. . . ."

Ieronim heaved a deep sigh and took hold of the rope again. We were by now approaching the bank.

We floated straight out of the darkness and stillness of the river into an enchanted realm, full of stifling smoke, crackling lights and uproar. By now one could distinctly see people moving near the tar barrels. The flickering of the lights gave a strange, almost fantastic, expression to their figures and red faces. From time to time one caught among the heads and faces a glimpse of a horse's head motionless as though cast in copper.

"They'll begin singing the Easter hymn directly . . ." said Ieronim, "and Nikolay is gone; there is no one to appreciate it. . . . There was nothing written dearer to him than that hymn. He used to take in every word! You'll be there, sir, so notice what is sung; it takes your breath away!"

"Won't you be in church, then?"

"I can't. . . . I have to work the ferry. . . ."

"But won't they relieve you?"

"I Don't know. . . . I ought to have been relieved at eight; but, as you see, they don't come! . . . And I must own I should have liked to be in the church. . . ."

"Are you a monk?"

"Yes . . . that is, I am a lay-brother."

The ferry ran into the bank and stopped. I thrust a five-kopeck piece into Ieronim's hand for taking me across and jumped on land. Immediately a cart with a boy and a sleeping woman in it drove creaking onto the ferry. Ieronim, with a faint glow from the lights on his figure, pressed on the rope, bent down to it, and started the ferry back. . . .

I took a few steps through mud, but a little farther walked on a soft freshly trodden path. This path led to the dark monastery gates, that looked like a cavern through a cloud of smoke, through a disorderly crowd of people, unharnessed horses, carts and chaises. All this crowd was rattling, snorting, laughing, and the crimson light and wavering shadows from the smoke flickered over it all. . . . A perfect chaos! And in this hubbub the people yet found room to load a little cannon and to sell cakes. There was no less commotion on the other side of the wall in the monastery precincts, but there was more regard for decorum and order. Here there was a smell of juniper and incense. They talked loudly, but there was no sound of laughter or snorting. Near the tombstones and crosses people pressed close to one another with Easter cakes and bundles in their arms. Apparently many had come from a long distance for their cakes to be blessed and now were exhausted. Young lay brothers, making a metallic sound with their boots, ran busily along the iron slabs that paved the way from the monastery gates to the church door. They were busy and shouting on the belfry, too.

"What a restless night!" I thought. "How nice!"

One was tempted to see the same unrest and sleeplessness in all nature, from the night darkness to the iron slabs, the crosses on the tombs and the trees under which the people were moving to and fro. But nowhere was the excitement and restlessness so marked as in the church. An unceasing struggle was going on in the entrance between the inflowing stream and the outflowing stream. Some were going in, others going out and soon coming back again to stand still for a little and begin moving again. People were scurrying from place to place, lounging about as though they were looking for something. The stream flowed from the entrance all round the church, disturbing even the front rows, where persons of weight and dignity were standing. There could be no thought of concentrated prayer. There were no prayers at all, but a sort of continuous, childishly irresponsible joy, seeking a pretext to break out and vent itself in some movement, even in senseless jostling and shoving.

The same unaccustomed movement is striking in the Easter service itself. The altar gates are flung wide open, thick clouds of incense float in the air near the candelabra; wherever one looks there are lights, the gleam and splutter of candles. . . . There is no reading; restless and lighthearted singing goes on to the end without ceasing. After each hymn the clergy change their vestments and come out to burn the incense, which is repeated every ten minutes.

I had no sooner taken a place, when a wave rushed from in front and forced me back. A tall thick-set deacon walked before me with a long red candle; the grey-headed archimandrite in his golden mitre hurried after him with the censer. When they had vanished from sight the crowd squeezed me back to my former position. But ten minutes had not passed before a new wave burst on me, and again the deacon appeared. This time he was followed by the Father Sub-Prior, the man who, as Ieronim had told me, was writing the history of the monastery.

As I mingled with the crowd and caught the infection of the universal joyful excitement, I felt unbearably sore on Ieronim's account. Why did they not send someone to relieve him? Why could not someone of less feeling and less susceptibility go on the ferry? "Lift up thine eyes, O Zion, and look around," they sang in the choir, "for thy children have come to thee as to a beacon of divine light from north and south, and from east and from the sea. . . ."

I looked at the faces; they all had a lively expression of triumph, but not one was listening to what was being sung and taking it in, and not one was "holding his breath." Why was not Ieronim released? I could fancy Ieronim standing meekly somewhere by the wall, bending forward and hungrily drinking in the beauty of the holy phrase. All this that glided by the ears of the people standing by me he would have eagerly drunk in with his delicately sensitive soul, and would have been spell-bound to ecstasy, to holding his breath, and there would not have been a man happier than he in all the church. Now he was plying to and fro over the dark river and grieving for his dead friend and brother.

The wave surged back. A stout smiling monk, playing with his rosary and looking round behind him, squeezed sideways by me, making way for a lady in a hat and velvet cloak. A monastery servant hurried after the lady, holding a chair over our heads.

I came out of the church. I wanted to have a look at the dead Nikolay, the unknown canticle writer. I walked about the monastery wall, where there was a row of cells, peeped into several windows, and, seeing nothing, came back again. I do not regret now that I did not see Nikolay; God knows, perhaps if I had seen him I should have lost the picture my imagination paints for me now. I imagine the lovable poetical figure solitary and not understood, who went out at nights to call to Ieronim over the water, and filled his hymns with flowers, stars and sunbeams, as a pale timid man with soft mild melancholy features. His eyes must have shone, not only with intelligence, but with kindly tenderness and that hardly restrained childlike enthusiasm which I could hear in Ieronim's voice when he quoted to me passages from the hymns.

When we came out of church after mass it was no longer night. The morning was beginning. The stars had gone out and the sky was a morose greyish blue. The iron slabs, the tombstones and the buds on the trees were covered with dew There was a sharp freshness in the air. Outside the precincts I did not find the same animated scene as I had beheld in the night. Horses and men looked exhausted, drowsy, scarcely moved, while nothing was left of the tar barrels but heaps of black ash. When anyone is exhausted and sleepy he fancies that nature, too, is in the same condition. It seemed to me that the trees and the young grass were asleep. It seemed as though even the bells were not pealing so loudly and gaily as at night. The restlessness was over, and of the excitement nothing was left but a pleasant weariness, a longing for sleep and warmth.

Now I could see both banks of the river; a faint mist hovered over it in shifting masses. There was a harsh cold breath from the water. When I jumped on to the ferry, a chaise and some two dozen men and women were standing on it already. The rope, wet and as I fancied drowsy, stretched far away across the broad river and in places disappeared in the white mist.

"Christ is risen! Is there no one else?" asked a soft voice.

I recognized the voice of Ieronim. There was no darkness now to hinder me from seeing the monk. He was a tall narrow-shouldered man of five-and-thirty, with large rounded features, with half-closed listless-looking eyes and an unkempt wedge-shaped beard. He had an extraordinarily sad and exhausted look.

"They have not relieved you yet?" I asked in surprise.

"Me?" he answered, turning to me his chilled and dewy face with a smile. "There is no one to take my place now till morning. They'll all be going to the Father Archimandrite's to break the fast directly."

With the help of a little peasant in a hat of reddish fur that looked like the little wooden tubs in which honey is sold, he threw his weight on the rope; they gasped simultaneously, and the ferry started.

We floated across, disturbing on the way the lazily rising mist. Everyone was silent. Ieronim worked mechanically with one hand. He slowly passed his mild lustreless eyes over us; then his glance rested on the rosy face of a young merchant's wife with black eyebrows, who was standing on the ferry beside me silently shrinking from the mist that wrapped her about. He did not take his eyes off her face all the way.

There was little that was masculine in that prolonged gaze. It seemed to me that Ieronim was looking in the woman's face for the soft and tender features of his dead friend.

Assignments

- Warm-up: Most readers have a hard time taking a read on Chekhov's faith journey. What do you think?
- Students should complete Concept Builder 27-A.
- Students should review the required reading(s) *before* the assigned chapter begins.
- Teachers may want to discuss assigned reading(s) with students.
- Teachers shall assign the required essay. The rest of the essays can be outlined, answered with shorter answers, discussed, or skipped.
- Students will review all readings for chapter 27.

Read this excerpt from Anton Chekhov's "The Bet," and respond to the following:

CONCEPT BUILDER 27-A
Active Reading

It was a dark autumn night. The old banker was walking up and down his study and remembering how, fifteen years before, he had given a party one autumn evening. There had been many clever men there, and there had been interesting conversations. Among other things they had talked of capital punishment. The majority of the guests, among whom were many journalists and intellectual men, disapproved of the death penalty. They considered that form of punishment out of date, immoral, and unsuitable for Christian States. In the opinion of some of them the death penalty ought to be replaced everywhere by imprisonment for life.

"I don't agree with you," said their host the banker. "I have not tried either the death penalty or imprisonment for life, but if one may judge à priori, the death penalty is more moral and more humane than imprisonment for life. Capital punishment kills a man at once, but lifelong imprisonment kills him slowly. Which executioner is the more humane, he who kills you in a few minutes or he who drags the life out of you in the course of many years?"

"Both are equally immoral," observed one of the guests, "for they both have the same object — to take away life. The State is not God. It has not the right to take away what it cannot restore when it wants to."

Among the guests was a young lawyer, a young man of five-and-twenty. When he was asked his opinion, he said: 'The death sentence and the life sentence are equally immoral, but if I had to choose between the death penalty and imprisonment for life, I would certainly choose the second. To live anyhow is better than not at all."

A lively discussion arose. The banker, who was younger and more nervous in those days, was suddenly carried away by excitement; he struck the table with his fist and shouted at the young man:

"It's not true! I'll bet you two millions you wouldn't stay in solitary confinement for five years."

"If you mean that in earnest," said the young man, "I'll take the bet, but I would stay not five but fifteen years."

"Fifteen? Done!" cried the banker. "Gentlemen, I stake two millions!"

"Agreed! You stake your millions and I stake my freedom!" said the young man.

And this wild, senseless bet was carried out! The banker, spoilt and frivolous, with millions beyond his reckoning, was delighted at the bet. At supper he made fun of the young man, and said:

'Think better of it, young man, while there is still time. To me two millions are a trifle, but you are losing three or four of the best years of your life. I say three or four, because you won't stay longer. Don't forget either, you unhappy man, that voluntary confinement is a great deal harder to bear than compulsory. The thought that you have the right to step out in liberty at any moment will poison your whole existence in prison. I am sorry for you."

The story is a frame story — a story within a story. The entire story, in other words, is a flashback to events 15 years ago. Eventually the story will return to the present. Why would the author begin the short story this way?

What is the purpose of having individuals in the party discuss the death sentence?

"The Bet"
Anton Chekhov

It was a dark autumn night. The old banker was walking up and down his study and remembering how, fifteen years before, he had given a party one autumn evening. There had been many clever men there, and there had been interesting conversations. Among other things they had talked of capital punishment. The majority of the guests, among whom were many journalists and intellectual men, disapproved of the death penalty. They considered that form of punishment out of date, immoral, and unsuitable for Christian States. In the opinion of some of them the death penalty ought to be replaced everywhere by imprisonment for life.

"I Don't agree with you," said their host the banker. "I have not tried either the death penalty or imprisonment for life, but if one may judge à priori, the death penalty is more moral and more humane than imprisonment for life. Capital punishment kills a man at once, but lifelong imprisonment kills him slowly. Which executioner is the more humane, he who kills you in a few minutes or he who drags the life out of you in the course of many years?"

"Both are equally immoral," observed one of the guests, "for they both have the same object — to take away life. The State is not God. It has not the right to take away what it cannot restore when it wants to."

Among the guests was a young lawyer, a young man of five-and-twenty. When he was asked his opinion, he said: "The death sentence and the life sentence are equally immoral, but if I had to choose between the death penalty and imprisonment for life, I would certainly choose the second. To live anyhow is better than not at all."

A lively discussion arose. The banker, who was younger and more nervous in those days, was suddenly carried away by excitement; he struck the table with his fist and shouted at the young man: "It's not true! I'll bet you two millions you wouldn't stay in solitary confinement for five years."

"If you mean that in earnest," said the young man, "I'll take the bet, but I would stay not five but fifteen years."

"Fifteen? Done!" cried the banker. "Gentlemen, I stake two millions!"

"Agreed! You stake your millions and I stake my freedom!" said the young man.

And this wild, senseless bet was carried out! The banker, spoilt and frivolous, with millions beyond his reckoning, was delighted at the bet. At supper he made fun of the young man, and said: "Think better of it, young man, while there is still time. To me two millions are a trifle, but you are losing three or four of the best years of your life. I say three or four, because you won't stay longer. Don't forget either, you unhappy man, that voluntary confinement is a great deal harder to bear than compulsory. The thought that you have the right to step out in liberty at any moment will poison your whole existence in prison. I am sorry for you."

And now the banker, walking to and fro, remembered all this, and asked himself: "What was the object of that bet? What is the good of that man's losing fifteen years of his life and my throwing away two millions? Can it prove that the death penalty is better or worse than imprisonment for life? No, no. It was all nonsensical and meaningless. On my part it was the caprice of a pampered man, and on his part simple greed for money. . . ."

Then he remembered what followed that evening. It was decided that the young man should spend the years of his captivity under the strictest supervision in one of the lodges in the banker's garden. It was agreed that for fifteen years he should not be free to cross the threshold of the lodge, to see human beings, to hear the human voice, or to receive letters and newspapers. He was allowed to have a musical instrument and books, and was allowed to write letters, to drink wine, and to smoke. By the terms of the agreement, the only relations he could have with the outer world were by a little window made purposely for that object. He might have anything he wanted — books, music, wine, and so on — in any quantity he desired by writing an order, but could only receive them through the window. The agreement provided for every detail and every trifle that would make his imprisonment strictly solitary, and bound the young man to stay there exactly fifteen years, beginning from twelve o'clock of November 14, 1870, and ending at twelve o'clock of November 14, 1885. The slightest attempt on his part to break the conditions, if only two minutes before the end, released the banker from the obligation to pay him two millions.

For the first year of his confinement, as far as one could judge from his brief notes, the prisoner suffered severely from loneliness and depression. The sounds of the piano could be heard continually day and night from his lodge. He refused wine and tobacco. Wine, he wrote, excites the desires, and desires are the worst foes of the prisoner; and besides, nothing could be more dreary than drinking good wine and seeing no one. And tobacco spoilt the air of his room. In the first year the books he sent for were principally of a light character; novels with a complicated love plot, sensational and fantastic stories, and so on.

In the second year the piano was silent in the lodge, and the prisoner asked only for the classics. In the fifth year music was audible again, and the prisoner asked for wine. Those who watched him through the window said that all that year he spent doing nothing but eating and drinking and lying on his bed, frequently yawning and angrily talking to himself. He did not read books. Sometimes at night he would sit down to write; he would spend hours writing, and in the morning tear up all that he had written. More than once he could be heard crying.

In the second half of the sixth year the prisoner began zealously studying languages, philosophy, and history. He threw himself eagerly into these studies — so much so that the banker had enough to do to get him the books he ordered. In the course of four years some six hundred volumes were procured at his request. It was during this period that the banker received the following letter from his prisoner: "My dear Jailer, I write you these lines in six languages. Show them to people who know the languages. Let them read them. If they find not one mistake I implore you to fire a shot in the garden. That shot will show me that my efforts have not been thrown away. The geniuses of all ages and of all lands speak different languages, but the same flame burns in them all. Oh, if you only knew what unearthly happiness my soul feels now from being able to understand them!"

The prisoner's desire was fulfilled. The banker ordered two shots to be fired in the garden.

Then after the tenth year, the prisoner sat immovably at the table and read nothing but the Gospel. It seemed strange to the banker that a man who in four years had mastered six hundred learned volumes should waste nearly a year over one thin book easy of comprehension. Theology and histories of religion followed the Gospels.

In the last two years of his confinement the prisoner read an immense quantity of books quite indiscriminately. At one time he was busy with the natural sciences, then he would ask for Byron or Shakespeare. There were notes in which he demanded at the same time books on chemistry, and a manual of medicine, and a novel, and some treatise on philosophy or theology. His reading suggested a man swimming in the sea among the wreckage of his ship, and trying to save his life by greedily clutching first at one spar and then at another.

The old banker remembered all this, and thought: "To-morrow at twelve o'clock he will regain his freedom. By our agreement I ought to pay him two millions. If I do pay him, it is all over with me: I shall be utterly ruined."

Fifteen years before, his millions had been beyond his reckoning; now he was afraid to ask himself which were greater, his debts or his assets. Desperate gambling on the Stock Exchange, wild speculation and the excitability which he could not get over even in advancing years, had by degrees led to the decline of his fortune and the proud, fearless, self-confident millionaire had become a banker of middling rank, trembling at every rise and fall in his investments.

"Cursed bet!" muttered the old man, clutching his head in despair. "Why didn't the man die? He is only forty now. He will take my last penny from me, he will marry, will enjoy life, will gamble on the Exchange; while I shall look at him with envy like a beggar, and hear from him every day the same sentence: 'I am indebted to you for the happiness of my life, let me help you!' No, it is too much! The one means of being saved from bankruptcy and disgrace is the death of that man!"

It struck three o'clock, the banker listened; everyone was asleep in the house and nothing could be heard outside but the rustling of the chilled trees. Trying to make no noise, he took from a fireproof safe the key of the door which had not been opened for fifteen years, put on his overcoat, and went out of the house.

It was dark and cold in the garden. Rain was falling. A damp cutting wind was racing about the garden, howling and giving the trees no rest. The banker strained his eyes, but could see neither the earth nor the white statues, nor the lodge, nor the trees. Going to the spot where the lodge stood, he twice called the watchman. No answer followed. Evidently the watchman had sought shelter from the weather, and was now asleep somewhere either in the kitchen or in the greenhouse.

"If I had the pluck to carry out my intention," thought the old man, "suspicion would fall first upon the watchman."

He felt in the darkness for the steps and the door, and went into the entry of the lodge. Then he groped his way into a little passage and lighted a match. There was not a soul there. There was a bedstead with no bedding on it, and in the corner there was a dark cast-iron stove. The seals on the door leading to the prisoner's rooms were intact.

When the match went out the old man, trembling with emotion, peeped through the little window. A candle was burning dimly in the prisoner's room. He was sitting at the table. Nothing could be seen but his back, the hair on his head, and his hands. Open books were lying on the table, on the two easy-chairs, and on the carpet near the table.

Five minutes passed and the prisoner did not once stir. Fifteen years' imprisonment had taught him to sit still. The banker tapped at the window with his finger, and the prisoner made no movement whatever in response. Then the banker cautiously broke the seals off the door and put the key in the keyhole. The rusty lock gave a grating sound and the door creaked. The banker expected to hear at once footsteps and a cry of astonishment, but three minutes passed and it was as quiet as ever in the room. He made up his mind to go in.

At the table a man unlike ordinary people was sitting motionless. He was a skeleton with the skin drawn tight over his bones, with long curls like a woman's and a shaggy beard. His face was yellow with an earthy tint in it, his cheeks were hollow, his back long and narrow, and the hand on which his shaggy head was propped was so thin and delicate that it was dreadful to look at it. His hair was already streaked with silver, and seeing his emaciated, aged-looking face, no one would have believed that he was only forty. He was asleep. . . . In front of his bowed head there lay on the table a sheet of paper on which there was something written in fine handwriting.

"Poor creature!" thought the banker, "he is asleep and most likely dreaming of the millions. And I have only to take this half-dead man, throw him on the bed, stifle him a little with the pillow, and the most conscientious expert would find no sign of a violent death. But let us first read what he has written here."

The banker took the page from the table and read as follows: "To-morrow at twelve o'clock I regain my freedom and the right to associate with other men, but before I leave this room and see the sunshine, I think it necessary to say a few words to you. With a clear conscience I tell you, as before God, who beholds me, that I despise freedom and life and health, and all that in your books is called the good things of the world.

"For fifteen years I have been intently studying earthly life. It is true I have not seen the earth nor men, but in your books I have drunk fragrant wine,

I have sung songs, I have hunted stags and wild boars in the forests, have loved women. . . . Beauties as ethereal as clouds, created by the magic of your poets and geniuses, have visited me at night, and have whispered in my ears wonderful tales that have set my brain in a whirl. In your books I have climbed to the peaks of Elburz and Mont Blanc, and from there I have seen the sun rise and have watched it at evening flood the sky, the ocean, and the mountain-tops with gold and crimson. I have watched from there the lightning flashing over my head and cleaving the storm-clouds. I have seen green forests, fields, rivers, lakes, towns. I have heard the singing of the sirens, and the strains of the shepherds' pipes; I have touched the wings of comely devils who flew down to converse with me of God. . . . In your books I have flung myself into the bottomless pit, performed miracles, slain, burned towns, preached new religions, conquered whole kingdoms. Your books have given me wisdom. All that the unresting thought of man has created in the ages is compressed into a small compass in my brain. I know that I am wiser than all of you. And I despise your books, I despise wisdom and the blessings of this world. It is all worthless, fleeting, illusory, and deceptive, like a mirage. You may be proud, wise, and fine, but death will wipe you off the face of the earth as though you were no more than mice burrowing under the floor, and your posterity, your history, your immortal geniuses will burn or freeze together with the earthly globe. You have lost your reason and taken the wrong path. You have taken lies for truth, and hideousness for beauty. You would marvel if, owing to strange events of some sorts, frogs and lizards suddenly grew on apple and orange trees instead of fruit, or if roses began to smell like a sweating horse; so I marvel at you who exchange heaven for earth. I don't want to understand you. To prove to you in action how I despise all that you live by, I renounce the two millions of which I once dreamed as of paradise and which now I despise. To deprive myself of the right to the money I shall go out from here five hours before the time fixed, and so break the compact."

When the banker had read this he laid the page on the table, kissed the strange man on the head, and went out of the lodge, weeping. At no other time, even when he had lost heavily on the Stock Exchange, had he felt so great a contempt for himself. When he got home he lay on his bed, but his tears and emotion kept him for hours from sleeping.

Next morning the watchmen ran in with pale faces, and told him they had seen the man who lived in the lodge climb out of the window into the garden, go to the gate, and disappear. The banker went at once with the servants to the lodge and made sure of the flight of his prisoner. To avoid arousing unnecessary talk, he took from the table the writing in which the millions were renounced, and when he got home locked it up in the fireproof safe.

Assignments

- Warm-up: What is the bet?
- Students should complete Concept Builder 27-B.
- Students should review reading(s) from the next chapter.
- Students should outline essay due at the end of the week.
- Per teacher instructions, students may answer orally, in a group setting, some of the essays that are not assigned as formal essays.

Does the lawyer change? Circle the words that describe him at the beginning of the novel and check the words that describe him at the end of the novel.

Melancholic

moody
anxious
rigid
sober
pessimistic
reserved
unsociable
quiet

Choleric

touchy
restless
aggressive
excitable
changeable
impulsive
optimistic
active

The Young Lawyer

Phlegmatic

passive
careful
thoughtful
peaceful
controlled
reliable
even-tempered
calm

Sanguine

sociable
outgoing
talkative
responsive
easy-going
lively
carefree
leadership

Critics Corner

If one really wants to understand Chekhov, one must realize that he was the moralist of the venial sin, the man who laid it down that a soul is damned not for murder, adultery or embezzlement but for the small, unrecognized sins of ill-temper, untruthfulness, stinginess and disloyalty. . . . As in Degas and Lautrec the whole beautiful theory of the art schools is blown sky-high, so in Chekhov the whole nineteenth-century conception of morals is blown sky-high. This is not morality as anyone from Jane Austen or Trollope would have recognized it, though I suspect that an orthodox theologian might have something very interesting to say about it. . . . Sin to him is ultimately a lack of refinement, the inability to get through a badly cooked meal without a scene.

— Frank O'Connor ("A Writer Who Refused to Pretend," *New York Times Book Review* (January 17, 1960).

What becomes of the traditional division of a story — prologue, exposition or development and finally dénouement or conclusion — in Chekhov's work? The "prologue" or introduction to the story is generally reduced to nil, or to a short sentence that immediately goes to the heart of the matter. . . . The Chekhov of the final years ended his stories and plays abruptly, on a sort of musical chord. There is, strictly speaking, no longer an ending at all. . . . The same form of ending is to be found in nearly all his works after 1894.

— Sophie Laffitte (*Chekhov, 1860–1904* (London: Angus & Robertson, 1973).

Assignments

- Warm-up: What stands out to you about Chekhov's writing style?
- Students should complete Concept Builder 27-C.
- Students should write rough draft of assigned essay.
- The teacher may correct rough drafts.

Does the lawyer change? Rate the lawyer's views on a subject before his voluntary incarceration and his attitude toward the same subjects after incarceration. Rate each subject from 1 to 5: 1 means "values not at all," 5 means "values very much."

Subject	Before Incarceration	After Incarceration
Money		
Prestige		
Friendship		
Family		
Solitude		
Education		
Faith in God		

What do you value? What do your parents value? What do your friends value? Rate each subject from 1 to 5: 1 means "values not at all," 5 means "values very much."

Subject	Me	My Family	My Friends
Money			
Prestige			
Friendship			
Family			
Solitude			
Education			
Faith in God			

Short Story Review

Short Story: "Easter Eve"
Author: Anton Chekhov

I.   Briefly describe the:

Protagonist — The protagonist is Ieronim. The reader does not obtain any physical description of Ieronim until the last few paragraphs, forcing the reader to concentrate on Ireonim's soul. Ieronim hungers after Christ and after his lost companion and mentor.

Antagonist — While there is no set "antagonist" in Checkov's short story, the loss of Ieronim's friend and mentor, Nikolay, serves to develop him in the same way that an antagonist would.

Other characters used to devolp the protagonist — The monastery devlops Ieronim — the lifestyle of a monastic set apart for the Lord that Ieronim desires but never can have. The narrator serves as a conduit for the vital information the reader wishes to know about Ieronim by asking him questions.

If applicable, state why any of the story's characters remind you of specific biblical characters. Ieronim has a Davidic hunger for the things of the Lord. He ponders the canticles that his friend Nikolay wrote to the Lord — they seem similar to the Psalms.

II. Setting

The setting is a ferry on the banks of the River Gvolta at dusk on Easter Eve. The narrator is awed by the beauty and light of the stars. He sees in the stars the same restlessness he sees in the pulsing water. Checkov creates an atmosphere of quiet, sacred expectation for the reader. He sees through the narrator's eyes the quivering river, the monastery waiting on the other side.

III. Point of View: First Person, Third Person, Third Person Omniscient

The point of view is first person. Checkov allows the reader to experience the situation as if he were a companion of the narrator.

IV. Brief summary of the plot.

The narrator rides on a ferry with Ireonim, and hears him describe his relationship with Nikolay. They arrive at the monastery. Nikolay longs to be accepted into the monastic order. The reader returns over the ferry and sees Nikolay's face.

Identify the climax of the short story —

The climax of the story occurs when Ieronim's face is revealed to the reader.

V.   Theme (The quintissential meaning/purpose of the story in one or two sentences):

The theme is that life is an unceasing struggle for a deeper walk with God. This is represented by Ieronim's struggle to join the monastery, and his lament for losing Nikolay.

VI. Author's worldview:

The author is a Christian theist.

How do you know this? What behavior does the character manifest to lead you to this conclusion?

Ieronim's ceaseless pursuit of God and longing after his presence reveals the author's Christian theistic bent.

VII.   Why did you like/dislike this short story?

I liked this short story. The powerful syntax and fascinating way of purporting a worldview intrigued me. Checkov has an incredibly concise way of portraying large concepts.

VIII.   The next literary work I read will be . . .

"A Doll's House" by Henrik Ibsen (Alouette)

Assignments

- Warm-up: Do you like Chekhov's short stories? Why? Why not?
- Students should complete Concept Builder 27-D.
- Students will re-write corrected copies of essay due tomorrow.

Detailed descriptions are vitally important to both of Chekhov's short stories. Write down ten things in your bedroom that you do not think your family has seen. Now ask your family if they have noticed these things. The ability to find and to describe details that others miss makes a short story much better.

1.

2.

3.

4.

5.

6.

7.

8.

9.

10.

The Ending of "The Bet"

"You have lost your reason and taken the wrong path. You have taken lies for truth, and hideousness for beauty. You would marvel if, owing to strange events of some sorts, frogs and lizards suddenly grew on apple and orange trees instead of fruit, or if roses began to smell like a sweating horse; so I marvel at you who exchange heaven for earth. I don't want to understand you.

"To prove to you in action how I despise all that you live by, I renounce the two millions of which I once dreamed as of paradise and which now I despise. To deprive myself of the right to the money I shall go out from here five hours before the time fixed, and so break the compact. . . ." — "The Bet"

The man spends his time in confinement educating himself. The day before the 15-year period concludes, the banker resolves to kill the lawyer to avoid paying him money. However, the banker finds a note written by the lawyer. The note declares that in his time in confinement he has learned to despise material goods for the fleeting things they are. Therefore, to demonstrate his contempt, he leaves five hours prior to when the bet would be up, thus losing the bet and unknowingly saving his own life.

Assignments

- Warm-up: Why does the protagonist leave before the end of the bet?
- Students should complete Concept Builder 27-E.
- Essays are due. Students should take the chapter 27 test.

Setting is the time and place in which a story occurs. It is used by the author to develop the characters and to advance the plot. Analyze the setting of "Easter Eve."

Setting of "Easter Eve"	
Physical Features	*The author toys with light and dark imagery to great effect. We see that the narrator is surrounded by "impenetrable darkness," which offsets the shimmering explosion of fireworks.*
Time	*Despite the religious overtones of Chekhov's tale — it is set on Easter day, and our attention is drawn to the joyous celebrations at the church — we see that the author delights in shifting the boundaries between reality and unreality.*
Geographical Location	
Activities of the Characters	

(1800–1890):
Realism (Part 4)

First Thoughts Henrik Ibsen (1828–1906) was a man who did not belong to his time but did advance the thinking of his time. He introduced a rare character — an assertive woman, some would say a thinking woman. Ibsen was a major Norwegian playwright of the late 19th century who introduced to the European stage a new sort of moral analysis that was uncommon in plays. He was the first modern European playwright. His plays were full of action, penetrating dialogue, and rigorous thought.

Chapter Learning Objectives In chapter 28 we examine one of the first, and certainly the most controversial, examples of realism in world literature.

As a result of this chapter study you will be able to . . .

1. Analyze the role the doctor performs in this play.

2. Describe setting in Ibsen's *A Doll's House*. What makes it unusual?

3. Define and discuss Ibsen's use of dramatic irony to advance the plot.

4. Search Scripture for all the references to marriage and the role of men and women in the marriage relationship.

5. Speculate on the end of the play. Do you think Nora will return? Why or why not?

Weekly Essay Options: Begin on page 273 of the Teacher Guide.

Reading ahead: "I Am Not Alone" and "Tiny Feet" by Gabriela Mistral, "A Very Old Man with Enormous Wings" by Gabriel García Márquez.

403

History connections: *World History* chapter 28, "German History."

A Doll's House
Henrik Ibsen

Background Not all revolutions are political; some revolutions are social revolutions or cultural revolutions. Ibsen's *A Doll's House* (1879), written while Ibsen sparked a cultural revolution of sorts in Europe. Married to the ardor of the 1848 European revolutions, a new modern perspective was emerging in the literary and dramatic world, challenging the romantic tradition. It is Ibsen who can be credited for mastering and popularizing the realist drama, which was revolutionary indeed.

Only William Shakespeare was more popular. Ibsen's plays were performed all over Europe.

A Doll's House was based on an event in Ibsen's own life. Ibsen's female friend Laura Kieler experienced a similar situation. Mrs. Kieler's husband fell ill and was advised to take a vacation in a warm climate — and Laura, like Nora does in the play, secretly borrowed money to finance the trip (which took place in 1876). Laura wrote a hot check, the bank refused payment, and she told her husband the whole story. He demanded a separation, removed the children from her care, and only took her back after she had spent a month in a public asylum.

Assignments

- Warm-up: Compare Ibsen's *A Doll's House* to controversial plays like *Hair* or *Jesus Christ Superstar*. When does a dramatist move from aesthetics to vulgarity or to blasphemy?

- Students should complete Concept Builder 28-A.

- Students should review the required reading(s) *before* the assigned chapter begins.

- Teachers may want to discuss assigned reading(s) with students.

- Teachers shall assign the required essay. The rest of the essays can be outlined, answered with shorter answers, discussed, or skipped.

- Students will review all readings for chapter 28.

Read this excerpt from Henrik Ibsen's *A Doll's House* (act 1), and respond to the following:

SCENE — A room furnished comfortably and tastefully, but not extravagantly. At the back, a door to the right leads to the entrance-hall, another to the left leads to Helmer's study. Between the doors stands a piano. In the middle of the left-hand wall is a door, and beyond it a window. Near the window are a round table, arm-chairs and a small sofa. In the right-hand wall, at the farther end, another door; and on the same side, nearer the footlights, a stove, two easy chairs and a rocking-chair; between the stove and the door, a small table. Engravings on the walls; a cabinet with china and other small objects; a small book-case with well-bound books. The floors are carpeted, and a fire burns in the stove.

It is winter. A bell rings in the hall; shortly afterwards the door is heard to open. Enter NORA, humming a tune and in high spirits. She is in outdoor dress and carries a number of parcels; these she lays on the table to the right. She leaves the outer door open after her, and through it is seen a PORTER who is carrying a Christmas Tree and a basket, which he gives to the MAID who has opened the door.]

Nora. Hide the Christmas Tree carefully, Helen. Be sure the children do not see it until this evening, when it is dressed. [To the PORTER, taking out her purse.] How much?

Porter. Sixpence.

Nora. There is a shilling. No, keep the change. [The PORTER thanks her, and goes out. NORA shuts the door. She is laughing to herself, as she takes off her hat and coat. She takes a packet of macaroons from her pocket and eats one or two; then goes cautiously to her husband's door and listens.] Yes, he is in. [Still humming, she goes to the table on the right.]

Helmer [calls out from his room]. Is that my little lark twittering out there?

Nora [busy opening some of the parcels]. Yes, it is!

Helmer. Is it my little squirrel bustling about?

Nora. Yes!

Helmer. When did my squirrel come home?

Nora. Just now. [Puts the bag of macaroons into her pocket and wipes her mouth.] Come in here, Torvald, and see what I have bought.

Helmer. Don't disturb me. [A little later, he opens the door and looks into the room, pen in hand.] Bought, did you say? All these things? Has my little spendthrift been wasting money again?

What is extraordinary about the setting is the ordinariness of the entire scene. Why is this an important element of the setting?

From this dialogue, what can you infer about the relationship between Helmer and his wife, Nora?

Realism

The second half of the 19th century was an age of faith in all knowledge, which would derive from science, and scientific objective methods, which could solve all human problems.

In the visual arts, this spirit is most obvious in the widespread rejection of romantic subjectivism and imagination in favor of realism — the accurate and apparently objective description of the ordinary, observable world. Realism was different from naturalism in degree, not in substance. Realism argued that if people were honest they would admit that God was not present at all. They entered the cosmic arena and let the chips fall where they may. They shared the same criticisms of other worldviews that naturalism held.

They did not Expect Him by Ilya Repin, c.1884 (PD-Art).

"Bonjour, Monsieur Courbet" by Gustave Courbet , 1854 (PD-US).

The Stone Breakers by Gustave Courbet , 1849 (PD-US).

Assignments

- Warm-up: Realism is only real if it is real. Let me explain. Hollywood depicts most of its characters as being lonely, separated, divorced nihilistic heathens. Sex outside of marriage is offered as normal and healthy. But the reality is that the "normal" life is the biblical life. Explain.

- Students should complete Concept Builder 28-B.

- Students should review reading(s) from the next chapter.

- Students should outline essay due at the end of the week.

- Per teacher instructions, students may answer orally, in a group setting, some of the essays that are not assigned as formal essays.

CONCEPT BUILDER 28-B
Realism

A Doll's House **is part of a new movement in literature, called realism. Realism was much like naturalism, except realism went beyond agnosticism — realism argued that if people were honest they would admit that God was not present at all. Realism entered the cosmic arena and let the chips fall where they may. Artistically, realism celebrated the "ordinary." The painting below is an early example of realism. Why?**

The Gleaners by Jean-François Millet, 1857 (PD-Art).

Critics Corner

A Doll's House

Review of premiere of "A Doll's House" (A Play in 3 Acts by Henrik Ibsen) at the Royal Theatre by C. Thrane in *Illustreret Tidende* (*Illustrated News*), Copenhagen, no. 1057, 21st volume (December 28, 1879): p. 145–148).

Henrik Ibsen's new play "A Doll's House" is a Christmas present of an usual kind, not suitable, however, to be enjoyed fleetingly and then put aside, but rich in content, and inviting reflection. The play is both entertaining and suspenseful and interesting, but these descriptions badly suit a work whose ethical gravity is so very prominent. The playwright stands like a clergyman and holds the mirror up to his congregation, only a little worried that one should find him much too strict and unbending. The theatre must, when "A Doll's House" is performed, make its "not for pleasure alone" twice as big.

In pure dramatic terms, the play is already a masterpiece. The focus of the action is accomplished to perfection; nothing is superfluous; every supporting role, every scene and every line serve to illuminate the main action, the relationship between the lawyer Helmer and his wife, Nora. We are invited into their "doll's home" and become witnesses to what seems to be a rare matrimonial happiness. Helmer wishes nothing more than that Nora shall be happy and content; he makes allowances for her childish little errors, he gives in, if at all possible, to her wishes and has only endearing terms and the friendliest words for her. And Nora in her turn loves him deeply. She is a childish creature, of sanguine temperament, and reminds us in some respects of Charles Dickens' "child-wife" Dora. But Helmer is no David Copperfield. He is surprised when his lark "speaks like a human being," but he does not put a price on it; he is prone to forgiving the extravagant "playbird" her sins, because they almost set her childishness in relief, and he wants to have her exactly as she is, dancing for him, dressing up,

declaiming, because that is how she shows herself in all the grace of her youth and her naivety. That the couple have had three children does not make the least difference; Helmer is an intelligent, clever businessman, but has, side by side with his practical talents, his own taste for the beautiful and the artistically balanced; this taste must at any cost be satisfied in the home, and Nora, whose whole personality is extremely suited to giving it nourishment, fulfils it in every way. This is how their lives are lived as a lovely game in this doll's home. Yet the strong sunlight does not lack the necessary shadow. Ghostlike, an intimate friend of both husband and wife wanders around, the half-dead Doctor Rank, who mocks life and the existence he knows he shall soon leave. Helmer perceives of this eerie figure almost aesthetically, as "the shadowy background for our sunlit happiness"; Nora, whom Rank loves, is very fond of him, as she often feels somewhat freer in conversation with him than with Helmer, who of course has to have everything his way. But neither Helmer nor Nora has any idea that Rank, who soon, as a farewell to their home, leaves his visiting card as a death sign, is the symbol that the doll's home itself contains the germ of its own demise. Nora is burdened by a secret. In the early days of her marriage Helmer became dangerously ill and nothing could cure him but a sojourn in the Mediterranean; a journey they could not afford; but Nora, who otherwise was a frivolous child, showed manly energy when it came to the life of her loved one, and executed an action, the only thing she, in her heart, is proud of, because it was an expression of the sacrifice of love: she took up a loan by writing a certificate of debt in her father's name — and her father had at the time already been dead for a few days. Nora had no concept of having committed an act that could be branded a crime; she has not been able to speak openly to her husband about taking up the loan, as she did not dare to reveal his true condition to him, and she was even less willing to write how things were to her absent father, who was on his deathbed, in fear of hastening his death; she knew that her father would give his consent, had he been asked, there was no time to lose — she acted and believed that she acted correctly, and her instinct tells her constantly that the laws could not be brought to bear on it. In this she was not wrong either — exactly because of the presumed consent — as long as the dubious circumstance did not step in to complicate it, that her father's death had happened before she wrote it; however, this was a point that it was perfect to exploit for those who wanted to hurt and worry her, and as it happens, the lender, the broken solicitor Mr. Krogstad, suddenly has a reason to bring the case to the doll home. Nora has earlier, when she proudly looked upon her action as the most beautiful and best, refused to confess the secret to Helmer: "Thorvald, with his male pride — how awkward and humiliating it would be for him to know that he owed anything to me. It would upset the whole balance of the relationship between us, our lovely, happy home would no longer be what it now is." In other words, she could not bear to show her true self; she had an instinctive feeling that it was as a doll that she was loved, and this happiness of love she was reluctant to disturb. And now Krogstad turns up and tells her that her action is a crime, and threatens to report it to Helmer. The moment seems to have arrived when she can no longer hesitate to reveal everything to her husband, but she finds it even more impossible than before. While on the one hand the usual lack of exchange of thoughts when it comes to deeper concerns restrains her, on the other, she regards with ideal sanguinity that if Helmer knew about the matter that threatens disgrace and misfortune, he will show his love from its noblest side; he will stand up as the knight of her honour, he will take the shame upon himself — the "wonderful" thing will happen, that he will love and admire the woman in her; but this sacrifice must not take place, she shall die without experiencing the "wonderful"

thing in order to save her husband's happiness and honour. One rarely gets to see such tragically devastating scenes as those that develop, while Nora still for a while tries to prevent that Krogstad's fatal letter falls into Helmer's hands. That the not quite faultless, but in her heart innocent and pure woman, in the middle of her home and at her husband's side, stands so alone and abandoned in all her anguish, is an unusually stirring sight; she feels that she has entered circumstances she cannot come to grips with and understand; Krogstad, who himself is guilty of falsehood, speaks to her in a confidential conversation, as when one criminal gives advice to another, and the unsuspecting Helmer lets her dance the tarantella for him — as a rehearsal for the next evening's costume ball — and fails to understand, when she gives expression to her despair and angst in the dance itself, that she is suffering spiritually and needs his help: "You've forgotten everything I've taught you," he says; "I see you need more guidance."

So far we have, without difficulty, followed the author's portrayal. It is so natural and often so ordinary that we give ourselves up to it and believe we see an image of something that often takes place. This pleasant home, these turtle doves, this nice aesthetic relationship, are altogether things we know well; we acknowledge the author for his insights into their souls, and have a feeling that poor Nora suffers too much; but everything could still turn out well. Many authors would not have hesitated to resort to some turnaround, whereby the characters in question found happiness after enduring sufferings, before the curtain came down for the last time. At least that is what often happened in the old days, when the authors preferred harmony to the strictest psychological consequence. But our author spares his audience as little as he does his characters; it is for the now approaching catastrophe that he has written the whole play; in that lies the lesson, he wants to preach, and it has to be admitted, that even if there is something about the ending, which opposes one's immediate emotion, even if what happens causes a swarm of doubts and objections, he has twisted the threads in such a way that one bows to them almost against one's wishes.

When Helmer learns what has happened from Krogstad's letter, he passes the test he is subjected to in the worst way possible. His egotism breaks out in all its force, and far from thinking about his wife's love or sacrificing himself in the name of her honour, he showers her with reproaches, and his only thought is to cover up everything for the eyes of the world. Still, this is not the worst. Because of a change in his own circumstances, Krogstad gives up all plans of exploiting the situation and offers Helmer the debt certificate on which Nora has signed her father's name. In his joy, he forgets everything Nora has done and suffered for his sake, which he earlier despaired about. He is merciful and magnanimous: "Do you think you are less dear to me because you don't have the judgment to act on your own? I wouldn't be a real man if your feminine helplessness didn't make you twice as attractive in my eyes. I have forgiven you, Nora; I swear to you, I have forgiven you." To him, Nora is still the one who visits the cake shop or eats macaroons against his express wish, yes, he feels, with the same pleasure as before, that offering his forgiveness gives him the right to start the game with his lovely doll all over again. "Don't worry about anything, Nora; just open your heart to me, and I shall be your will and your conscience." With this portrayal, the author passes a hard judgment on men, and the question begs asking, if Helmer really has shown any signs in the preceding action that he would reveal such moral turpitude in this the most serious of moments. His is not a deep nature, he is pretty egoistical, with a touch of sensuality, but his faults towards Nora are close to being of the negative kind, of not acting; he did not want to change what appealed to him so much, he did not want to interfere, where he saw no reason to; he seemed, rather, like quite a good and amiable man. The author, however, saw in the little testimonies what was to come out in the big one. Helmer's whole married life was a witness to the fact he has never loved his wife, but had just "been in love with her," and that he has never had the slightest idea about the moral meaning of marriage. You don't overcome such a big step in your maturing development in a moment, and instead of revealing a better nature, he merely reveal his own self and shows the abyss, which throughout the marriage, has stood between him and his wife. Nora understands this, Nora whose ideal longing for love receives its death blow, and the wonderful happens: having matured to a clear understanding during these days of misfortune, she sees in Helmer merely a stranger, and she sheds her love like the jewellery she has just taken off. The relationship has suddenly been turned around: she is the superior partner, she is the one who judges, and the sentence is this, that she cannot continue in a marriage, which is not a marriage, and she leaves her home, husband and children. It is this, which to weak, mortal people's feelings, is too harsh. So be it, that the dissonant ending is almost unbearable — of course, the author refuses to worry about this aesthetic consideration — but is not the dissonance itself a result of the fact that the action cannot immediately be justified? The ethic of marriage demands that both partners are equally respected as people, but what does it say about the offended wife's duties, when it comes to her children? It might have been better for the play, if these children did not exist. Even as regards Helmer, the punishment seems far worse than the crime; and one must not forget that Nora, if we leave out the one misdeed, was a child-wife, who in many ways showed that she was not very open to seriousness and reason; her faults were many; she was used to making herself guilty of many small untruths, she taught the children falsehood, she was imprudent and wasteful; her ideal nature she kept hidden, almost wilfully. How can she then let her husband take the whole responsibility, she who herself probably helped him continue on the less than praiseworthy road? Was it not time for her, who had become so emancipated, to begin to teach him? She herself feels that, to learn to distinguish truth from untruth and right from wrong, she must leave this home which led her astray; but could she not also achieve that in her home, if duty told her to stay there. However, that is not her duty, according to the author, and she cannot stay with the stranger, who has deserved his punishment as the one, who in his capacity as a husband, has the greatest responsibility in the marriage and who so frivolously has played with his wife's soul. If it is the author's intention that a bridge never can be built over the abyss between the married couple, this is certainly a big question. The last words between them were about "the most wonderful," about the possibilities that "a life together could become a marriage" and Helmer's last exclamation "The most wonderful?!" happens as "a hope wells up in him";

however, at the same time there is the sound of a gate slamming shut downstairs — it is Nora leaving the house, and the sound does not augur well. But this symbolism, which perhaps, however difficult it may be to believe, is a small concession to a theatrical effect, does not have the meaning which the author leads us towards in the middle of the play. We saw in Dr. Rank a warning of the imminent misfortune and thus we are also obliged to take note of lucky warnings: such a one is pretty obvious in what happens to Mrs. Linde and the solicitor, Krogstad, who loved each other in the days of their youth and parted from each other and after great trials find each other again and enter the union of marriage. It seems, as if Nora for the time being will begin a working life just like Mrs. Linde before her, and Nora will possibly, after a few years, like her friend, take the first step towards a reconciliation. In the theatre, we want everything to be this tangible and are thus very dissatisfied with being referred to the future; but during difficult circumstances one must be happy with a mere wink, and the author cannot be annoyed that the audience member grabs hold of this and becomes preoccupied with it; because although the moral cannot be preached pressingly enough, it is human to want an expiation of the crime, and that true happiness at one stage will make its triumphant march into this home which still had the advantage over so many other homes, that it was a home of beauty.

The play, which on the whole is performed well, has given occasion to two theatrical achievements of great interest and importance: Mr. E. Poulsen's Helmer and Mrs. Hennings' Nora. That Mr. Poulsen understands Ibsen as only the few do, he has often shown; Helmer is perhaps his most perfect role in the Ibsen repertoire. No nuance, no subtlety in the transitions escape his attention, and he executes his role with such a truthfulness that his portrayal utterly convinces. If we at certain times are close to thinking better of Helmer than he actually deserves, some of the reason lies in the fact that his whole personality carries the stamp of the sense of beauty that Helmer possesses, in too high a degree. The actor does not lead us astray, however, and stresses strongly enough the egotism and the sense of superiority in the middle of the childish games with Nora. The portrayal in the last act of the light champagne intoxication, the erotic atmosphere and all the changing emotions from rage to joy is especially masterly; the performances have a flight of their own, and the many details are brought together to a large and full picture. Mrs. Hennings, who in her capability as an ingénue so often has had to play less important roles or characters, which distinguished themselves as not being characters, has as Nora been given one of the most arduous roles, one which has a very unusual character development. That this artist would be able to portray the role as the "child wife" with excellence, was of course a given; on the other hand she prepared a surprise by following through and portraying the whole character with the greatest assurance. Her nimbleness and grace, which are so necessary for this role, did not fail at any point, and she acted with such fine nuances and such a sensitivity that the whole growth from child wife to a particular personality had a natural quality. And thus the audience also showed their enjoyment at seeing her talents so excellently used on a large scale (Translated to English by May-Brit Akerholt, http://www.ibsen.net/index. gan?id=11183655&subid=0).

Assignments

- Warm-up: Did you like this play? Why or why not?
- Students should complete Concept Builder 28-C.
- Students should write rough draft of assigned essay.
- The teacher may correct rough drafts.

Nora is not only the most remarkable character in this play, but some also think she is without equal in Western literature. Trace her development as a character.

A helpless, dependent female

An independent, modern woman

Student Essay:
Themes in *A Doll's House*

"You've never loved me, you've only found it pleasure to be in love with me." (Act 3)

A Doll's House, by Henrik Ibsen, portrays a woman who questions her duty to her husband and seeks to escape the stifling confines of her marriage. There are three themes present in this book — women are no less than men; though lying and cheating may be helpful now, in the long run, they have serious consequences; and relationships only prosper when there are no secrets.

The first theme clearly revealed in "A Doll's House" was that women are no less than men. Torvald Helmer exhibited the traditional view of women all throughout the book. He thought that men are greater and women. Helmer: "I'm in the power of a man without scruples; he can do what he likes with me — ask what he wants of me — order me about as he pleases, and I dare not refuse him. And I'm brought so pitifully low all because of a shiftless woman!" (Act 3) However, Nora, Torvald's wife, persistently displayed her view that women are no less than men. She argued against Helmer every time he said something condescending about women. Helmer: "But no man would sacrifice his honor for the one he loves." Nora: "Thousands of women have." (Act 3) Throughout the book, Nora showed that she was no less than her husband. This theme was rather easy to notice because it contradicts what the majority of contemporary audiences think.

The second theme was that though lying and cheating may be helpful now, in the long run, they have serious consequences. Nora forged her father's name when she was borrowing money. Krogstad: "Your father died on the twenty-ninth of September. But look at this — your father has dated his signature the second of October. Isn't that a curious thing, Mrs Helmer? . . . It really was you father himself who wrote his name there?" Nora: "No, it was not. I wrote Papa's name." (Act 1) At the moment when she forged the signature, she received the money she needed and lived happily; but later in the story, readers see that it was a foolish mistake. Nora could have been taken to court because of that mistake. All throughout the book, she was trying to make sure that Krogstad got the job in banking, or else she would have to face the court because it was she that forged the signature. Krogstad: "Mrs Helmer, you obviously don't realize what you've been guilty of . . . it's the law that you'll be judged by if I produce this paper in court." (Act 1)

The final theme depicted in *A Doll's House* was that relationships cannot prosper when there are secrets. During the eight years that Torvald and Nora were married, Nora never told Torvald her secret that she borrowed money. This made their relationship shaky because Nora would always be trying to hide something from him. When Krogstad's letter revealing Nora's actions arrived in the mail, Nora did everything she could to stop Torvald from reading it. Nora: "What do you want out there?" Helmer: "I'm just seeing if the post's come." Nora: "No, no Torvald — don't do that." Helmer: "Why not?" Nora: "Please don't Torvald — there's nothing there." (Act 2) Also, Nora has been keeping her true feeling hidden for the eight years she has been married to Torvald. This has kept her a distance away from having a prosperous relationship with Torvald. She finally told him that she was never happy and felt like she lived in a doll's house, hence the title *A Doll's House*. Nora: "I mean when I passed out of Papa's hands into yours. You arranged everything to suit your own tastes, and so I came to have the same tastes as yours . . . or I pretended to. I'm not quite sure which . . . perhaps it was a bit of both — sometimes one and sometimes the other. Now that I come to look at it, I've lived by performing tricks for you, Torvald. That was how you wanted it. You and Papa have committed a grievous sin against me: it's you fault that I've made nothing of my life. . . . I've been your doll-wife here, just as at home I was Papa's doll-child." (Act 3) Torvald and Nora's marriage did not prosper because there were secrets.

A Doll's House, by Henrik Ibsen, portrays a woman who questions her duty to her husband and seeks to escape the stifling confines of her marriage. There are three themes present in this book — women are no less than men; though lying and cheating may be helpful now, in the long run, they have serious consequences; and relationships only prosper when there are no secrets. (Hannah)

Assignments

- Warm-up: Develop two or three themes of this play.
- Students should complete Concept Builder 28-D.
- Students will re-write corrected copies of essay due tomorrow.

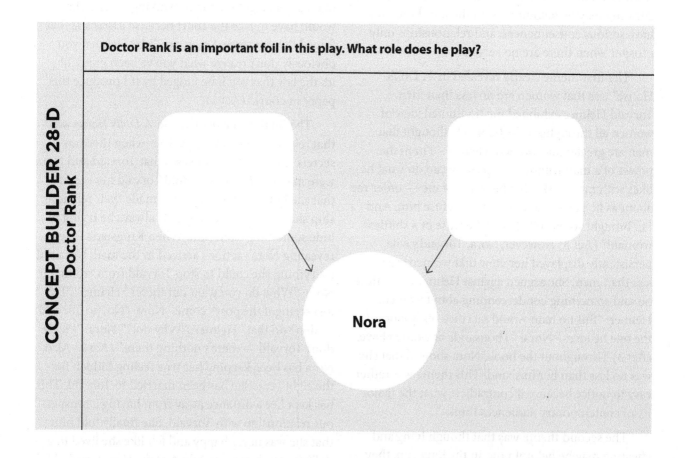

CONCEPT BUILDER 28-D
Doctor Rank

Doctor Rank is an important foil in this play. What role does he play?

Nora

Student Essay: Nora

NORA: "Yes, Torvald, we may be a wee bit more reckless now, mayn't we? Just a tiny wee bit!"

Nora, protagonist of Henrik Ibsen's iconoclastic play "A Doll's House," stands apart from other literary figures of her era. As Nora steps through the door at the beginning of the play, so the modern woman walks through the door of literature. Nora's character development takes place in three stages throughout the play. First, Nora embraces discontent with her current life; second, she turns to conceal her discontent; and third, she releases her discontent on her world with disastrous results.

Nora becomes discontent with her current life.

NORA: [humming and smiling with an air of mystery]. Hm, hm! Aha!

MRS. LINDE: Because you couldn't have borrowed it.

NORA: Couldn't I? Why not?

MRS. LINDE: No, a wife cannot borrow without her husband's consent.

NORA: [tossing her head]. Oh, if it is a wife who has any head for business — a wife who has the wit to be a little bit clever.

MRS. LINDE: I don't understand it at all, Nora.

NORA: There is no need you should. I never said I had borrowed the money. I may have got it some other way. [Lies back on the sofa.] Perhaps I got it from some other admirer. When anyone is as attractive as I am. . . ."

Nora tells her friend with a sense of urgency that her borrowing money for an Italy trip was necessary for her husband's health. The reader feels that it was Nora who needed the change — Nora who was suffering from a nervous complaint. The reader feels tension building as Nora appears to glory in her deception. Nora becomes a second Madame Bovary, turning to wrongdoing in order to prove her strength.

Next, Nora attempts to conceal her discontent under a forefront of wit. Her borrowing of money becomes her "little secret."

HELMER: Not — not happy! NORA: No, only merry. And you have always been so kind to me. But our home has been nothing but a playroom. I have been your doll-wife, just as at home I was papa's doll-child; and here the children have been my dolls. I thought it great fun when you played with me, just as they thought it great fun when I played with them. That is what our marriage has been, Torvald.

In the final scene when Nora determines to leave Torvald, he is shocked that she could have kept such a secret. But Nora reveals the key to her secrecy — to her, married life was nothing but a game. Nora's demise into suicidal thoughts and depression occurs when she realizes that she can no longer play her game. She is forced to face reality, and is left with nothing , not even a sense of who she is.

Finally, Nora releases her discontent on her world:

HELMER: That you have not. What duties could those be?

NORA: Duties to myself.

HELMER: Before all else, you are a wife and a mother.

NORA: I don't believe that any longer. I believe that before all else I am a reasonable human being, just as you are — or, at all events, that I must try and become one. I know quite well, Torvald, that most people would think you right, and that views of that kind are to be found in books; but I can no longer content myself with what most people say, or with what is found in books. I must think over things for myself and get to understand them.

Nora's discontent is released upon her responsibility with disastrous results. Her brewing contempt for a life as a wife and mother leaves her callous to the effects of her desertion of husband and children. Nora places identity above God and above the people she is called to love. Ibsen's portrait of a woman who has no love other than herself is embraced by the culture as the "modern woman" admired by contemporaries such as Gustav Flaubert and Simone de Beauvoir. (Alouette)

Assignments

- Warm-up: How would you describe Nora in your own words?
- Students should complete Concept Builder 28-E.
- Essays are due. Students should take the chapter 28 test.

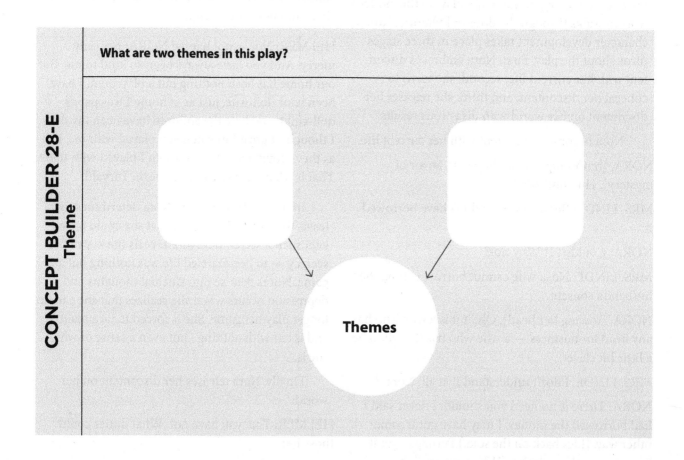

CONCEPT BUILDER 28-E
Theme

What are two themes in this play?

Themes

(1890–Present):
Modern Age (Part 1)

First Thoughts Nobel prize winner Gabriela Mistral (1889–1957) is one of Chile's most beloved writers. After the tragic death of a person very close to her, Mistral basically lived a life of self-imposed isolation. Mistral often spoke out for social justice for the disenfranchised poor.

Chapter Learning Objectives In chapter 29 we examine two Latin American writers and understand their use of magic realism.

As a result of this chapter study you will be able to . . .

1. Gabriela Mistral always yearned for, but never experienced motherhood. She turned her heartbreak into stunning poetry that offers encouragement to others struggling in hopelessness. Find evidence of this in these poems and in at least one other poem by Mistral.

2. Discuss what the tiny feet represent in "Tiny Feet."

3. Analyze the narrative technique Márquez employs.

4. Give examples of magic realism in "A Very Old Man with Enormous Wings," which appeared in his 1972 Gabriel García Márquez's *Leaf Storm and Other Stories*.

5. As a young law student, García Márquez read Kafka's *The Metamorphosis*. It greatly influenced his short story "A Very Old Man with Enormous Wings." Compare these two literary pieces.

Weekly Essay Options: Begin on page 273 of the Teacher Guide.

Reading ahead: *The Löwenskölds Ring* by Selma Lovisa Lagerlöf.

417

Gabriela Mistral

I Am Not Alone

The night, it is deserted
from the mountains to the sea.
But I, the one who rocks you,
I am not alone!
The sky, it is deserted
for the moon falls to the sea.
But I, the one who holds you,
I am not alone!
The world, it is deserted.
All flesh is sad you see.
But I, the one who hugs you,
I am not alone!

Tiny Feet

A child's tiny feet,
Blue, blue with cold,
How can they see and not protect you?
Oh, my God!
Tiny wounded feet,
Bruised all over by pebbles,
Abused by snow and soil!
Man, being blind, ignores
that where you step, you leave
A blossom of bright light,
that where you have placed
your bleeding little soles
a redolent tuberose grows.
Since, however, you walk
through the streets so straight,
you are courageous, without fault.
Child's tiny feet,
Two suffering little gems,
How can the people pass, unseeing.

usa.publiboda.com/zona-latina/latin-love-poems/gabriela-mistral.html.
Translated by Mary Gallwey, www.poetseers.org/nobel-prize-for-literature/gabriela-mistral-1945/gabriela-mistral-poems/1-2-2/.

Assignments

- Warm-up: What does: "The sky, it is deserted/ for the moon falls to the sea./ But I, the one who holds you,/ I am not alone!" mean?

- Students should complete Concept Builder 29-A.

- Students should review the required reading(s) *before* the assigned chapter begins.

- Teachers may want to discuss assigned reading(s) with students.

- Teachers shall assign the required essay. The rest of the essays can be outlined, answered with shorter answers, discussed, or skipped.

- Students will review all readings for chapter 29.

CONCEPT BUILDER 29-A
The Modern Poem

The following poems by Gabriela Mistral are modern poems. Modern literature manifests the following characteristics: first, human emotion and kindness are primary, God's participation is secondary. Next, characters are often isolated and depressed. In what ways are the following poems "modern"?

I Am Not Alone	Tiny Feet
The night, it is deserted from the mountains to the sea. But I, the one who rocks you, I am not alone! The sky, it is deserted for the moon falls to the sea. But I, the one who holds you, I am not alone! The world, it is deserted. All flesh is sad you see. But I, the one who hugs you, I am not alone!	A child's tiny feet, Blue, blue with cold, How can they see and not protect you? Oh, my God! Tiny wounded feet, Bruised all over by pebbles, Abused by snow and soil! Man, being blind, ignores that where you step, you leave A blossom of bright light, that where you have placed your bleeding little soles a redolent tuberose grows. Since, however, you walk through the streets so straight, you are courageous, without fault. Child's tiny feet, Two suffering little gems, How can the people pass, unseeing.
I am not alone — on the contrary — this author feels very much alone! She has her feelings, nature, and other people, but noticeably absent is a loving God.	

www.poemhunter.com/gabriela-mistral/.

"A Very Old Man With Enormous Wings"
Gabriel García Márquez

On the third day of rain they had killed so many crabs inside the house that Pelayo had to cross his drenched courtyard and throw them into the sea, because the newborn child had a temperature all night and they thought it was due to the stench. The world had been sad since Tuesday. Sea and sky were a single ash-gray thing and the sands of the beach, which on March nights glimmered like powdered light, had become a stew of mud and rotten shellfish. The light was so weak at noon that when Pelayo was coming back to the house after throwing away the crabs, it was hard for him to see what it was that was moving and groaning in the rear of the courtyard. He had to go very close to see that it was an old man, a very old man, lying face down in the mud, who, in spite of his tremendous efforts, couldn't get up, impeded by his enormous wings.

Frightened by that nightmare, Pelayo ran to get Elisenda, his wife, who was putting compresses on the sick child, and he took her to the rear of the courtyard. They both looked at the fallen body with a mute stupor. He was dressed like a ragpicker. There were only a few faded hairs left on his bald skull and very few teeth in his mouth, and his pitiful condition of a drenched great-grandfather took away and sense of grandeur he might have had. His huge buzzard wings, dirty and half-plucked were forever entangled in the mud. They looked at him so long and so closely that Pelayo and Elisenda very soon overcame their surprise and in the end found him familiar. Then they dared speak to him, and he answered in an incomprehensible dialect with a strong sailor's voice. That was how they skipped over the inconvenience of the wings and quite intelligently concluded that he was a lonely castaway from some foreign ship wrecked by the storm. And yet, they called in a neighbor woman who knew everything about life and death to see him, and all she needed was one look to show them their mistake.

"He's an angel," she told them. "He must have been coming for the child, but the poor fellow is so old that the rain knocked him down."

On the following day everyone knew that a flesh-and-blood angel was held captive in Pelayo's house. Against the judgment of the wise neighbor woman, for whom angels in those times were the fugitive survivors of a spiritual conspiracy, they did not have the heart to club him to death. Pelayo watched over him all afternoon from the kitchen, armed with his bailiff's club, and before going to bed he dragged him out of the mud and locked him up with the hens in the wire chicken coop. In the middle of the night, when the rain stopped, Pelayo and Elisenda were still killing crabs. A short time afterward the child woke up without a fever and with a desire to eat. Then they felt magnanimous and decided to put the angel on a raft with fresh water and provisions for three days and leave him to his fate on the high seas. But when they went out into the courtyard with the first light of dawn, they found the whole neighborhood in front of the chicken coop having fun with the angel, without the slightest reverence, tossing him things to eat through the openings in the wire as if weren't a supernatural creature but a circus animal.

Father Gonzaga arrived before seven o'clock, alarmed at the strange news. By that time onlookers less frivolous than those at dawn had already arrived and they were making all kinds of conjectures concerning the captive's future. The simplest among them thought that he should be named mayor of the world. Others of sterner mind felt that he should be promoted to the rank of five-star general in order to win all wars. Some visionaries hoped that he could be put to stud in order to implant the earth a race of winged wise men who could take charge of the universe. But Father Gonzaga, before becoming a priest, had been a robust woodcutter. Standing by the wire, he reviewed his catechism in an instant and asked them to open the door so that he could take a close look at that pitiful man who looked more like a huge decrepit hen among the fascinated chickens. He was lying in the corner drying his open wings in the sunlight among the fruit peels and breakfast leftovers that the early risers had thrown him. Alien to the impertinences of the world, he only lifted his antiquarian eyes and murmured something in his dialect when Father Gonzaga went into the chicken coop and said good morning to him in Latin. The parish priest had his first suspicion of an imposter when he saw that he did not understand the language of God or know how to greet His ministers. Then he noticed that seen close up he was much too human: he had an unbearable smell of the outdoors, the back side of his wings was strewn with parasites and his main feathers had been mistreated by terrestrial winds, and nothing about him measured up to the proud dignity of angels. The he came out of the chicken coop and in a brief sermon warned the curious against the risks of being ingenuous. He reminded them that the devil had the bad habit of making use of carnival tricks in order to confuse the unwary. He argued that if wings were not the essential element in determining the different between a hawk and an airplane, they were even less so in the recognition of angels. Nevertheless, he promised to write a letter to his bishop so that the latter would write his primate so that the latter would write to the Supreme Pontiff in order to get the final verdict from the highest courts.

His prudence fell on sterile hearts. The news of the captive angel spread with such rapidity that after a few hours the courtyard had the bustle of a marketplace and they had to call in troops with fixed bayonets to disperse the mob that was about to knock the house down. Elisenda, her spine all twisted from sweeping up so much marketplace trash, then got the idea of fencing in the yard and charging five cents admission to see the angel.

The curious came from far away. A traveling carnival arrived with a flying acrobat who buzzed over the crowd several times, but no one paid any attention to him because his wings were not those of an angel but, rather, those of a sidereal bat. The most unfortunate invalids on earth came in search of health: a poor woman who since childhood has been counting her heartbeats and had run out of numbers; a Portuguese man who couldn't sleep because the noise of the stars disturbed him; a sleepwalker who got up at night to undo the things he had done while awake; and many others with less serious ailments. In the midst of that shipwreck disorder that made the earth tremble, Pelayo and Elisenda were happy with fatigue, for in less than a week they had crammed their rooms with money and the line of pilgrims waiting their turn to enter still reached beyond the horizon.

The angel was the only one who took no part in his own act. He spent his time trying to get comfortable in his borrowed nest, befuddled by the hellish heat of the oil lamps and sacramental candles that had been placed along the wire. At first they tried to make him eat some mothballs, which, according to the wisdom of the wise neighbor woman, were the food prescribed for angels. But he turned them down, just as he turned down the papal lunches that the pentinents brought him, and they never found out whether it was because he was an angel or because he was an old man that in the end ate nothing but eggplant mush. His only supernatural virtue seemed to be patience. Especially during the first days, when the hens pecked at him, searching for the stellar parasites that proliferated in his wings, and the cripples pulled out feathers to touch their defective parts with, and even the most merciful threw stones at him, trying to get him to rise so they could see him standing. The only time they succeeded in arousing him was when they burned his side with an iron for branding steers, for he had been motionless for so many hours that they thought he was dead. He awoke with a start, ranting in his hermetic language and with tears in his eyes, and he flapped his wings a couple of times, which brought on a whirlwind of chicken dung and lunar dust and a gale of panic that did not seem to be of this world. Although many thought that his reaction had not been one of rage but of pain, from then on they were careful not to annoy him, because the majority understood that his passivity was not that of a her taking his ease but that of a cataclysm in repose.

Father Gonzaga held back the crowd's frivolity with formulas of maidservant inspiration while awaiting the arrival of a final judgment on the nature of the captive. But the mail from Rome showed no sense of urgency. They spent their time finding out if the prisoner had a navel, if his dialect had any connection with Aramaic, how many times he could fit on the head of a pin, or whether he wasn't just a Norwegian with wings. Those meager letters might have come and gone until the end of time if a providential event had not put and end to the priest's tribulations.

It so happened that during those days, among so many other carnival attractions, there arrived in the town the traveling show of the woman who had been changed into a spider for having disobeyed her parents. The admission to see her was not only less than the admission to see the angel, but people were permitted to ask her all manner of questions about her absurd state and to examine her up and down so that no one would ever doubt the truth of her horror. She was a frightful tarantula the size of a ram and with the head of a sad maiden. What was most heartrending, however, was not her outlandish shape but the sincere affliction with which she recounted the details of her misfortune. While still practically a child she had sneaked out of her parents' house to go to a dance, and while she was coming back through the woods after having danced all night without permission, a fearful thunderclap rent the sky in tow and through the crack came the lightning bolt of brimstone that changed her into a spider. Her only nourishment came from the meatballs that chari-table souls chose to toss into her mouth. A spectacle like that, full of so much human truth and with such a fearful lesson, was bound to defeat without even trying that of a haughty angel who scarcely deigned to look at mortals. Besides, the few miracles attrib-uted to the angel showed a certain mental disorder, like the blind man who didn't recover his sight but grew three new teeth, or the paralytic who didn't get to walk but almost won the lottery, and the leper whose sores sprouted sunflowers. Those consolation miracles, which were more like mocking fun, had

already ruined the angel's reputation when the woman who had been changed into a spider finally crushed him completely. That was how Father Gonzaga was cured forever of his insomnia and Pelayo's courtyard went back to being as empty as during the time it had rained for three days and crabs walked through the bedrooms.

The owners of the house had no reason to lament. With the money they saved they built a two-story mansion with balconies and gardens and high netting so that crabs wouldn't get in during the winter, and with iron bars on the windows so that angels wouldn't get in. Pelayo also set up a rabbit warren close to town and have up his job as a bailiff for good, and Elisenda bought some satin pumps with high heels and many dresses of iridescent silk, the kind worn on Sunday by the most desirable women in those times. The chicken coop was the only thing that didn't receive any attention. If they washed it down with creolin and burned tears of myrrh inside it every so often, it was not in homage to the angel but to drive away the dungheap stench that still hung everywhere like a ghost and was turning the new house into an old one. At first, when the child learned to walk, they were careful that he not get too close to the chicken coop. But then they began to lose their fears and got used to the smell, and before they child got his second teeth he'd gone inside the chicken coop to play, where the wires were falling apart. The angel was no less standoffish with him than with the other mortals, but he tolerated the most ingenious infamies with the patience of a dog who had no illusions. They both came down with the chicken pox at the same time. The doctor who took care of the child couldn't resist the temptation to listen to the angel's heart, and he found so much whistling in the heart and so many sounds in his kidneys that it seemed impossible for him to be alive. What surprised him most, however, was the logic of his wings. They seemed so natural on that com-pletely human organism that he couldn't understand why other men didn't have them too.

When the child began school it had been some time since the sun and rain had caused the collapse of the chicken coop. The angel went dragging himself about here and there like a stray dying man. They would drive him out of the bedroom with a broom and a moment later find him in the kitchen. He seemed to be in so many places at the same time that they grew to think that he'd be duplicated, that he was reproducing himself all through the house, and the exasperated and unhinged Elisenda shouted that it was awful living in that hell full of angels. He could scarcely eat and his antiquarian eyes had also become so foggy that he went about bumping into posts. All he had left were the bare cannulae of his last feathers. Pelayo threw a blanket over him and extended him the charity of letting him sleep in the shed, and only then did they notice that he had a temperature at night, and was delirious with the tongue twisters of an old Norwegian. That was one of the few times they became alarmed, for they thought he was going to die and not even the wise neighbor woman had been able to tell them what to do with dead angels.

And yet he not only survived his worst winter, but seemed improved with the first sunny days. He remained motionless for several days in the farthest corner of the courtyard, where no one would see him, and at the beginning of December some large, stiff feathers began to grow on his wings, the feathers of a scarecrow, which looked more like another misfortune of decreptitude. But he must have known the reason for those changes, for he was quite careful that no one should notice them, that no one should hear the sea chanteys that he sometimes sang under the stars. One morning Elisenda was cutting some bunches of onions for lunch when a wind that seemed to come from the high seas blew into the kitchen. Then she went to the window and caught the angel in his first attempts at flight. They were so clumsy that his fingernails opened a furrow in the vegetable patch and he was on the point of knocking the shed down with the ungainly flapping that slipped on the light and couldn't get a grip on the air. But he did manage to gain altitude. Elisenda let out a sigh of relief, for herself and for him, when she watched him pass over the last houses, holding himself up in some way with the risky flapping of a senile vulture. She kept watching him even when she was through cutting the onions and she kept on watching until it was no longer possible for her to see him, because then he was no longer an annoyance in her life but an imaginary dot on the horizon of the sea (salvoblue.homestead.com/wings.html).

Assignments

- Warm-up: What would you do if an angel suddenly appeared in your chicken coop?
- Students should complete Concept Builder 29-B.
- Students should review reading(s) from the next chapter.
- Students should outline essay due at the end of the week.
- Per teacher instructions, students may answer orally, in a group setting, some of the essays that are not assigned as formal essays.

Written material, even a poem, provides the reader with much information. The reader then uses this information to make inferences. What do these images infer?

The night, it is deserted from the mountains to the sea.	*The speaker is alone.*
But I, the one who hugs you,	
A child's tiny feet, Blue, blue with cold, How can they see and not protect you? Oh, my God!	
Man, being blind, ignores that where you step, you leave A blossom of bright light, that where you have placed your bleeding little soles	
How can the people pass, unseeing.	

Magical Realism

Magic realism a genre of fiction in which magical elements blend with the real world. The story explains these magical elements as real occurrences, presented in a straightforward manner that places the "real" and the "fantastic" in the same stream of thought. Within the story itself, fantasy and reality interact until fantasy seems reality, and reality fantasy.

As literary critic Franz Roh writes, "We recognize the world, although now — not only because we have emerged from a dream — we look on it with new eyes. We are offered a new style that is thoroughly of this world, that celebrates the mundane. This new world of objects is still alien to the current idea of realism. It employs various techniques that endow all things with a deeper meaning and reveal mysteries that always threaten the secure tranquility of simple and ingenuous things. This [art offers a] calm admiration of the magic of being, of the discovery that things already have their own faces, [this] means that the ground in which the most diverse ideas in the world can take root has been reconquered — albeit in new ways. For the new art it is a question of representing before our eyes, in an intuitive way, the fact, the interior figure, of the exterior world." (Franz Roh, "Magic Realism: Post-Expressionism" (1925), www.public.asu.edu/~aarios/resourcebank/definitions/.)

Assignments

- Warm-up: What contemporary movie exhibits magic realism?
- Students should complete Concept Builder 29-C.
- Students should write rough draft of assigned essay.
- The teacher may correct rough drafts.

An ode is a sad poem/song of remembrance to honor a loved one. Read "An Ode to a Cricket" by Jim Stobaugh, then write your ode to a beloved cricket. It must be at least ten lines long.

Oh little cricket!
We miss you so.
Your steady hum
Is gone forever!
Oh little one.
Where is your hum?
It greeted us on the morning.
Said good-bye to us in the afternoon.
Hum, hum, hum.
What took you from us?
A thoughtless student tennis shoe?

A cold autumn breeze?
Miss girl cricket?
We don't know but . . .
We miss you so.
Oh little cricket.

Your ode to a cricket:

Student Essay

Gabriela Mistral completed many accomplishments in her life. She was a schoolteacher, a poet, was the Chilean consul in three European countries, participated in the cultural committee of the League of Nations and above all, she was the first female Latin American to receive a Nobel Prize. Sadly, although her poetry is sprinkled with an obvious desire for children, one accomplishment she would never achieve was motherhood. However, because of this she is able to write beautiful poems giving encouragement to others who have also suffered from disappointment sometime in their life.

In her poem "I Am Not Alone," Mistral depicts a caring mother who is reminding a little child in the darkness of night, that even when the world seems deserted, the child is not abandoned.

. . . The world is deserted.

All flesh is sad you see.

But I, the one who hugs you,

I am not alone!

The poem brilliantly portrays the comforting warmth of the mother's embrace, which penetrates through the shadows of night like a candle. And interestingly, not only is the child comforted by the mother, the mother also gains encouragement and strength by being with the child.

Another powerful example of Mistral's encouragement to others is seen in "Those Who Do Not Dance." The poem is written to those who have a handicap and feel as though they can not participate in the activities of others.

A crippled child

Said, "How shall I dance?"

Let your heart dance

We said.

Then the invalid said:

"How shall I sing?"

Let your heart sing

We said. . . .

The poem ends saying the entire valley is "dancing together under the sun." It reminds the reader to look at the world through other perspectives. She seems to be saying that instead of just limiting "dancing" to movement, one should view it as an action that can not only take place through the body, but through the heart as well. It expresses a wonderful picture of the beauty of God's creation as a whole. This takes on great meaning, especially to those who might not be as talented in certain areas as others are.

Even in her poem "Tiny Feet," which tells the story of a neglected child, Mistral offers hope. Although the child walks through the cold, with torn and weary feet, it is followed by a bright light, indicating a greater unseen plan for the child.

Since, however, you walk

through the streets so straight,

you are courageous, without fault. . . .

Although the child walks alone, apparently unnoticed, someone sees and notices the courage that shines through even during desperate times.

Gabriela Mistral was a Christian, and must have sought much comfort from God and His Word, overflowing into her poetry. "I Am Not Alone" almost parallels the 23rd Psalm:

Yea, though I walk through the valley of the shadow of death, I will fear no evil: for thou art with me; thy rod and thy staff they comfort me (Psalm 23:4; KJV).

Perhaps Mistral's belief in a sovereign God is what allowed Mistral to take feelings of emptiness, such as an abandoned child, handicaps, or the darkness of night, and still finds the good in the situation, giving the characters — and the reader — a sense of faith that their situation will get better, and that there is a purpose there for them. (Lauren)

Assignments

- Warm-up: To what extent is Mistral making political statements with her poetry?
- Students should complete Concept Builder 29-D.
- Student will re-write corrected copies of essay due tomorrow.

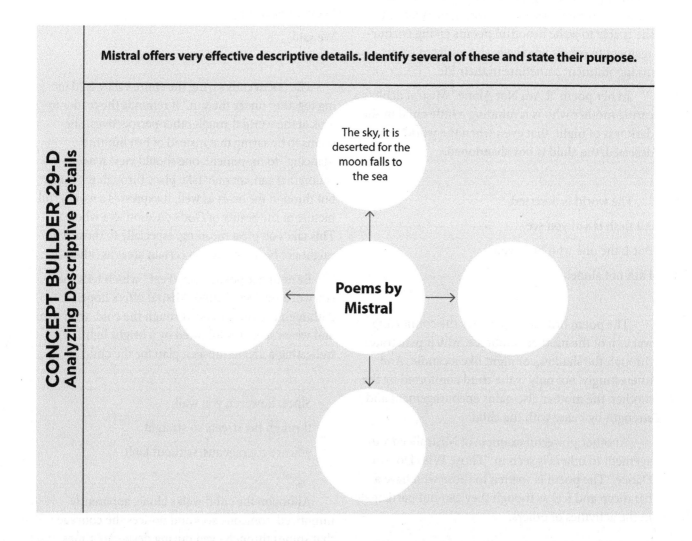

CONCEPT BUILDER 29-D
Analyzing Descriptive Details

Mistral offers very effective descriptive details. Identify several of these and state their purpose.

The sky, it is deserted for the moon falls to the sea

Poems by Mistral

Student Essay

Gabriel García Márquez wrote "A Very Old Man with Enormous Wings" in 1968. It is a story about a family who finds an old man lying in the mud outside their house. The man has wings, and the people take him to be an angel. They keep the angel with them, first locked in a chicken coop and then around the house, until one day he flies away. Márquez wrote this story using magic realism, a style of writing that contains supernatural elements while depicting things plainly as they appear without focusing extensively on emotions. Three examples of magic realism in the story are the angel, the spider woman, and the miracles of the people's ailments.

The angel's appearance in the story is a fantastic element, but he is depicted as a simple man with wings. Instead of describing the angel with qualities that people would normally associate with angels, Márquez chose to plainly state the simple facts.

[Pelayo and Elisenda] looked at the fallen body with a mute stupor. He was dressed like a ragpicker. There were only a few faded hairs left on his bald skull and very few teeth in his mouth, and his pitiful condition of a drenched great-grandfather took away any sense of grandeur he might have had. His huge buzzard wings, dirty and half-plucked were forever entangled in the mud.

Because he is using magic realism, Márquez didn't even bother to address the question of who he was, where he came from, or how he got there. He only wrote of what the people saw.

In the case of the spider woman, Márquez did write about who the woman used to be. When she was very young, she sneaked out of her house against her parents' permission to go to a dance. On the way back home, she was struck with a "lightning bolt of brimstone" that changed her into a huge spider. Once again, there is no explanation of why or how she was transformed, only the events that occurred and her appearance.

Another example of magic realism in "A Very Old Man with Enormous Wings" is the miracle ailments of the people who went to see the angel. They thought that by touching him or by rubbing his feathers on them they would be cured. Instead, unusual miracles occurred.

Besides, the few miracles attributed to the angel showed a certain mental disorder, like the blind man who didn't recover his sight but grew three new teeth, or the paralytic who didn't get to walk but almost won the lottery, and the leper whose sores sprouted sunflowers. Those consolation miracles, which were more like mocking fun, had already ruined the angel's reputation when the woman who had been changed into a spider finally crushed him completely.

As is characteristic of this story, these strange happenings are described as commonplace. Instead of being fantastic abilities that the angel possessed, they are merely a side-note.

By his use of magic realism, Márquez trivialized supernatural occurrences and made them ordinary and realistic. By describing the angel, spider woman, and miracles that affected people in the way that he did, Márquez turned an unbelievable story into one that, aside from outlandish events, almost seems normal. (Kory)

- Warm-up: To what effect does Marquez use magic realism?
- Students should complete Concept Builder 29-E.
- Essays are due. Students should take the chapter 29 test.

CONCEPT BUILDER 29-E
Keen Observers

Mistral is a keen observer of her surroundings. She is always on the lookout for things, images that connect with an idea. By giving these images — tiny feet — she communicates a ton of information.

In the following poem by Emily Dickinson, notice how a small, insignificant event deeply affected her. A simple event — a bird walking down a walk — becomes a metaphor for Dickinson's life.

A bird came down the walk:
He did not know I saw;
He bit an angle-worm in halves
And ate the fellow, raw.

And then he drank a dew
From a convenient grass,
And then hopped sidewise to the wall
To let a beetle pass.

He glanced with rapid eyes
That hurried all abroad, —
They looked like frightened beads, I thought;
He stirred his velvet head

Like one in danger; cautious,
I offered him a crumb,
And he unrolled his feathers
And rowed him softer home

Than oars divide the ocean,
Too silver for a seam,
Or butterflies, off banks of noon,
Leap, splashless, as they swim.

Remember two seemingly insignificant events that changed your life.

Event	Details	My Own Thoughts
Last Thanksgiving my grandmother told me how much she loved me. I did not know it, but she was dying of cancer. She did not live until Christmas.	My grandmother was looking right at me and she smiled as she said, "I really love you!"	I remember thinking how strange that was. My grandmother does not normally tell me she loves me at the end of a meal! I remember enjoying the thought of her love, but I did not think anything about it. How I wish I would have told her that I loved her, too!

Chapter 30

(1890–Present):
Modern Age (Part 2)

First Thoughts

Selma Ottiliana Lovisa Lagerlöf (1858–1940) was born in Marbacka, Sweden, in 1858. She had been writing poetry ever since she was a child, but she did not publish anything until 1890, when a Swedish newspaper gave her the first prize in a literary competition and published excerpts from her first novel, *Gösta Berlings Saga*. After several minor works she published *Jerusalem*, but it was with *The Wonderful Adventures of Nils*, a book for children, that she became recognized worldwide. *The Löwenskölds Ring*, one of her best psychological novels, was written in 1925. She was awarded the Nobel Prize in Literature in 1909.

Chapter Learning Objectives

In chapter 30 we read the works of the first female to win the Nobel Prize. It is a story of generational sin, but, indirectly, a story of redemption.

As a result of this chapter study you will be able to . . .

1. Discuss the narrative technique in *The Löwenskölds Ring*.

2. Analyze the purpose of General Löwenskölds' ring.

3. List the themes in the novel.

4. Generational sin is a popular subject. Give at least one other example and draw parallels between the two works.

5. Discuss Marit Eriksdotter and her purpose in the novel.

Weekly Essay Options: Begin on page 273 of the Teacher Guide.

Reading ahead: *The Stranger* by Albert Camus.

431

Student Essay:
Themes in *The Löwenskölds Ring*

Even though *The Löwenskölds Ring* is part of a three-book trilogy written by Selma Lagerlöf, it is a complete story in itself. Several well-developed themes emerge and confirm this.

The Löwenskölds Ring opens with the death of a well-admired general, who wears a golden ring on his left ring finger. This grand general is greatly admired by the townspeople. "That same old general gave the Lowenskolds their name, property and title, and as long as any of them were still living at Hedeby his portrait hung between the windows in the large upstairs drawing room. The huge painting extended from the floor to ceiling, and at first glance you took it to be no less than Charles the Twelfth himself, in a blue greatcoat and huge chamois gloves, his enormous cavalry boots placed firmly on the checkerboard floor; but when you moved closer you could see quite plainly that this was an entirely different kind of man" (Lagerlöf 7–8). Upon first glance of the picture, a viewer may have imagined the man in the portrait as a great ruler, or perhaps a king. But upon closer examination, the man's identity is seen, and the reader sees that all men, regardless of how great they may be in man's eyes, are really just men. "In any case, the longer you looked at the painting, the more you accepted the man's appearance" (Lagerlöf 8). This is the first theme of *The Löwenskölds Ring*. Although most of the characters throughout the story view the general with much respect, nearly as much respect as would be given to a king, the narrator reminds the reader that the general was human. The villagers and various paintings portrayed the general as a king-like figure, with respect and command over all. However, in reality, this man was just an ordinary person, despite his greatness, stature, power, or might. He was not a better man, but just an everyday person put in an esteemed and respected position.

The second theme emerges once the general's ring is stolen by Bard Bardsson. "Since the theft of the ring, he has led a totally lonely life of Job-like trials and tribulations, and now wants to repent before he dies" (Lagerlöf 110). In the afterword, following the story, Bard's life after stealing the ring is seen in great detail and its events confirm how sin affects multiple people. Bard's house burned down, he lost his livestock, his crops were destroyed, and his wife committed suicide, almost exactly what happened to the biblical character of Job. He had thought the ring would bring many benefits to his family, but it did the opposite, and brought much suffering and disaster upon Bard's family and possessions. The consequences of Bard's sins spread quickly and many were affected.

But Bard was not the only individual to suffer from the robbery. Later, as the general's son is searching for the thief, he captures three men. These men are "tried" through dice rolling. The idea was that the individual who rolled the lowest roll would be guilty. However, all men roll double sixes and leave innocent. However, they are later arrested and hung after an edict stated their rolls meant death. These men are another example of how sin affects other individuals than just the sinner. These men were, in fact, innocent, but Bard's sin resulted in them losing their lives. Once again, other people than Bard were affected by Bard's robbery.

The author may not have intended, but the three innocent men, who rolled dice, serve vital roles in a theme besides the idea of sin affecting individuals. This theme deals with whether or not man can determine his own fate. "At the physical middle of the story and at its thematic core as well, is a scene, depicted with masterful subtlety and irony, which epitomizes all the previous innuendos with regard to our human difficulty in claiming responsibility for our actions, and accepting the extent to which we determine our own fate" (Lagerlöf 112). The afterword to the 1991 Norvik Press edition of *The Lowenskold Ring* speaks of this theme and the scene from which the theme is derived. This scene is the same scene as above, where the three men are rolling dice to see who is guilty. "Then the sheriff picked up the dice and requested that the judge and several others roll them to check that they were all right. . . . These tiny objects that had been the undoing of so many men, were they now to be seen as worthy of interpreting the will of God? (Lagerlöf 58–59). Because neither the thief had admitted his crime, nor the thief had been captured, the sheriff and judge decided to take control of the situation. They believed dice could reveal the thief, but this "simple" method failed. The men had all rolled double-sixes, and according to the judge and the sheriff, were thus innocent. However, things soon changed.

Although the three men had initially been "proven" innocent by the dice, their fate was changed. The authorities in the city of Stockholm issued a statement clearly stating the three men were not innocent, but in fact guilty. Thus, the men were hanged.

Lagerlof uses this scene to demonstrate how man cannot determine his own fate. The three men, when they were rolling the dice, probably thought they were in sole control of what happened next. However, as seen above, these men's rolls were overruled by the authorities in Stockholm. This hints at the absurdity of man thinking he controls his own destiny. Men seem to forget outside forces such as other people, or God, play a major role in determining fate. Man is not in sole control of himself, but is just one factor in the realm of factors.

Such three powerful themes emerge in *The Löwenskölds Ring*. After the ring is stolen, great evil comes upon the thief, his family, his possessions, and multiple other individuals, hinting at how sin affects not just the sinner, but those around him. In addition, the author dispels the views of grandeur and magnificence of the general, showing him to be an ordinary man put in a special position. Finally, the dice rolling and the edict from Stockholm demonstrate how man cannot control his own fate, but is affected by outside forces beyond one's control. And all three rings caused by a simple act of robbery. (Chris)

Assignments

- Warm-up: Do you believe in generational curses?
- Students should complete Concept Builder 30-A.
- Students should review the required reading(s) *before* the assigned chapter begins.
- Teachers may want to discuss assigned reading(s) with students.
- Teachers shall assign the required essay. The rest of the essays can be outlined, answered with shorter answers, discussed, or skipped.
- Students will review all readings for chapter 30.

Discuss the narrative technique in *The Löwensköld Ring* and why the author employs it.

Omniscient Narration

First Person

First person allows the author to personalize the tale and thereby quickly involve the reader in the story.

The Wonderful Adventures of Nils
Selma Lagerlöf

Lagerlöf wrote *The Wonderful Adventures of Nils* when she was commissioned to do so from the National Teachers Association in 1902 to write a geography reader for the public schools. "She devoted three years to nature study and to familiarizing herself with animal and bird life. She has sought out hitherto unpublished folklore and legends of the different provinces. These she has ingeniously woven into her story." (From translator Velma Swanston Howard's introduction.)

THE ELF

Sunday, March twentieth

Once there was a boy. He was — let us say — something like fourteen years old; long and loose-jointed and towheaded. He wasn't good for much, that boy. His chief delight was to eat and sleep; and after that — he liked best to make mischief.

It was a Sunday morning and the boy's parents were getting ready to go to church. The boy sat on the edge of the table, in his shirt sleeves, and thought how lucky it was that both father and mother were going away, and the coast would be clear for a couple of hours. "Good! Now I can take down pop's gun and fire off a shot, without anybody's meddling interference," he said to himself.

But it was almost as if father should have guessed the boy's thoughts, for just as he was on the threshold — ready to start — he stopped short, and turned toward the boy. "Since you won't come to church with mother and me," he said, "the least you can do, is to read the service at home. Will you promise to do so?" "Yes," said the boy, "that I can do easy enough." And he thought, of course, that he wouldn't read any more than he felt like reading.

The boy thought that never had he seen his mother so persistent. In a second she was over by the shelf near the fireplace, and took down Luther's Commentary and laid it on the table, in front of the window — opened at the service for the day. She also

Image from the cover of *The Wonderful Adventures of Nils*. Art by Mary Hamilton Frye, 1906 (PD-US).

opened the New Testament, and placed it beside the Commentary. Finally, she drew up the big arm-chair,

435

which was bought at the parish auction the year before, and which, as a rule, no one but father was permitted to occupy.

The boy sat thinking that his mother was giving herself altogether too much trouble with this spread; for he had no intention of reading more than a page or so. But now, for the second time, it was almost as if his father were able to see right through him. He walked up to the boy, and said in a severe tone: "Now, remember, that you are to read carefully! For when we come back, I shall question you thoroughly; and if you have skipped a single page, it will not go well with you."

"The service is fourteen and a half pages long," said his mother, just as if she wanted to heap up the measure of his misfortune. "You'll have to sit down and begin the reading at once, if you expect to get through with it."

With that they departed. And as the boy stood in the doorway watching them, he thought that he had been caught in a trap. "There they go congratulating themselves, I suppose, in the belief that they've hit upon something so good that I'll be forced to sit and hang over the sermon the whole time that they are away," thought he.

But his father and mother were certainly not congratulating themselves upon anything of the sort; but, on the contrary, they were very much distressed. They were poor farmers, and their place was not much bigger than a garden-plot. When they first moved there, the place couldn't feed more than one pig and a pair of chickens; but they were uncommonly industrious and capable folk — and now they had both cows and geese. Things had turned out very well for them; and they would have gone to church that beautiful morning — satisfied and happy — if they hadn't had their son to think of. Father complained that he was dull and lazy; he had not cared to learn anything at school, and he was such an all-round good-for-nothing, that he could barely be made to tend geese. Mother did not deny that this was true; but she was most distressed because he was wild and bad; cruel to animals, and ill-willed toward human beings. "May God soften his hard heart, and give him a better disposition!" said the mother, "or else he will be a misfortune, both to himself and to us."

The boy stood for a long time and pondered whether he should read the service or not. Finally, he came to the conclusion that, this time, it was best to be obedient. He seated himself in the easy chair, and began to read. But when he had been rattling away in an undertone for a little while, this mumbling seemed to have a soothing effect upon him — and he began to nod.

It was the most beautiful weather outside! It was only the twentieth of March; but the boy lived in West Vemminghög Township, down in Southern Skåne, where the spring was already in full swing. It was not as yet green, but it was fresh and budding. There was water in all the trenches, and the colt's-foot on the edge of the ditch was in bloom. All the weeds that grew in among the stones were brown and shiny. The beech-woods in the distance seemed to swell and grow thicker with every second. The skies were high — and a clear blue. The cottage door stood ajar, and the lark's trill could be heard in the room. The hens and geese pattered about in the yard, and the cows, who felt the spring air away in their stalls, lowed their approval every now and then.

The boy read and nodded and fought against drowsiness. "No! I don't want to fall asleep," thought he, "for then I'll not get through with this thing the whole forenoon."

But — somehow — he fell asleep.

He did not know whether he had slept a short while, or a long while; but he was awakened by hearing a slight noise back of him.

On the window-sill, facing the boy, stood a small looking-glass; and almost the entire cottage could be seen in this. As the boy raised his head, he happened to look in the glass; and then he saw that the cover to his mother's chest had been opened.

His mother owned a great, heavy, iron-bound oak chest, which she permitted no one but herself to open. Here she treasured all the things she had inherited from her mother, and of these she was especially careful. Here lay a couple of old-time peasant dresses, of red homespun cloth, with short bodice and plaited shirt, and a pearl-bedecked breast pin. There were starched white-linen head-dresses, and heavy silver ornaments and chains. Folks don't care to go about dressed like that in these days, and several times his mother had thought of getting rid of the old things; but somehow, she hadn't had the heart to do it.

Now the boy saw distinctly — in the glass — that the chest-lid was open. He could not understand how this had happened, for his mother had closed the chest before she went away. She never would have left that precious chest open when he was at home, alone.

He became low-spirited and apprehensive. He was afraid that a thief had sneaked his way into the cottage. He didn't dare to move; but sat still and stared into the looking-glass.

While he sat there and waited for the thief to make his appearance, he began to wonder what that dark shadow was which fell across the edge of the chest. He looked and looked — and did not want to believe his eyes. But the thing, which at first seemed shadowy, became more and more clear to him; and soon he saw that it was something real. It was no less a thing than an elf who sat there — astride the edge of the chest!

To be sure, the boy had heard stories about elves, but he had never dreamed that they were such tiny creatures. He was no taller than a hand's breadth — this one, who sat on the edge of the chest. He had an old, wrinkled and beardless face, and was dressed in a black frock coat, knee-breeches and a broad-brimmed black hat. He was very trim and smart, with his white laces about the throat and wrist-bands, his buckled shoes, and the bows on his garters. He had taken from the chest an embroidered piece, and sat and looked at the old-fashioned handiwork with such an air of veneration, that he did not observe the boy had awakened.

The boy was somewhat surprised to see the elf, but, on the other hand, he was not particularly frightened. It was impossible to be afraid of one who was so little. And since the elf was so absorbed in his own thoughts that he neither saw nor heard, the boy thought that it would be great fun to play a trick on him; to push him over into the chest and shut the lid on him, or something of that kind.

But the boy was not so courageous that he dared to touch the elf with his hands, instead he looked around the room for something to poke him with. He let his gaze wander from the sofa to the leaf-table; from the leaf-table to the fireplace. He looked at the kettles, then at the coffee-urn, which stood on a shelf, near the fireplace; on the water bucket near the door; and on the spoons and knives and forks and saucers and plates, which could be seen through the half-open cupboard door. He looked at his father's gun, which hung on the wall, beside the portrait of the Danish royal family, and on the geraniums and fuchsias, which blossomed in the window. And last, he caught sight of an old butterfly-snare that hung on the window frame. He had hardly set eyes on that butterfly-snare, before he reached over and snatched it and jumped up and swung it alongside the edge of the chest. He was himself astonished at the luck he had. He hardly knew how he had managed it — but he had actually snared the elf. The poor little chap lay, head downward, in the bottom of the long snare, and could not free himself.

The first moment the boy hadn't the least idea what he should do with his prize. He was only particular to swing the snare backward and forward; to prevent the elf from getting a foothold and clambering up.

The elf began to speak, and begged, oh! so pitifully, for his freedom. He had brought them good luck — these many years — he said, and deserved better treatment. Now, if the boy would set him free, he would give him an old coin, a silver spoon, and a gold penny, as big as the case on his father's silver watch.

The boy didn't think that this was much of an offer; but it so happened — that after he had gotten the elf in his power, he was afraid of him. He felt that he had entered into an agreement with something weird and uncanny; something which did not belong to his world, and he was only too glad to get rid of the horrid thing.

For this reason he agreed at once to the bargain, and held the snare still, so the elf could crawl out of it. But when the elf was almost out of the snare, the boy happened to think that he ought to have bargained for large estates, and all sorts of good things. He should at least have made this stipulation: that the elf must conjure the sermon into his head. "What a fool I was to let him go!" thought he, and began to shake the snare violently, so the elf would tumble down again.

But the instant the boy did this, he received such a stinging box on the ear, that he thought his head would fly in pieces. He was dashed — first against one wall, then against the other; he sank to the floor, and lay there — senseless.

When he awoke, he was alone in the cottage. The chest-lid was down, and the butterfly-snare hung in its usual place by the window. If he had not felt how the right cheek burned, from that box on the ear, he would have been tempted to believe the whole thing had been a dream. "At any rate, father and mother will be sure to insist that it was nothing else," thought he. "They are not likely to make any allowances for that old sermon, on account of the elf. It's best for me to get at that reading again," thought he.

But as he walked toward the table, he noticed something remarkable. It couldn't be possible that the cottage had grown. But why was he obliged to take so many more steps than usual to get to the table? And what was the matter with the chair? It looked no bigger than it did a while ago; but now he had to step on the rung first, and then clamber up in order to reach the seat. It was the same thing with the table. He could not look over the top without climbing to the arm of the chair.

"What in all the world is this?" said the boy. "I believe the elf has bewitched both the armchair and the table — and the whole cottage."

The Commentary lay on the table and, to all appearances, it was not changed; but there must have been something queer about that too, for he could not manage to read a single word of it, without actually standing right in the book itself.

He read a couple of lines, and then he chanced to look up. With that, his glance fell on the looking-glass; and then he cried aloud: "Look! There's another one!"

For in the glass he saw plainly a little, little creature who was dressed in a hood and leather breeches.

"Why, that one is dressed exactly like me!" said the boy, and clasped his hands in astonishment. But then he saw that the thing in the mirror did the same thing. Then he began to pull his hair and pinch his arms and swing round; and instantly he did the same thing after him; he, who was seen in the mirror.

The boy ran around the glass several times, to see if there wasn't a little man hidden behind it, but he found no one there; and then he began to shake with terror. For now he understood that the elf had bewitched him, and that the creature whose image he saw in the glass — was he, himself (www.gutenberg.org/cache/epub/10935/pg10935.html).

Assignments

- Warm-up: What is the lesson Lagerlof is teaching in "The Elf"?
- Students should complete Concept Builder 30-B.
- Students should review reading(s) from the next chapter.
- Students should outline essay due at the end of the week.
- Per teacher instructions, students may answer orally, in a group setting, some of the essays that are not assigned as formal essays.

Who is Marit Eriksdotter and what is her purpose in the novel?

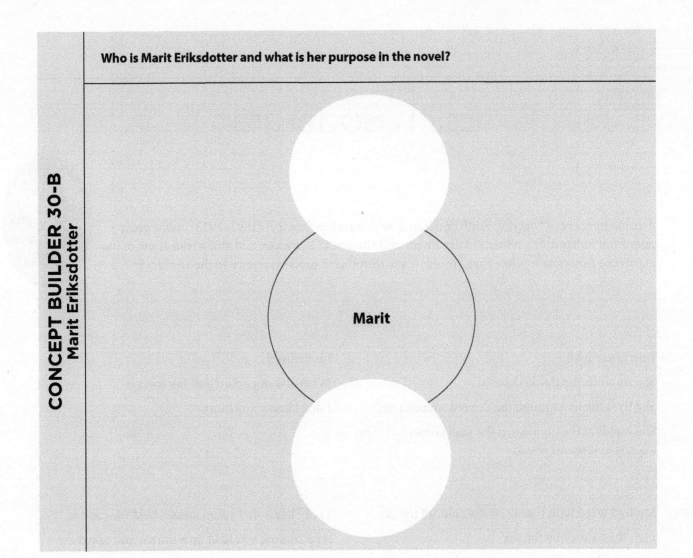

Marit

Edith Södergran

A contemporary of Lagerlöf, Edith Södergran, who wrote in Swedish (1892–1923), was a great poet from Finland. She refused to use rhyme and rhythm in her verse, and along with some of the expatriate Americans — like Ezra Pound — she introduced modern poetry to the world.

Pain Governs All

Pain governs all,
She smooths the thinker's brow,
She fixes the jewel round the desired woman's neck,
She stands at the door when the man comes out from
his beloved . . .
What else does pain give her lovers?
I don't know any more.

www.kirjasto.sci.fi/sodergra.htm.

Love

My soul was a light blue dress the color of the sky;
I left it on a rock by the sea
and naked I came to you, looking like a woman.
And like a woman I sat at your table
and drank a toast in wine, inhaling the scent of
some roses.
You found me beautiful, like something you saw in
a dream,
I forgot everything, I forgot my childhood and my
homeland,
I only knew that your caresses held me captive.
And smiling you held up a mirror and asked me
to look.
I saw that my shoulders were made of dust and
crumbled away,
I saw that my beauty was sick and wished only to —
disappear.
Oh, hold me tight in your arms so close that
I need nothing.

www.poemhunter.com/poem/love-1956/.

Assignments

- Warm-up: From these two poems, what is Södergran's favorite subject matter?
- Students should complete Concept Builder 30-C.
- Students should write rough draft of assigned essay.
- The teacher may correct rough drafts.

What two themes clash in this novel?

Student Essay: Redemptive Theme

The Löwenskölds Ring, written by Selma Lagerlöf, tells the story of the Lowenskold family and their heirloom ring, which is passed down from generation to generation. However, after the ring is stolen from General Lowenskold's grave, a never-ending series of disasters plagues the Lowenskolds over several generations. *The Löwenskölds Ring* has several very important themes, including generational sin, greed, and forgiveness.

Generational sin is perhaps the most dominant theme in this novel. All characters, innocent and guilty, suffer from the Löwensköld tragedy. Bard Bardsson, the first character introduced, seems to be an honest, simple man, with good intentions on his mind. After noticing that the general's burial vault is open, Bardsson is plagued by the fear that someone will walk in and rob the body. He and his wife go to the vault, intending to make sure no one takes the Löwensköld ring:

> They stood irresolute and at a loss what to do, staring down into the vault. They ought, indeed, to have gone home now, but something mysterious, which neither of them dare to allude to, kept them rooted to the spot. . . . They raised the lid, and then it was impossible to restrain their longing for the treasure. They took the ring off the withered finger, replaced the lid on the coffin, and stole out of the vault in dead silence."

Bardsson's actions set off a chain of disaster that haunts over three generations, including the execution of three innocent men and the destruction of relationships. Tragically, even those innocent people who are not related to the Löwenskölds undergo consequences. The general's ghost haunts one housekeeper, several women lose their husbands in strange accidents, and the town is generally plagued with a mysterious, oppressive force.

The same "mysterious" force that drew Bardsson and his wife into the vault captivates the General's own nephew, the Baron. The ring is truly a cursed object:

> For the first time, the young baron saw the general's features. It was the face of an old man — he recognized it at once from the portrait in the drawing room. But there was none of the peacefulness of death there — a furious greed shone in the eyes, and on the lips trembled an uncanny smile of triumph and of certainty of victory. . . . He was overwhelmed with terror. In unreflecting anguish, he dashed open the door of his parents' room and . . . cried out: "Father! Mother! The General!" and fell on the floor in a dead swoon.

After the disasters have finally run their course, it is up to the next generation to rebuild. Characters such as Karl Arthur, General Löwensköld's grandson, are forced to sacrifice love, happiness, and safety for the Löwensköld ring.

Greed also ties into Lagerlof's idea of generational sin. General Löwensköld is the epitome of greed, for it is he who executes three men who have been proven innocent:

> "Paul Eliasson has thrown double sixes, which is the highest throw!"
> Then arose a great commotion among the crowd, but no rejoicing. No one believed that there had been any fraud about the matter — that was impossible — but everyone was uneasy, for the judgment of God

had not been clearly manifest. Were all three prisoners equally innocent? . . . Captain Lowenskold was seen to hurry excitedly toward the judge. He was trying to explain that nothing had been decided; but the judge turned brusquely away from him.

In the end, the truly innocent men are executed, for the General Löwensköld is very keen on having someone pay for wronging him, whether it is the guilty party or not. In his mind, blaming someone is the only thing that will settle this dispute. His authority has been insulted, and the general is determined to make someone pay.

In spite of all the disturbing themes in *The Löwenskölds Ring*, there is a very redemptive theme: forgiveness. In the case of Marit, the daughter of Eric Ivasson, there is great redemption. Thirty years after the wrongful execution of her father, fiancée, and brother, ironically her son has made friends with a Lowenskold. He approaches Marit:

Marit looked at Adrian Löwensköld, a handsome boy with a gentle, friendly expression. Her heart began to beat — she always felt hurt and frightened when she saw a Löwensköld. (Julia)

Assignments

- Warm-up: In what way does this book have a hint of redemption?
- Students should complete Concept Builder 30-D.
- Students will re-write corrected copies of essay due tomorrow.

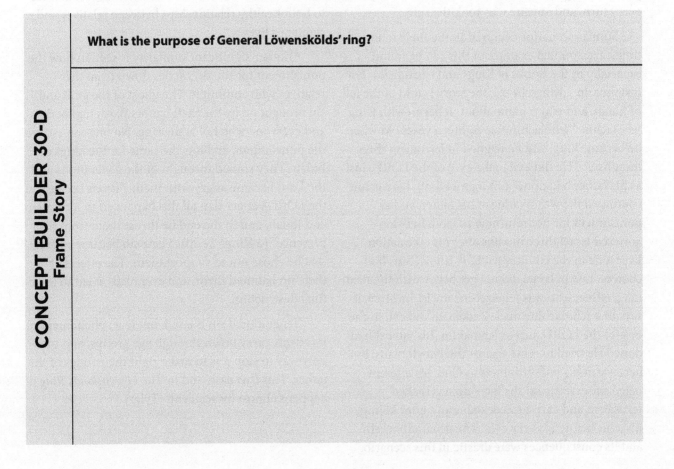

CONCEPT BUILDER 30-D
Frame Story

What is the purpose of General Löwenskölds' ring?

Student Essay: Generational Sin

In the book *The Löwenskölds Ring*, Bard Bardsson robs the grave of a very famous general under King Charles the Twelfth. The tomb contained an extremely valuable ring, worth an entire estate, that the general had wanted buried with him. After the crime was exposed as Bard lay dying, his son Ingilbert, though he had never done such a thing before, stole the ring for a second time, and carried it with him until he was discovered. This was generational sin, as two generations of the same family committed the same crime. With the crime, however, came the punishment, for both age groups. The ghost of the general was said to haunt the family at every turn, and anyone who took the ring.

Similar scenarios occurred in the Bible many times. Exceptional example of this can be found especially in the Books of Kings and Chronicles. For instance, in 2 Kings 14–25, the story is told of the fall of Judah, and why it came about. It began with King Jehoiachin: "Jehoiachin was eighteen years old when he became king, and he reigned in Jerusalem three months. . . . He did evil in the eyes of the LORD, just as his father had done" (2 Kings 24:8–9). Jehoiachin continued the wrongdoing of his father, and as punishment for not returning to God, Babylon annexed Israel three months after his coronation. Everyone in the country paid for Jehoiachin's bad choices. Life in Israel did not get better with the next king, either, who was Jehoiachin's uncle. In 24:19, it says that Jehoiachin's uncle Zedekiah "did evil in the eyes of the LORD, just as Jehoiakim [his father] had done." He tried to rebel against the Babylonians, but because of his unfaithfulness to God, his attempt failed miserably, and the Babylonians sacked Jerusalem and carried Zedekiah away, after killing his sons before his very eyes. The generational sin and its consequences were drastic in this scenario.

Although in scale the stories are very different, there are some important connections between the two. The first is how easily sin is transmitted between generations. Ingilbert had never stolen anything, he was a quite normal person, but upon hearing of the wrong of his father, he committed the same wrong without a second thought! The same happened with Jehoiachin, his father Jehoiakim, and his uncle Zedekiah. They continued down their sinful path, without regard for God. It doesn't seem to make sense, since good would come from repentance, but it shows just how powerful family connections and ideas are. Family values are critical to both healthy relationships between relatives and righteous lives.

Another significant similarity is seen in how the punishment for the sin carries down from the relatives who commit it. The ghost of the guilt and sin brought on by the theft haunts Bard, Ingilbert, and everyone who holds the ring. No one can escape the punishment, and it is the same for the kings of Judah. They sinned throughout the generations and the Lord became angry with them. "It was because of the LORD's anger that all this happened to Jerusalem and Judah, and in the end he thrust them from his presence" (2 Kings 24:20). Their sin became so great that he chose not to support them. The effects of their sin haunted them, and eventually it led to their final destruction.

Generational sin is a sad, but true, phenomenon. Its effects carry down through age groups, and the only way to stop it is to make right the wrongs of the father. This isn't easy, and in *The Löwenskölds Ring* it happens almost by accident. (Tyler)

Assignments

- Warm-up: What is generational sin and is it real?
- Students should complete Concept Builder 30-E.
- Essays are due. Students should take the chapter 30 test.

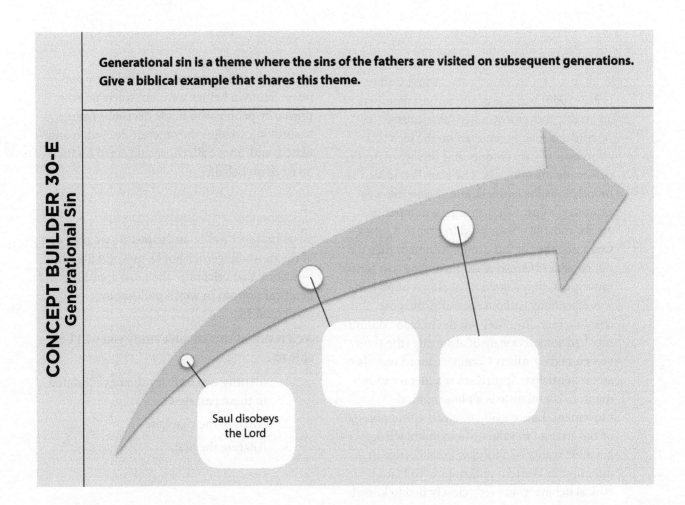

CONCEPT BUILDER 30-E
Generational Sin

Generational sin is a theme where the sins of the fathers are visited on subsequent generations. Give a biblical example that shares this theme.

Saul disobeys the Lord

Chapter 31

(1890–Present)
Modern Age (Part 3)

First Thoughts Albert Camus (1913–1960) was one of the earliest members of an artistic movement called "absurdism." Absurdism mainly centered on the idea that awareness of the certainty and finality of death makes life meaningless. The post-World War II mood of disillusionment and skepticism was expressed in peculiar terms by a number of artists, most of whom lived in France. Camus was a member of this group. Although they did not consider themselves as belonging to a formal movement, they shared a belief that human life was essentially without meaning, purpose, and absolute morality. They felt the human community had sunk to a state of absurdity (the term was coined by Albert Camus). Camus was also an existentialist. Absurdism is a literary movement. Existentialism is a philosophical movement. Existentialism rejects epistemology or the attempt to validate human knowledge as a basis for reality — a fundamental change in direction in Western philosophy. To Plato, ethical behavior was very closely tied to knowledge. Plato argued that if one knew the right thing to do, one would do it. Existentialism argued that that was not so. People made decisions based on need and function rather than knowledge. People were quite capable of making an evil decision if it suited their purposes. Human beings were not solely or even primarily people who made decisions from a basis of knowledge; they merely desired, manipulated, and, above all, chose and acted on their own selfish behalf.

Chapter Learning Objectives
In chapter 31 we read one of the most dangerous books in world literature — a book that celebrates the most appealing and heretical notions in world philosophy: existentialism.

As a result of this chapter study you will be able to . . .

1. Identify two or three themes exhibited in these passages.

2. Analyze the chaplain.

3. Analyze the plot.

Weekly Essay Options: Begin on page 273 of the Teacher Guide.

Reading ahead: *All Quiet on the Western Front* by Erich Maria Remarque.

History connections: *World History* chapter 31, "World War I: A World Tragedy."

Existentialism

Camus was an existentalist. Existentialism, in the spirit of Immanual Kant, bases reality on subjectivity, not on epistemology (knowledge) or metaphysics (religion). Existentialism rejects epistemology or the attempt to validate human knowledge as a basis for reality — a fundamental change in direction in Western philosophy.

He seemed so certain about everything, didn't he? And yet none of his certainties was worth one hair of a woman's head. He wasn't even sure he was alive, because he was living like a dead man. Whereas it looked as if I was the one who'd come up empty handed. But I was sure about me, about everything, surer than he could ever be, sure of my life and sure of the death I had waiting for me. Yes, that was all I had. But at least I had as much of a hold on it as it had on me. I had been right, I was still right, I was always right. I had lived my life as one way and I could just as well have lived it another. I had done this and I hadn't done that. And so? It was as if I had waited all this time for this moment and for the first light of this dawn to be vindicated. Nothing, nothing mattered, and I knew why. So did he. Throughout the whole absurd life I'd lived, a dark wind had been rising toward me from somewhere deep in my future, across years that were still to come, and as it passed, this wind leveled -whatever was offered to me at the time, in years no more real than the ones I was living. What did other people's deaths or a mother's love matter to me; what did his God or the lives people choose or the fate they think they elect matter to me when we're all elected by the same fate, me and billions of privileged people like him who also called themselves my brothers? Couldn't he see, couldn't he see that? Everybody was privileged. . . . (Albert Camus, *The Stranger*, p. 120–121, Random House Digital, Inc., books.google.com/ books?isbn=0679720200).

Then, in the dark hour before dawn, sirens blasted. They were announcing departures for a world that now and forever meant nothing to me. . . . And I felt ready to live it all again too. As if that blind rage had washed me clean, rid me of hope; for the first time, in that night alive with signs and stars, I opened myself to the gentle indifference of the world. Finding it so much like myself — so like a brother, really — I felt that I had been happy and that I was happy again (Albert Camus, *The Stranger*, New York: Vintage Books, 1942, p. 153–154).

It might look as if my hands were empty. Actually, I was sure of myself, sure about everything, far surer than he; sure of my present life and of the death that was coming. That, no doubt, was all I had; but at least that certainty was something I could get my teeth into — just as it had got its teeth into me. I'd been right, I was still right, I was always right. I'd passed my life in a certain way, and I might have passed it in a different way, if I'd felt like it. . . . I, too, felt ready to start life all over again. It was as if that great rush of anger had washed me clean, emptied me of hope, and, gazing up at the dark sky spangled with its signs and stars, for the first time, the first, I laid my heart open to the benign indifference of the universe. To feel it so like myself, indeed, so brotherly, made me realize that I'd been happy, and that I was happy still (Albert Camus, *The Stranger*, p. 92–93, books.google.com books?id= ECYOAAAAQAAJ).

Read this excerpt from Albert Camus' *The Stranger* (chapter 1), then respond to the following:

CONCEPT BUILDER 31-A
Active Reading

MOTHER died today. Or, maybe, yesterday; I can't be sure. The telegram from the Home says: YOUR MOTHER PASSED AWAY. FUNERAL TOMORROW. DEEP SYMPATHY. Which leaves the matter doubtful; it could have been yesterday.

The Home for Aged Persons is at Marengo, some fifty miles from Algiers. With the two o'clock bus I should get there well before nightfall. Then I can spend the night there, keeping the usual vigil beside the body, and be back here by tomorrow evening. I have fixed up with my employer for two days' leave; obviously, under the circumstances, he couldn't refuse. Still, I had an idea he looked annoyed, and I said, without thinking: "Sorry, sir, but it's not my fault, you know."

Afterwards it struck me I needn't have said that. I had no reason to excuse myself; it was up to him to express his sympathy and so forth. Probably he will do so the day after tomorrow, when he sees me in black. For the present, it's almost as if Mother weren't really dead. The funeral will bring it home to me, put an official seal on it, so to speak.

I took the two-o'clock bus. It was a blazing hot afternoon. I'd lunched, as usual, at Céleste's restaurant. Everyone was most kind, and Céleste said to me, "There's no one like a mother." When I left they came with me to the door. It was something of a rush, getting away, as at the last moment I had to call in at Emmanuel's place to borrow his black tie and mourning band. He lost his uncle a few months ago.

I had to run to catch the bus. I suppose it was my hurrying like that, what with the glare off the road and from the sky, the reek of gasoline, and the jolts that made me feel so drowsy. Anyhow, I slept most of the way. When I woke I was leaning against a soldier; he grinned and asked me if I'd come from a long way off, and I just nodded, to cut things short. I wasn't in a mood for talking.

The Home is a little over a mile from the village. I went there on foot. I asked to be allowed to see Mother at once, but the doorkeeper told me I must see the warden first. He wasn't free, and I had to wait a bit. The doorkeeper chatted with me while I waited; then he led me to the office. The warden was a very small man, with gray hair, and a Legion of Honor rosette in his buttonhole. He gave me a long look with his watery blue eyes. Then we shook hands, and he held mine so long that I began to feel embarrassed. After that he consulted a register on his table, and said: "Madame Meursault entered the Home three years ago. She had no private means and depended entirely on you." I had a feeling he was blaming me for something, and started to explain. But he cut me short.

What is the narrative point of view?

Given the opening comments, what sort of man is Mersault?

448

Modernism

If the worldview deism suggested that God was out to lunch, modernism, a cousin of naturalism, suggested that God was absent altogether.

Modernism, in its broadest definition, is cultural tendencies originally arising from wide-scale and far-reaching changes to Western society in the late 19th and early 20th centuries. The world, including America, had rapidly changed from an agrarian to an urban society in one short generation.

Modernism fervently believed in science and technology. It was an optimistic vision of the future.

It was also a revolt against the conservative values of limitation and pragmatism. The trademark of modernism was its rejection of tradition. Modernism rejected the lingering certainty of Enlightenment epistemology and also rejected the existence of a compassionate, all-powerful Creator God in favor of human progress. The first casualty of this Quixotic thinking was Judeo-Christian morality. Examine this modernist sculpture. In what ways does it capture the hopelessness of a Modernist vision?

Assignments

- Warm-up: I am fond of saying that the best symbol for modernism is the Ferris wheel invented during early modernism: phenomenal technology, entertaining, but it takes the participant nowhere but in circles. What do I mean?

- Students should complete Concept Builder 31-B.

- Students *should* review reading(s) from next chapter.

- Students should outline essays due at the end of the week.

- Per teacher instructions, students may answer orally, in a group setting, some of the essays that are not assigned as the formal essay.

Existentialism is a worldview that advances the following components:

1. ____	Evil is trivialized	A. Mersault is constantly discussing how he feels, what he thinks. He does so with a perfunctory indifference to everyone around him, including the reader.
2. ____	Truth is subjective	B. Truth to Mersault is what he wants and needs. He has created a "whatever" world for himself.
3. ____	Environment, interior and exterior, is paramount	C. Mersault shows no remorse for murdering the stranger on the beach.

Student Essay:

Camus's Existential Worldview

"You will never be happy if you continue to search for what happiness consists of. You will never live if you are looking for the meaning of life."

— Albert Camus (classiclit.about.com/cs/profileswriters/p/aa_acamus.htm)

The Stranger, written by Albert Camus, is a book about Meursault's feelings after his mother's death and his crime. Meursault's feelings about life exhibit Albert Camus's existential worldview.

Existentialism, a philosophical movement, attempts to validate human knowledge as a basis for reality. Existentialists believe that man makes decisions based on need and function rather than knowledge. These decisions can be good or evil; it just depends on if it suits one's needs. Existentialists have quite a selfish view. Every action they do is for their own behalf. They believe that human nature is made through life choices and worldly desire is futile. Existentialists view the world as hostile and indifferent. Camus's protagonist Meursault displays these qualities.

Meursault believes that he was right, is right, and will always be right. This clearly shows the selfish beliefs of Camus. "I had been right, I was still right, I was always right." Also, Meursault says he took one path in life, but he could have just as well taken any other path. He believes that human nature is made through life choices. He could have had another way of life if he had made different choices. "I had lived my life as one way and I could just as well have lived it another. I had done this and I hadn't done that."

Meursault shows that Camus does not care for worldly desires. He does not even care for the world around him. "What did other people's deaths or a mother's love matter to me; what did his God or the lives people choose or the fate they think elect matter to me when we're all elected by the same fate, me and billions of privileged people like him who also called themselves my brothers?"

Camus also writes about the indifference of the world. He even relates the indifference to himself. Camus portrays his view through Meursault that human life is unexplainable and apathetic. "I opened myself to the gentle indifference of the world. Finding it so much like myself — so like a brother, really — I felt that I had been happy and that I was happy again." (Hannah)

Assignments

- Warm-up: What evidence of existentialism do you find in *The Stranger*?
- Students should complete Concept Builder 31-C.
- Students should write rough draft of assigned essay.
- The teacher may correct rough draft.

Meursault is psychologically detached from the world around him. Events that would be very significant for most people, such as a marriage proposal or a parent's death, do not matter to him, at least not on a sentimental level. He simply does not care that his mother is dead, or that Marie loves him.

Meursault is also honest, which means that he does not think of hiding his lack of feeling by shedding false tears over his mother's death. In displaying his indifference, Meursault implicitly challenges society's accepted moral standards, which dictate that one should grieve over death. Because Meursault does not grieve, society sees him as an outsider, a threat, even a monster. At his trial, the fact that he had no reaction to his mother's death damages his reputation far more than his taking of another person's life.

Meursault is neither moral nor immoral. Rather, he is amoral — he simply does not make the distinction between good and bad in his own mind. When Raymond asks him to write a letter that will help Raymond torment his mistress, Meursault indifferently agrees because he "didn't have any reason not to." He does not place any value judgment on his act, and writes the letter mainly because he has the time and the ability to do so.

In short, Mersault is the opposite of heroes like El Cid, Odysseus, and Aeneas. Which heroes do you find more appealing? Why?

Student Essay:
Gentle Indifference of the World

"I opened myself to the gentle indifference of the world. Finding it so much like myself — so like a brother, really — I felt that I had been happy and that I was happy again." This is the summation of the existentialist paragon as described by Albert Camus in *The Stranger*. This ideal involves the complete and total rejection of any absolutes in life such as meaning and truth, and the embrace of a world of relatives, in which every decision is as good as any other.

The road to the existentialist ideal paved by Camus begins with disillusionment. In nearly every other philosophy, there is an aspect of searching: a quest to find the meaning and purpose of life. The existentialist gives up this quest as hopeless from the start, believing wholeheartedly in the meaninglessness of life. Others pull their hair out trying to find absolutes, but the existentialist is able to relax in a serene assurance of relatives.

The serenity of this assurance is this: that in a world of relatives, void of any absolute right or wrong, every decision is as good as any other. ... In this freeing system, the existentialist exchanges a moral compass for the natural guiding mechanism of human desire to direct his life. There is no remorse, because what is done is done, and it was the best possible thing that could have been done.

... Through this dark wind, Camus further establishes the meaninglessness of choices. In the end, a "wind" will level all of the highs and lows of everyone's life into the same "terrain." Thus, according to existentialism, everyone's lives are worth exactly the same, and have all been spent just as well, regardless of choices. ...

Thus, Camus's paragon of existentialism is the image of perfect freedom, of a person free from the chains of morality and the burden of meaning. With this release there comes a serenity unmatchable by any other philosophy. "I opened myself to the gentle indifference of the world. Finding it so much like myself — so like a brother, really — I felt that I had been happy and that I was happy again." (Austin)

Assignments

- Warm-up: What is the "gentle indifference of the World"?
- Students should complete Concept Builder 31-D.
- Students will re-write corrected copies of essay due tomorrow.

Two important foils, Marie (*The Stranger*) and Gretchen (*Faust*), are treated poorly by their male friends. Compare these two women.

Issue	Marie	Gretchen
View of ultimate reality	*Marie is an existentialist, an atheist*	*Gretchen is a Christian theist*
Relationship with their friends		
Purpose in the written work		
How she fares in the written work		

Jean-Paul Sartre

Sartre believed that there were two kinds of existentialists; first, those who were Christians, and second, the atheistic existentialists, which is what Jean-Paul Sartre, a contemporary and kindred spirit of Camus, saw himself as. What they had in common is that they thought that existence preceded essence. This thought denied orthodox Western Christian thought that argues that people have an essence, or soul, separate form their bodies. This notion expressed Sartre in broad relief, the philosophical bent of this thoroughly modern existentialist. Existentialism is a worldview/philosophy that argues that each individual is his own world. Existence precedes essence.

Freedom is existence and in it existence precedes essence. This means that what we do, how we act in our life, determines our character. It is not that someone tells the truth because he is honest, but rather he defines himself as honest by telling the truth again and again.

Sartre in one sense is a quintessential modern. He invites the reader to think through his life in a rational way. On the other hand, his writings presage post-modernism. Post-modernism is opposed to universal rationalism or objective views of knowledge. Postmodernism purports to be a movement that is centered in the subjective and relative.

Assignments

- Warm-up: Why is someone like Jean-Paul Sartre such a great threat to the 21st-century Christian? At what points does his worldview clash with Christianity? Discuss why Sartre's worldview would be so appealing to a naturalist.

- Students should complete Concept Builder 31-E.

- Essay is due. Students should take the chapter 31 test.

Match each quote with its context.

1. ___	Maman died today. Or yesterday maybe, I don't know. I got a telegram from the home: "Mother deceased. Funeral tomorrow. Faithfully yours." That doesn't mean anything. Maybe it was yesterday.	A. Mersault is speaking to the chaplain.
2. ___	A moment later she asked me if I loved her. I said that sort of question had no meaning, really; but I supposed I didn't. She looked sad for a bit, but when we were getting our lunch ready she brightened up and started laughing, and when she laughs I always want to kiss her.	B. Mersault is thinking about his eternal destiny.
3. ___	But, apparently, he had more to say on the subject of God. I went close up to him and made a last attempt to explain that I'd very little time left, and I wasn't going to waste it on God.	C. Mersault is discussing Marie and his relationship with her.
4. ___	It was as if that great rush of anger had washed me clean, emptied me of hope, and, gazing up at the dark sky spangled with its signs and stars, for the first time, the first, I laid my heart open to the benign indifference of the universe. To feel it so like myself, indeed, so brotherly, made me realize that I'd been happy, and that I was happy still. For all to be accomplished, for me to feel less lonely, all that remained to hope was that on the day of my execution there should be a huge crowd of spectators and that they should greet me with howls of execration.	D. Mersault is reacting to his mother's death.

(1890–Present):
Modern Age (Part 4)

First Thoughts

All Quiet on the Western Front is still one of the greatest European bestsellers of the 20th century. It is also one of the greatest, if not the greatest, anti-war novels ever written. The story of Paul Baumer is the story of a generation of disillusioned Europeans. "We had taken no root and the war swept us away. . . ."

Chapter Learning Objectives

In chapter 32 we are confronted again with the horror that was World War I.

As a result of this chapter study you will be able to . . .

1. Discuss what the boots of Paul's dead comrade represents.

2. Explore the way Remarque employs naturalism in his novel.

3. Please obtain and read works by Nelly Sachs (1891–1970), Nobel Prize winner in Literature.

4. Analyze why Remarque thinks this generation is lost.

Weekly Essay Options: Begin on page 273 of the Teacher Guide.

Reading ahead: *Nectar in a Sieve* by Kamala Markandaya.

457

World War I

Recently, while my wife and her mother vigorously reconnoitered and then exploited local shopping opportunities in a Scottish Highland community, my father-in-law and I walked around the same quaint village. In the center of this small community — no more than 1,200 people — there was the obligatory war monument. We see the same sort of thing in America, so I was not at first particularly impressed. For instance, in my hometown there is a memorial to American Civil War union dead in the center of our town square. In fact, there is a list of American World War veterans on the wall at our local post office, too. While waiting for stamps, I read through the names many days. The ones who died have a small, impressive golden star next to their name. Only two names have stars.

However, on the monument in the central square of this beautiful Scottish village, there were 128 names — 128 gold stars among approximately the same number of names in my post office. These were names of the dead, not the participants. A community that was then about 850 people had 128 dead casualties in World War I. The reality is that double that number was permanently maimed. Indeed, on one summer day in 1916, at the Somme, some towns lost their entire local soccer team and most of the volunteer fire company. Suppose there were about 425 men who lived in this community in 1914. By 1918, over 250 of them had been killed or wounded. Can you imagine the impact World War I had on this small, unpretentious Scottish community? It lost almost half its male population. As I traveled across Scotland, this story was repeated time and time again. This carnage is unique to European communities; in American history there is nothing to compare with it.

For the last time, during World War I, the British army recruited its regiments by county and town, but the trend was exaggerated in the Kitchener armies recruited for World War I. The British army made a promise very early, when they weren't sure how many volunteers they were going to get, that if a volunteer joined a group, the group would be kept together. And, the phrase was: "Join up with your pals or your chums, your friends." This certainly maintained morale and increased recruitment numbers. That is, it improved morale until they were all killed together on some nameless battlefield in France.

Of the 65 million men who participated in the war, more than 10 million were killed and more than 20 million wounded. The term "World War I" did not come into general use until after World War II. Before that, the war was known as the "Great War." World War I was the first total war. No war had been quite like it. All the participating countries mobilized all their resources to achieve victory on the battlefield. The home front, then, became as important as the battlefield. In fact, in some places in France, the home front was only a few miles behind the war front.

What caused this conflagration to spread all over the world?

By 1900, the world was changing with increasing speed and pronounced intensity that before then seemed to be fanciful. Space, time, and physical dimensions had been transformed in a way that a century before no one could have imagined. Telephone defied time and space in taking the human voice instantly across time and space. Cities were lit by electricity all the time. Literally, there was less darkness by 1900 than any previous century. It did not take 80 days to travel around the world; 80 hours was a possibility. Indeed, there were limitless possibilities — mankind could even travel under the ocean.

People were moving from the farm to the city. Advances in medicine and surplus crops assured that there was a substantial population explosion. By 1914, countries had a surplus number of young men to contribute to the war engine. The expansion of education, the expansion of entertainments, the emergence of the film industry, and newsreels all brought to masses of people visions of worlds they had never thought were available. All this progress conspired to give people realistic reasons to hope things would be better than they were today.

It could also mean intense frustration for those poor people who did not participate in this progress. Inequality and injustice among classes had always existed. However, with the advent of a national media, people now knew about it, and it suddenly mattered more than it had. People wanted more things and more control over their lives.

The industrial revolution had increased productivity and made possible a flourishing military. Europe knew the industrial basis of military power. In order to provide for the steel and the machinery necessary to stand up to the powers of the day, countries knew they had to grow economically if they were to have military power, and the converse was also true. If they wished to have military power they needed to build a strong, thriving industrial infrastructure. Nations — no matter how large — that did not have strong industrial bases lost wars: Russia with its massive army and large land mass lost to lowly Japan in 1905. The same was true 30 years earlier when industrial Germany defeated agrarian France in the Franco-Prussian War of 1870. This fundamental anxiety plagued all European nations and contributed in no small way to the War when it finally came less than two decades into the new century.

Once a nation felt it was threatened, it had to move quickly to meet the challenge. In the European industrial states, the nation that mobilized first usually won the resulting war. Thus, small conflict could easily become big world wars.

In a backwater part of the Balkans that is exactly what happened.

In the summer of 1914, a Serbian nationalist — a citizen of the aging Austria-Hungarian Empire — assassinated the Archduke Francis Ferdinand, the heir to the throne of Austria-Hungary. Perhaps foolishly, Germany issued a blank check to Austria-Hungary and said it would support her no matter what. Russia, whose ally was Serbia, said the same thing. Then everyone rushed to declare war on each other so that they could mobilize first. Quickly, a local, insignificant conflict became a world war.

An ethnic civil war became a world war because of alliances and coalitions. The Allied Powers fought the Central Powers. The Allied Powers included the United Kingdom, France, Belgium, Serbia, Montenegro, and Russia. The Central Powers consisted of Germany and Austria-Hungary. Japan joined the Allied Powers in 1914. The Ottoman Empire joined the Central Powers in 1914, as did Bulgaria in 1915. The same year, Italy entered the war on the Allied side. Although the United States initially remained neutral, it joined the Allies in 1917. The conflict eventually involved 32 countries, 28 of which supported the Allies.

While this new war was a world war in scope and sequence, most of the fighting occurred along a front in western Europe called the "Western Front." On the Western Front, within two months after the War began (in August 1914), there was a stalemate. Across intersecting trenches that ran north and south across France and Belgium, warring armies faced each other in open defense. At great cost in men and material, each side laid siege to the other's system of trenches. After millions of men died to prove that these trenches were mostly impregnable, warring armies settled down to a sort of draconian war where the nation with the most survivors at the end of the carnage would win.

A broad outline of the events as they unfolded in 1914–1918 includes the following. Most of the battles during World War I occurred on land. Besides one sea battle, the Battle of Jutland, and submarine warfare, there was not much of a sea war in World War I. Naval forces were used primarily to blockade hostile coasts. Airplanes were used extensively in World War I.

At first, Germany had a two-front war: the Western Front and the Eastern Front. On the Western Front, German armies fought the British Expeditionary force, France, Belgium, and the United States (in 1917). Most of the fighting on this front took place in northeastern France. Such names as Ypres, Verdun, and Sommes were names that haunt Western nations even today. Trenches ran from the North Sea to the border of Switzerland. Some of the trenches were miles apart; others were yards apart. On the Eastern Front, German and Austria-Hungarian armies faced the Russians. It was not long before the Central Powers had soundly defeated Russia and could concentrate totally on the western Allies.

While most of the most important action occurred in Europe, there were ancillary conflicts all over the world. For instance, the aborted Gallipoli Campaign in 1915 pitted the British and French against the Turks. The Turks won.

Since France, England, and Germany had colonial empires in Africa, Asia, and the Middle East, conflicts occurred in these areas, too. In Africa, England and Germany fought a long and arduous campaign that the British finally won. Likewise, in the Middle East, the British finally won the campaign in Syria and Iraq. All these conflicts, however, paled in the face of the war in Europe.

When the war finally came to an end on November 11, 1918, and the Central Powers were defeated, the political order and geographical map of Europe had been radically transformed. The Versailles Treaty, the treaty that ended the war, changed the future of the world. The German, Austria-Hungarian, Russian, and Ottoman empires had collapsed and new countries (e.g., Poland) were created. World War I was also partially the cause of the Russian Revolution. The humiliating terms imposed by the Versailles Treaty on Germany became a rallying cry for the Nazis who rose to power in the 1920s and ultimately precipitated a Second World War.

Assignments

- Warm-up: Why is this an ironic statement: "World War I was the war to end all wars."
- Students should complete Concept Builder 32-A.
- Students should review the required reading(s) *before* the assigned chapter begins.
- Teachers may want to discuss assigned reading(s) with students.
- Teachers shall assign the required essay. The rest of the essays can be outlined, answered with shorter answers, discussed, or skipped.
- Students will review all readings for chapter 32.

CONCEPT BUILDER 32-A
Symbolism

Paul and his friends steal a pair of boots from a dead Englishman. What do the boots come to symbolize?

$\longrightarrow$

Critics Corner

Many critics have hailed Remarque for writing *All Quiet on the Western Front* so objectively, without a trace of nationalism, political ill will, or even personal feelings. Even when a character's inner world is revealed, it always seems to be that person's inner life — not the author's. In 1929, as noted in this guidebook in The Author and His Times, the Nazis attacked the book not on literary but on political grounds, and a few reviewers accused Remarque of sensationalism. In America, magazine and newspaper reviews immediately hailed Remarque as the new Stephen Crane and his novel as an updated *Red Badge of Courage*.

Academic critics, however, have paid little attention to *All Quiet*. German critics were displeased at Remarque's departure from the intellectualism of traditional German fiction, and European and American critics were put off by its being a bestseller — how could anything so popular possibly be worthwhile?

Remarque succeeded in transcending his own personal situation; he touched on a nerve of his time, reflecting the experiences of a whole generation of young men on whom the war had left an indelible mark.

— Christine R. Barker and R.W. Last, *Erich Maria Remarque*, 1979.

Anyone who was sufficiently in the thick of it for a long period, on one side or the other, might have written this grim, monotonous record, if he had the gift, which the author has, of remembering clearly, and setting down his memories truly, in naked and violent words.

— *All Quiet on the Western Front*,[book review], New Statesman, vol. 25, no. 5, 1929; quoted in Barker and Last, *Erich Maria Remarque*, 1979.

[Lewis Milestone's 1930 film *All Quiet on the Western Front*] was one of the few serious attempts at a realistic approach to the World War. . . . The drama was kept within the bounds of its theme: a critical recapitulation of the slaughter of innocents. . . . Many instances were eloquent and moving indictments of the emotional and physical destructiveness of war: the sequence of the dead boy's cherished boots being taken over by his comrade, and the celebrated closing scene of the hand of the young soldier reaching out from the trenches for a butterfly only to fall limp on being shot."

— Lewis Jacobs, *The Rise of the American Film*.

Assignments

- Warm-up: Why does Paul despise the schoolmaster and the training sergeant?
- Students should complete Concept Builder 32-B.
- Students should review reading(s) from the next chapter.
- Students should outline essay due at the end of the week.
- Per teacher instructions, students may answer orally, in a group setting, some of the essays that are not assigned as formal essays.

CONCEPT BUILDER 32-B
Paul Baumer

Does Paul Baumer change? Circle the words that describe him at the beginning of the novel and check the words that describe him at the end of the novel.

Paul Baumer

Melancholic	Choleric
moody	touchy
anxious	restless
rigid	aggressive
sober	excitable
pessimistic	changeable
reserved	impulsive
unsociable	optimistic
quiet	active

Phlegmatic	Sanguine
passive	sociable
careful	outgoing
thoughtful	talkative
peaceful	responsive
controlled	easy-going
reliable	lively
even-tempered	carefree
calm	leadership

A Band of Brothers

All of the following foils (characters who develop the protagonist) are some of the important influences on Paul Baumer.

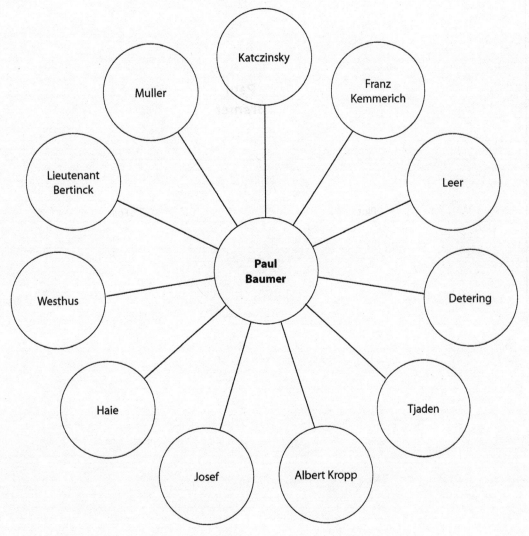

Assignments

- Warm-up: Why were the friendships between most of these men so enduring?
- Students should complete Concept Builder 32-C.
- Students should write rough draft of assigned essay.
- The teacher may correct rough drafts.

The Setting

World War I

**Paul
Bremer**

Plot

Foils

Student Essay:
Naturalism

All Quiet on the Western Front is a novel written by Erich Maria Remarque about a man in the German army in World War I. Throughout his novel, Remarque expresses naturalism. Naturalism is a worldview that sees life as being hopeless. The world, nature, and God are all indifferent to the naturalist, and even malicious. There are many instances of this worldview in the novel, but three in particular are the artillery shells, the excess of graphic violence, and the grove of trees.

The artillery shells represent naturalism because one never knows where they will fall. It is a matter of chance whether one will live or die. Remarque writes about this characteristic in chapter 6.

The front is a cage in which we must await fearfully whatever may happen. We lie under the network of arching shells and live in a suspense of uncertainty. Over us Chance hovers. If a shot comes, we can duck, that is all; we neither know nor can determine where it will fall.

The world in this case is indifferent to the plights of the soldiers. It doesn't care if they live or die and kills them randomly.

Another example is the violence in the novel. Remarque describes in detail the horrors of war. A young recruit gets hit in chapter 4.

The man on the ground is a recruit. His hip is covered with blood; he is so exhausted that I feel for my water-bottle where I have rum and tea. Kat restrains my hand and stoops over him. . . .

We lay the hip bare. It is one mass of mincemeat and bone splinters. The joint has been hit. This lad won't walk any more.

Violence is one of the characteristics of naturalism.

In chapter 8, Paul takes in the beauty of a grove of trees.

But the most beautiful are the woods with their line of birch trees. Their colour changes with every minute. Now the stems gleam purest white, and between them airy and silken, hangs the pastel-green of the leaves; the next moment all changes to an opalescent blue, as the shivering breezes pass down from the heights and touch the green lightly away; and again in one place it deepens almost to black as a cloud passes over the sun.

Nature, similar to the shells, is naturalistic because of its indifference to the violence around it. It doesn't care about the troubles of people. (Kory)

Assignments

- Warm-up: Based on Paul's description of the front, what part of the experience do you think would be the hardest to bear? What could provide consolation?

- Students should complete Concept Builder 32-D.

- Students will re-write corrected copies of essay due tomorrow.

Alienation
and Despair

Themes

Student Essay: Lost in Time

"Remarque is proposing the view that human existence can no longer be regarded as having any ultimate meaning. Baumer and his comrades cannot make sense of the world at large for the simple reason that it is no longer possible to do so, not just for this group of ordinary soldiers, but for a substantial proportion of his entire generation. Remarque refuses to lull his readers into a false sense of security, into thinking that God is in his heaven and all is right with the world" (Barron's Notes, Christine R. Barker and R.W. Last, *Erich Maria Remarque*, 1979). In this quote, Christine Barker and R.W. Last from Barron's Notes give their opinion on the main theme of *All Quiet on the Western Front*. In one aspect, they are correct. In another, their reasoning is flawed.

The first half of the above quote is quite accurate. "Remarque is proposing the view that human existence can no longer be regarded as having any ultimate meaning. Baumer and his comrades cannot make sense of the world at large for the simple reason that it is no longer possible to do so, not just for this group of ordinary soldiers, but for a substantial proportion of his entire generation." In this portion of the quote, Barker and Last argue that Remarque presents a world with no purpose for man. It is a world where man has no ultimate meaning. And Remarque does present such a world. "I am young, I am twenty years old; yet I know nothing of life but despair, death, fear, and fatuous superficiality cast over an abyss of sorrow. I see how peoples are set against one another, and in silence, unknowingly, foolishly, obediently, innocently slay one another. I see the keenest brains of the world invent weapons and words to make it yet more refined and enduring. . . . Through the years our business has been killing — it was our first calling in life. Our knowledge of life is limited to death. What

will happen afterwards? And what shall come out of us?" (Remarque 264) Here, the main character Baumer makes a confession. He says he only knows life as death, suffering, and fear, since he has been in the army for so many years. This constant barrage of death has worn down this character. Now, he is astonished at war and how men fight against each other and the brightest minds make weapons for killing. This essentially leads him to the conclusion that life is really about suffering, as he asks, "What shall come out of us?" The main character seems to think his generation will only be good at killing and destroying, nothing else. Years of fighting in the trenches of war and seeing death firsthand have convinced this soldier that his life has no true meaning.

In addition to losing his self-value, Baumer lost value for his generation as a whole. "For us lads of eighteen they ought to have been mediators and guides to the world of maturity, the world of work, of duty, of culture, of progress-to the future. We often made fun of them and played jokes on them, but in our hearts we trusted them. The idea of authority, which they represented, was associated in our minds with a greater insight and a more human wisdom. But the first death we shattered this belief." (Remarque 12) Here, Baumer writes how he thought his generation would progress, become more mature, and better the world through fighting for their county. But as he experienced death and the constant suffering of war, he lost this vision. Baumer also lost any meaning whatsoever regarding what his generation was here to do. Thus, Baumer viewed his generation as a "lost generation."

In the second portion of Barker and Last's quote, the claim Remarque "refuses to lull his reader into a false sense of security, into thinking that God is in his heaven and all is right with the world." Barker and Last are correct in saying Remarque does not mention God, because the characters of *All Quiet on the Western Front*, do not have faith in or believe in a God. But the reason for this ignoring of God, that Barker and Last give, is quite disturbing. Essentially, they argue God gives a false sense of security, and is really far away, and out of human affairs, if he even exists. But is this the real God?

" 'For I know the plans I have for you,' declares the LORD, 'plans to prosper you and not to harm you, plans to give you hope and a future' " (Jer. 29:11). This verse from the Bible speaks of how God is intertwined in human affairs. God is not some lofty, high God that sits in his throne in heaven and laughs pitifully on man. Instead, God is actively involved in human affairs. Jeremiah writes how God knows the plans he has for us. God has a will and a direction for our lives, which means there is ultimate meaning in each and every human life. And then Jeremiah writes what kind of plan God has for humans. God gives each human a hope and a reason to live for the future. And God will not harm humans or chastise humans. God's will ultimately comes out for the better. Sure, there will be struggles, trials, and tribulations along the way, but these are ways to build up one's character and faith. God is not a mean, angry God that has no interest in humans. Instead, he is interested in humans and helps us along our way.

In the end, Remarque does present a meaningless world. Baumer begins his life as a soldier with a vision of glory and fame for himself and his generation. But with the onset of war, and the reality of death and the constant suffering, this view of life erodes. Soon, Baumer sees the world as a cold, ruthless place, where man is just here. Humans have no ultimate meaning or goal in life. And just as Barker and Last's quote says, Remarque does not mention God. But Remarque does not refuse to lead his reader into a false sense of security, since God is not a false security. God is a safe, and secure being to which every human can go for love and safety. (Chris)

Assignments

- Warm-up: What images from the novel linger in your mind? Explain why these images made an impression on you.

- Students should complete Concept Builder 32-E.

- Essays are due. Students should take the chapter 32 test.

Situational irony is an unexpected event that occurs in spite of other circumstances. When John Hinckley attempted to assassinate Ronald Reagan, all of his shots initially missed the president; however, a bullet ricocheted off the bullet-proof presidential limousine and struck Reagan in the chest. Thus, a vehicle made to protect the president from gunfire was partially responsible for his being shot. Why is the ending of *All Quiet on the Western Front* an example of situational irony?

Situational Irony

Paul Bremer Dies

(1890–Present)
Modern Age (Part 5)

First Thoughts Kamala Purnaiya Taylor, who often writes under the name Kamala Markandaya, was born in India, in 1924. Her family was Brahmin, the highest caste in Hindu society. Markandaya made an effort to know not just the city in which she lived, but also the rural areas. She was educated at the University of Madras in Chennai, India, and worked briefly for a weekly newspaper before emigrating to England in 1948. There she met her husband, with whom she lived in London until her death in 2004. They have one daughter. Markandaya has made England her home, but she has made many visits to India over the years, returning to stay in touch with her culture and to find inspiration and information for her fiction. As a writer, Markandaya is respected for her accessible writing style and the range of experience expressed in her novels. Critics generally commend her portrayals of personal relationships, social consciousness, and the desire for independence.

Chapter Learning Objectives In chapter 33 we visit a South Asian village and recall again the most basic of human needs and potential in great adversity.

As a result of this chapter study you will be able to . . .

1. Discuss the central theme of this novel and how it is related to the protagonis

2. Discuss the style that is employed in this novel.

3. State the central theme of this novel and how it is related to the protagonist.

4. Analyze the character Biswas.

Weekly Essay Options: Begin on page 273 of the Teacher Guide.
Reading ahead: *Cry, the Beloved Country* by Alan Paton.

 History connections: *World History* chapter 33, "World War II and Beyond."

Kamala Markandaya

Kamala Markandaya (1924–May 16, 2004) was a pseudonym used by Kamala Purnaiya Taylor. A native of Mysore, India, Markandaya moved to Britain, though she still labeled herself an Indian expatriate long afterward.

Known for writing about culture clash between Indian urban and rural societies, Indian rich and poor societies, Markandaya's first published novel, *Nectar in a Sieve*, was a bestseller.

"While the sun shines on you and the fields are green and beautiful to the eye, and your husband sees beauty in you which no one has seen before, and you have a good store of grain laid away for hard times, a roof over you and a sweet stirring in your body, what more can a woman ask for?"

— *Nectar in a Sieve*

Assignments

- Warm-up: The author uses a flashback technique. The novel begins with Rukmani as an old woman remembering her life. Why did the author use this technique?
- Students should complete Concept Builder 33-A.
- Students should review the required reading(s) *before* the assigned chapter begins.
- Teachers may want to discuss assigned reading(s) with students.
- Teachers shall assign the required essay. The rest of the essays can be outlined, answered with shorter answers, discussed, or skipped.
- Students will review all readings for chapter 33.

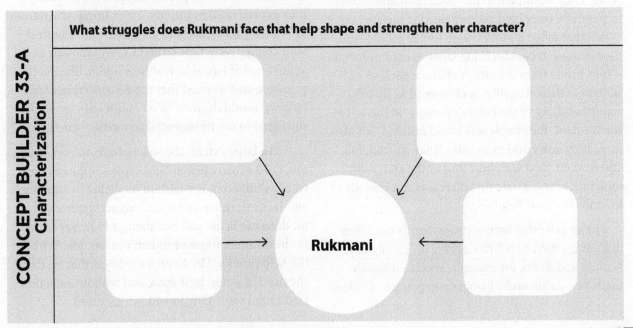

CONCEPT BUILDER 33-A
Characterization

What struggles does Rukmani face that help shape and strengthen her character?

Rukmani

The Family
Emauddin Hoosain

An extended family structure was common among Indian families. Often as many as three generations lived in the same house. This resulted in problems such as lack of privacy, inadequate resources, family disputes, and dependence on diminishing food supplies produced on ever-less-fertile land.

Although there were not enough resources available to the family, its members lived with some contentment and peace. Rukmani (Ruku) and Nathan were devoted to each other until Nathan's death. They encouraged and supported each other. Nathan was a compassionate and loving husband. Ruku adjust quickly to the role of a homemaker. The belief among Indians was that a woman's place was in the home, bringing up children, preparing meals, keeping house, and maintaining religious and cultural traditions. In addition, Ruku planted a vegetable garden and on occasions helped Nathan in the rice field.

Ruku and Nathan worked hard to achieve their goals. They attempted to put aside food and money to purchase their land and provide for their family. When that failed and they were forced off the land, they worked at backbreaking labor to earn money to return home from the city. A characteristic of Indians is their frugality, as evidenced in Ruku's astute handling of the family's meager finances. To some extent, the couple was broad minded, but also incredibly naive and unworldly. They trusted Puli, shared their food with him, and in the end, Ruku took him home, aware that there was not enough food for her own family.

In an extended family, strong family ties often discourage members from leaving the family unit. Nathan and Ruku, for example, tried to dissuade their sons Arjun and Thambi from going to Ceylon, even though their land and meager resources could not support them. As with most Indian peasant fathers, Nathan wanted his sons to stay and work the land, but they were reluctant to do so because they recognized that the family's situation would not improve and their opportunities were better elsewhere. This provides an example of how changing, industrialized economies alter extended family structures that tend to exist in agricultural, peasant economies. Selvam had similar thoughts about the land, but when he decided to work for Kenny his parents did not stop him because he was not going to leave the family's home as his elder brothers had done. In many ways, villagers were also an extension of the family helping one another during births, deaths, marriages, and drought or monsoon.

Ruku and Nathan were hopeful that their situation would improve. Nathan aspired to buy a house like that of his fatherin-law and abandoned certain traditional Hindu practices such as revering the cobra. Ruku was proud. Despite the sufferings they experienced in the city, for example, she refused to beg. Her resilience and great reluctance to deal with change sometimes irked Kenny who saw her acceptance of fate as a weakness. Ruku, like many peasants, was worried that the construction of the tannery would destroy their traditional way of life; she failed to see its potential economic benefits.

To a large extent, she was right. However, she, too, unlike many peasants, accepted some modern ways exhibited in her faith in medicine to cure hers and Ira's infertility. However, this acceptance of modern medicine was her attempt to preserve the tradition and culture of Indian peasant life. Without the help provided by Kenny, she knew that neither she nor Ira would bear sons, and without sons their traditional way of life would be destroyed.

Assignments

- Warm-up: Why is the family so important to Rukmani?
- Students should complete Concept Builder 33-B.
- Students should review reading(s) from next chapter.
- Students should outline essays due at the end of the week.
- Per teacher instructions, students may answer orally, in a group setting, some of the essays that are not assigned as the formal essay.

CONCEPT BUILDER 33-B
Character Analysis

Choose from the options at left to best define these three characters from the novel.

Character	Rukmani	Nathan	Biswas
Protagonist (the main character) Antagonist (the opponent of the protagonist) Foil (a character who develops the protagonist)			
Dynamic (Changes) Static (Does not change)			
Internal Conflict External Conflict			

Student Essay: Why Christians Should Learn about Hinduism

Christians should learn about Hinduism not only to understand the people and their rituals, but also to be able to use this knowledge for spreading the gospel.

Christians should learn about Hinduism because it gives them more understanding of the people and their practices. If a Christian, who does not know the beliefs of Hinduism, visits India, where bulls and cows roam the streets freely; he may think that this is a land of wildlife. However, this is not true. One of the Hindu beliefs is that bulls and cows are sacred. They are to be worshiped and not to be killed. Rats and other insects are also considered sacred animals. The Christian may think this is crazy, but knowing the people and their practices can aid in understanding their way of life.

It is commonly heard and said that knowledge is useless without application. The same goes with the knowledge of Hinduism. A Christian should not only know about Hinduism, but also use that knowledge to his advantage when he is sharing the gospel to Hindu followers. Knowing that Hindus believe that there is an impersonal universal spirit called Brahma whose goal is for the extinction of individuality and the establishment of one goal, a Christian can immediately look up a Bible verse that will contradict this belief. Before a Christian preaches, he should know his audience. By studying Hindu beliefs, Christians can share the gospel with them more easily.

Christians should learn about Hinduism not only to understand the people and their rituals, but also to be able to use this knowledge for spreading the gospel. (Hannah)

Assignments

- Warm-up: What can a Christian say to a Hindu that would encourage him/her to commit his/her life to Jesus?

- Students should complete Concept Builder 33-C.

- Students should write rough draft of assigned essay.

- The teacher may correct rough draft.

Characters in *Nectar in a Sieve* are followers of Hinduism. Hinduism developed in India between 1400 and 500 B.C. as a blending of the beliefs of the Aryan (Persian) invaders and the Hindi people. Hinduism is a polytheistic religion. These gods are the separate forms of a single god called Brahma (or universal spirit). The three Hindu deities most worshiped are Vishnu, Shiva, and Shakti. Hindu worship practices center less around public group activities than on private rituals, usually performed in the home for important events like marriages, births, and deaths. Among the important beliefs of Hinduism is *samsara*, the idea that all life is a series of births, deaths, and rebirths, influenced by the moral purity of a person's behavior and attention to religious rituals, called *karma*. Karma is sometimes explained as the law of moral cause and effect. By following proper rituals, doing good deeds, and maintaining purity of thought and action, people can improve and be reborn into a higher, more spiritual kind of life. Hinduism places great emphasis on performing one's duty to the gods as well as to other people. One's duty is, in turn, dependent on one's place in society. Hindu society has traditionally been divided into groups, called castes, based on heredity, which determine a person's occupation and status. How does Hinduism affect Rukmani?

1.

2.

3.

Student Essay

Rukmani: Complex Character

Nectar in a Sieve's most predominate theme is change, something that is reflected in both the protagonist and her personal struggles. Written by Kamala Markandaya, it is the story of Rukmani, an Indian peasant woman. Rukmani, called Ruku, marries as a very young girl, to a man she does not know, and must become a wife and mother when she is still a child. She adjusts to the life of a peasant and, once her children are grown, must watch as her daughter becomes a prostitute and her six sons are gradually drawn away from traditional Indian values into the industrialized world of the white man.

Ruku marries out of a family of privilege into hardship. Her husband Nathan is a farmer, and rather poor. Although her family was never wealthy, they could afford to hire servants, and Ruku was given an education. Now, as a farmer's wife, she cannot afford to hire help. At the young age of 12, Ruku must leave her childhood, taking on the responsibilities of marriage, motherhood, and a household. She must cook, clean, prepare food, and take care of her husband. These enormous responsibilities are both frightening and exciting to her:

> "I was ignorant of the slightest things, and no ornament either. Kali and Janaki between them had to show me how to milk the goat, how to plant seed, how to churn butter from milk, and how to mull rice. What patience indeed my husband must have had; to put up with me uncomplainingly during those early days of our married lives!"

Ruku experiences the changes typical of a young woman in her time. Getting used to change becomes a necessity in her life. By the end of the story, her sons have grown and started their own lives, leaving her with an all but empty household until her daughter is forced to return. Rukmani's husband brings their daughter home because she cannot bear children. Ruku is forced to face even more painful change as her daughter turns to prostitution because of her seeming worthlessness as a barren woman.

Despite all these family changes, Ruku refuses to allow her beliefs to change. In other words, she clings to the traditional Indian beliefs that she was brought up with, beliefs that some Westerners might consider backward. But the author gives Ruku enough depth and foresight to assure the reader that she is not ignorant. These beliefs and traditions are the only comforting, constant, fixed things in her life:

> Deepavali, the Festival of Lights, approached. It is a festival mainly for the children, but of course everyone who can takes part. . . . As it grew dark we lit the tapers and wicks and encircled our dwelling with light. A feathery breeze was stirring, setting the flames leaping and dancing, their reflections in the black glistening oil cavorting too. Selvam, the youngest . . . stood a safe distance away, legs apart and obviously ready to run.
> . . . "Go and play," I said to him. "Deepavali comes but once a year and this is the first time we have brought fireworks. Do not lose the opportunity."

Other changes, like industrialization, however, prove more difficult for Rukmani to accept. When the tannery comes to her town, she is deeply resistant to its effects on the village and its people. She comments,

"Change I had known before, and it had been gradual. But the change that now came into my life, into all our lives, blasting its way into our village, seemed wrought in the twinkling of an eye."

To her, the tannery is destructive to their peaceful way of life, causes prices to increase, and encourages people to choose wayward paths. Although she eventually takes her husband's advice to be flexible, she does so only because she has little choice:

"It is true, one gets used to anything. I had got used to the noise and the smell of the tannery; they no longer affected me. I had seen the slow, calm beauty of our village wilt in the blast from town, and I grieved no more; so now I accepted the future and Ira's lot in it, and thrust it from me; only sometimes when I was weak, or in sleep while my will lay dormant, I found myself rebellious, protesting, rejecting, and no longer calm."

Several commentators have suggested that Nectar in a Sieve is a chronicle not of Ruku's life and the changes she came to accept, but of India itself and the changes that occurred during British colonization. When the British people imposed their Western views on the people of India, the Hindus watched their traditions fade away, and they grieved first, and then accepted the change. Just as Ruku found herself sometimes rebellious and restless, India too rebelled. The people recognized opportunity, but they hesitated to forsake the customs and values that defined their culture.

Nectar in a Sieve is truly a mesmerizing book. Rukmani is a complex character, something that Markandaya strove to create. Her complexity allows this novel's depth to reach unbelievable heights. (Julia)

Assignments

- Warm-up: Give a character sketch of Rukmani.
- Students should complete Concept Builder 33-D.
- Students will re-write corrected copies of essay due tomorrow.

Generalizations are broad statements about a particular subject that are consistent with facts and observations. Support the following generalization with facts and observations.

↓

Fact:

↓

Fact:

Rukmani was a very strong, capable woman.

Student Essay

Change in *Nectar in a Sieve*

"Change I had known before, and it had been gradual. . . . But the change that now came into my life, into all our lives, blasting its way into our village, seemed wrought in the twinkling of an eye."

Nectar in a Sieve, by Kamala Markandaya, is a story of a simple peasant woman in a primitive village in India whose whole life was a gallant and persistent battle to care for those she loved. Throughout this book, change was a major theme. Change could be seen in the surroundings and in the people.

The first of the surrounding changes can be seen in Rukmani's marriage. Her father was a prestigious headman, but he soon lost his power. "Don't speak like a fool, the headman is no longer of consequence. There is the Collector, who comes to these villages once a year, and to him is the power, and to those he appoints; not to the headman." Because of this surrounding change, Rukmani was married to a poor tenant farmer. Her setting changed from living with her stable family to living with her impecunious husband.

The second surrounding change came from Rukmani's daughter's marriage. Rukmani found it hard to live without her daughter under her roof. "The stars were pale in the graying night before I lay down beside my husband. Not to sleep but to think. For the first time since her birth, Ira no longer slept under our roof." An even greater change occurred when Ira, Rukmani's daughter, was sent home from her husband because she was barren. Rukmani was shocked, sad, and shattered.

The time when Rukmani's two sons went to work for the tannery began the third surrounding change. Both Rukmani and her husband opposed the notion of working for the tannery, but their sons did not heed to their advice. "A few days later he began working at the tannery, and before long Thambi, my second son, had joined him. . . . Nathan and I both tried to dissuade him, but without avail. My husband especially had been looking forward to the day when they would join him in working on the land; but Thambi only shook his head."

Family changes were not the only surrounding changes, but there were also devastating weather changes. One year, the rains were extremely heavy, causing all the crops to be flooded. Rukmani and her family had to change their eating habits to compensate for the lack of food. "I went out to see if anything could be saved of the vegetables but the shoots and vines were battered and broken, torn from their supports and bruised; they did not show much signs of surviving. The corn field was lost." In another year, the weather was so dry that all the crops withered. "That year the rains failed. . . . Before long the shoots of the paddy were tipped with brown; even as we watched, the stain spread like some terrible disease, choking out the green that meant life to us." The changing weather constantly put strains on Rukmani and her family.

Perhaps the greatest surrounding change that happened in the story was Rukmani and Nathan's journey to find their son. Because of their inability to pay for their land, Rukmani and Nathan left to find their son, hoping that they could stay with him. However, this was a long and difficult journey. All their belongings and money were stolen along the way. "It was only then that we remembered, with trepidation, our bundles. . . . We went to it, but the bundles had vanished. . . . The coins were gone. I felt my bodice and again in my waistband, I shook out the folds of my sari, but there was no doubt the money was gone." On an even worse note, when they actually arrived at their son's house, they were told by his wife that he had left long ago and never came back. Soon after the end of this journey, Nathan died. Rukmani then decided to just journey back to her homeland. This was one of the greatest portrayals of the theme of change in the book.

Not only did the surroundings change in *Nectar in a Sieve*, but the people also changed. Rukmani, the narrator and protagonist, underwent great change throughout the story. She started with a rather decent life with her parents, but after her marriage, the problem of a shortage of food and money plagued her everyday life. Rukmani suffered through numerous amounts of hardships, from her crops failing to her daughter becoming a prostitute. However, as Rukmani was beaten and broken, she never gave up. She constantly gave fights against these troubles and somehow managed to survive. After each trial, she became mentally stronger and kept pushing for the end. Rukmani developed from a newlywed to a capable mother.

Nectar in a Sieve, by Kamala Markandaya, is a story of a simple peasant woman in a primitive village in India whose whole life was a gallant and persistent battle to care for those she loved. The theme of change was entwined in many different parts of the story. (Hannah)

Assignments

- Warm-up: Do you enjoy change?
- Students should complete Concept Builder 33-E.
- Essay is due. Students should take the chapter 33 test.

CONCEPT BUILDER 33-E Sequencing	*Nectar in a Sieve*, like most fictional novels, follows a chronological pattern. Place the events in the correct order as they occur.
	____ A The older Rukmani thinks back over her life.
	____ B Rukmani and Nathan search out Murugan in the city.
	____ C Kenny has raised money to construct a hospital, and says he will train Selvam to assist him.
	____ D At the age of 12, Rukmani and Nathan marry.
	____ E Rukmani gives up her savings to provide for her family after heavy rains destroy their crops.

(1890-Present):
Modern Age (Part 6)

First Thoughts Our brief journey through world literature fortunately ends on a note of hopefulness. *Cry, the Beloved Country* is a story of love, forgiveness, and redemption. Without a doubt it is one of the most moving and hopeful novels written. Alan Paton, caught in the injustice of Apartheid South Africa, writes a story that invites the reader to examine his own heart and to find a way to forgive anyone who has wronged or damaged him.

Chapter Learning Objectives In chapter 34, analyze a remarkable novel of hope, forgiveness, and trust.

As a result of this chapter study you will be able to . . .

1. Discuss the point of view that Paton uses.

2. Identify one or two themes in *Cry, the Beloved Country*.

3. Discuss Paton's development of protagonist Reverend Stephen Kumalo.

Weekly Essay Options: Begin on page 273 of the Teacher Guide.

Theme: Forgiveness

Forgiveness is the major theme of Paton's novel. Another person who plumbed the depth of forgiveness was the Christian apologist Corrie ten Boom. Corrie ten Boom was born into a loving Christian family in the Netherlands. Corrie was living with her older sister and her father in Haarlem (a section of Amsterdam) when Holland surrendered to the Nazis in World War II (1940). She was 48, unmarried, and worked as a watchmaker in the shop that her grandfather had started in 1837. Her family were committed Christians and harbored many Jewish fugitives. Eventually Corrie and her family were arrested and sent to prison. Within ten days Corrie's father died from illness, but Corrie and her older sister Betsie remained in a series of prisons and concentration camps. Although the concentration camp would have been the end of many people's faith (concentration camp survivor Elie Wiesel, for instance, said "I lost my faith in the fires of Auschwitz."), the months Corrie and her sister Betsie spent in the camp became an opportunity for ministry and hope. Eventually, Betsie died. In *The Hiding Place*, years later, Corrie described how she struggled with and overcame the hate that she had for the man who betrayed her. Corrie found a way to forgive those who had wronged her. Read this letter she wrote to the man who caused her to lose the people closest to her.

Dear Sir,

Today I heard that most probably you are the one who betrayed me. I went through ten months of concentration camp. My father died after nine days of imprisonment. My sister died in prison, too.

The harm you planned was turned into good for me by God. I came nearer to Him. A severe punishment is awaiting you. I have prayed for you, that the Lord may accept you if you will repent. Think that the Lord Jesus on the Cross also took your sins upon Himself. If you accept this and want to be His child, you are saved for eternity.

I have forgiven you everything. God will also forgive you everything, if you ask Him. He loves you and He Himself sent His Son to Earth to reconcile your sins, which meant to suffer the punishment for you and me. You, on your part, have to give an answer to this. If He says: "Come unto Me, give Me your heart," then your answer must be: "Yes, Lord, I come, make me your child." If it is difficult for you to pray, then ask if God will give you His Holy Spirit, who works the faith in your heart.

Never doubt the Lord Jesus' love. He is standing with His arms spread out to receive you.

I hope that the path which you will now take may work for your eternal salvation.

We do not know whether or not the man committed his life to Christ, but Corrie had done all she could. Discuss the theological importance of forgiving those who have wronged you. Include in your discussion the role of repentance with forgiveness: consider what God requires before He extends forgiveness.

Assignments

- Warm-up: Has anyone wronged you and you felt that you could not forgive him/her?

- Students should complete Concept Builder 34-A.

- Students should review the required reading(s) *before* the assigned chapter begins.

- Teachers may want to discuss assigned reading(s) with students.

- Teachers shall assign the required essay. The rest of the essays can be outlined, answered with shorter answers, discussed, or skipped.

- Students will review all readings for chapter 34.

CONCEPT BUILDER 34-A
Character Analysis

Choose from the options at left to best define these three characters from the novel.

Character	Reverend Stephen Kumalo	James Jarvis	John Kumalo
Protagonist (the main character) Antagonist (the opponent of the protagonist) Foil (a character who develops the protagonist)			
Dynamic (Changes) Static (Does not change)			
Internal Conflict External Conflict			

Critics Corner

Alan Paton . . . needs no introduction to Americans. *Cry, the Beloved Country* was published in 1948, and ever since he has been cited as one of the premier South African writers of his time: perhaps of all time. . . . He is 78 years old now and his voice is slow and deliberate, but the words offer years of careful thought. He has lived through changes in government, people, and publishing, and witnessed the economic growth of his nation. And, perhaps more than any other living South African author, he has chronicled these changes for the world to read.

> — Andrew Sussman, "Three Writers," *Publishers Weekly*, 1982
> (www.pinkmonkey.com/booknotes/barrons/cryblvd58.asp)

Cry, the Beloved Country may be longer remembered than any other novel of 1948, but not because it fits into any pattern of the modern novel. It stands by itself; it creates rather than follows a tradition. It is at once unashamedly innocent and subtly sophisticated. It is a story; it is a prophecy; it is a psalm. It is passionately African, as no book before it had been; it is universal.

> — Lewis Gannett, Introduction, *Cry, the Beloved Country*, 1948

Cry, the Beloved Country is a great novel, but not because it speaks out against racial intolerance and its bitter effects. Rather the haunting milieu of a civilization choking out its own vitality is evoked naturally and summons our compassion. There are no brutal invectives, no blatant injustices to sear the reader's conscience, no vicious hatred, no righteously unleashed passion. It is a great compliment to Paton's genius that he communicates both a story and a lasting impression without bristling, bitter anger.

> — F. Charles Rooney, "The 'Message' of Alan Paton," *Catholic World*, 1961,
> in *Paton's Cry, the Beloved Country: The Novel, The Critics, The Setting*,
> Sheridan Baker, editor (New York: Charles Scribner's Sons, 1968).

The mainspring of this unusual book is saintliness. The hero, an old Zulu minister, the Reverend Stephen Kumalo, is a feat of characterization rare in the modern novel: a convincing portrait of a saintly man.

> — Charles J. Rolo, "Reader's Choice," *The Atlantic Monthly*, 1948, in *Paton's
> Cry, the Beloved Country: The Novel, The Critics, The Setting*, Sheridan
> Baker, editor (New York: Charles Scribner's Sons, 1968).

Paton succeeds to a remarkable degree in portraying a segment of South African life during a brief period immediately following the end of World War II. And he succeeds, to an even more remarkable degree, in endowing this regional portrait with universal significance. He accomplishes this by incorporating into the actualities of South Africa's physical and social setting a fundamental theme of social disintegration and moral restoration. This theme is worked out through two complementary, or counterpointed, actions: Stephen Kumalo's physical search for his son Absalom, and James Jarvis' intellectual search for the spirit of his son Arthur. In each case, the journey, once undertaken, leads to an inner, spiritual awakening. . . .

[There is] a dominant style associated with the book. This is the pattern of speech with a marked poetic quality accorded to Kumalo and the African characters generally, and also to some extent employed in the lyric passages voiced from outside the action. This quality can be viewed as an artistic re-creation, in English, of the sound and syntax of spoken Zulu. But to be more precise, it is an artistic amalgam: a melting-pot of African and other speech patterns analogous to the tribal melting-pot in industrial Johannesburg. Thus, the language of *Cry, the Beloved Country* is a poetic invention designed to carry over into English the effects of the sound and idiom of African speech.

At least as many readers were drawn to *Cry, the Beloved Country* by the freshness of its language and the pleasure of its rhythms as by its insights into social dilemmas and complex relations among races. In contrast to the commonplace language of journalism they found Paton's language fresh and lively.

— Edward Callan, Alan Paton, 1968 (Ibid)

Assignments

- Warm-up: Why is *Cry the Beloved Country* a great book?
- Students should complete Concept Builder 34-B.
- Students should review reading(s) from the next chapter.
- Students should outline essay due at the end of the week.
- Per teacher instructions, students may answer orally, in a group setting, some of the essays that are not assigned as formal essays.

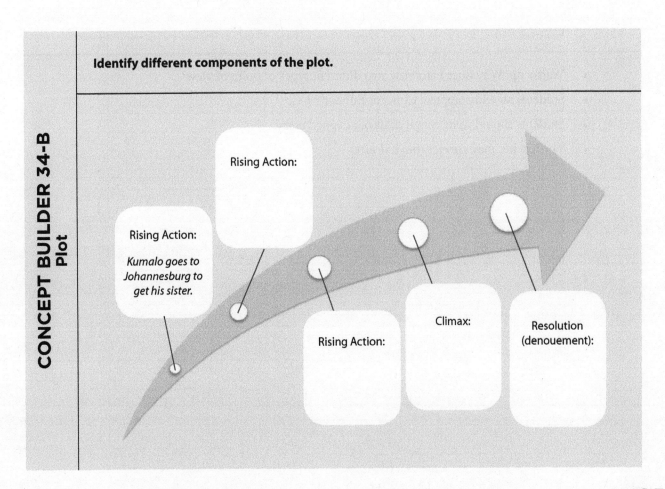

CONCEPT BUILDER 34-B
Plot

Identify different components of the plot.

Rising Action:

Rising Action:

Kumalo goes to Johannesburg to get his sister.

Rising Action:

Climax:

Resolution (denouement):

Point of View

Two kinds of third-person narration are used in *Cry, the Beloved Country*. First, Paton uses third-person omniscient narration. The opening and closing paragraphs of most chapters are omniscient narration. In other parts of the novel the point of view is limited omnisicient — the narrator uses the perspective — the eyes and ears and mind — of one specific character. That character is usually the protagonist Stephen Kumalo, but there are places in the novel where the focus shifts, and readers experience the story through the eyes of Mrs. Lithebe or James Jarvis.

Paton accomplishes two things by using a combination of omniscient and limited omniscient point of view. First, reader empathy of Stephen Kumalo is greatly enhanced by limited omniscient narration. At the same time, omniscient narration encourages readers to examine South African society at large.

Assignments

- Warm-up: Why does Paton use two different types of point of view?
- Students should complete Concept Builder 34-C.
- Students should write rough draft of assigned essay.
- The teacher may correct rough drafts.

There are several opposing themes that are warring for the souls of men in this book.

CONCEPT BUILDER 34-C
Themes

Decay —

Kamulo's homeland is deteorating

Hope —

Even though Absalom will be executed there is hope that someday justice will prevail

Death —

Absalom dies

487

Student Essay: Change in Characters

In *Cry, The Beloved Country*, several characters experience change in their personality and outlook on life. All these characters change because of the internal conflicts they experience within themselves. Two characters experience essentially the same internal conflict, while a third experiences a different argument.

The storyline of *Cry, The Beloved Country* revolves around a reverend's journey from his rural village to a modern city. While in the city, he learns his son has been arrested and is on trial for murder. Sadly, his son is convicted of murder and sentenced to death by hanging. "I sentence you, Absalom Kumalo, to be returned to custody, and to be hanged by the neck until you are dead." (Paton 236) After these words spoken by the judge, Stephen Kumalo and his son Absalom both experience the same internal conflict.

Both men are distraught upon hearing the death sentence pronounced. Absalom is especially struck by the news because it is his own life. "The Judge rises, and the people rise. But not all is silent. The guilty one falls to the floor, crying and sobbing. And there is a woman wailing, and an old man crying, *Tixo, Tixo*. No one calls for silence, though the Judge is not quite gone. For who can stop the heart from breaking?" (Paton 236-237) Absalom, like many probably would, was deeply saddened and depressed, knowing his death was not far away. Naturally, then, he struggled with accepting his fate. "At those dread word the boy fell on the floor, he was crouched in the way that some of the Indians pray, and he began to sob, with great tearing sounds that convulsed him. For a boy is afraid of death. . . . I am afraid, he cried. I am afraid. . . . Au! Au! I am afraid of the hanging, he sobbed, I am afraid of the hanging." (Paton 241)

This is Absalom's struggle within his mind, one he battles throughout the rest of the novel.

Strangely, though saddened and distressed at first, Absalom comes to accept his fate and is even joyous about his circumstances, as seen in one of his letters written home. "My dear Father and Mother: I am hoping you are all in health even as I am. They told me this morning there will be no mercy for the thing that I have done. So I shall not see you or Ndotsheni again. This is a good place. I am locked in, and no one may come and talk to me. But I may smoke and read and write letters, and the white men do not speak badly to me." (Paton 274) Ironically, though knowing his last day is rapidly approaching, Absalom is calm. His maturity from the day of his sentencing to this letter has grown, and he is able to approach death peacefully.

Absalom's sentencing also deeply affected his parents, as seen above, in the courtroom. "And there is a woman wailing, and an old man crying, *Tixo, Tixo*." (Paton 236-237) Since their son has just been given the death penalty, the parents are also deeply saddened. But the father soon overcomes his sadness and is able to give comfort to his son. "Be of courage my son. . . . Be of courage, my son. . . . Still kneeling, the father took his son's hands, and they were not lifeless any more, but clung to his, seeking some comfort, some assurance. And the old man held them more strongly, and said again, be of good courage, my son." (Paton 241) Perhaps Absalom's father's faith in God allowed him to encourage his son. Like Absalom, Kumalo's maturity is also seen, as he moves from sorrow in the courtroom to being able to comfort his son in the jail cell.

Both Kumalo and James Jarvis came from the same rural village. Jarvis was a farmer in the fertile fields of the valley. Being a farmer, Jarvis had plenty of time to think, ponder, and analyze the world.

And the people were ignorant, and knew nothing about farming methods. Indeed, it was a problem almost beyond solution. Some people said there must be more education, but a boy with education did not want to work on the farms, and went off to the towns to look for more congenial occupation. . . . Some said there was too little land anyway, and that the natives could not support themselves on it, even with the most progressive methods of agriculture." (Paton 163) One day, while farming, Jarivs realized how less food was being grown this year. Jarvis blamed this on things like fewer people working, the educated individuals leaving, and problems with giving land to natives. However, Jarivs forgot to notice the current injustice in his country. "Jarvis turned these old thoughts over in his mind as he climbed to the tops, and when he reached them he sat down on a stone and took off his hat, letting the breeze cool him." (Paton 163) This is Jarvis' internal struggle, the battle to admit there were injustices in his country and racial prejudice between natives and whites.

Only until Jarvis journeyed to the big city of Johannesburg did he begin to accept reality. Jarvis went to the big city because his son had been killed by Absalom. While rummaging through his son's belongings, Jarvis made a very interesting discovery. See, Jarvis and his son saw racial prejudice differently. "My son and I didn't see eye to eye on the native question, John. In fact, he and I got quite heated about it on more than one occasion. But I'd like to see what he wrote." (Paton 170) And Jarvis did look through his son's writings. "Jarvis say, deeply moved. . . . Whether because there was some quality in the ideas, that too he could not say, for he had given little time to the study of these particular matters." (Paton 188) Jarvis's son had written on the racial prejudice in South Africa and made some interesting points. Among these included the fact that Christians in South Africa argued everyone was equal but practiced inequality. Likewise, they believed God gave everyone certain talents, but they prevented the natives from using their talents.

After reading his son's works, Jarvis' view of the world began to change. He realized natives were not treated as equals and the Christians in power were being hypocrites. His long-held views of the world began to shatter and break apart.

Jarvis, Absalom, and Kumalo all experience deep internal struggles in *Cry, The Beloved Country.* Absalom and Kumalo both struggle with accepting Absalom's death sentence. Still, they are able to mature and Absalom is able to face death with courage while his father is able to encourage his son. Jarvis also has difficulty acknowledging the racial differences and prejudices in his country. However, after reading his son's works and writings, this view begins to break apart, and Jarvis begins to see the world as it really is. (Chris)

Assignments

- Warm-up: Is there someone you need to forgive?
- Students should complete Concept Builder 34-D.
- Students will re-write corrected copies of essay due tomorrow.

Identify three components of the setting. There are multiple answers.

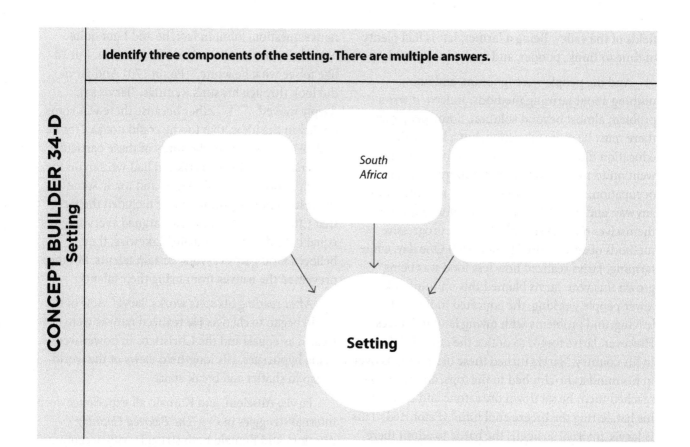

South Africa

Setting

Student Essay:
Fear and Forgiveness

"Aye, and cry aloud for the man who is dead, for the woman and children bereaved. Cry, the beloved country, these things are not yet at an end" (from chapter 11).

In the novel by Alan Paton, *Cry, the Beloved Country*, Paton writes of fear and reconciliation. Fear is prevalent in the society, and this fear rules the lives of all. In the end of the novel one can see the reconciliation that happens as forgiveness comes.

Throughout the novel, Paton portrays the theme of fear — fear of others, fear of self, fear of life. Kumalo, a South African priest in a small town, encounters fear everywhere he goes in Johannesburg. He even sees fear in himself, "his head aches, he is afraid." Kumalo's sister is fearful because of what she has done wrong in her life, "Have no doubt it is fear in her eyes." When he talks to his son's fiancé, she has fear in her, "And she smiled at him uncertainly, with something that was fear." Kumalo fears for his son's death by execution. So Kumalo goes into the mountains to sit, and pray, and wait for the moment when his son will be executed, for the murder of the son of Jarvis, a distant, white neighbor. Everyone has a sense of fear that is almost ingrained in them. They fear what others would say or do if others knew what they have done or are doing.

The second theme that Paton portrays is reconciliation and forgiveness. Kumalo forgives his sister for her actions. Kumalo forgives his brother for allowing Kumalo's son to suffer the consequences on his own and not punishing his brother's son for his wrong influence. Jarvis, the father of the man whom Kumalo's son murdered, forgives Kumalo for Kumalo's son's actions. In doing so he also forgives Kumalo's son. Jarvis eventually realizes that Kumalo could not have stopped the death of his son since he was not even there. Once he comes to this realization he begins to not only forgive but to also help Kumalo and other blacks in his valley. Throughout the story forgiveness must be given and received.

Throughout the novel, Paton shows the frightened people and shows the need for forgiveness and reconciliation. One cannot change others and so one must just forgive what they have done against you. One cannot be afraid of all at once, so one must chose what is most prevalent and think of that only. (Matthew)

Assignments

- Warm-up: Would if matter if all the principal characters were women?
- Students should complete Concept Builder 34-E.
- Essays are due. Students should take the chapter 34 test.

Two kinds of third-person narration are used in *Cry, the Beloved Country*. One type of third-person narration is by an omniscient or all-knowing viewer who sees everything. The opening and closing paragraphs of most chapters are of this type and so are the chapters composed of a dozen or more bits and pieces of the dialog of many different people. In other parts of the novel the point of view is what is called third person limited — the narrator has you focus on events through the eyes and ears and mind of Stephen Kumalo, but there are places in the novel where the focus shifts, and you find yourself looking through the eyes of Mrs. Lithebe or James Jarvis. First, he lets you get to know, care about, and appreciate Stephen Kumalo as a person. Second, he presents an overview of what many people in South Africa are thinking and saying, whether they are black or white, Afrikaans or English. Match the different kinds of narration (Barron's Booknotes AOL.COM).

1. ___	And now for all the people of Africa, the beloved country. God save Africa. But he would not see that salvation. It lay afar off, because men were afraid of it. Because, to tell the truth, they were afraid of him, and his wife, and Msimangu, and the young demonstrator. And what was there evil in their desires, in their hunger? That man should walk upright in the land where they were born, and be free to use the fruits of the earth, what was there evil in it? . . . They were afraid because they were so few. And such fear could not be cast out, but by love.	A. Omniscient Narration
2. ___	I see only one hope for our country, and that is when white men and black men . . . desiring only the good of their country, come together to work for it. . . . I have one great fear in my heart, that one day when they are turned to loving, they will find we are turned to hating.	B. First-person Narration

What is your favorite quote in this novel?

Glossary of Literary Terms

Allegory—A story or tale with two or more levels of meaning—a literal level and one or more symbolic levels. The events, setting, and characters in an allegory are symbols for ideas or qualities.

Alliteration—The repetition of initial consonant sounds. The repetition can be juxtaposed (side by side; e.g., simply sad).

Allusion—A casual and brief reference to a famous historical or literary figure or event.

Analogy— The process by which new or less familiar words, constructions, or pronunciations conform to the pattern of older or more familiar (and often unrelated) ones; a comparison between two unlike things. The purpose of an analogy is to describe something unfamiliar by pointing out its similarities to something that is familiar.

Antagonist—In a narrative, the character with whom the main character has the most conflict. In Jack London's "To Build a Fire" the antagonist is the extreme cold of the Yukon rather than a person or animal.

Archetype—The original pattern or model from which all other things of the same kind are made; a perfect example of a type or group.

Argumentation—The discourse in which the writer presents and logically supports a particular view or opinion; sometimes used interchangeably with *persuasion*.

Aside—In a play, an aside is a speech delivered by an actor in such a way that other characters on the stage are presumed not to hear it; an aside generally reveals a character's inner thoughts.

Autobiography—A form of nonfiction in which a person tells his/her own life story. Notable examples of autobiography include those by Benjamin Franklin and Frederick Douglass.

Ballad—A song or poem that tells a story in short stanzas and simple words with repetition, refrain, etc.

Biography—A form of nonfiction in which a writer tells the life story of another person.

Character—A person or an animal who takes part in the action of a literary work. The *main* character is the one on whom the work focuses. The person with whom the main character has the most conflict is the *antagonist*. He is the enemy of the main character (*protagonist*). Characters introduced whose sole purpose is to develop the main character are called foils.

Classicism—An approach to literature and the other arts that stresses reason, balance, clarity, ideal beauty, and orderly form in imitation of the arts of Greece and Rome.

Conflict—A struggle between opposing forces; can be internal or external; when occurring within a character is called *internal conflict*. An *external conflict* is normally an obvious conflict between the protagonist and antagonist(s). Most plots develop from conflict, making conflict one of the primary elements of narrative literature.

Crisis or Climax—The moment or event in the *plot* in which the conflict is most directly addressed: the main character "wins" or "loses" and the secret is revealed. After the climax, the *denouement* or falling action occurs.

Dialectic—Examining opinions or ideas logically, often by the method of question and answer.

Discourse, Forms of—Various modes into which writing can be classified; traditionally, writing has been divided into the following modes:

Exposition: Writing which presents information

Narration: Writing which tells a story

Description: Writing which portrays people, places, or things

Persuasion (sometimes also called *Argumentation*): Writing which attempts to convince people to think or act in a certain way

Drama—A story written to be performed by actors; the playwright supplies dialogue for the characters to speak and stage directions that give information about costumes, lighting, scenery, properties, the setting, and the character's movements and ways of speaking.

Dramatic monologue—A poem or speech in which an imaginary character speaks to a silent listener.

Elegy—A solemn and formal lyric poem about death, often one that mourns the passing of some particular person.

Essay—A short, nonfiction work about a particular subject; *essay* comes from the Old French word *essai*, meaning "a trial or attempt"; meant to be explanatory, an essay is not meant to be an exhaustive treatment of a subject; can be classified as formal or informal, personal or impersonal; can also be classified according to purpose as either expository, argumentative, descriptive, persuasive, or narrative.

Figurative Language—See *metaphor, simile, analogy*

Foil—A character who provides a contrast to another character and whose purpose is to develop the main character.

Genre—A division or type of literature; commonly divided into three major divisions, literature is either poetry, prose, or drama; each major genre can then be divided into smaller genres: *poetry* can be divided into lyric, concrete, dramatic, narrative, and epic poetry; *prose* can be divided into fiction (novels and short stories) and nonfiction (biography, autobiography, letters, essays, and reports); *drama* can be divided into serious drama, tragedy, comic drama, melodrama, and farce.

Gothic—The use of primitive, medieval, wild, or mysterious elements in literature. Gothic novels feature writers who use places like mysterious castles where horrifying supernatural events take place; Poe's "The Fall of the House of Usher" illustrates the influence of Gothic elements.

Harlem Renaissance—Occurring during the 1920s, a time of African-American artistic creativity centered in Harlem in New York City; Langston Hughes was a Harlem Renaissance writer.

Hyperbole—A deliberate exaggeration or overstatement.

Idyll—A poem or part of a poem that describes and idealizes country life.

Irony—A method of humorous or subtly sarcastic expression in which the intended meanings of the words used is the direct opposite of their usual sense.

Journal—A daily autobiographical account of events and personal reactions.

Kenning—Indirect way of naming people or things; knowledge or recognition; in Old English poetry, a metaphorical name for something.

Literature—All writings in prose or verse, especially those of an imaginative or critical character, without regard to their excellence and/or writings considered as having permanent value, excellence of form, great emotional effect, etc.

Metaphor—(*Figure of speech*) A comparison which creatively identifies one thing with another dissimilar thing and transfers or ascribes to the first thing some of the qualities of the second. Unlike a *simile* or *analogy*, metaphor asserts that one thing is another thing—not just that one is like another. Very frequently a metaphor is invoked by the verb *to be*.

Meter—A poem's rhythmical pattern, determined by the number and types of stresses, or beats, in each line; a certain number of *metrical feet* make up a line of verse; (pentameter denotes a line containing five metrical feet); the act of describing the meter of a poem is called *scanning*, which involves marking the stressed and unstressed syllables, as follows:

> **Iamb**: A foot with one unstressed syllable followed by one stressed syllable, as in the word *abound*.
>
> **Trochee**: A foot with one stressed syllable followed by one unstressed syllable, as in the word *spoken*.
>
> **Anapest**: A foot with two unstressed syllables followed by one stressed syllable, as in the word *interrupt*.
>
> **Dactyl**: A foot with a stressed syllable followed by two unstressed syllables, as in the word *accident*.

Motif—A main idea element, feature; a main theme or subject to be elaborated on.

Narration—The way the author chooses to tell the story:

> **First Person Narration**: A character refers to himself or herself, using "I." This is a creative way to bring humor into the plot.
>
> **Second Person Narration**: Addresses the reader and/or the main character as "you" (and may also use first person narration, but not necessarily).
>
> **Third Person Narration**: Not a character in the story; refers to the story's characters as "he" and "she." This is probably the most common form of narration.
>
> **Limited Narration**: Only able to tell what one person is thinking or feeling. Omniscient Narration: Charles Dickens employs this narration in most of his novels.
>
> **Reliable Narration**: Everything this Narration says is true, and the Narrator knows everything that is necessary to the story.
>
> **Unreliable Narrator**: May not know all the relevant information; may be intoxicated or mentally ill; may lie to the audience. Example: Edgar Allan Poe's narrators are frequently unreliable.

Onomatopoeia—Use of words which, in their pronunciation, suggest their meaning. "Hiss," for example, when spoken is intended to resemble the sound of steam or of a snake. Other examples include these: *slam, buzz, screech, whirr, crush, sizzle, crunch, wring, wrench, gouge, grind, mangle, bang,* and *pop.*

Parallelism—Two or more balancing statements with phrases, clauses, or paragraphs of similar length and grammatical structure.

Plot—Arrangement of the action in fiction or drama— events of the story in the order the story gives them. A typical plot has five parts: *Exposition, Rising Action, Crisis or Climax, Falling Action,* and *Resolution* (sometimes called *Denouement*).

Précis—Summary of the plot of a literary piece.

Protagonist—The enemy of the main character (*antagonist*).

Rhetoric—Using words effectively in writing and speaking.

Setting—The place(s) and time(s) of a story, including the historical period, social milieu of the characters, geographical location, descriptions of indoor and outdoor locales.

Scop—An Old English poet or bard.

Simile—A figure of speech in which one thing is likened to another dissimilar thing by the use of like, as, etc.

Sonnet—A poem normally of fourteen lines in any of several fixed verse and rhyme schemes, typically in rhymed iambic pentameter; sonnets characteristically express a single theme or idea.

Structure—The arrangement of details and scenes that make up a literary work.

Style—An author's characteristic arrangement of words. A style may be colloquial, formal, terse, wordy, theoretical, subdued, colorful, poetic, or highly individual. Style is the arrangement of words in groups and sentences; *diction* on the other hand refers to the choice of individual words; the arrangement of details and scenes make up the *structure* of a literary work; all combine to influence the tone of the work; thus, diction, style, and structure make up the *form* of the literary work.

Theme—The one-sentence, major meaning of a literary piece, rarely stated but implied. The theme is not a moral, which is a statement of the author's didactic purpose of his literary piece. A thesis statement is very similar to the theme.

Tone—The attitude the author takes toward his subject; author's attitude is revealed through choice of details, through diction and style, and through the emphasis and comments that are made; like theme and style, tone is sometimes difficult to describe with a single word or phrase; often it varies in the same literary piece to suit the moods of the characters and the situations.

Book List for Supplemental Reading

(Comprehensive list comprised of American, British, and other authors from around the world)

Note: Not all literature is suitable for all students; educators and students should choose literature appropriate to students' age, maturity, interests, and abilities.

Jane Austen, *Emma*

Charlotte Brontë, *Jane Eyre*

Thomas Bulfinch, *The Age of Fable*

Pearl S. Buck, *The Good Earth*

John Bunyan, *Pilgrim's Progress*

Agatha Christie, *And Then There Were None*

Samuel T. Coleridge, "Rime of the Ancient Mariner"

Joseph Conrad, *Heart of Darkness*

James F. Cooper, *The Last of the Mohicans*

Clarence Day, *Life with Father*

Charles Dickens, *Great Expectations; A Christmas Carol; Oliver Twist*

Arthur C. Doyle, *The Adventures Of Sherlock Holmes*

Alexander Dumas, *The Three Musketeers*

Anne Frank, *The Diary of Anne Frank*

Edith Hamilton, *Mythology*

Nathaniel Hawthorne, *The House of the Seven Gables*

Thor Heyerdahl, *Kon-Tiki*

J. Hilton, *Lost Horizon*

Homer, *The Odyssey, The Iliad*

W. H. Hudson, *Green Mansions*

Victor Hugo, *Les Miserables*

Zora Neale Hurston, *Their Eyes Were Watching God*

Washington Irving, *The Sketch Book*

Rudyard Kipling, *Captains Courageous*

Harper Lee, *To Kill a Mockingbird*

Madeline L'Engle, *A Wrinkle in Time*

C. S. Lewis, "The Chronicles Of Narnia"

Jack London, *The Call Of The Wild*

George MacDonald, *The Curate's Awakening*

Sir Thomas Malory, *Le Morte d'Arthur*

Guy de Maupassant, *Short Stories*

Herman Melville, *Moby Dick*

Edgar Allan Poe, *Poems & Short Stories*

E. M. Remarque, *All Quiet on the Western Front*

Anne Rinaldi, *A Break With Charity: Story of the Salem Witch Trials*

Carl Sandburg, *Abraham Lincoln*

William Saroyan, *The Human Comedy*

Sir Walter Scott, *Ivanhoe*

William Shakespeare, "Hamlet," "Macbeth," "Romeo and Juliet"

George Bernard Shaw, "Pygmalion"

Sophocles, "Antigone"

Harriet Beecher Stowe, *Uncle Tom's Cabin*

John Steinbeck, *Of Mice and Men; The Grapes of Wrath*

R. L. Stevenson, *Treasure Island*

Irving Stone, *Lust For Life*

Booth Tarkington, *Penrod*

J.R.R. Tolkien, "The Lord of the Rings Trilogy"

Mark Twain, *The Adventures of Tom Sawyer*

Jules Verne, *Master of the World*

Booker T. Washington, *Up From Slavery*

H. G. Wells, *Collected Works*

FOR OLDER STUDENTS

Chinua Achebe, *Things Fall Apart*

Aristotle, *Poeticus*

Edward Bellamy, *Looking Backward*

Jorge Luis Borges, *Various Short Stories*

Stephen V. Benet, *John Brown's Body*

Charlotte Brontë, *Wuthering Heights*

Camus, *The Stranger*

Chaucer, *The Canterbury Tales*

Miguel de Cervantes, *Don Quixote*

Fyodor Dostovesky, *Crime And Punishment*

F. Scott Fitzgerald, *The Great Gatsby*

John Galsworthy, *The Forsythe Saga*

Lorraine Hansberry, *Raisin In The Sun*

Thomas Hardy, *The Return Of The Native*

Write Articulately.

Think Critically.

Live Biblically

Integrate **3** Years of
High School Literature
with History

2 Hours a Day
Yields **9**
Course Credits

Master Books®
A Division of New Leaf Publishing Group
www.masterbooks.net

American **LITERATURE**	British **LITERATURE**	World **LITERATURE**	AMERICAN HISTORY	BRITISH HISTORY	WORLD HISTORY
Teacher 978-0-89051-672-0	Teacher 978-0-89051-674-4	Teacher 978-0-89051-676-8	Teacher 978-0-89051-643-0	Teacher 978-0-89051-645-4	Teacher 978-0-89051-647-8
Student 978-0-89051-671-3	Student 978-0-89051-673-7	Student 978-0-89051-675-1	Student 978-0-89051-644-7	Student 978-0-89051-646-1	Student 978-0-89051-648-5

Coursework designed by Dr. James Stobaugh: ordained pastor, certified secondary teacher, SAT coach, recognized homeschool leader and author.